THE PAPERS OF
WOODROW WILSON

VOLUME 32
JANUARY 1–APRIL 16, 1915

SPONSORED BY THE WOODROW WILSON
FOUNDATION
AND PRINCETON UNIVERSITY

THE PAPERS OF

WOODROW WILSON

ARTHUR S. LINK, *EDITOR*

DAVID W. HIRST, *SENIOR ASSOCIATE EDITOR*

JOHN E. LITTLE, *ASSOCIATE EDITOR*

ANN DEXTER GORDON, ASSISTANT EDITOR

PHYLLIS MARCHAND AND MARGARET D. LINK,
EDITORIAL ASSISTANTS

Volume 32
January 1-April 16, 1915

PRINCETON UNIVERSITY PRESS
PRINCETON, NEW JERSEY
1980

Note to scholars: Princeton University Press
subscribes to the Resolution on Permissions of
the Association of American University Presses,
defining what we regard as "fair use" of copyrighted works. This Resolution, intended to encourage scholarly use of university press publications and to avoid unnecessary applications
for permission, is obtainable from the Press or
from the A.A.U.P. central office. Note, however,
that the scholarly apparatus, transcripts of
shorthand, and the texts of Wilson documents
as they appear in this volume are copyrighted,
and the usual rules about the use of copyrighted materials apply.

Publication of this book has been aided by a
grant from the National Historical Publications
and Records Commission.

Printed in the United States of America
by Princeton University Press
Princeton, New Jersey

INTRODUCTION

THIS volume begins with the aftermath of the American note to Great Britain of December 26, 1914, protesting against alleged British violations of neutral trading rights. Soon afterward, the State Department strongly supports the right of an American to purchase a German ship, *Dacia*, lying in an American harbor, and sail her to Germany with a cargo of cotton. Anglo-American tempers flare when Sir Edward Grey, British Foreign Secretary, lashes back in a memorandum to Wilson that virtually accuses him of unneutrality and of being under German-American influence.

Anglo-American tension recedes when the German government, on February 4, 1915, announces that the English Channel and all waters surrounding the British Isles are "within the zone of war" and that, after February 18, all enemy vessels encountered in this area would be sunk by submarines, even though it might not be possible to save passengers and crews. Moreover, the announcement added, neutral vessels would not be safe on account of the use of neutral flags by belligerent ships. Wilson replies at once that the United States will hold Germany to "a strict accountability" for the illegal destruction of American ships and lives on the high seas.

Wilson and Bryan try to extricate themselves from the cross fire by proposing a compromise. The Germans would give up the submarine campaign, while the British would permit the free entry of food for civilians into Germany. Grey seems receptive but then rejects the proposal when the Germans insist upon free entry for all products on the free list of the Declaration of London.

Tension between Germany and the United States mounts dangerously in the following weeks. Count von Bernstorff, the German Ambassador in Washington, gives a memorandum to the press accusing the United States of violating the spirit of "true neutrality" by permitting the private sale of munitions to the Allies. Worse still, an American citizen is killed when a submarine torpedoes a British liner, *Falaba*, without warning on March 28, 1915.

Leaders in the administration now square off in a momentous debate. Counselor Lansing argues that the sinking of *Falaba* is an atrocious act and the killing of her passengers and crew nothing less than murder. Bryan replies that no American should threaten his country's peace by traveling on belligerent ships; in any event, the United States should agree to arbitrate the

Falaba case. Wilson agrees in principle with Lansing but is deeply moved by Bryan's appeals. Wilson is still in deep perplexity about what to do as this volume ends.

Meanwhile other events and crises absorb Wilson's attention. Egged on by the Germans, Colonel House goes to England, France, and Germany on a futile peace mission. Mexico remains in a state of virtual chaos; on one occasion Wilson threatens to hold Carranza personally responsible if he permits mobs to sack Mexico City. At about the same time—mid-January 1915— a crisis erupts in the Far East. The Japanese government presents twenty-one demands to China, adherence to which will make the latter virtually a protectorate of Japan. While Japanese troops in Manchuria mobilize and the Tokyo government bullies the Chinese, Bryan, ever the peacemaker and trusting the assurances coming from Tokyo, proposes a compromise that will yield much to the Japanese. Wilson intervenes, takes personal charge of the negotiations, and turns American policy strongly in support of China. The crisis is at its height when this volume ends.

Meanwhile, Wilson, in January 1915, begins to recover from the profound depression caused by the death of Ellen Axson Wilson. He denounces the Republicans in a highly partisan address at a Jackson Day Dinner in Indianapolis on January 8. Most important, in mid-March he meets a lovely widow, Edith Bolling Galt, and is entranced by her. They are already warm friends by the time that this volume ends.

"VERBATIM ET LITERATIM"

In earlier volumes of this series we have said something like the following: "All documents are reproduced *verbatim et literatim*, with typographical and spelling errors corrected in square brackets only when necessary for clarity and ease of reading." The following essay explains our textual methods and review procedures.

We have never and do not intend to print critical, or corrected, versions of documents. We print them exactly as they are, with a few exceptions which we always note. We never use the word *sic* except to denote the repetition of words in a document; in fact, we think that a succession of *sics* simply defaces a page.

We usually repair words in square brackets when letters are missing. As we have said, we also repair words in square brackets for clarity and ease of reading. Our general rule is to do this when we ourselves cannot read the word without stopping to determine its meaning. Jumbled words and names misspelled beyond recognition of course have to be repaired. We are usually able to correct the misspelling of a name in the footnote identifying the person. Moreover, all misspelled names, place names, names of ships, etc., are corrected in the Indexes.

However, when an old man writes to Wilson saying that he is glad to hear that Wilson is "comming" to Newark, or a semiliterate farmer from Texas writes phonetically, we see no reason to correct spellings in square brackets when the words are perfectly understandable. We do not correct Wilson's misspellings unless they are unreadable, except to supply in square brackets letters missing in words. For example, for some reason he insisted upon spelling "belligerent" as "belligerant." Nothing would be gained by correcting "belligerant" in square brackets.

We think that it is very important for several reasons to follow the rule of *verbatim et literatim*. Most important, a document has its own integrity and power, particularly when it is not written in perfect literary form. There is something very moving in seeing a Texas dirt farmer struggling to express his feelings in words, or a semiliterate former slave doing the same thing. Second, in Wilson's case it is crucially important to reproduce his errors in letters that he typed himself, since he always typed badly when he was in an agitated state. Third, since style is the essence of the person, we would never correct grammar or make tenses consistent, as one correspondent has urged us to do. Fourth, we think that it is obligatory to print typed documents *verbatim et literatim*. For example, we think that it is very important that we print exact transcripts of Charles L. Swem's copies of Wilson's letters. Swem made many mistakes (we correct them in footnotes from a reading of his shorthand books), and Wilson let them pass. We thus have to assume that Wilson did not read his letters before signing them, and this, we think, is a significant fact. Finally, printing letters and typed documents *verbatim et literatim* tells us a great deal about the educational level of the stenographical profession in the United States during Wilson's time.

We think that our series would be worthless if we produced unreliable texts, and we go to some effort to make certain that the texts are authentic.

Our typists are highly skilled and proofread their transcripts carefully as soon as they have been typed. The Editor sight proofreads documents once he has assembled a volume and is setting the annotation. The editors who write the notes read through documents several times and are careful to check any anomalies. Then, once the manuscript volume has been completed and all notes checked, the Editor and Senior Associate Editor orally proofread the documents against the copy. They read every comma, dash, and character. They note every absence of punctuation. They study every nearly illegible word in written documents.

Once this process of "establishing the text" is completed, the manuscript volume goes to our editor at Princeton University Press, who checks the volume carefully and sends it to the printing plant. The volume is set by linotype by two typographers who have been working on the Wilson volumes for years. The galley proofs go to the proof room, where they are read orally against copy. And we must say that the proofreaders at the Press are extraordinarily skilled. Some years ago, before we found a way to ease their burden, they used to query every misspelled word, absence of punctuation, or other such anomalies. Now we write "O.K." above such words or spaces on the copy.

We read the galley proofs three times. Our copyeditor gives them a sight reading against copy to look for remaining typographical errors and to make sure that no line has been dropped. The Editor and the Senior Associate Editor sight read them against documents and copy. We then get the page proofs, which have been corrected at the Press. We check all the changes twice. In addition, we get *revised* pages and check them twice.

This is not the end. Our indexer of course reads the pages word by word. Before we return the pages to the Press, she comes in with a list of queries, all of which are answered by reference to the documents.

Our rule in the Wilson Papers is that our tolerance of error is zero. No system and no person can be perfect. We are sure that there are errors in our volumes. However, we believe that we have done everything humanly possible to avoid error; the chance is remote that what looks at first glance like a typographical error is indeed an error.

We are indebted to Professors John Milton Cooper, Jr., William H. Harbaugh, and Richard W. Leopold and to Katharine E. Brand for reading the manuscript of this volume and for helpful suggestions. We continue to benefit from the careful work of Judith May, our editor at Princeton University Press.

THE EDITORS

Princeton, New Jersey
July 6, 1979

CONTENTS

ILLUSTRATIONS

Following page 268

Wilson in the Oval Office
Library of Congress

At a Baseball Game with Helen Bones
Princeton University Library

The Secretary of State is Amused
(Bryan with Albert S. Burleson)
Library of Congress

Walter Hines Page
Library of Congress

Edward Mandell House
Library of Congress

Constantin Theodor Dumba
Library of Congress

Count Johann Heinrich von Bernstorff
Library of Congress

Jean Jules Jusserand
Library of Congress

ABBREVIATIONS

ALI	autograph letter initialed
ALS	autograph letter signed
CC	carbon copy
CCL	carbon copy of letter
CCLS	carbon copy of letter signed
CLS	Charles Lee Swem
CLSsh	Charles Lee Swem shorthand
CLST	Charles Lee Swem typed
EBW	Edith Bolling Wilson
EMH	Edward Mandell House
FR	*Papers Relating to the Foreign Relations of the United States*
FR-LP	*Papers Relating to the Foreign Relations of the United States, The Lansing Papers*
FR-WWS 1914	*Papers Relating to the Foreign Relations of the United States, 1914, Supplement, The World War*
FR-WWS 1915	*Papers Relating to the Foreign Relations of the United States, 1915, Supplement, The World War*
Hw	handwriting, handwritten
HwC	handwritten copy
HwLS	handwritten letter signed
JPT	Joseph Patrick Tumulty
JRT	Jack Romagna typed
MS	manuscript
RG	record group
RL	Robert Lansing
T	typed
T MS	typed manuscript
TC	typed copy
TCL	typed copy of letter
TL	typed letter
TLI	typed letter initialed
TLS	typed letter signed
TS	typed signed
WHP	Walter Hines Page
WJB	William Jennings Bryan
WW	Woodrow Wilson
WWhw	Woodrow Wilson handwriting, handwritten
WWsh	Woodrow Wilson shorthand
WWT	Woodrow Wilson typed
WWTLI	Woodrow Wilson typed letter initialed
WWTLS	Woodrow Wilson typed letter signed

ABBREVIATIONS FOR COLLECTIONS AND REPOSITORIES

Following the National Union Catalog
of the Library of Congress

A-Ar	Alabama Department of Archives and History, Montgomery

BIA	Bureau of Insular Affairs
CLO	Occidental College
CtY	Yale University
CSt-H	Hoover Institution on War, Revolution and Peace
DLC	Library of Congress
DNA	National Archives
FO	British Foreign Office
GFO-Ar	German Foreign Office Archives
MH	Harvard University
MH-Ar	Harvard University Archives
Nc-Ar	North Carolina State Department of Archives and History
NjP	Princeton University
NNC	Columbia University
OCAJA	American Jewish Archives, Cincinnati
PRO	Public Record Office
RSB Coll., DLC	Ray Stannard Baker Collection of Wilsoniana, Library of Congress
ScCleU	Clemson University
SDR	State Department Records
ViU	University of Virginia
WC, NjP	Woodrow Wilson Collection, Princeton University
WDR	War Department Records
WHi	State Historical Society of Wisconsin
WP, DLC	Woodrow Wilson Papers, Library of Congress

SYMBOLS

[Feb. 17, 1915]	publication date of a published writing; also date of document when date is not part of text
[*Oct. 7, 1914*]	composition date when publication date differs
[[Jan. 8, 1915]]	delivery date of speech if publication date differs
* * * *	text deleted by author of document

THE PAPERS OF
WOODROW WILSON
VOLUME 32
JANUARY 1–APRIL 16, 1915

THE PAPERS OF
WOODROW WILSON

From Richard Heath Dabney

Dear Woodrow: University of Virginia, New Year's Day, 1915.

First, let me wish you a happy New Year, and many happy returns of your recent birthday. I don't know that any man with as many burdens upon his shoulders as you have *can* be exactly *happy*. But, at any rate, I earnestly hope that some of the burdens may be lifted and that you may be as happy as is possible under the circumstances.

And now let me speak of a matter which may prove somewhat of a nuisance to you, but which may possibly also assist you in the solution of one of the great problems that confront you & the world.

Every thoughtful man must hope that the settlement of the world after the war will be of such a nature that so horrible a catastrophe may not occur again. It is perhaps Utopian to dream of "the Parliament of Man, the Federation of the World"; and yet it seems to me that we must all strive to move in that direction. Raleigh Minor[1] has just completed the manuscript of a book[2] in which he makes the bold attempt to draw up a constitution for such a federation. In parallel columns he has the Constitution of the United States and the proposed Constitution of the United Nations; and he gives in the body of the work his reasons for proposing each article & clause of this latter constitution. I have not read anything except the constitution, but have talked with him about it, and believe that he has produced something which will at least serve as a basis for a plan to be laid for discussion before the nations when peace at last comes. It may well be that you will be asked to assist the warring nations to a settlement, and I believe that Raleigh's book will help you in the formulation of a plan. He is writing to you tonight on the subject, and if it should turn out that you could find time to examine his manuscript, it is possible that you might approve it sufficiently to write an introduction recommending his plan as at least worthy of the consideration of thoughtful & philanthropic men.

As you may know, Raleigh has not only republished, with changes bringing them up to date, some of his father's books, but has also written a highly praised volume on The Conflict of Laws.[3] I regard him as a man of very unusual ability.

With renewed good wishes for your success & happiness, I remain   Faithfully & affectionately,   R. H. Dabney.

ALS (WP, DLC).
[1] Raleigh Colston Minor, Professor of Law at the University of Virginia, son of Wilson's law professor, John Barbee Minor.
[2] *A Republic of Nations: A Study of the Organization of a Federal League of Nations* (New York, 1918).
[3] *Conflict of Laws; or, Private International Law* (Boston, 1901).

Robert Lansing to William Jennings Bryan

Dear Mr. Secretary: [Washington] January 1, 1915.

Reverting to our conversation the other day relative to the unjustifiable charges of partiality for Great Britain and her allies in the enforcement of neutrality by this Administration, which are publicly made by Germans and their American sympathizers, I have been considering the means which might be employed to meet these charges which are undoubtedly believed to be true by many of our citizens.

I assume

(1st) that the answer should be made for publication in the press in order that it may reach those who have read the charges;

(2nd) that the answer should traverse the charges *seriatim*;

(3rd) that the answer should have an official character; and

(4th) that the answer should not be addressed to private individuals who have made complaint to the President or the Secretary of State.

The following means suggest themselves:

First. An address in the Senate by the Chairman of the Committee on Foreign Relations setting forth the charges and answers in detail.

Second. A letter to the Secretary of State from the Chairman of the Committee on Foreign Relations or from the Chairman of the Committee on Foreign Affairs setting forth the charges and asking to be advised as to the facts and the action of the Department.

Third. A public statement by the Secretary of State based upon the fact that numerous communications have been received by the Department showing misapprehension of the facts and the law and consequent unjust criticism of the action of the Government in performing its neutral obligations.

Fourth. A request by the Secretary of State upon the Counselor for the Department for a memorandum setting forth the charges made and the facts and law relative to the several charges for transmittal to the President or the Chairman of the Foreign Relations or Foreign Affairs Committees.

Fifth. An oral statement by the President in a public address or otherwise in which the charges are taken up separately and answered in detail.

As to which means would best accomplish the purpose (i.e., a clear public statement of the facts and a refutation of the several complaints which have been made) I express no opinion. That is largely a question of political expediency and of the degree of official character with which the statement should be impressed. In determining it the fact should be borne in mind that any answer to the charges made is in the nature of a defense of the conduct of the Government and that the charges are not official but are made by private persons in letters and publications. On the other hand, thousands have read and believe the charges. I do not think that unofficial denials and refutations will change this belief. The answers to be effective must be explicit and emanate from an official source.

In regard to the *first* means suggested (a speech in the Senate) I fear that it would not be given the same weight as a statement issued by the President or by the Secretary of State.

In regard to the *fifth* means (an oral statement by the President) I am not sure that it could be done in an address since it would be difficult to enter into the details of fact which constitute conclusive answers to the charges. There can be no doubt of course but that an utterance by the President would have the greatest influence in dispelling the misapprehensions which exist; on the other hand, I cannot but question whether the charges should be dignified to such an extent. However, that is a matter, upon which I do not presume to make suggestions.

Whatever course is adopted I do not think that it would be wise to answer by letter to a private individual or even to a Senator or Representative unless he acted as Chairman of one of the Committees charged with the conduct of our foreign affairs. To do so would hardly comport with the dignity of the Government and would establish a dangerous precedent. If one correspondent was answered, it would be difficult to avoid answering others making different complaints. Furthermore silence as to some charges might be construed into admission of their truth.

Appended are the principal charges which have been published

against the Government by those in the United States who advocate the cause of Germany and Austria.[1]

[Robert Lansing]

CCL (WP, DLC).
[1] This memorandum is printed in *FR-LP*, 1, 187-88. It substantially summarized the charges in H. Münsterberg to WW, Nov. 19, 1914, Vol. 31.

Sir Cecil Arthur Spring Rice to Sir Edward Grey

Washington. 1 January 1915.

Private. President writes:

"I beg you will convey to His Majesty my warm thanks for his
generous thought of me[1] while himself beset by so many serious
and perplexing matters of State and that you will express my
sincere personal regard. No one wishes more truly and earnestly
than I do for most cordial relations of mutual friendship and
helpfulness between the people of British Empire and people of
United States, or for most cordial understanding and mutual
trust and esteem of those who represent or speak for them, and
no one will strive more constantly or watchfully than I for maintenance of such feelings and understandings. I know your own
feelings in these matters and congratulate myself that it is
through you that matters of delicacy and temporary debate may
be (group undecypherable). With warm regard and best wishes
for New Year that it may bring peace and lasting settlements
and quick healing" &c.

I have taken occasion of a meeting with his friendly consent
to speak of publication of Note in London in form given to it
as unfriendly. President's letter has no doubt reference to this
although immediate occasion was his birthday.

T telegram (E. Grey Papers, FO 800/85, PRO).
[1] George V to WW, Dec. 28, 1914, T telegram (SDR, RG 59, 811.001W69/108,
DNA).

From Edward Mandell House

Dear Governor: New York City. January 2nd, 1915.

Mr. Curtis came over from Philadelphia today to lunch with
me.

I think you would be perfectly safe in tendering him a place
on the Trades Commission. In my opinion, he would not accept
it, and if he did he would make a desirable member.

He suggested George W. Norris of Philadelphia as being the

most suitable person he knew for a place on that Commission. Norris, as you know, is the man that McAdoo wanted you to place on the Federal Reserve Board. I understand he has had large business experience and is now Commissioner of Wharves, Docks and Ferries.

Wilson Howe has just left. I have discouraged the South American venture and I think he will drop it.

I am to see "Jones" [Bernstorff] on Monday and I will report if he has anything important to say.

Affectionately yours,   E. M. House

TLS (WP, DLC).

From the Diary of Nancy Saunders Toy

Jan. 2, 1915

This time only the negro servant, Henderson, was awaiting me as my train rolled into the station. He took my things and led the way to the automobile where I found Helen Woodrow Bones. She gave me a sweet, friendly welcome and put me *au courant* with the family news as we drove to the White House. There Margaret welcomed me. The President had gone for a morning game of golf with Dr. Grayson. The two girls came to my room for a talk while I was waiting for my trunk, and with its arrival and their departure I unpacked and dressed for luncheon.

In the Red Room, where the family gathers before meals I found Mr. & Mrs. Sayre, and in a few minutes the President came in followed by Dr. Grayson. He looked better than I have ever seen him physically and acknowledged later in reply to a question from Helen that he had never felt better in his life. But in his talk and manner the old buoyancy had gone and I missed it during my whole visit. Also there was more formality beneath the unvarying friendliness of voice and manner. Was it, as John Hay said about Roosevelt, "the Kingly shadow falling upon him?" Or, what is more likely, the schooling in self-control which Mrs. Wilson's death has forced upon him?

At table he talked about golf: "I don't often swear, but today I just had to." "I was worse than you," chimed in Dr. G. The P. announced that some man wanted to print his History of the United States serially in a lot of daily papers. Should he do it? he asked the family. "Is there any money in it?" this gaily from Margaret. "Oh yes, but that's the reason why I don't want to do it while I am President." Then the talk fell to his books and he declared that he had never written but *two real* books in his life, "Congressional Government" and "Mere Literature," with the latter he had a great deal of fun, keeping it for hours of relaxation. "But your history!" exclaimed Jessie. "Oh that I wrote merely to learn the history of the United States," he said, and continued: "The worst book of history that I have ever read is Sir George Trevelyan's 'American Revolution.' How absurd at this day to believe that the English were all wrong and that we were all right."

At dinner the President seemed very sad. Immediately afterwards he took up a book of Essays by A. G. Gardner[1] and read aloud a delightfully clear rendering of Bryan.[2] Then he turned over the leaves and began an Essay on Morley which was interrupted by Dr. Mitchell who dropped in after a visit to Mrs. Sayre —interrupted for only a minute for the P. said, "I have nearly finished this, and you must hear it whether you want to or not." After the doctor's departure the P. said: "I already feel as if Morley were dead. He lives absolutely in the past and can't adjust himself to the very changed environment of the present. He was never a man of action at his best; a man of reflection, of theories which he shrank from putting into action when he had the chance."

[1] Alfred George Gardiner, *Prophets, Priests and Kings* (London, 1908).
[2] Gardiner's sketch of Bryan was a friendly but not uncritical one; it characterized the Commoner as a great moral crusader but not a profound intellect.

Sunday, Jan. 3d.

This morning the P. went to church accompanied by Margaret and myself. I suggested walking home but the P. hates walking and asked if I should enjoy it always followed by four Secret Service men. In the afternoon Helen and I went with him for a 2½ hours motor ride. He talked much about Mrs. Wilson, about my mother and about religion. This began with a question from Helen—did I not enjoy Dr. Fitch's sermons very much? I said I had heard him only once and then he aroused my opposition by declaring that in this break-down of civilization, these hugenesses of suffering, life would not be worth living did we not believe that God was behind everything and working out his own plan. I do not believe that and still I think life is worth living, I added. The P. took up my challenge. His views are those of Dr. Fitch's. "*My* life would not be worth living," he declared, "if it were not for the driving power of religion, for *faith*, pure and simple. I have seen all my life the arguments against it without ever having been moved by them." 'Did you never have a religious Sturm und Drang period?' I asked. "No, never for a moment have I had one doubt about my religious beliefs. There are people who *believe* only so far as they *understand*—that seems to me presumptuous and sets their understanding as the standard of the universe. Why shouldn't Helen's dog, Hamisch here set up *his* understanding as a standard! I am sorry for such people."

After dinner that evening Mr. Tumulty came in. "Good," whispered Margaret, "now we shall have some talk about politics." Mr. T. plunged right in, "Governor," he said, "did you write that English Note?" (This was the Note to the English Govt. in protest against holding up our ships bound for neutral ports.) The President: "Bryan brought me that note in an entirely rough and unliterary form, threatening, too. I drew my pen through certain offensive passages, wrote out new statements on the margin and between the lines, handed it back to him, and suggested that he should re-write it. Three days passed and I was wondering what had become of that note when Bryan brought it to me exactly in the form in which I had given it to him and pointing to the marginal notes *made in my own handwriting* said that he had made those corrections, and was I now satisfied. Nothing else had been done." What did you say? I asked. "Nothing," answered the P. "What *was* there to say!" Mr. Tumulty, after a moment's silence: "All the same, Governor, I believe you wrote that note in its final form, the first two paragraphs anyhow."

Norman Hapgood says that the President is falling more and more under Tumulty's influence, and Tumulty, he thinks, inspired the political part of his Indianapolis speech, but this episode would show that he doesn't know everything the President does.[1] After T. went away, the P. fell to talking about Bryan. It began this way: he took down a book of lectures he had made six years ago at Columbia College on "The Constitution." He was then President of Princeton. "Let's read my chapter on the President," he said. "I haven't read these lectures since I delivered them," and thus we had the piquant experience of hearing the President of the United States read what was an ideal Executive written by the President of a college when he had no idea what Fate had in store for him. He closed the book with a sigh, and I asked, does that mean that you are discouraged? *Are* you discouraged? "Yes," he said simply, "I am discouraged by the eternal talk with senators one by one. The ideal form of leadership in this country (and I am going to write a book about it one of these days) would be the leadership in the Senate. Now I have to talk with senators one by one—what they say on the floor all the country knows—what I say to them nobody hears.

The President should be a mere figure-head like the King of England. The leader of the Party should be the leader in Congress and should be heard in debate fully." Dont you want under existing conditions to be President again? I asked. "I wish with all my heart that it wouldn't be necessary," he said. "I should be much happier doing anything else. If I run again for the Presidency, it will be only to keep Bryan out. I feel like a pig when I sit in my chair and look at him and think, I mustn't let *him* be President. For he would make a very bad President: he would be ruinous to the country, ruinous to his own reputation. He always wants to think the best of everybody but he's the worst judge of character I ever knew, a spoilsman to the core and a determined enemy to civil service reform. Do you think," he said addressing me, "that McAdoo could be elected if he were nominated?" No, Mr. President, I answered. I do not. Whereupon I spoiled my chance of any member of the Wilson family ever liking me again. But the P. went on quietly: "It is the senators who break down the President, generally the senators of his own party. The Democratic senators have no idea of team work like the Republicans. There are always more freaks in the Democratic Party, more men with radical ideas, and each one holds to his own little idea which he thinks will save the nation, and will not submit to leadership. They are very hard to manage, too. Martine is a hopeless man. I've given him up long ago. O'Gorman is always smiling and Jesuitical. He sat in this very chair some weeks ago and talked with me for an hour, and I made about as much impression upon *him* as I did upon the chair."

HwC (RSB Coll., DLC).
    1 Mrs. Toy added this sentence to her diary later. Wilson spoke in Indianapolis on January 8.

To Richard Heath Dabney

My dear Heath: The White House January 4, 1915
    Thank you with all my heart for your New Year's letter. It was cheering merely to hear from you, and more cheering still to get such a message of friendship from you and of thoughtfulness for my welfare. You may be sure that all the good wishes are reciprocated many fold.
    I am interested in what you tell me of Mr. Raleigh Minor's work, very much interested, but I could not venture at this time to give public sanction to any suggestion, as I am sure Mr. Minor will realize upon reflection. It is imperative that I should stand aloof at present for fear of seeming to press a matter which

must be handled with the utmost delicacy and can be carried only the first practicable step.

But I will write to him about it, and am very much complimented that he should desire my opinion about his important manuscript.

In haste   Affectionately yours,   Woodrow Wilson

TLS (Wilson-Dabney Corr., ViU).

From Paul Samuel Reinsch

Personal.

Dear Mr. President: Peking, January 4, 1915.

Even in these distant parts we are following with deep interest the development of the attitude of the United States towards the great struggle, in the belief that our country may be able, when the proper psychological moment comes, to exercise a powerful influence towards suggesting a rational solution of the present troubles. If all the woe and sacrifice of this war could secure for the world a more adequate international organization, ensuring that the affairs of the world should be governed by law, and handled in an open, above-board fashion foreign to the older diplomacy, a great good would come out of this fearful tragedy.

You have probably often thought of the considerations I shall here suggest, and you may already have decided that action along this line is not feasible, yet I venture to submit them to you merely as an indication of how deeply our great responsibilities and opportunities are felt by those far from the seat of action and decision.

The desideratum would be an agreement among the Allies on the following points: that at the conclusion of the war armed forces and military expenditures are to be reduced to no more than one-half of the scale they had reached in 1914; that the organization of civilized society be strengthened by providing The Hague Court with an executive supported by the armies and navies of the Allied Powers; that a world-wide government of law be thus instituted, under which all nationalities would have full freedom to develop (as, witness, the French in Canada).

Some such program being announced as inalterable would provide the only justifiable motive for the use of force: namely, the establishment of a more efficient and beneficent organization of civilized life. One hopeful thing about this struggle is that an alliance of very diverse nations is fighting on either side and that the very war involves international cooperation on a large

scale. If notice were given to Germany of this purpose, together
with a decision that the territorial status quo ante would be
observed after the war, but that Germany and her allies would
have to assume an indemnity for damages which would increase
enormously with the duration of the war, a basis might be provided for the general acceptance of such a program.

As I am setting these things down, I realize their triteness
and the great difficulties in the way of their realization, yet if
it were possible that the good offices of the United States and
of other neutrals could be exercised in this direction at the right
time, some real step in advance would undoubtedly be accomplished.

With the highest regards and with every wish for your continued well being, I remain, dear Mr. President,

Faithfully yours,   Paul S. Reinsch

TLS (WP, DLC).

From the Diary of Nancy Saunders Toy

Monday, Jan. 4th.

Today Margaret & I went to the Senate where a small page
came up to tell us who the various senators were. We had hoped
to hear some debate on the Merchant Marine Bill, but the Republican senators were busily engaged in obstructing by long
speeches on Emergency appropriations. We then went down to
the House where we had no better luck. Coming back to the
White House I found Gen. & Mrs. Crozier[1] having tea with Mr.
& Mrs. Sayre, and after a few words with them I started to Mrs.
Hanna's[2] where I had an appointment with Mr. A. Maurice Low.[3]
He was enthusiastic over Mr. Muirhead's[4] scheme to open an
office in New York for the object of confuting German misstatements about the war, but he agreed with me that the propaganda
should rather throw its energies to gaining Irish sympathy for
the Allies.

At dinner the P. spoke of his annoyance because the Note to
England had leaked out and was published in the papers before
he was ready to publish it. "I wish I knew where that leak was,"
he said. I repeated Mr. Rhodes's account of a similar leak during
McKinley's administration which was traced to John W. Foster.
When I laughed at M.'s unwillingness that afternoon to let it be
known that she was the President's daughter in order to facilitate
our getting our seats, the P. declared that he felt so much like
M. that when telephoning he could not bring himself to say, "this

is the President"—instead he always said, "this is Wilson." After dinner the P. read us his chapter on the Senate from the book of the night before, but I was too sleepy to enjoy or understand.

¹ Brigadier General William Crozier, Chief of Ordnance, U.S.A., and Mary Williams Crozier.
² Charlotte Augusta Rhodes Hanna, widow of Senator Marcus Alonzo Hanna.
³ Alfred Maurice Low, chief American correspondent of the London *Morning Post*.
⁴ James Fullarton Muirhead, at this time the London correspondent of the New York *Nation*.

Remarks at a Press Conference

January 5, 1915

Mr. President, I notice there is a little discussion of an extra session.

Not by me.

Predicting some of the problems—probable failure of the rural credits bill. Mr. Glass of Virginia—

Nobody is thinking about a special session.

The morning papers are treating it rather seriously.

Well, they can dismiss it from their minds. There is nothing in it.

What is the status of rural credits, Mr. President?

I can't tell you because it is very mixed. I don't know, even after my interview with Mr. Glass, what the likelihood is of an agreement by the committee. There has been considerable disagreement in the committee on certain features of the bill—a natural disagreement. Just whether it will be reported out or not, I don't know.

Mr. President, do you find greater demand for rural credit legislation at this session than you had expected?

No.

You don't regard it as one of the legislative necessities of the session?

As a matter of fact, an extraordinary amount of relief was afforded in the granting of rural credits by the Federal Reserve Act. Before the recess of Congress, before this short session, a number of men who represented the agricultural interests of the country were very emphatic in their statement that they thought that a great deal had been done and that the proposition had been a good deal relieved, the necessity had been a good deal relieved, but that doesn't slacken their desire to go forward. It's wise to go forward only when we can get a thoroughly satisfactory bill.

The failure of rural credits in this session wouldn't be considered a reason for an extra session?

> It would be a reason for taking it up very early in the next session.

Would the failure of the ship purchase bill—would that be regarded in the same way?

> That is another matter, because we are in pressing need of shipping facilities, and we must get them. So that that might make a different case. But I don't expect that to be a failure.

Doesn't it seem apparent, Mr. President, that private capital is ready to go into it with confidence?

> There is plenty of capital. That is not the difficulty. The difficulty is the subject of adequate security which is recognized as adequate throughout the investing community. That is all the trouble about it. There is capital. . . .

Mr. President, is it a fair inference from what you said just now that failure of that bill might make an extra session possible?

> I never go on hypotheses. That is an hypothesis I deplore.

Mr. President, in connection with that rural credits bill, has anything come to your attention to show that there is almost a deliberate effort to conceal the advantages which the Federal Reserve Act provides for rural credit?

> Well, I don't like to express an opinion about those things. I try not to be suspicious.

Mr. President, have you decided to hold the hearing on the immigration bill?

> No hearing has been proposed, sir.

I thought it had been proposed?

> Mr. Forster. Some time ago.

And I understood that Mr. Hammerling[1] was coming again and urging you—

> I simply wasn't informed. I hadn't heard anything of the proposal recently.

Mr. President, I notice in the *Post*[2] this morning a dispatch from London, probably Associated Press, indicating that the United States Government might send a representative to the Vatican to cooperate there, with other representatives there, with a view to helping the efforts of the Pope to bring about peace.

> I took that as one of the many ways in which the *Post* amuses itself, sir. Of course it is ridiculous.

[1] Louis Nicholas Hammerling, president of the American Association of Foreign Language Newspapers.
[2] The *Washington Post*.

Mr. President, that is an Associated Press dispatch.

I don't know where those things are invented. I think not very far away from Washington.

Mr. President, do you regard the preamble of the Philippine bill[3] as an essential feature of that measure?

Essential in this sense: I think it is straightforward to declare purposes, to declare the point of view, the general line of policy upon which the bill is conceived—essential in that particular. Of course, the bill will work just as well because the substance, the effective substance will be there. But the preamble is a very important part.

You weren't influenced, Mr. President, by anything Mr. Taft said,[4] were you?

Well, with apologies to Mr. Taft, I must—I mean, I have not read what he said. But Mr. Taft has often very frankly avowed his views on that subject so far as he could which, from the headlines, there was nothing that he had not said before.

The point would be, with reference to that preamble, though, that it is representative of American sentiment. There is actual damage done by those references in the Philippines.

So it is alleged.

Yes, sir.

Of course. But the allegations of the effect in the Philippines have been so many that it is a matter of judgment which are well founded.

Mr. President, some time ago, when you told us that you were opposed to the literacy test in the immigration law, you said that it was because it was not a fair test of quality of citizenship.

---

[3] H.R. 18459. The preamble of the bill read as follows:

"Whereas it was never the intention of the people of the United States in the incipiency of the War with Spain to make it a war of conquest or for territorial aggrandizement; and

"Whereas it is, as it has always been, the purpose of the people of the United States to withdraw their sovereignty over the Philippine Islands and to recognize their independence as soon as a stable government can be established therein; and

"Whereas for the speedy accomplishment of such purpose it is desirable to place in the hands of the people of the Philippines as large a control of their domestic affairs as can be given them without, in the meantime, impairing the exercise of the rights of sovereignty by the people of the United States, in order that, by the use and exercise of popular franchise and governmental powers, they may be the better prepared to fully assume the responsibilities and enjoy all the privileges of complete independence." *Cong. Record*, 63d Cong., 2d sess., p. 16027.

[4] Former President Taft testified in opposition to the Philippine bill before the Senate Committee on the Philippines on January 2. In the course of his extensive remarks, he quoted from Wilson's *Constitutional Government* in support of his contention that the Filipinos were not yet prepared for self-government. *New York Times*, Jan. 3, 1915.

I mentioned that to a couple of senators after you said that, and it was one of them who helped frame the literacy test. In the first place, it was never intended to be a test for quality but a device to keep out certain kinds of people. He asked if you were just opposed to the method of restriction?

> Well, if he will ask me, I will tell him.

Could you tell us about anything—whether you are opposed to the restriction?

> I am not going to discuss the general policy. That leads chiefly—I feel I would have to hire a hall. It would take an hour. . . .

Mr. President, there was a paragraph in one of the papers to the effect that the President of France is to transmit to the French Academy some letter which he received from you. Could you tell us about that?

> Well, that is simply this: Monsieur Brieux was in this country as a representative of the French Academy, a very old body, the representatives—the chief literary men in France. He came over to bring greetings and make an address to the American Academy of Letters, which is a recent body and has by no means as much prestige as the French Academy. And he brought with him a letter to me from the President of France, a personal letter, simply because the President of France was a member of the French Academy and I am a member of the American Academy. It was—it had nothing in it but conventional salutations. It was not a personal letter. And I have replied, and he will transmit that letter to the French Academy. It is altogether just a matter between literary fellows.

Mr. President, it has been stated, in this matter of the passport fraud, which has been brought personally to your attention, that you have had something to do with the procedure followed in the investigation?

> No, it has merely been brought to my attention, as everything else is. It is in the hands of the district attorney in New York.

Any development, Mr. President, in the controversy with Great Britain?

> Not any, sir.

Mr. President, will your Indianapolis speech be of a political character?

> Decidedly. It will be political.

Mr. President, are you planning to prepare anything in advance on that?

No. I have suffered all my life under the incapacity of writing a speech. It is just about as dry as sawdust if I write it, so I always speak extemporaneously. But the speech is going to be delivered in the afternoon, so there will be time enough for telegraphic transmission, at any rate.

How about the Trade Commission, Mr. President?

No further progress.

Mr. President, could you take us enough into confidence on that speech, on your ideas in advance on that speech, to say what topics will be taken up?

[No answer recorded.]

Mr. President, it has been said with a good deal of definiteness that you have decided upon three members of the Trade Commission?

That is not true, sir, except in this sense—that I have made three lists and torn them up.

JRT transcript (WC, NjP) of CLSsh (C. L. Swem Coll., NjP).

To Edward Mandell House

My dear Friend: The White House January 5, 1915

The letter to Zimmerman is absolutely all right[1] and I have requested our Ambassador to deliver it. I am sincerely obliged to you, as always.

You spoke to me the other day about a letter you had received from Hammond,[2] the man about whom I talked to you when you were here in connection with what Tumulty has been telling me. At Tumulty's suggestion, I am writing to ask if you would be willing to send Hammond's letter to us to be kept with the other evidences of his methods of work.

In haste, with the warmest affection,

Faithfully yours, Woodrow Wilson

TLS (E. M. House Papers, CtY).

[1] EMH to A. Zimmermann, Jan. 3, 1915, TLS (Weltkrieg No. 2, geheim, Vermittlungsaktionen, 4272 D955746-48, GFO-Ar). It read:

My dear Herr Zimmermann:

Your letter of December 3rd came to me a few days ago.

I have had many conversations with the German and British Ambassadors here in regard to the beginning of peace parleys. These discussions have lead me to believe that if an indemnity to Belgium could be agreed upon and a plan for settlement made which would insure permanent peace, conversations could now begin.

The President thinks that some result might be more easily brought about through me in an unofficial way, because there would be no embarrassment to anyone and no formal commitments.

If you could give me any assurances in this direction, I would leave immediately for England where I have reason to believe I would get a sympathetic hearing.

I stand ready to start at any time upon receipt of either a letter or cable from you indicating that Germany would be willing to begin the discussion upon such terms.

His Imperial Highness, the Crown Prince, was quoted as saying that this was a stupid war. No one knows better than I how true this is. Knowing the situation from many different angles that are not available to any of the belligerants, I can confidently say that there is a general misunderstanding of motives and purposes, which might readily be cleared away if the principals could discuss the situation frankly.

The President bids me thank you for your kindly personal allusions to him. He would consider it a great privilege to be instrumental in serving Europe in this hour of trial.

With warm regards and good wishes, I am, my dear Herr Zimmermann,
Sincerely yours,   E. M. House

2 House sent this letter, probably from John Hays Hammond, prominent mining engineer, to Wilson. It is missing.

To Seth Low

Personal.

My dear Mr. Low: The White House January 5, 1915

I have been very much gratified by the contents of your letter of December twenty-ninth. I am very much pleased at what you tell me of Mr. Rockefeller's attitude, and I want to say that I think the Commission was wise not to go to Colorado just yet. Its work will certainly be best done quietly and by well-considered stages.

Cordially and sincerely yours,   Woodrow Wilson

TLS (S. Low Papers, NNC).

To Raleigh Colston Minor

My dear Professor Minor: [The White House] January 5, 1915

I have your letter of January first.[1] Heath Dabney had already written me about the interesting work upon which you have been engaged and I want to express my very great interest in it.

I should despair of finding time to give any book the careful examination which such a manuscript as yours deserves, and my feeling is that I ought at present to express no opinion about any comprehensive plan of world peace. Such an expression of opinion on my part just now would, I think, be more irritating to the belligerent powers than helpful to the cause of practical and immediate peace.

I none the less congratulate you on the serious study you have devoted to this profoundly important subject.

Cordially and sincerely yours,   Woodrow Wilson

TLS (Letterpress Books, WP, DLC).
1 It is missing.

From Edward Mandell House

Dear Governor: New York City. January 5th, 1915.

When I was talking with Dr. Frederic Howe the other day he expressed such a high opinion of Mr. Gilbert E. Roe[1] that I asked him to bring him to call yesterday.

He impressed me more strongly than anyone I have yet seen in connection with the Trades Commission. He seems a man of marked ability, and I would suggest that you meet him before making your final selection.

He is about fifty years old, in vigorous health, has had no objectionable practice, so I hear, and his name would be enthusiastically received by both progressives and progressive republicans.   Affectionately yours,   E. M. House

TLS (WP, DLC).
[1] Gilbert Ernstein Roe, former law partner and still a close friend and political associate of Senator Robert M. La Follette. After moving to New York in 1899, he had from 1905 to 1910 been in law partnership with William F. McCombs. Most recently he had been active in reform politics in New York City and State.

From Paul Oscar Husting

PERSONAL

Dear Mr. President: Mayville, Wisconsin Jan. 5, 1915.

Trusting that you will pardon my intrusion, I take the liberty of writing to you in regard to matters political in Wisconsin, which I believe of sufficient importance to be deserving of your attention.

No doubt, you are aware that we have a strong German-American population in Wisconsin. For some time past, indeed, ever since the beginning of the war in Europe, the republican press as well as members of the republican party have been industriously seeking to prejudice the German-Americans against your administration and the democratic party, claiming that the administration is favoring the enemies of Germany and discriminating against Germany. Of course, in doing this, our republican friends do not hesitate to misrepresent the facts, and in many instances, are making charges and statements that are entirely without foundation. These charges and statements, however, are given wide currency and there appears to be no concerted movement on our part, or rather on the part of the democratic party, to challenge the truth of these charges or to explain the misstatements. In consequence, a good many people honestly believe that practices are being winked at or even being approved of by the administration that are without precedent in our international dealings with other nations under like or similar circumstances. From time to time, I have run across democrats of German extraction who are giving some credence to these charges or mis-statements and I fear that unless steps are taken to counteract this campaign of misrepresentation and falsehood that the party may suffer material and perhaps lasting injury.

I visited Milwaukee the other day and had a conference on this subject with Mr. Nieman of the Milwaukee Journal. He suggested that this matter be brought to your attention forthwith.

In discussing this matter, Mr. Nieman agreed with me that the best way to counteract this movement would be to institute a campaign of public discussion and education relating to the shipment of contraband of war between nations. In short, to enlighten the people on this subject and to show them that what has and is being done in this nation, at this time, is in strict accord with the laws of nations according to past usuages and practices. I am firmly of the belief that whatever feeling has been aroused against the administration is due to a lack of information or ignorance on the subject, rather than to any other cause, because the people of this state and the German-Americans in particular have had a very friendly feeling for the administration and, in fact, warmly supported you in the last election. In the fall campaign, I had a special opportunity to note their enthusiastic endorsement of your Mexican policy in keeping this nation out of war.

Mr. Nieman expects to visit Washington within the next four weeks and I expect to accompany him if possible. If you think it worth while, would you kindly suggest with whom we might take up this subject for discussion when we visit Washington?

With assurances of high personal respect and esteem, I remain,   Very truly yours,   Paul O Husting

TLS (WP, DLC).

From the White House Staff

The White House. January 5, 1915.

Miss Mabel Boardman telephoned to ask if the President could see Miss Jane Addams and Miss McDowell[1] of Chicago on Monday next. Miss Addams and Miss McDowell wish to see the President in reference to immigration legislation.

oкeh   W.W.

TL (WP, DLC).
[1] Mary Eliza McDowell, for many years director of the University of Chicago Settlement in the stockyards district of Chicago.

From the Diary of Nancy Saunders Toy

Tuesday. Jan. 5th [1915].

A day brimful of excitement. In the morning Dr. Grayson took Mr. Sayre & myself to the Navy Yard, introduced us to Capt. Berry[1] who took us over the Mayflower and through the gun-building house where nearly all the guns in the Navy are made and afterwards through Capt. Taylor's[2] shop where he builds the models for the battleships—a great genius. At luncheon I told the President of my interview with Maurice Low about Mr. M.'s proposal. "Low would be the very man for that job," said the P. "You may tell Mr. Muirhead that I said so." "Father," objected Margaret, "do you think that would be discreet?" Silence for a moment. Then the P. said quietly, "perhaps not." Another silence which I broke by remarking irrelevantly that I had never heard Tipperary. "I have the record upstairs," said M. "We'll put it on the Victor after lunch." "What! In the White House!" exclaimed Helen. And then I made the biggest *break* of my life. "Who wants to sing Tipperary," the Sun asks, "with Daniels Secretary of the Navy!"[3] I have never seen the President angry before. I never want to see him angry again. His fist came down on the table: "Daniels did *not* give the order that Tipperary should not be sung in the Navy. He is surrounded by a network of conspiracy and of lies. His enemies are determined to ruin him. I can't be sure who they are yet, but when I do get them— God help them."

[1] Lieutenant Commander Robert L. Berry, commanding officer of the presidential yacht *Mayflower*.

[2] David Watson Taylor, chief of the Bureau of Construction and Repair, U.S.N.

[3] In early December 1914, the commandant of the Naval Training Center at Newport, R.I., was reported in the newspapers as having ordered the men in training not to sing the British military song "It's a Long, Long Way to Tipperary." When reporters brought the matter to Daniels's attention on December 5, he denied any knowledge of the affair beyond the newspaper accounts, but opined that it would have been correct for the officer to issue such an order on an "official occasion." *New York Times* and *New York Herald*, Dec. 6, 1914. For Daniels's account of the incident, see Josephus Daniels, *The Wilson Era: Years of Peace—1910-1917* (Chapel Hill, N. C., 1944), pp. 575-77.

Wednesday, Jan. 6th.

At breakfast this morning the President announced that he was to receive a deputation of Suffragists after luncheon. "Suffrage for women," he said, "will make absolutely no change in politics—it is the home that will be disastrously affected. Somebody has to make the home and who is going to do it if the women don't?" At luncheon he read aloud from Gardner an essay on himself[1]—that was *too* delightful. The Suffragists came and went without a crumb of comfort, and I said my goodbyes and went too with many crumbs of comfort.

1 Alfred George Gardiner, *Pillars of Society* (London, 1913), pp. 104-13. Gardiner's brief but lively character sketch was well suited to a dramatic reading. A typical passage follows:

"Mr. Wilson does great things with an extreme economy of effort. His speeches have the quality of acts. . . . It is not that he scorns oratory in its place. It is the instrument through which one touches the general heart to fine issues. But when he comes to business he dismisses rhetoric. He is that rare combination, a thinker who loves action, a scholar and a man of affairs, one who reads Greek and writes shorthand, who combines a luminous idealism with the practicality of a plumber and a sunny smile with a ruthless purpose. His courage mounts to any task; but he has a scrupulous tidiness in small things. When he has finished writing he wipes his pen and puts the cloth back in the drawer. He has great energy; but it is not the boisterous energy of Mr. Roosevelt. It is disciplined. 'After all,' he says, 'life doesn't consist in eternally running to a fire.' He has, what Mr. Chamberlain never had, what Mr. Lloyd George, with all his fine intuitions and democratic sympathies, has not—a considered philosophy of politics. It is a philosophy warmed with a generous humanity and a sincere vision."

Remarks to a Delegation of Democratic Women[1]

January 6, 1915

Mrs. Armes and ladies: I am most unaffectedly complimented by this visit that you have paid me. I have been called on several times to say what my position is in the very important matter that you are so deeply interested in. I want to say that nobody can look on at the fight you are making without great admiration, and I certainly am one of those who admire the tenacity and the skill and the address with which you try to promote the matter that you are interested in. But I, ladies, am tied to a conviction, which I have had all my life, that changes of this sort ought to be brought about state by state. If it were not a matter of female suffrage, if it were a matter of any other thing connected with suffrage, I would hold the same opinion. It is a long-standing and deeply matured conviction on my part, and, therefore, I would be without excuse to my own constitutional principles if I lent my support to this very important movement for an amendment to the Constitution of the United States.

Frankly, I do not think that that is the wise or the permanent way to build. I know that you perhaps unanimously disagree with me, but you will not think the less of me for being perfectly frank in the avowal of my own convictions on that subject; and certainly that avowal represents no attitude of antagonism, but merely an attitude of principle.

I want to say again how much complimented I am by your call and also by the confidence that you have so generously expressed in me, Mrs. Armes. I hope that in some respects I may live to justify that confidence.

T MS (WP, DLC).
[1] A delegation of approximately one hundred women called on Wilson to ask his support for an equal suffrage amendment to the Constitution which was before the House of Representatives. Lucy Hamilton Kerr (Mrs. George A.) Armes, president of the District of Columbia branch of the Wilson and Marshall League, headed the delegation.

To Stephen Seymour Thomas

My dear Mr. Thomas: [The White House] January 6, 1915

The portrait came in perfect order and has been hung in the place which Mrs. Wilson had chosen for it. I hope that everyone will like it as much as I do. It seems to me a stunning piece of work and I know that Mrs. Wilson admired it very much indeed. It will certainly be one of the ornaments of the House.

I am delighted to hear that there is a chance that we should get a glimpse of Mrs. Thomas[1] and you on your way to California. Pray let us know several days in advance so that we may be sure to make a leisure space in which we may really see you.

All unite with me in the warmest good wishes of the season.
                    Cordially and sincerely yours,   Woodrow Wilson

TLS (Letterpress Books, WP, DLC).
[1] Helen Montmorency Haskell Thomas.

To Ralph Adams Cram

My dear Mr. Cram: [The White House] January 6, 1915

May I not thank you very warmly for your generous letter in response to mine?[1] I feel, in view of what you tell me of the conditions existing, almost like chiding myself for suggesting anything to you about finding employment for my friend. I hope you will not make it a burden nor a real obligation, but that you will feel only that any advice you may be able to give or any suggestion that might occur to you would be very acceptable.

It was a real pleasure to hear from you again and I want you to know how sincerely I value the confidence expressed in your letter. A man daily struggling with perplexing questions needs to be heartened in this way and finds the heartening very grateful.
                    Cordially and sincerely yours,   Woodrow Wilson

TLS (Letterpress Books, WP, DLC).
[1] Wilson had written to Cram asking him to help Mrs. Hulbert. Wilson's letter is missing. Cram's letter is R. A. Cram to WW, Jan. 4, 1915, ALS (WP, DLC).

From William Jennings Bryan

My Dear Mr. President: Washington January 6, 1915.

The House Committee on Foreign Affairs is hearing arguments in favor of the Bartholdt resolution[1] and a number of the members of the Committee have called in regard to the Administration's opinion of the resolution. I have told them that any action looking to interference with the right of belligerents to buy arms here would be construed as an unneutral act, not only because the effect of such action would be to assist one party at the expense of the other, but also because the *purpose* of the resolution is plainly to assist one party at the expense of the other. They may make inquiry in regard to your position on the question or the Department's position. Do you think it wise to make any statement yourself or have any statement made by the Department? I have no doubt that the Chairman of the Committee would be glad to ask the opinion either of yourself or of the Department and that the position taken would be controling in the Committee.

With assurances of high respect, I am, my dear Mr. President,
Very sincerely yours,   W. J. Bryan

TLS (WP, DLC).

[1] H.J. Res. 378, introduced by Congressman Richard Bartholdt on December 7, 1914, which prohibited the export of all munitions of war from the territory or any seaport of the United States. *Cong. Record*, 63d Cong., 3d sess., p. 12.

From Newton Diehl Baker

My dear Mr President: Cleveland January 6, 1915

You must be too busy to read all the welter of writing about the War in the magazines and books nowadays, but Lowes Dickinson's "The War and the Way Out," in the December Atlantic, is the product of a mind naturally lucid and by long, high thinking freed from many illusions. I am sure you would enjoy it. The use of armed forces as an international police is of course not a new suggestion but it is put rather more persuasively than I have seen elsewhere. This war would almost be worth while if it could lead to a new Holy Alliance, based on such a policy, and with Prince Metternich and his kind too dead to pervert it as they did the old one.

With the prayer that the New Year will bring you health and peace, believe me   Heartily yours,   Newton D. Baker

ALS (WP, DLC).

To William Jennings Bryan

My dear Mr. Secretary:　　The White House January 7, 1915

I hope that when the opportunity offers you will be kind enough to say to the House Committee on Foreign Affairs that I entirely agree with your judgment that "any action looking to interference with the right of belligerents to buy arms here" taken at the present time "would be construed as an unneutral act." My opinion is very clear, as I think the opinion of everyone must be who is fully cognizant of all the implications that would attend such action.

Cordially and faithfully yours,　Woodrow Wilson

TLS (W. J. Bryan Papers, DNA).

To Mark Sullivan

Personal.

My dear Mr. Sullivan:　　The White House January 7, 1915

I am sincerely glad you brought to my attention what you have been thinking about Mr. Crane.[1] I have the warmest admiration and affection for him.

I would be very glad to head the list of those who wish to present him a portrait of himself.

I doubt whether it would be feasible to get John Sargent, though it may be that just at this time he would welcome an opportunity to get away from the turmoil in Europe. If he cannot be obtained, the best man I know of is Mr. S. Seymour Thomas, who has done some capital work. Mr. Thomas is just about transferring his studio from New York, where he has been for the last year, to San Francisco, but I have no doubt he could be obtained for this purpose.

As for an honorary degree, I have, as you know, lost my standing at Princeton, but I should think it would be entirely proper for you to write to President Lowell of Harvard. The University of Virginia does not give honorary degrees. If you chose, you could in writing to President Lowell refer to me and say that I was very much interested in the matter and would be glad if he would refer to me if he wished to make any inquiries about Mr. Crane in regard to which I could be of service.

Cordially and sincerely yours,　Woodrow Wilson

TLS (M. Sullivan Papers, DLC).
[1] M. Sullivan to WW, Jan. 5, 1915, TLS (WP, DLC).

To John Sharp Williams

Personal.

My dear Senator: [The White House] January 7, 1915
   Thank you for letting me see Mr. Ward's letter about the immigration bill.[1]
   I find myself in a very embarrassing situation about that bill. Nothing is more distasteful to me than to set my judgment against so many of my friends and associates in public life, but frankly stated the situation is this: I myself personally made the most explicit statements at the time of the Presidential election about this subject to groups of our fellow-citizens of foreign extraction whom I wished to treat with perfect frankness and for whom I had entire respect. In view of what I said to them, I do not see how it will be possible for me to give my assent to the bill. I know that you will appreciate the scrup[l]e upon which I act.
              Cordially and sincerely yours,   Woodrow Wilson

TLS (Letterpress Books, WP, DLC).
   [1] J. S. Williams to WW, Jan. 4, 1915, TLS (WP, DLC). WW returned Ward's letter.

To William Joel Stone

My dear Senator: [The White House] January 7, 1915
   Following up our conversation of the other day, I take the liberty of sending you a list of the charges which have been made in various quarters by those who think we have not been dealing fairly with questions of neutrality, charges made chiefly by those who have a very strong sympathy with the cause of Germany and Austria in the existing war.
   I think the plan we agreed upon[1] will be the best way to clear away the mists that have been accumulating around this subject.
       With the warmest regard,
              Faithfully yours,   Woodrow Wilson

TLS (Letterpress Books, WP, DLC).
   [1] It was to have Stone, as chairman of the Foreign Relations Committee, write a letter to Bryan, listing the charges of unneutral acts against the Central Powers; for Bryan to reply; and then to publish their exchange. It was widely printed at the time in question and answer form, e.g., *New York Times*, Jan. 25, 1915. It is reprinted in *FR-WWS 1914*, pp. vi-xiv.

From William Jennings Bryan

My dear Mr. President: Washington January 7, 1915.

The situation in Hayti is still embarassing and we have apparently made no progress.

We came very near making an agreement with Zamor, but, at the last moment he refused and this refusal continued until he was just about to leave the office when it was too late to do anything.

The new man, Theodor, showed some disposition to make an agreement but his Secretary of Foreign Affairs was unfortunate in the language used in their Congress and was roughly treated, and since then matters have been at a standstill.

There is now an insurrection in the north which is making progress toward Port au Prince. The army which Theodor sent out against the insurrectionists went over to the insurrectionists without a fight and it now looks as if Theodor's tenure of office may be brief.

The important matter of interest, however, is the Bank. It is a French institution but the stock is owned largely by Americans—the French being next in influence in the bank. There are some small German holders.

The Bank removed a half-million dollars in gold from the vaults and took it to New York on a U. S. Government ship recently; and the Haytien Government has been trying to get hold of the rest of the money in the Bank. The financial affairs of the country are in bad shape.

I am sending you a copy of the contract which the Bank made with the Government[1] from which you will see that the Bank receives certain exclusive privileges. The Government is threatening to do things in violation of this contract, having already authorized an issue of money, which is contrary to the contract of the Bank. The Bank is attempting to secure some settlement and these negotiations are now going on.

We have instructed the Minister there, Bailly-Blanchard, to look after the protection of the lives of Americans and other foreigners employed in the Bank.

I enclose, with the Bank contract, a memorandum stating what the Bank would like to have done.[2] I believe that there will be no peace and progress in Hayti until we have some such arrangement as we have in Santo Domingo, and, as you remember, we have proposed that to them but have not felt like compelling acceptance of the plan. There is probably sufficient ground for intervention, but I do not like the idea of forcible interferance on purely business grounds.

I would like to know how far you think we ought to go in forcing the Bank's views and interests. If the revolution proceeds it may reach a point where we can propose a plan similar to that adopted in Santo Domingo—namely, send a Commission down there to bring the leaders together into agreement upon a provisional President, with a view of holding an election to be supervised by us—the choice of the people to be recognized and supported, as in Santo Domingo.

This, to be effective, would have to be accompanied by some agreement in regard to customs which seem to be the source of trouble, because an insurrection always aims at the control of as many custom houses as possible, for from these they draw their revenue.

I thought while you were on the train you might find time to read over the enclosures and form an opinion as to the course to be pursued. The success of this Government's efforts in Santo Domingo would, it seems to me, suggest the application of the same methods to Hayti whenever the time is ripe.

The morning paper reports that the Mole St. Nicholas is being used by Germans as a base of supplies. We have not received direct word of this from our Minister. If word is received I take it for granted it will be necessary for us to make some urgent representations and possibly ask for the control of Mole St. Nicholas during the war.

Wishing you a pleasant journey and safe return, with assurances of high respect I am, my dear Mr. President,

Yours very sincerely,   W. J. Bryan

TLS (WP, DLC).
1 This enclosure is missing.
2 "Memorandum re the National Bank of the Republic of Haiti . . . ," printed in FR 1915, pp. 496-98. It described the situation and made no recommendations for action by the United States Government.

Remarks from a Rear Platform in Richmond, Indiana

January 8, 1915.

I haven't made a speech for so long that I fear I don't know how. You know, I have been confined for a couple of years at hard labor and am out on parole for a day or two. I have to hurry back for fear I will forfeit the parole. But I do want to say this, my fellow citizens, that it is a very genuine pleasure to me to get abroad again and stir among the people I so dearly love. Because the one thing we have to think about down in Washington is the best thing to do for you and the thing that you want us to do for you, and that is a mighty hard thing to find out, particularly when you are not thinking about your own affairs and are constantly thinking about what is none of your business, namely, what is going on on the other side of the water. I say that in playfulness, but I mean it half in earnest. It does not do, my friends, to divert our attention from the affairs of this great country. The duty which this country has to perform to the rest of the world largely depends upon the way in which it performs its duty to itself.

I have always thought, with regard to individuals, that if a man was true to himself he would then be true to other persons; and I believe that that applies to a great country like ours—that a nation that is habitually true to its own exalted principles of action will know how to serve the rest of mankind when the opportunity offers. That is a very deep philosophy of life which it is very thoroughly worthwhile living up to. We have a great many things to do in this country that we can do only if we keep our equilibrium, only if we think and speak justly about one another, only if we try to do the just thing from day to day in the daily tasks.

We have been trying at Washington to remove some of the shackles that have been put upon American business; but after you have removed the shackles you must determine what you are going to do with your liberty. And there are many tasks to perform for mankind. There are many things to be bettered in this world, which we must set ourselves to make better. So what I want to say to you now is merely this: Let us seek sober, common counsel about our own affairs, and then, when the time comes when we can act upon a larger field, there will be no mistake as to what America will do for the peace of the world, having found her own peace and having established justice in her own land.

I am sincerely glad to see you. I did not expect to make a speech to you. I am merely giving you in the few words I have uttered what lies deep in my heart.

T MS (WP, DLC).

A Jackson Day Address in Indianapolis

[[Jan. 8, 1915]]

Governor Ralston, ladies, and gentlemen: You have given me a most royal welcome, for which I thank you from the bottom of my heart. It is rather lonely living in Washington. I have been confined for two years at hard labor, and even now I feel that I am simply out on parole. You notice that one of the most distinguished members of the United States Senate[1] is here to see that I go back. And yet, with sincere apologies to the Senate and House of Representatives, I want to say that I draw more inspiration from you than I do from them.

They, like myself, are only servants of the people of the United States. Our sinews consist in your sympathy and support, and our renewal comes from contact with you and with the strong movements of public opinion in this country. That is the reason why I, for one, would prefer that our thoughts should not too often cross the ocean, but should center themselves upon the policies and duties of the United States. If we think of the United States, when the time comes we shall know how this country can serve the world. I will borrow a very interesting phrase from a distinguished gentleman of my acquaintance[2] and beg that you will keep your moral powder dry.

But I have come here on Jackson Day. If there are Republicans present, I hope they will feel the compelling influences of such a day. There was nothing mild about Andrew Jackson; that is the reason I spoke of the "compelling influences of the day." Andrew Jackson was a forthright man, who believed, everything he did believe in, in fighting earnestly. And, really, ladies and gentlemen, in public life, that is the only sort of man worth thinking about for a moment.

If I was not ready to fight for everything I believe in, I would think it my duty to go and take a back seat. I like, therefore, to breathe the air of Jackson Day. I like to be reminded of the old militant hosts of Democracy which I believe have come to life again in our time.

The United States had almost forgotten that it must keep its fighting ardor in behalf of mankind when Andrew Jackson became President; and you will notice that, whenever the United States forgets its ardor for mankind, a Democrat is elected President.

The trouble with the Republican party is that it has not had a new idea for thirty years. I am not speaking as a politician; I am speaking as a historian. I have looked for new ideas in the record, and I haven't found any proceeding from the Republican ranks.

They have had leaders from time to time who suggested new ideas, but they never did anything to carry them out. And I

[1] Senator Kern.
[2] John R. Mott. See C. R. Crane to WW, Jan. 10, 1915, n. 1.

suppose there was no harm in their talking, provided they could not do anything. And, therefore, when it was necessary to say that we had talked about things long enough, which it was necessary to do, and the time had come to do them, it was indispensable that a Democrat should be elected President.

I would not speak with disrespect of the Republican party. I always speak with great respect of the past. The past was necessary to the present, and was a sure prediction of the future. The Republican party is still a covert and a refuge for those who are afraid, for those who want to consult their grandfathers about everything. And you will notice that most of the advice taken by the Republican party is taken from gentlemen old enough to be grandfathers, and that when they claim that a reaction has taken place they react with the re-election of the oldest members of their party. They won't trust the youngsters. They are afraid the youngsters may have something up their sleeves.

You will see, therefore, that I have come to you in the spirit of Jackson Day. I got very tired staying in Washington and saying sweet things. I wanted to come out and get in contact with you once more and say what I really thought.

But, my friends, what I particularly want you to observe is this—that politics in this country does not depend any longer upon the regular members of either party. There are not enough regular Republicans in this country to take and hold national power; and I must immediately add there are not enough regular Democrats in this country to do it, either. This country is guided and its policy is determined by the independent voter; and I have come to ask you how we can best prove to the independent voter that the instrument he needs is the Democratic party, and that it would be hopeless for him to attempt to use the Republican party. I do not have to prove it; I admit it.

What it seems to me is perfectly evident is this—that, if you made a rough reckoning, you would have to admit that only about one third of the Republican party is progressive; and you would also have to admit that about two thirds of the Democratic party is progressive. Therefore, the independent progressive voter finds a great deal more company in the Democratic ranks than in the Republican ranks.

I say a great deal more because there are Democrats who are sitting on the breeching strap; there are Democrats who are holding back. There are Democrats who are afraid. I dare say they were born that way. It is their temperament. And I understand and respect the conservative temperament. I claim to be an animated conservative myself, because, by a conservative I understand to mean a man not only who preserves what is best, but who sees that, in order to preserve it, you dare not stand still, but must move forward. For the virtue of America is not statical; it is dynamic. All the forces of America are forces in action or else they are first forces of inertia—

(Governor Ralston: "Ladies and gentlemen, I appeal to you in the rear part of the hall to keep quiet. It is too difficult for the President to speak, and we shall have to clear the outside hall if quiet is not preserved.")

I have no doubt the gentlemen out there have just as interesting things to say as I have, but it would be just as well if it were one at a time.

What I want to point out to you—and what I believe that this whole country is beginning to perceive—is this: That there is a larger body of men in the regular ranks of the Democratic party who believe in the progressive policies of our day, and mean to see them carried forward and perpetuated, than there is in the ranks of the Republican party. How can it be otherwise, gentlemen? The Democratic party, and only the Democratic party, has carried out the policies which the progressive people of this country have desired.

There is not a single great act of this present great Congress which has not been carried out in obedience to the public opinion of America, and the public opinion of America is not going to permit any body of men to go backward with regard to these great matters.

Let me instance a single thing: I want to ask the businessmen here present if this is not the first January in their recollection that didn't bring a money stringency for the time being because of the necessity of paying out great sums of money by way of dividends and the other settlements which come at the first of the year. I have asked bankers if that happened this year, and they say, "No; it did not happen; it could not happen under the Federal Reserve Act." We have emancipated the credits of this country. And is there anybody here who will doubt that the other policies that have given guarantees to this country that there will be free competition are policies which this country will ever allow to be reversed?

I have taken a long time, ladies and gentlemen, to select the Federal Trade Commission, because I wanted to choose men, and be sure that I had chosen men, who would be really serviceable to the businessmen of this country, great as well as small, the rank and file. These things have been done, and will never be undone. They were talked about, and talked about with futility, until a Democratic Congress attempted and achieved them.

But the Democratic party is not to suppose that it is done with the business. The Democratic party is still on trial. The Democratic party has to prove to the independent voters of this country, not only that it believes in these things, but that it will continue to work along these lines, and that it will not allow any enemy of these things to break its ranks. This country is not going to use any party that can not do continuous and consistent teamwork. If any group of men should dare to break the solidarity of the Democratic team for any purpose or from any motive, theirs will be a most unenviable notoriety and a responsibility which will bring deep bitterness to them. The only party that is serviceable to a nation is a party that can hold absolutely together and march with the discipline and with the zest of a conquering host.

I am not saying these things because I doubt that the Democratic party will be able to do these things, but because I believe that, as leader for the time being of that party, I can promise the country that it will do these things. I know my colleagues at Washington; I know their spirit and their purpose; and I know that they have the same emotions, the same high emotions as to public service that I have.

I want at this juncture to pay my tribute of respect and of affectionate admiration for the two great Democratic senators from the State of Indiana.[3] I have never had to lie awake of nights wondering what they were going to do. And the country is not going to trouble itself, ladies and gentlemen, to lie awake nights and wonder what men are going to do. If they have to do that, they will choose other men, and that is the whole of the business. Teamwork all the time is what they are going to demand of us, and that is our individual as well as our collective responsibility. That is what Jackson stands for. If a man will not play in the team, then he does not belong to the team. You see, I have spent a large part of my life in college, and I know what a team means when I see it; and I know what the captain of a team must have if he is going to win. So it is not an idle figure with me.

Now, what is there to do? You say, "Has not this Congress carried out a great program?" Yes, it has carried out a great program. It has the most remarkable record that any Congress since the Civil War has had; and I say since the Civil War be-

---

[3] Kern and Benjamin Franklin Shively.

cause I haven't had time to think about those before the Civil
War. But we are living at an extraordinary moment. The world
has never been in the condition that it is now, my friends. Half
the world is on fire. Only America among the great powers of the
world is free to govern her own life; and all the world is looking
to America to serve its economic needs; and while this is happening, what is going on?

Do you know, gentlemen, that the ocean freight rates have
gone up in some instances to ten times their ordinary figure, and
that the farmers of the United States—those who raise grain
and those who raise cotton, those things that are absolutely
necessary to the world as well as to ourselves—cannot get any
profit out of the great prices that they are willing to pay for
these things on the other side of the sea, because the whole
profit is eaten up by the extortionate charges for ocean carriage?
And in the midst of this, the Democrats proposed a temporary
measure of relief in the shipping bill.

The merchants and the farmers of this country must have
ships to carry their goods, and, just at the present moment, there
is no other way of getting them than through the instrumentality
that is suggested in that shipping bill. And I hear it said in Washington on all hands that the Republicans in the United States
Senate mean to talk enough to make the passage of that bill impossible.

These self-styled friends of business, these men who say the
Democratic party does not know what to do for business, are
saying that the Democrats shall do nothing for business. I challenge them to show their right to stand in the way of the release
of American products to the rest of the world. Who commissioned them, a minority, a lessening minority? For they will be
in a greater minority in the next Senate than in this. You know,
it is the peculiarity of that great body that it has rules of procedure which make it possible for a minority to defy the nation.
And these gentlemen are now seeking to defy the nation and
prevent the release of American products to the suffering world,
which needs them more than it ever needed them before. Their
credentials as friends of business and friends of America will
be badly discredited if they succeed.

If I were speaking from a selfish, partisan point of view, I
should wish nothing better than that they could show their true
colors as partisans and succeed. But I am not quite so malevolent
as that. Some of them are misguided; some of them are blind;
most of them are ignorant. I would rather pray for them than
abuse them. But the great voice of America ought to make them

understand what they are said to be attempting to do now. I say they are "said to be attempting," because they do not come out and tell me what they are attempting. I don't know why. I would express my opinion of them in parliamentary language; I would express it, I hope, none the less plainly because couched in terms of courtesy. This country is bursting and gasping, and they are seeing to it that its jacket is not only kept tight, but is riveted with steel.

Now, the Democratic party does know how to serve business in this country, and its future program is a program of service. We have cleared the deck. We have laid the lines now upon which business that was doing the country harm shall be stopped and the economic control which was intolerable shall be broken up. We have emancipated America, but America must do something with her freedom. There are great bills pending in the United States Senate just now that have been passed by the House of Representatives, which are intended as constructive measures in behalf of business—one great measure which will make available the enormous water powers of this country for the industries of the country; another bill which will unlock the resources of the public domain, which the Republicans desire to save locked up so that nobody could use them.

The reason I say the Republicans have not had a new idea in thirty years is that they have not known how to do anything except sit on the lid. Now, if you can release the steam so it will drive great industries, it is not necessary to sit on the lid. And what we are trying to do in the great conservation bill is to carry out for the first time in the history of the United States a system by which the great resources of the country can be used, instead of being set aside so that no man can get at them. I shall watch with a great deal of interest what the self-styled friends of business try to do with these bills.

Now, don't misunderstand me. There are some men on that side of the chamber who understand the value of these things and are standing valiantly by them, but they are a small minority. The majority that is standing by them is on our side of the chamber, and they are the friends of America. But there are other things we have to do.

Sometimes, when I look abroad, my friends, and see the great mass of struggling humanity on this continent it goes very much to my heart to see how many men are at a disadvantage and are without guides and helpers. Don't you think it would be a pretty good idea for the Democratic party to undertake a systematic method of helping the workingmen of America? There is a very simple way in which they could help the workingmen. If we were simply to establish a great federal employment bureau, it would do a great thing. By the federal agencies which spread all over this country, men could be directed to those parts of the country, to those undertakings, to those tasks where they could find profitable employment. The laborer of this country needs to be guided from opportunity to opportunity.

Just the other day, we were told that in two states of the Union, 30,000 men were needed to gather the crops. It was suggested in a cabinet meeting that the Department of Labor should have printed information about this in such form that it could be posted up in the postoffices all over the United States, and that the Department of Labor should get in touch with the labor departments of the states, so that notice could go out from them.

What was the result? Those 30,000 men were found, and were sent to places where they got profitable employment. I don't know of any one thing that has happened in my administration that made me feel happier than that—that the job and the man had been brought together. Now, it won't cost a great deal of money, and it will do a great deal of service if the United States were to undertake to do such things systematically, and all the year round; and I, for my part, hope that it will do that. If I were writing an additional plank for the Democratic platform, I would put that in.

And there is another thing that needs very much to be done. I am not one of those who doubts either the industry or the learning or the integrity of the courts of the United States, but I do know that they have a very antiquated way of doing business.

I do know that the United States, in its judicial procedure, is many decades behind every other civilized government in the world; and I say that it is an immediate and an imperative call upon us to rectify that, because the speediness of justice, the inexpensiveness of justice, the ready access to justice, is the greater part of justice itself.

If you have to be rich to get justice, because of the cost of the process itself, then there is no justice at all. And so I say there is another direction in which we ought to be very quick to see the signs of the times and help those who need to be helped.

Then, there is something else. The Democrats have heard the Republicans talk about the scientific way in which to handle the tariff, though the Republicans have never given any exhibition of a knowledge of how to handle it scientifically. If it is scientific to put additional profits into the hands of those who are already getting the greater part of the profits, then they have been exceedingly scientific. It has been a science of selfishness; it has been a science of privilege.

But that kind of science I do not care to know anything about, except enough to stop it. But if by scientific treatment of the tariff they mean adjustment to the actual trade conditions of America and the world, then I am with them; and I want to call their attention, as they apparently have not noticed it, to the fact that the bill which creates the new trade commission does that very thing. We were at pains to see that it was put in there. That commission is authorized and empowered to inquire into and report to Congress, not only upon the conditions of trade in this country, but upon the conditions of trade, the cost of manufacture, the cost of transportation—all the things that enter into the question of the tariff—in foreign countries as well as in the United States, and into all those questions of foreign combinations which affect international trade between Europe and the United States. It has full powers which will guide Congress in the scientific treatment of questions of international trade. Being by profession a schoolmaster, I am glad to point that out to a class of uninstructed Republicans, though I had not always taught in the primary grades.

At every turn, the things that the Republicans, that is, the progressive Republicans, have proposed that were practical, the Democrats either have done or are immediately proposing to do. If that is not a bill of particulars to satisfy the independent voters of the country, I would like to have one produced. There are things that the Progressive program contains which we, being constitutional lawyers, happened to know cannot be done by the Congress of the United States. That is a detail which they seem to have overlooked. But so far as they can be done by state legislation, I, for one, speaking for one Democrat, am heartily in favor of their being done, because Democrats do not congregate merely in Washington. They congregate also in the state capitals, and they congregate there in very influential numbers and with very influential organizations.

Just before I came away from Washington, I was going over some of the figures of the last elections, the elections of November last. The official returns have not all come in yet. I don't know why they are so slow in getting to us, but, so far as they have come in, they have given me this useful information—that, taking the states where senators were elected and where senators were not elected; taking the election of governors, and where governors were not elected; taking the returns for the state legislatures; or for the congressional delegations—the Democrats, reckoning state by state, would, if it had been a presidential year, have had a majority of about eighty in the Electoral College.

Fortunately or unfortunately, this is not a presidential year, but the thing is significant to me for this reason. A great many people have been speaking of the Democratic party as a minority party. Well, if it is, it is not so much a minority party as the Republican party, and, as between minorities, I think we can claim to belong to the larger minority. The moral of that is merely what I have already been pointing out to you—that neither party, in its regular membership, has a majority. Now, I don't want to make the independent voter too proud of himself, but I have to admit that he is our boss, and I am bound to admit that the things he wants are, so far as I have seen them mentioned, things that I want.

I am not an independent voter, but I hope I can claim to be an independent person; and I want to say this distinctly: I do not love any party any longer than it continues to serve the immediate and pressing needs of America. I have been bred in the Democratic party, I love the Democratic party, but I love America a great deal more than I love the Democratic party. When a party thinks it is an end in itself, then I rise up and dissent.

It is a means to the end, and its power depends, and ought to depend, on its showing that it knows what America needs and is ready to give it what it needs. That is the reason I say to the independent voter: "You have got us in the palm of your hand. I do not happen to be one of your number, but I recognize your supremacy because I read the election returns." And I have this ambition, my Democratic friends—I can avow it on Jackson Day: I want to make every independent voter of this country a Democrat. It is a little cold and lonely out where he is, because, though he holds the balance of power, he is not the majority, and I want him to come in where it is warm. I want him to come in where there is a lot of good society, good companionship, where there are great emotions. That is what I miss in the Republican party; they don't seem to have any great emotions. They seem to think a lot of things, old things, but they don't seem to have any enthusiasm about anything.

Now, there is one thing that I have a great enthusiasm about— I might almost say a reckless enthusiasm—and that is human liberty. The governor has just now spoken about watchful waiting in Mexico. I want to say a word about Mexico, not so much about Mexico as about our attitude toward Mexico. I hold it as a fundamental principle, and so do you, that every people has the right to determine its own form of government; and, until this recent revolution in Mexico, until the end of the Díaz reign, 80 per cent of the people of Mexico never had a "look-in" in determining who should be their governors or what their government should be. Now, I am for the 80 per cent. It is none of my business, and it is none of your business, how long they take in determining it. It is none of my business, and it is none of yours, how they go about the business. The country is theirs. The government is theirs. The liberty, if they can get it, and Godspeed them in getting it, is theirs. And, so far as my influence goes while I am President, nobody shall interfere with them.

That is what I mean by a great emotion of sympathy. Do you suppose that the American people are ever going to count a small amount of material benefit and advantage to people doing business in Mexico against the liberties and the permanent happiness of the Mexican people? Haven't European nations taken as long as they wanted and spilt as much blood as they pleased in settling their affairs, and shall we deny that to Mexico because she is weak? No, I say! I am proud to belong to a strong nation that says: "This country, which we could crush, shall have just as much freedom in her own affairs as we have. If I am strong, I am ashamed to bully the weak. In proportion to my strength is my pride in withholding that strength from the oppression of another people." And I know when I speak these things—not merely from the generous response which they have just called from you, but from my long-time knowledge of the American people—that that is the sentiment of the American people.

With all due respect to editors of great newspapers, I have to say to them that I never take my opinions of the American people from their editorials. So that, when some great daily not very far from where I am temporarily residing, thundered with rising scorn against watchful waiting, Woodrow sat back in his chair and chuckled, knowing that he laughs best who laughs last—knowing, in short, what were the temper and the principles of the American people. If I did not at least think that I knew, I would emigrate, because I would not be fit to stay where I am. There may come a time when the American people will have to judge whether I know what I am talking about or not. I didn't intend to start anything then. That was merely prefatory to saying that at least for two years more I know what I am talking about. And there is great comfort in the thought that the next Congress of the United States is going to be very safely Democratic, and that, therefore, we can altogether feel as much confidence as Jackson did. Then we know what we are about. You know, Jackson used to think that every man who disagreed with him was an enemy of the country. I have never gone quite that far in my thoughts, but I have ventured to think that they didn't know what they were talking about, knowing that my fellow Democrats expected me to live up to the full stature of Jackson's Democracy.

And so I feel, my friends, in a very confident mood today. I feel confident that we do know the spirit of the American people, that we do know the program of betterment which it will be necessary for us to undertake, that we do have a very reasonable confidence in the support of the American people.

I have been talking with businessmen recently about the present state of mind of American business. There is nothing the matter with American business except a state of mind. I understand that your chamber of commerce here in Indianapolis is working now upon the motto, "If you are going to buy it, buy it now." That is a perfectly safe maxim to act upon. It is just as safe to buy it now as it ever will be, and if you start the buying there will be no end to it, and you will be a seller as well as a buyer. I am just as sure of that as I can be, because I have taken counsel with men who know. I never was in business, and therefore I have none of the prejudices of business. But I have looked on and tried to see what the interests of the country were in business, and I have taken counsel with men who did know; and their counsel is uniform—that all that is needed in America now is to believe in the future. And I can assure you, as one of those who speak for the Democratic party, that it is perfectly safe to believe in the future.

We are so much the friends of business that we were for a little time the enemies of those who were trying to control business. I say for a little time, because we are now reconciled. They have graciously admitted that we had the right to do what we did, and they have very handsomely said that they were going to play the game.

I believe, and I always have believed, that American businessmen were absolutely sound at heart, but men immersed in business do a lot of things that opportunity offers to do which in other circumstances they would not do. And I have thought all along that all that was necessary to do was to call their attention sharply to the kind of reforms in business that were necessary, and that they would acquiesce, and I believe that they have heartily acquiesced. And there is all the more reason, therefore, why we should be confident in the future. And what a future it is, my friends!

Look abroad upon the troubled world! Only America at peace.

Among all the great powers of the world, only America is saving her power for her own people! Only America is using her great character and her great strength in the interests of peace and of prosperity!

Do you not think it likely that the world will some time turn to America and say: "You were right, and we were wrong. You kept your heads when we lost ours; you tried to keep the scale from tipping, but we threw the whole weight of arms in one side of the scale. Now, in your self-possession, in your coolness, in your strength, may we not turn to you for counsel and for assistance"?

Think of the deep-wrought destruction of economic resources, of life, and of hope that is taking place in some parts of the world, and think of the reservoir of hope, the reservoir of energy, the reservoir of sustenance that there is in this great land of plenty. May we not look forward to the time when we shall be called blessed among the nations, because we succored the nations of the world in their time of distress and of dismay?

I, for one, pray God that that solemn hour may come, and I know the solidity of character, I know the exaltation of hope, I know the high principle with which the American people will respond to the call of the world for this service. And I thank God that those who believe in America, who try to serve her people, are likely to be also what America herself from the first intended to be—the servant of mankind.[4]

Printed in *Cong. Record*, 63d Cong., 3d sess., pp. 1279-82 (a CLS transcript); with numerous corrections from the complete text in the *Indianapolis News*, Jan. 9, 1915.

[4] There are WWsh notes for and a WWT outline of this address, both dated Jan. 8, 1915, in WP, DLC.

From Edward Mandell House

Dear Governor: New York City. January 8th, 1915.

I have a letter from Brown [Spring Rice] which is partly in cypher but which translated reads:

"I have now received the answer from E.G. who is very much obliged for your message. He said before that the main thing was security and that Jones [Bernstorff] had authority to say what he did. Unfortunately, careful enquiry and especially news brought back lately by American travellers on the Continent, show without any question that these so called offers were not sincere, and indeed, have been publicly and emphatically repudiated quite lately in the highest quarters.

The only result of entering into any sort of conversations on this subject would be to expose all concerned to a very humiliating rebuff. Texas [England] is singled out for especial attacks of a most virulent character and hopes are now being held out that Texas and the United States will fall out to the benefit of Maine [Germany].

Were there any hopes of a good, satisfactory and durable settlement he could consult his friends about the question, but at present, the only result would be to add to the bitterness which is already so bad.[1]

Please let me know when you will be here."

I wish to call your attention to the second sentence in which he says that the main thing is security that Jones had authority to say what he did. If Zimmermann replies to my letter favorably, then we will have word from the Government of Maine itself, which would surely answer this objection.

You will notice also that E.G. says that if there were any hopes of a satisfactory and durable settlement, he would consult his friends.

It is now clearly up to us to get something definite from Maine and then we can test the sincerity of Texas. What they say about American travellers, seems to me puerile and is hardly worthy of being used as an argument in a matter as momentous as this.

I have a feeling that things will perhaps move more rapidly soon and that something sufficiently definite will develop by January 30th to warrant my leaving on that date.

I am wondering whether or not you have seen the Senate Foreign Relations Committee upon the other matter.[2] As soon as I hear that you have, I will come to Washington to go along with it further.   Affectionately yours,   E. M. House

TLS (WP, DLC).
[1] Spring Rice was paraphrasing E. Grey to C. A. Spring Rice, Jan. 2, 1915, T telegram (E. Grey Papers, FO 800/85, pp. 17-18, PRO).
[2] The proposed Pan-American treaty.

From William Jennings Bryan

My Dear Mr. President: Washington January 9, 1915.

I enclose a statement[1] which, with your approval, I will give out to the press, in regard to the demands made upon us to protest against the invasion of Belgium by Germany. Mr. Lansing prepared a memorandum to which I made some amendments and this statement is the result of our conference on the subject.

If you will return Mr. Lansing's letter and this statement with such corrections as you wish to make, I will give the statement out early next week.

With assurances of high respect, I am, my dear Mr. President,
Very sincerely yours, W. J. Bryan

TLS (SDR, RG 59, 763.72111/1396½, DNA).
1 Robert Lansing, "*Proposed Statement for the Press*," T MS dated Jan. 9, 1915 (SDR, RG 59, 763.72111/1396½, DNA). It was a legalistic argument to the effect that the United States had no obligation under The Hague Conventions to protest against Germany's violation of Belgian neutrality. Wilson made a few literary changes. The memorandum is printed in *FR-LP*, I, 189-90.

From Franklin Knight Lane

My dear Mr. President: Washington January 9, 1915.

That was a bully speech, a corker! You may have made a better speech in your life but I never have heard of it. Other Presidents may have made better speeches but I have never heard of them. It was simply great because it was the proper blend of philosophy and practicality. It had punch in every paragraph. The country will respond to it splendidly. It was jubilant, did not contain a single minor note of apology and the country will visualize you at the head of the column. You know, this country and every country wants a man to lead it of whom it is proud, not because of his talent but because of his personality,—that which is as indefinable as charm in a woman, and I want to see your personality known to the American people just as well as we know it who sit around the Cabinet table. Your speech glows with it, and that is why it gives me such joy that I can't help writing you as enthusiastically as I do.

Sincerely yours, Franklin K. Lane

TLS (WP, DLC).

From Edward Mandell House

Dear Governor: New York City. January 9th, 1915.

That was a splendid, militant, democratic speech that you made at Indianapolis yesterday and it will do great good.

I have heard many comments upon it already and it has put your followers into a better frame of mind than they have been for a long time. Affectionately yours, E. M. House

TLS (WP, DLC).

From the Diary of Chandler Parsons Anderson

January 9, 1915.

Met the President at the White House, Executive Offices, at
5.15 p.m. by appointment, for a conference with regard to my
views about the various international questions arising out of
the war affecting the United States. After some conversation
about personal matter, I told him that on the eve of my departure
from London Sir Edward Grey had made certain statements to
me with the view of having them repeated to the President in
an informal way, and without committing them to writing. With
the President's permission I reproduced from memory as accu-
rately as the lapse of time would permit, the chief points mentioned by Sir Edward Grey as follows: He had expressed himself
emphatically as of the opinion that the time had not yet come
for peace overtures or even the discussion of possible terms of
peace, nevertheless, he had no objection to having it known by
the President that certain essential points would undoubtedly be
insisted upon by the Allies, assuming that they were in a position to insist at the end of the war. At the head of the list was
reparation for Belgium so far as reparation was possible, and
how that could be accomplished was a question which had not
yet been worked out. So far as the other Allies were concerned,
Great Britain wanted nothing but would hope to find some way
of relieving herself of the increasing burden of naval expenditures. I gathered from what he said that this meant the elimination of the German fleet, if that were not already accomplished
during the progress of the war, and possibly a general international program for disarmament. He spoke of having the United
States undertake the police work of Europe. Nothing was said
about recompense for the British Colonies, but I understood that
he intended to speak for the whole Empire. France, he said,
would require the restoration of Alsace and Lorraine and a money
indemnity. What more, if anything, would be required, he did
not say. I had spoken with Sir Edward of the possibility that
some difficulty would be presented in transferring both of these
provinces to France on account of the germanization of Lorraine
since 1871, and that this might renew instead of removing the
sore spot in European politics. I had asked if it might not be
possible to put the province of Lorraine on the footing of Lux-
emburg, or else permit the population of the province to decide
their political future by popular vote. Sir Edward Grey said that
those suggestions would require consideration. The President at
this point said that he had felt that in making terms of peace it

would be unwise for the belligerents to reproduce under any new arrangement a situation similar to that presented by Alsace-Lorraine and my suggestion about how this might be avoided seemed to meet with his approval. Russia, Sir Edward Grey said, would desire Constantinople and the Dardanelles. He did not say that Great Britain had agreed to this, but he left it to be understood that she would. Whether or not any understanding had already been reached among the Allies with regard to terms of peace was not stated, but he said that the tri-partite agreement between Great Britain, France, and Russia that neither one of them would conclude or even discuss terms of peace with their enemies independently of the others, which was made on September 5, 1914, and subsequently adhered to by Japan and Servia, had been proposed and requested by Russia, and not by Great Britain as was commonly supposed. The President expressed much interest on these points, and said in regard to Constantinople that he had anticipated that it would either be neutralized or would be taken by Russia, and that in his opinion Great Britain's traditional policy against permitting Russia access to the Mediterranean was based on theoretical rather than practical dangers to British interests.

I stated to the President that Sir Edward Grey had not expressed any view as to what Japan would wish, but I gathered from what he said that it was the desire of the British Government to localize Japanese activities in order to keep down the bill which they might present at the close of the war, and that this view had been confirmed by the great satisfaction expressed in official circles of Great Britain that the German fleet off the Falkland Islands had been defeated by the British fleet without the assistance of the Japanese fleet, about which there was some doubt when the news was first received. In this connection the President spoke of the Japanese official statement that in taking Kiao-Chow their intention was not to hold it indefinitely, and he asked if I had any information as to the views of the British Government on that subject. I told him that Sir Edward Grey had said nothing about that, but I recalled that either in Parliament or in some public discussion of the question, it was stated that Japan by the terms of that statement had not precluded itself from changing its position if changed conditions later gave ground for it. The President said that he remembered that this aspect of the situation had also been called to his attention. Nothing was said about Servia, or the Balkan States or Italy, except that I told him that I had been positively informed by a member of an international banking house, whose name I mentioned, and who had authorized me to make use of the information in a confidential way, that a loan was being negotiated for the Italian Government in London and the United States, and that one of its essential terms was a written assurance that Italy would come into the war on the side of the Allies early in the present year, and that the same was true about Roumania. We spoke of the effect of this, in relieving some of the difficulties with regard to trade between the United States and Italy, and that brought us to the general question of the interference by Great Britain with American trade.

I told the President that Sir Edward Grey had made one statement upon this point which he said could not be made officially, and would have to be left to its own inherent probability for its justification, and that was that the Danish Government was becoming very apprehensive that Denmark might be involved in the war by reason of the enormous quantity of war material which was being sent into Denmark and which was greatly in excess of the requirements of that country, and all of which was greatly desired by Germany. The same situation in a lesser degree was developing in Holland. The danger was that the time would come when Germany would say to these countries that inasmuch as they had on hand more of these materials than they could possibly use for their own purposes, it was an unfriendly act on their part to refuse their exportation to Germany; that pressure would be brought upon them to remove the embargo against reexportation under which Great Britain had permitted these supplies to be imported into these countries, and that these countries might find it impossible to refuse Germany's demand without being forced into war. The President admitted that this situation presented a very interesting and difficult question. I explained to him that the situation had grown up from the position our Government had taken with regard to trade in war materials in neutral countries, and that if the result above suggested did come about, Great Britain would feel that we were in large measure responsible for that result. I pointed out briefly that the negotiations between the United States and Great Britain about our trade in contraband had developed along the following lines: The United States had at first insisted that Great Britain should adopt the Declaration of London as the law governing the subject during this war; that Great Britain had refused for reasons which our Government had finally admitted were justifiable; that Great Britain had insisted that under the special conditions prevailing in this war, it was impossible to rely on precedents because in Germany all material and supplies available for military uses were in effect under the control of the Government; in other words, that the entire population of Germany was organized into a military system; that for this reason Great Britain felt justified in treating as absolute contraband certain classes of supplies which under other circumstances might be regarded as conditional contraband, and in applying the doctrine of continuous voyage and ultimate destination to conditional contraband going to neutral countries contiguous to the belligerents; and furthermore that Great Britain felt that under these circumstances there was no difference in principle between seizing contraband consigned directly to Germany and contraband either absolute or conditional consigned to neutral countries adjoining Germany in the absence of proof or a guarantee that such supplies would not be exported from that country to Germany. The United States joined issue with Great Britain on these contentions as a matter of international law, with the result that the seizure and detention of all such cargoes was made the subject of claims for damages by the United States. Then and in order to avoid any unnecessary interference with American trade with neutral countries, Great Britain entered into separate arrangements with the neutral countries through which it was feared the contraband trade was reaching Germany, which agreements provided that an embargo should be adopted preventing the exportation of such articles to Germany. Under this arrangement Great Britain hoped to be able to discontinue any further interference with all cargoes consigned to these countries, but in order to make this plan effective in relieving interference with American trade, the cooperation of the United States was necessary on three points: First, that all shipments should be fully and completely listed in the ship's manifest; second, that shipments should be consigned in such a way that they could not be diverted from neutral countries, and third, that the United States Treasury Order adopted at the beginning of the war prohibiting the giving of any information about the character of shipments until thirty days after the departure of the vessel, should be revoked. As regard the last point, I explained that the revocation of this order would be equally to the advantage of American and British interest because the lack of information about shipments made it necessary for Great Britain to stop and search all vessels, whereas full information would in most cases avoid such delay.

The President said that on my presentation of the situation there were no very important questions of principle involved in the differences between the two Governments because our objections were directly [directed] chiefly against the manner in which Great Britain was interfering with neutral trade rather than against the right of Great Britain to exercise the supervision which she claimed over commerce with the enemy. I said that this was the case at the present time, and that our objections would very largely be met by better administrative methods on the part of Great Britain in enforcing the rights which they asserted. I said further that even if we did not agree as to what those rights were, the only practical question was the recovery of damages for losses suffered in consequence of illegal interference by Great Britain, and that there were very few cases in which we could properly take up the question of damages before the prize court had acted, and that the prize court itself had jurisdiction to award damages in all cases in which the seizure was held to be improper. In any event we must recognize that even if an important difference in principle should arise the question of what was the correct rule of international law must be settled either by agreement or failing that, by arbitration, inasmuch as such questions of difference were of a legal nature and under our general arbitration treaty with Great Britain, we had agreed to submit to arbitration all questions of a legal nature which it may not be possible to settle by diplomacy.

I then reminded the President of the points made by me in my memorandum of October 21st last, indicating the policy which I thought should be adopted in dealing with this situation,[1] a copy of which memorandum was forwarded to him by Mr. Page at that time. The President did not recall this memorandum, and I restated some of the points which in the memorandum are stated as follows:[2]

The President said that of course where the difference was one involving a question of a legal nature, that all we could do was to submit the question to judicial decision, and that for this reason he had publicly stated in commenting upon the recent

[1] "Memorandum of reasons why the United States should acquiesce without protest but reserving all rights in regard to Great Britain's interference with shipments from the United States to neutral countries of supplies available for war purposes, the ultimate destination of which is Germany," dated Oct. 21, 1914, T MS (C. P. Anderson Papers, DLC). As the title suggests, Anderson followed the line of argument presented in the above diary entry, stressing the point that virtually all goods destined for Germany were in effect war materials and that, in any case, Great Britain had too much at stake in the conflict to permit such materials to reach Germany by any means whatever. He also warned that, if the United States made a "quarrel" with Great Britain over this subject, it "would lose not merely its extraordinary opportunity for usefulness as a peacemaker when that time comes, but also the opportunity of working in close friendship and harmony with Great Britain in the reorganization of world influences which will follow this war."

[2] Here follows a blank space.

note of protest (December 24 [26], 1914) to Great Britain, that the course pursued by Great Britain was furnishing the grounds for a demand for very large damages in the future.

I said in regard to protests, that it seemed to me that one distinction which had not been made, but perhaps might be made with advantage, was the difference between the public interests and the private interests involved in this situation. So far as the private interests were concerned, they consisted of the trade of American citizens based upon war conditions dealing largely in contraband, which Great Britain was determined to keep out of Germany and Austria, and as pointed out in my memorandum, Great Britain would not desist from stopping that sort of trade even at the risk of a quarrel with us, and all that we could hope to accomplish in cases of seizure and detention was to miminize [minimize] the loss so far as possible, and lay the foundation for a claim for damages on behalf of the American shippers; that Great Britain was entirely ready to admit without protest or formal objection on our part in each case, that whatever rights the United States had under the rules of international law should be understood as reserved without prejudice for future adjustment by agreement or judicial decision; and that in accomplishing this, we would accomplish everything that could be done at present on behalf of the private interests. Having done this, we were free to consider our future course with reference primarily to public interest, in distinction from private interests, and that national interests would best be served by reserving all disputed questions for future settlement, instead of trying to force an immediate acceptance of our theory of the law, by threatening our displeasure and unfriendly action at a time when Great Britain was fighting for national existence. Such a position might easily involve us in a quarrel with Great Britain, and certainly would have important consequences after the war. Moreover we should go slow in establishing precedents which would be prejudicial if applied to ourselves hereafter as a belligerent instead of as a neutral. The President apparently agreed to all of this, and said that although he had not been able to devote his personal attention to the details of carrying out the policy of this Government, he felt that the policy he had laid down was exactly in accordance with the views I had expressed, and that if there were any instances which could be pointed out by me or by the American Embassy in London, in which that policy was not being followed, he hoped that Mr. Page and I would not hesitate to discuss them freely with the Department of State.

Incidently, during the course of the discussion, I told him that Sir Edward Grey had made a very interesting comment on the effect of the war on the internal governmental situation in the several countries involved. He had said that up to this time capital had ruled the world; that this war showed that the capitalists had made a mess of it, and that capital itself was being destroyed to such an extent that it had practically disappeared and would have to be recreated before it could play its former part in the economical subdivisions of the state; that being so, he predicted that when the war was over, labor might rule in place of capital, and would take control of the state in order to provide employment for itself. The President said that this point of view was exceedingly interesting to him, and had not occurred to him, but that on first impressions, it seemed to be in line with our own form of democratic government where the people were the ruling power. I told him further that Sir Edward Grey had expressed the hope that this would be the outcome in Germany, because a more democratic form of Government there was greatly to be desired, as an effective protection against a continuance of Germany's present military policy.

In response to some questions by the President, I gave him an account of the impressions gathered during my trip and of the general conditions in the belligerent countries which I had visited. I told him among other things that so far as I had been able to observe, Germany was not short of food, and probably would not be, although I thought that conditions were otherwise in Austria. I also said that I thought the war would be over before the middle of this summer, and that the Allies would win.

T bound diary (C. P. Anderson Papers, DLC).

To Mary Allen Hulbert

Dearest Friend,   The White House 10 January, 1915.

If you will send on to me the omitted receipts that you meant to put into the little article you sent me, I will have them inserted and copied with the rest on a typewriter, and I will then send it to Mr. Bok, of the Ladies' Home Journal and ask him to give it his personal attention.[1] I have had my own articles rejected too often to predict what he will say or do about it; but I think he ought to accept it and I hope with all my heart he will. You have evidently been too shy to let yourself *go* in writing it, and it lacks the personal touch which I am sure you could give it, if you were not afraid to try; but it ought to commend itself to an editor who really wishes to help beginning hostesses. It was no burden at all to go through it, of course. I am more than glad to help in any way I can. God knows there are few enough ways in which I can! And *please* do not think that you could ever write too often or too long letters! They bring me a certain sort of subtle pain, because I can read between their lines and see just how and how much you are suffering, in spite of the fine spirit that keeps you up. I can see the excitement, of distress, of uncertainty, of plans that will not yet form themselves, of fear lest you will not be equal to the ordeal, and, more than that, that Allen will suffer more than your mother's heart likes to think of. I sympathize with all my heart, and understand by every instinct that is in me: and sympathy with those to whom we are bound by sincere affection and intimate understanding involves suffering when there is suffering to comprehend and share. But I want your letters. I know just what outlet they give you, and I am so glad that they do give you an outlet. I am glad you saw the real quality of the Tedcastles. They are true stuff; and will be, I venture to predict, of more practical service to you than many others whose place and influence are larger and greater. Mr. Tedcastle is an intensely practical and sensible man. He has made his own way up from the bottom, with extraordinary courage and resourcefulness. And he *likes* to help, if he can see a way. You need not feel shy with them for a moment, and you need hold nothing back. How I hope that in your talk *something* definite and practicable began to form itself by way of a plan! This happens to be just about as hard a time to find things to do that will afford profitable employment as has been within many a year: the Republicans say because of the policy of the Democrats with regard to business! Do not in any case lose patience, or lose heart. The thing cannot be worked out in a day, but I have the faith to believe that it will be worked out; and that, as you have yourself suggested, it may all prove to have been for the best so far as Allen is concerned. It was necessary that he should be put on his mettle. It will make a man of him; and happy days will come yet.

Strangely, though I feel the pain at my heart whenever I think of you, there is a certain relief in having my thoughts drawn away from the present deep anxieties of public business and from myself. I welcome almost any demand on my time or energy that diverts my mind from myself. How it amuses me to read what the papers say, or imply, about my personal ambitions! I care no more what happens to me personally in politics than I care what happened a thousand years ago to some man struggling in the dark against hostile forces that have long ago spent themselves and been forgotten. My thoughts lose their vivacity when they are turned upon myself, though I can still keep them quick when they handle business. And there are the dear ones about me, for whom I do care intensely. But their interests do not depend upon my remaining in public life, could be better served, no doubt, if I were to leave it.

We are all well. My trip to Indianapolis got me out of the daily rut a bit. It was good to get my blood moving in a speech again. All unite with me in affectionate messages.

Your devoted friend,   Woodrow Wilson

WWTLS (WP, DLC).
¹ Mrs. Hulbert had sent him a handwritten draft of an article, "Around the Tea Table—Afternoon Tea." Wilson had the article typed and then edited it carefully in his own hand. Mrs. Hulbert sent the recipes later. All the foregoing documents are in WP, DLC. Wilson had them retyped before sending them to Bok.

From Charles Richard Crane

Dear Mr President   [New York] January 10 1915

This is my Sunday sermon. The speech was all right and evidently reached the audience to whom it was addressed. I am sure such experiences will do you nothing but good and hope that you will go out in the fresh air of the free world more often. My recent visit in Washington convinced me more than ever of the artificial, reactionary and depressing atmosphere that you and your cabinet have to live in. You must get out and so must Houston and Lane. You need the experience and so does the country. The Washington atmosphere reminds me of the remark of an old friend who lived in New Orleans that, somehow, everything he liked was unhealthy, immoral or expensive.

Of course the friendly word to the "progressives" will be bitterly resented around here but not West of the Hudson river. They are trying hard to make themselves believe here that the progressive movement is to be "a long time dead." When Senator La Follette was governor he had a regular habit of going directly to the constituents of any member of the legislature who was fighting his program and I hope sooner or later you can make some remarks in both Reed's and Hitchcock's territory. There is no doubt you would get fine receptions in both places.

I am sure that a little gentle exercise in the open political air will do you only good.

And thank you for the wonderful evening with you and Mott.¹

I am glad that you are to see Miss Addams. She is a wise progressive. Faithfully Charles R. Crane

ALS (WP, DLC).
¹ On January 6. There is a brief handwritten outline, dated January 6, 1915, of topics to be discussed at this meeting in the J. R. Mott Papers (CtY-D). It reveals that Mott assured Wilson of appreciation in all parts of Europe of his attitude, particularly as revealed in his utterances on neutrality. Mott reported that an immense amount of thinking and study was taking place about the outcome of the war and what should follow its end. All eyes were on America, or, as Sir Edward Grey put it, "America is needed." Mott suggested that it was most important not to limit America's rendering her great service by premature action or by departing from strict neutrality: it was wise to "keep [our] moral powder dry." The war must be fought out, but with "due regard for princ[iples] of justice and kindness" and a "firm stand for rights." At the conclusion of the war, the United States would have "a unique opportunity" because of the exhaustion of the belligerents.

To Newton Diehl Baker

My dear Mr. Mayor: [The White House] January 11, 1915

Thank you for calling my attention to Mr. Lowes Dickinson's article. I shall look it up at once. I saw some mention of it somewhere and had intended to do so anyhow. Now that you have read it and vouched for its interest, I shall be the more eager.

Thank you for your helpful thought of me.

In haste

Cordially and faithfully yours, Woodrow Wilson

TLS (Letterpress Books, WP, DLC).

To Edward Mandell House

My dear Friend: The White House January 11, 1915

Your praise of anything that I do or say is always very sweet to me, and I thank you with all my heart for what you say about the speech at Indianapolis. I would rather have your judgment than that of anybody I know.

I am going to write you a line soon about the Argentine business. I am not quite ready to report yet, though the thing is in course.

But are you not coming down this week?

Always Affectionately yours, Woodrow Wilson

P.S. I received the letter I asked you for and am sincerely obliged to you for sending it.

TLS (E. M. House Papers, CtY).

To Franklin Knight Lane

My dear Lane: [The White House] January 11, 1915

I don't know when I have been more cheered than by your generous praise of my speech at Indianapolis. It sent my barometer up many points and I thank you with all my heart.

Always   Faithfully yours,   Woodrow Wilson

TLS (Letterpress Books, WP, DLC).

From Robert Lansing

Dear Mr. President: Washington January 11, 1915.

I enclose herewith some notes on Sir Edward Grey's reply of January 7th.[1] They are intended merely as preliminary comments on the British defense of the action of which we complain, and as a possible suggestion of the evidence required to meet Sir Edward's positions.

My general impression of the document is that the tone is conciliatory and that the presentation of the British case is adroit, though transparently illogical in many particulars to one familiar with the facts. It appears to be drafted with the purpose of allaying public irritation in this country without giving any assurance that trade conditions with neutral countries will be relieved.

It seems to me that in acknowledging the note Mr. Page, while expressing gratification at its temperate tone, and stating that comment would be withheld until the complete British reply had been received, should be instructed to urge the delivery of such reply as soon as possible in view of the existing doubt as to British action in the future and the consequent demoralizing effect on American commerce.

I have submitted a copy of the enclosed to Secretary Bryan and I am sending you a copy with his approval.

Very sincerely yours,   Robert Lansing.

TLS (WP, DLC).
   [1] "Notes," T MS dated Jan. 10, 1915 (SDR, RG 59, 763.72112/699½, DNA), pointing out the alleged inconsistencies, inaccuracies, and unresponsiveness of the British preliminary reply. The "notes" are printed in *FR-LP*, I, 262-65. The British preliminary reply is printed in *FR-WWS 1915*, pp. 299-302.

Remarks at a Press Conference

January 12, 1915

Has the administration at this time in mind pressing any one of the employment bureau bills now before the House committee?

Well, I haven't in mind, to tell you the truth, any additional legislation at this short session, because it is so obviously too short a session in which to accomplish a careful piece of legislation.

Mr. President, in view of what has already been done in the departments about the matter, is legislation on the subject really necessary?

I think it is. We are doing and can do a great deal, and of course we will continue to do so, but I think for the proper co-ordination of it all, legislation is necessary.

You could accomplish that legislation within the next two years?

Yes, I am confident we could.

If the legislation can be accomplished within the next two years, a platform declaration on the subject will hardly be necessary.

I suppose not. I simply put it the way I did in my speech because I was not authorized to commit anybody but myself. But I have not heard any dissenting opinions.

Mr. President, an effort has been made in some of the papers this morning to show that the British note is unsatisfactory in some respects to the American government?

I saw an article headed "Note Unsatisfactory to Wilson," or something like that. I thought of writing to the editor and asking him how he found out. He didn't ask me, and nobody had asked me, and I have not expressed an opinion, because I haven't studied the note yet. It is merely preliminary, anyway.

You are not likely to send any reply until the full text is received?

No, we couldn't until the full text is here.

Mr. President, there has been some question as to whether or not we in Indianapolis interpreted your speech correctly on the point of your candidacy.

I said at the time I did not intend to start anything. But, honestly, I wasn't thinking about that; I was thinking about the judgment sooner or later that would be expressed by the country upon the party.

Mr. President, despite your desire not to start anything, it seems to have started something.

Yes, sir, so I noticed.

Mr. Mitchell Palmer puts forward the suggestion that if the candidacy is intended it can be done by repealing a section of the Baltimore platform; do you regard that as necessary?

You must permit me, gentlemen, not to talk about myself. I don't know how.

Mr. President, how much of an appropriation would it require,

probably, for the purposes of the federal employment bureau?
    I haven't gone into that. I do not know.
Could such a bureau be used effectively, Mr. President, to divert
a good deal of the immigration to the land instead of to the big
industrial centers?

> Yes, undoubtedly it could. One of the things that I have had
> at heart for a great many years has been some means by
> which we could guide immigrants to the places where they
> could find the most suitable employment—employment best
> suited to what they had done at home and what they knew
> best how to do. That has never been supplied except by
> private agencies. Certain societies have interested them-
> selves in that, but they have not had the access or the
> authority that would enable them to guide the immigrant.

There was a report by a Mr. Husband about a year ago to the
Secretary of Labor,[1] following his investigation in Russia, in
which he said one of the greatest problems was to place the
Russian peasant, who had been on the land over there, in the
proper environment here.

> And a great many of the Portuguese and Italian immigrants
> are admirably suited: they have been accustomed to truck
> gardening and intensive cultivation of various sorts.

They pointed out, in that connection, that one of the important
deficiences was the lack of rural credit facilities for these people
who came over here.
    You mean to give them credit to buy land and settle?
Yes.

> That is being done by private individuals; there is a notable
> scheme in the Carolinas.[2]

Mr. President, are you willing yet to let us know what action
you are going to take with regard to the immigration bill?

> No; I am willing that you should form a shrewd guess. But
> the bill, of course, hasn't come out of conference yet, and
> the final form of it is not determined.

But the provision which is objectionable to you remains in the
bill.

[1] "Report of W. W. Husband, Special Immigrant Inspector, Regarding Immigration from Eastern Europe," printed as an appendix to *Annual Report of the
Commissioner General of Immigration to the Secretary of Labor . . . 1914*
(Washington, 1915), pp. 391-406.
[2] A reference to several farm colonies, composed largely of immigrants, established since 1905 near Wilmington, N. C., by Hugh MacRae, a wealthy busi-
nessman of that city. See Paul K. Conkin, *Tomorrow a New World: The New
Deal Community Program* (Ithaca, N. Y., 1959), pp. 277-79, and Robert W.
Vincent, "Successful Immigrants in the South," *World's Work*, XVII (Nov. 1908),
10908-11.

Necessarily, I suppose, because both houses approved it. . . .
Is there anything you can tell us about Mexico, Mr. President?

No, sir, except that once again things seem to be quieting there. I suppose you know that certain arrangements have been made at the border. They have been fighting too near the edge.

Mr. President, can you develop a little more the idea of the Trade Commission taking up the work of a tariff commission?

No, that has to be developed by the commission itself. The powers are there; and the powers had been partly granted, you may remember, only very partially, to the Bureau of Corporations. It is a matter of development. Some of the later reports of the Bureau of Corporations show an admirable method of exhibiting the conditions of particular lines of business.

Isn't there a bureau in the Commerce Department that has that power.

The Bureau of Foreign and Domestic Commerce has, inferentially, those powers. It handles questions upon which it reports, and its reports are naturally the source of a great deal of information with regard to foreign trade conditions.

Mr. Underwood, when the tariff bill was in process, laid some stress upon the powers which had been granted to these bureaus.

Yes, he did. I don't think that there is any lack of power now. It merely is a question of development.

Would it be the idea, Mr. President, to have all these separate organizations (of course, the Bureau of Corporations goes out of existence) study along the same lines and have independent reports?

Of course, their independence is almost inevitable, because the function of the Bureau of Foreign and Domestic Commerce is to send agents to foreign countries and study the opportunities there for American merchants, and then get American merchants in touch with those opportunities. It is an active sort of business of promotion, which is different in kind from the business of scientific study. What they report will naturally be very serviceable to the men who are making a more scientific study of it on the Trade Commission.

Is there any progress on the Trade Commission, Mr. President?

I think I am nearing a solution.

Are you expecting the passage of the Philippine bill this session, Mr. President?

Well, under the rules of the Senate one can never tell what one expects, but I hope for its passage at this session. I haven't heard anything to the contrary.

T MS (C. L. Swem Coll., NjP).

To Paul Oscar Husting

My dear Senator: The White House January 12, 1915

Allow me to acknowledge with deep interest your letter of January fifth. I feel to the full what you urge about the mistaken sentiment growing up among German-Americans. I feel it, indeed, so strongly that I have already taken steps which I hope will lead to a public correction of many of the mistaken views which are now prevalent.

I am very much interested to know that you are coming to Washington soon with Mr. Nieman and hope that I shall have a glimpse of you both while you are here. I would be very much obliged if you would take up the question which your letter deals with with Mr. Robert Lansing, the Counsellor of State who has been specially charged with handling questions of that sort.

Cordially and sincerely yours,   Woodrow Wilson

TLS (P. O. Husting Papers, WHi).

From William Jennings Bryan, with Enclosure

My dear Mr. President: Washington January 12, 1915.

I am sending you a copy of the telegram in reply to the preliminary note from Great Britain. It was prepared by Mr. Lansing and is all we think needs to be said at this time.

As a matter of precaution, however, I will ask you to take the trouble to look it over and then send this copy to the State Department telegraph room *with any corrections that you have to make.*

If you have no corrections to make you can telephone me and I will release the telegram.

With Assurances of high respect I am my dear Mr. President,

Yours very sincerely,   W. J. Bryan

TLS (WP, DLC).

ENCLOSURE[1]

January 12, 1915.

Your number 1434 January 7th, 8 P.M. Please prepare a note to Sir Edward Grey in reply to his note of January 7th in the sense of the following:

We appreciate the friendly spirit in which the American note of December 28th[2] was received by the British Government and we have no doubt that the cordial relations between the two governments will continue throughout the pending diplomatic discussion. The Government of the United States notes with satisfaction that His Majesty's Government agree with the principles of international law as set forth in the American note. As this note is being carefully examined by the British Government with a view to making a further reply in detail it would seem premature for me to answer at the present time the remarks of Sir Edward Grey. It is the intention of this Government to consider the points raised by Sir Edward Grey in connection with the further reply of the British Government promised by him. Please impress upon Sir Edward Grey ⟨the urgency of hastening⟩ *our hope that* the reply of the British Government *may be delivered to us in full as soon as possible* in order that the irritation in this country may not be increased by a delay in presenting the British position, which may be understood by the American public as an intentional prolongation of the discussion.[3]

CC telegram (WP, DLC).
[1] Wilson deleted the words in angle brackets and added those in italics.
[2] The note, dated December 26, 1914, was presented to the Foreign Office on December 28.
[3] On second thought, Wilson deleted this last sentence entirely. The note, printed in *FR-WWS 1915*, pp. 305-306, was sent as WJB to WHP, Jan. 12, 1915, T telegram (SDR, RG 59, 763.72112/594, DNA).

Two Letters from William Jennings Bryan

My dear Mr. President: Washington January 12, 1915.

Senator Stone told me this morning that Senator Root had asked him to delay calling up the Nicaragua treaty until Mr. Paul Fuller could be heard. From what Senator Stone said it would seem that Mr. Fuller had presented an objection to the treaty on the ground that the present Government does not represent the people.

I remember that you spoke of being impressed by a conversation you had with Fuller, but I thought it was with reference to the Platt Amendment part of the treaty. There are some powerful influences working against the treaty the most potent being the influence of the former President, Zelaya[1] who, according to our information, ruled the land despotically and plundered it systematically.

If you think best I can telegraph Mr. Fuller to come down, although I think we have fully considered the view which he seems to have presented to Mr. Root.

The canal route is valuable to us and the Fonsica Bay site still more valuable and if we are not to negotiate with the existing government it looks as though it would be an invitation [to] them to have another revolution, with no probability that the Government issuing from the next revolution would be any more authoritative than the present.

With assurances of high respect I am, my dear Mr. President,
Yours very sincerely,   W. J. Bryan

[1] José Santos Zelaya, President and dictator of Nicaragua, 1893-1909.

My dear Mr. President: Washington January 12, 1915.

Another matter that I had intended to speak to you about this morning was the statement explaining why we have taken no action on the invasion of Belgium by Germany.

I sent you a few days ago a copy of the statement that we (Mr Lansing & I) have prepared and which I will give out if you approve.

With assurances of high respect I am, my dear Mr. President,
Yours very sincerely,   W. J. Bryan

TLS (WP, DLC).

To William Jennings Bryan

My dear Mr. Secretary,   [The White House] 12 January, 1915.

I find myself regretting that it is necessary to say anything on this subject.

This note is entirely sound and conclusive from the lawyer's point of view; but I fear that it will make the impression of a technical defense against the charge that we have not performed a duty suggested by moral considerations and the general sense of thoughtful men throughout the world.

Will you not think of it again in this light, and give me your final impression?[1]   Faithfully,   W.W.

WWTLI (SDR, RG 59, 763.72111/13971½, DNA).
[1] Lansing twice later urged the advisability of issuing some sort of statement

on the American government's failure to protest against the invasion of Belgium: RL to WJB, Jan. 13 and 23, 1915, *FR-LP*, 1, 191-94. However, he finally agreed that it would not be wise to issue the statement. See RL to WJB, Feb. 10, 1915, printed as an Enclosure with WJB to WW, Feb. 12, 1915.

From the Diary of Colonel House

Washington, January 12, 1915.

I took the 12.08 for Washington. I found Samuel Huston Thompson of the Department of Justice and H. C. Wallace on the train. At Baltimore, Davies and Harris, Director of the Census,[1] met me so altogether, I had no rest.

McAdoo and Grayson were at the station to meet me. After I had dressed for dinner I went into the President's study and in a few minutes he came in. We had exactly twelve minutes conversation before dinner, and during those twelve minutes it was decided that I should go to Europe on January 30th. I had practically decided before I came to Washington that this was necessary, and I was certain, when I gave my thoughts to the President, he would agree with me it was the best thing to do.

I thought we had done all we could do with the Ambassadors at Washington, and that we were now travelling in a circle. It was time to deal directly with the principals. I had a feeling we were losing ground and were not in as close touch with the Allies as we had been, and that it was essential to take the matter up directly with London and afterward with Berlin.

There were no visitors for dinner. After dinner the President read from A. G. Gardiner's sketches of prominent men until half past eight when Senator La Follette came.[2] When he left the President resumed his reading. I was surprised that he preferred to do this rather than discuss the matters of importance we had between us. He evidently had confidence in my doing the work I came to Washington for, without his help.

T MS (E. M. House Papers, CtY).
[1] William Julius Harris.
[2] La Follette reported on his meeting with Wilson in a letter to Gilbert E. Roe, written that same evening:

"It is ten o'clock, and I have just come from an interview with the President. He sent for me . . . and I spent an hour with him. He said that he had two or three sets of men under consideration for the Trade Commission and he wanted to know about you. I cannot at this time go into detail nor is it necessary. . . . Suffice it to say that you are most seriously under consideration beyond any question, and I hazard the opinion that you are in great danger of being struck by lightning.

"He also wanted to discuss with me matters of legislation, and urged me to come and talk with him about legislation from time to time without waiting to be called, as he believed we had much the same point of view and desires regarding service to the public." Printed in Belle Case La Follette and Fola La Follette, *Robert M. La Follette* (2 vols., New York, 1953), 1, 516.

To William Jennings Bryan

My dear Mr. Secretary: [The White House] January 13, 1915

I return herewith the papers you were kind enough to send me some days ago about the situation in Hayti. The more I think about that situation the more I am convinced that it is our duty to take immediate action there such as we took in San Domingo. I mean to send commissioners there who will seek and obtain an interview with the leaders of the various contending factions of the republic and say to them as firmly and definitely as is consistent with courtesy and kindness that the United States cannot consent to stand by and permit revolutionary conditions constantly to exist there. They ought, as in San Domingo, to insist upon an agreement for a popular election under our supervision and to be told that the result of that election would be upheld by the United States to the utmost.

Is not this your judgment?

Cordially and faithfully yours,   Woodrow Wilson

TLS (Letterpress Books, WP, DLC).

To Benjamin Ryan Tillman

My dear Senator: The White House January 13, 1915

You have treated me as I wish to be treated and in offering me your advice about the financial situation of the Government you have honored me and done me a real service.[1]

You may be sure that nothing has been more on my mind than the very topics you so forcibly touch upon.

It is true that the budget plan which I have had so much at heart has seemed lately to fall into the background, if not entirely to disappear, but that is only because other subjects have so forced themselves into the foreground and so absolutely absorbed my attention that I was obliged to turn to them and neglect other things. Apparently, my mind is not big enough to contain all the subjects now to be dealt with at one and the same time.

I have been having conferences recently with Congressman Fitzgerald, the Chairman of the House Committee on Appropriations, and am planning a conference with him and the Secretary of the Treasury with a view to doing whatever it is possible to do to check the appropriations at every point where it is possible to check them. Your letter is a spur to duty which I cheerfully respond to. I do not know what I can accomplish but you may be sure I will accomplish what I can.

　　With warmest regard,

　　　　　Cordially and sincerely yours,　Woodrow Wilson

TLS (B. R. Tillman Papers, ScCleU).
　¹ B. R. Tillman to WW, Jan. 11, 1915, TLS (WP, DLC).

To Benjamin Ide Wheeler

　　　　　　　　　　　　　　　　　　[The White House]
My dear President Wheeler:　　　　　　January 13, 1915

　It is very gracious of you to remind me of your kind desire to have me speak on your Charter Day¹ and I sincerely hope that it will be possible. Amidst the anxieties of the European conflict and its effects on the United States, I cannot be certain of anything and am obliged, much against my will, to postpone even yet for a while the making of any detailed programme.

　I hope you will not think it ungracious on my part if I say that I do not think that any man ought while President of the United States to accept an honorary degree. I have very firm convictions on that subject and much as I would be honored by a degree from the University of California, I feel that it is my duty to say that I could not accept one at this time.

　I hope sincerely that it will be possible to meet your wishes and you may be sure I will form detailed plans just as soon as practicable.

　　　　　Cordially and sincerely yours,　Woodrow Wilson

TLS (Letterpress Books, WP, DLC).
　¹ B. I. Wheeler to WW, Jan. 6, 1915, TLS (WP, DLC).

From the Diary of Colonel House

　　　　　　　　　　　　　　　　　　January 13, 1915.

　After breakfast this morning the President and I strolled from the elevator to his study in which time I told him of my plans for the day. That is, I should see the South American Ambassadors, the British Ambassador and Mr. Bryan. I considered it important for us to decide what reason to give Spring-Rice for my going over. He thought it was best to tell him I wanted to go over to try out the Germans, and the President said, "of course if you stop over in London and see the British Government in the meantime, that would be expected, and could not offend the sensibilities of the British Ambassador." . . .

It was now time to meet my engagement with the Chilean Ambassador and I had to leave. I found the Chilean Ambassador very cordial, but he had not heard from his Government regarding the President's proposal. I told him the Senate would adjourn in about sixty days, and would not meet again for nearly a year, and that it was important for him to get into communication with his Government again and ask them to send a response. I informed him of the favorable responses from both Brazil and Argentine, but before preceding to a further discussion of the convention, we wished to hear from Chile. The President requested me to say to him that he had approached Senator Stone of the Foreign Relations Committee, and had found him sympathetic, and he felt sure there would be no difficulty from that source.

I went from Phillips to see the Brazilian Ambassador to inform him also that the President had taken the matter up with the Senate Foreign Relations Committee, and he would soon call them together for a more intimate discussion of the details of the convention. Da Gama was pleased with this procedure and thought it was wise for the President to get the Senate in line before any public announcement was made.

I returned to the White House for lunch, and while the President was dressing for his golf, I told of my morning's work.

After lunch McAdoo and I had a talk. He remained with me for more than two hours. The Shipping Bill, the New York situation and his own personal affairs filled the time until I had to leave for Phillips'.

I was the first to arrive, then came Spring-Rice and later, Jusserand and Bakhmeteff. I had asked Sir Cecil to inform the other two Ambassadors of our conversation in the morning and to get them into a receptive frame of mind. He evidently had not done so, and he was not particularly nice in helping me out. It was rather awkward at first. Both Jusserand and Bakhmeteff were violent in their denunciation of the Germans and evinced a total lack of belief in their sincerity. They thought my mission would be entirely fruitless.

Later, I brought them around to the view that at least it would be well worth while to find how utterly unreliable and trecherous the Germans were by exposing their false pretenses of peace to the world. That suited them better, and it was not a great while before we were all making merry, and they were offerring me every facility to meet the heads of their governments. I found them somewhat sensitive about my going to London and Berlin; each thought Petrograd and Paris should also be visited. I agreed to this, but made a mental reservation that it would be late in the Spring before I could get as far as Russia. . . .

I met Mr. Bryan at the State Department and drove him to his home. I told him of my conversations with the South Americans, and he asked if it would be proper now for him to take up the discussion with the[m]. I told him it was although I felt certain in my own mind, the President would prefer his not doing so, since it is his purpose to finish this work himself.

I gave Mr. Bryan a summary of my day's work with the European Ambassadors and of what the President desired me to do. He was distinctly disappointed when he heard I was to go to Europe as the peace emissary. He said he had planned to do this himself and in the following way: Germany and Spain have not ratified the peace treaties which he has been making with the other nations, and he thought if this was given as an excuse, he could go to Germany and could bring about a general discussion of mediation and peace parleys.

I replied that the President thought it would be unwise for anyone to do this officially, and that his going would attract a great deal of attention, and people would wonder why he was there for such a purpose when the matter could have been done quite as well from Washington. He answered that my going would create just as much of a sensation, because of my well known relations with the President. I reminded him that heretofore I had been successful in escaping such notoriety. His reply was that I had never gone abroad while a great world war was in progress. By this time we had arrived at his home in Calumet Place, and he insisted upon my getting out and pursuing the conversation further, a thing I hesitated to do, because I knew how footless it was. He was generous enough to say that if he did not go in an official way, I was the one best fitted to go in an unofficial way. I hope he may be right, for I am leaving with much trepidation. The undertaking is so great, and the difficulties are so many, that to do it alone and practically without consultation or help from anyone, is as much of a task as even I, with all my willingess to assume responsibility, desire.

The President was waiting for me when I returned to the White House and we had nearly a half hour's talk before dinner. He was, of course, interested in my day's work and remarked: "your experience with the three Ambassadors shows that it is fortunate you have them back of you." What he meant was that I need not be disturbed by them further, for they were out of my path, for the present.

He was disturbed by Mr. Bryan's ambition, and said he believed he, Bryan, would prefer not to have peace if it could not be brought about through himself. He corrected himself after making this statement and said it was unfair to Mr. Bryan, but what he meant to say was that Mr. Bryan was so anxious to do it himself that the idea obsessed him. He declared that if necessary he would allow Mr. Bryan to resign from the Cabinet before he would let him undertake such a delicate mission, for which he felt he was so unfitted. I expressed a willingness to have Mr. Bryan or anyone else go in my stead. However, I thought if Mr. Bryan was the best man in the world for the mission, his reputation in Europe would bar him from consideration. The President said he would talk with him about it and tell him his mind was irrevocably made up.

McAdoo, Col. Edward Brown of Atlanta, a kinsman of Mrs. Wilson, and John Wilson, a kinsman of the President, from Franklin, Pa. were at dinner. After we finished dinner we inspected the portrait of the President by Seymour Thomas. The crowd were equally divided as to its merits. Eleanor insisted upon her father standing in front of the portrait so that a comparison could be made. Instead of doing as she wished, he made all sorts of contortions, sticking his tongue in his cheek, twisting his mouth into different positions, rolling his eyes, dropping his jaw, and doing everything a clown would do at a circus. She tried composing his features with her hand, and whenever she would touch his chin he would let it drop on his shirtfront, and when she lifted it, he would raise his eyes to heaven. He had us all laughing immoderately, and Eleanor gave it up.

We started up the marble stairway to the study, the President and McAdoo leading. McAdoo walked as bow-legged as his long legs could possibly be bowed, and the President not only walking bowlegged, but pigeon-toed. In this way they walked up the entire flight, much to the amusement of the rest of us. John Wilson said it would make his legs ache for a week just from looking at the position of the President.

We went into the oval sitting room and the President read A. G. Gardiner's sketch of Joseph Chamberlain.[1] The President said Chamberlain was his *bête noir*, that he disliked his character intensely and thought him intellectually dishonest.

At nine o'clock Chandler Anderson came at the President's request to tell him of a recent conversation with Sir Edward Grey, and of the message which Sir Edward had sent directly to the President by word of mouth, and which he did not care to have in writing. There was nothing in it that I had not already

---

[1] Gardiner, *Pillars of Society*, pp. 12-20.

learned from Spring-Rice, except that England would probably not object to Russia taking Constantinople, and that Russia had suggested that the Allies agree not to make peace terms separately.

When Anderson left, it was ten o'clock and after before the President and I got down to work. We agreed upon a code to be used between us in sending cable messages while I am abroad. I thought he should write me a letter of instructions, something that I need not let go out of my hands, but which I might show in the event it was necessary for me to go to countries where I was not well known.

Together we outlined what this letter should contain, and he is to send me a draft of it in a day or two for me to look over and make suggestions which seem pertinent. He said he would write it himself on his little typewriter, so that not even his confidential stenographer would know of it.

I told of my plans more in detail, and asked if he desired me to go to Russia to make the treaty between the United States and Russia. He hated to ask me to go to Russia in winter, but he thought it would be of great advantage, and he expressed a lack of confidence in the ability of Mayre[2] to do such work.

We talked of his difficulties with the Senate, and he was inclined to tell them if they did not accept his leadership, he would not become a candidate in 1916. I strongly urged against taking any such action. Later he said, "You are the only one in the world to whom I can open my mind freely, and it does me good to say even foolish things and get them out of my system."

He urged me to remain another day, but I told him the German Ambassador was in New York, and I had arranged to see him there tomorrow. We then bade each other an affectionate good-bye. Grayson went with me to the train, and he alarmed me somewhat by saying that the President's kidneys were not acting as well as they should. There was nothing serious as yet, but he was watching him closely. He thought he was worrying too much and should take more diversion.

[2] George Thomas Marye, appointed Ambassador to Russia on July 1, 1914.

Two Letters to William Jennings Bryan

My dear Mr. Secretary: The White House January 14, 1915

I return the English preliminary note with Mr. Lansing's memoranda, and wish to make this suggestion, as I did hurriedly over the telephone the other day:

The two governments being apparently in substantial agreement about the principles involved, it would seem to me best that the whole argument should be directed to practicable methods of handling the whole matter with the least possible delay, unfairness, or friction, and with a view to bringing the British practices to some basis of uniformity and consistency upon which our merchants could reckon. My feeling is that it is not worth while debating details with them. But this is only a judgment preliminary like the note itself.

Cordially and faithfully yours,   Woodrow Wilson

TLS (SDR, RG 59, 763.72112/699½, DNA).

My dear Mr. Secretary: The White House January 14, 1915

I have your note about the Nicaragua treaty. I am very sorry that Senator Root's request has been complied with. It occurs to me that it would be well, as you suggest, to have a talk with Mr. Paul Fuller yourself with regard to this matter. He seemed to me when he talked to me about it to be unusually well informed. The interview, besides, might afford you an opportunity to ascertain whether it was possible for Mr. Fuller to suggest someone as familiar as himself with the Spanish language who could fill the place we wish to fill of informal agent and spokesman at Mexico City. I should prefer to reserve Mr. Fuller himself for larger and more lasting functions.

In haste, always
Cordially and faithfully yours,   Woodrow Wilson

TLS (W. J. Bryan Papers, DNA).

Arch Wilkinson Shaw[1] to Joseph Patrick Tumulty, with Enclosure

Dear Mr. Tumulty: Chicago January 14, 1915

In my conversation with the President, I gathered that he was not averse to making a statement defining his attitude towards business and suggesting what business men might expect of the Administration. With Congress in session, however, I know that his days are fully occupied and that he may not find time to prepare a statement reflecting his views.

I have ventured, therefore, to write an account of my talk with him. As I explain in the introductory paragraphs, I have tried to convey his viewpoint—to interpret his ideas rather than to reproduce his actual utterances. The latter I would be unable to do, of course, and I say as much in the introduction, in order to relieve the President of responsibility for any awkward phrasing. At the same time, I cannot help feeling that the interview is the only form in which the President's attitude can be clearly and forcibly conveyed to the business men of the country. They are accustomed to direct, man-to-man speaking. To interject my own personality by putting the President's views in the third person would subtract too much from their force.

The result of my efforts I am enclosing. There is both need and occasion, just now, I think, for the President to speak a positive word of reassurance to business men, through some medium which has always been identified with their interests and which they know has no partisan bias or purpose in any message which it presents. Despite all favorable conditions, business has not picked up as decidedly as I, and so many others like me, had hoped and expected. Some such statement as I inclose would create his confidence in conditions which individual business men must feel before they go ahead. When you read it, I trust you will be of the same opinion and that the President will incline to see it in the same light.

You are at liberty, of course, to edit the interview as you see fit, either before or after it comes under the President's eye. If you will wire me that there is a strong probability of the President's approving the interview, I will hold one form of the February issue and give you several days to consider it.

Yours very truly,　A. W. Shaw.

P.S. I found the Blythe interview in The Saturday Evening Post[2] intensely interesting. I thought it presented the human side of the President in admirable fashion.

TLS (WP, DLC).
　[1] President of the A. W. Shaw Co. of Chicago, publishers of *System: The Magazine of Business* and other business publications.
　[2] Printed at Dec. 5, 1914, Vol. 31.

ENCLOSURE

What follows here is the substance of a talk I had with President Wilson, Monday, January fourth. I had gone to Washington convinced that nothing stood between the country and an immediate resumption of business activity except a general feeling of uncertainty. An inquiry covering many trades and industries had made it plain that the legislative and executive program of the Administration formed an important factor—if not the chief factor—in this state of suspended initiative. Why this should be so was not entirely evident. The organization of the federal reserve bank system precluded any chance of a money stringency. The war in Europe had minimized the effects of the new tariff. The Trade Commission law had been accepted as constructive legislation, though the scope of its influence and usefulness to business would depend in part on the character of its membership. Such legislation as Congress had under consideration would hardly account for the prevailing tendency to distrust the future.

Still, confidence was lacking. Over-caution would certainly continue to be the rule in business unless the mental fog which seemed to obscure the Government's intentions could be cleared up. Here, I felt, SYSTEM might help. If the President's attitude was what I conceived it to be and if he would consent to make a statement of his position and his purposes, I believed that the fog could be dispelled and business could safely drive ahead again at its normal 100% gait.

I went to Washington, therefore, on the day appointed. The President received me and verified my belief. His viewpoint, as I understand it, I shall try to convey here, though my effort will be to interpret his ideas rather than to reproduce his actual utterances. It would be much more effective, I know, if I could recall his exact words and preserve the incisive clarity of his speech. My excuse must be that I am first of all a business man accustomed to get the gist of a conversation rather than to remember its exact phrasing. The main purpose will be served, however, if I can make the President's attitude clear and can make every reader of SYSTEM feel what I feel today—that for two years at least business-baiting will not be a popular diversion at the Capitol and that once again "the way to resume is to resume."

Any discussion in which Mr. Wilson has a part gets quickly to the point. We were hardly seated before I found myself voicing my belief that the fundamental difficulty with business just now is fear.

"That," he agreed, "is exactly as I think. It is fear, but fear of what?"

"Fear of the results likely to come from recent and pending legislation," I ventured. "To use an expression of the street, it is largely a 'hang-over' from the uncertainty attending the discussion of the problems which the country faced last year.

The President does not evade an issue—even a potentially disagreeable one.

"You mean," he asked, "that it is fear of the Democratic party —fear of the incompetence of the Democratic party to interpret public opinion correctly? This lack of confidence in our ability to enact intelligent and adequate laws, you think, is at the bottom of our current pessimism?"

"It might be that," I answered. "At all events, the fear exists. And that fear is the only thing that I can see which would interfere with a revival of activity. It seems to me, Mr. President, that the prevailing business situation is peculiar. Like a gasoline motor whose electrical circuit has just been broken, there is no lack of fuel. The fumes of business are thick and rich. It needs only a spark to touch them off and start the machinery going. Once started, it would keep on, gathering power at every revolution. That spark, I believe, you could supply, if you would go direct to the average business man and talk to him in terms of his own experience. The trouble is that he has been absorbed in the inside problems of his business—in establishing the policies and the routine of his store or factory. By and large, he has not taken as much interest in the external problems of his business—in its contact with the law, with the government and with public opinion—as have the farmer and the workingman. Lacking this experience in forecasting the effects of legislation and in adjusting his policies to conditions not wholly understood, he moves slowly or does not move at all."

"That is true," the President assented. "Business men have come to me singly and in delegations to protest against bills which Congress was considering and to plead that Congress be allowed to adjourn without enacting further laws to hamper trade and industry. To all of them I put the same question: 'Is any of this legislation such that it will interfere directly with the activities of any honest business man?' Their answer invariably was 'No'—that the thing they dreaded was the indirect effect upon all business—the disturbed conditions which had always accompanied or followed any legislative action concerned with business. What I did not understand then and cannot understand now is the reason for such apprehension. Why is it not better to so organize our machinery of trade that all business men, as well as the public generally, shall be protected against the practices of dishonest men? It seems to me that it is wiser and safer and more efficient to do this—to establish standards of fair conduct and right relations in business and to define unfair and mischievous practices—than to continue in a state of uncertainty which puts hobbles on the honest manufacturer and trader and provides the dishonest man with opportunities."

The President paused, as if to find the most convincing way of putting his next thought into words.

"So far as I can see," he said finally, "the business man can now rest assured of two things:

"For the first time in our recent history, he is safe from unfair methods of competition, whether it be the competition of dishonest men or that of normally honest men so entangled in the web of organizations which they do not control, that they cannot apply their personal standards of honor and justice in their every-day dealings.

"For at least two years, also, the business man is free to go ahead without needing to forecast or discount the effect of new legislation. The laws already enacted are, in my view of them, so comprehensive that they will need no additions or amendments for some time.

"You suggested that the present disposition to mark time in business is an after-effect of last year's legislation. Such conditions as existed then probably never will prevail again. An accumulation of problems left by previous administrations had to be settled. Then the war in Europe intervened to jeopardize the results. With so many hostile circumstances arrayed against us, it was a marvel that the decrease in the volume of trade and industry should have been so slight. Such a combination of domestic problems alone is not likely to occur again. There was revision of the tariff; there was a radical change in our banking laws; there was the trust problem; all waiting to be threshed out and solved without hurting business. There was the depressing influence also of the Inter-State Commerce Commission's first refusal to grant a general rate increase to the railroads, with its consequent curtailment of their buying in innumerable lines. Finally there was the explosion in Europe to upset the credit and the financial machinery not of the United States alone, but of the whole world.

"All these, you will say, are problems of 1914. They are; and except for the war they have been settled to the advantage of constructive business men. Why, then, should they, with their keen practical minds, and with the courage and initiative they show in their undertakings, allow mere memories of past apprehensions to disturb or depress the activities of 1915? The most ardent protectionist could not ask for a higher tariff wall than that erected by the war. The recent rate decision of the Inter-State Commerce Commission has reassured the railroads and their dependent industries. The new banking law has given us for the first time an elastic currency equal to the demands of the most active periods like crop-moving times and dividend-paying seasons. I would like to ask business men if this is not the first January within their recollection that did not bring a temporary money stringency due to the necessity of disbursing great sums by way of dividends and other settlements which come at the first of the year. I have asked bankers if that happened this year, and they said: 'No, it did not happen. It could not happen under the federal reserve act.' That would look as though we had emancipated the credits and the business operations of the country from a periodic cause of alarm. Why should anybody doubt that the other policies which have given guarantees to the country that there will be free competition in business are policies which the country will never allow to be reversed?"

"It is possible," I suggested, "that the average business man does not understand what your trust legislation means and what it is going to accomplish. He has accepted the new currency law because he understands it. He feels that it gives the capital of the country an elasticity and a mobility which insure him an adequate supply of money—all he has a right to command—at all seasons and at whatever place he needs to use it. 'Tight money' and excessive interest rates, he perceives, are things of the past. About the trust legislation, however, he is not so clear."

"Yet it seems simple enough to me," Mr. Wilson answered. "What is the effect of this trust legislation, after all? Does it not mean that while the old law of 1890 stands, two important steps have been taken to adjust it to business as it is done today and as it will develop tomorrow? The Clayton law does no more than define certain points in trading practice which have been disputed. Having them settled and fixed should certainly make it easier for business to avoid unfair practices and their penalties hereafter. That, it seems to me, is clear gain. The effect of the Trade Commission should be even more vital and far reaching because it provides a body of men—the majority practical business men—to interpret the facts and apply the laws. Not the least service the Trade Commission should perform is to interpret business men to the law as well as the law to business.

"The net result of the trust legislation, then, should be real freedom for the honest business man—freedom to go ahead with his enterprises, knowing that he is protected not only against unfair methods but also against misconstruction of his motives and actions when the law is applied. Fields that he has been afraid to enter, projects which he has hesitated to undertake because of competition with enormous aggregations of capital, he can now consider. He is free at last to go ahead and match his manufacturing or selling ability against the field, with the assurance at least that the best man or the best goods will prevail.

"I believe, I always have believed," the President continued, "that American business men were absolutely sound at heart. But men immersed in business do a lot of things that opportunity offers to do, which in other circumstances they would not do. I have thought all along that all that was necessary to do was to call their attention sharply to the kind of reforms in business which were necessary, and they would acquiesce. I believe they have heartily acquiesced. Business men who have come to Washington to protest against the passage of the Clayton law have generally been favorable to the idea of a trade commission. Their objection to the Clayton law was that its definitions of unfair trading practices were at once too inclusive and too specific. Certain of its sections defining practices which we know are absolutely bad and indefensible are not nearly so specific or inclusive as corresponding sections of the 'Seven Sisters' laws of New Jersey. Yet I have still to hear of the first serious complaint of the workings of those laws since they became operative. At first I was inclined to think that various other practices had become obviously unfair and detrimental and that it would be best to define them as such in the Clayton law. As I talked with business men and students of legislation, however, I came to agree with them that these unfair practices would be reached through the Trade Commission law. In its final form, I believe, the Trade Commission law reaches every unfair method or device not specifically defined in the Clayton law or in prior court decisions. In fact, the Trade Commission has powers which will make it a great constructive force in all business legislation. It has authority to inquire into and report to Congress not only upon all the conditions of trade in this country, but also upon the conditions of trade, the cost of manufacture and the cost of transportation in foreign countries.

"As I see things, every fundamental condition in the United States is favorable to business. I never was in business, and I have none of the prejudices of business, but I have looked on and tried to see what the interests of the country were in business. I have taken counsel with men who know, and their counsel is uniform. All that is needed in America now is to believe in the future; and I can assure you as one of those who speak for the Administration that it is perfectly safe to believe in the future. There is only one unsettled factor—the war in Europe. Even there, I believe, the dangerous period required for a readjustment of the financial and credit mechanism has passed, and that effect of the war which is commercially favorable is just beginning."[1]

T MS (WP, DLC).
[1] This article was not published.

From Edward Mandell House

Dear Governor: New York City. January 15th, 1915.

I have a letter from Gerard and among other things he says:

"Prospects of peace seem very dim, but in about three months from now the plain people in every land are going to be very sick of this business, and then unless one side has some startling success, (which all hope for in the Spring) peace will come grudgingly.

The Germans are a little irritated just now at our sale of munitions to the Allies. Also because of an extraordinary order issued by our State Department that American Ambassadors shall not inspect or visit prisons, camps etc. They naturally feel that we cannot protect their interests in France, England and Russia without such inspection and they are quite sore because Chandler Anderson, from our Embassy in London, was allowed to come here and inspect places where English were confined, but when I (and this was an express condition of allowing Anderson here) sought to send someone from here to look at English camps, we were met by this order.

The Emperor has been sick for a few days, but neither I nor anyone else saw him. They say he is quite angry at Americans over the sale of arms, but I do not think he would shut up Krupps factory if we were at war with Japan and during the Spanish War, many munitions from Germany found their way to Spain."

Affectionately yours, E. M. House

Mr. Charles Crane has just telephoned me that he has bought Vonnoh's picture of Mrs. Wilson and daughters. He says he will discuss with me the disposition of it later.

TLS (WP, DLC).

From William Jennings Bryan, with Enclosures

My Dear Mr. President: Washington January 15, 1915.

I am very glad that you approve of the idea of sending a commission to Haiti; I believe the time is ripe for it. You may be interested to know the fruit borne by the telegram sent to Santo Domingo. Arias had tendered his resignation and threatened to make trouble.¹ After receiving your instructions at the Cabinet Meeting I sent a telegram, of which the enclosed is a copy. I also told the Santo Domingo Minister here,² who is a nephew of the President,³ to say to the President that he ought to accept the resignation of Arias whenever it was tendered and then notify him that if he made any trouble he would be put out of the country immediately and that this Government would furnish whatever force was necessary to help the President maintain order. The enclosed telegram just received indicates that the situation has improved materially.

I think as soon as we are in position in Haiti to take similar action, Haiti can be put on the highway to prosperity. Now as to the commission: Why would it not be a good plan to send Governor Fort and Smith down to Haiti to act in conjunction with Bailly-Blanchard? Having had that experience in Santo Domingo they would be able to lay the matter before Haiti more clearly and emphatically than a new commission could. Fort entered into the work with great enthusiasm and seemed to appreciate the responsibility entrusted to him. He is an impressive fellow and I believe that he, Bailly-Blanchard and Smith would make a good commission. Smith could act as Secretary and Bailly-Blanchard knows the French language perfectly. What do you think?

With assurances of high respect, I am, my dear Mr. President,
Very sincerely yours,   W. J. Bryan

TLS (SDR, RG 59, 839.00/1660a, DNA).
   ¹ General Desiderio Arias, Minister of War of the Dominican Republic. About his resignation and threat to join the opposition, see J. M. Sullivan to WJB, Jan. 9, 1915, FR 1915, p. 279.
   ² Enrique Jiménez.
   ³ Juan Isidro Jiménez.

E N C L O S U R E   I

Washington, January 12, 1915.

You may say to President Jimínez that this Government will support him to the fullest extent in the suppression of any insurrection against his Government. The election having been held and a Government chosen by the people having been established no more revolutions will be permitted. You may notify both Horacio Vasquez¹ and Arias that they will be held personally responsible if they attempt to embarass the Government.

The people of Santo Domingo will be given an opportunity to develop the resources of their country in peace. Their revenues will no longer be absorbed by graft or wasted in insurrections. This Government meant what it said when it sent a Commission there with a proposal looking to permanent peace and it will live up to the promises it has made. Reasonable delay in carrying out the proposed reforms is not objectionable but the changes advised are the reforms necessary for the honest and efficient administration of the Government and the early and proper development of the country. There should be no unnecessary delay therefore in putting them into operation. Keep us advised. A naval force will be sent whenever necessary.

  copied to President   Bryan

T telegram (SDR, RG 59, 839.00/1660a, DNA).
  1 Leader of the principal opposition party in the Dominican Republic, usually known as the *Horacistas*.

ENCLOSURE II

Santo Domingo. January 13, 1915

  Arias has withdrawn resignation and situation better.
                                   Sullivan.

T telegram (SDR, RG 59, 839.002/25, DNA).

From Jacob Henry Schiff

Dear Mr. President: New York, Jan. 15, 1915.

  Concerning the Immigration Bill recently passed by the Congress, may I respectfully submit that it ought not to be finally enacted into law by the attachment of your signature.

  While, with the repeated utterances that have emanated from you heretofore, I am led to believe that you do not favor several of the important provisions in the Bill, to me it appears that the literacy test is the most obnoxious part of the measure, which should never be placed upon the statute books of this country. If enacted, it will in time exclude tens and hundreds of thousands of the class of people who have done in the past most for the up-building of our country into the great and strong nation it now is, and if we shall now change our traditional policy in this respect, we shall only make more true in our own case the words of the poet: "Woe to the land where cities grow and men degenerate."

With the firm belief that you will again guide the country aright in this, and with great esteem, I am, dear Mr. President,
                    Yours most faithfully,   Jacob H. Schiff

TLS (WP, DLC).

From Samuel Gompers

My dear Mr. President: Washington, D. C., Jan. 15, 1915.

The Executive Council of the American Federation of Labor is now meeting in this city. My colleagues and I are greatly desirous of being accorded the opportunity of presenting to you in person a few matters of great importance to the interests of those whom we have the honor to represent. Therefore if you could grant us an interview this afternoon or any time tomorrow, we would be deeply appreciative.[1] Our week's session will adjourn tomorrow afternoon.

Thanking you in advance for your courtesy, I have the honor to remain,   Very sincerely yours,   Saml. Gompers.

TLS (WP, DLC).
    [1] Wilson saw them on January 16 at 6 P.M. See Remarks at a Press Conference, Jan. 19, 1915.

From Joseph Patrick Tumulty

                    The White House, January 15, 1915

Assuming that the immigration bill will reach the President tomorrow or Monday, what date will be set for the hearing? I suggest Friday in the East Room.   J.P.T.

OKeh.   W.W.

TL (WP, DLC).

From Elmer Truesdale Merrill[1]

My dear Wilson: Chicago Jan. 15, 1915.

I don't suppose you really mind the occasional cuffs dealt by the "DamNation" (as one of my colleagues persists in calling that excellent weekly) in the effort to preserve its exaltedly austere attitude. Its struggles after intellectual equilibrium often amuse me. I am sure they also do you. Perhaps I shouldn't enjoy it half so well on the whole, if I didn't frequently feel the need of applying to it the prefix quoted above. But it's comment on your Indianapolis speech, especially at the end, was really too silly!²

I read your address with great interest and approval, and believe you did well to make it. I hope you'll do so some more. We people need to be talked to by our chief magistrate. To be sure we can read his messages to Congress (I never *could* those of your predecessors, but I can yours), but that isn't enough. Needless to say, I'm not urging any Chatauqua circuits!

I was particularly touched by your invitation to people of my political attitude to "come in out of the cold." It was really this that is the excuse for my writing now. You so happily managed to make your hearty invitation sound personal to each shivering mugwump. Doubtless you have been flooded with other replies already. I was really touched; it was such a compliment to be asked in by this particular personage. It was kind of you—very kind—and I know you meant it. But I, for one, am like the chick-adee in the nursery-rhyme that you would have learned, if you had been brought up in New England—the bird that the compassionate little girl wanted brought in by the fire and provided with some warm clothing. I am really-truly more comfortable and easy out in the snow. It is my native atmosphere. I don't really enjoy the pattern of your wall-paper, when it runs all around and above me. I'd rather look in at the window at it. So I can better compare it with the pattern of clouds and stars in the blue heaven. I'm afraid if I were inside that it would not seem like heaven—those walls and that ceiling. (But I am really glad that you like better to be inside.) And though I like you firstrate, I am a bit afraid of your family-circle. There are so many people there, and they make so much noise that is quite unintelligible to me. I don't believe I could think there, and I'm quite sure I shouldn't feel like singing.

And after all, you so candidly pointed out the power that rests in the hands of these poor people out in the cold, that this might well lead one to be content to stay there. Doubtless that is rank individualism; but I fancy that the millenium is to be the triumph of individualism instead of collectivism, or socialism, or democracy, or whatever you choose to call it, and that the Divine Governor even now looks in that aspect upon the members of the *civitas Dei*. Even if we can't bring the millenium in quite yet, perhaps it is well not to shut out of mind the concept of it, but for some of us to wander in the outer sunlight (it really isn't darkness, you know!).

At all events, I am not a democrat (with either the big or the little D). I am in ultimate theory an individualist, and in present working theory (so far as I can teach and work it) an aristocrat —but with humane tendencies.

So you see I really can't come in. You were kind to ask me: be more kind in allowing me to decline: but be sure that I will help on the good in all the ways I can. And let me say how often, and with what hearty and affectionate sympathy and approval, I think of you and your great work, and what joy it gives me, and what hope for the future of the country, to hear it almost universally praised by the men not of your political party who yet have brains and hearts and consciences.

And so believe me always, Mr. President, your loyal and grateful and appreciative fellow-citizen, and, my dear Wilson, your faithful friend,   Elmer Truesdale Merrill.

ALS (WP, DLC).
¹ An old friend from Wilson's teaching days at Wesleyan University, 1888-90. Merrill had been Professor of Latin at the University of Chicago since 1908.
² "The President's Speech," New York *Nation*, c (Jan. 14, 1915), 41. "If to stir up criticism and create a buzz of comment be the test of a successful political speech," it began, "then President Wilson's Jackson Day speech at Indianapolis must be set down as a distinct success." It speculated that the speech had been intended, at least in part, to rally the spirits of Wilson's "somewhat dejected party followers." It attacked Wilson's contention that the Republican party had not had a new idea in thirty years. Not only had progressive Republicans had at least as much as the Democrats to do with devising and enacting the progressive legislation of recent years, but the Republican party had also performed a signal service in scotching the Democratic "new idea" of the free coinage of silver. It also criticized some of Wilson's phraseology, in particular his characterization of the current struggle for power among the revolutionary leaders in Mexico as a struggle for "liberty." On a more favorable note, the editorial praised Wilson's sensitivity to the political reality that neither the Democrats nor the Republicans could hope to win coming elections without the aid of the independent voter. However, it doubted that many of the voters who had voted the Progressive ticket in 1912 would accept Wilson's invitation to come into the Democratic fold.
The editorial concluded with another critical comment:
"If the President's admirers feel any disappointment in his first political speech, after so long a silence, it is mainly because Woodrow Wilson essayed for a day to be Andrew Jackson. That is a rôle which he is not well fitted to play. Its temper is not congenial to him. And the effect upon the national audience of his attempting to assume the part is plainly surprise mixed with irritation."

To William Jennings Bryan

My dear Mr. Secretary   [The White House] 16 January, 1915.

The suggestion seems to me an admirable one. I hope you will ask Governor Fort and Mr. Smith to serve, as they did in the other case, with such admirable results.

                    Faithfully Yours,   W.W.

WWTLI (SDR, RG 59, 838.00/1382, DNA).

To Edward Mandell House, with Enclosure

Dear Friend,   [The White House] 16 January, 1915.

Here is a despatch I want you to see at once. This is the only copy except that in the hands of the Secretary of State. You need not return it. It seems to me to mean a great deal.

Do you not think that it would be well for you to write Page a confidential letter at once, telling him what to expect? If you think it would be opened at the other end before being delivered, send it to me and I will see that it is sent in the pouch from the State Department.

Another letter will follow this very soon.

In haste,   Affectionately Yrs.,   W.W.

WWTLI (E. M. House Papers, CtY).

E N C L O S U R E

London, January 15, 1915.

No. 1474. January 15, p.m. VERY CONFIDENTIAL. The following despatch is sent in the special cypher explained in the Secretary's autograph letter to me of September:

Confidential for the Secretary. To be deciphered by himself. I lunched today with General French[1] who came here secretly for a council of war. He talked of course in profound confidence.

He says the military situation is a stalemate. The Germans cannot get to Paris or to Calais. On the other hand it will take the allies a year, perhaps two years and an incalculable loss of men to drive the Germans through Belgium. It would take perhaps four years and unlimlted [unlimited] men to invade Germany. He has little confidence in the ability of Russian aid in conquest of Germany. Russia has whipped Austria and will whip Turkey but he hopes for little more from her.

Speaking only for himself and in the profoundest confidence he told me of a peace proposal which he said the President, at Germany's request, has submitted to England. He tells me that this proposal is to end the war on condition that Germany gives up Belgium and pays for its restoration. French's personal opinion is that England would have to accept such an offer if it should be accompanied with additional offers to satisfy the other allies, such, for example, as the restoration to France of Alsace-Lorraine and the agreement that Russia shall have Constantinople.

I had an agreeable and friendly acquaintance with General French before the war and he has sent me several personal messages from the front. But I cannot help suspecting that he had a further purpose than a mere friendly talk in telling me these things. He seemed so much surprised when I confessed that I had not heard of such a proposal that I felt that possibly he held back something else that he had it in mind to say for the President.

He was solicitous to find out my opinion whether this peace proposal has been made in good faith or whether it was probably a German move to affect public opinion in the United States.

Colonel Squier had an interview today with Lord Kitchener whose military opinion coincides with General French's.

American Ambassador, London.

T telegram (E. M. House Papers, CtY).
1 Field Marshal Sir John Denton Pinkstone French.

To Oscar Wilder Underwood

My dear Mr. Underwood: The White House January 16, 1915

I am told that there is a resolution now pending before both Houses of Congress for the purchase of Monticello, the home of Mr. Jefferson, and that back of it lies a very strong sentiment in both houses. Certainly my own interest in it is very deep and very sincere. I most earnestly hope that there will be some interval in the business of the House which can be used for the passage of this most interesting piece of legislation, which I think will meet the approval of the whole nation.

Cordially and sincerely yours,   Woodrow Wilson

TLS (O. W. Underwood Papers, A-Ar).

To Jacob Henry Schiff

My dear Mr. Schiff: The White House January 16, 1915

Thank you for your letter of January fifteenth. What you say about the pending immigration bill makes a great impression upon me, for it certainly states one of the most serious doubts with regard to the whole bill. You may be sure that what you say will have my most serious consideration.

Sincerely yours,   Woodrow Wilson

TLS (J. H. Schiff Papers, OCAJA).

To Edward Mandell House

Dear Friend,   [The White House] 17 January, 1915.

Here is a draft of the letter. Please criticise it freely. Pull it about, alter and add to it as you think best, and send it back to me to be put into final shape against your visit next week.[1]

Page's despatch which I sent you last night puts hope into me in a very definite way.

In haste,   Affectionately Yours,   W.W.

WWTLI (E. M. House Papers, CtY).
[1] See WW to EMH, Jan. 29, 1915.

To Mary Allen Hulbert

Dearest Friend,   The White House 17 January, 1915.

We have had an exciting day: the climax of it came at half past four this afternoon when my dear Jessie gave birth to a fine boy,[1] a little beauty, weighing seven and three quarters pounds. And so none of us can think straight. I forget where the keys of the typewriter are as I absent-mindedly try to write this. I can only say that both mother and child are doing splendidly, and that the happy father is due to arrive in a few minutes. My own heart is full of the pity that the sweet, sweet mother could not have been here to share her daughter's joy!

You have not sent the receipts yet, and the article waits for them.

All join me in affectionate messages.

Your devoted friend,   Woodrow Wilson

WWTLS (WP, DLC).
[1] Francis Bowes Sayre, Jr.

Two Letters from Edward Mandell House

Dear Governor: New York City. January 18th, 1915.

I am returning you the draft of the letter you sent me under cover of your note of January 17th.

There is not a sentence or a word I would change in it for it reads like a classic. You can never know how deeply I appreciate your confidence and friendship and I shall endeavor to merit them both.

I have written to Page as you suggested[1] and will send it to him by Sir Horace Plunkett who sails on Wednesday.

That which strikes me most in Page's despatch is the glaring indiscretion of the Generals in question. It makes me feel more strongly than ever how necessary it is for us to keep our own counsel.

I have it in mind to go over to Washington on Sunday afternoon, reaching there in time to be with you in the evening. I shall do this unless I hear from you to the contrary.

Affectionately yours,   E. M. House

1 EMH to WHP, Jan. 18, 1915, TLS (W. H. Page Papers, MH). House responded to Page's No. 1474 by explaining that he had had informal talks with the ambassadors in Washington of the belligerent nations and also had had direct communication with Zimmermann, which had led Wilson and him to believe that peace conversations might now be initiated in an unofficial way. Toward this end, he would sail for London on January 30.

Dear Governor: New York City. January 18th, 1915.

Seth Low called yesterday to tell me that things in Colorado were going well and that he thought he could see daylight there.

He has had several talks with young Rockefeller who has changed his views to this extent that he now no longer talks of what is "consistent with the good of our stockholders."

In a few days, Low expects to be able to publish your letter to the Committee and other correspondence looking to the direction of the settlement.

Mr. Low asked me if I thought it would be useful to you to have the cooperation of the Chamber of Commerce in the Shipping Bill. He thought this might be arranged provided certain changes in the bill could be agreed upon. He thought if the Chamber of Commerce, which was now unanimously opposed to the bill, could be brought to endorse it, that it would bring to its support many Senators who are now against it.

I asked him to give me the changes that he would suggest and this morning he sends me the enclosed.[1]

Affectionately yours,   E. M. House

TLS (WP, DLC).
1 The enclosure is missing.

To Edward Mandell House[1]

My dear Friend: The White House January 18, 1915

I am very grateful to you for consenting to go to Europe at this time to ascertain what our opportunities as neutrals and as disinterested friends of the nations at war are in detail with respect to the assistance that we can render, and how those opportunities can best be made use of; and I beg that you will let this letter serve both as your introduction to those whom it may be necessary for you to consult and as your commission to speak as my personal, though private, representative.

You know as I do that it is the earnest desire of our fellow-countrymen of all classes to minister to the relief of the suffering in Europe wherever it is possible and legitimate for them to do so; and, more than that, to put themselves and their resources at the service of all the belligerents in whatever way the rules and practices of neutrality permit for the purpose of mitigating the distresses and lessening the friction and the dislocations of a time of war. I would esteem it a very generous service on your part if you would be kind enough to make inquiry in every quarter open to you as to what would in the circumstances be our best course of action in these matters.

A great many of us feel that our efforts so far have in some degree lacked order and effective cooperation. I would very much like to know if there is any way in which we can effect a better coordination in what we are already doing, whether there are other objects to which it is our duty to turn our attention, and whether I can personally or officially do anything that would helpfully direct or assist such work.

We cannot answer these questions satisfactorily from this side of the water. They can be answered only by some one person who has made himself familiar with the situation as a whole and in all its parts. I know no one who can do this better than you can. It gives me the greatest satisfaction to be able to commission you thus informally to do it.

With warmest regard,

Faithfully yours,   Woodrow Wilson[2]

TLS (E. M. House Papers, CtY).
  [1] House was to use the following letter as a cover for his mission.
  [2] There is a WWsh draft of this letter in WP, DLC.

From Oscar Wilder Underwood

My dear Mr. President: Washington, D. C. January 18, 1915.

I received your letter of the sixteenth instant this morning, in reference to the bills pending before Congress for the purchase of Monticello. I am in accord with the views expressed in your letter in reference to the matter and hope that the bills can be considered before the end of the session. I will be glad to confer with the gentlemen having this legislation in charge and call your letter to their attention.[1]

Sincerely yours,   O W Underwood

TLS (WP, DLC).
 [1] House Joint Res. 390, "creating a commission and authorizing said commission to acquire by purchase the property known as Monticello, and embracing the former home of Thomas Jefferson and the park surrounding the same, consisting of 700 acres of land . . . ," was introduced in the House by Representative James Hay of Virginia on December 17, 1914. The Committee on Rules reported the resolution with an amendment on February 24, 1915, but no further action was taken before the end of the session. James E. Martine had introduced a similar resolution in the Senate on February 17 but it never emerged from committee. *Cong. Record*, 63d Cong., 3d sess., pp. 329, 3928-29, 4553. For the complex story of the efforts to purchase Monticello from its owner, Representative Jefferson Monroe Levy of New York, see Merrill D. Peterson, *The Jefferson Image in the American Mind* (New York, 1960), pp. 380-384.

From Dudley Field Malone

PERSONAL and URGENT

Dear Mr. President: Port of New York January 18, 1915.

. . . I am writing you particularly to add emphasis to the importance of the visit of Dr. Francis Kelley[1] with me on Wednesday morning. Without any regard to the merits of the controversy that has been going on with more or less acrimony over the Mexican problem, this fact remains: That there are hundreds of thousands of perfectly sincere, honest American Catholics, who are members of the Democratic party, or independents, and who voted gladly for you and the Democratic party in the last national election, but who are being filled up with arguments contrary to the views and purposes of your administration. Dr. Kelley can do more than any other man in this country to tell the truth and correct this situation, and restore confidence in the minds of these people as to the truly patriotic, American purposes of your administration's policy in Mexico. Dr. Kelley is most friendly, and will talk frankly and in confidence; and I hope it will be possible for us to have sufficient time for both of you to discuss a situation of critical importance.

With my affectionate remembrance to all in the family, and especially to Jessie and your little grandson, believe me to be,

Yours most faithfully,   Dudley Field Malone

TLS (WP, DLC).
 [1] The Rev. Dr. Francis Clement Kelley, founder and president of the Catholic Church Extension Society of the United States of America.

Sir Cecil Arthur Spring Rice to Sir Edward Grey

Washington [Jan. 18, 1915]

Private. My telegram of December 29th.

Mr. Morgan[1] saw President to-day. The latter was quite willing M. should take any action "in furtherance of trade" including advancement to Russia. He says President is still most anxious to get shipping bill through but that Congress will certainly delay it for at least some time. M. could manage private purchase of German ships if His Majesty's Government desired it. President's personal sentiments to us are friendly and he is opposed to proposal for restricting sale of contraband: but he is much afraid of German vote.

T telegram (E. Grey Papers, FO 800/85, PRO).
[1] J. Pierpont Morgan, Jr.

Remarks at a Press Conference

January 19, 1915

Mr. President, I understand that you have sent a letter to Attorney General Gregory in regard to the rise of food prices?[1]

I merely asked him to investigate for the purpose of finding out if there was anything illegal, really, at the bottom of it. Of course, only illegal things are being investigated. The investigation has already begun.

In that connection, Mr. President, will you regard the possibility of an embargo on war materials?

Of course there is no authority lodged anywhere to place an embargo.

Could not that authority be conferred by legislative action?

It would have to be conferred that way, if at all.

Isn't that unconstitutional?

I can't answer that question. I have never looked into it.

Mr. President, is there anything you can tell us about your recent conference with Mr. Gompers?

Mr. Gompers brought the executive committee of the American Federation of Labor here on Saturday afternoon merely to go over the various things in which they were interested. One of them was the immigration bill. Another was the seamen's bill. I don't recollect any other particular topics. Those are the ones most particularly talked about, and they left me a memorandum.[2]

Any suggestion of additional legislation?

No, except the seamen's bill. Oh, yes—I beg your pardon—

they did. They expressed their interest in further legislation on employers' liability and workmen's compensation, but we didn't go into that. That was merely a suggestion.

In a general way, Mr. President, you had already expressed sympathy with this program, except one or two features of the immigration bill.

Yes. They were coming to urge it upon me so much as to keep it fresh in my recollection—their interest in it. . . .

Mr. President, do you still regard the passage of the ship purchase bill—of its passage—as certainly probable?

I think it is extremely probable.

With some amendments?

Oh, I dare say with some amendments, but no amendments going to the essential features of the bill.

Mr. President, did Mr. Underwood say that they would hold night sessions from now on to facilitate the passage of legislation in the House?

No, he did not. He didn't speak of legislation.

Mr. President, do you regard it as essential to the shipping bill that the shipping board be made up of cabinet members, as provided for? Some of the Progressives said it should be nonpolitical and nonpartisan.

I discussed that. I think the arrangement in the bill is much the more to be preferred than any other.

Mr. President, does that cover the point of the time of government ownership? They also suggested that the bill ought to read that if the venture was successful, government ownership should be continued.

I don't want to discuss out of court, so to speak, the details of the bill, because I don't know just what is in the minds of the gentlemen up there.

Mr. President, some of your callers have suggested that, because of the European situation, you might not make the Panama Exposition trip?

I see the papers have been talking about that. That is nothing new. I have felt obliged to say all along that, while I confidently expected to go, of course it was possible that a situation might arise that would make it necessary for me to stay here. . . .

Mr. President, in that connection, have you any intimation at all of any likelihood of peace, come this spring?

No. I wish I could say yes. There are no signs as yet.

The morning papers, Mr. President, say that the Democratic caucus last night endorsed the rural credits legislation as passable. Does that mean this session?

Not necessarily. That depends on how soon the shipping bill passes.

Mr. President, last summer, when the ship registry bill passed, there was an expression of desire to encourage the American merchant marine. The question was brought up as to whether the seamen's bill and similar legislation might have a deterrent effect in keeping American capital out of it. Has that been brought up lately?

No, that is a question which has been debated all along. There have been two sides to it.

Mr. President, does the apparent reluctance of the British government to allow the [*Dacia*] to make the first try[3] interfere in any way with your resolution of the shipping bill?

No, I don't think it is a parallel instance.

Mr. President, there is much interest in the baby.

He is all right.

Have you any views as to when you will hear from Great Britain on the note?

No, we have not. I haven't heard anything except the preliminary note.

JRT transcript (WC, NjP) of CLSsh (C. L. Swem Coll., NjP).
[1] WW to T. W. Gregory, Jan. 18, 1915, TLS (Letterpress Books, WP, DLC).
[2] It is missing.
[3] On about December 28, 1914, Edward Nicklas Breitung, American-born but of German ancestry, a mining operator of Marquette, Mich., purchased the steamship *Dacia*, then at Port Arthur, Tex., from the Hamburg-America Line. He transferred the vessel to American registry on January 4, intending to use it to transport cotton to Europe. If successful, he planned to purchase other German ships then in American ports for the same purpose. By January 19, Breitung's actions had led to considerable comment in the American press and had created a furor in Great Britain. Moreover, the State Department had by this time received formal protests from the British and French ambassadors and from Sir Edward Grey. For further details and the dénouement of this affair, see Arthur S. Link, *Wilson: The Struggle for Neutrality, 1914-1915* (Princeton, N. J., 1960), pp. 179-87.

To Elmer Truesdale Merrill

My dear Merrill: [The White House] January 19, 1915

I thank you for your letter with all my heart. It was like you in every particular, full of your habitual independence of judgment and of attitude, and also full of a fine spirit. For my part I am just as sure of you while you remain outside as I would be if you came inside. I wish I had time to write you a letter which would be some adequate return for the pleasure which your letter gave me. It was a delightful glimpse of an old friend whose friendship and confidence I value very highly indeed, and such messages go far to keep a fellow in heart.

Cordially and faithfully yours,   Woodrow Wilson

TLS (Letterpress Books, WP, DLC).

To George Sibley Johns

Personal.

My dear Johns: [The White House] January 19, 1915

Thank you for your letter of the fifteenth about German-American sentiment.[1] It contains just the kind of information that is most valuable and important to me.

As a matter of fact, I keep personally in very close touch with the Department of State and I want to say that throughout Mr. Bryan has shown the most generous and evidently genuine desire that I should share the responsibilities of that department with him in the fullest measure, and he has invariably shown a willingness to be guided by my view when our views differed, which has been not often.

The editorial you sent me was certainly pitched in the right tone and contained the right judgment.[2] It is hard to work these things out, but you may be sure we will do the best that can be done when half the world is on fire.

It is always a great pleasure to hear from you.

Cordially and faithfully yours,   Woodrow Wilson

TLS (Letterpress Books, WP, DLC).

[1] G. S. Johns to WW, Jan. 15, 1915, TLS (WP, DLC). Johns summarized for Wilson a recent conversation with an unnamed German-born citizen of St. Louis whom he characterized as very intelligent and disposed to be judicious and fair. This informant believed that "the best German-American sentiment" so far saw no ground for criticism either of the Wilson administration or of Wilson personally. He warned, however, that the German-American community was "vigilantly watching" the conduct of the administration in the dispute with England over interference with neutral trade. Furthermore, he asserted that the German Americans distrusted Bryan, partly because of his free silver campaign of 1896, but mostly because of lack of confidence in his ability to handle the difficult questions raised by the war.

[2] An undated clipping from the *St. Louis Post-Dispatch*. The editorial, "Great Britain's Vicious Plea," commenting on the British preliminary reply, said that the United States Government could not accept the "preposterous doctrine" that German wrongs excused British violations of international law. "Nothing could be more vicious and destructive of civilization and international law than the theory that one wrong justifies another. . . . There is no form of piracy or brutality practiced by the lowest people in the scale of civilization that would not be justified under this dictum."

From William Jennings Bryan, with Enclosure

My dear Mr. President: Washington January 19, 1915.

I send you a flimsy of a telegram which I have just received from London. It is the only flimsey made and the original is locked up. It was shown to the Solicitor and Chandler Anderson who was with him, also to Phillips but neither of them nor I have kept a flimsey for fear it might get out. I thought I would send it over to you and then call you up by phone between half-past eight and nine and get your opinion over the private wire.

With assurances of high respect I am, my dear Mr. President,
Yours very sincerely,   W. J. Bryan

We are in a very delicate position. If we maintain the American position it will irritate Gt B. If we surrender it we will irritate our own people

TLS (WP, DLC).

E N C L O S U R E

London. January 18, 1915.

1486. FOR SECRETARY AND THE PRESIDENT. STRICTLY CONFIDENTIAL. VERY CONFIDENTIAL.

Your 966, January fifteenth.[1]

I have had more than an hour's talk with Sir Edward Grey. He confirms what Haldane told me about the DACIA but he does not confirm what Haldane said about other German ships in the last sentence of my 1473, January fifteenth.[2] About this they are not agreed and the Cabinet will have further discussion. It will be prudent to disregard the last sentence above referred to.[3] Apparently Haldane went beyond what had been agreed on by the Cabinet. My inquiry whether British Government would object to purchase and transfer of German-interned ships to ply between American and British ports brought from Sir Edward Grey the most ominous conversation I have ever had with him.

He explained that the chief weapon that England has against any enemy is her navy and that the navy may damage an enemy in two ways: by fighting and by economic pressure. Under the conditions of this war economic pressure is at least as important as naval fighting. One of the chief methods of using economic pressure is to force the German merchantships off the seas. If, therefore, these be bought and transferred to a neutral flag this pressure is removed.

He reminded me that he was not making official representations to the United States Government and for that reason he was the more emphatic. If the United States without intent to do Great Britain an injury but moved only to relieve the scarcity of tonnage should buy these ships it would still annul one of the victories that England has won by her navy. He reminded me of the fast rising tide of criticism of the United States about the transfer of the DACIA and he declared that this has intensified and spread the feeling against us in England on account of our note of protest. He spoke earnestly, sadly, ominously, but in the friendliest spirit.

The foregoing only confirms the following paragraphs which I wrote yesterday and held till I could see Grey today. There is a steadily deepening and spreading feeling throughout every section of English opinion that the German influence in the United States has by this temptation to buy these interned ships won us to the German side. The old criticism of the President for not protesting against the violation of The Hague Treaty by Germany when she invaded Belgium is revived with tenfold its first earnestness. This is coupled with our protest against shipping as showing an unfriendly spirit. But both these criticisms were relatively mild till the DACIA was transferred to the American flag. That transfer added volume and vehemence to all preceding criticisms and is cited in the press and in conversation everywhere as proof of our unfriendliness. They regard the DACIA as a German ship put out of commission by their navy. She comes on the seas again by our permission which so far nullifies their victory. If she come here she will, of course, be seized and put into the Prize Court. Her seizure will strike the English imagination in effect as the second conquest of her first from the Germans and now from the Americans. Popular feeling will, I fear, run as high as it ran over the TRENT affair; and a very large part of English opinion will regard us as enemies.

If another German ship should follow the DACIA here I do not think that any Government could withstand the popular demand for her confiscation; and if we permit the transfer of a number of these ships there will be such a wave of displeasure as will make a return of the recent good-feeling between the two peoples impossible for a generation. There is no possible escape from such an act being regarded by the public opinion of this Kingdom as a distinctly unfriendly and practically hostile act.

I not only read and hear this at every turn—I feel it in the attitude of people towards me and towards our Government. For the first time I have felt a distinctly unfriendly atmosphere. It has the quality of the atmosphere just before an earthquake.

The Government is studiously polite and still genuinely friendly. But there are warnings that it may not be able to maintain its old-time friendly attitude if a whirlwind of anti-American feeling sweep over the Kingdom and over its Allies. Nine men out of every ten you meet in London today are convinced that the DACIA is proof that the Germans have won us to their support. I can not exaggerate the ominousness of the situation. The case is not technical but has large human and patriotic and historic elements in it.   American Ambassador London.

T telegram (WP, DLC).
   1 WJB to WHP, Jan. 15, 1915, *FR-WWS 1915*, p. 679, stating that "American interests" contemplated purchasing a German merchant vessel lying in an American harbor "for trade exclusively between this country and British ports," and requesting that Page ascertain the attitude of the British government.
   2 WHP to WJB, Jan. 15, 1915, *ibid.*, pp. 679-80, relaying the British cabinet's decision concerning *Dacia*: if *Dacia* fell into British hands, her cargo would be purchased at the price already offered by the German buyers; however, the legitimacy of the transfer of the ship would be decided by the British prize court.
   3 "Lord Haldane said further that if the *Dacia* were used, under *bona-fide* American register, in coastwise trade or in trade with South America, his Government would not object. I asked him if this remark would apply to other German ships now interned in the United States and he replied yes." *Ibid.*, p. 680.

From Charles William Eliot

Dear President Wilson: Cambridge, Mass. 19 January, 1915
   I hope very much that you will veto the Burnett Bill. The literacy test in that Bill is a restrictive measure merely; since it affords no sound test whatever of the real desirability of the immigrant. Any restriction on the immigration of healthy, industrious, liberty-seeking people is, I believe, at once uneconomic and ungenerous. Freemen who have secured liberty for themselves and their children ought to be generous in welcoming less fortunate people to the same privilege. The supreme selfishness of the attitude of the labor leaders on Immigration ought to put them out of court altogether. Many of them are recent immigrants themselves.
   I am, with high regard,
                     Sincerely yours,   Charles W. Eliot

TLS (WP, DLC).

From Edward Mandell House

Dear Governor: New York City. January 20th, 1915.

Thank you for your letter of the 18th which I can use as an excuse for going to Europe if we find it necessary.

I do not believe that there will be any notice taken of my going. A great many people necessarily know that we are sailing on the Lusitania and not one has yet asked, or shown any curiosity as to the purpose of our trip.

You will notice it is already in the papers via Washington. I believe it would be better not to give any excuse unless necessary for the reason that all the relief societies in Europe would be alert and waiting for me.

I shall leave on the 12.08 Sunday, hoping to be with you at 5.40 as usual.   Affectionately yours,   E. M. House

P.S. I had a long talk with Bernstorff today, but nothing important developed. He seemed glad that I was leaving so soon. Dumba comes tomorrow.

TLS (WP, DLC).

To William Hughes

My dear Senator: [The White House] January 21, 1915

I took up with the Postmaster General the matter[1] which you and Mr. Kitchin pressed upon me so earnestly the other day and I find that you were both of you under a false impression with regard to at least a part of the matter.

You will remember that we bound ourselves in our platform to appoint, wherever it was possible to do so, residents of Porto Rico to the offices in that island, and the redemption of this pledge has been very earnestly pressed upon us by Governor Yager. Mr. Burleson called Mr. Reilly's[2] attention to this at the time he proposed Mr. Bibeau[3] and said that it was our desire and policy to appoint a resident of Porto Rico if possible.

I may say to you confidentially that in the Postmaster General's opinion the man of whom you spoke who was proposed for the office would not be a suitable appointment. We have, however, a very earnest recommendation for a resident of Porto Rico from the Governor General.

I agree with the Postmaster General that if this man proposed by the Governor General is indeed fitted for the post, it is really our duty under the pledge of the platform to appoint him, and

I feel confident that you and Mr. Kitchin will agree that that is the best solution in the light of all the circumstances.

    Always

        Faithfully and cordially yours,   Woodrow Wilson

TLS (Letterpress Books, WP, DLC).
  [1] The appointment of the postmaster of San Juan, P. R.
  [2] Thomas Lawrence Reilly, Democratic congressman from Connecticut.
  [3] Henry C. Bibeau of Meriden.

To Hester Eloise Hosford

My dear Miss Hosford: [The White House] January 21, 1915

    Your letter of January eighteenth[1] interests me very much indeed.

    You would be quite right in saying that I do hope by my peace policies to establish such standards in the action of this country that will enable the United States to serve as an unimpeachably just example of the way in which the relations between different countries should be regarded and handled.

    You would be also entirely right in saying not only that no discriminations had ever been made by this administration on the ground of religious belief, but that I regard religious toleration as one of the most invaluable fruits of civilization, indispensable to the peaceful and prosperous life of a people and the just conduct of their affairs.

    I am very glad indeed that you gave me the privilege of expressing an opinion about these points that have interested you.

        Cordially and sincerely yours,   Woodrow Wilson

TLS (Letterpress Books, WP, DLC).
  [1] H. E. Hosford to WW, Jan. 18, 1915, TLS (WP, DLC).

From Joseph Patrick Tumulty

                The White House January 21, 1915.

    At the beginning of the hearing on the Immigration Bill[1] in the East Room tomorrow (Friday) morning at 10:00 o'clock, will the President announce that the time of the hearing will be 2½ hours, to be equally divided between those who wish the bill approved, and those who wish the bill vetoed; that during the first hour the President will hear those in favor of the bill, this time to be controlled by Mr. Frank Morrison, Secretary of the American Federation of Labor; that the next hour and fifteen minutes the President will hear those who wish the bill to be vetoed, this time to be controlled by Representatives Gallivan, Sabath and Goldfogle; that at the conclusion of the two hours and fifteen minutes, the closing 15 minutes will be given to those who favor the bill, the time to be controlled by Mr. Morrison.

Will the President also please announce that he would prefer that speakers be not interrupted? Also that if any of those present have prepared briefs he will be glad to go over them if they are left with his Secretary?

For the information of the President, there is attached hereto lists of those who have asked to be heard. These lists have been furnished Mr. Morrison and Representatives Gallivan, Sabath and Goldfogle.

IMMIGRATION BILL HEARING—JANUARY 22, 1915.

(For the Bill)[2]

William A. Pike of Philadelphia.[3]

George Kirkpatrick, General Secretary, New Jersey Federation of Patriotic Fraternities, Camden, New Jersey.

Frank Morrison, Secretary, American Federation of Labor, Washington.

Dr. Thomas W. Salmon, National Committee for Mental Hygiene, New York.

Allan D. Crone, Secretary, North Point Council No. 93, J.O.U.A.M.,[4] Baltimore, Md.

George W. McFarland, Chairman, National Legislative Committee, Daughters of Liberty, Trenton, N. J.

J. H. Patten, representing the Farmers National Congress and the Farmers National Union.

Representatives of the Railroad Brotherhoods.

Professors Lee,[5] Fairchild and Ross.

Samuel Friedman, Chairman, American Anti-Congestion League, New York, (*Not known whether for or against.*)

(Against the Bill)

Representative Henry M. Goldfogle.

Representative Adolph J. Sabath.

Representative James A. Gallivan.

Louis Marshall, New York City.[6]

Louis Hammerling, New York City.

Charles Edward Russell, Washington, D. C.[7]

Paul Kennaday, Secretary, Friends of Russian Freedom—delegation of prominent citizens—New York City.

James F. McNaboe, Secretary, National Liberal Immigration League, New York City.

Joseph Smolinski, Washington, D. C.[8]

James M. Curley, Mayor of Boston.

Rabbi Stephen S. Wise, New York City.

Ezekiel Leavitt, Editor, Boston Jewish Voice, Boston.

Marcus Braun, Editor, Fair Play, New York City.

Hon. Bourke Cockran.

Leon Sanders, President, Hebrew Sheltering and Immigrant Aid
    Society of America, New York City.

Michael Leveen, Grand Master, Independent Order of King Solo-
    mon, Newark, New Jersey.

Frank Leveroni, Boston, Mass.[9]

E. M. Grella, Italian Press Publishing Association, New York City.

Louis J. Shapiro, (National Liberal Immigration League), Nor-
    folk, Va.

Meyer L. Brown, General Secretary, Jewish National Workers'
    Alliance of America, New York City—represented by Dr.
    Isaac A. Hourwich.

Julius I. Peyser, representing the Executive Committee of the
    Independent Order B'nai B'rith.

Myer Cohen, representing the Board of Delegates of Civil Rights
    of the Union of American Hebrew Congregations.

Representative J. Hampton Moore.

Judge Sanders, New York.[10]

Rabbi Heller, Boston.[11]

Rabbi Levy, Philadelphia.[12]

Rabbi Taitlebaum, New York.[13]

Rabbi Silverstone, Washington.[14]

Samuel Tausig[15] and small delegation from New York City—
    request of Representative Walter M. Chandler.

Samuel Friedman, Chairman, American Anti-Congestion League,
    New York City, (*Not known whether for or against*).

Randolph Dodge, representing the *Civic* Service House at Boston.

Emanuel Nardi, of Philadelphia, Chairman of Committee of five
    representing the Italian-American Alliance of the United
    States—request of Representative Logue.

Herman Bernstein, of New York.

T MS (WP, DLC).

[1] There is a T transcript of the hearing, dated Jan. 22, 1915, in WP, DLC.

[2] The following individuals will be identified only if not previously identified
or not sufficiently identified in the document itself. Not all the persons here
named actually appeared at the hearing.

[3] Secretary of the Order of Independent Americans, of Philadelphia.

[4] Junior Order United American Mechanics, an anti-Catholic, nativistic
fraternity.

[5] Joseph Lee of Boston, who, though never a professor, was an influential
social worker and a key figure in the Immigration Restriction League. Fairchild
and Ross have been identified elsewhere in this series.

6 Lawyer, civic and Jewish communal leader, with a long-time interest in defending the cause of immigrants.

7 Well-known muckraker and frequent candidate for public office in New York on the Socialist ticket.

8 Clerk in the office of the Adjutant General in Washington. It is not known what organization he represented at the hearing.

9 Lawyer, active in Italian-American charitable organizations.

10 "Judge Sanders" is the same Leon Sanders, listed above, who was a former judge of the New York Municipal Court.

11 Isaac Heller, not a rabbi but president of the Hebrew Immigrant Aid Society of Massachusetts.

12 Louis Edward Levy, also not a rabbi, but rather a prominent scientist and inventor of Philadelphia and president of the Association for the Relief and Protection of Jewish Immigrants.

13 Rabbi Aaron Teitelbaum, secretary of the Union of Orthodox Rabbis of the United States and Canada and a member of the executive committee of the Central Relief Committee, an organization to aid Jews suffering as a result of the war.

14 Gedalia Silverstone, chief rabbi of the Orthodox congregations of Washington.

15 Tausig cannot be identified.

From Edward Mandell House, with Enclosure

Dear Governor: New York City. January 21st, 1915.

I am enclosing you a copy of a letter which has come from the Chilian Ambassador this morning.

Everything now seems to be in shape for you to go ahead. I believe the country will receive this policy with enthusiasm and it will make your Administration notable, even had you done but little else.

I told Bernstorff yesterday that as long as such raids as that on Yarmouth and the other coast towns continued, my mission would be hopeless. He promised to protest to his government, but he remarked that the military were now in authority and the civil authorities could do but little.

Affectionately yours,   E. M. House

TLS (WP, DLC).

E N C L O S U R E

Eduardo Suárez-Mujica to Edward Mandell House

Confidential.

My dear Sir: Washington. January 19th, 1915.

I have tried to communicate with you at the White House but I knew that unfortunately you were in New York.

I wished to inform you that I have since two days the expected reply from Chile. It is favourable in principle and praises the idea [a]s a generous and panamerican one.

Although it is sometimes not little difficult to find the proper expressions to render an idea agreeable to several parties, I hope we shall succeed when the moment of discussing the development of our first accord comes.

Mr. Bryan has told me lately to be in full acquaintance with the matter; and under this understanding I assume I can communicate with him in your absence.

I am, my dear Mr. House,

Very sincerely yours,   Edo. Suárez-Mujica.

TCL (WP, DLC).

From Edward Mandell House, with Enclosure

Dear Governor: New York City. January 21st, 1915.

This is a copy of a letter which came to me from Brown [Spring Rice] this morning. Of course he means a message from E.G.

After receiving it, I telephoned him under my code name and he is to send his kinsman tonight with the message, so I may have it tomorrow.

I take it that it concerns the recent raids by Maine [Germany], and I fear that it is to say that no negociations can be begun while such things happen.

Smith [Dumba] called today. He said he considered such raids senseless and harmful, and that he intended to inform his people as to his views.   Affectionately yours,   E. M. House

TLS (WP, DLC).

E N C L O S U R E

20-1-15.

I have received an answer from our friend in London which I shall be ready to communicate when you come. When is that likely to be?

It relates to the present state of public opinion in London as to which you may be glad to receive and transmit information, and to other matters which would be of interest to your friend.

I am likely to be here for some time as it is difficult for me to go to New York at the present moment but I hope you will be able to come here before leaving.

T MS (WP, DLC).

From Mary Eloise Hoyt

My dearest cousin,   [Baltimore] Jan. 21, 1915.

I am just so happy about the boy! Baby-lover as I am, I should have been grateful for boy or girl—but I know a boy will be more of a companion for you. And, besides, from his own point of view, he would, naturally, choose to be a boy; I cannot imagine any creature with spirit and energy really liking to be a woman, can you? We put up with our fate and try to be as nice as possible under the circumstances but if we had been permitted to do the choosing! And all this reminds me of one of Ellen's dearest confidences. "Mary, Woodrow is really the loveliest person. You know he has always wanted a boy. But now he says he does not want *a* boy he wants *the* boy, and, of course, he might not get *the* boy, so he is satisfied." I hope, dear cousin, this will be *the* boy, but those of us who really know his grandfather do not expect Master Francis Sayre to be a more admirable person. Bless the dear little seven pounds of him, how little, at this moment, he cares about all our hopes and expectations; does he yell very much? I hear that his first cry bore witness to good lungs. I feel he has found a pretty good place for himself; I should not mind a bit having Frank and Jessie for parents, should you? But I fear that he will be cross when he realises that he might have been named for his grandfather! . . .

With dearest love to all,

Affectionately yours,   Mary Hoyt

ALS (WP, DLC).

To William Jennings Bryan, with Enclosure

[The White House]

My dear Mr. Secretary,   22 January, 1915.

Here are my suggestions for additions to the note to Page. I have made very slight and immaterial changes in the note as you dictated it, as you will see; and have merely prepared some elaborations.   Faithfully Yours,   W.W.

WWTLI (SDR, RG 59, 763.72112/796a, DNA).

ENCLOSURE[1]

Amembassy London   January 20, 1915.

Confidential, to be deciphered by the Ambassador himself. Answering your two telegrams in regard to the irritation and apparent change in public opinion regarding the United States you will please ⟨say to Sir Edward that⟩ *discuss the matter again with Sir Edward Grey in effect as follows*: We regret exceedingly to learn that the British public entertains any doubt as to the strict neutrality of this Government or as to the support given by the general public to the Government's position. This is probably due to the fact that a portion of the British public is quite naturally uninformed as to the character of our population.

⟨We have here representatives of all the principal nations of Europe.⟩ While the English element predominated in the original stock the immigration in latter years has been largely from other countries. Germany and Ireland, for instance, have contributed very materially during the last half century and among those *who are* the children of foreign born parents the German element now predominates. This element is not only numerous but it has a strong representation in financial, mercantile life and agriculture. Congressman Bartholdt is a naturalized American with a long service in Congress. A considerable portion of the voters of his district are naturalized Germans or of German descent. ⟨This statement is made to show the character of our population. Various influences have operated to irritate the different sections of our country and elements of our people.⟩ *There need be no fear that his proposals will be adopted; but they are a sample of our difficulties. Notwithstanding such influences the vast majority of the American people are genuinely friendly in their attitude towards Great Britain. Mere debate and newspaper agitation will not alter that attitude; but acts which seem to them arbitrary, unnecessary, and contrary to the recognized rules of neutral commerce may alter it very seriously, because the great majority of them are trying in good faith to live within those rules and they are sensitive about nothing more than about their legitimate trade.*

It is worth while to enumerate some of the chief causes of irritation on this side the water, because they are causes which can be removed and which this Government would be glad to cooperate to remove.

First, *the* interruption in exports *has very seriously* affected

---

[1] Words in italics inserted by Wilson; words in angle brackets deleted by him.

cotton, which is the staple product of the southern states. Cotton for a while was very low the price being probably not more than half of the ordinary price. As a fall of one cent in cotton means a loss of eighty millions of dollars to the cotton-growing states, they estimated their loss at three or four hundred millions of dollars. The price has risen as ships have been *slowly* secured, but *the number of bottoms is still wholly inadequate and* the scarcity of ships has resulted in a rise of freight rates of four, five, six, and even seven hundred per cent. This double tax upon the leading industry of a whole section has aroused a complaint which is being voiced by members of congress and senators from that section. *Moreover it has seriously affected the whole financial situation of the country inasmuch as cotton is the crop with which the foreign balances against this country have usually been paid at this season of the year*

Next, the copper situation has been embarassing. A large number of people were thrown out of employment in the mining districts just as winter was coming on and the senators and members from the mountain states have been kept busy ⟨looking after⟩ *meeting* complaints⟨.⟩ *and making explanations to those most affected.*

Third, the export of arms, ammunition and horses to the allies is, of course, known and the protests made by German-Americans and by a portion of the Irish-Americans, while entirely without justification, is not unnatural. It is difficult for people to think logically when their sympathies are aroused. The Government has done all in its power to make the situation plain and has today issued a lengthy letter answering numerous criticisms that have been made.[2] ⟨There is no likelihood of the Bartholdt bill being reported or passed, but there is no doubt that the interference with merchandise exported from the United States to neutral countries has caused widespread irritation.⟩

The Dacia case has received a great deal of newspaper notoriety because of predictions as to what would be done with her. Breitung, seeing that there was a chance to profit by the high freight rates, decided to buy a ship. He first tried to buy an English ship and then a French ship but as his correspondence shows he failed to secure a ship ⟨in⟩ *from* either country. He then bought the Dacia, paying for it about three-fourths of what it cost fourteen years ago when it was built. He secured a cargo of cotton and intended to sail for Bremen. When he was informed that it would be ⟨safer⟩ *wiser* to go to Rotterdam he

---

2 That is, the Stone-Bryan exchange.

changed the route and planned to sail to Rotterdam. The inquiries which have come to the State Department have come from the owners of the cotton, rather than from the owner of the ship. The Government has had nothing to do with the transaction further than to make inquiries for interested parties. Whether the ship is taken into the prize court or not is a question between the British Government and the owner of the ship, but, if it is taken into the prize court the court will of course decide upon the evidence produced and so far as we know the evidence will support the *bona fides*[3] of the transactions. If the evidence shows that the sale was made in good faith the transfer cannot be objected to according to the rules recognized by both Great Britain and the United States ⟨and a⟩. A change in these rules at this time could not be made by the United States and it would seem to be an inopportune time for Great Britain to change them. Great Britain fears that the Dacia might be made a precedent and that other German interned ships would be bought in case the Dacia sale was not contested. That is true and yet the precedent would only stand in case the sales were *bona fide*[4] in which case they would come within the rules. The chief point presented in your despatch is that Great Britain is trying to bring pressure to bear upon Germany by preventing the sale of interned German ships. This is perfectly legitimate so long as the pressure is exerted according to the international law, but the pressure becomes illegitimate if well settled rules are violated, and a well-settled rule would be violated if an attempt was made to prevent a *bona fide*[5] sale.

⟨It is only fair too to ask Great Britain to remember that a violation of the rules in regard to bona fide sales puts a pressure upon the commerce of the United States more than upon Germany. The loss suffered by Germany through the internment of these ships is small compared with the loss suffered by the United States because of its inability to secure ships to carry its merchandise. Is it not worth while for Great Britain to consider not only the present but the future effect of the condition which she is creating here. This nation has depended largely upon foreign ships to carry her commerce—Great Britain enjoying a larger share of this than any other nation. The war has not only deprived us to some extent of the British and French ships but because of their domination of the ocean has deprived us entirely of German ships.⟩

[3] Italicized in Bryan's text.
[4] *Ibid.*
[5] *Ibid.*

The point which should be made very clear to the British authorities as our view and purpose in the whole matter if such purchases are made is that as a matter of actual fact such purchases do not constitute a restoration of German commerce to the seas. Such ships would not and could not be used on the former routes or with the former and usual cargoes and would serve as German commerce in no particular. They would serve only the trade of the United States with neutral countries and within the limits necessarily set by war and all its conditions. The withdrawal of so many ships from the seas is so far a curtailment of the commerce of the United States. The United States cannot in the circumstances sell articles to Germany which the rules of war or the circumstances now existing forbid. The owners of the ships bought from German owners cannot use them on the routes or to the ports which would serve their former owners as the carriers of German commerce. They would be used on new routes and for the release of American merchandise to new ports. They would represent an extension of American commerce, not a renewal of German. This cannot be justly or even plausibly regarded as an effort to relieve the present economic pressure on Germany or to recreate anything that Great Britain had a right to destroy. America must have ships and must have them for these uses. She will build them if she cannot find them for sale. The legitimate restoration of American commerce may be delayed but it cannot be prevented. It cannot be part of the purpose of the British government to put an intolerable economic pressure on the United States, as might very easily be the result if its attitude as reflected in your note is maintained. It is not unlikely that this great hardship will suggest legislation looking to the encouragement of American shipping. Already provision has been made for the transfer and register of foreign bottoms and congress is considering a measure authorizing the Government to take part in a corporation for the operation of ships. These measures have been the outgrowth of six months of war. Is it not worth while to consider the possibilities of the future? If this Government must undertake the building of enough ships to carry its commerce while idle ships lie in its harbors will there not be an excess of ships when the war is over? You may assure Sir Edward that this Government will adhere conscientiously to its course of neutrality. It will not intentionally deviate a hair's breadth from the line but it is powerless to prevent the increasing criticism which has been aroused by acts which have, from the American standpoint, seemed unnecessarily severe for the enforcement of belligerent rights. Say to Sir Edward that we shall take up and consider each question upon its merits and appreciate the candid and friendly spirit which the Foreign Office has manifested. We hope that both Governments may be successful in lessening the criticism and moderating the language of individual citizens.

We are struck by the very encouraging fact that in the principles which they both recognize in such matters the two governments are practically in agreement. What is lacking is merely the adoption of some practical method by which individual cases of dispute or question may be reduced to a negligible minimum. It ought to be possible for two governments so genuinely friendly and so nearly of one mind with regard to the principles involved to agree upon means by which good faith and entire compliance with the proper restrictions of a time of war and of national defence can be determined with the smallest possible number of seizures and trials in prize courts. We earnestly invite attention to the feasibility of devising and settling upon such methods and would not only welcome but earnestly desire practical suggestions looking to that end. The English government can thus be assured of compliance with all its just regulations and of freedom from even the risk of friction and hostile sentiment as between the two months.[6]

T MS (SDR, RG 59, 763.72112/796a, DNA).
[6] This telegram was sent as WJB to WHP, Jan. 23, 1915, T telegram (SDR, RG 59, 763.72112/796a, DNA), and is printed in *FR-WWS 1915*, pp. 684-87. There is a WWsh draft of Wilson's long additions in WP, DLC.

To Charles William Eliot

My dear Doctor Eliot: The White House January 22, 1915

Thank you for your letter of the nineteenth of January about the immigration bill. I am to hold a hearing on the bill this morning and must keep my mind open to both sides, but my present judgment is with yours.

Cordially and sincerely yours,   Woodrow Wilson

TLS (C. W. Eliot Papers, MH-Ar).

From William Jennings Bryan

My dear Mr. President: Washington January 22, 1915.

We have received and read the note as you have prepared it. Will have it put into the private cipher. I think the changes which you made are important. You used more of what I suggested than I had expected you to use. It was written hurriedly and only in the form of suggestions for consideration.

Mr. Lansing and I have been conferring in regard to the general situation, and we are inclined to think that it would go a long way toward releiving the fear that is expressed in GREAT BRITAIN if an announcement was made on your authority that the Government had no thought of purchasing German ships under the authority which the shipping bill is intended to confer. I believe that a large part of the alarm in Great Britain arises over the fear that if the Dacia sale is allowed to stand the Government would expect to use it as a precedent and proceed to buy the German ships. That was Jusserand's fear and you remember how agitated he was at the time. While I think that private individuals have a right to purchase these ships if the purchase is bona fide, I do not think that our Government could afford to raise an international question by purchases made by a corporation in which the Government had a controlling interest —or even a large interest.

If you said—or authorized me to say:—"To avoid misunderstanding and misrperesentation [misrepresentation] of the Government's purpose, the press is informed that in case the shipping bill is passed the corporation authorized by that bill, being partly owned by the Government, will not, in the purchase of ships, acquire any vessel whose purchase would raise any international question or issue."—I believe it would do much to calm the fears across the ocean and it would also remove one of the objections which is made against the shipping bill by its opponents in Congress.

As we could not afford and, therefore, have no intention of raising an issue by purchasing German ships, would it not be worth while to remove the fears that are based upon the possibility of such a purchase? A failure to answer these objections and put them to rest stimulates speculation and causes excitement. If such a statement could be made before the new note reaches London it would smooth the way for the strong statement which you have prepared and which I presume you want me to say is sent at your direction.

With assurances of high respect I am, my dear Mr. President,
Yours very sincerely,   W. J. Bryan

TLS (WP, DLC).

From Edward Mandell House

Dear Governor: New York City. January 22nd, 1915.

The most inportant [important] thing that Brown [Spring Rice] told me verbally was that public opinion in Texas [England] was beginning to resent what they considered our pro Maine [Germany] attitude, and that they think if this sentiment grows, it would be impossible for New Jersey [the Allies] to accept your good offices.

You will see what the despatch contains and we can then discuss it Sunday evening.

Affectionately yours, E. M. House

TLS (WP, DLC).

From Edward Mandell House, with Enclosure

Dear Governor, New York, January 22, 1914 [1915].

I am inclosing you this dispatch that Brown [Spring Rice] has sent to me this morning by his kinsman. I will write you further during the day. Affectionately yours E. M. House

ALS (WP, DLC).

E N C L O S U R E

PERSONAL MEMORANDUM.[1]

Your message received.

It will give me great pleasure to see him and talk to him freely. Of course he understands that all that can be promised here is that if Germany seriously and sincerely desires peace I will consult our friends as to what terms of peace are acceptable.

Before however setting out on his journey it is as well that he should be informed as to the state of public opinion here. I fear it is becoming unfavourably and deeply impressed by the trend of the action taken by the United States Government and by its attitude towards Great Britain. What is felt here is that while Germany deliberately planned a war of pure aggression, has occupied and devastated large districts in Russia, Belgium and France, inflicting great misery and wrong on innocent populations, the only act on record on the part of the United States is a protest singling out Great Britain as the only Power whose conduct is worthy of reproach.

The following facts are taken to be indicative of the general attitude of Government and Congress in the United States.

1. Soon after the war the United States Government issued an order prohibiting the publication of manifests with the apparent object of making it more difficult for the Allies to trace and seize contraband.

2. An American Banking House was prevented from issuing a loan to one of the Allies.

3. Although Japan during the war with Russia had been allowed to import finished parts of submarines made in the United States and though the best advice was to the effect that such an export was legal, yet the United States Government prohibited the export to Great Britain of parts of submarines less finished than in the case of Japan. Whatever the cause the impression remains that there was discrimination.

4. The United States Government is using every possible means to secure the passage of a bill through Congress which would authorise the purchase of the ships now interned as a consequence of war. We are being pressed to recognise the purchase and transfer of German merchant vessels to the United States flag under conditions which are far more liberal than those allowed by the German regulations. If these purchases are made it is evident that the German shipping lines, which are practically Government institutions, will be enabled to sell for advantageous prices to the United States Government their ships now useless to them and a cause of barren expenditure: and thus to acquire credits for use during the war, by drawing on American funds. It is even urged openly and apparently with the consent of members of the Government, that these ships when purchased should be used in furtherance of the commercial interests of Germany under the protection of the American flag. It is not to be wondered at that although some time ago German commercial circles, especially shipping circles, were urging peace on the German government that they have now ceased to do so.

5. United States Congress has now before its Committee a bill which is supported by the United pressure of the German societies, organised throughout the United States, and by the German members of Congress under the open direction of the German Ambassador, to do what has never been done in any previous war and is absolutely contrary to American precedent, namely to put an embargo on the export of munitions of war. There can be no question, indeed there is none, that such a measure would work to the advantage of the power which had prepared for war and to the disadvantage of those who, like us, had not

prepared for it. But the United States Government has taken no public steps to discourage it.

I have no doubt whatever that the desire of the President, if he intervenes, is to be absolutely neutral and impartial, and that his feelings are equally friendly to both parties in the struggle. Mr. Page's personal qualities make it a real pleasure for me to do business with him. But what the public sees are the facts which I have just stated which they see as I have described them whatever be their real explanation or significance.

At the beginning of the war there was no doubt a distinct and purely American sentiment which was stirred by the wrong done to Belgium and which approved of our action in going into the war. This feeling was no doubt genuine and widespread and founded rather on ideals of conduct than on race, history or language. But we feel that the German Americans regard themselves as Germans first of all, that they have organised themselves as partisans, that they work actively in America as everywhere else, by all means in their power for the success in Europe of the German arms, and that they aim one way or another at making their influence felt in the press, in business and in every branch of the Government. Upon their action and upon the success which has attended it so far Germany founds hopes that the attitude of the United States Government will be increasingly disadvantageous to the Allies and, it may be added, more especially to Great Britain. Prospects are held out that the United States on whom as on all other neutrals the indirect consequences of the war in some ways bear hardly, will cut off the supplies of munitions of war on which the Allies are in need and at the same time insist that the door be kept open for supplies of contraband to Germany, with the object of bringing the war to an end by the complete victory of the latter.

I can hardly believe that such a policy is deliberately desired by any but the German-Americans in the United States. There is however an impression in Europe that there is a danger of the United States Government insensibly drifting into such a policy. If this apprehension is realised then there can be no hope of a speedy conclusion of the war. Germany will not relax her hold on Belgium and as for Great Britain, not to speak of the Allies, she cannot give up the restoration of Belgium unless and until she has exhausted all her resources and has herself shared Belgium's fate.

This is what people here are beginning to feel and I should like him to know it. The feeling has not yet found widespread public expression but it is there and it is growing. In the struggle for existence in which this country is at stake much store is set in England on the goodwill of the United States, and people cannot believe that the United States desire to paralyze the advantage which we derive from our sea power while leaving intact to Germany those military and scientific advantages which are special to her.

I think it is only fair that he should be warned that should people in England come to believe that the dominant influence in United States politics is German, it would tend to create an untoward state of public opinion which we should greatly regret.

The above is purely personal and must be so regarded: but I think it is my duty under the circumstances to give this personal and friendly warning as to the probable trend of public sentiment.

T MS (WP, DLC).

1 Spring Rice considerably expanded and altered this telegram, at times sharpening the criticisms, at others muting them. The telegram sent (E. Grey to C. A. Spring Rice, Jan. 18, 1915, T telegram [E. Grey Papers, FO 800/85, pp. 56-57, PRO]) reads as follows:

"PERSONAL.

"Your personal telegram of January 14.

"I will gladly see President's friend and talk freely to him, but he must realize that I cannot promise to do more than consult our Allies as to terms of peace if there is evidence that Germany seriously desires peace.

"Public opinion here is becoming unfavourable and I fear deeply impressed by the attitude of the United States Government and the trend of action in the United States.

"It is felt that, while Germany planned a war of aggression, has occupied Belgian, French, and Polish territory, and inflicted great misery and wrong there, the only act of the United States Government on record is a protest singling out Great Britain as the only Power of all those at war whose conduct is open to reproach.

"American feeling is said to be stirred mainly about Belgium; except for Belgium, Great Britain would not have gone to war with the united spirit she has shown; yet Great Britain is in fact the only belligerent to whom United States action has been unfavourable.

"(1). The prohibition of the publication of manifests necessarily helped Germany to get supplies and made it more difficult for Great Britain to intercept contraband.

"(2). The prohibition to export parts of submarines was imposed though the highest legal advice, I am informed, was to the effect that such export was legal and though parts even in more finished state had been exported to Japan in the Russo-Japanese war. It is urged that such export to Japan was by inadvertence, but the impression of discrimination remains.

"(3). Pressure is now being applied to us to recognize the purchase and transfer of German merchant vessels to the United States flag under conditions contrary even to German Admiralty Prize regulations. These purchases, if persisted in, will enable the great German shipping lines to sell their ships at very advantageous prices and acquire large credits with which to start again after the war. Some time ago there were indications that German commercial circles, especially shipping, were urging the German Government to make peace. We have heard no more of this recently.

"(4). There is a movement in the United States to do what has not been done in any previous war and put an embargo on the export of munitions of war to belligerents to the disadvantage of Great Britain and those who had not prepared for war and the consequent advantage of Germany who had prepared for it.

"I do not doubt the President's intention to be neutral and that his feeling is friendly, and the friendliness of Mr. Page here makes all my dealings with him a real pleasure, but the public see only the facts I have stated above.

"We feel that the sentiment in favour of Belgium that approved Great Britain's entry into the war was distinctly and solely American, and therefore detached though genuine and widespread; but we feel that German-Americans regard themselves as Germans in America, are organized as partizans, work actively in America for German success in Europe as every where, and that in one way or another they have succeeded in influencing the executive and legislature. Upon their action and the success that has so far attended it, Germany founds hopes of an attitude on the part of the United States that will be increasingly disadvantageous to Great Britain; and sees a prospect that the United States, being like all neutrals chafed by the indirect consequences of the war, will insist upon the door being kept open for supplies of contraband to Germany, while cutting off supplies of particular munitions of war that are necessary to the Allies, thus bringing the war to an end by German victory.

"That this is a policy intended or an end desired by any but Germans in the United States I do not believe, but there seems a danger that the country may drift into such a policy insensibly. If this apprehension is realized, the war cannot be a short one, for Germany will harden as regards Belgium and Great Britain cannot give up the restoration of Belgium till all her resources are exhausted and she herself has shared Belgium's fate, and this is not likely to be soon accomplished.

"I should like President's friend to know all this, because it is what people here are beginning to feel; it has not yet found public expression, because we are engaged in a struggle in which the very existence of this country is at stake and much store is set by the goodwill of the United States, and people cannot believe that the United States desire to paralyze the advantage that we derive from sea-power while leaving intact the other military and scientific advantages that are special to Germany. But if people come to think that Germans in the United States are the dominant influence there in politics, there will be an outburst of resentment here, which, though it be of no help to us, will be irrepressible."

From Nancy Saunders Toy

My dear Mr. President,   Cambridge [Mass.]. 22 Jan. 1915

I am not afraid of lèse majesté tonight. I am too oppressed. You will say "it wearies me," and it wearies *me* too. But in sooth, *I* know why *I* am sad. I am overwhelmed with such a sense of disaster that write to you I must, not to the President but to our old friend, Mr. Wilson, without waiting for your consent via Helen. If you had heard all that I have heard these last two days, you wouldn't blame me. I think—from your warm friends, the country's without—variableness—or shadow of turning—friends who are not sleeping at night on account of this Merchant Marine Bill. Mr. Rhodes (*has* he any ulterior motive? and you know he has a contempt for Senator Lodge) gives me leave to quote him as saying that if the Administration buys those German ships, it will place the country in serious danger of a war with England. Three other men, *our* kind, are gravely anxious, and O Mr. President, think of my overhearing this in a book-shop yesterday! As I came up, one man was saying: "Well, every man has his Waterloo, and this Bill is going to be Wilson's. It's going to ruin him—that he won't care particularly about—but he will care if it ruins the Democratic Party and puts his country in jeopardy." "It will be an awful tragedy," said the other man, "because there's no principle behind it. It's merely a blunder. But you know this Bill is permissive and not mandatory, and I have a feeling that when Wilson realizes that there are only German ships to buy, that the Germans will get thirteen millions from the transaction, thereby prolonging the war and making this country take the gravest sort of risks, he'll hold the Bill over until after the war." "It's the most extraordinary proposition I ever heard," said the first man, "when you think that no Government in the world owns its Merchant Marine."

Ah well, I know "the Court" has decided this case, but when there is fresh evidence, there can be another trial before the Supreme Court of a fresher mind—can't there?—and why shouldn't a mind be fresher with breezes from all sides blowing?

Your sincere friend   Nancy Toy

ALS (WP, DLC).

Sir Cecil Arthur Spring Rice to Sir Edward Grey

Washington 22nd January, 1915

Confidential. Chan[d]ler Anderson called to-day. He has seen President, Minister of Commerce, Counsellor of State Department &c. He confessed that condition of affairs here is chaotic and no one has central control except President. He brings, however, message to me for you that United States Government while bound to make a public statement of its claims and to satisfy public opinion will not depart from principle that legal remedy must be exhausted before diplomatic intervention takes place.

They understand that His Majesty's Government are doing much for free trade and appreciate difficulties as to piling up stores in neutral countries. They must however leave no doubt in mind of members of Congress that they intend to urge their claims.

Questions at issue are mainly those as to right of belligerent to take ships into port and detain them for search, which right accrues owing to new and unprecedented conditions, which, he acknowledges, United States Government ought to regard from point of view of a possible future belligerent and not only in light of past precedents.

Important point for us is to keep as few ships detained as possible and explain reasons for detention (as in fact you are doing).

In your answer please lay stress on total figures of trade of neutrals. Press argues that imports from here must increase owing to forced cessation of trade with Germany. Please do not mention his name.

T telegram (FO 382/2, No. 8655, PRO).

Two Letters from William Jennings Bryan

My dear Mr. President: Washington January 23, 1915.

I have had several conversations recently with the Japanese Ambassador. He is very anxious that we shall make another effort to bring the Japanese question to an end.

You will recall that it was agreed we should attempt to secure the ratification of a treaty which would guarantee to the Japanese now in the country equal treatment with other aliens and thus prevent any other state from passing such laws as California has passed.

In the original treaty proposed by them there was a clause which would have invalidated the California law insofar as it affected the right of inheritance. I explained to him that any attempt to interfere with the California law would, in all probability, prevent the ratification of the treaty and it was finally omitted. It was the fact that it was omitted that lead the new Government over there to withdraw the proposition.

Ambassador Chinda now renews the proposition in another form. The enclosed draft,[1] as you will notice, only relates to the future. In Article III you will find the provision:

> "* * * that the settlement of the question regarding Chapter 113," (California anti-alien law.) "shall be sought independently of the present convention, and that nothing contained in this Convention shall in any wise or manner affect such settlement."

I told him that I thought objection might be raised to this treaty on the ground it did not settle the question, but while he did not say so I think that his idea is that if we can get a treaty ratified which will prevent any future legislation against the Japanese and it will be easier to settle this question.

In other words—that, having removed the fear of other legislation, the acuteness of this question will be over.

He also says that he believes simultaneously with this treaty a treaty could be signed such as we have signed with the thirty other countries, providing for investigation in all cases, and he is quite anxious that such a treaty shall be negotiated between his country and ours. I think such a treaty would go a long way toward answering the "jingos" who are always insisting upon our getting ready for a war with Japan.

I have explained to the Ambassador that it would be impossible to have this treaty ratified at this session and that, that being the case, it would not be wise to negotiate it before the conclusion of Congress. There is no immediate action necessary, therefore, and you can consider it at your leisure and let me know what you think of the proposal. Believing, as I do, that the states should not be permitted to raise international issues (which they cannot settle by themselves) I am favorable to the principle set forth in the proposed Convention, and I do not believe we will find any permanent settlement of the Japanese question short of some such action.

With assurances of high respect I am, my dear Mr. President,
Yours very sincerely,   W. J. Bryan

TLS (SDR, RG 59, 811.52/299a, DNA).
1 A typed draft. Bryan summarizes it very well in his letter.

My dear Mr. President: Washington January 23, 1915.

I am enclosing a personal statement from the British Ambassador which I think you will find interesting.[1] I was talking with him the other day and he asked me if I would like to know what the British papers were saying and I told him I would— and this letter is intended to furnish the information.

You will notice the stress that they lay upon the purchase of German ships. The fact that the bill authorizes the purchase of ships, without excepting the interned German ships, is the basis for their fears.

You will notice from a clipping[2] which I also enclose, that Lodge is basing his opposition to the shipping bill—or at least making it one of his objections—upon the possibility of the purchase of these ships. Lodge, as you know, is very pro-British, and both he and Gardner have defended an increase in the army and navy on the ground that we may have war with Germany.

I have just talked with Senator Walsh of Montana[3] and he tells me that Lodge has introduced an amendment to the shipping bill prohibiting the purchase of the German ships. He says it will either be necessary to vote for that amendment or else defend the right of the Government to buy those ships. His own position is that the Government has a right to buy the ships. He thinks that even an announcement that the ships are not to be bought under the provisions of this shipping bill would hardly be sufficient because they would ask—"*Why not put the prohibition in the bill if there is no intention of buying?*"

The question is not logical and I think if an announcement was made that the authority would not be used to purchase ships from belligerents it would be sufficient, because the Democrats could say that it was not necessary to support the President's word in such a matter by adopting an amendment. And they could object to the adoption of the Lodge amendment because after what he has said in regard to the belligerents his amendment would be accepted as an endorsement of his views and not merely upon its legal effect. It being unnecessary to put that provision in the bill, its adoption would naturally be attributed to other motives and the most natural motive would be that expressed by the man who introduced it, who is anything but neutral in his attitude.

I only send this to reinforce the suggestion made in the letter of yesterday in regard to the advisability of an immediate statement on the subject. Senator Walsh says they may have to vote on this amendment Monday. In view of the controversy that has arisen it might be wise to make the statement even more specific than the one I suggested—that is, have it specifically state that the authority would not be used by us *to purchase ships of belligerents*.

With assurances of high respect I am, my dear Mr. President,
Yours very sincerely,   W. J. Bryan

TLS (SDR, RG 59, 763.72111/1577, DNA).
1 It was a revised version, without any significant change in the substance, of the Enclosure printed with EMH to WW, Jan. 22, 1915.
2 It is missing.
3 Thomas James Walsh, Democrat.

From Thomas Jones Pence

My dear Mr. President: Washington, D. C. January 23, 1915.

I am sending herewith copies of three of the Bulletins[1] issued from our Headquarters during the past ten days for use by the rural press. In two of these Bulletins I have attempted to set forth the best parts—eliminating of course the very personal references to yourself—of the editorials regarding your Indianapolis speech. I do not recall any utterance delivered in my time that has received such generous praise from influential and representative daily papers. Of course, I have not attempted to quote from the great weekly press.

No doubt you have observed a very decided tendency on the part of a large section of the metropolitan press and some of the larger papers of the big cities to be hypercritical of you. Where they do not attempt to discredit you, they strike at others high in the Administration. This newspaper policy has the appearance of being concerted. Pardon me for saying it, but you did not arrive at your present high position by reason of the kindness and courtesy of the metropolitan press and the big dailies. From a newspaper standpoint, the American people became acquainted with you through the rural press and the small dailies that are powerful in creating public opinion in this nation.

I think our list of this class of papers is the most complete ever assembled. We have on our list approximately 11,000 papers, to which we mail our press matter. These represent all the weeklies and small dailies, independent as well as Democratic. In many instances we send our service to republican papers.

With my very best wishes,   Sincerely,   Thos J Pence

TLS (WP, DLC).
1 These enclosures are missing.

Robert Lansing to Joseph Patrick Tumulty

Personal.

Dear Mr. Tumulty: Washington January 23, 1915.

I had yesterday an hour's conference with Commissioner Davies, Senator-elect Hustings of Wisconsin and Mr. Nieman, the editor of a Milwaukee paper, in regard to the general German-American situation in this country, and the steps necessary to prevent or offset the present propaganda against the administration.

I was very much impressed with Mr. Nieman's views, particularly the plan which he suggested to meet the situation. I know that you are as fully alive as I am to the serious political effect of the present movement, unless it is checked, and in view of the sound, practical, common-sense point of view of Mr. Nieman, I would suggest that if you can arrange an interview for him with the President that you do so. I believe that in a quarter of an hour he can present the case and suggest the remedy.

Very sincerely yours,   Robert Lansing.

OKeh   W.W.

TLS (WP, DLC).

From the Diary of Colonel House

The White House, January 24, 1915.

I left today on the 12.08 for Washington. There was no one I knew on the train and I had a quiet and restful trip. Dr. Grayson met me in a White House car. The President was waiting for me and we immediately began to work, and remained at it continuously for more than an hour, delaying dinner ten or fifteen minutes, which is a most unusual thing for the President to do.

He read me long letters from the two Pages, Walter and Thomas Nelson, covering the English and Italian situations. He said, "Your being my most trusted friend causes you a lot of trouble." I replied: "Not nearly so much trouble as pleasure."

He insisted upon arranging for my expenses abroad and for those of my secretary, Miss Denton. I let him know how trustworthy she was, so he would not think me indiscreet in writing through her about matters of an important and confidential nature. He asked me to tell Sir Edward Grey his entire mind so he would know what his intentions were about everything, and he wished me to mention his relations with Mr. Bryan and the conduct of the State Department under him. He said, "Let him know that while you are abroad I expect to act directly through you and to eliminate all intermediaries."

He approved all I had in mind to say to Sir Edward and to the Germans. He said: "There is not much for us to talk over for the reason we are both of the same mind and it is not necessary to go into details with you."

I asked if it would be possible for him to come to over to [sic] Europe in the event a peace conference could be arranged and in the event he was invited to preside over the conference. He thought it would be well to do this and that the American people would desire it.

There was no one at dinner excepting Dr. E. P. Davis of Philadelphia, who is attending Jessie (Mrs. Sayre). I brought the new baby a pair of pearl pins which seemed to please them. Margaret and I had a peep at the baby after dinner. The President will not consent to it's being named for him. He thought the child was sufficiently handicapped by being born in the White House.

The President read to us for awhile from A. G. Gardiner's, "Pillars of Society" and then he and I had a talk of about an hour before we went to bed. I suggested the the [sic] Mexican problem could best be solved now by calling in the A.B.C. Powers and ourselves. The President thought this an excellent idea and that it was merely a question of when to put it in operation. I offered to see the Ambassadors tomorrow if he thought well of it. He believed this would be too soon for conditions were not quite ready in Mexico for such a move, and he was afraid the A.B.C. Ambassadors would not want to move so quickly.

We discussed at considerable length the shipping bill and its probable effect on our international relations. He still believes trouble may be avoided by using proper discretion.

I put to him many questions which it was necessary for him to answer, such as the German and Austrian query as to parts of submarines being sent to Canada. Etc. We went to bed around eleven o'clock.

Telephonic Messages[1]

January 25, 1915.

To Mr. Moore,[2] President of the Panama Pacific Exposition in San Francisco:

It appeals to the imagination to speak across the continent. It is a fine omen for the Exposition that the first thing it has done is to send its voice over from sea to sea. I congratulate you on the fine prospects for a successful Exposition. I am confidently hoping to take part in it after the adjournment of Congress. May I not send my greetings to the management and to all whose work has made it possible and made it the great event it promises to be, and convey my personal congratulations to you?

To Mr. Thomas A. Watson in San Francisco (Dr. Alexander Graham Bell listening in on the line at New York.) (Mr. Watson was Dr. Bell's electrician and mechanic at the time of the invention of the telephone and was the first person to hear a word spoken over a telephone.):

I consider it an honour to be able to express my admiration for the inventive genius and scientific knowledge that have made this possible and my pride that this vital cord should have been stretched across America as a new symbol of our unity and our enterprise. Will you not convey my cordial congratulations to Mr. Bell? And I want to convey to you my personal congratulations, sir.

To Dr. Bell in New York:

May I not congratulate you very warmly on this notable consummation of your long labours and remarkable achievements?

You are justified in feeling a great pride in what has been done. This is a memorable day, and I convey to you my warm congratulations, sir.

The President also congratulated Mr. Vail[3] (at Jekyll Island), President of the A.T.&T. Company.

T MS (WP, DLC).
1 Celebrating the completion of the first transcontinental telephone line. The hookup for the ceremonies included Boston; New York; Washington; Jekyll Island, Ga.; and San Francisco. The first persons to speak were Alexander Graham Bell and Thomas Augustus Watson, in commemoration of the first telephonic communication between them in 1876. For further details, see the *New York Times*, Jan. 26, 1915.
2 Charles Cadwell Moore.
3 Theodore Newton Vail.

From William Williams Keen

My dear Mr. President: Philadelphia Jan. 25th, 1915.

You know how earnestly and loyally I supported you on the repeal of the proviso in the Panama Tolls matter. I wish sincerely that I could do the same as to the Ship Purchase Bill, but as I look upon it it is playing with fire near a powder magazine. I do not know a single person in this community who is not dead opposed to it as not only futile, but vicious from an economic point of view, and perilous from a political point of view. The case of the "Dacia" is bad enough, but why should we buy a fleet of Dacias ten times more perilous because Government owned? It seems to me that we are hunting trouble when we already have a superabundance both at home and abroad.

Very respectfully, Your obedient servant,   W. W. Keen

TLS (WP, DLC).

From the Diary of Colonel House

January 25, 1915.

I was not well and had an uneasy and unhappy night. However, I got up for breakfast at eight and had a few minutes talk with the President. I had Hoover request Billy Phillips to come to the White House on his way to the State Department. He arrived soon after nine, and I asked him to arrange passports for Loulie and maid, Miss Denton and myself. Phillips is disturbed at the growing dissatisfaction of our Government among the belligerents. He is also fearful of the shipping bill. I asked him to return this afternoon at six and I would ask the President to see him.

I went to Phillips' at ten o'clock to meet the British Ambassador. He seemed pleased that I was holding to my intention to leave on Saturday. I again requested that he arrange with Sir Edward Grey by cable an engagement immediately upon my arrival. He said Sir Edward left Saturday afternoons and did not return until Monday morning, but if I thought best, he knew Sir Edward would remain in town. I did not consider this necessary, for my boat would probably get in Saturday and I would not be in London until Sunday, therefore Monday would be time enough. He is cabling Sir Edward to ask me for lunch on Monday.

Spring-Rice talked optimistically in one minute, and pessimistically the next, absolutely contradicting himself. He is arranging by cable to have me passed through the Customs with the minimum amount of trouble. He warned me that we should probably encounter sentiment in England hostile to my mission, with the belief that it was possibly actuated by a desire to help Germany.[1] He said there was a party there [Great Britain] which would seize upon any excuse for an early peace, and that they ressembled the "Copperheads" of the North during our Civil War. I replied that he need not worry about my giving them comfort.

I went to the White House and laid down until lunch. After lunch I told the President of my interviews with Phillips and Spring-Rice. . . .

Lansing came at 5.45 and McAdoo at the same time. I gave Lansing the right of way, McAdoo promising to come in after dinner. Lansing and I had a satisfactory talk concerning departmental affairs. I urged him to get more and better help so he could give his entire time to deciding problems, rather than working the[m] out.

The President came in before he left and the three of us talked for a few minutes about the Chinese-Japanese difficulties which are becoming acute because of Japan's demands upon China for concessions etc.[2] Trouble may grow out of this and I advised great caution. We are not at present in a position to war with Japan over the "open door" in China.

We discussed the advisability of issuing a statement regarding our neutrality as to Belgium.

Phillips was in the Blue Room awaiting us when Lansing left. He explained the arrangements he had made concerning money for my expenses. I dislike taking money even for them. I have never been paid by either a State or National Government for my services, and while I am not being paid for them now, I have heretofore paid my expenses. I do not feel able to meet the expenses of such a trip as this, and it lifts a load from me to have the Government pay them. It was agreed that $4000.00 should be placed to my credit at once. I have a feeling this will last for six months.

Phillips also gave me a Department Code. I asked him to have the Department delegate to me one of the secretaries from each of the Embassies in London, Paris and Berlin, and upon receipt of a cable from me he will do this.

After Phillips left, the President and I went to his study to work out the code we had agreed upon. I suggested he frame a message and that we work it out. This was done and I have a memorandum of it as we coded it.

There were no visitors at dinner excepting Dr. Grayson, John Wilson and myself. . . .

McAdoo came in later, and we talked at length about the shipping bill, New York appointments, etc. etc. The President was impatient for me to come back to the study. He told McAdoo he had to talk with me. I went in at nine o'clock and we talked until 10.15. We covered a multitude of subjects. The reforming of the National Committee, Woolley's plan for linking up the Progressives and progressive newspapers, and everything else I had on my list to discuss with him.

It then came time to say goodbye. The President's eyes were moist when he said his last words of farewell. He said: "Your unselfish and intelligent friendship has meant much to me," and he expressed his gratitude again and again, calling me his "most trusted friend." He declared I was the only one in all the world to whom he could open his entire mind.

I asked if he remembered the first day we met, some three and a half years ago. He replied "yes, but we had known one another always, and merely came in touch then, for our purposes and thoughts were as one." I told him how much he had been to me; how I had tried all my life to find someone with whom I could work out the things I had so deeply at heart, and I had begun to despair, believing my life would be more or less a failure, when he came into it, giving me the opportunity for which I had been longing.

He insisted upon going to the station with me. He got out of the car and walked through the station and ticket office and then to the train itself, refusing to leave until I entered the car. It is a joy to work for such an appreciative friend.

1 That was what Spring Rice himself believed. "The Government wishes to be neutral," he wrote to Sir Edward Grey on January 23, "but the prevailing

feeling is fear of the German vote, and this peace mission is most probably promoted by the German and Austrian Governments, and possibly part of a bargain." C. A. Spring Rice to E. Grey, Jan. 23, 1915, T telegram (E. Grey Papers, FO 800/85, pp. 64-65, PRO).

2 The Japanese government had just submitted a series of demands to the Chinese government which, if accepted, would have seriously impaired Chinese sovereignty. One set, known as Group V, would have made China virtually a protectorate of Japan. Subsequent documents in this and the following volume will illustrate the development of what historians call the far eastern crisis of 1915 and the role that Wilson and his advisers played in it. For the fullest account, see Link, *Struggle for Neutrality*, pp. 267-308.

Remarks at a Press Conference

January 26, 1915

Mr. President, there seems to be an organized effort on the part of the Republicans to defeat the shipping bill. I was wondering whether you had anything to say about the responsibility of holding up legislation.

No, sir; I think that will be very obvious.

Mr. President, the treatment which is being accorded the ship purchase bill endangers the passage of some of the appropriation bills, doesn't it?

No, sir.

At this session?

I did not say at this session.

I was coming to that.

No, I don't honestly think that it imperils their passage at this session.

Do you think, then, that both the appropriation bills and the ship purchase bill will pass?

Yes, sir, I do.

That would obviate the danger of an extra session?

Yes, sir.

But, if either fails, do you regard an extra session as—

I don't go on a hypothesis. "Sufficient unto the day is the evil thereof."

Mr. President, do you think there is any effort being made to force you to have an extra session?

None that I am aware of, sir. I have the good fortune to be insensible to pressure.

Mr. President, when the immigration bill goes back to the House, will it be accompanied by a memorandum?

What makes you think it will go back. If I sign it, it will not have to go back. If it goes back, it will be accompanied by a memorandum.

Won't you tell us which way it is going, Mr. President?

No; I have a conference tomorrow with members of the two houses.

Mr. President, the chief opposition to the shipping bill seems based on the belief that we are going to buy ships of some nations and get into trouble. Have you any assurances that we will not?

Of course, that is a matter that is not necessarily involved in the bill at all. They always question the discretion of the administration; so there is nothing new in that.

Is it possible to put into a bill in exact words an exclusion of the right to purchase certain ships; in other words, differentiate between one ship and another?

No. Of course, literally speaking it would be possible, but it would be a very questionable practice.

The Lodge amendment provides for prohibiting the purchase of belligerent vessels. I wonder how that would appeal to you.

It appeals to me just exactly as it is going to appeal to the majority in the Senate.

Senator Simmons says that the belligerent ships will be purchased only on assurance that the transfers will be recognized. Is that with authority?

I dare say he has conferred with the Department of State.

Mr. President, there is a group of private bankers in New York who are arranging to finance the neutrals; and, in connection with that, it is said that no systematic scheme of aiding South American trade will be adopted until it is known what will be the policy of the administration in respect of the enforcement of contracts. Do you happen to know about that?

No, I don't know anything about that.

Mr. President, some of the Republican senators—Senator Root and Borah and others—lately have had a good deal to say in opposition to the method of caucus legislation in the dark, and they say there hasn't been any real discussion on the floor, because the Democrats have made up their minds in advance—they are not open to conviction. And they place that alongside your stand in the campaign in favor of open discussion. I wonder if you could let any light on that?

I could let a great deal, but I am not going to. . . .

Mr. President, the inquiry that is being made into the number of people out of work in New York City by the Department of Labor—is that to be extended to other cities?

It is being extended to other cities, if we can get the facilities. You see, we haven't an appropriation for that purpose, and the investigation is possible through such agencies as the immigration bureaus at certain ports, which wouldn't be possible with the present appropriations elsewhere. Wherever it is possible, it will be looked into.

You don't intend to ask for an appropriation to furnish machinery for that purpose?

No, it hardly seems to me necessary in view of the very careful investigation that is being made by municipal authorities. It would be merely in many instances to check their inquiries, to see whether they were correct or not.

As it was explained, the purpose of that was to meet some of the statements that have issued from partisan sources. In order to make the inquiry satisfactory to you, it would have to come through sources of your own.

I don't understand that those statements which are said to be partisan proceeded from municipal authorities. They proceeded from other sources and were largely guesswork. In one statement, with regard to the country as a whole, there were more men out of employment than there are men ever in employment in the United States, in the industry spoken of, I mean, which does not seem to be likely. That would mean that all that were ever in employment in that industry were out of employment, and some more besides. They don't look up the statistics of employment before they invent the statistics of unemployment. It would be prudent for them to do so.

The ordinary political census would be accepted?

If conducted in a systematic way; I should feel that we have no right to question it. As a matter of fact, I am told—I don't know this officially—that the municipal lodging houses in New York are not full. Notwithstanding that, we have opened some of the accommodations at Ellis Island to those out of employment to sleep overnight, and they are carried back and forth, you know, on the boat; and there is no great crowd there. From those indications, it wouldn't look as if the distress is as extreme as has been feared.

Are the avenues of employment gradually being opened in New York?

I am told they are. A gentleman was telling me only yesterday he thought that, slowly but steadily, was taking place.

Do you see other evidences of a return to more satisfactory business conditions?

A great many, taking the country at large; a great many, and there is no depression west of the Mississippi.

Can you point us to some of these circumstances?

I can't offhand. The newspapers, Mr. Tumulty suggests. We

get letters indicating the same things. Again, by such statements as are made to me by such men as the editor of *System*, for example, who was here the other day, and who spoke in very confident terms.

Anything on Mexico, Mr. President?

No, sir; things are still fermenting down there.

Is there anything with regard to the rural credit situation?

There is a unanimous desire to pass it, but you see how the ways are blocked. That is all that is standing in the way of it.

There has been no agreement, so far as you are concerned, on the bill, has there?

Not a final agreement, no, sir.

T MS (C. L. Swem Coll., NjP).

A Talk to the Washington Y.M.C.A.

January 26, 1915.

Mr. Chairman[1] and gentlemen: I hesitate to stand here and detain you from your dinner, but I could not decline the invitation of the committee to come and express my very deep interest in this association. I have expressed my interest in the Young Men's Christian Association on a great many occasions, but every time I express it, it seems to me the feeling grows in me that nothing is more valuable to a city than an association like this. I have said on another occasion that I can almost assess the character of a community by the manner in which it supports or does not support its Young Men's Christian Association,[2] because there is such a splendid mixture of objects in a Young Men's Christian Association.

The supreme object, of course, is to exhibit the spirit of Christ, and to show what His example will do in a world that needs that example so much. Then, flowing out of that, naturally there comes all the delight of association and of comradeship and of mutual helpfulness. Men do not often help each other for their own individual sakes. There has got to be some motive bigger than the man himself to make him a good comrade, even, and a generous friend. The man who serves only himself is going to serve within a very narrow circle, indeed, and will serve grudgingly, only as he sees some material or obvious advantage. The only thing that can move a man to great service of any sort is something bigger than himself. That is the reason that the Christian motive, the motive of the love of Christ, is the supreme motive.

My father used to tell me that the old casuists, the old students of conscience, used to maintain that all sin was reducible to egotism, that an egotist makes himself the center of the universe. If you make yourself the center of the universe, all your perspective is skewed. There is only one moral center of the universe, and that is God. If you get into right relations with Him, then you have your right perspective and your right relation and your right size. But if you make everything related to yourself, you have the wrong size, at any rate in your own estimation, and the whole thing is so out of drawing that nobody would recognize the picture as you draw it of yourself. All the relations of life, therefore, are dependent upon knowing the truth —knowing where you stand and how you stand in your relationships. When you once get that reckoning—of course, nobody gets it perfectly—but in proportion as you get that reckoning, you know where you are and how to steer, where you are going, and where you want to go, and how you are related to your fellow men.

All of these things are delightfully illustrated in the variety of the purposes and life of the Young Men's Christian Association. They are released in the physical energies; they are released in the social amenities; they are released in the religious work; they are released in the work for others outside of the Association, as, for example, the work in the slums and for young boys in the boy's clubs. The more character a man has to spend, and the less he spends it on himself, the richer he grows, not only, but the richer the community grows. This is a sort of nursery in which the things that benefit the community most are planted and nourished. The social motive is, in the last analysis, in its highest exhibition, also the Christian motive.

I do not want to moralize, but we cannot too often realize, gentlemen, how deep the foundations of life are. By life I do not mean the physical life. That is relatively a matter of indifference; but the life that *is* the life—the spiritual life. For it is the spiritual life, if you will only admit that word, by which we judge everybody. We do not judge a merchant by his written contract. We judge him by his character. That is the best guarantee of that contract, and we do not willingly enter into contractual relations with him unless we have got the moral bond that we know exists in his integrity. After all, your final test is a spiritual test, whether you want to use that handsome word or not. You are judging the spirit of the man—what is behind his eyes, what is implied in his words, what is illustrated in his conduct.

I have long ago received, with amiability, I hope, the professions of all sorts and conditions of men, but after I have heard their professions I wait patiently to see their performance, and I do not pass any judgment until I see that performance. As a witty man said, "If you wish me to consider you witty, I must really trouble you to make a joke." So if a man wishes me to consider him loyal, for example, I must really trouble him to show his quality when he is put to the test. And if he cannot show his quality when put to the test, I may not say anything the next time he comes around and professes his loyalty, but I will do a lot of thinking. I wonder within my own head if he really thinks that I am deceived, if he really thinks I am as innocent as I look.

That is the rigid and stern standard to which we hold each other, whether we realize it or not. You know the slang expression, "He is a bad actor!" You are not speaking of the stage. You mean he does not do what he says; and the minute you find he does not do what he says, then it is all up so far as your trustfulness and admiration and willing dealings with him are concerned.

I think of a Young Men's Christian Association as a place where young men, and men not so young, get their assessment and their standard by which they can assess other men, and then spread that impression and that standard throughout the community. They get their measure of men and their measure of themselves, and there isn't any better clearinghouse for that kind of assessment than among the younger men of any community. The only men that serve the world now are young men and men who never grow old—men in whose systems the steam goes strong all the time and who do not get so stiff that their whole machinery buckles up. Those are the men, and I have seen some men retain that splendid vivacity of character away on into the nineties, and be just as young at ninety as they were at nineteen. It does not always happen, perhaps, it does not often happen, but a Young Men's Christian Association is a good place for a man of any age, provided he has not grown old.

I want to express my thanks to the committee for giving me the pleasure of expressing once more my faith in this great institution.

T MS (WP, DLC).

1 Walter Winter Warwick, Assistant Comptroller of the Treasury, and a member of the board of managers of the Washington Y.M.C.A.

2 In his address to the Nashville Y.M.C.A., printed at Feb. 24, 1912, Vol. 24.

From Edward Mandell House

Dear Governor: New York City. January 26th, 1915.

I did not notice until this morning that you had forgotten to sign the letter. I am returning it to you as quickly as possible so there may be no delay.

I have already seen Hapgood and he has since seen his friend, Lamont, so that matter has been attended to.[1] I told Hapgood that later you might possibly say something through his paper.

My! How I hated to leave you last night. Around you is centered most of the interest I have left in life, and my greatest joy is to serve you. Your words of affection at parting touched me so deeply that I could not tell you then, and perhaps can never tell you, just how I feel.

Affectionately yours,   E. M. House

TLS (WP, DLC).
[1] Undoubtedly a reference to a loan from Thomas William Lamont, a Morgan partner, to Hapgood to sustain *Harper's Weekly*.

From Francis Clement Kelley

                                           Chicago January,
My dear Mr. President: Twenty-sixth, Nineteen Fifteen.

Since my return to Chicago, I have had before me the promise I made to write you in detail concerning the Mexican situation. I have almost finished at the present time; and hope to send the papers to Mr. Malone for his criticisms tomorrow night.

In the meantime, some important information came to me today, which I believe you should know. There is talk in San Antonio of a meeting of Mexicans, to be called "A Pacification Junta." I received this information from the Archbishop of Morelia, who asked my advice as to whether or not the Bishops should be represented, or attend the meeting.

In a conversation with Mr. Fuller, I believe I suggested something of that kind; and it was also suggested to me afterward by one of the ex-cabinet ministers of Mexico. It appears, however, that an actual move is being made in San Antonio. Today I wired the Archbishop of Morelia to know if the meeting could not be postponed until about the 20th of February, to give me time to make some plans in connection with it. I had in mind also communicating with you, because such a meeting could be turned to do very useful work for Mexico and very useful work in aiding you to find a solution for Mexican difficulties.

In line with my assurance to you that I desired to be a help and that I appreciated the sympathetic interest you showed, I communicate the news of this meeting to you and place myself at your disposal to co-operate in drawing out of it, if possible, some assistance for that unfortunate country.

It is my present plan, if the meeting is postponed, to be in San Antonio when it occurs; and I suggest that it might not be a bad idea if Mr. Fuller could be there at the same time.

Faithfully yours,   Francis C. Kelley

TLS (WP, DLC).

From Walter Hines Page

Dear Mr. President: London. *July*[1] [Jan.] 26, 1915

I think (I cannot quite know) that the extracts from this week's *Spectator*,[2] which I send in this letter, are inspired by some Department of the Government. The *Spectator*, you know, is friendly to us; and to me, who know something at least of the currents of opinion here, these read very like a friendly warning. They surely confirm the several long telegrams that I sent during the week about the ominous state of public opinion here. You will observe that the *Spectator* does not accuse us of definite acts of hostility but only of an unsympathetic lack of understanding.

I think I can present the English case as they feel it—long story as it is:

They find themselves forced into this horrible war—the fate of Great Britain and of the Empire itself at stake—at a time when they were on the eve of celebrating 100 years of peace with us —us, who have taken their institutions by inheritance and developed them and with whose civilization we have so much in common. This comes happily at a time when a man is President who understands the origin and meaning and kinship of the two peo-

---

[1] WW italics.

[2] An editorial, "A Great Danger," and several brief items of editorial comment from the London *Spectator*, Jan. 23, 1915. The "great danger," according to the editor, was that Britain was at that moment "drifting towards the danger of a collision with the United States." The chief reason, he said, was "the want of the understanding of the situation, both military and moral, which is shown by the American Government and by large sections of the American people." Both failed to realize that Great Britain, engaged in a struggle for its very existence, could not be expected to make concessions to a neutral nation which might have seemed reasonable and prudent in peacetime. The editor pointed out that the American government had been similarly intractable about trade with the Confederacy. He concluded with the parting shot that American policy seemed most often determined by mercenary motives. The brief editorial items stressed much the same themes but added the charge that the American government was yielding to pressure from the German government and its propaganda.

ples and the general similarity of their aims—a broad man and a fair man. Of course the U. S. will be neutral, but it will be sympathetic also: at least it will not put obstacles in our way.

Forthwith they were surprised by our request that they adopt the Declaration of London *in toto*—a document that they had fully discussed in a quiet time and had deliberately declined to adopt—decided that they could not. We not only asked them to adopt it once, but we insisted on it—twice, thrice, four times, reminding them that Germany wd. adopt it, thus adding a tinge of insult (as they saw it) to a suspicious insistence.

Then we grudgingly accepted (if we have accepted at all) their addition of copper to the contraband list. Our hesitancy could not in the least affect the question of its addition but could only embarrass them somewhat in carrying it into effect.

Then, without discussion or notice, we forbade the publication of ships' manifests till they were a month old.

In all these, we were clearly within our rights. But every one of them (and there is a long list of such acts) we did give the enemy an advantage. Our acts began, therefore, to seem to them to be influenced somehow or other for the benefit of Germany.

All the while the definitely organized German propaganda was going on in the U. S. The German Government has always had a practically open contempt for the U. S.—the systems of the two peoples are polewide in difference; but the Germans wish to win favour in the U. S. only to embarrass England—not at all for love of the U. S. It must be German influence then—a supposition which the talk of buying the interned German ships seemed to make practically certain. Then when the *Dacia* was bought—Q.E.D.—I told you so!

Thus public opinion and public feeling have run—run to this present ominous and almost angry mood. But these things (and these sorts of things) are not all: I am not sure that they have had, by themselves, as great an effect as another series of events or revelations.

The other influences have been a sort of dense lack of sympathy—a lack of understanding of the dire predicament the Kingdom is in—a lack of understanding, in any proper proportion, what the war is or means. . . .

The *method* of the Dp't[3] quite as much as the acts of our Gov't (acts, all within our rights) thus seem to British opinion to show our Government's lack of understanding of the meaning of this war and lack of sympathy such as corresponds at all with the

---

[3] The State Department.

protestations we made as the peace celebration came within sight.

I do not better know how to explain the genesis of this great change of feeling. They know and they are grateful for the sympathy of the vast majority of our people. But they are already persuaded that our State Dp't, so easily used by anybody who has a complaint, has been (unconsciously) won by the Germans. . . .

In this mood & stress & necessity & fever we come and (as if things were as usual & everybody in good health & the day fine) we say: "Ah, this young fellow accused of a crime against a girl—his family may raise an embarrassing fuss if he be convicted. Can't you somehow let him off?" Or, "just one load of cotton, please, the Texas cotton men are *so* hard up. We won't count this as a precedent"—this, when half the cotton mills here are idle for lack of a market, when every fortune is going into the war as well as 2,000,000 of the youth of the Kingdom, and every woman is a nurse. John Bull has a fever. He is sore pressed. He is courteous yet. But it isn't a time to bother him with things that can wait, nor a time to be asking little everyday favours.

They say we show no consideration—or little—of the dire plight the war has put them in. They do not ask for any breach of neutrality—only for a courteous recognition now and then of our old friendship, some nod or token or word—or some silence —which will mean: "We won't trouble you now with unnecessary things."

They've no time now, even if they had inclination to be dishonest with us. They've no time even to look after their own trade. But our State Dp't set this embassy, the consul-general & his consuls a little while ago investigating the exports of copper from this Kingdom because somebody had informed the Dp't that the Gov't having stopped American copper here and bought it at the English price was issuing licenses for copper to be sent to Sweden—to be sold for a higher price: *i.e.* stopping our copper to make money on it.

Of course no facts were found to warrant such a charge; but I am very much afraid—in spite of the secrecy I insisted on —that this piece of spying was discovered. That, they think, was hardly friendly to a sick man. They say we do not show that we know the real condition of John Bull's household under this stress. Or, if we do know, this is not good neighborly conduct while he is so ill and so seriously engaged.

This is a long way to Tipperary—all these incidents to explain the rise of a popular mood. But this is the way it has come; and I think I have given you the processes whereby it has been engendered and I have, I think, fairly given you the English point of view.

On this showing you can say truly that we've done nothing to deserve such a change of feeling. We haven't gone beyond our rights. True, but it isn't yet a case of rights. It's a case of feeling. They are deeply wounded by what they regard as our lack of appreciation of their condition and struggle—wounded and hurt. This is as dangerous a mood as a feeling of definite enmity. . . .

I keep thinking of the outcome—for us. The Germans have always despised us. (I mean the ruling Prussian and his Government.) This will come out when the war ends. The French are fond of us. Since we have no friction with them, they will end as our friends. The English feel akin to us—really closely akin. (That's one thing the matter now!) They will come out of the war, I am afraid, hurt by us—feeling that we haven't dared be friendly, feeling that we are afraid of the Germans. This can be prevented—in great measure at least—by our manner our manners and our method. It's worth some trouble to prevent. A mere senseless popular prejudice may be a most dangerous thing for years and years and keep people from doing much good in the world. Therefore, holding absolutely and firmly to all essentials

Don't let's argue side-issues with them—e.g. whether ships shall be searched at sea or in a port, wh. is not of the essence of the question, & wh. touches a tender spot because wherever a British warship *stops* in these waters, a submarine torpedo get her. Their chief defense is motion.

Don't let's seem to accuse them of crimes they have no time (even if they had inclination) to commit—*e.g.* deliberately to sell copper at a high price when they stop ours & buy it at a low price.

Don't let's omit the sick-room courtesies while John Bull has a fever

Don't let's bother him with requests for special favours till he gets well. He's not only sick but he's most devilish busy. And if we could manage sometimes to speak to him on other subjects than those that touch our purse & say, with a kind tone, "You needn't tuck your tail, John, we're not going to twist it *now,*" the old fellow wd. really feel better. For, after all's said & done, he's the best friend we have in the world; and (if we wish to indulge a thought of thrift) he & we are the only citizens of this planet who are going to come out of this raging storm really stronger than before it came.   Yours heartily,   Walter H. Page

ALS (WP, DLC).

From Lucius William Nieman

My dear Mr. President: Milwaukee Jan. 26, 1915.

I forgot to ask you for a companion statement from the state department, dealing with the complaints of friends of the allies. This would greatly strengthen the answer to the partisans of Germany. In no other way could the difficulties of our government be so strikingly brought home to the crowd on both sides. To be useful, this statement should come soon and should not be confined to the case of Belgium, but should also take up minor matters. I went somewhat into details with Mr. McAdoo and Mr. Tumulty.

Very sincerely yours,   L. W. Nieman.

TLS (WP, DLC).

From the Diary of Josephus Daniels

January Tuesday 26 1915

"I desire you, Mr. Secretary, to convey to the Admiral who discussed administration policies in New York last night,[1] that he should confine his remarks to questions asked him by committees of Congress." These were the words used by the President to me when the Cabinet met to-day. He was aroused and indignant. In the afternoon I conveyed the message to Admiral Knight who was much perturbed. He is obsessed by the belief that the Navy Department should be organized on the German system and in order to bring about that plan is guilty of doing injustice to the service and criticizing the administration's policy. He averred that he was loyal to the administration & never dreamed that what he said would be construed into a criticism of the Secretary's or President's policy.

I told him if he was right in saying the Department was not organized for readiness for war, he, the War College, the General Board, the Aids and the Secretary were incompetent and should be removed.

In the Cabinet, the President expressed faith that the ship bill would pass, decided to change Friday night cabinet meetings to day meetings, combatted the suggestion that we might declare it was not the purpose to buy the German merchant ships interned, but that we should insist upon our right even though we should not exercise it. "England is trying its old game of bluff" was Burleson's opinion. Bryan was rejoiced to get news that gave the lie to the oft repeated story that nuns had been violated in Mexico. Some Republican Catholics had been using that canard againt the administration. Goethals had told President he could not be certain the canal would be ready in March. Decided to postpone celebration till July. When will Senate filibuster end. "Reps[.] are not open to reason" said W.

Bound diary (J. Daniels Papers, DLC).

[1] Rear Admiral Austin Melvin Knight, senior naval member and president of the Naval War College. In a speech to the Efficiency Society in New York, he declared that the organization of the Navy Department provided for every contingency except that of war. None of its bureaus had responsibility for keeping the navy in readiness, for preparing war plans, or for conducting war. To fill this need, he urged creation of a new "Division of Strategy and Operations" standing above the existing bureaus and reporting directly to the Secretary of the Navy. Knight also criticized what he called the policy of "economy first" regarding naval expenditures and advocated the creation of a "Council of National Defense," headed by the President, for the "co-ordination of national resources for national defense." *New York Times*, Jan. 26, 1915.

To William Joel Stone

My dear Senator: [The White House] January 27, 1915

That was a splendid speech you delivered in caucus.[1] I have heard a great many speak of it and I want to say that it shows not only a great heart, but a sound and statesmanlike conception of how a party must act in order to govern a great country and really determine legislative policy.

I think you know, my dear Senator, my feeling towards you, and everything that you do serves to enhance it.

Cordially and sincerely yours,   Woodrow Wilson

TLS (Letterpress Books, WP, DLC).

[1] Stone spoke on January 23 in a caucus of Democratic senators on the ship purchase bill. "There can be no middle ground," he said. "Either you are with the Administration or against it. The issue is clear cut. It is a fight between the people on one side and special interests on the other. . . . I intend to follow the leadership of Woodrow Wilson, and not that of Elihu Root or Henry Cabot Lodge. The purpose of the obstructionists is plain. They are seeking to kill the Democratic Party. . . ." As a result of Stone's speech, the thirty-seven Democrats present voted unanimously to approve an amended ship purchase bill and to make it a party measure binding upon all Democratic senators. *New York Times*, Jan. 24, 1915. See also, Link, *Struggle for Neutrality*, pp. 146-47.

To Edward Mandell House

Dear Friend,   The White House 27 January, 1915.

This is just a line to tell you that I yesterday deposited with the Commercial National Bank here $4000, to be placed to your credit at the Fifth Avenue Branch of the Guaranty Trust Company. Perhaps you had better see that it arrived and was properly credited.

My thoughts are constantly with you and it keeps my heart warm and strong to think in any circumstances of your friendship.   Affectionatel[y] Yours,   Woodrow Wilson

WWTLS (E. M. House Papers, CtY).

Edward Thomas Williams to William Jennings Bryan, with Enclosure

[Washington] January 27, 1915.

MEMORANDUM

THE CRISIS IN CHINA.

Dear Mr. Secretary:

The telegrams[1] attached and the press telegrams printed in the morning papers disclose *in part only* the demands made upon China by Japan, but what is revealed shows a serious crisis in Far Eastern affairs threatening not only China's peace but America's interests.

Four only of the twenty-one demands are known but these are such as to show

(1) an infringement of China's neutrality,

(2) a violation of the "Open Door" agreement between the United States and Japan,

(3) a disregard for the Root-Takahira agreement between the United States and Japan,

(4) a denial of Japan's professed desire for peace in the Far East.

(1) The territorial concessions leased to Germany and Austria are four: to Germany, Kiaochow, one settlement tract at Tientsin, and another at Hankow; and to Austria, a settlement at Tientsin. *In all these the sovereignty of China has never been surrendered.* The lands are leased for purposes of residence and trade. The inhabitants of these settlements are of many nationalities and are made up not merely of the subjects of the leasing powers. If China revokes the leases under Japanese threats she

is forced into an unneutral attitude. If China refuses and Japan takes these unfortified settlements by force she can do so only by crossing the neutral territory of China. Having done this already in Shantung it becomes easier to do it again, but in doing so she brings the horrors of war into the midst of international colonies.

(2) The "Open Door" declarations, to which Japan has subscribed are agreements, made at the request of the United States, among the powers having treaties with China, and *registered in our archives* with the avowed objects of preserving China's territorial integrity and administrative entity and guaranteeing equality of opportunity in China for the trade of all nations.

The demand that no concessions be granted to any power but Japan or the less offensive demand for special and exclusive concessions in certain provinces is a clear violation of these agreements and is aimed at American trade as well as that of other countries. Especial antagonism to American investments in China has been shown by Japan in recent years.

(3) In November, 1908, *Japan sought an exchange of views with* the United States which resulted in the Root-Takahira notes in which the two governments agreed "to preserve the common interests of all powers in China by supporting by all pacific means at their disposal the independence and integrity of China and the principle of equal opportunity for commerce and industry of all nations in that empire" and furthermore that "should any event occur threatening the status quo as above described or the principle of equal opportunity as above defined it remains for the two governments to communicate with each other in order to arrive at an understanding as to what measures they may consider it useful to take."

Japan's present action not only violates the pledge as to the preservation of "the common interests of all powers," but practically repudiates the pledge to consult the United States and is the more regrettable since the United States *in August last* intimated an expectation that it would be consulted in case further action in China should be found by Japan to be desirable.

In our own interest and in that of the powers who have at our request entered into the "Open Door" agreements, it seems to be our duty to ask explanation from Japan and insist firmly upon our rights.

I believe that any lack of firmness will but encourage further disregard of our rights.

Our present commercial interests in Japan are greater than those in China, but the look ahead shows our interest to be a strong and independent China rather than one held in subjection by Japan.

China has certain claims upon our sympathy. If we do not recognize them, as we refused to recognize Korea's claim, we are in danger of losing our influence in the Far East and of adding to the dangers of the situation.   E.T.W.

TLI (SDR, RG 59, 793.94/211, DNA).
[1] They were P. S. Reinsch to WJB, Jan. 23, 24, and 26, 1915, T telegrams (SDR, RG 59, 793.94/209, 210, and 211, DNA), all printed in paraphrased or expurgated texts in *FR 1915*, pp. 79-80. The telegram of January 26 is printed as an Enclosure below.
[2] Emphases by Wilson.

ENCLOSURE

Peking January 26, 1915.

STRICTLY CONFIDENTIAL. My telegram January twenty-three, seven P.M., January twenty-four, two A.M. The Legation is informed in strict confidence by a high official that the Japanese demands include not only predominant special interests in impairment of China's sovereignty and of Open Door in Shantung, Kiangsu, Chekiang, Anhui and Kiangsi in addition to Manchuria, but also such further reservations in behalf of Japanse interests as would in effect make subject to their veto all future concessions to other nationalities throughout China. In view of the active antagonism against all American enterprise in China shown by Japanese Legation as reported in despatches three forty August eighteenth[1] and four seventy-eight December twenty-second[2] this would effectively work the exclusion of American participation in economic and industrial development of China.

In insisting upon these demands the Japanese Minister[3] stated to the Minister of Foreign Affairs[4] that a considerable body of the Japanese public regards with disfavor the present administration of China but might be *conciliated*[5] *by compliance with their wishes and he added that in that case the Japanese Government could give President Yuan assurances of immunity from the activities of the Chinese rebels residing in Japan.*

The opinion prevails here among Chinese and foreigners that the unconscionable demands of Japan are prompted by *the desire* of the Okuma Cabinet *to score popular success* in Chinese affairs with a view to general elections in March. This finds confirmation in the following reliably quoted statement of Japanese Minister to the President: *"The ambition* of a large section of the

Japanese nation *to utilize the present crisis* throughout the world forces my Government *to take the most far-reaching action.*"

The reports that Japan's action is impelled [by] China's seeking an alliance with Germany are, in my opinion, utterly unfounded and fantastic: this Government has been almost absurdly zealous to avoid any manner of commitment to either party in the war. It is no less preposterous to charge with truculence a Government which has been even weakly compliant towards Japanese pretensions hitherto. It cannot be doubted, however, that among all classes of the Chinese people there is *intense distrust and resentment towards Japan and that insistence upon the present demands might very probably aggravate that feeling into an uncontrollable anti-Japanese or anti-foreign popular outbreak.*

Unless, therefore, means can be found to induce Tokyo Government to withdraw or very substantially moderate the demands already categorically made, the Chinese Government will be confronted with the dilemma either of complying and thus not only forfeiting a great measure of its political and economical independence and sacrificing the interests of the Powers in maintaining Open Door but also incurring the danger of a popular uprising; or on the other hand of refusing and thus exposing itself to either the direct use of force or the instigation of rebellions by Japan.

In view not only of the special relationship of Great Britain to Japan but also of the particular impairment of British interests in China especially in the Yangtze Valley which would result from realization of Japan's plan as now understood here, I venture earnestly to renew suggestion that representations be made to that government as to the desirability of seeking from its Ally a full statement of all demands which she is taking advantage of the present situation to urge upon China with a view to abating such of them as may prove inconsistent with purposes of the Anglo-Japanese alliance.   Reinsch

T telegram (SDR, RG 59, 793.94/211, DNA).

[1] J.V.A. MacMurray to WJB, Aug. 18, 1914, TLS (SDR, RG 59, 893.00/2184, DNA).

[2] Printed at that date in Vol. 31.

[3] Eki Hioki.

[4] Sun Pao-ch'i, who resigned on January 28 and was succeeded by Lu Cheng-hsiang.

[5] All emphases by Wilson.

Two Letters to William Jennings Bryan

My dear Mr. Secretary,   [The White House] 27 January, 1915.

This memorandum[1] is illuminating, *and* a bit discouraging. But I believe that step by step all these things can be cleared up and misunderstandings removed.

Faithfully Yours,   W.W.

WWTLI (SDR, RG 59, 763.72111/1577, DNA).
[1] That is, Spring Rice's letter to Bryan paraphrasing Grey's telegram.

My dear Mr. Secretary,   [The White House] 27 January, 1915.

This[1] is, of course, something that (or, at least, something like what) we must at the opportune time seek to do for Japan, whose friendship we so sincerely desire and to whom we so sincerely desire to do justice.

But there are many things to consider first: among the rest her present attitude and intentions in China and her willingness or unwillingness to live up to the obligations she has assumed towards us with regard to the open door in the East.

I would be very much obliged if you would ask Mr. Lansing to prepare for our discussion a memorandum explicitly setting forth just what obligations in this sense she did undertake.[2]

Faithfully Yours,   W.W.

WWTLI (SDR, RG 59, 811.52/300, DNA).
[1] See WJB to WW, Jan. 23, 1914 (first letter of that date).
[2] No evidence that Lansing responded in writing to Wilson's request can be found in the various collections and archives. However, the first long note to Japan on the twenty-one demands (see WW to WJB, March 12, 1915, n. 1) went into Japanese treaty obligations to the United States and the degree to which Chinese acceptance of the demands would abridge American rights under treaties between China and the United States and other international agreements.

From William Joel Stone

Dear Mr. President: [Washington] January 27 1915.

I thank you for your very kind note of today. It is sufficient to say that you must know that I greatly appreciate such a compliment from you. I am almost vain enough to wish that it might be given to The Republic,[1] although it would perhaps be better not to do that. It would be gratifying to me, but I cannot escape some fear that in other respects it would not be wise.

Sincerely yours,   Wm. J. Stone.

TLS (WP, DLC).
[1] The St. Louis *Republic*, one of the leading Democratic newspapers of the Middle West.

From Henry Lee Higginson

Dear Mr. President: Boston. January 27, 1915.

I have just been talking with a man from the middle West, who has lived there many years and who is interested in the farms and the general business of the country. He lives in the Mississippi Valley. He says that people are feeling pretty well, but not so well as he had expected. They have been paying their debts, which is always a satisfaction, but he says that they are apprehensive about the war and about our being drawn in. Of course the chance comes through the shipping bill, so he says.

I have been passing the day examining the accounts of one of the very great railroad systems and noting that, with all the huge expenses, which have been carefully trimmed, the company is netting but twenty per cent. of the gross earnings of the system. It is not enough, and it leaves the Road, which is about the best in the country, in a rather dangerous position. A little more business, and the net would be fair, a little less business and the Road will be in the hands of receivers.

This keeps people on the anxious seat, and investors are buying securities yielding 3½ per cent. because they do not know about the railroads or the industrial enterprises. No doubt you have noticed the figures of the Steel Company, which anybody might have guessed beforehand, and they are much worse than the guess. It brings up again my prayer for quiet and no interference with the legitimate operations of trade. In our State the great railroad systems are to be put in order, and the poor stockholders—and they are poor for the most part—are the sufferers. Of course blame is due to certain people, but that is not what we are considering today, but how to overcome the evils.

You would hardly believe how fear of the shipping bill unsettles people's minds and takes away their courage. We all wish that our merchants should have more ships at their command, and wish that we might have a splendid fleet of vessels, but any purchase made today would be at a very high rate if full value were paid, and the moment the war is over, the rates will fall very much, because England is building so many vessels. They tell us about the very high rates for freight paid in sending goods to Europe, but our people do not pay them; it is the consumers of goods who pay them; and just as no American is grieving at seeing wheat at $1.45 and other commodities in the same ratio, just so nobody should be grieved to see the rates on American ships very high, and we also need not grieve much if Europe pays high freight on goods which they receive. In short, that burden is not on our shoulders but on the shoulders of others, and it does not impede trade one bit. More than that, there are a great many ships on the Great Lakes that are coming out very soon and could be brought out now if the Welland Canal were opened, and many ships now used for coastwide trade can be used for foreign trade, and coal &c. can be transported by railroad.

I will not take up the question of whether the Government can manage shipping as well as private individuals can, for that is of less consequence; but it seems to everyone whom I see of the greatest consequence that we should not sin against the laws in taking ships from any one of the four belligerents and putting our flag over them during wartime. If it does not breed a war, it will breed unpleasant disputes and again agitate people so that they will not go on with their industries. People have been inclined to do a little more and a little more, and are getting on their feet. This is true of some branches of trade, but not of others. But the moment there is any agitation, they shrink back, as we have seen in these last few days.

Peace will breed confidence, and confidence will breed prosperity, for we have an abundance of money and ability. The balances between here and Europe are on our side. Everything is all right if people only feel so, but they will not feel so so long as there is any possibility of disturbance.

Day after day I watch the changes and the moods of people, and as I am not in the crowd of busy men, I can judge the more fairly. If we could have no legislation and nothing except routine business, no new regulations, no shipping bill, we should gradually get into a more prosperous condition. It is hard enough to keep our feet and our heads with this horrible war going on, and no man can guess what the result will be. Personally, I regard it as a struggle between the spirit of democracy and that of autocracy. Our people do not care to be told exactly what they shall do, and the Germans do not mind it. Therefore, it seems to me that it is our fight as well as theirs, and I am very reluctant to do anything which will hamper the Allies in finishing the war and stopping that spirit. I see no dislike for the Germans; I do see a great dislike for their spirit.

If the war is once over, and we want to have the government interested in shipping, I shall have nothing to say. But, of all things, I do not wish to sin against the letter or the spirit of the law which keeps us from buying ships from any of the belligerent nations.

You will forgive me for writing you, and I am

Very respectfully yours,   Henry L. Higginson

TLS (WP, DLC).

Thomas Dixon, Jr., to Joseph Patrick Tumulty

Dear Mr Tumulty: [New York] Jan 27, 1915

Please thank the President for me & say that I will be sure to make the journey to Washington to see him next Wednesday the 3rd Feb.[1]

Please write me the hour of my appointment.

Sincerely   Thomas Dixon

ALS (WP, DLC).

[1] Dixon conferred with Wilson at the White House for half an hour on February 3. His object was to persuade Wilson to view the just-completed motion picture, "The Birth of a Nation," based on Dixon's novel and play, *The Clansman* (1905), and directed by David Wark Griffith. Dixon told Wilson that he had a favor to ask of him—not as President, but as a scholar and student of history—that he view this motion picture because it made clear for the first time that a new universal language had been invented. Wilson said that he could not go to a theater because he was still in mourning, but that, if Dixon would set up his projector in the White House, he would invite the cabinet members and their families to come and see it. Wilson insisted that the White House showing not be mentioned in any way in the press. Thomas Dixon, Jr., "Southern Horizons: An Autobiography" (MS in possession of Mrs. Thomas Dixon, Jr.), pp. 424-26. Dixon did not inform Wilson about the subject of "The Birth of a Nation." As he later wrote to Tumulty: "Of course, I didn't dare allow the President to know the *real big purpose back of my film—which was to revolutionize Northern sentiments by a presentation of history that would transform every man in my audience into a good Democrat!* . . . What I told the President was that I would show him the birth of a new art—the launching of the mightiest engine for moulding public opinion in the history of the world." T. Dixon, Jr., to JPT, May 1, 1915, TLS (WP, DLC).

To the House of Representatives

The White House, 28 January, 1915.

It is with unaffected regret that I find myself constrained by clear conviction to return this bill (H.R. 6060, "An act to regulate the immigration of aliens to and the residence of aliens in the United States") without my signature. Not only do I feel it to be a very serious matter to exercise the power of veto in any case, because it involves opposing the single judgment of the President to the judgment of a majority of both the Houses of the Congress, a step which no man who realizes his own liability to error can take without great hesitation, but also because this particular bill is in so many important respects admirable, well conceived, and desirable. Its enactment into law would undoubtedly enhance the efficiency and improve the methods of handling the important branch of the public service to which it relates. But candor and a sense of duty with regard to the responsibility so clearly imposed upon me by the Constitution in matters of legislation leave me no choice but to dissent.

In two particulars of vital consequence this bill embodies a radical departure from the traditional and long-established policy of this country, a policy in which our people have conceived the very character of their government to be expressed, the very mission and spirit of the nation in respect of its relations to the peoples of the world outside their borders. It seeks to all but close entirely the gates of asylum which have always been open to those who could find nowhere else the right and opportunity of constitutional agitation for what they conceived to be the natural and inalienable rights of men;[1] and it excludes those to whom the opportunities of elementary education have been denied, without regard to their character, their purposes, or their natural capacity.[2]

Restrictions like these, adopted earlier in our history as a nation, would very materially have altered the course and cooled the humane ardors of our politics. The right of political asylum has brought to this country many a man of noble character and elevated purpose who was marked as an outlaw in his own less fortunate land, and who has yet become an ornament to our citizenship and to our public councils. The children and the compatriots of these illustrious Americans must stand amazed to see the representatives of their nation now resolved, in the fullness of our national strength and at the maturity of our great institutions, to risk turning such men back from our shores without test of quality or purpose. It is difficult for me to believe that the full effect of this feature of the bill was realized when it was framed and adopted, and it is impossible for me to assent to it in the form in which it is here cast.

The literacy test and the tests and restrictions which accompany it constitute an even more radical change in the policy of the nation. Hitherto we have generously kept our doors open to all who were not unfitted by reason of disease or incapacity for self-support or such personal records and antecedents as were likely to make them a menace to our peace and order or to the wholesome and essential relationships of life. In this bill it is proposed to turn away from tests of character and of quality and impose tests which exclude and restrict; for the new tests here embodied are not tests of quality or of character or of personal fitness, but tests of opportunity. Those who come seeking opportunity are not to be admitted unless they have already had one of the chief of the opportunities they seek, the opportunity of education. The object of such provisions is restriction, not selection.

If the people of this country have made up their minds to

limit the number of immigrants by arbitrary tests and so reverse the policy of all the generations of Americans that have gone before them, it is their right to do so. I am their servant and have no license to stand in their way. But I do not believe that they have. I respectfully submit that no one can quote their mandate to that effect. Has any political party ever avowed a policy of restriction in this fundamental matter, gone to the country on it, and been commissioned to control its legislation? Does this bill rest upon the conscious and universal assent and desire of the American people? I doubt it. It is because I doubt it that I make bold to dissent from it. I am willing to abide by the verdict, but not until it has been rendered. Let the platforms of parties speak out upon this policy and the people pronounce their wish. The matter is too fundamental to be settled otherwise.

I have no pride of opinion in this question. I am not foolish enough to profess to know the wishes and ideals of America better than the body of her chosen representatives know them. I only want instruction direct from those whose fortunes, with ours and all men's, are involved.[3]   Woodrow Wilson.

Printed in *Message from the President of the United States Vetoing H.R. 6060 . . .* (Washington, 1915).

[1] Provisions (repeating many of those of the Immigration Act of 1903) excluding, among others, all anarchists or other persons who believed in or advocated the forcible overthrow of governments or the assassination of public officials. Wilson specifically referred to the new clauses forbidding the entry of aliens "who disbelieve in or are opposed to organized government" and "persons who are members of or affiliated with any organization entertaining and teaching disbelief in or opposition to organized government." He was also undoubtedly disturbed by the failure to include in the immigration bill of 1915 the following exception in the Act of 1903: "*Provided*, That nothing in this Act shall exclude persons convicted of an offense purely political, not involving moral turpitude." Wilson showed keen interest in amendments offered by Senators Thomas and O'Gorman exempting from the literacy test persons coming to the United States to escape racial, religious, or political persecution, amendments which failed of adoption. See C. R. Nixon to JPT, Jan. 27, 1915, TLS (WP, DLC). The text of the Burnett bill and Wilson's veto message are printed in 63d Cong., 3d sess., House Doc. No. 1527.

[2] This was the famous "literacy test" provision of Section 3 which provided that, with some limited exceptions, all aliens over the age of sixteen, physically capable of reading, had to prove as a condition of their admission to the United States that they could read a selected passage in English or any other language or dialect, including Hebrew or Yiddish.

[3] There is a WWsh draft of this message, dated Jan. 26, 1915, and a WWT undated draft, both in the C. L. Swem Coll., NjP.

To Edward Mandell House, with Enclosure

Dear Friend,   [The White House] 28 January, 1915.

I hurry the enclosed to you, for your information, not for your discouragement! Is not the last paragraph amazing?

Affectionately,   W.W.

WWTLI (E. M. House Papers, CtY)

ENCLOSURE

Berlin (via Rome). January 24, 1915.

1418, January 24, 3 p.m. STRICTLY CONFIDENTIAL.

I do not think that people in America realize how excited the Germans have become on the question of the selling of munitions of war by Americans to the Allies. A veritable campaign of hate has been commenced against America and Americans. The following is from today's TAGEBLATT, the newspaper of greatest circulation:

"It is but a demand of the inexorable logic of war to pay back the English in their own coin. Since they do not hestitate an instant to cut us off from all importations in order to overpower through hunger and need the German people, whom they cannot conquer in open sea or land battle, so is it for the German Empire absolutely necessary to do every possible injury to English commerce. The official publication of the German Government concerning the American delivery of the above material shows clearly that matters cannot go on as they have up to now. Rightly is the question put forward whether, if not the neutrality of the American Government, at least the neutrality of the American people is broken by the unpermissible commerce of war material with France and England. It is impossible to permanently look on at this traffic and not to do everything which lies in our power to divide in this commerce from abroad sun and light equally among all the warring Nations. If possible airships and submarine boats can bring this about, it would be the height of misplaced consideration *to force* (to forego?) their assistance."

Under Secretary of Foreign Affairs Zimmerman showed me a long list, evidently obtained by an effective spy system, of orders placed with American concerns by the Allies. He said that perhaps it was as well to have the whole World against Germany, and that in case of trouble there *were five hundred thousand trained Germans in America who would join the Irish and start a revolution.*[1] I thought at first he was joking but he was actually serious. The fact that our six Army observers are still here in Berlin and not sent to the front is a noteworthy indication. Zimmerman's talk was largely ridiculous and impossible as it seems to us it would not surprise me to see this maddened Nation in arms go to lengths however extreme.   Gerard

T telegram (E. M. House Papers, CtY).
[1] Italicization by Wilson. He also marked this entire paragraph in the margin.

Two Letters to William Jennings Bryan

My dear Mr. Secretary,   [The White House] 28 January, 1915.

The last paragraph of Gerard's despatch is nothing less than amazing. Such distempers of the mind make the discussion of peace seem painfully difficult.

Faithfully Yours,   W.W.

WWTLI (CLO).

Confidential

My dear Mr. Secretary,   [The White House] 28 January, 1915.

You will remember that when you and Mr. Lansing and I discussed the Pan-American agreement you asked me to send you a copy and to add a fourth Article, embodying the substance of our recent peace treaties.

I have literally not had time until to-day, to set about this, and now that I have begun I find myself at a loss as to just how to phrase it. Will you not be kind enough to complete what I have here (in the enclosed) begun and let me have it at your early convenience in order that we may push forward this important business?[1]   Faithfully Yours,   Woodrow Wilson

WWTLS (SDR, RG 59, 710.11/190½, DNA).
[1] Bryan completed Article IV, the text of which is embodied in the Enclosure with WW to WJB, Jan. 29, 1915.

To Thomas Nelson Page

My dear Mr. Ambassador: [The White House] January 28, 1915

Your letter of January fifth[1] has served to illuminate many things for me and I thank you for it most sincerely. All light of this kind is extremely valuable for my present guidance, for, of course, I am looking for the right opportunity to influence, if I may, the course of events towards peace.

Let me say how great a comfort it is to me to have someone upon whose insight and capacity to deal with delicate matters I can have such complete reliance.

Things go normally enough here and I hope that the excitements generated in this country by the war are in some measure subsiding, though it is still very difficult to convince those Americans whose hearts are still on the other side of the water that the government is pursuing a consistent and impartial course of neutrality.

Will you not convey to Mrs. Page[2] my warm regards, and believe me

Cordially and faithfully yours,   Woodrow Wilson

TLS (Letterpress Books, WP, DLC).
[1] T. N. Page to WW, Jan. 5, 1915, TLS, enclosing T. N. Page to WW, Jan. 1, 1915, TLS, both in WP, DLC.
[2] Florence Lathrop Field Page.

To Jessie Kennedy Dyer

My dear Jessie: [The White House] January 28, 1915

Your letter of January twenty-first[1] was very welcome. I always wish when I get your letters that I had time to answer them satisfactorily and were not shut in to the few lines I have time to write, but those few lines you may always be sure carry the most affectionate messages from all of us.

Jessie and the baby are doing famously well; nothing untoward has marred the eleven days since the baby was born, and everything looks bright for them. The baby's name, as perhaps you know through the newspapers, is to be Francis, after his father. They wanted to name him after me but I thought he was entitled to a name of his own and persuaded them not to give him my name.

Jessie sends you her love, and we are all so glad to hear that your children are getting along so happily.

Affectionately yours,   Woodrow Wilson

TLS (Letterpress Books, WP, DLC).
[1] Jessie K. Dyer to WW, Jan. 21, 1915, ALS (WP, DLC).

From Edward Mandell House

Dear Governor: New York City. January 28th, 1915.

I am enclosing you a revised code[1] as I find that nearly all the ones we had are in the regular code book, meaning something else, which would cause confusion.

I have selected words beginning with w's, y's and z's for the reason that these letters are not in the code at all.

I had a satisfactory talk with Bernstorff today. He said he notified his government of my coming, but he has not received a reply which he considers favorable, believing if they did not desire to talk with me, they would notify him.

I have asked him, however, to cable Zimmermann to communicate with me through our two Embassies in Berlin and London. I told Bernstorff something of the contents of your letter of instruction. He thought it admirable and believed that upon the lines you have laid down, at least preliminary conversations may be begun.   Affectionately yours,   E. M. House

TLS (WP, DLC).
¹ It is missing in WP, DLC; there is a copy in the House Papers, CtY.

From Herman Bernstein

New York, Jan. 28, 1915.

Pray accept my warmest congratulations upon one of your greatest acts   your brilliant message vetoing restrictive immigration bill will doubtless be applauded by liberal and broadminded Americans and they are in the majority   By your courage you have saved America from committing herself to a policy of narrow selfishness and retrogression.   Herman Bernstein.

T telegram (WP, DLC).

A Memorandum by Edward Thomas Williams

[Washington] January 28, 1915.

Comment on telegram of January 26, 8 p.m., page 2.

The conditional promise of immunity from the activities of revolutionaries tends to confirm the reports that at present Japan is encouraging such activities.

The explanation given that Count Okuma's demands are made with a view to influencing the Japanese elections only makes the situation more serious since it shows that the Japanese people want a war of conquest. The Minister's admission that a large section of the people want to utilize the present world situation points in the same direction.

Telegram, January 27, 8 p.m., page 1.¹

The phrase "administrative powers in South Manchuria" means the "expulsion of Chinese officials from those provinces." It is a blow at the "administrative entitiy" of China, to the preservation of which Japan is pledged and can be viewed only as a step towards annexation.

Japan's violation of all her pledges to Korea warns us, however, not to expect her to fulfill her engagements when apparent self interest dictates their repudiation.

"Special rights" as to "iron deposits throughout China" will prevent acceptance by Americans of offer of mining rights in

Fukien and will probably prevent China's manufacture of armament and building of ships except as Japan may permit.

T MS (SDR, RG 59, 793.94/211, DNA).
¹ P. S. Reinsch to WJB, Jan. 27, 1915, 8 p.m., T telegram (SDR, RG 59, 793.94/214, DNA). Williams summarizes and comments on it in the next three paragraphs.

An Address to the American Electric Railway Association[1]

[[Jan. 29, 1915]]

Mr. President,[2] ladies and gentlemen: It is a real pleasure to me to be here and to look this company in the face. I know how important the interests that you represent are. I know that they represent some of the chief channels through which the vigor and activity of the nation flow. I am also very glad, indeed, to have you come and look at some portion, at any rate, of the Government of the United States. Many things are reported and supposed about that government, and it is thoroughly worth your while to come and see for yourselves.

I have always maintained that the only way in which men could understand one another was by meeting one another. If I believed all that I read in the newspapers, I would not understand anybody. I have met many men whose horns dropped away the moment I was permitted to examine their heads. For, after all, in a vast country like this the most difficult thing is a common understanding. We are constantly forming get-together associations, and I sometimes think that we make the mistake of confining those associations, in their membership, to those who are interested only in some one particular group of the various industries of the country. The important thing is for the different enterprises of the country to understand one another; and the most important thing of all is for us to comprehend our life as a nation and understand each other as fellow citizens.

Now, it seems to me that I can say, with a good deal of confidence, that we are upon the eve of a new era of enterprise and of prosperity. Enterprise has been checked in this country for almost twenty years, because men were moving amongst a maze of interrogation points. They did not know what was going to happen to them. All sorts of regulations were proposed, and it was a matter of uncertainty what sort of regulation was going to be adopted. All sorts of charges were made against business,

¹ Delivered at the New Willard Hotel.
² C. Loomis Allen, president of the Newport News and Old Point Railway & Electric Co. and president of the association, 1914-15.

as if business were at fault, when most men knew that the great majority of businessmen were honest, were public-spirited, were intending the right thing, and the many were made afraid because the few did not do what was right.

The most necessary thing, therefore, was for us to agree, as we did by slow stages agree, upon the main particulars of what ought not to be done, and then to put our laws in such shape as to correspond with that general judgment. That, I say, was a necessary preliminary, not only to a common understanding, but also to a universal cooperation. The great forces of a country like this cannot pull separately; they have got to pull together. And, except upon a basis of common understanding as to the law and as to the proprieties of conduct, it is impossible to pull together. I, for one, have never doubted that all America was of one principle. I have never doubted that all America believed in doing what was fair and honorable and of good report. But the method—the method of control by law against the small minority that was recalcitrant against these principles—was a thing that it was difficult to determine upon; and it was a very great burden, let me say, to fall upon a particular administration of this government to have to undertake practically the whole business of final definition. That is what has been attempted by the Congress now about to come to a close. It has attempted the definitions for which the country had been getting ready, or trying to get ready, for half a generation. It will require a period of test to determine whether they have successfully defined them or not; but no one needs to have it proved to him that it was necessary to define them and remove the uncertainties, and that, the uncertainties being removed, common understandings are possible and a universal cooperation.

You, gentlemen, representing these arteries of which I have spoken, that serve to release the forces of communities and serve, also, to bind community with community, are surely in a better position than the men perhaps of any other profession to understand how communities constitute units—and even a nation constitutes a unit; and that what is detrimental and hurtful to a part, you, above all men, ought to know is detrimental to all. You can not demoralize some of the forces of a community without being in danger of demoralizing all the forces of a community. Your interest is not in the congestion of life, but in the release of life. Your interest is not in isolation, but in union—the union of parts of this great country, so that every energy in those parts will flow freely and with full force from county to county throughout the whole nation.

What I have come to speak of this afternoon is this unity of our interest, and I want to make some—I will not say "predictions," but to use a less dangerous though bigger word—prognostications. I understand that there is among the medical profession diagnosis and prognosis. I dare say the prognosis is more difficult than the diagnosis, since it has to come first; and not being a physician, I have all the greater courage in the prognosis. I have noticed all my life that I could speak with the greatest freedom about those things that I did not understand; but there are some things that a man is bound to try to think out, whether he fully comprehends them or not. The thought of no single man can comprehend the life of a great nation like this, and yet men in public life, upon whom the burden of guidance is laid, must attempt to comprehend as much of it as they can. Their strength will lie in common counsel; their strength will lie in taking counsel of as many informed persons as possible in each department with which they have to deal; but some time or other the point will come when they have to make a decision based upon a prognosis. We have had to do that in attempting the definitions of law which have been attempted by this Congress. And now it is necessary for us, in order to go forward with the confident spirit with which I believe we can go forward, to look ahead and see the things that are likely to happen.

In the first place, I feel that the mists and miasmic airs of suspicion that have filled the business world have now been blown away. I believe that we have passed the era of suspicion and have come into the era of confidence. Knowing the elements we have to deal with, we can deal with them; and with that confidence of knowledge, we can have confidence of enterprise. That enterprise is going to mean this: Nobody is henceforth going to be afraid of or suspicious of any business merely because it is big. If my judgment is correct, nobody has been suspicious of any business merely because it was big; but they have been suspicious whenever they thought that the bigness was being used to take an unfair advantage. We all have to admit that it is easier for a big fellow to take advantage of you than for a little fellow to take advantage of you. Therefore, we instinctively watch the big fellow with a little closer scrutiny than we watch the little fellow. But, bond having been given for the big fellow, we can sleep o'nights. Bond having been given that he will keep the peace, we do not have to spend our time and waste our energy watching him. The conditions of confidence being established, nobody need think that, if he is taller than the rest, anybody is going to throw a stone at him simply because he is a favorable target—always provided there is fair dealing and real service.

Because the character of modern business, gentlemen, is this: The number of cases in which men do business on their own individual, private capital is relatively small in our day. Almost all the greater enterprises are done on what is, so far as the managers of that business are concerned, other people's money. That is what a joint-stock company means. It means, "Won't you lend us your resources to conduct this business and trust us, a little group of managers, to see that you get honest and proper returns for your money?" And no man who manages a joint-stock company can know for many days together, without fresh inquiry, who his partners are, because the stock is constantly changing hands, and the partners are seldom the same people for long periods together. Which amounts to saying that, inasmuch as you are using the money of everybody who chooses to come in, your responsibility is to everybody who has come in or who may come in. That is simply another way of saying that your business is, so far forth, a public business, and you owe it to the public to take them into your confidence in regard to the way in which it is conducted.

The era of private business in the sense of business conducted with the money of the partners—I mean of the managing partners —is practically passed, not only in this country, but almost everywhere. Therefore, almost all business has this direct responsibility to the public in general: We owe a constant report to the public, whose money we are constantly asking for in order to conduct the business itself. Therefore, we have got to trade, not only on our efficiency, not only on the service that we render, but on the confidence that we cultivate. There is a new atmosphere for business. The oxygen that the lungs of modern business takes in is the oxygen of public confidence, and if you have not got that, your business is essentially paralyzed and asphyxiated.

I take it that we are in a position now to come to a common understanding, knowing that only a common understanding will be the stable basis of business, and that what we want for business hereafter is the same kind of liberty that we want for the individual. The liberty of the individual is limited with the greatest sharpness where his actions come into collision with the interests of the community he lives in. My liberty consists in a sort of parole. Society says to me, "You may do what you please until you do something that is in violation of the common understanding, of the public interest; then your parole is forfeited. We will take you into custody. We will limit your activities. We will penalize you if you use this thing that you call your liberty against our interest." Business does not want, and ought not to ask for, more liberty than the individual has. And I have always in my own thought summed up individual liberty, and business liberty, and every other kind of liberty, in the phrase that is common in the sporting world, "A free field and no favors."

There have been times—I will not specify them, but there have been times—when the field looked free, but when there were favors received from the managers of the course; when there were advantages given; inside tracks accorded; practices which would block the other runners; rules which would exclude the amateur who wanted to get in. That may be a free field, but there is favor, there is partiality, there is preference, there is covert advantage taken of somebody, and while it looks very well from the grandstand, there are men whom you can find who were not allowed to get into the track and test their powers against the other men who were racing for the honors of the day.

I think it is a serviceable figure. It means this: That you are not going to be barred from the contest because you are big and strong, and you are not going to be penalized because you are big and strong. But you are going to be made to observe the rules of the track and not get in anybody's way, except as you can keep ahead of him by having more vigor and skill than he has. When we get that understanding, that we are all sports, and that we are not going to ask for, not only, but we are not going to condescend to take, advantage of anything that does not belong to us, then the atmosphere will clear so that it will seem as if the sun had never shone as it does that day. It is the spirit of true sportsmanship that ought to get into everything, and men who, when they get beaten that way, squeal do not deserve our pity.

Some men are going to get beaten because they have not the brains; they have not the initiative; they have not the skill; they have not the knowledge; they have not the same capacity that other men have. They will have to be employees; they will have to be used where they can be used. We do not need to conceal from ourselves that there are varieties of capacity in the world. Some men have heads, but they are not particularly furnished. I overheard two men one day talking about a third man, and one of them referred to his head. "Head?" the other said, "Head? That isn't a head; that's just a knot the Almighty put there to keep him from raveling out!" We have to admit that there are such persons. Now, liberty does not consist in framing laws to put such men at the front and demand that they be allowed to keep pace with the rest; because that would hold the whole process of civilization back. But it does consist in saying no matter how featherweight the other man is, you must not arbitrarily interfere with him; that there must be an absolutely free field and no favor to anybody.

There are, therefore, I suppose, certain rules of the game. I will mention what seem to me some of them. I have already mentioned one of them by way of illustration. First of all is the rule of publicity: not doing anything under cover; letting the public know what you are doing and judge of it according as it is. There are a great many businesses in this country that have fallen under suspicion because they were so secretive, when there was nothing to secrete that was dishonorable. The minute I keep everything in my pocket and will not show anybody what is there, they conjecture what may be in my pocket; whereas, if I turn my pockets inside out, the conjecture is, at any rate, dissipated. There is no use inviting suspicion by secretiveness. If a business is being honorably done and successfully done, you ought to be pleased to turn it inside out and let the people whom you are inviting to invest in it see exactly how it is done and with what results. Publicity, which is required in sport, is required in business. Let's see how you are running the game!

Then, in the second place, is giving a full equivalent for the money you receive, the full equivalent in service; not trying to skimp in the service in order to increase profits above a reasonable return, but trying to make the profits proportioned to the satisfaction of the people that you serve. There isn't any more solid foundation for business than that. If you thoroughly satisfy the people you are serving, you are welcome to their money. They are not going to grudge it, because they will feel that they are getting a *quid pro quo*; they are getting something such as was promised them when their money was asked of them.

Then, in the third place, this game requires something more than ordinary sport. It requires a certain kind of conscience in business, a certain feeling that we are, after all, in this world because we are expected to make good according to the standards of the people we live with. That, after all, gentlemen, is the chief compulsion that is laid on all of us. I am not aware of being afraid of jail; I do not feel uneasy when I pass a penitentiary; but I would feel extremely uneasy if I knew I had done something which some fine, honorable friend of mine would condemn if it passed before him. I would look carefully at his eyes to see if he suspected anything, and I would feel unhappy until I had made a clean breast of it with him. That is what we are afraid of, and that is what we ought to be afraid of. We are sustained by the moral judgments of honorable men; and there isn't anything else in this world that I know of that is worthwhile. How honors must hurt a man if he feels that they have been achieved dishonorably! They then are an arrow in his heart, not a quickening or a tonic to his spirit in any respect. If he feels that he has cheated the people who trusted him, then, no matter what fortunes he piles up, they never can contribute to his peace of mind for a moment. So I say that conscience in business is the motive spring of the whole thing—the pride of doing the thing as it ought to be done.

I ask every man in this room who employs other men if he would not pay the best salary he has if he could be assured that the man he employed was of that quality. You know that is the sort of men that you want—the men who will take a pride in doing the thing right and have a clean conscience toward you who employ them. Now, all of us are employees of the public. It doesn't make any difference what our business is, or how small it is, we are, so far as we get money for it, employees of the public. And our clear, clean consciences towards our employers are the basis of our success and, it goes without saying, the basis of our happiness.

Then, the fourth rule, as it seems to me, is the rule of having the spirit of service. I know a lot of cant is talked about that, and I get very sick of the cant, as I dare say you do; but when I talk about the spirit of service I am not meaning a sentiment. I am not meaning a state of mind. I am meaning something very concrete—that you want to see to it that the thing that you do for the public and get money for is the best thing of that kind that can be done. That is what I mean by the spirit of service. I have known many a man who gave up profit for mental satisfaction. I know men in this city—there are men in the scientific bureaus of this government whom I could cite—who could make very big salaries, but who prefer the satisfaction of doing things that will serve the whole community, and doing them just as well as they possibly can be done. I, for one, am proud of the scientific bureaus of this government. There are men in them of the most self-sacrificing spirit and of the highest scientific efficiency, who do things on a petty salary which some other men would not do at all; for if you have to pay a man a salary to produce the best product of his brain, then he scales the product down to the salary. Here are men who scale the product up to the highest standards of scientific ideals! They have hitched their wagons to a star, and the star is apt to lift their names above the names of the rest of us. So I say that if your earning capacity is the capacity to earn the public confidence, you can go about your business like freemen. Nobody is going to molest you, and everybody is going to say, "If you earn big profits; if you have treated the people from whom you are making your profits as they ought to be treated; if you treat the employees whom you use in earning those profits as they ought to be treated; if your methods of competition are clean and above reproach; why, then, you can pile those profits as high as the Rockies, and nobody will be jealous of it." Because you will have earned them in a sense that is the handsomest sense of all.

It is in this spirit that we all ought to regard the laws, that we all ought to criticise the laws, and that we all ought to co-operate in the enforcement of the laws. Government, gentlemen, is merely an attempt to express the conscience of everybody, the average conscience of the nation, in the rules that everybody is commanded to obey. That is all they are. If the government is going faster than the public conscience, it will presently have to pull up. If it is not going as fast as the public conscience, it will presently have to be whipped up. Because the public conscience is going to say, "We want our laws to express our character"; and our character must have this kind of solidity underneath it—the moral judgment of right and wrong. The only reason we quarrel with reformers sometimes is because they are, or suppose that they are, a little more enlightened than the rest of us, and they want us all of a sudden to be just as enlightened as they are, and we cannot stand the pace. That is all that makes us uneasy about reformers. If we could get our second wind, if we could keep up the pace as long as they do, we might be able to run as fast as they do, but we are more heavily weighted with clay than they are. We cannot go as fast. And we like companionship. We want to wait for the rest of them. We do not want to be in a lonely advance, climbing some heights of perfection where there is no good inn to stop at overnight.

That, gentlemen, is the homely and, I dare say, obvious lesson which I have meant to give utterance to this afternoon. I think that I understand what you are after. I hope that you understand what we are after. All I ask is that if anything is being done that ought not to be done, the fault in it be conclusively pointed out and the way to correct the mistake be explicitly shown. There is an old rule that ought to obtain in politics as in everything else, and it is expressed in a very homely way. It is the rule of "Put up or shut up." Some one said, "If you wish me to consider you witty, I must really trouble you to make a joke." If you wish me to consider you wise, I must really trouble you to show the concrete proof; to show how the thing can be done; to show how it can be better done. Because nobody is fool enough to suppose that the way he has determined that the thing ought to be done is necessarily the best way to do it. But it is the best way to do it until you show a better way. That is a perfectly obvious rule. So, again, I say it is the rule of "Put up or shut up." And I do not mean that in any sort of disrespect. The market for ideas is a highly competitive market, and the rules of competition are necessarily fair. There is only one test for an idea and that is, "Is it good?" You may for the time being dress it with such rhetoric that it will look good—and the best thing that characterizes countries like our own is that every man who has an idea is constantly invited to the platform; there is nothing better for an idea by way of test than exposure to the atmosphere. If you let enough people hear it stated often enough, it will certainly seek its proper level.

That is the reason I believe in free speech. I have been subjected to free speech myself, and it is hard to endure sometimes, because the office of the President seems to be the clearinghouse for original ideas. I am brought more original ideas *per diem*, I dare say, than any other person in the country and, therefore, pay the penalty of freedom of speech. Perhaps my mind does not register original ideas readily enough, because some of them do not register at all. I am perfectly willing to admit that that is the fault of the register, not the fault of the idea. All I have to say to you is that, if you have ideas, the register is entirely at your service.[3]

Printed in *Address of the President of the United States . . . January 29, 1915* (Washington, 1918).
[3] There is a WWsh outline and a WWT outline of this speech, dated Jan. 27, 1915, in WP, DLC.

A Letter and a Telegram to Edward Mandell House

My dear Friend,   The White House. 29 January, 1915.

It gives me peculiar pleasure to give you my commission to go, as my personal representative, on the mission you are now so generously undertaking, a mission fraught with so many great possibilities, and which may, in the kind providence of God, prove the means of opening a way to peace.

It is altogether right and fortunate that you are to act only as my private friend and spokesman, without official standing or authority; for that will relieve both you and those with whom you confer of any embarrassment. Your conferences will not represent the effort of any government to urge action upon another government, but only the effort of a disinterested friend, whose suggestions and offers of service will not be misunderstood and may be made use of to the advantage of the world.

The object of this letter is not merely to furnish you with an informal commission but also to supply you with what I know you desire, a definite statement of our attitude with regard to the delicate and important matters you are to discuss and the sort of service we wish to render.

Please say, therefore, very clearly to all with whom you may confer that we have no thought of suggesting, either now or at any other time, the terms and conditions of peace, except as we may be asked to do so as the spokesmen of those whose fortunes are involved in the war. Our single object is to be serviceable, if we may, in bringing about the preliminary willingness to parley which must be the first step towards discussing and determining the conditions of peace. If we can be instrumental in ascertaining for each side in the contest what is the real disposition, the real wish, the real purpose of the other with regard to a settlement, your mission and my whole desire in this matter will have been accomplished.

I do not know how better to express my conception of your mission than by saying that it is my desire, if they will be so gracious as to permit me to do so, to supply through you a channel of confidential communication through which the nations now at war may make certain that it is right and wise and consistent with their safety and dignity to have a preliminary interchange of views with regard to the terms upon which the present conflict may be brought to an end and future conflicts rendered less likely. There is nothing to which we wish to bind them. It has occurred to us that to ascertain each other's present views in this informal way might be less embarrassing to them than to ascertain them in any other way; that they might possibly be glad to avail themselves of our services, offered in this way, rather than run the risk of missing any honourable opportunity to open a way to peace; and that they would be willing to make use of us the more readily because they might be sure that we sought no advantage for ourselves and had no thought or wish to play a part of guidance in their affairs. The allies on both sides have seemed to turn to the United States as to a sort of court of opinion in this great struggle, but we have no wish to be the judges; we desire only to play the part of disinterested friends who have nothing at stake except their interest in the peace of the world.

Your sincere friend,   Woodrow Wilson[1]

WWTLS (E. M. House Papers, CtY).
    ¹ There is an undated WWsh draft of this letter in WP, DLC, and a WWT
draft (the one that Wilson had earlier sent to House for his approval) in the
EBW Papers, DLC.

The White House Jany 29, 1915.

Of course you know my heart goes with you   God bless you
and speed you   Woodrow Wilson

T telegram (E. M. House Papers, CtY).

To William Jennings Bryan, with Enclosure

Dear Mr. Secretary,   [The White House] 29 January, 1915.

Here are the four articles of agreement complete. I am sorry
not to have had time to send them before.

                         Faithfully Yours,   W.W.

WWTLI (SDR, RG 59, 710.11/198½, DNA).

E N C L O S U R E

I.

That the contracting parties to this solemn covenant and
agreement hereby join one another in a common and mutual
guarantee of territorial integrity and of political independence
under republican forms of government.

II.

That, to this end, and as a condition precedent to the foregoing
guarantee of territorial integrity, it is covenanted and agreed between them that all disputes now pending and unconcluded between any two or more of them with regard to their boundaries
or territories shall be brought to an early and final settlement
in the following manner, unless some equally prompt and satisfactory method of settlement can be agreed upon and put into
operation in each or any case within three months after the signing of this convention and brought to a decision within one year
after its inception:

Each of the parties to the dispute shall select two arbiters and
those thus selected and commissioned shall select an additional
arbiter or umpire; to the tribunal thus constituted the question
or questions at issue shall be submitted without reservation; and
the decisions and findings of this tribunal shall be final and conclusive as between the parties to the dispute and under the terms

of this convention as to the whole subject-matter submitted. The findings of such tribunal or tribunals shall be arrived at and officially announced and accepted within not more than one year after the formal constitution of the tribunal; and the tribunal shall be constituted not more than three months after the signing and ratification of the convention.

III.

That the high contracting parties severally pledge themselves to obtain and establish by law such control of the manufacture and sale of munitions of war within their respective jurisdictions as will enable them absolutely to control and make them responsible for the sale and shipment of such munitions to any other of the nations who are parties to this convention.

IV.

That the high contracting parties further agree, First, that all questions, of whatever character, arising between any two or more of them which cannot be settled by the ordinary means of diplomatic correspondence shall, before any declaration of war or beginning of hostilities, be first submitted to a permanent international commission for investigation, one year being allowed for such investigation; and, Second, that, if the dispute is not settled by investigation, to submit the same to arbitration, provided the question in dispute does not affect the honour, independence, or vital interests of the nations concerned or the interests of third parties; and the high contracting parties hereby agree, where this has not already been done, to enter into treaty, each with all of the others severally, to carry out the provisions of this Article.

WWT MS (SDR, RG 59, 710.11/198½, DNA).

To Lucius William Nieman

My dear Mr. Nieman: [The White House] January 29, 1915

Thank you for your letter of January twenty-sixth.

I doubt if the complaints of the friends of the Allies have been formulated with anything like the explicitness that the complaints of the friends of Germany are formulated, but I shall see what can be done by way of a satisfactory statement and reply.

Thank you sincerely for the suggestion.

Faithfully yours,   Woodrow Wilson

TLS (Letterpress Books, WP, DLC).

To Robert Lansing

My dear Mr. Lansing: The White House January 29, 1915

The enclosed letter[1] is from a genuine friend of peace and Americanism and who is intelligently active in trying to correct the gross misapprehensions and prejudices which have prevailed among some of our fellow-citizens of German extraction. I think that his suggestion in the enclosed letter is a very interesting and important one. I am writing to ask if the "complaints of the friends of the Allies" have been formulated in a way which would give us an opportunity to treat them as we have treated the complaints of the other side. Perhaps this could be done in connection with the letter about Belgium.

Cordially and sincerely yours,   Woodrow Wilson

TLS (SDR, RG 59, 763.72111/1675½, DNA).
[1] L. W. Nieman to WW, Jan. 26, 1915.

Three Letters from Edward Mandell House

Dear Governor: New York City. January 29th, 1915.

The despatch you send me is astounding. I told you last year of the highly nervous condition of those people, and present troubles are evidently putting them over the border line. I have known from the beginning that our hardest task would be there.

I think it essential that you inform Walter [Bernstorff], through Wallace, that it is not your wish for me to visit any country that does not indicate in advance that my coming would be welcome. I have told Walter that I would expect word from Wolf [Zimmermann] soon after my arrival in London, and have told him the way to get it to me. But I think the above message should come directly from you.

I have a letter from Winkle [Spring Rice] this morning saying that he had word from White [Grey] that he would see me at any time after my arrival that I would indicate. This puts that matter in satisfactory shape.

I will appreciate it if you will have me kept fully informed by cable concerning the happenings and information that have a bearing upon the situation. I would suggest that the cablegrams be sent saying "For the information of the Ambassador and and [sic] Beverly."

Please add the word Beverly for my name and also let the State Department do so when cabling to London.

I think it would be well to keep me fully informed as to conditions in other capitals so that I may know conditions. News is so censored that there will be no chance for even the general information that one gets here.

Wolf's outbreak indicates the necessity of our holding to the friendship of Zenobia [Britain].

Affectionately yours,   E. M. House

Dear Governor: New York City. January 29th, 1915.

The $4000.00 has been received at the Guaranty Trust Company.

I am sure you know I am deeply grateful for this additional proof of your consideration for me.

Affectionately yours,   E. M. House

TLS (WP, DLC).

New York January 29, 1915.

Good-bye, dear friend, and may God sustain you in all your noble undertakings. When I think of the things you have done, of the things you have in mind to do, my heart stirs with pride and satisfaction. You are the bravest, wisest leader, the gentlest and most gallant gentleman and the truest friend in all the world.   Your devoted and affectionate,   E. M. House

ALS (WP, DLC).

From Jane Addams

My dear Mr. Wilson: Chicago January 29, 1915

May I express my admiration of the message which accompanied your veto of the Immigration Bill, and assure you of the affection and warm appreciation with which your action has been received by many thousand immigrants and their friends.

I wish you might have heard some of our cosmopolitan callers who came to Hull-House last night, express their gratitude for your action.   Sincerely yours,   Jane Addams

TLS (WP, DLC).

From Frank Trumbull

Dear Mr. President: White Sulphur, W. Va., Jan. 29th, 1915.

Will you permit me to congratulate you because of your veto of the Immigration Bill? I have just finished the perusal of it with a feeling of exhilaration. It is admirable in expression, statesmanlike in quality, and although a veto—really augments the notable constructive acts of an administration not yet two years old.

With high regard,

Very sincerely yours, Frank Trumbull

TLS (WP, DLC).

To Frank Trumbull

My dear Mr. Trumbull: [The White House] January 30, 1915.

I thank you warmly for your kind letter of January 29th. Your generous words are, indeed, very gratifying and pleasing.

Cordially and sincerely yours, Woodrow Wilson

TLS (Letterpress Books, WP, DLC).

From William Hitz[1]

Sir: Washington, D. C. January 30, 1915.

Several months ago I had the honor of proposing Mr. Louis D. Brandeis of Boston for non-resident membership in the Cosmos Club of Washington, which proposal was duly seconded and put into the proper course of consideration.

It now seems likely that action upon this nomination will be taken on Monday night February 1st, or shortly thereafter, and several members of the Club have started an opposition to Mr. Brandeis which bids fair to be successful unless his friends come strongly to his support.

The grounds of opposition to Mr. Brandeis are stated to be that he is a reformer for revenue only; that he is a Jew; and that he would be a disturbing element in any club of gentlemen.

Letters of objection have been written by members of the Club having no acquaintance whatever with Mr. Brandeis, and who have been requested to object by other persons not members of the Club.

Because of the injustice done Mr. Brandeis by these covert attacks to which he cannot reply, I have ventured to hope that you might deem it not improper as a member of the Club to write a word to the Committee on Admissions in support of the nomination of Mr. Brandeis.

If the matter could be brought to a vote of the whole Club there would of course be no apprehension as to the result, but a small Committee on Admissions proceeding entirely in secret is so irresponsible a tribunal as to be capable of reaching any sort of conclusion.

If Mr. Brandeis were aware of any considerable opposition to his election, he would undoubtedly require his friends to withdraw his name, but he has not learned of it, and, of course, he does not know that I am taking the liberty of bringing the matter to your attention.

Very respectfully yours,   Wm Hitz

TLS (WP, DLC).
1 Lawyer of Washington.

To Mary Allen Hulbert

Dearest Friend,   [The White House] 31 January, 1915.

Of course you understand why I have not written: it has simply been impossible: there was not time in the twenty-four hours, there was not force enough in my nerves to suffice for the things that had to be done; it was humanly out of the question to add anything more. But in the midst of it all my thought has been full of you and your fortunes; my sympathy and my anxiety have been without limit.

Let me speak first of your practical suggestions. As you have probably seen by the papers, it is not going to be possible to hold the exercises at Panama until midsummer. It would not be safe to try to put the battleship fleet through just yet because of the constant slides and settlings. So that trip is off for all of us for the present. As for the forest service, I have not had time since your last letter came to look into the rules that govern that or to determine whether there is anything there that I could open to Allen that would be worth his taking. I will look into it at once, and hope with all my heart that something will be disclosed. How I would love to do what you suggest, if I legally may! We will see.

How brave you are, and how capable, when an emergency arises! And with what spirit you carry it off,—those trying expeditions to Nantucket, the negociations for the sales, and all the rest. It is fine. You *think* that you show me your weak side in your letters: in reality your strength shows more clearly than any weakness; and the appeal to my sympathy is all the more poignant. Nothing can happen that will really conquor you. And it is as fine as it is extraordinary that you should grow physically stronger and better amidst it all. It makes me happy to hear that.

And it makes me still more happy to hear that you are unexpectedly making friends. You have a genius for friendship,—that's the reason. It is they who are fortunate, not you!

I am blessed in keeping well, too. Heavy as the burden is every day, and apparently more and more heavy as the days come and go, I have so far not suffered physically from the load. I am only very sad. And yet the dear daughters are as sweet and companionable as ever lovely women were, and I have nothing to complain of,—only a great deal to grieve about.

With affectionate messages from all of us,

Your devoted friend,   Woodrow Wilson

WWTLS (WP, DLC).

To Nancy Saunders Toy

Dear Friend,   The White House 31 January, 1915.

Of course you did not like the Indianapolis speech[1] (that palpable lapse of taste, "Woodrow &c." was only a silliness of the moment; was not in the notes; was produced by the psychology of the stump, no doubt, and admits of no excuse); I instinctively knew that you would not: any more than you would like a real fight, or anything that wore the aspect of partisanship. But there is a real fight on. The Republicans are every day employing the most unscrupulous methods of partisanship and false evidence to destroy this administration and bring back the days of private influence and selfish advantage. I would not, if I could, imitate their tactics; but it is no time for mere manners. The barriers of taste may be overstepped in stating the truth as to what is going on: it must be displayed naked. All that I said was true, to my knowledge, though I did not shade it or trace the lines of it artistically or with literary restraint. The struggle that is on, to bring about reaction and regain privilege is desperate and absolutely without scruple. It cannot be met by gentle speeches or by presidential utterances which smack of no bias of party. A compact and fighting party must be lead against them. I think you cannot know to what lengths men like Root and Lodge are going, who I once thought had consciences but now know have none. We must not suffer ourselves to forget or twist the truth as they do, or use their insincere and contemptible methods of fighting; but we must hit them and hit them straight in the face, and not mind if the blood comes. It is a blunt business, and lacks a certain kind of refinement, but so does all war; and this is a war to save the country from some of the worst influences that ever debauched it. Please do not read the speeches in which I use a bludgeon. I do not like to offend your taste; but I cannot fight rottenness with rosewater. Lend me your indulgence. At any rate forgive me, if you can do nothing else.

As for the shipping bill, it does, as you perceive, permit us to commit blunders, fatal blunders, if we are so stupid or so blind; but it is not a blunder in itself, and, if we use ordinary sense and prudence, it need lead us into no dangers. The only dangers it involves have already been created by the ship registry bill and the war risk insurance measure, for which the Republicans hastened to vote, some coming back to Washington to advocate what the shipping interests wanted who had been absent from their seats for weeks. But the shipping interests do not want this bill. They will do nothing themselves without a subsidy, unless, that is, they are given government money out of the taxes to use as they think best for themselves; if they cannot get that, and of course they cannot, they do not mean to let the development take place, because the control of ocean carriage and of ocean rates will pass out of their hands. We are fighting as a matter of fact the most formidable (covert) lobby that has stood against us yet in anything we have attempted; and we shall see the fight to a finish; trying, when we have won, to act like men who know very familiarly the dangers of what they are about to undertake. It pleases me that you should be so generously distressed at the possibility of our doing what will lead to disaster or even danger; but those who speak to you of these risks have a very poor opinion of our practical sense, and are unconsciously misled by what the press represent, for their own purposes, as the main object of the measure when it is not its object at all. One would suppose that this was a bill to authorize the government to buy German ships. There would be just as stiff a fight against it, and from the same quarters, if it merely conferred the power to build ships.

The path is indeed strewn with difficulties at every turn, in this and in many other matters, and God knows I have no serene confidence in my own judgment and discretion: but of one thing I am resolved, to break the control of special interests over this government and this people. Pardon the seriousness of this letter. These are critical things in which much is wrapped up. All join me in most affectionate messages.

Your sincere friend,   Woodrow Wilson

WWTLS (WP, DLC).
1 Nancy S. Toy to WW, Jan. 13, 1915, printed as an addendum in this volume.

From Andrew Carnegie

Dear Mr. President   New York, Jany 31 1915.
   My desire for your continued success is the only excuse I have
to offer.
   The purchase of interned German ships by you would inevitably cause disapointment, chagrin, coldness toward our country
by the Allies even if you could successfully hold that you had kept
the letter of the law, which is doubtful. It is the spirit not the
letter of the law which tells in this crisis
   True you have disclaimed *any intention* to impair your policy
of neutrality which still leaves an open vent.
   If you buy the German ships you know this will directly advantage Germany and disadvantage the Allies   You would sin
against knowledge. No reply expected
                    Your friend Ever   Andrew Carnegie
ALS (WP, DLC).

To the Admissions Committee of the Cosmos Club

My dear Sirs: [The White House] February 1, 1915
   I hope I am not taking an unjustified liberty in writing to urge
very warmly upon you the admission to the Cosmos Club of
Mr. Louis D. Brandeis of Boston. I know Mr. Brandeis and hold
him in the highest personal esteem, and believe that his admission to the Club would not only be an act of justice to him, but
would add a member of very fine quality to its list.[1]
                    Sincerely yours,   Woodrow Wilson
TLS (Letterpress Books, WP, DLC).
   [1] Brandeis was admitted to membership.

To Henry Lee Higginson

My dear Major Higginson: [The White House] February 1, 1915
   Thank you for your letter of January twenty-seventh. It dis-
cusses matters to which we are, of course, devoting a great deal
of careful thought here.
   I think it is obvious that the shipping bill does make it possible to do very foolish things, but I hope that it is true that the
country need give itself no concern about the possible consequences, for we are very keenly alive to the difficulties we might
get into if ships were purchased from the belligerents and shall

be very slow to do anything that involves such dangers as are disclosed.

As a matter of fact, the ship registry bill already passed involves the same dangers and, unfortunately, those dangers may be made realities by the action of individuals over which the Government has no control.

In haste

Cordially and sincerely yours,   Woodrow Wilson

TLS (Letterpress Books, WP, DLC).

To Jane Addams

Personal

My dear Miss Addams: [The White House] February 1, 1915

Allow me to thank you for your kind letter of the twenty-ninth of January. I appreciate your words of approbation.

Sincerely yours,   Woodrow Wilson

TLS (Letterpress Books, WP, DLC).

From Lindley Miller Garrison

My dear Mr President: Washington. Feb. 1. 1915

Mr Breckinridge has just come from his visit to you.[1] I am satisfied, from what he tells me, that he correctly represented to you the matter as it developed and the situation as it existed. I had abstained from coming to you in person because the matter lay in my mind undecided, and unless I had determined to do something affirmative there was no occasion to burden you with my personal affairs and personal attitude.

What you have said to Mr. Breckinridge has decided me.

I cannot contemplate permitting anything personal to myself to lead me into doing that which would seem unfair or prejudical to another who had placed trust in me. In all honesty I did not assess my own position as having any such importance.

I now understand that you feel and so expressed yourself to Mr Breckinridge that the effect of my retirement before the end of my term would be very detrimental to the party: and I therefore should serve out my term.

If this is your feeling, I will do so. I want to avoid embarrasing you in any serious way and want you to feel entirely free to so indicate to me if, for any reason, this is not your feeling.

I feel that rehashing the matter can be productive of no beneficial result, if I have correctly interpreted your feeling and I
have met it by my response. I will however be very pleased to
see you and go over the situation if you so desire, and will make
an appointment to suit your convenience.

Sincerely yours   Lindley M. Garrison

ALS (WP, DLC).
[1] See the entry from H. S. Breckinridge's diary, dated Feb. 4, 1915, printed as
an addendum in this volume.

Paul Samuel Reinsch to William Jennings Bryan

Peking February 1, 1915

Strictly confidential.

More precise information now obtained in reference to the
Japanese demands indicates that the fragmentary advices contained in my telegrams January 23, 7 P.M., January 24, 2 A.M.,
January 26, 8 P.M., January 27, 8 P.M., January 29, 1 A.M.[1]
though subject to correction in detail were nevertheless substantially accurate and rather understated their effect in subverting
Chinese administrative integrity and the equality of commercial
opportunity. The following are now known to be among the most
significant of the specific demands: First, That the Chinese
must undertake "to permit the joint organization of Chinese
police force in important places or to engage a large number of
Japanese to assist in police matters." Second, That half of the
arms required by China must be purchased in Japan or in the
alternative that joint Sino-Japanese arsenals must be established
for the manufacture of arms.

Third, That "educational, political, financial and military advisers" must be engaged from among Japanese subjects. Fourth,
That all mining rights in Manchuria and Inner Mongolia to be
given to Japan. Fifth, Hanyeping Iron and Coal Company is to
be organized as a joint Chinese and Japanese Company and that
the Chinese Government must "engage not to permit foreigners
to operate mines in the neighborhood of the Company's mines
[and] not to allow any enterprise which might affect the Company's interests directly or indirectly without the consent of
Tokyo."[2]

The concession of these and other similar demands would
make China politically and in a military sense a protectorate of
Japan and *establish a Japanese monopoly in the commercial resources of China most requisite for military purposes.*[3]

With respect to these demands the Japanese authorities are attempting to stifle publicity. It is announced here that comment in the Japanese press has been prohibited: Reuter despatches from Tokyo quoting the highest authority describe the demands as overtures which violate no treaty and contemplate no infringement upon China's territory but they evade the question of administrative integrity. The local Reuter correspondent has refused to transmit to England *and* [an] identical dementi which the Japanese Minister asked him to telegraph as based upon the highest authority but for which he declined to permit the Japanese Legation to be quoted. Japanese Minister has also protested against inaccuracies in the report telegraphed by the acting correspondent of the Associated Press but has refused to specify any of the inaccuracies complained of and it is believed than [that] a similar protest has been lodged with the management of the Associated press. In view of these efforts to escape or prejudice the public opinion of other countries it is a question whether the United States ought not in its own interests as well as in those of China which it has hitherto loyally championed to assume the responsibility of asking the Chinese Government to disregard the injunction of secrecy and make it officially cognizant of the facts in this regard of the substance of which it is already actually advised in order that the American Government may be enabled to adopt such measures as may be appropriate for the protection of its interests guaranteed by existing international agreements. I believe that the Chinese Government would readily make such a communication if assured that the Government of the United States would assume moral and consequent political responsibility for insistence upon the disclosure of matters affecting its rights.

In my opinion such a direct application to the Chinese Government would constitute a supplement to an understanding with Great Britain for the purpose of influencing Japan towards a course of moderation and equity. All aspects of the crisis indicate that the British Government holds the key of the situation. I am convinced that British interests and their official representation here would alike welcome the support of the United States in opposing Japanese domination in China even though that support were to take a somewhat imperative form. *And considering not only the value attached to the friendly character of American neutrality but also the coercive power which rests with our country as an accessible base of supplies I suggest the British Government would not be disposed to ignore an intimation from our government that it could not regard with indif-*

ference the usurpation of political military and economic domi-
nation of China by Japan nor dissociate Great Britain from
responsibility for such a situation created by its Ally under
circumstances incidental to purposes professedly dictated by the
Anglo-Japanese Alliance.

Should the British Government take the position which we
would seem warranted in anticipating the result would almost
certainly be a quietus upon the present Japanese designs which
could not be carried out without the acquiescence of her Ally.[4]
In the alternative Japan would risk an estrangement possibly
leading to the dissolution of that Alliance. In either case, the
Alliance would be purged of the danger of being employed as
a means of nullifying any moderating influence which Great
Britain might otherwise bring to bear in the event of Japan's
desiring for any reason to impose upon the United States the
military ascendency which would have been made feasible by a
command of the immense material resources of China and encouraged by success in a policy of aggression.   Reinsch.

T telegram (WP, DLC).
   [1] The first four telegrams have been cited. The last was P. S. Reinsch to
WJB, Jan. 29, 1915, T telegram (SDR, RG 59, 793.94/215, DNA); printed in *FR
1915*, p. 81, giving further information about the Japanese demands.
   [2] He was listing the most important demands in Group V.
   [3] This and the following emphases by Wilson.
   [4] Bryan spoke to Spring Rice soon afterward, saying that he was anxious
about Japan's reported demands on China and that the United States ought to be
informed if extensive demands were being made on China. Bryan added that he
had induced the Governor of California to prevent further anti-Japanese legislation as he was "most anxious that nothing should occur to inflame public
opinion." C. A. Spring Rice to E. Grey, Feb. 4, 1915, printed telegram (FO
371/2322, p. 73, PRO). The Foreign Office made inquiries in Tokyo, and the
British Ambassador replied that the substance of the Japanese demands would
be communicated to the United States Government at once. C. Greene to E.
Grey, Feb. 6, 1915, printed telegram (FO 371/2322, p. 110, PRO). This telegram
was repeated to Peking and Washington.

Remarks at a Press Conference

February 2, 1915

Mr. President, can you say anything about the shipping bill?
   That needn't bother you.
It does.
   Well, you must not let it.
It doesn't bother us, Mr. President, we just want to know about it.
   It is going through all right.
With some changes, Mr. President?
   No changes of any sort that are not consistent with the
   principle of the bill.

Will these changes be of a character to meet some of the progressive Republican objections?

I hope so, but, so far as I can learn, they are not asking anything that is not perfectly consistent with the principle.

They ask a provision in it that will prohibit the purchase of ships from belligerents.

I think you have misapprehended their wish, so far as I can learn it. Their wish is to declare a policy, not to surrender a right. I don't find anybody who wishes to waive the rights that the country may have.

Senators Kenyon and Norris have proposed certain amendments with reference to the purchase of belligerents ships.[1]

So I understand; I did not see the text of them. I don't know just what terms they're in.

Do you feel now, Mr. President, that the progressive Republicans will support the bill?

They have supported it all along, in the sense that they were in favor of the principle of it and merely wanted some modifications in details that, so far as I know, were not inconsistent.

Mr. President, do I gather from what you have said that there will be no objection to saying that German ships shall not be bought as a matter of policy, but reserving the right?

I am not expressing an opinion of what amendments would be acceptable, or unacceptable; that belongs to the other end of the avenue. I am just trying to give the situation so far as I see it.

Mr. President, Senator Norris insists that the ships should not be resold or released at the end of the period of profit. He insists that when the lines become profitable they should not be put in private hands. That seems to be rather vital.

There is nothing in the bill saying they shall be. It will take action of Congress, you know.

[1] Wilson earlier that morning had conferred with Senators George W. Norris, William S. Kenyon, and Moses E. Clapp to see if there was any possibility that the ship purchase bill might be amended so as to win their support. Clapp made it clear that he would never vote for the measure. Kenyon and Norris, however, indicated that they might vote for the bill with certain amendments. Norris insisted that it must include a proviso such as one he had introduced in the Senate on January 28: "That no vessel shall be purchased under this act, which sails under the flag of any nation at war with any other nation which is at peace with the United States, unless prior to such purchase an understanding or agreement shall have been reached that will avoid any international difficulty or dispute regarding such purchase." *Cong. Record*, 63d Cong., 3d sess., p. 2543. The exact nature of the amendments introduced by Kenyon on January 29 (*ibid.*, p. 2538) is not known, but he probably agreed with Norris on the subject of the purchase of belligerent ships. See the *New York Times*, Feb. 3, 1915, and Link, *Struggle for Neutrality*, pp. 154-55.

They insist that there should be something in the bill saying that they shouldn't be.

> That, you see, would not bind future Congresses. Future Congresses are at liberty to pursue what policy they please. Nothing that you can put in this bill by way of details can stand in the way of repeal by future Congresses. One Congress cannot bind another.

Another point that was made, Mr. President, was that they wanted the organization of the government line taken out of the control of the cabinet and put, rather, in a nonpartisan board.

> As I understand it, the bill as it is now framed provides for a board of five, two of them *ex officio* and three of them appointed outside the cabinet; so that point is already covered. That was the bill as it came out of the Democratic conference.

Are you advised, Mr. President, as to what the program at the Capitol will be? Will this bill maintain its right of way, or will it be displaced temporarily?

> I am not informed, I am sorry to say. I don't think it will be displaced; if so, it will be only temporarily.

If these amendments are made acceptable to the progressive Republicans, still that will not do away with the objection of the other branch of the Republican family, will it?

> No, I suppose not.

So that the filibuster will continue until it is broken in some other way?

> I suppose so; but I don't know, of course.

Mr. President, have you been advised that the acceptance of the amendments desired by the progressive Republicans might lose some Democratic votes?

> No, I have not.

Do you understand that this so-called bolt of the seven Democrats[2] is a permanent position on this bill?

> No, I do not understand that.

2 During the Senate debate on the ship purchase bill on February 1, Senator James P. Clarke of Arkansas suddenly moved to send the bill back to the Commerce Committee. Senator Stone, the administration spokesman, countered by attempting to table Clarke's motion. In the ensuing vote on the motion to table, Clarke, John H. Bankhead of Alabama, Johnson N. Camden of Kentucky, Thomas W. Hardwick of Georgia, Gilbert M. Hitchcock of Nebraska, James A. O'Gorman of New York, and James K. Vardaman of Mississippi voted with the Republicans to defeat the administration Democrats. The regular Democrats then had to filibuster to prevent a vote on Clarke's motion until the Senate agreed to adjourn. During the following two days it became clear, not only that the seven rebels had carefully planned their strategy, but that they had no intention of altering their stand against the ship purchase bill. See *ibid.*, pp. 153-55.

Mr. President, I was told at the Treasury Department yesterday that the congestion of grain and cotton and other products in American ports to relieve which the bill was framed, in the first place, it was said, has been very much relieved now, and that the necessity for it was largely passed over.

Where did they tell you that?

In the customs division of the Treasury Department.

That is news to me.

They said that the country had passed the emergency point; that the grain was nearly normal.

They know more than anybody else knows. I don't mean to be disrespectful to the customs division. . . .

You had some visitors yesterday, Mr. President, who were presumed to have made some suggestions to you about peace.

Did I?

That is what we understood.

I didn't mean to contradict you; I had forgotten who came to see me.

The editor of the *Christian Science Monitor*.[3]

Oh, yes. He didn't make any suggestions about peace. He came for what was to my mind a very welcome purpose: simply to know what was the truth about certain things he had been in doubt about. No, he didn't have any suggestions at all.

There is nothing working now that you can see that is helpful?

I am sorry to say I don't see anything definite working. There is a very strong and growing hope and sentiment, I think, all over the world for peace, but I don't see anything definite.

I don't suppose you gave much consideration to the plans of Representative Bartholdt?

He hasn't presented them to me.

In the first place, Mr. President, on this ship bill you gave as one of the purposes of the ship line to open up new lines of trade, with South America, etc. Would it be practicable to build ships for that purpose, or would we need them immediately?

Of course, we shall build ships, and there is no reason to suppose that they can't be built, of the type we wish. You see, people haven't thought very carefully what sort of ships we will need. We will need ships of what are called the tramp type—ships built entirely for cargo and not necessarily running on fixed trips.

[3] Frederick Dixon.

None of those German ships are of that type, are they?

None, so far as I know.

Mr. President, can you say anything of the Trade Commission this week?

I hope I shall before the end of the week.

Mr. President, have you any information as to the available supply of ships of the tramp type?

I have not. I think they have at the Treasury Department—a partial list; I don't know that they have made a systematic census.

Mr. President, do you expect to meet the Democratic National Committee when it meets here next month?

Well, it hasn't resolved to meet here next month. I got a letter from Mr. McCombs only yesterday[4] saying that that interview that was given out in his name was absolutely a piece of fiction.

Does that refer, Mr. President, to the story with regard to your candidacy or to the plans?

It refers to the whole thing. So his letter stated to me.

Mr. President, I got it directly from him.

I think you must have got it in a different form. Mr. McCombs did discuss with me[5] the propriety or the advisability of having such a meeting, but he did not state it as a plan, and it is not a plan, an adopted plan. That is what I mean, that the statement of facts, not what was being considered, but the statement of facts, was unfounded.

I think he said, Mr. President, when he came out that the idea was to have a dinner or a banquet of some sort here.

That is what he suggested to me here.

As an anniversary of your administration.

He did state that to me as an idea, but, as he said to me, not as a plan.

Mr. President, have any of the belligerent powers expressed either directly or indirectly an opinion with regard to the policy involved in the shipping bill?

I think we are apt to get into a tangle about that. No government has made any representations to us on that subject. Of course, it has been a subject of conversation with the representatives of different governments, and I dare say that it is those conversations that have given rise to the idea that something formal was up, some protest. There has been no

4 W. F. McCombs to WW [Jan. 31, 1915], ALS (WP, DLC).
5 Wilson and McCombs conferred at the White House on January 30.

protest. Of course, we can't meet these gentlemen without discussing what we are all interested in, but they were not authorized to make any protests.

Were they speaking by direction of their government, informally, do you know?

I think not, so far as I know.

They couldn't make a protest on anything that has not passed Congress.

No, you can't make a protest on anything that hasn't happened, either. It is, of course, what is usually called academic.

T MS (C. L. Swem Coll., NjP).

From Henry Lee Higginson

Dear Mr. President: Boston. February 2, 1915.

Thank you very much for your letter of February 1st, which is a great relief. If the shipping bill could be put over to another season, and then receive careful consideration as to all its provisions, and win or lose the opinion of the whole country, it would seem to many of us wise.

A ship registry bill always seemed to me dangerous.

Still further, I hear directly from the Cunard people today that the Cunard officers in England have cabled to their officers here not to send any more ships laden with goods yet, as the wharves are blocked at all the ports by the great quantity of goods which they have not yet been able to move. They are doing their best just as we are.

I do believe that the ships will come as fast as the goods can be cared for there. Norway has a very large quantity of shipping which we might buy if it seemed worth while; but I dread buying ships at the top of the market, and have great confidence in the laws of trade—that if the ships are much wanted at higher rates, they will appear, and then the rates will drop. But we do not pay the freight,—it is the consumer.

It is a very great comfort to me to receive your letter of February 1st,—and be sure that we shall not get into trouble, for, of all things, we want peace.

The men and women here are busy with the unemployed, to whom we wish to give work, and indeed we must do so if we are to go on quietly. Everybody is straining himself to that end.

I am, with great respect,

Very truly yours   H. L. Higginson

TLS (WP, DLC).

Edward Thomas Williams to William Jennings Bryan

Dear Mr. Secretary: [Washington] February 2d. 1915.

I have been ill since last Thursday, and my physician still forbids my going out. I am sorry to be away from the Department at this time when the Far Eastern question is pressing for attention.

I do not know what course you have decided to take, or whether you feel it necessary to take any action at all, but with your permission I should like to make one or two suggestions.

If Minister Reinsch has been correctly informed—and I have no reason to doubt that he has been—we have now about one-half of the twenty-one demands upon China that have been made by Japan, and they confirm all that Mr Reinsch has said of the danger to our interests which they threaten. Some of the possible dangers are viz.—

(1) The interference with the Customs may affect the revenues which are pledged for the payment of the Boxer Indemnity.

(2) Special rights in Shantung and Fukien are likely to result in the serious injury of our trade in those provinces by the adoption of the unfair tactics employed in Manchuria, where our cotton goods trade has been almost entirely destroyed.

(3) The control of the iron industry, especially of the arsenals and of the manufacture of arms, may affect the contract with the Bethlehem Steel Cor. for a loan to reconstruct the arsenals and with which to build certain war vessels.

(4) The demand for a Japanese military adviser fore-shadows the control of China's military policy and in connection with (3) the control of her navy and will make it impossible for the U. S. to lend China the naval officers as promised.

(5) The demand for a Japanese Educational Adviser strikes directly at the work upon which we have prided ourselves. Even while I was in charge at Peking an attempt was made to get our Indemnity College (Tsing Hua) under control of the Ministry of education which at that time was filled with Japanese-educated officials of Japanese leanings. I protested that the college must remain under the control of the Foreign Office, and the matter was dropped.

(6) China has a National Police Force. Japanese control of this force gives Japan command of a large well-drilled army, the force used to detect and suppress the revolutionary risings.

Connected with it is the Secret Service, a wonderful intelligence service, which will give Japan accurate knowledge of the condition of every district in the Republic.

With such beginnings, it is not difficult to foresee the course which events are likely to take, and with control of such resources, Japan, which is not restrained by the scruples of the West, and which declines to enter into peace pacts, becomes a greater menace than ever to the U. S. She has given us fair warning that she will not tolerate what she considers race discrimination against her people.

I suggest that we ought to call the attention of the Chinese Government to the published reports of demands that affect our interests and our Treaty Rights and protest against the grant of concessions that violate those rights. To assure ourselves that nothing of the sort is intended China ought to make public the demands that all the world may judge.

Great Britain probably has her blind eye on the telescope and does not desire to see the danger signal. Nevertheless, if we can get the demands made public, she will undoubtedly be glad and aid in bringing about a modification of them.

If we can succeed in reducing the demands, it seems to me that we ought to insist upon China's putting her house in order and making herself able to defend herself. We can and ought to assist her in this, and in so doing we shall be building up a strong defence for ourselves.   E.T.W.

TLI (WP, DLC).

An Address to the United States Chamber of Commerce[1]

[[Feb. 3, 1915]]

Mr. President,[2] ladies and gentlemen: I feel that it is hardly fair to you for me to come in in this casual fashion among a body of men who have been seriously discussing great questions; and it is hardly fair to me, because I come in cold, not having had the advantage of sharing the atmosphere of your deliberations and catching the feeling of your conference. Moreover, I hardly know just how to express my interest in the things you are undertaking. When a man stands outside an organization and speaks to it, he is too apt to have the tone of outside commendation, as who should say, "I would desire to pat you on the back and say 'Good boys; you are doing well!'" I would a great deal rather have you receive me as if, for the time being, I were one of your own number.

[1] In the New Willard Hotel.
[2] John Henry Fahey, publisher of the *Boston Traveler* and other newspapers; president of the United States Chamber of Commerce, 1914-15.

Because the longer I occupy the office that I now occupy, the more I regret any lines of separation; the more I deplore any feeling that one set of men has one set of interests and another set of men another set of interests; the more I feel the solidarity of the nation—the impossibility of separating one interest from another without misconceiving it; the necessity that we should all understand one another, in order that we may understand ourselves.

There is an illustration which I have used a great many times. I will use it again, because it is the most serviceable to my own mind. We often speak of a man who cannot find his way in some jungle or some desert as having "lost himself." Did you never reflect that that is the only thing he has not lost? *He* is *there*. He has lost the rest of the world. He has no fixed point by which to steer. He does not know which is North, which is South, which is East, which is West; and if he did know, he is so confused that he would not know in which of those directions his goal lay. Therefore, following his heart, he walks in a great circle from right to left and comes back to where he started—to himself again. To my mind, that is a picture of the world. If you have lost sight of other interests and do not know the relation of your own interests to those other interests, then you do not understand your own interests, and have lost yourself. What you want is orientation—relationship to the points of the compass, relationship to the other people in the world, vital connections which you have for the time being severed.

I am particularly glad to express my admiration for the kind of organization which you have drawn together. I have attended banquets of chambers of commerce in various parts of the country and have got the impression at each of those banquets that there was only one city in the country. It has seemed to me that those associations were meant in order to destroy men's perspective, in order to destroy their sense of relative proportions. Worst of all, if I may be permitted to say so, they were intended to boost something in particular. Boosting is a very unhandsome thing. Advancing enterprise is a very handsome thing, but to exaggerate local merits in order to create disproportion in the general development is not a particularly handsome thing or a particularly intelligent thing. A city cannot grow on the face of a great state like a mushroom on that one spot. Its roots are throughout the state, and unless the state it is in, or the region it draws from, can itself thrive and pulse with life as a whole, the city can have no healthy growth. You forget the wide rootages of everything when you boost some particular region.

There are dangers which probably you all understand in the mere practice of advertisement. When a man begins to advertise himself, there are certain points that are somewhat exaggerated, and I have noticed that men who exaggerate most, most quickly lose any proper conception of what their own proportions are. Therefore, these local centers of enthusiasm may be local centers of mistake if they are not very wisely guided, and if they do not themselves realize their relations to the other centers of enthusiasm and of advancement.

The advantage about a Chamber of Commerce of the United States is that there is only one way to boost the United States, and that is by seeing to it that the conditions under which business is done throughout the whole country are the best possible conditions. There cannot be any disproportion about that. If you draw your sap and your vitality from all quarters, then the more sap and vitality there is in you, the more there is in the commonwealth as a whole, and every time you lift at all you lift the whole level of manufacturing and mercantile enterprise. Moreover, the advantage of it is that you cannot boost the United States in that way without understanding the United States. You learn a great deal. I agreed with a colleague of mine in the cabinet the other day that we had never before in our lives attended a school to compare with that we were now attending for the purpose of gaining a liberal education.

Of course, I learn a great many things that are not so, but the interesting thing about that is this: things that are not so do not match. If you hear enough of them, you see there is no pattern whatever; it is a crazy quilt, whereas, the truth always matches, piece by piece, with other parts of the truth. No man can lie consistently, and he cannot lie about everything if he talks to you long. I would guarantee that if enough liars talked to you, you would get the truth; because the parts that they did not invent would match one another, and the parts that they did invent would *not* match one another. Talk long enough, therefore, and see the connections clearly enough, and you can patch together the case as a whole. I had somewhat that experience about Mexico, and that was about the only way in which I learned anything that was true about it, for there had been vivid imaginations and many special interests which depicted things as they wished me to believe them to be.

Seriously, the task of this body is to match all the facts of business throughout the country and to see the vast and consistent pattern of the facts. That is the reason I think you are to be congratulated upon the fact that you cannot do this thing without common counsel. There isn't any man who knows enough to comprehend the United States. It is a cooperative effort, necessarily. You cannot perform the functions of this Chamber of Commerce without drawing in, not only a vast number of men, but men, and a number of men, from every region and section of the country. The minute this association falls into the hands, if it ever should, of men from a single section or men with a single set of interests most at heart, it will go to seed and die. Its strength must come from the uttermost parts of the land and must be compounded of brains and comprehensions of every sort. It is a very noble and handsome picture for the imagination, and I have asked myself before I came here today, what relation you could bear to the Government of the United States, and what relation the government could bear to you?

There are two aspects and activities of the government with which you will naturally come into most direct contact. The first is the government's power of inquiry, systematic and disinterested inquiry, and its power of scientific assistance. You get an illustration of the latter, for example, in the Department of Agriculture. Has it occurred to you, I wonder, that we are just upon the eve of a time when our Department of Agriculture will be of infinite importance to the whole world? There is a shortage of food in the world now. That shortage will be much more serious a few months from now than it is now. It is necessary that we should plant a great deal more; it is necessary that our lands should yield more per acre than they do now; it is necessary that there should not be a plow or a spade idle in this country if the world is to be fed. And the methods of our farmers must feed upon the scientific information to be derived from the state departments of agriculture, and from that taproot of all, the United States Department of Agriculture. The object and use of that department is to inform men of the latest developments and disclosures of science with regard to all the processes by which soils can be put to their proper use and their fertility made the greatest possible. Similarly with the Bureau of Standards. It is ready to supply those things by which you can set norms, you can set bases, for all the scientific processes of business.

I have a great admiration for the scientific parts of the government of the United States, and it has amazed me that so few men have discovered them. Here in these departments are quiet men, trained to the highest degree of skill, serving for a petty remuneration along lines that are infinitely useful to mankind; and yet in some cases they waited to be discovered until this Chamber of Commerce of the United States was established.

Coming to this city, officers of that association found that there were here things that were infinitely useful to them and with which the whole United States ought to be put into communication.

The Government of the United States is very properly a great instrumentality of inquiry and information. One thing we are just beginning to do that we ought to have done long ago: we ought long ago to have had our Bureau of Foreign and Domestic Commerce. We ought long ago to have sent the best eyes of the government out into the world to see where the opportunities and openings of American commerce and American genius were to be found—men who were not sent out as the commercial agents of any particular set of businessmen in the United States, but who were eyes for the whole business community. I have been reading consular reports for twenty years. In what I came to regard as an evil day, the congressman from my district began to send me the consular reports, and they ate up more and more of my time. They are very interesting, but they are a good deal like what the old lady said of the dictionary, that it was very interesting but a little disconnected. You get a picture of the world as if a spotlight were being dotted about over the surface of it. Here you see a glimpse of this, and here you see a glimpse of that, and through the medium of some consuls you do not see anything at all. Because the consul has to have eyes, and the consul has to know what he is looking for. A literary friend of mine said that he used to believe in the maxim that everything comes to the man who waits, but he discovered after a while, by practical experience, that it needed an additional clause, "provided he knows what he is waiting for." Unless you know what you are looking for, and have trained eyes to see it when it comes your way, it may pass you unnoticed. We are just beginning to do, systematically and scientifically, what we ought long ago to have done—to employ the Government of the United States to survey the world in order that American commerce might be guided.

But there are other ways of using the Government of the United States—ways that have long been tried, though not always with conspicuous success or fortunate results. You can use the Government of the United States by influencing its legislation. That has been a very active industry, but it has not always been managed in the interest of the whole people. It is very instructive and useful for the Government of the United States to have such means as you are ready to supply for getting a sort of consensus of opinion which proceeds from no particular quarter and originates with no particular interest. Information is the very foundation of all right action in legislation.

I remember once, a good many years ago, I was attending one of the local chambers of commerce of the United States at a time when everybody was complaining that Congress was interfering with business. If you have heard that complaint recently and supposed that it was original with the men who made it, you have not lived as long as I have. It has been going on ever since I can remember. The complaint came most vigorously from men who were interested in large corporate development. I took the liberty to say to that body of men, whom I did not know, that I took it for granted that there were a great many lawyers among them, and that it was likely that the more prominent of those lawyers were the intimate advisers of the corporations of that region. I said that I had met a great many lawyers from whom the complaint had come most vigorously, not only that there was too much legislation with regard to corporations, but that it was ignorant legislation. I said, "Now, the responsibility is with you. If the legislation is mistaken, you are on the inside and know where the mistakes are being made. You know not only the innocent and right things that your corporations are doing, but you know the other things, too. Knowing how they are done, you can be expert advisers as to how the wrong things can be prevented. If, therefore, this thing is handled ignorantly, there is nobody to blame but yourselves." If we on the outside cannot understand the thing and cannot get advice from the inside, then we will have to do it with the flat hand and not with the touch of skill and discrimination. Isn't that true? Men on the inside of business know how business is conducted, and they cannot complain if men on the outside make mistakes about business if they do not come from the inside and give the kind of advice which is necessary.

The trouble has been that when they came in the past—for I think the thing is changing very rapidly—they came with all their bristles out; they came on the defensive; they came to see, not what they could accomplish, but what they could prevent. They did not come to guide; they came to block. That is of no use whatever to the general body politic. What has got to pervade us like a great motive power is that we cannot, and must not, separate our interests from one another, but must pool our interests. A man who is trying to fight for his single hand is fighting against the community and not fighting with it. There are a great many dreadful things about war, as nobody needs to be told in this day of distress and of terror, but there is one thing about war which has a very splendid side, and that is the consciousness that a whole nation gets that they must all act as a unit for the nation. And when peace is as handsome as war, there will be no war. When men, I mean, engage in the pursuits of peace in the same spirit of self-sacrifice and of conscious service of the community with which, at any rate, the common soldier engages in war, then shall there be wars no more. You have moved the vanguard for the United States in the purposes of this association just a little nearer that ideal. That is the reason I am here, because I believe it.

There is a specific matter about which I, for one, want your advice. Let me say, if I may say it without disrespect, that I do not think you are prepared to give it right away. You will have to make some rather extended inquiries before you are ready to give it. What I am thinking of is competition in foreign markets as between the merchants of different nations.

I speak of the subject with a certain degree of hesitation, because the thing farthest from my thought is taking advantage of nations now disabled from playing their full part in that competition, and seeking a sudden selfish advantage because they are for the time being disabled. Pray believe me that we ought to eliminate all that thought from our minds and consider this matter as if we and the other nations now at war were in the normal circumstances of commerce.

There is a normal circumstance of commerce in which we are apparently at a disadvantage. Our antitrust laws are thought by some to make it illegal for merchants in the United States to form combinations for the purpose of strengthening themselves in taking advantage of the opportunities of foreign trade. That is a very serious matter for this reason: There are some corporations, and some firms, for all I know, whose business is great enough, and whose resources are abundant enough, to enable them to establish selling agencies in foreign countries; to enable them to extend the long credits, which in some cases are necessary in order to keep the trade they desire; to enable them, in other words, to organize their business in foreign territory in a way which the smaller man cannot afford to do. His business has not grown big enough to permit him to establish selling agencies. The export commission merchant, perhaps, taxes him a little too highly to make that an available competitive means of conducting and extending his business.

The question arises, therefore, how are the smaller merchants, how are the younger and weaker corporations, going to get a foothold as against the combinations which are permitted and even encouraged by foreign governments in this field of competition? There are governments which, as you know, distinctly encourage the formation of great combinations in each particular field of commerce in order to maintain selling agencies and to extend long credits, and to use and maintain the machinery which is necessary for the extension of business. And American merchants feel that they are at a very considerable disadvantage in contending against that. The matter has been many times brought to my attention, and I have each time suspended judgment. I want to be shown this: I want to be shown how such a combination can be made and conducted in a way which will not close it against the use of everybody who wants to use it. A combination has a tendency to exclude new members. When a group of men get control of a good thing, they do not see any particular point in letting other people into the good thing. What I would like very much to be shown, therefore, is a method of cooperation which is not a method of combination. Not that the two words are mutually exclusive, but we have come to have a special meaning attached to the word "combination." Most of our combinations have a safety lock, and you have to know the combination to get in. I want to know how these cooperative methods can be adopted for the benefit of everybody who wants to use them, and I say, frankly, if I can be shown that, I am for them. If I cannot be shown that, I am against them. I hasten to add that I hopefully expect I *can* be shown that.

You, as I have just now intimated, probably cannot show it to me offhand, but, by the methods which you have the means of using, you certainly ought to be able to throw a vast deal of light on the subject. Because the minute you ask the small merchant, the small banker, the country man, how he looks upon these things, and how he thinks they ought to be arranged in order that he can use them, if he is like some of the men in country districts whom I know, he will turn out to have had a good deal of thought upon that subject and to be able to make some very interesting suggestions whose intelligence and comprehensiveness will surprise some city gentlemen, who think that only the cities understand the business of the country. As a matter of fact, you do not have time to think in a city. It takes time to think. You can get what you call opinions by contagion in a city, and get them very quickly, but you do not always know where the germ came from. And you have no scientific laboratory method by which to determine whether it is a good germ or a bad germ.

There are thinking spaces in this country, and some of the

thinking done is very solid thinking indeed—the thinking of the sort of men that we all love best, who think for themselves, who do not see things as they are told to see them, but look at them and see them independently; who, if they are told they are white when they are black, plainly say that they are black—men with eyes and with a courage back of those eyes to tell what they see. The country is full of those men. They have been singularly reticent sometimes, singularly silent, but the country is full of them. And what I rejoice in is that you have called them into the ranks. For your methods are bound to be democratic in spite of you. I do not mean democratic with a big "D," though I have a private conviction that you cannot be democratic with a small "d" long without becoming democratic with a big "D." Still that is just between ourselves. The point is that when we have a consensus of opinion, when we have this common counsel, then the legislative processes of this government will be infinitely illuminated.

I used to wonder, when I was governor of one of the states of this great country, where all the bills came from. Some of them had a very private complexion. I found upon inquiry—it was easy to find—that practically nine tenths of the bills that were introduced had been handed to the members who introduced them for some constituent of theirs, had been drawn up by some lawyer whom they might or might not know, and were intended to do something that would be beneficial to a particular set of persons. I do not mean, necessarily, beneficial in a way that would be hurtful to the rest—they may have been perfectly honest—but they came out of cubbyholes all over the state. They did not come out of public places where men had got together and compared views. They were not the products of common counsel, but the products of private counsel—a very necessary process if there is no other, but a process which it would be a very happy thing to dispense with if we could get another. And the only other process is the process of common counsel.

Some of the happiest experiences of my life have been like this. We had once, when I was president of a university, to revise the whole course of study. Courses of study are chronically in need of revision. A committee of, I believe, fourteen men was directed by the faculty of the university to report a revised curriculum. Naturally, the men who had the most ideas on the subject were picked out and, naturally, each man came with a very definite notion of the kind of revision he wanted, and one of the first discoveries we made was that no two of us wanted exactly the same revision. I went in there with all my war paint on to get the revision I wanted, and, I dare say, though it was perhaps more skillfully concealed, the other men had their war paint on, too. We discussed the matter for six months. The result was a report which no one of us had conceived or foreseen, but with which we were all absolutely satisfied. There was not a man who had not learned in that committee more than he had ever known before about the subject, and who had not willingly revised his prepossessions; who was not proud to be a participant in a genuine piece of common counsel. I have had several experiences of that sort, and it has led me, whenever I confer, to hold my particular opinion provisionally, as my contribution to go into the final result, but not to dominate the final result.

That is the ideal of a government like ours, and an interesting thing is that if you only talk about an idea that will not work long enough, everybody will see perfectly plainly that it will not work; whereas, if you do not talk about it, and do not have a great many people talk about it, you are in danger of having the people who handle it think that it will work. Many minds are necessary to compound a workable method of life in a various and populous country; and, as I think about the whole thing and picture the purposes, the infinitely difficult and complex purposes which we must conceive and carry out, not only does it minister to my own modesty, I hope, of opinion, but it also fills me with a very great enthusiasm. It is a splendid thing to be part of a great wide-awake nation. It is a splendid thing to know that your own strength is infinitely multiplied by the strength of other men who love the country. It is a splendid thing to feel that the wholesome blood of a great country can be united in common purposes, and that, by frankly looking one another in the face and taking counsel with one another, prejudices will drop away, handsome understandings will arise, a universal spirit of service will be engendered; and that, with this increased sense of community of purpose, will come a vastly enhanced individual power of achievement; for we will be lifted by the whole mass of which we constitute a part.

Have you never heard a great chorus of trained voices lift the voice of the prima donna as if it soared with easy grace above the whole melodious sound? It does not seem to come from the single throat that produces it. It seems as if it were the perfect accent and crown of the great chorus. So it ought to be with the statesman. So it ought to be with every man who tries to guide the counsels of a great nation. He should feel that his voice is lifted upon the chorus, and that it is only the crown of the common theme.

Printed in *Address of the President of the United States before the United States Chamber of Commerce* . . . (Washington, 1915).

To J. B. Phinney[1]

My dear Mr. Phinney: [The White House] February 3, 1915

I am very sorry if it has seemed to you that there was any discourtesy or lack of appreciation on my part in the matter of your wife's generous act in deeding me a piece of property in Dade City. I can assure you that I did deeply appreciate her kindness and was certainly not guilty of any intentional discourtesy or lack of appreciation.

I know that both Mrs. Phinney and you will appreciate the scruple which makes me feel that it is impossible while I occupy office to accept gifts of such value. I beg that you will express to Mrs. Phinney my gratitude for her kindness and the hope that she will have a deed to herself made out, which I can execute and return to her, for the property. I am sure that you understand that this does not indicate in the least that I do not value in the highest degree such an act of generous friendship.
Cordially and sincerely yours,   Woodrow Wilson

TLS (Letterpress Books, WP, DLC).
[1] Civil engineer and surveyor of Dade City, Fla.

To Theodore Marburg

My dear Mr. Marburg: The White House February 3, 1915

I am sure I do not need to tell you how absolutely the Secretary of State and I are for peace and anything that promotes it, but I feel obliged to say in reply to your letter of January twenty-ninth[1] that I think it would be unwise for a member of the administration to appear at a public meeting called for the advocacy of some particular measure of international organization just at this juncture. I feel that we might be in danger of irritating the very persons whom we now wish to serve if we proposed a harness for them which they are not yet in a humor to wear.
Cordially and sincerely yours,   Woodrow Wilson

TLS (WP, DLC).
[1] T. Marburg to WW, Jan. 29, 1915, TLS (WP, DLC), asking Wilson's assistance in persuading Bryan to appear with William Howard Taft at a public meeting to further the cause of "a true international court of justice."

From William Squire Kenyon

Dear Mr. President: Washington, D. C. February 3, 1915.

I have met with an embarrassment in the shipping bill matter, which I suggested to you, but did not discuss at any great length.

I told my colleague, Senator Cummins, a few days ago I would vote to recommit the bill. It was my feeling at that time that this was the only thing to do to get the bill back in a legislative status where we could propose our amendments. Of course, having made that agreement, I was in honor bound to keep it. From my standpoint it seemed to me that I could carry out the agreement to vote to recommit with instructions to report the bill with certain amendments. However, in discussing that matter with Senator Cummins, he feels that this would be a breach of faith, and I realize that on a question of breach of faith the opinions of both parties to the conversation should have weight. He feeling that way, however, I have felt it my duty to vote for the straight recommittal. There will be enough votes, as I understand it, however, to commit with instructions.

When the bill is returned with these amendments, as I now understand these amendments to be, I shall support the bill and vote for it on its final passage.

I wanted to acquaint you with the situation as you have been kind enough to talk it over with me, and I wanted you to know the reason for my voting to recommit.

Sincerely yours,   Wm. S Kenyon.

TLS (WP, DLC).

To John Rogers Commons

[The White House]

My dear Professor Commons: February 4, 1915

I wish I knew where to send this letter more directly than by way of Wisconsin, but perhaps it will reach you in time to reply to your kind suggestion[1] that you would like to discuss with me the bills which have been prepared in line with the conclusions of the Industrial Relations Commission. If you could arrange to be here Wednesday morning of next week, I could arrange for an hour at that time. I wish with all my heart it might be more, but apparently an hour is the utmost that I can devote to one subject in these crowded days. We could discuss the general features of the legislation and you might, if you would be so kind, leave with me copies of the bills which I might examine in the evening.

Cordially and sincerely yours,   Woodrow Wilson

TLS (Letterpress Books, WP, DLC).
  [1] Commons' letter to Wilson, if he wrote one, is missing.

To William Squire Kenyon

My dear Senator: [The White House] February 4, 1915

I am sincerely obliged to you for your kind and candid letter of yesterday. You may be sure that I honor your scruple in the matter of your promise to Senator Cummins. My own feeling is very clear to the effect that no promise is binding which is made without a full knowledge of the conditions under which the promise would be fulfilled, and that one can perfectly honorably withdraw from such a promise if the conditions are not what he supposed them to be; but I say this not in the least, you may be sure, by way of criticism, only by way of comment.

Cordially and sincerely yours,   Woodrow Wilson

TLS (Letterpress Books, WP, DLC).

To Daniel Moreau Barringer

My dear Moreau: The White House February 4, 1915

It always distresses me not to be able to agree with you,[1] but I do entirely disagree with you about the best manner of handling the merchant marine business. I am entirely opposed in principle to subsidies. They amount to this, that money taken from the taxpayers is given into private hands to be used for private profit without regard to the regulation of the service or the study of the interests of the public in general.

It is a serious matter to use public money for commercial development at all, but if it is used, it seems to me that it should be used under the direct control of those who are responsible to the people for the taxation.

You see, my dear fellow, therefore, that we unfortunately differ in the principle of the thing.

You may be sure, however, that your letters are none the less welcome when I disagree with you than when I agree with you.

Always   Faithfully yours,   Woodrow Wilson

TLS (WC, NjP).
[1] D. M. Barringer to WW, Feb. 2 (two letters) and 3, 1915, TLS (WP, DLC).

To Nancy Saunders Toy

Dearest Friend,   The White House 4 February, 1915.

Helen (who is with old friends in Dayton, Ohio, waiting for the floods again) has sent me your letter of the twenty-eighth of January.[1] I have just read it, and hasten to reply to it myself, for

I will not leave you a moment longer than I can't help under the impression that I could in any circumstances doubt your loyalty or that your judgment of me would always err, if it erred at all, on the side of generosity. I am painfully aware that I am liable to make mistakes, big mistakes; and it is the privilege not only, but the duty of a friend to tell me that I have made them, when the evidence seems against me. That is a proof of loyalty, not a disproof of it! If, in answer to criticism I reply in what may seem rather grim earnest, it is because I am realizing now, as I have not realized before, even during the fight on the currency bill, that the influences that have so long dominated legislation and administration here are making their last and most desperate stand to regain their control. They are mustering every force they have in this very fight on the shipping bill. It is a very grim business, in which they will give no quarter and in which, so far as I am concerned, they will receive none. If they cannot be mastered, we shall have to have a new struggle for liberty in this country, and God knows what will come of it. Only reform can prevent revolution.

It is not to be wondered at that you do not see the inside of these things, as I am forced to. The wonder would be if you did. And it is a real service to me to be told what is being said by the thoughtful people about you. They are exceedingly critical; but so much the better, if they are fair. There is no harm done in their speaking out their minds or my hearing what they say. It is the necessary tonic and test of men in public life.

No, no! *Please* don't worry about that! I want to be told exactly what is in your mind; and I shall always understand exactly the spirit in which you utter it. Even if it hurts, it will not wound my heart. Things are desperately hard here, but there is no sense in trying to make them soft; for they cannot be. A man must eat meat.

Your letters are always the most welcome thing the postman could bring. Please give my warmest regards to Mr. Toy, and believe me always (though in haste),

Your sincere and loyal friend,   Woodrow Wilson

WWTLS (WP, DLC).
  1 It is missing.

To Edward William Bok

My dear Mr. Bok,   The White House 4 February, 1915.

Will you do me the favour of reading the enclosed, to see if it is worthy of your acceptance for the *Journal*, or whether you think it indicates that the writer, with a few directions and instructions, might be useful to you.

It was written by Mrs. Mary A. Hulbert, at present at #49 Gloucester St., Boston, Mass. She is a women of great refinement, of a very unusually broad social experience, and of many exceptional gifts, who thoroughly knows what she is writing about, whether she has yet discovered the best way to set it forth or not. She is one of the most gifted and resourceful hostesses I have known; but has now fallen upon hard times.

Among other things that she really knows, she really does thoroughly know old furniture and all kinds of china worth knowing.

Pardon me, if I have been guilty of an indiscretion in sending this direct to you. I am throwing myself upon your indulgence in my desire to help a splendid woman.

With much regard,
        Cordially and sincerely Yrs.,   Woodrow Wilson

P.S. Mrs. Hulbert has a great collection of recipes which housekeepers would like to have. Does a serial cook book sound like nonsense?[1]   W.W.

WWTLS (WP, DLC).
  [1] Apparently nothing came of this suggestion. However, D. Appleton and Co. of New York published Mrs. Hulbert's *Treasures of a Hundred Cooks* in 1927.

To Dudley Field Malone

My dear Dudley: [The White House] February 5, 1915

Alas, I am afraid that there is nothing anyone can do outside the Senate to remedy the present condition there which threatens the prestige and success of the party more, perhaps, than anything that has happened. I thank you with all my heart for offering,[1] and I know that you stand ready, to do yeoman's work. I certainly will let you know if anything occurs to me that can be done.   Faithfully yours,   Woodrow Wilson

TLS (Letterpress Books, WP, DLC).
  [1] D. F. Malone to WW, Feb. 3, 1915, T telegram (WP, DLC).

A Memorandum by Lindley Miller Garrison

[c. Feb. 5, 1915]
        Private *mem.*

At Cabinet Feb. 5, 1915, some talk about proper rule of international law for us to insist on in our relations to Gt Britain in the matter of purchase & transfer of flag of interned or belliger-ent ships. It was suggested we make some statement public about this—some talk about Germanys position, &c.

I tho't matter of great importance & suggested that study be made of it. Mr Lansing present, Mr Bryan being away. It was suggested we make simultaneous statement to Gt Britain ab't this & to Germany ab't War Zone admiralty order. I suggested that public statement would crystalize sentiment here & be treated as a declaration of Am. right which must be held invio-lable & hence we must be prepared to back up by force if defied &c. The P. seemed to agree with my position. Spoke of boys drawing line in sand & daring other to cross.

Lane-Burleson rather strong for statement.

Lansing came to my Dept late in day & suggested unavoida-bility of statement—wanted me to go to P. &c.

Hw MS (received from Harvey Mortimer).

From Robert Lansing

Dear Mr. President: Washington February 5, 1915.

I enclose a copy of a letter which I wrote to the German Am-bassador this afternoon enclosing a copy of the alleged declara-tion of the Admiralty at Berlin;[1] to this I received a reply, a copy of which I also enclose.[2]

I think it would be well to have this declaration conveyed to us officially before taking any action upon it,[3] not alone because of the propriety of such a course, but also because I think a protest in regard to it should only be drawn after careful deliber-ation. It seems to me that this action presents a most delicate situation which will have to be handled with extreme care.

If it meets your convenience I would like a few moments of your time tomorrow to present my views in regard to a public statement relative to the transfer of belligerent vessels in our ports. I have grave doubts as to the expediency of such a course.

Very sincerely yours,   Robert Lansing.

TLS (WP, DLC).

[1] RL to J. H. von Bernstorff, Feb. 5, 1915, CCL (SDR, RG 59, 763.72/13405e, DNA), inquiring about a wireless report from Berlin in the *Washington Post* of February 5 to the effect that the German Admiralty had announced that the English Channel and the waters surrounding the British Isles were a war zone. See RL to WW, Feb. 7, 1915, n. 1.

[2] Bernstorff's reply is missing in the State Department files.

[3] The official announcement came in over the wire later in the day. It was J. W. Gerard to WJB, Feb. 4, 1915, T telegram (SDR, RG 59, 763.72/1434, DNA), printed in *FR-WWS 1915*, p. 94.

A Draft of a Note to Germany[1]

Draft Feby 6/15

American Ambassador, Berlin.   Robert Lansing.

Please immediately address a note to the German Government ⟨in the sense of⟩ *to* the following *effect*:

The Department ⟨has⟩ *having* had its attention directed to ⟨a report in the press that⟩ *the proclamation of* the German Admiralty *issued* on February fourth ⟨issued a declaration⟩ that the waters around the British Isles, including the whole of the English Channel, are to be ⟨a war zone after the eighteenth instant⟩ *considered as comprised within the seat of war*; that ⟨every enemy ship⟩ *all enemy merchant vessels* found in ⟨this war zone⟩ *those waters after the eighteenth instant* will be destroyed *although it may not always be possible to save crews and passengers*;[2] and that neutral ships are in danger, as on account of the misuse of neutral flags ordered by the British Government on January thirty-first and the hazards of naval warfare, it cannot always be avoided that attacks meant for enemy ships endanger neutral ships. The declaration adds that shipping around the Shetland Islands in the eastern basin of the North Sea and in a strip of at least thirty miles in breadth along the Dutch coast is endangered in the same way.

⟨Assuming that the report is officially confirmed.⟩ The Government of the United States ⟨would⟩ *feels con[s]trained to inform the government of Germany in all frankness that it would* view with grave concern the critical situation in the relations between this country and Germany which ⟨would⟩ *might* arise if ⟨a⟩ *the* German naval force, in carrying out the policy ⟨set forth⟩ *foreshadowed* in the Admiralty's declaration, should destroy any merchant vessel of the United States or cause the death of American citizens.

The German Government must be aware that the sole right of a belligerent in dealing with neutral vessels on the high seas is limited to visit and search, unless a blockade is proclaimed and ⟨efficiently⟩ *effectively* maintained, which ⟨has not been done⟩ *this Government does not understand to be proposed* in the present case. To declare or exercise a right to attack and destroy any vessel entering a prescribed area of the high seas without first determining its belligerent nationality and the contraband character of its cargo would be ⟨a wanton⟩ *an* act ⟨unparalleled⟩ *so unprecedented* in naval warfare⟨.⟩ *that this Government is reluctant to believe that the Government of Germany itself in this case contemplates it as possible.*[3] ⟨A⟩ *No* neutral vessel ⟨and an⟩

and innocent cargo can ⟨not⟩ be impressed with enemy character by traversing any portion of the high seas. The suspicion that enemy ships are using improperly a neutral flag creates no presumption that all ships under neutral flags are of enemy nationality because they are within the prescribed area.

If the Imperial German Government should act upon such presumption and destroy on the high seas an American vessel or the lives of American citizens, the Government of the United States could not but view the act as a flagrant violation of neutral rights, ⟨as one⟩ *seriously* offensive, if not ⟨hostile,⟩ *deliberately unfriendly* to the United States.

If such a deplorable situation should arise the Government of the United States would be constrained to hold the Imperial German Government to a strict accountability for ⟨the⟩ *such an* unwarranted act of their naval authorities and to take ⟨the measures⟩ *any steps it might be* necessary to *take to* safeguard American lives and property and to secure to American citizens the full enjoyment of their rights on the high seas.

The Government of the United States, in view of these considerations, expresses the confident hope and expectation that the Imperial German Government *can &* will give assurance that ⟨the lives of⟩ American citizens and their vessels will not be molested by the naval forces of Germany other than by visit and search though the vessels may be traversing the sea area ⟨prescribed⟩ *delimited* in the declaration of the German Admiralty.

T MS (WP, DLC).
    1 Words in angle brackets in the following document deleted by Wilson; words in italics inserted by him.
    2 Wilson wrote the foregoing words in shorthand.
    3 *Ibid.*

From Robert Lansing

Confidential

Dear Mr. President,   Washington February 7, 1915.

I call your attention to the enclosed Associate Press report of the memorandum of the German Government explanatory of the declaration of the German Admiralty. Ambassador Gerard notified us that he had *mailed* this memorandum and yesterday he was directed to telegraph it immediately. I assume, however, that the A.P. report is accurate.

The memorandum impresses me as a strong presentation of the German case and removes some of the objectionable features of the declaration, if it is read without explanitory statements.

In my opinion it makes the advisability of a sharp protest, or of any protest at all, open to question.[1]

As the provisions of the declaration do not come into operation until the 18th instant, there is ample time to consider the subject.

Very sincerely yours   Robert Lansing.

ALS (WP, DLC).

[1] After detailing British violations of international law, the announcement went on:

"In certain directions they [the neutral powers] have also aided the British measures, which are irreconcilable with the freedom of the sea, in that they have obviously, under the pressure of England, hindered by export and transit embargoes the transit of wares for peaceful purposes to Germany.

"The German government has in vain called the attention of neutral powers to the fact that it must face the question of whether it can longer persevere in its hitherto strict observance of the rules of the London declaration, if Great Britain were to continue its course and the neutral powers were to continue to acquiesce in these violations of neutrality, to the detriment of Germany.

"For her violations of international law Great Britain pleads the vital interests which the British empire has at stake, and the neutral powers seem to satisfy themselves with a theoretical protest.

"Therefore, in fact, they accept the vital interests of belligerents as sufficient excuse for every method of warfare.

"Germany must now appeal to these same vital interests, to its regret. It therefore sees itself forced to military measures aimed at England in retaliation against the English procedure. Just as England has designated the area between Scotland and Norway as an area of war, so Germany now declares all the waters surrounding Great Britain and Ireland, including the entire English channel, as an area of war, and thus will proceed against the shipping of the enemy. For this purpose, beginning February 18, 1915, it will endeavor to destroy every enemy merchant ship that is found in this area of war, without its always being possible to avert the peril that thus threatens persons and cargoes.

"Neutrals are therefore warned against further intrusting crews, passengers, and wares to such ships. Their attention is also called to the fact that it is advisable for their ships to avoid entering this area, for even though the German naval forces have instructions to avoid violence to neutral ships, in so far as they are recognizable, in view of the misuse of neutral flags ordered by the British government and the contingencies of naval warfare, their becoming victims of torpedoes directed against enemy ships cannot always be averted.

"At the same time it is specifically noted that shipping north of the Shetland Islands, in the eastern area of the North Sea, and in a strip of at least 30 sea miles in width along the Netherlands coast, is not imperilled.

"The German government gives such early notice of these measures that hostile, as well as neutral ships, may have time accordingly to adapt their plans for landing at ports in this area of war. It is to be expected that the neutral powers will show no less consideration for the vital interests of Germany than for those of England, and will aid in keeping their citizens and the property of the latter from this area.

"This is the more to be expected, as it must be to the interest of the neutral powers to see this destructive war end as soon as possible." Clipping of an AP wireless dispatch from Berlin dated Feb. 6, 1915. The memorandum is printed in *FR-WWS 1915*, pp. 96-97.

To Paul Samuel Reinsch

Personal and Confidential.

My dear Mr. Reinsch: [The White House] February 8, 1915

I thank you sincerely for your letter of January fourth, as for all your letters which have served to illuminate many matters for me.

I particularly appreciate your suggestions about the things that we ought to be thinking about as a basis for a satisfactory international settlement. They have made a permanent impression on me. Just at present it is impossible to see in which direction an open road lies.

I have thought a great deal about the present situation in China, in view of the Japanese demands, and have been doing what I could indirectly to work in the interest of China. I have had this feeling, that any direct advice to China or direct intervention on her behalf in the present negotiations would really do her more harm than good, inasmuch at it would very likely provoke the jealousy and excite the hostility of Japan, which would first be manifested against China herself. I have been trying to play the part of prudent friend by making sure that the representatives of Great Britain realized the gravity of the situation and just what was being attempted. For the present, I am watching the situation very carefully indeed, ready to step in at any point where it is wise to do so.

With the warmest appreciation of your services and congratulating ourselves on having a representative at Peking who comprehends and can interpret each turn of the game,

Cordially and sincerely yours,   Woodrow Wilson

TLS (Letterpress Books, WP, DLC).

From Oscar Wilder Underwood

My dear Mr. President: Washington. D. C. February 8, 1915.

I have called on Senator Martin in reference to our conversation of this morning, relative to the status of the shipping bill.

Senator Martin says he has not expressed the opinion that the passage by the House of the Weeks bill,[1] with the Gore shipping bill[2] attached as an amendment, would improve the parliamentary situation in the Senate or expedite the passage of the bill. He agrees with the view I expressed this morning as to the status of the bill under the Senate rules. He believes that the passage of the bill by the House would have a good effect on the country, but does not believe the bill can be passed in the Senate at this session of Congress.

After seeing Senator Martin, I advised with the Speaker, Mr. Kitchen,[3] Judge Alexander, and Mr. Henry. They were unanimous in their opinion that action by the House at this time would not expedite the passage of the bill. We are of one mind that if the Senate passes the bill any time before the first of March, we can pass it in the House, but do not think it wise to disturb the present legislative condition in the House where no effective result would be accomplished by our doing so.

Sincerely yours,   O W Underwood

TLS (W. G. McAdoo Papers, DLC).

¹ S. 5259, "to establish one or more United States Navy mail lines between the United States and South America," introduced in the Senate by John Wingate Weeks, Republican of Massachusetts, on April 14, 1914. The bill was amended to allow service to Europe also and was passed by the Senate on August 3. It was referred to the House Committee on Naval Affairs on August 4, but was not brought up for debate on the floor until February 16, 1915. At this time the House Rules Committee proposed drastically to amend it to include a version of the Gore shipping bill (see n. 2 below). *Cong. Record*, 63d Cong., 2d sess., pp. 6662-63, 13134-41, 13276; *ibid.*, 3d sess., pp. 3875-3923.

² S. 7552, introduced by Senator Thomas Pryor Gore of Oklahoma on February 3, 1915. In general, the Gore bill closely followed the administration's ship purchase bill (S. 6856), but made much more detailed and explicit the legal and financial restrictions upon the federal shipping board and the corporation to be created under its auspices. The most important addition in the Gore bill was a proviso that "during the continuance of the present European war no purchases shall be made in a way which will disturb the conditions of neutrality." The entire Gore bill, with a few minor changes, became Sections 5 to 15 of the amended Weeks bill introduced in the House on February 16 (see n. 1 above). In addition, the House Rules Committee added a Section 16, which stated that, two years after the conclusion of the European war, all vessels purchased or constructed under the auspices of the shipping board and corporation would be turned over to the Navy Department, which in turn could lease them to private firms or individuals. For the text of the combined Weeks-Gore bill, see *ibid.*, pp. 3875-76.

³ That is, Claude Kitchin, Democratic congressman from North Carolina.

From Theodore Marburg

Dear Mr President,   Wilmington North Carolina Feb 8 1915

The letter of Feb 3 with wh. you have honored me reveals to me the fact that I failed in my original letter to point out that the international court we have in mind is the Court of Arbitral Justice adopted in principle by all the participants in the Second Hague Conference and warmly espoused since then by Germany, England and France.

I trust this explanation will cause you to waive your objections to the Secretary's participation in a public meeting to be called in support of the project and to plead our cause with him. We feel that the present moment, when the horrors of war are borne in upon the minds and hearts of people as never before, when the nerves of the world are exposed and when moreover European countries are each inclined to conciliate the United States, is possibly the most opportune time actually to get the court established under our leadership. Mr Taft shares this view.

In our stroll last evening before turning in we were reminded of you by passing the rectory where you formerly lived. Wilmington is greatly improved by admirable streets everywhere; they have saved the superb live-oaks which make the town so attractive.

I am, with great respect,

Yours Sincerely   Theodore Marburg

ALS (WP, DLC).

From John Rogers Commons

My dear Mr. President: Madison, February 8, 1915

I have received your letter of February 4th, on my return from New York this morning, stating that you could arrange for a meeting on Wednesday morning of this week with reference to some features of the legislative measures now under consideration by the Commission on Industrial Relations. Unfortunately the Commission has been delayed in deciding upon these measures, and, as we learn that Congress will probably not act upon labor measures during the present session, we have decided to postpone action. I hope that we can have an appointment with you at a later date.

Sincerely yours,   John R Commons

TLS (WP, DLC).

Remarks at a Press Conference

February 9, 1915

Mr. President, is this situation (filibuster over ship bill) certain to bring on an extra session?

No, I don't think it is.

How do you reason it out?

Why, I reason it out that nothing is certain.

Is that the most hopeful view of the situation, Mr. President?

I was at first jesting. I don't see that it is necessary to come to that conclusion, what little I know about it.

Senator Williams told us yesterday that he thought it was "inescapable," to use his word. I wondered whether that was your opinion.

No, it is not. I don't feel the force of that conclusion yet.

Mr. President, you will not consent to the dropping of the shipping bill, will you?

No.

Mr. President, there have been some publications with regard to Mr. House's alleged mission in Europe and the character of the credentials he carries from you. Can you tell us something?

> He doesn't carry any credentials, and his mission is a very simple one. In the first place, he often goes abroad just at this time. He is going abroad a little earlier than usual, because there are a great many things we want to keep in touch with—the relief situation and everything of that sort. There is no formal mission of any kind. The papers have been imagining that.

The credentials that he carries are merely letters of introduction?

> Letters of introduction—that is all.

Has he any particular itinerary mapped out?

> Not that I know of. He didn't when he left.

Mr. President, the same article under a London dateline said that there have been some conferences between the representatives of Russia and Austria and the United States all bearing upon this question of a possible peace. Is that true?

> No, sir, it is not.

Has there been any discussion by the representatives of other nations with reference to the prisoner situation.

> There may have been; if so, I don't know.

Mr. President, is it a common practice for belligerents to use neutral flags, as the *Lusitania* used our flag the other day, for the purpose of deception?

> It has been very common, yes, sir.

There is no basis for a protest, then, in that sort of practice?

> I would rather you gentlemen would not quote me on that subject, but I am perfectly willing to show you my mind about it, on that understanding. There is no rule of international law that prevents it. Of course, it involves manifest risks and embarrassments; but there is no basis, so far as I now know, for anything like a protest by one government to another. Besides, it wasn't a government ship; it was a privately owned ship. My information is that it is not an uncommon practice, though I must admit that I didn't know it until recently.

Does the German declaration of a war zone furnish ground for a protest?

> There we are waiting for what Mr. Gerard has promised us—a more extended explanation of just what is intended by the German proclamation, and, not having received that, I don't feel that I know what it is they have in mind. The brief proclamation as published, of course, bristles with things one would like to know more about.

The German Ambassador's explanation of the subject[1] has been somewhat reassuring, hasn't it?

Yes, he intended it to be so.

Do you so regard it?

Well, that is as you look at it. I wouldn't like to express any opinion about that.

Mr. President, the mere fact that there may not be any rule in international law regarding this flag incident, any precedent for it—that does not preclude your right to make it a matter of protest in the circumstances?

Again speaking in the same way, without being quoted, it does not at all prevent our making representations as to the troubles that might arise if the practice were resorted to very often. I don't mean troubles between the two countries, but the embarrassments to neutral commerce.

There is some suggestion of drawing up a law in Congress to meet the situation.

That wouldn't touch the situation; it would have to be an international agreement.

Mr. President, do you attach any significance to England's long delay in answering our note of protest?

No, I think it is entirely the absorption of her Foreign Office in other matters.

We can't answer her preliminary note until her final one?

No, because when she sent the preliminary note, she promised a final one, as if expecting us to wait for it. . . .

Mr. President, does this German blockade lessen the necessity for government ships of ours?

It isn't a blockade.

It amounts to the same thing.

No, it doesn't. That is where you are mistaken. It isn't even a paper blockade. It is a warning. It is interpreted by them as being a warning as to danger existing in that zone. It is not a blockade.

Mr. President, is there anything about Mexico that you can tell

[1] Ambassador Bernstorff issued a statement on February 6 giving his interpretation of the German war zone proclamation, adding, however, that he had not yet been instructed on the subject. He argued that the proclamation contained no new doctrine in regard to enemy or neutral merchant shipping. It was merely an explicit reminder of what had in fact been the case since the beginning of the war. The only new element in the situation was the danger to neutral shipping created by the British use of neutral flags on their vessels. He declared that the German government did not "profess to close even the English Channel to neutral commerce and she does not intend to molest or seize American vessels laden with foodstuffs for the civilian population of enemy countries." *New York Times*, Feb. 7, 1915.

us? The situation down there seems to have been stirred up again by some trouble with the foreign diplomats.

They haven't been having any active troubles. They have just been left high and dry a bit by having no foreign office to deal with in the City of Mexico. There has been no intimation of the slightest danger to them.

Mr. Duval West[2] is in town now, I believe; is he to go back to Mexico on any mission?

He came up to consult with Mr. Bryan about some Mexican affairs. I don't know anything further about that.

Mr. President, one of the arguments which have been advanced against the ship bill is the condition of congestion in foreign ports, the inability to unload the ships that are going over there now. Have you any information about the situation abroad in that respect?

Such information as I have does not verify that statement.

Will the United States embassy, or what remains of it, remain in the City of Mexico, Mr. President?[3]

Yes, we expect it to—unless all the foreign representatives go.

Wouldn't it be a matter of delicacy to accept Carranza's invitation to go to Veracruz?

It would be a matter of extreme delicacy, yes. Of course, all our relations with any of the various Mexican authorities now are private relations, not public, not formal.

Do you expect to get the Trade Commission this week?

I hope so, sir; I always hope so at the beginning of the week.

T MS (C. L. Swem Coll., NjP).

[2] A lawyer in San Antonio, Tex. For details of his career and his appointment as special agent to Mexico, see Larry D. Hill, *Emissaries to a Revolution: Woodrow Wilson's Executive Agents in Mexico* (Baton Rouge, La., 1973), pp. 309-11.

[3] General Álvaro Obregón reoccupied Mexico City for the *Carrancistas* on January 28, and shortly thereafter Carranza announced the formal transfer of the capital of Mexico to Veracruz. As one historian has pointed out, there were at this time at least four towns, not including Mexico City, each controlled by a different revolutionary faction, which had been proclaimed the capital of Mexico. Meanwhile, shortages of food, water and other supplies, widely reported to have been deliberately created by Obregón and Carranza, were rapidly reducing Mexico City to a desperate condition. See Charles C. Cumberland, *Mexican Revolution: The Constitutionalist Years* (Austin, Tex., 1972), pp. 192-95, and Link, *Struggle for Neutrality*, pp. 266, 456-58.

From William Jennings Bryan

My dear Mr. President: Washington February 9, 1915.

Mr. Duval West of Texas, whom you met this morning will start tomorrow night for Texas.

It will be necessary for you to give him a letter designating him as your special representative to visit Mexico and acquaint himself with the situation there that you may be more fully informed. And I think it might be well for you to write a second letter for his own private direction, telling him explicitly what you would like to have him do. One letter he can use for his authority and the other he can keep for his own guidance.

He will select a Secretary who can act as interpreter and stenographer. He seems to be a cool, levelheaded man and I am hopeful that he will be able to gain a clear understanding of the situation down there and bring back a report which will be helpful to you.

With assurances of high respect I am, my dear Mr. President,
Yours very sincerely,   W. J. Bryan

If you will send these letters to me I will deliver them.

TLS (WP, DLC).

To Duval West

Private.

My dear Mr. West: [The White House] February 9, 1915

I do not believe that it is necessary for me to give you detailed suggestions as to your mission in my behalf in Mexico, for I know you have talked the matter over, I hope quite fully, with the Secretary of State.

My wish in general is this: To have you meet and, as far as possible, assess the character and purposes of the principle men down there of the several groups and factions, in the hope that you may be able to form a definite idea not only as to their relative strength and their relative prospects of success, but also as to their real purposes.

Above all, I want to find out just what prospects of a settlement there are and what sort of settlement it would be likely to be. If the settlement contemplated is not seriously intended for the benefit of the common people of the country, if the plans and ambitions of the leaders center upon themselves and not upon the people they are trying to represent, of course it will not be a permanent settlement but will simply lead to further distress and disorder. I am very anxious to know just what the moral situation is, therefore, and just what it behooves us to do to check what is futile and promote what promises genuine reform and settled peace.

With the best wishes for your success and with genuine appreciation of your kindness in undertaking this mission,
    Cordially and sincerely yours,   Woodrow Wilson

TLS (Letterpress Books, WP, DLC).

From Edward Mandell House[1]

Dear Governor: London, England. February 9th, 1915.

We arrived here Saturday afternoon and I immediately arranged a private conference with White [Grey] for eleven o'clock Sunday morning. We talked steadily for two hours and then he insisted upon my remaining for lunch, so I did not leave until two thirty.

We discussed the situation as frankly as you and I would have done in Washington, and, as far as I could judge, there was no reservation. He said several times, "I am thinking aloud so do not take what I say as final, but merely as a means of reasoning the whole subject out with you."

I gave him your book which pleased him and he regretted that the only thing he could give you in return was a book he had written on angling.

We went into every phase of the situation, he telling me frankly the position Wilmot [the Allies] was in, their difficulties, their resources and their expectations. That part of it is not as encouraging as I had hoped, particularly in regard to Irritancy [Italy] and Principal [Rumania] (See Department Code). There is no danger of their going with Zadok [Germany], but there is considerable doubt whether they will go with Wilmot. Zadok's success has made them timid and there is also difficulty in regard to Conform [Bulgaria]. (D.C.) Up to now it has been impossible to harmonize the differences between Conform and Recliners [Serbia] (D.C.) Zadok is making tremendous efforts at present to impress Irritancy and Principal and to keep them from participating. If the differences between Conform and Recliners could be adjusted, Principal would come in at once, and so probably would Grogshops [Greece] (D.C) but they are afraid to do so as long as Conform is not satisfied.

The difficulty with Winter [Russia] is not one of men, but of transportation. They have not adequately provided for this while Zadok has to the smallest detail. It prevents them from putting at the front and maintaining more than Motiveless Heartening

[1] EMH to WW, Feb. 8, 1915, T telegram (WP, DLC), briefly conveyed the gist of this letter.

Magnesian to Strung Magnesian [one and a half to two million men] (D.C.)

The most interesting part of the discussion was what the Frighted Slivering [final terms of the settlement] (D.C.) might be and how the difficult question of Bluebird [armaments] could be adjusted. I made a suggestion along these lines that seemed to strike him favorably and which he desired to think over and discuss with the others at interest. I thought that the question of the Pinkroot Sayer [relative strength] (D.C) of the Blurred and Messenger [armies and navies] to be hereafter Liberals [maintained] should not be gone into at all for it would be impossible of adjustment.

My suggestion was that they should cease the Limkins of Medallion and the Confluent of Tricking [warship building and the manufacture of munitions] for a period of ten years and not go into the question further. At the end of that period everything would be obsolete and then a further period could be agreed upon. This taken together with a general guarantee of Slothful Inscient [territorial integrity] would about accomplish what we all have in mind.

He went into the discussion of what Winter and Warren [France] would demand. I told him if Warren insisted upon Banks [Alsace-Lorraine], I would suggest that a counter proposition should be made to neutralize them in some such way as Legitimize [Luxembourg] now is. This would prevent the two from touching anywhere and they could only get at one another by sea.

He thought that Winter might be satisfied with Determents [Constantinople] and we discussed that in some detail.

I let him know that your only interest was in bringing them together and that you had no desire to suggest Slivering [terms], and that what I was saying was merely my personal view expressed to him in confidence and as between friends.

There was one thing that White was fairly insistent upon and that was that we should come into some general guaranty for worldwide Nodal [peace]. I evaded this by suggesting that a separate convention should be participated in by all neutrals as well as the present belligerents and which should lay down the principles upon which civilized warfare should in the future be conducted. In other words, it would merely be the assembling at The Hague and the adopting of rules governing the game. He did not accept this as our full duty, but we passed to other things.

Gentlemen [Delcassé] is now here and so also is Propounder

of Frigidity [Russian Minister of Finance].[2] White is to talk to them concerning our conversation. We agreed that it would not do for any Miller [negotiations] whatever to be carried on between Zadok and Zenobia [Britain] without fully informing Wilmot for reasons which are obvious.

The great difficulty with Winter is that it is hard to know who is the proper person to discuss such subjects with. White told me frankly he did not know. There is something of the same difficulty with Zadok. It is not altogether certain that Dante [the Kaiser] is supreme, nor is it certain that Alto [Bethmann Hollweg], Othello [Jagow] and Wolf [Zimmermann] have sufficient authority to be taken into these discussions.

I am to meet White tomorrow at lunch at Yucca's [W. H. Page's] and it may be that I will have another cablegram to send you. There is some difficulty about the cablegrams. Yucca has been insistent upon signing them with me because he says they will not pass the Censor unless his name is attached. Of course, one of the first things I arranged with White was to have everything for or from me go through promptly. I could send them through the Conchiform Gambol [the Foreign Office], but I do not like to do this as it might seem to indicate to them that Yucca was not in our full confidence, which might impair his usefulness.

Please do not worry about what the American papers say concerning me or my mission. My name has not been mentioned on this side in any paper. Almost every paper in London has sent its representative to me, but, upon my assertion that I was here for rest and quiet and would be exceedingly obliged if they would not make foolish speculations or mention my name, they have acquiesced. An Associated Press despatch from Washington came through yesterday as far as the Censor. White immediately sent it to me and I advised that it be killed.

I am making a point to influence opinion over here favorably to you and to America. There has been considerable criticism of us and I was told that at a public meeting the other day when the name of the United States was mentioned there was some hissing. I find, though, that intelligent people over here are wholly satisfied with your course. I took tea yesterday with one of the editorial writers of the Times and dined with the Managing Editor last night.[3] Tonight I dine with our friend A. G. Gardiner. I shall write you about that later.

Affectionately yours,   E. M. House

[2] Petr L'vovich Bark.

[3] George Geoffrey Robinson (he later legally changed his surname to Dawson), editor of *The Times*.

P.S. One of the many interesting things White told me was that the Triable [war] was costing the Claver [belligerents] about Gatherer Magnesian [$40,000,000] a day, but that even this stupendous cost would be worth while from an economic viewpoint, provided it did not continue longer than six months more and provided Ensnarles [disarmament] plans were carried out.

Feb. 10th. I had a delightful evening with Gardiner. I think now he will be able to write of you in a way that will be helpful.

TLS (WP, DLC).

A Memorandum by Lindley Miller Garrison

Private *mem.*   [c. Feb. 9, 1915]

Feb 9, Cabinet: Question of making statement again brought up. I against same unless we were prepared to back up by going to war if defied. Bryan also against &c.

Hw MS (received from Harvey Mortimer).

From Edward William Pou[1]

Dear Mr. President: Washington, D. C. Feby 9, 1915.

I do not call to see you unless I have some matter which should be called to your attention because I think I know how completely your time is taken up.

I am writing this note to say that I hope you will call the 64th Congress in extra session immediately after March 4th if the Senate does not vote on the Shipping Bill. I have taken the pains to interview all of the members from North Carolina. Of the ten members eight are heartily with you for certain. There may be two votes against the bill upon a roll call in the House. The chances are that there will be just one.

Both as a member of the House and a member of the Committee on Rules I stand ready to help you put this measure through.   Cordially & Sincerely yrs,   Edwd W. Pou.

ALS (WP, DLC).
[1] Democratic congressman from North Carolina since 1901.

To James Watson Gerard[1]

Washington, February 10, 1915.

Please address a note immediately to the Imperial German Government to the following effect:

[1] The only earlier draft of the following dispatch is the one printed at Feb-

The Government of the United States, having had its attention directed to the proclamation of the German Admiralty issued on the fourth of February, that the waters surrounding Great Britain and Ireland, including the whole of the English Channel, are to be considered as comprised within the seat of war; that all enemy merchant vessels found in those waters after the eighteenth instant will be destroyed, although it may not always be possible to save crews and passengers; and that neutral vessels expose themselves to danger within this zone of war because, in view of the misuse of neutral flags said to have been ordered by the British Government on the thirty-first of January and of the contingencies of maritime warfare, it may not be possible always to exempt neutral vessels from attacks intended to strike enemy ships, feels it to be its duty to call the attention of the Imperial German Government, with sincere respect and the most friendly sentiments but very candidly and earnestly, to the very serious possibilities of the course of action apparently contemplated under that proclamation.

The Government of the United States views those possibilities with such grave concern that it feels it to be its privilege, and indeed its duty in the circumstances, to request the Imperial German Government to consider before action is taken the critical situation in respect of the relations between this country and Germany which might arise were the German naval forces, in carrying out the policy foreshadowed in the Admiralty's proclamation, to destroy any merchant vessel of the United States or cause the death of American citizens.

It is of course not necessary to remind the German Government that the sole right of a belligerent in dealing with neutral vessels on the high seas is limited to visit and search, unless a blockade is proclaimed and effectively maintained, which this Government does not understand to be proposed in this case. To declare or exercise a right to attack and destroy any vessel entering a prescribed area of the high seas without first certainly determining its belligerent nationality and the contraband character of its cargo would be an act so unprecedented in naval warfare that this Government is reluctant to believe that the Imperial Government of Germany in this case contemplates it as

---

ruary 6. After editing this draft, Wilson then made a new WWT draft (he did not dictate it to Swem) and sent it to the State Department where it was copied on a "Telegram Sent" form and wired to Berlin. The WWT draft is missing. The Wilsonian phrasing and tone of the note as sent will be at once apparent to the reader. Bryan had returned to Washington on February 8 and he probably went over the revised draft with Wilson, as, indeed, Lansing might have done also.

possible. The suspicion that enemy ships are using neutral flags improperly can create no just presumption that all ships travers- ing a prescribed area are subject to the same suspicion. It is to determine exactly such questions that this Government under- stands the right of visit and search to have been recognized.

This Government has carefully noted the explanatory state- ment issued by the Imperial German Government at the same time with the proclamation of the German Admiralty, and takes this occasion to remind the Imperial German Government very respectfully that the Government of the United States is open to none of the criticisms for unneutral action to which the Ger- man Government believe the governments of certain other neutral nations have laid themselves open; that the Government of the United States has not consented to or acquiesced in any measures which may have been taken by the other belligerent nations in the present war which operate to restrain neutral trade, but has, on the contrary, taken in all such matters a position which warrants it in holding those governments respon- sible in the proper way for any untoward effects upon American shipping which the accepted principles of international law do not justify; and that it, therefore, regards itself as free in the present instance to take with a clear conscience and upon ac- cepted principles the position indicated in this note.

If the commanders of German vessels of war should act upon the presumption that the flag of the United States was not being used in good faith and should destroy on the high seas an Amer- ican vessel or the lives of American citizens, it would be difficult for the Government of the United States to view the act in any other light than as an indefensible violation of neutral rights which it would be very hard indeed to reconcile with the friendly relations now so happily subsisting between the two govern- ments.

If such a deplorable situation should arise the Imperial Gov- ernment can readily appreciate that the Government of the United States would be constrained to hold the Imperial German Government to a strict accountability for such acts of their naval authorities and to take any steps it might be necessary to take to safeguard American lives and property and to secure to Amer- ican citizens the full enjoyment of their acknowledged rights on the high seas.

The Government of the United States, in view of these con- siderations, which it urges with the greatest respect and with the sincere purpose of making sure that no misunderstanding may arise and no circumstance occur that might even cloud the intercourse of the two governments, expresses the confident hope and expectation that the Imperial German Government can and will give assurance that American citizens and their vessels will not be molested by the naval forces of Germany otherwise than by visit and search, though their vessels may be traversing the sea area delimited in the proclamation of the German Admiralty.

It is added for the information of the Imperial Government that representations have been made to His Britannic Majesty's Government in respect to the unwarranted use of the American flag for the protection of British ships.[2] End quote.

Bryan

T telegram (SDR, RG 59, 763.72/1434, DNA).
2 It pointed out that, in the present circumstances, any general use of the American flag by British ships "would be a serious and constant menace to the lives and vessels of American citizens" and requested the British government to do all in its power to restrain British vessels from deceptive use of the American flag in the war zone. WJB to WHP, Feb. 10, 1915, *FR-WWS 1915*, pp. 100-101.

To Duval West

My dear Mr. West: [The White House] February 10, 1915

I am sincerely obliged to you for your disinterested kindness in undertaking to visit Mexico as my personal representative.

The situation there has become so complicated that I feel that I have lost the threads of it and that it is very necessary for me to know just what the developments have been and just what the outlook is for an early settlement.

I would be very much obliged if you would acquaint yourself with the situation very fully and report to me at your convenience.

Pray let this letter serve as your introduction to the leading men of Mexico. I commend you to their interest and courtesy.

With the most cordial wishes for a successful mission,
Cordially and sincerely yours,   Woodrow Wilson

TLS (Letterpress Books, WP, DLC).

From Robert Lansing

Personal

Dear Mr. President: Washington February 10, 1915.

I return herewith the letter from Mr. Nieman which you were good enough to let me see in which he urges the issuance of a statement of the Government's reasons for failure to protest against Germany's conduct as a belligerent.

Confirmatory of Mr. Nieman's opinion as to the advisability of a statement of this sort Mr. McKelway, the correspondent of *Harper's Weekly*, called upon me yesterday and said that he wished that the Government's position could be made public, as recent articles in periodicals showed that "since Colonel Roosevelt set the ball rolling it was still in the public mind." (the metaphor of a "ball" being "in the public mind" I disavow).

Personally I have felt that criticism on this subject was dying out, but as both Mr. Nieman and Mr. McKelway are better judges of public opinion than I am, I presume that I am wrong.

I am handing to Secretary Bryan today a memorandum for a statement on our position together with a letter explaining the reasons for the treatment of the subject adopted.[1]

I also enclose a reported statement of Sir Edward Grey,[2] appearing in yesterday's papers, which will have a tendency to encourage the critics to renewed activity.

Very sincerely yours,   Robert Lansing.

TLS (WP, DLC).

[1] RL to WJB, Feb. 10, 1915, printed as an Enclosure with WJB to WW, Feb. 12, 1915, enclosing "Memorandum for a Statement . . . ," printed in *FR-LP*, I, 201-10.

[2] An unidentified newspaper clipping which summarized the comments of Albert Henry George Grey, 4th Earl Grey (not Sir Edward Grey, as Lansing states above) while presiding at a meeting in London. Lansing had underscored the following direct quotation: "The neutral Powers who signed The Hague conventions missed a great opportunity by not protesting against the violations of the international regulations that occurred in this war, which undoubtedly would have led to a diminution of its horrors."

From Walter Hines Page

Dear Mr. President: London, Feb. 10. 1915

At my lunch-table to-day House and I sat down with Sir Edw. Grey and Sir Wm. Tyrrell for more than two hours. House delivered his message—put himself at Sir Edward's service, if a way appeared to prepare an approach to peace and put you at his service if any practical plan can be made to ripen—all admirably done and cordially received. The Allies will not *propose* peace till they have won some more convincing military victory; but they will listen now to any proposal from the other side and England at least will heartily welcome any sincere proposal wh. will include the restoration of Belgium and security for the future. All other conditions are details. These two are the English essentials. The other Allies, of course, will demand something—the Black Sea, Alsace-Lorraine etc., but presumably nothing insuperable.

The question is, Can House get a proposal or any approach to a proposal from Germany? I have no doubt that an invitation direct from the Government to go to Berlin will reach him next week. My feeling is that when he gets there he will receive no direct proposal but an indication of the possibility of talking a proposal out of the English. Then he will get some tentative hints —the brush will be cleared away a little. At another sitting or on another visit, a tentative proposal (somewhat short of accept- ability) will be made. Then, if the Allies win some decisive- looking fight or if the economic pinch become severe enough, presently a proposal will be made sufficiently definite to warrant a conference. They are going to come to it. Recent events make this clear to me for the first time—unless these late new stages of bitterness make it possible for the military party in Germany to fight it out to the last man and the last cartridge; and this seems incredible.

The hitch (assuming that Russia and France can be led along through the early stages) will be when they begin to discuss methods of safeguarding the world from another such catas- trophe. That's the rub; and there precisely will be our chance for a master-stroke, if indeed anybody can do *that* stroke. It sounds like foolishness while the roar of cannon is heard along two great battle-lines of nearly 1000 miles. I hardly dare dream that it can come now, but it must come if Europe is to hold the civilization her best men have reached—if there is really to be any hope of the progress of mankind on this side the world. The dogma of Might can be overthrown only by limiting armies and navies. Armies and navies can be limited only by an agreement that has behind it the power to enforce it—a sort of Federation of the states of Europe, which Federation must, in the last resort, control some sort of force—an army & a navy big enough to coerce any one or two States. That sounds foolish. But some such foolishness must come. Then if search & capture at sea of all merchant ships be forbidden and contraband be abolished, there will be less need & excuse for navies. If no commerce can be hindered or destroyed, there's no need of a navy to protect commerce. One other idea & the Trinity of Prevention is com- plete: the private financial exploiter of weak and backward countries must not call in the power of his Government to collect his usury or even his proper dividends. He must take his own risks.

If, in the discussions that will speedily follow peace, we commit ourselves to these ideas and insist on them (or some better formulation of ideas making for the same ends), and if in the meantime we keep ourselves in the confidence of the Allies, we may, with all the other neutrals, possibly bring about such a Confederation. Germany will have to be dragooned into it—or previously whipped into it. I doubt if any other Great Power can or would stand against a strong formulation of such a pro- gramme. The Neutrals must demand it. A corollary, of course, wd. be the prohibition of the private manufacture of arms etc.

But peace first—such a peace as only the belligerents them- selves must make. Nobody can see beyond his nose. *E.g.* if Ger- many take Warsaw, that will kindle their military hope anew and probably very considerably postpone the end, tho' it cannot pos- sibly change the result. If German submarines can really destroy any considerable number of British merchantmen, that will have a similar effect. Moreover, if none of these things happen and the present deadlock continue, will the two sides agree on what constitutes security against a recurrence of this war—unless one or the other win some spectacular victory? And this deadlock kind of warfare doesn't yield spectacular results.

I have moods when I wonder whether Germany is not more or less deliberately going to provoke all the neutrals (the U. S. in particular) to give her an excuse to surrender. "All the world against us, inspired by envy, of course there's no use in our wasting life in such a contest: we've always wanted peace any- how etc." Then they can say that it wasn't England that whipped 'em, nor France nor Russia, nor all three of them, but that they desisted only when opposed by the whole world. This seems a fantastic kind of absurdity & crime. But the Germans have com- mitted every other conceivable mistake. What is sacred about this huge mistake that they shd. not make that too?

As matters stand now any proposal by England for peace wd. loose a storm here such as no Government could weather. To discuss or even to accept an acceptable proposal from the other side—that wd. be a welcome task—very. Everything rests here: viz. what will Germany propose? sincerely and directly propose? And I think that everything will hang there to the end. For England is now making such preparations for continuing the war as no Power on earth ever before made. She is going at it as if she knew France and Russia wd. one day quit and she wd. have to continue the war alone. Men, small arms, big guns, food, aircraft, watercraft from submarine (2 a week) to dread- naughts. She is working at a rate to produce our navy every 14 months. She will be stronger on both land and sea in another year (and in money) than any nation on earth ever was. Those Germans who know things must know this. If they do know it, they must find some way out of an ultimate crushing defeat.

They'll tell House when they come to it—unless they prefer to run amuck and get us into it as a way to save their face. They have given up hope of winning American sympathy. They are having poor success getting American copper and food. American hostility is possibly the only American thing they can now utilize. (That's the German way of thinking—perhaps.) Through all thought and speculation about it there runs a large Perhaps— except only about the final result. That is certain.

But the uncertain thing is whether it will end as a drawn battle or be prolonged to a decisive defeat. Nobody can yet tell that. And here this idea comes in: If it were definitely known by England that in the discussion that must follow the laying down of arms, all the moral power of the world—our power in particular —wd. be actively and strenuously exerted for the making of a programme of forcible security for the future—in that event England might consent to end the war as a drawn contest and trust to the subsequent discussion and world-wide agreement to secure safety for the future.

All probable or possible events make it necessary that we shd. keep our good feeling with this Kingdom and this people intact, which is the task that engages me day in and day out—a task that can be helped by care and consideration along the whole line. God grant it!

Yours most faithfully Walter H. Page

16. Feb. '15.

P.S. I have today talked long with Hoover, of the Belgium Commission, an American and a man of uncommonly good judgment. He is just back from 10 days in Berlin where he talked with the Chancellor and with most of the members of the Government. Hoover (he is very strongly pro-British and he knows the determination and the resources of the British) is very decidedly of the opinion that the war will end as a drawn battle, neither side having won any decided advantage and each side, therefore, obliged to keep and to strengthen its armies and navies. He sees no early destruction of militairism. If it come at any early time, it will come as an after-discussion and after-agreement. He doesn't expect to live to see it.

This, you will recall, is General French's view. The trench has made the whipping of one army by another of anything like equal strength impossible. When they have all put their new armies in the field and have lost a considerable proportion of them and gained no substantial advantage—then they'll talk peace, but peace on the old war footing.

There may be no such thing as starving out Germany or any resourceful nation. They can probably produce enough to live on. They already have a substitute for copper, which they are using, and for gasoline—very good substitutes. They can turn most corners in this way.

The hope of a Confederation of practically unarmed nations may rest only on the moral pressure of the less belligerent nations—or, it may not come for an indefinite time, perhaps never as long as Kings and captains survive.

I write you this as a good way to show how your mind—if you are here, studying the thing never so diligently—changes from week to week. This week you dare hope what next week seems absurd. In fact the future will turn on the fortunes of the war. If either side could win a clear-cut victory, you could think out the results. If neither can, you can only guess. The trench seems to be a deadlock device. If it turn out really to be so, the war will end when both sides have reached the mood that recoils from more slaughter; and it will end with each side's getting not what it wants, but what it can.

Most men here, I observe, guess Aug. as the earliest date. But it's a guess.   W.H.P.

ALS (WP, DLC).

Remarks to the National Council
of the Boy Scouts of America[1]

February 11, 1915.

Gentlemen, I am sincerely glad to have the pleasure of this visit from you, and to have an opportunity to express my very sincere interest, not only in the organization of the Boy Scouts, but in the objects that that organization has. From all that I know of it, and from all that I have been able to observe personally, it is an admirable organization, devoted to the objects that I myself thoroughly believe in.

There is only one rule in the world, and it applies to all professions, and that is that you are expected to "make good." No excuses are allowed in this school of life, and the only way to make good is to keep faith. That is the reason I like the idea of the Boy Scouts—because of their secure notion of being responsible to society. They are responsible to the people who live around them to help maintain the standards of order and fidelity upon which the community depends.

You are recruits in the ranks that we all stand in, and that is to serve the country in some way that will tell, and that has nothing particular to do with our own personal benefit. The man who devotes himself exclusively to the development of his own character will succeed in nothing except to make of himself a prig. But if he devotes himself to helping other people, his character will not only take care of itself but it will grow to a very noble stature.

I have always maintained that, in the language of manufacture, character is a by-product. If you set out to develop it because you love it for yourself, you will be an ass. If you disregard the consequences to yourself in order to serve other people, you will make a noble gentleman, and that I believe is fundamental and sacred in an organization of this sort.

I congratulate you for belonging to it and hope you will honor it in every way by your conduct and allegiance. Now I understand I am to have the pleasure of shaking hands with you and then to present the medals—or to present the medals first.

T MS (WP, DLC).
¹ Wilson spoke to the council and a group of scouts in the East Room of the White House. Following his remarks, he presented Boy Scout medals to several boys from the Washington area. *Washington Post*, Feb. 12, 1915.

To Robert Lansing

My dear Mr. Lansing:　　　The White House February 11, 1915

Thank you sincerely for your letter of February tenth in regard to Mr. Nieman's suggestion. I am going to take the liberty of sending Mr. Nieman a copy of it.

　　　　　　　　　Faithfully yours,　Woodrow Wilson

TLS (SDR, RG 59, 763.72111/1680½, DNA).

To Robert Lansing, with Enclosure

My dear Mr. Lansing:　　　The White House February 11, 1915

It is a pleasure to read letters like the enclosed. They are so exactly in line with the facts and the right way of dealing with them. Thank you for letting me see it.

　　　　　　　　　Cordially and sincerely yours,　Woodrow Wilson

TLS (SDR, RG 59, 763.72111/1690½, DNA).

ENCLOSURE

Jacob McGavock Dickinson[1] to Robert Lansing

My dear Mr. Lansing: Chicago February Sixth, 1915.

Recent international developments are giving very great concern to all thoughtful and patriotic people. It seems to me that it will be a prudent and safe course to make a clear, firm and timely declaration in case the newspaper reports as to the attitude of Germany in respect to neutral ships shall be confirmed.

A reproduction in the Chicago Tribune today of editorials from German papers shows clearly that their understanding is that Germany will proceed to enforce what it calls a blockade by destruction of ships by means of submarines. This, in the nature of things, means that there can be no reasonable steps taken in advance to ascertain the nationality of the ships attacked. The reason for this course seems to be founded upon the alleged statement that the British Government has secretly authorized its ships to use the flags of neutral nations. The paper this morning indicates that our State Department will inquire into this. It seems to me that this fact, however it may be, can have no bearing on the question. The British Government by such a course cannot take away our right to hold the German Government responsible if it attacks and destroys the property and lives of Americans under our flag. We probably would have ground to protest against such action of the British Government, but such action could not warrant the German Government in such destruction. It is at most a paper blockade, and is to be carried out not by stopping and examining ships, and determining their nationality, or by taking them into a Prize Court where all questions can be adjudicated, but by destroying them without the possibility of ascertaining the true nationality.

If any Government should do this under such circumstances, it would be a wanton and unjustifiable attack, and would call for immediate action on our part.

My reading and my own observation of personal affairs have lead me to the conclusion that a clear and firm declaration in advance generally tends to obviate such extreme action as will force a collision, while on the other hand a failure so to do often brings about the very thing that we most desire to avoid. In this nations and individuals are the same, and a timely and explicit warning is wholesome with both. I have seen many personal difficulties avoided by taking a clear, firm and just stand in the beginning, and have seen them brought about because aggressions have advanced slowly, step by step, and to a point which they would not have reached if the consequences had been clearly understood.

Therefore it seems to me that if it shall become clear that Germany may in the course of events, in pursuance of this policy, destroy American ships while legitimately under the protection of the American flag, we should now make a clear and firm declaration as to what our attitude will be. In my judgment it should be that we will protect our flag at all hazards.

Now you know I am a Peace man. I say this in the interest of Peace and as a Peace measure, for I have often seen for the want of such timely action affairs drift gradually into a condition where drastic action becomes unavoidable.

We are in a most delicate situation, and it requires not only justice but firmness to keep us out of complications. We cannot expect, however just we may be, to escape severe criticism, and that from people and newspapers of all the belligerents.

The papers report much severe criticism of Secretary Bryan in Germany and some in England. This cannot be avoided. It is about the best evidence that the recent position taken by him in his letter[2] was correct. I think it was eminently correct. If it had pleased one side it would not have stood the test. The fact that there are those in both England and Germany who severely criticized it, is no evidence of it being unsound, but is evidence of the highly excited condition in which those people are. Any neutral that pursues a just course is bound to excite more or less the antagonism of both contending parties. You will recall how this was in respect of the attitude of England during the Civil War. Both the North and South criticized it. I do not refer to her example then as a proper one to follow, but merely to illustrate how hard it is for a neutral country to avoid the hostility of contending parties. Many of them think that those who are not actively for them are against them. This is the human nature of the thing, and it often manifests itself in governmental action. While there is some disposition to make party capital out of the action of our Government, I believe that the overwhelming judgment in this country is that the Administration has acted in the main wisely in our foreign relations, including those with Mexico. Even those who at one time advocated a more strenuous attitude toward Mexico now realize that it is fortunate for our country that in the midst of this great international turmoil we have not a Mexican war on our hands.

While such a war in and of itself would not be serious, there is no telling in these complicated conditions what reflex action it might have and what it might lead to. Therefore we breathe easier because we have no such war.

I did not intend to inflict so long a letter upon you but I, in common with many with whom I talk, am deeply disturbed over the situation, and am most anxious that we shall not become involved in any way in this European trouble. I know that the Department of State has information that the people at large have not, and for this reason accept and support whatever course it may take as the wise one, for I am convinced that the Secretary of State is filled with the utmost desire to maintain our neutrality in all honorable ways.

With cordial remembrances to Mrs. Lansing[3] and General and Mrs. Foster,[4] I am,

Yours sincerely,   J. M. Dickinson

TLS (SDR, RG 59, 763.72111/1689½, DNA).
    [1] Secretary of War, 1909-11; at this time a lawyer of Chicago.
    [2] To Senator Stone. See WW to W. J. Stone, Jan. 7, 1915, n. 1.
    [3] Eleanor Foster Lansing.
    [4] Ex-Secretary of State John Watson Foster and Mary Parke McFerson Foster. The Lansings resided at the Fosters' home in Washington.

To Lucius William Nieman

Personal.

My dear Mr. Nieman: [The White House] February 11, 1915

I handed your letter of January twenty-sixth to Mr. Lansing, the Counselor of the Department of State, and here is his reply which I send for your information.

I am not sure that the paper he refers to can be drawn in such a way as to be satisfactory to those who have been hypercritical in this matter, but we can at any rate make a very clear case.

Cordially and faithfully yours,   Woodrow Wilson

TLS (Letterpress Books, WP, DLC).

To Edward William Pou

My dear Mr. Pou: The White House February 11, 1915

Your generous letter of February ninth has just been laid before me. I hasten to send you my most cordial and heartfelt thanks. Letters such as that keep a man in heart, no matter what the circumstances.

Cordially and sincerely yours,   Woodrow Wilson

TLS (E. W. Pou Papers, Nc-Ar).

A Telegram and a Letter from Edward Mandell House

London, Feb. 11 [1915]

Had another conference with Sir Edward Grey at which Walter Page was present. Nothing new developing. The French Minister of Foreign Affairs[1] does not believe Germany sincere. Both Sir Edward Grey and the French Minister of Foreign Affairs thought probably Germany playing for advantage in order to impress (confluence) [conform, i.e., Bulgaria][2] as they think Allies have not achieved sufficient military success to insure acceptance of their demand for permanent peace. They are determined not to enter into any peace negotiations unless permanence is insured. They regard with favor my visit to Germany so as to test Germany's sincerity. I have not heard from Germany, though Wallace cables that Bernstorff has asked his Government to indicate that my coming will be agreeable. The difficulty is to get conversations started. Neither trusts the other and neither desires to place themselves at a disadvantage. The (nutations) [outlook] is fairly hopeful provided I can get to Germany by invitation and provided Germany does nothing foolish to create fresh irritation.

Did you receive my dispatch of February 8th?

Edward House

Transcripts of WWsh decode of T telegram (WP, DLC; WC, NjP).
  [1] Théophile Delcassé.
  [2] All of Wilson's encodes and decodes of cables to and from House have been read against the copies in the House Papers. Significant differences in the House versions will be noted in square brackets.

Dear Governor: London, England. February 11th, 1915.

Yucca [W. H. Page] had White [Grey] and me to lunch yesterday. I have cabled you the essentials of the conference.

White was again insistent upon our taking part in a final Nodal Guernsey [peace conference]. (D.C.) I told him it was impossible for us to enter into such a pact, but that we would be glad to take part in a Goatishly Demits [separate convention] including all the Merchantly [neutrals] looking to the laying down of Progenitor for Culmen Trifle [principles of civilized warfare].

Yucca thought we could do the other, even though it was breaking a precedent. I was sorry he took this stand for the reason that it might give White encouragement which I felt sure would not be justified.

I also thought it well to let White know that you were not

trying to inject yourself into the situation for any personal or political advantage, that your whole thought was to serve and to help bring about Nosebag Nodal [worldwide peace]. My reason for telling him this was that people antagonistic to you are saying both at home and here that you are endeavoring to obtain political and personal advantage by bringing about Nodal and I had reason to believe that White had heard this talk.

I think Wilmot [the Allies] will not consent to Frighted Nodal Namation [final peace terms] until they have had a try at Zadok [Germany] during the Ruin Cooperates [coming spring]. I explained to White, however, that it was not too early to get the machinery in order and that if it developed that Zadok would give now Slivering [terms] that would be acceptable, it would be foolish to sacrifice so many useful lives.

If Zadok does not indicate that my coming is welcome, then it will prove that Wilmot is right in believing them Ingrowing [insincere]. In that event it will not do for me to remain too long in Zenobia [Britain] because it will Flatuous Shape in Zadok [it will cause suspicion in Germany]. I shall therefore probably go to Irritancy [Italy] and stay until the time is more propitious, keeping in touch, however, with both Climature [Berlin] and Lazier [London]. If I go to Climature and find nothing can be accomplished, then again, it will be best to go to Lazier and wait.

It seems to me that as much care must be used in not doing as in doing.

If Zadok Dealers [drops] any more Mutineers [bombs] on Mismates [Paris] by Utilla (Zeppelins) or otherwise, or if she Resulted Lovage [sinks ships] as threatened without notice or protection of their Doloroso or Nile [crews and passengers], then matters will have to remain in statu quo until such time as they may agree to discontinue such practices, because this Gray [government] would not be able to sustain themselves before their people by co[u]ntenancing Nodal Miller [peace conversations].

Affectionately yours,   E. M. House

TLS (WP, DLC).

From Champ Clark

Washington, D. C.

My Dear Mr. President: February 11, 1915.

Since seeing you[1] I have "felt out" the situation and have come to two conclusions:

1. The Ship Bill can be passed through this House.
2. It cannot be passed through the next House—*provided* the

Republicans line up solidly against it. I feel fairly certain that these conclusions are correct.

I also believe that the only way to get it through this Congress is for you & your Senatorial supporters to accept the amendment now proposed in the Senate which will bring into line the 7 opposing Democrats.[2] In that way pass it through the Senate, send it to us & we will pass it speedily.

Whenever you need information as to what the House thinks on any subject, Hon. John N. Garner of Texas, "Jack" as we name him, is a first rate man to inquire of. He is exceedingly able and active & has a wonderful way of finding out things.

I hope you will pardon this intrusion upon your time and patience, as I thought you ought to know the result of my observations.

There is not a Democrat in the House who does not fear the political effect of another extraordinary Session of Congress.
Sincerely Your Friend,   Champ Clark

ALS (WP, DLC).
[1] Wilson called on the Speaker at his home (an unprecedented step for a President) on the evening of February 9.
[2] Clark presumably referred to one of several proposed amendments to the ship purchase bill either restricting (if not forbidding) the purchase of ships of belligerent nations or seeking to insure that the federal government would not remain in the shipping business following the conclusion of the war. One of the dissident Democrats, Thomas W. Hardwick of Georgia, stated—in response to a direct question in the Senate on February 5—that he would support the bill if amended in these two ways. *Cong. Record*, 63d Cong., 3d sess., p. 3093.

To Karl Edwin Harriman[1]

My dear Mr. Harriman: [The White House] February 12, 1915

Thank you sincerely for your kind note of February tenth.[2] I am sincerely glad that Mrs. Hulbert's article has proved usable. I am sure she will prove serviceable to the Journal as she finds out the best way to serve it.

Thank you for the cordial message of your letter.
Sincerely yours,   Woodrow Wilson

TLS (Letterpress Books, WP, DLC).
[1] Managing editor of the *Ladies' Home Journal*.
[2] It is missing.

From William Jennings Bryan, with Enclosure

My dear Mr. President: Washington February 12, 1915.

I enclose a memorandum prepared by Counselor Lansing relative to the criticisms of the government for its failure to protest against Germany in invading Belgium, etc.; also his letter to me which accompanied the memorandum. I am strongly of the opinion that it would be unwise to publish a statement covering all of these protests. I sent you some time ago a brief statement which was intended merely to explain why this government made no protest. If it is considered necessary to make any statement—which I think doubtful—I think the brief statement covers all that we should say. Mr. Lansing, as explained in his letter, believes thst [that] it is not wise to make any statement at all. If the memorandum covers all these questions, as his memorandum does, it is quite sure to be regarded by the friends of the Allies as a defense of the German position, although not so intended. Our attitude, being that of absolute neutrality, it is not wise in my judgment to make any explanations which would indicate a siding with either the Allies or the Germans on act[s] done during the war, except, of course, where our own rights are affected and where we must act for the protection of our citizens. I shall be glad to take this matter up with you personally if you desire, but at present I would agree with Mr. Lansing that it is better not to make any statements at all.

With assurances of high respect, I am, my dear Mr. President,
Yours very sincerely,   W. J. Bryan

TLS (W. J. Bryan Papers, DNA).

E N C L O S U R E

Robert Lansing to William Jennings Bryan

Dear Mr. Secretary: Washington February 10, 1915.

I submit herewith for your consideration a memorandum[1] for a public statement by letter or otherwise relative to the criticisms which have been made of the failure of this Government, as a party to the Hague Conventions, to protest against alleged violations of those conventions by Germany.

I confess that I am by no means satisfied with the tone of the memorandum submitted. It is a cold legal statement of our position. It sounds almost brutal in that it evinces no humanitarian motives, no solicitude for the suffering. While I feel that the arguments are sound and will appeal to those who realize that a government must regulate its conduct by law even at the expense of sentiment, I am not at all sure that the average citizen, who feels abhorrence at a belligerent's disregard of the rules of civilized warfare, will be convinced that this Government had no right or duty to protest against such practices.

While, as you know, I have felt that the pressure of criticism was such as to require some explanation of the Government's continued silence, I now have some doubts as to whether it is expedient. The presentation of our reasons, in spite of the fact that I have endeavored in the last few paragraphs of the statement to consider the subject from the standpoint of international justice, sounds selfish and cold-blooded. I may be super-sensitive and misjudge its effect on public opinion, but I consider it my duty to express to you the uncertainty which I feel as to how far this statement will go in quieting the complaints which have been made. It is in fact possible that it may cause controversy and arouse additional criticism of the Government on the ground that it has adopted a low standard of conduct.

As to whether the need of explanation is sufficiently great to overcome the possible results I am not willing to give an opinion.

I should also direct your attention to the fact that it has seemed to me inexpedient to enter into a full discussion of the nature of the undertakings of the contracting powers in the Hague Conventions. It would require technical treatment and could not in my judgment be put in a form suitable for popular consumption. In view of the facts in each case and the treaty provisions applicable it does not seem necessary.

I have, however, raised the question toward the close of the memorandum in order that it may not be charged that the Department considers the Hague Conventions to be joint in nature and thereby be held to have possibly admitted a legal right to protest in every case of treaty violation by a belligerent, whether or not it affects American rights.

While the several character of these Conventions can, I believe, be conclusively shown by argument as a matter of law, the practical reason for holding this position is the one emphasized. If the Conventions are *joint* undertakings, which must be held if the general right to protest against a violation by a belligerent can be maintained, then the nullifying articles in the Conventions apply equally to belligerents and neutrals and all the provisions become inoperative in the present war in case one or more of the belligerents has failed to ratify. In such a case (and hardly a Convention is not defective in this particular) a neutral contracting power not only is deprived of a general right to protest a violation, but also loses the special right to protest if its rights or those of its nationals are impaired. Thus, nothing is to be gained by maintaining the joint nature of the agreements.

On the other hand, if the Conventions are *several* in nature, the nullifying articles would be construed as effective between belligerents, but as having no force in matters involving the relations between a belligerent and a neutral. Thus, by adopting this view as to the nature of the Conventions, the United States, while it would have no general right to protest, would have the special right to do so in case its rights or those of its citizens, as defined by the Conventions, were affected by a belligerent's violation of a treaty provision.

From the point of view of expediency as well as of legality the position, that the agreements entered into at The Hague are several and not joint in nature, would conserve American neutral rights as well as relieving this Government of a duty to intervene diplomatically when the rights of other powers appear to be impaired by the breach of a Hague Convention.

Very sincerely yours,   Robert Lansing.

TLS (SDR, RG 59, 763.72111/1679½, DNA).
1 It is printed in *FR-LP*, I, 201-10. Lansing characterizes it well in his letter.

From Edward Mandell House

Dear Governor: London, England. February 12th, 1915.

I had lunch with Tyrrell yesterday and the conversation was most interesting. He was as frank with me as if talking to his Chief.

He told me of a strategic Magdala Elided [military move][1] which they are soon to make, but which is of such importance that I do not dare to even let you have it by code. He told me, too, that he considered this one of the gravest crises in the history of the world, and the only hope he had of its being solved successfully lay with you and White [Grey].

Winter [Russia] and Warren [France], he thought, would not be helpful in directing the Redolence (D.C.) [peace settlement] upon Condign and Kilted Latinism [broad and humane lines]. That it would be a question of whether the nations of the earth would take the wrong road or the right, and without your and White's direction, they would surely take the wrong.

He said in this Contort [cabinet] there were only two that would be helpful, Fends [the Prime Minister] and Leavens Crick [Lord Haldane]. He thought it providential that you had sent me over here at this time, that it would insure your playing an important part in this great tragedy, no matter what stand Zadok [Germany] took.

I had felt, after my first interview with White that this was true, as far as you are concerned, for as Tyrrell put it, "White will be the dominating influence when the end comes," and I think I can now clearly see that this is true.

It is my purpose to try, if I can once get to Zadok, to bring about the same feeling for you there. I have not much confidence in my ability to do this, but you may be assured, that my every effort will be bent in that direction.

Affectionately yours, E. M. House

P.S. I lunch on Monday with the Editor of the Westminster Gazette,[2] the most influential Government paper here, and on Tuesday with Mr. Strachey,[3] Editor of the Spectator, the most anti-American paper in England. These meetings should bring some good results.

TLS (WP, DLC).
[1] A project to land a British expeditionary force at Salonika for an invasion of Serbia. This plan was shelved in favor of a more limited army-navy campaign to seize control of the Dardanelles and the Gallipoli peninsula in order to open the sea lanes to Russia.
[2] John Alfred Spender.
[3] John St. Loe Strachey.

From William Gibbs McAdoo, with Enclosure

Dear Mr. President: Washington February 12, 1915.

I enclose copy of an order I issued to-day, revoking the previous order about the publication of statistical information concerning ships' manifests.

Faithfully yours, W G McAdoo

TLS (WP, DLC).

E N C L O S U R E

Treasury Department, February 12, 1915.

To Collectors and Other Officers of the Customs:

T.D. 34868 of October 28, 1914, relative to the making public of information regarding outward cargoes and the destination thereof is hereby revoked and collectors of customs may permit publication of such information relative to outward cargoes as was permitted prior to said instructions.

W. G. McAdoo, Secretary.

T MS (WP, DLC).

From John Randolph Thornton

Mr. President: Washington, D. C. 12th Feb., 1915.

It is not my custom to offer unsolicited advice to you and I have never done so before except when I wrote you on 16th December, 1912, to please not commit yourself to any one to the effect that you would not become a candidate to succeed yourself.

I said in that letter that my excuse for writing it was because I was a Democrat and interested in the continuation of the Democratic Party in power after the expiration of your present term of office and that continuance might depend on your renomination.

My excuse for again presenting you with gratuitous advice is the same as before, my desire to see such courses adopted as in my judgment will conduce to the future success of the Democratic Party and such courses avoided as in my judgment may conduce to its future failure.

It is my understanding that at the present time you are deliberating as to the propriety of calling an extra session of Congress on account of the failure of the Shipping Bill in the present session.

I feel it my duty as a Democrat to say to you as the head of the party that in my judgment the political effect on the Democratic Party of a failure to pass the Government Appropriation Bills during the present session and the attendant necessity of calling an extra session to pass them, would be most disastrous.

I am assuming as a fact what every member of the Senate recognizes as a fact, the impossibility of passing the Shipping Bill during this session, owing to the ability of the Republican minority to prevent its passage by their filibustering methods; and they could have prevented it even without the deplorable action of seven Democrats in forsaking their party associates in this crisis.

I am also assuming that there would be the gravest doubt about the passage of the Bill in the House at an extra session, with the chances against its passage, judging from what I hear from the Democratic members of the present House who will also be members of the next House.

But even if final success could be achieved in the extra session, it would be purchased in my opinion at the cost of grave injury to the Democratic Party.

We cannot blind our eyes to the intense desire of the business interests of the country to have a cessation of Congress in order to permit an adaptation to the conditions imposed by recent legislation; and until Congress finally adjourns these business interests do not know what further legislation may be sought to be enacted; and this very uncertainty is and will continue to be a disturbing element.

They have your assurance that the constructive administration measures for the proper regulation of business have been completed and they have confidence in your statement in so far as it reflects your views, but they do not know what will be sought to be done by others without Administration sanction, if the opportunity will be given, as it will be given in an extra session, the length of which cannot be foretold.

It must be borne in mind that some Senators think the enactment of various measures other than the Shipping Bill would be popular in sections of the country in which they live, and possibly some think their personal political fortunes might be enhanced by having some measures passed with which their names would be linked.

Such might be quite willing to see an extra session called in the hope that thereby their personal interests might be advanced; but I do not consider such to be safe or impartial advisers.

Possibly there are others who for their own purposes might be willing to advise you in a way they think you might wish to be advised without reference to their own convictions as to what was best for the Party interest.

I wish you to be assured that if there are some in either or both classes, I am not among them, for I have no axe to grind and I am actuated by my convictions as to what is best for the Democratic Party.

My convictions on this question as now expressed to you are the same I have entertained for several weeks past and have expressed to various Senators, including the majority leader, Senator Kern.

I was one of the Democrats who voted in the caucus three weeks ago to reverse our previous unanimous caucus decision to pass the Appropriation Bills first, by now agreeing to keep the Shipping Bill to the front to the exclusion of everything else.

But I told several of my brother Senators directly after, and told Senator Kern three days after, that in so voting I was not deceiving myself or trying to do so; that I believed it would result in no Shipping Bill being passed and the consequent necessity for an extra session to pass the Appropriation Bills, which in my judgment would be disastrous to the Democratic Party, and I told him that in acting as I did, I was subordinating my own wishes and judgment to the wishes and judgment of the head of the Party, and only four days ago I told Senator Simmons that if the newspaper statement that he would advise you to call an extra session in order to pass the Shipping Bill was correct, then I wished to say to him that as a Democrat with the good of the Party only at heart, I entered my solemn protest against any such advice, as in my judgment an extra session was not to the interest of the Democratic Party.

I beg to assure you that a great majority of the Democrats of the Senate think the same way and would so express themselves if they were willing to express their true convictions.

It seems to me that under present conditions, you are given the opportunity for splendid campaign material on your Western tour[1] by claiming that by their filibustering tactics the Republicans prevented the passage during the regular session of a bill that was intended for the good of the entire country, barring some special shipping interests, relying on the well-known objections of the country at large to a special session and thereby postponing action on the matter until next fall.

Now I know of course that you consider the Shipping Bill as one that will do great good to the country if enacted; and it may be that you consider the country and the Party will be benefited by its enactment, even at the expense of an extra session that may and probably will be prolonged until next fall; and I recognize that you have greater facilities than myself for properly guaging the sentiment of the country on this question.

Yet with the convictions that I have on the subject I have felt justified in stating my views, feeling assured as I do that they will be received by you in the same spirit in which they are offered, even though you may disagree with them.

Very truly and respectfully,   J. R. Thornton

Addendum: Since dictating above I see a newspaper statement to the effect that you had fully determined to call an extra session if the Shipping Bill fails at this session; and of course if I knew this was authentic, I would not presume to try to change your mind; but I know that newspaper statements are not always reliable.   Thornton

TLS (WP, DLC).
[1] Wilson planned to go to San Francisco to open the exposition there. He canceled the trip on account of the press of diplomatic affairs.

From Mary Allen Hulbert

Dearest Friend: [Boston] Feb. 12 [1915].

Allen has gone, and I am happier than I have been in many a day, in spite of that fact. He is *awake* at last. And gave me a promise before leaving, regarding his habits of life (that he had for some time been fulfilling). Oh! my dear friend, God *is* good. Pray with me that he will bless my boy, my darling son.

I have been ill with a touch of grippe that has pulled me down a bit, but am better. Again, will you forgive my tragic letters? As my late unlamented used to say, "Mary you take things so *hard*." I'm just an emotional old woman. A dear woman friend telephoned yesterday to inquire for me, and the "sob in my voice" reached her fine ear. In half an hour came some beautiful roses, and later her dear cheerful self to sit with me through the first lonely afternoon. My friends are so *good* to me. A *wonderful* thing has come out of the Tea Table article, not, I fear, because of its real merit, but because of *you*—a check from the H. J.[1] for $50.00. It looks *very* large to me, and gives me a sense of power out of all proportion with my ability.

I may go to Hot Springs to visit friends after going to Nantucket to complete the sale of the furniture & to Pittsfield to move furniture here but will let you know of my movements as soon as I make definite plans. Allen did not receive the letter, and if you have not had time to send one to the steamer, can you, will you send it to him addressing Allen S. H. Hotel Grunewald, New Orleans.

He is *much* more reticent than Mother, and I am looking forward to his doing great things "on his own." Do you know any one in Quito? He is to look up information as to credits, packing of shoes and any number of things for the Chamber of Commerce here. Forgive me, forgive me, the hateful letters I write, but if you *will* be a safety valve you'll have to shriek a little. I hear there is a war in Europe. (I do not mean to be flippant).
Your devoted friend   M.A.H.

ALI (WP, DLC).
1 *The Ladies' Home Journal.*

To Edward Mandell House

[The White House, Feb. 13, 1915]

Your messages of eighth and eleventh received and read with the greatest interest.

You have laid the right foundations of confidence and of comprehension of the nature and spirit of your mission.

I will do what I can to stimulate the interest of Germany from this end through Bernstorff.

Regretted the necessity of sending the note about unauthorized use of flag. It could not be avoided because such use of flag plays directly in the hands of Germany in her extraordinary plan to destroy commerce.

(Later) Have just learned this afternoon through Wallace that Bernstorff is perfectly confident letter of invitation is on its way to you. He has referred to your contemplated visit repeatedly in his correspondence with his government and feels sure it is expected. He understands the necessity for actual invitation and is cabling again tonight asking about what his government has done or intends to do.   Wilson.

T transcript of WWsh telegram (WC, NjP).

From Edward Mandell House

[London] February 13th, 1915.

Wolf [Zimmermann] writes that I shall be cordially received.[1] He demurs at question of indemnity of Belgium, but says he hopes for interview in which we may discuss matters more satisfactorily than by correspondence.

After two hour private conference with White [Grey] it was concluded to delay answer until after Wednesday when I shall have conference with Prime Minister.

T telegram (E. M. House Papers, CtY).
[1] Zimmermann's letter is printed as an Enclosure with EMH to WW, Feb. 18, 1915.

From Frederick Leonard Blackmon[1]

PERSONAL

Dear Mr. President: Washington, D. C. Feb. 13, 1915.

I am taking the liberty of writing you with reference to the proposed ship purchase bill. I have stood by your administration all along with the exceptions of the Alaskan Railroad and Immigration bills. I voted for the Immigration bill during President Taft's administration and voted to pass it over his veto. I also voted for the bill in this Congress and I did not feel that I could be consistent and not vote to pass it over your veto.

I am opposed to the ship purchase bill because I believe it is a step in the direction of Government ownership of railroads and other public service corporations. This is my objection to the bill. I do not mean to say, however, that I will not vote for it because if the Republicans in the House make a partisan fight upon you as has been done in the Senate I would feel strongly inclined to waive my opposition to the measure. There is a very strong sentiment against this bill in the House. I have not made a canvass of the new House, but from the expressions I hear I doubt seriously if you could pass this bill in the next Congress. Should you call an extra session for the purpose of passing this bill, and we should fail to do it, I think this would be disastrous to the party.

Unless Mr. Underwood is a candidate for 1916 for President of the United States I expect to support you for the Democratic nomination and I believe that the country will demand that you run again. Feeling as I do toward you I am prompted to write this letter and I trust you will not think I am presumptuous in undertaking to give you my views on this subject.

Yours very respectfully,   Fred L. Blackmon

TLS (WP, DLC).
1 Democratic congressman from Alabama.

To Mary Allen Hulbert

Dea[r]est Friend,   The White House 14 February, 1915.

I know that I can count always upon your understanding that, whether I write or not, I have not for a moment lost sight of what is happening to you or slackened my sympathy in the least degree; but somehow, notwithstanding my confidence of that, I feel deeply uneasy when public affairs crowd out all possibility of my sending you the messages I have it in my heart to send when you are in distress. The last two weeks have been like a fever. We do not, either of us, put politics in our letters (sufficient unto the day is the evil thereof), but no one who did not sit daily here with me, each anxious twenty-four hours through, could possibly realize the constant strain upon our vigilance and upon our judgment entailed by the rapidly varied conditions both "on the Hill" (that is, in Congress) and in the war area. Together, England and Germany are likely to drive us crazy, because it looks oftentimes as if they were crazy themselves, the unnecessary provocations they invent. To keep cool heads and handle each matter composedly and without excitement as it arises, seeking to see each thing in the large, in the light of what is likely to happen as well as in the light of what is happening now, involves a nervous expenditure such as I never dreamed of, and drives every private matter into the background to wait for a time of exemption from these things which never comes. I go to bed every night absolutely exhausted, trying not to think about anything, and with all my nerves deadened, my own individuality as it were blotted out.

And yet not for a moment do I forget my dear friends or lose my heart's touch of them. I am as keenly sensitive to what they are going through as I could be if I saw and spoke with them every day. I know you understand all this, but I like to say it again and again in so many words, so that it may stand out among the eternal verities the more sharply.

Did you get a little cheque from the LADIES HOME JOURNAL? I enclose the nice letter[1] the managing editor wrote me about your article. Encouraging, is it not? It made me very happy that you were to get this little encouragement, to give you confidence that you may work along the new vein. Do you think you could plan out some series of popular expositions of the most interesting kinds of china and the most interesting styles of furniture, with picturesque suggestions of their origins and of their historical associations, so as to feed the imagination of the cillector [collector] a bit? The idea has just occurred to me. Does it suggest anything interesting to you? It is possible it might interest the HOME JOURNAL people, since they are hospitable.

I enclose a letter for Allen's use.[2] I hope it is what you had in mind. I *could* not turn to it when you first suggested it, and now I do not know how to send it to him direct. You will know where to reach him, will you not, from time to time on his journey?

Ah! how I wish I could help, directly and efficiently! You will let me know any ways in which I can that may occur to you, will you not?

I am very well, though worn out. I never knew before that it was possible, when necessary, for a man to lose his own personal existence, seem even to himself to have no individual life apart from his offi[ci]al duties. But it is possible. It has happened, —to me!

All join me in affectionate messages. Let us hear, please, everything you are willing to tell us, or would like to talk about.

Your devoted friend,   Woodrow Wilson

WWTLS (WP, DLC).
[1] It is missing.
[2] It is also missing.

From Lindley Miller Garrison

My dear Mr. President: Washington Feb 14. 1915

Your note just received.[1] I had come to the identical conclusion reached by you, and had determined yesterday not to go. I had intended to so advise you on Tuesday at Cabinet.

We are truly in times when no one can tell "what a day will bring forth."

If I can ease your burden in any way or aid in carrying it I would like the privilege of doing so.

Sincerely yours   Lindley M. Garrison

ALS (WP, DLC).
[1] It is missing.

To Edward Mandell House

[The White House] February 16 [15], 1915.

The following from a despatch from Gerard dated Eleventh.

"It is my conviction from knowledge secured here from various sources that if a reasonable peace proposition were offered to Germany a great many men of great influence would be inclined to use their efforts to induce Germany to accept the proposition. The terms would naturally develope from general discussion once negotiations were begun by all parties and the Allies should be the first to put forth the intimation which should take the form of a secret intimation. If peace does not come immediately a new and protracted phase of war will commence.

"It is my belief that if you seize the present opportunity you will be the instrument of bringing about the greatest peace that has been signed. But it will be fatal to hesitate or wait a moment. Success is dependent on prompt action."

Gerard proposes a method but not the right one. I only wish you to know his impression. I will put him in direct communication with you later. He says I did not send my cypher yesterday without reason. Have you had any intimation of any kind from Berlin?   Wilson.[1]

T decode (E. M. House Papers, CtY).
[1] There is a WWT coded draft and a partial shorthand draft of this telegram in WP, DLC.

To John Randolph Thornton

My dear Senator: [The White House] February 15, 1915

I thank you sincerely for your frank and grave letter of the twelfth of February. I have read it with the greatest interest and it has made a deep impression on me.

Cordially and sincerely yours, Woodrow Wilson

TLS (Letterpress Books, WP, DLC).

Two Letters from William Jennings Bryan

My dear Mr. President: Washington February 15, 1915.

I am enclosing three communications which we have received from the German Ambassador in regard to the food situation and the war zone.[1]

The situation is growing more and more delicate and under the proposed war zone plan we are liable, at any time, to have a disaster over there which will inflame public opinion—and we are not in position to meet this outburst of public opinion unless we have done all that we can do to prevent it.

I am led to believe from Conversations with the German and Austrian Ambassadors that there would be a chance of securing the withdrawal of the military zone order in return for favorable action on the food question.

I do not know in what direction your mind is moving on the subject but I feel myself more and more inclined in the opinion that the British position is without justification. The German Government is willing to give assurances that the food imported will not be taken by the Government and is even willing that American organizations shall distribute that food. This, it seems to me, takes away the British excuse for attempting to prevent the importation of food.

You will notice in the last note the bitterness of the tone in which the German Government speaks of the attempts to starve the non-combatants.[2] If I am not mistaken the efforts to bring this "economic pressure"—as they call it—upon women and children of Germany will offend the moral sense of our country and, of course, still further arouse those who are inclined to sympathize with Germany.

I am constrained to believe that it is worth while for us to make an attempt to adjust the difficulty by setting one of these propositions off against the other. I mean that we should see whether

Great Britain will withdraw her objection to food entering Germany—the same to be distributed there through American instrumentalities, in return for the withdrawal of the German order in regard to the war zone.

If we can secure the withdrawal of these orders it will greatly clear the admosphere [atmosphere] and if we cannot do it I believe that we are approaching the most serious crisis that we have had to meet.

As soon as you have time to consider this will you please let me know your wishes? I shall be at home this evening until nine or half-past and, of course, can remain at home longer if necessary, although I have promised to go out for a little while later in the evening to attend a meeting of the Alumni of the Nebraska University. I will telephone you between nine and half-after and if you have reached a decision we might send a communication to Great Britain tonight. If anything can be done no time should be lost in acting.[3]

With assurances of high respect I am, my dear Mr. President,
Yours very sincerely,   W. J. Bryan

TLS (WP, DLC).
[1] They are missing in WP, DLC. The first was the explanatory memorandum cited in RL to WW, Feb. 7, 1915. The second was J. H. von Bernstorff to WJB, Feb. 13, 1915, TLS (SDR, RG 59, 763.72112/839, DNA), printed in FR-WWS 1915, pp. 102-103, reporting that the German government had rescinded its order impounding certain grains and was prepared to give absolute assurances that imported food would not be used by the armed forces. The third was J. H. von Bernstorff to WJB, Feb. 15, 1915, TLS (SDR, RG 59, 763.72/1519, DNA), printed in FR-WWS 1915, pp. 104-105, warning that, on account of British methods of naval warfare, no neutral vessels would be safe in the war zone.
[2] "The new German method of naval warfare is imposed and justified by the murderous character of the English method of naval warfare, which seeks to condemn the German people to death by starvation through the destruction of legitimate trade with neutral foreign countries."
[3] They got off a telegram to Page on the following day (WJB to WHP, Feb. 16, 1915, [T telegram SDR, RG 59, 763.72/1457a, DNA]), repeating the note from the German Embassy of February 15 and referring to earlier communications from Berlin. The main portion of the telegram was written by Wilson (T MS, W. J. Bryan Papers, DNA):
"In giving these notes to Sir Edward Gray for his information, please make clear to him informally the position in which this government finds itself. It cannot escape the conviction that a policy which seeks to keep food from non-combatants, from the civil population of a whole nation, will create a very unfavorable impression throughout the world. It will certainly create, is already showing signs of creating, a strong revulsion of feeling in this country and the result might very easily be such a condemnation of that policy by American opinion, in view of the explicit assurances of the German notes sent herewith, as to be very embarrassing to this government if it took an inactive position. In the interest of the absolute good feeling that subsists between us these considerations should be very frankly stated."

My dear Mr. President: Washington February 15, 1915.

I am enclosing a copy of the note from Great Britain.[1] We have had it printed and you will therefore be saved time in reading it. I am taking a copy home tonight to read.

With assurances of high respect, I am, my dear Mr. President,
Very sincerely yours,   W. J. Bryan

TLS (WP, DLC).
[1] E. Grey to WHP, Feb. 10, 1915, printed telegram (WP, DLC); printed in FR-WWS 1915, pp. 324-34. A response to the American note of December 26, 1914, it was a long defense of British maritime economic warfare.

From Edward Mandell House

Dear Governor,   [London] February 15th, 1915.

Thank you for your long cablegram which came yesterday.

I am still undecided as to what to do about Berlin. The difficulties are these: This Government have to be extremely careful about giving us any encouragement whatever. They do not dare say what they actually feel, not only because it might make England's position misunderstood in Germany, but also because it would meet with a storm of disapproval here, for the reason that no one believes that anything like the kind of terms that England will demand will be met now.

As a matter of fact, there is no desire whatever, excepting among a very small circle, for anything out of the war excepting a permanent settlement and evacuation and indemnity to Belgium, but no one believes that Germany is ready for such terms.

Germany, on the other hand, is now almost wholly controlled by the militarists. There is a peace party there, as there is here, and both strangely enough are conducting the civil governments.

Those here are much more powerful to act than those in Germany, where I believe they have but little real power. As long as the military forces of Germany are successful as now, the militarists will not permit any suggestion of peace.

They are undertaking at the moment an enveloping movement against Warsaw, and if this is successful, it is their purpose, I think, to practically let their eastern campaign end there. They will entrench themselves strongly and then they will move all their forces to the west, hoping to break through and finally reach Paris.

If they are successful, the effect will be to keep both Roumania and Italy neutral. If they are not successful, it will have a tendancy to bring then [them] in on the side of the Allies.

So, for the moment, I am advised here to let matters develop somewhat further, and this coincides with my judgment.

White [Grey] explained to me the other day, the strategical military move about which Tyrrell told me briefly. I find it is not of immediate consequence and I greatly doubt whether it can be put into effect for many months, if at all. There are too many complications to be met to make it of immediate service.

Neither side has used much military imagination, but they depend largely upon the usual tactics with a tendancy everywhere to play safe.

I have a feeling, too, that it is just as well for me not to go to Germany until the present irritation in regard to your recent note has blown somewhat over. However, I shall be guided largely in this matter by our conference on Wednesday.[1]

I am formulating in my own mind, and am unravelling it from time to time to White and others in authority, to see how far it is feasible, a plan for a general convention of all neutral and belligerent nations of the world, at which you will be called upon to preside and which should be called upon your invitation.

It could meet concurrently with the peace conference, or if peace is not then in sight by August, it could be called and it might be used as a medium of bringing about peace between the belligerents. This convention, of course, would not deal with any of the controversies between the belligerents, but it would go into *the rules of future warfare and the rights of neutrals.*

It would be of far reaching consequence—more far reaching in fact than the peace conference itself.

I believe it could be arranged for the belligerents to take part in such a conference, or at least, sanctioning its assembling before this conflict ends, provided there seems to be no prospect of its ces[s]ation by the first of August. However, I will write you at greater length when it has more fully developed.

Affectionately yours,   E. M. House

Feby 16. Your second cable has just come. Gerard has not yet gotten me in direct touch by cable.

TLS (WP, DLC).
[1] House was to have lunch with Page, Grey, and Prime Minister Asquith on February 17.

From Charles William Eliot

Private

Dear President Wilson: Cambridge, Mass. 15 February, 1915

My dear friend Major Higginson has just sent me a copy of a letter you wrote him on February 1st, about the Shipping Bill.

It gives me hope that you will promote effective changes in the Bill, or cease to support it.

You recognize that the Bill makes it possible for the Administration to do foolish things. Is not the passage, under pressure from the Administration, of a Bill which contains such possibilities a bad precedent? Suppose that another Roosevelt should become President of the United States!

You think it reasonable that the country should trust your Administration not to do foolish things. I submit that the question—"Can you not trust *me*?" is never a satisfactory answer to the man or the party that objects to another's demanding or possessing illegitimate and dangerous powers. If, however, you continue to feel that the answer—"Cannot the country trust me?" ought to be sufficient in the present case, would not your position before the anxious country be strengthened by your saying publicly—"I know that this Bill contains powers for possible mischief; but my Administration does not propose to avail itself of those powers."

I ought to confess that my interest in your disposition of the Shipping Bill is intensified by my belief that your relation to the Shipping Bill up to this date seems likely to make a breach in the Democratic party, to contribute to the alienation from you of the great mass of the business men of the country, and to make probable the return of the Republican party to power in 1916. These results all seem to me calamitous.

Sincerely yours,   Charles W. Eliot

TLS (WP, DLC).

Remarks at a Press Conference

February 16, 1915

Are you in favor of [cloture], Mr. President?

I am.

Are you in favor of the Norris amendment to the cloture system which would abolish caucuses also, practically?

I haven't seen it.

It provides that no one shall vote by cloture rule whose freedom of action is tied by the caucus rule.

I have no comment on that. There are various ways of making one man the Senate of the United States.

Do you favor a general cloture rule, or one to fit this particular case?

I favor a reasonable cloture rule in general. I don't mean one that will cut off reasonable debate, but one that will cut off obstruction.

Mr. President, isn't it a fact, as it is reported in some newspapers, that you are keeping the ship purchase bill before the Congress in the face of advice to the contrary from leading Democrats who are unnamed?

No, sir.

There is no such advice?

There is such advice from Democrats, but not from those who are unnamed. Everybody knows who they are.

This wouldn't mean the seven gentlemen?

I didn't necessarily mean them, either. There is no such thing as you evidently have in mind.

Mr. President, the *Post* says you favor an extra session?

Who says so?

The *Post*, to revise the tariff.

The *Post* has executive information that nobody else has, not even myself.

Mr. President, are there any suggestions of an extra session that might be scheduled on the tariff that has information showing that there are schedules that would be well to revise?

No, sir.

The tariff is working satisfactorily?

It is working absolutely satisfactorily.

Is there any need of an extra session to devise new revenue legislation?

No, sir.

If the ship purchase bill and the appropriation bills are passed, there will be absolutely no need of an extra session?

None whatever.

If either fails?

I will cross that bridge when I get to it. I don't expect either to fail. As a matter of fact, that is the reason I don't face that "if" again. Sufficient unto the day is the "if" thereof.

Are you going to be able to break the filibuster, Mr. President, or satisfy the Republicans?

No, sir. I don't think I am, but I think the Senate is.

JRT transcript (WC, NjP) of CLSsh (C. L. Swem Coll., NjP).

To Champ Clark

My dear Mr. Speaker: [The White House] February 16, 1915

It was fine the way you rallied the men last night.[1] It has cheered me very much and I want to send you this line of cordial thanks.   Faithfully yours,   Woodrow Wilson

TLS (Letterpress Books, WP, DLC).
   1 In the House Democratic caucus, which considered the Weeks-Gore shipping bill during the evening of February 15 and the early morning of the next
day, Representative Robert N. Page of North Carolina (a brother of Walter H.
Page) offered an amendment putting a definite terminus on governmental operation of merchant ships following the conclusion of the war. Speaker Clark
then addressed the meeting, declaring that, while he personally was opposed
to governmental ownership of merchant ships, he foresaw that the Democratic
party would again be condemned to "wander in the wilderness" if it did not
give its leader the bill that he wanted. He also warned that an extra session
of Congress would be a disaster for the party. In the test vote on the amendment in the early morning, it was defeated 118 to 38. The caucus then proceeded to approve the Weeks-Gore bill. *New York Times*, Feb. 16, 1915.

To David Franklin Houston

My dear Houston: [The White House] February 17, 1915
   May I not congratulate you and wish you many happy returns
of your birthday? I want you to know how happy I have been to
be associated with you in the work of the administration. There
is no one whose judgment I trust more or in whose ability I have
greater confidence. The way in which you have conducted your
department has been a constant pleasure to me. You have been
a tower of strength and I thank you with all my heart.
          Cordially and faithfully yours,   Woodrow Wilson

TLS (Letterpress Books, WP, DLC).

To William Charles Adamson

My dear Judge: [The White House] February 17, 1915
   May I not send you a line of warm thanks and appreciation for
your work in getting the shipping bill through the caucus and
the Congress?[1] You are certainly a fine soldier and I am your
sincere admirer.
          Cordially and sincerely yours,   Woodrow Wilson

TLS (Letterpress Books, WP, DLC).
   1 The House adopted the Weeks-Gore bill, 215 to 121, in the early morning of
February 17.

To Frederick Leonard Blackmon

                                        [The White House]
My dear Mr. Blackmon: February 17, 1915
   Your letter of February thirteenth was not only welcome, but
I am sincerely obliged to you for writing to me so frankly. I
shall certainly give the views you express very serious considera-
tion.

My own feeling is that the ship purchase bill does not involve what you fear, but is the only immediately feasible method of relieving the country from the control of interests which are selfishly profiting by its necessities.

Cordially and sincerely yours,   Woodrow Wilson

TLS (Letterpress Books, WP, DLC).

To Joshua Willis Alexander

The White House
My dear Judge Alexander: February 17, 1915

The shipping bill fight was admirably conducted and certainly the conclusion of it ought to be deeply gratifying to everybody who wants to see the party serve the country in a disinterested fashion. May I not express my sincere admiration of the part that you played and my genuine appreciation?

Cordially and sincerely yours,   Woodrow Wilson

TLS (photostat in RSB Coll., DLC).

From Edward Mandell House

[London, February 17, 1915]
Your dispatch quoting Gerard received.

Had short private conference with Sir Edward Grey yesterday (16th). I have had a long conference today at which the Prime Minister and Walter Page were present. They [again] advised my not going to Germany until the present enveloping movement in the East is decided.

I feel that it is essential to conform to their wishes for they are accepting you as their medium of communication with Germany, and it is very important that they continue to do so. I am urging this government to make a compromise proposal regarding Germany's threat against merchantmen.

See Walter Page's dispatch.[1] I am keeping in touch with Zimmermann.   Edward House.

T transcript of WWsh decode (WP, DLC).
   [1] Printed as an Enclosure with WJB to WW, Feb. 18, 1915 (third letter of that date).

From William Jennings Bryan

My dear Mr. President: Washington February 17, 1915.

I wrote you a few days ago in regard to Harry Walker[1] and a man whom O'Gorman wanted appointed[2] and asked whether it would be advisable to try and make some exchange with O'Gorman.[3]

You answered disapproving[4] but I was left in doubt as to just what part of the proposition you objected to.

Would you be kind enough to indicate—first, whether you have any objection to the appointment of Harry Walker; second, whether your objection is to the appointment of the man recommended by O'Gorman; or, third, whether your objection was to the attempt to make an exchange of appointments with O'Gorman.

Mr. House has brought Harry Walker's name to my attention several times and, as you know, I have been anxious on my own account to find him something and this may be an available place. O'Gorman, however, desires it for a man by the name of O'Sullivan who is a graduate of Princeton.

I shall appreciate a line outlining your wishes in the matter.

With assurances of high respect I am, my dear Mr. President,

Yours very sincerely,   W. J. Bryan

TLS (W. J. Bryan Papers, DNA).
[1] Harry Wilson Walker, long-time Washington correspondent of various newspapers.
[2] Thomas Cullen O'Sullivan, Princeton 1914.
[3] Bryan's letter to Wilson is missing.
[4] Wilson's letter is also missing.

From David Franklin Houston

Dear Mr. President: Washington February 17, 1915.

I am deeply touched by your thoughtfulness and your cordial and generous expressions. I have the unique experience of being reminded by the President of the United States that I have a birthday. I had overlooked the matter, and for the first time in twenty years, so far as appears at the present moment, Mrs. Houston has failed to react. I shall take peculiar pleasure, I may say even malicious pleasure, in handing her your note.

It has been a privilege for me to be a part of your administration in these difficult and inspiring times. I have been very happy in my work under your liberal supervision and am receiving compensation much out of proportion to my service. I am not as old as some people, but I had scarcely expected to live to see an administration in power which by its standards and practices would contribute as much to the higher life of the nation as yours has or would secure the enactment into law of as many great measures.   Faithfully yours,   D. F. Houston.

TLS (WP, DLC).

From James Keeley[1]

My dear Mr. President: [Chicago, Feb. 17, 1915]

You and the burdens you are carrying for all of us have been on my mind for the last few days. I have felt that the average man does not realize the tremendous load you are bearing and what it all means: the depressing isolation of power, the abuse of those who set self interest in the seat which should be occupied by the common good, the torturing self examination as to the exact justice of one's own acts, the penalty one has to pay for power.

The acclaim of history is fine but present sympathetic understanding and support are more helpful to the man who is making history—particularly when its making is so difficult.

So I have written an editorial[2] which I hope will serve at least two purposes: To cause the average careless citizen to stop and think of the cross you are carrying for him and to further emphasize the point I have been trying to make for the last few days, that if we are at war among ourselves at home we are in more danger than if the nation were an active belligerent.

Faithfully Yours   J Keeley

ALS (WP, DLC).
   [1] Editor of the *Chicago Herald.*
   [2] "A Man of Burdens," *Chicago Herald*, Feb. 17, 1915.

To Charles William Eliot

Personal and Confidential.

My dear Doctor Eliot: The White House February 18, 1915

I have your valued favor of the fifteenth of February and am sincerely obliged to you for its candid advice.

My difficulty in this whole matter has been this: Our rights as neutrals in the matter of the purchase of ships from citizens of belligerent countries is, I believe, susceptible of clear establishment in any impartial tribunal. Just now the United States stands as the chief custodian of neutral rights and I do not think that any branch of the Government should say anything officially that would seem to be equivalent to even a temporary renunciation of those rights. That is the reason why I have thought that the only course open to us was to ask the public to trust us on the principle that no administration that had not lost its head would be likely to do anything that would bring extraordinary risks to the country itself and add to the perplexities and hostilities of a terrible season of war like this.

I think that you will see the nature of the quandary.

Cordially and sincerely yours,   Woodrow Wilson

TLS (C. W. Eliot Papers, MH-Ar).

To Thaddeus Austin Thomson

[The White House]

My dear Mr. Minister: February 18, 1915

It has given me genuine concern that the pressure of business upon the Congress of the United States should have been such and the constitutional limits of the present session so sharp that it has apparently become impossible to ratify in the present session the proposed treaty of the United States with Colombia. My personal interest in that treaty has been of the deepest and most sincere sort. I believe that it constitutes a just and honorable understanding between two friendly peoples and it is my earnest desire and purpose that it should be pressed to a ratification. The more the matter is studied the more evident it becomes that such a treaty is based upon equity and is the natural outcome of genuine friendship between the two countries.

Cordially and sincerely yours,   Woodrow Wilson

TLS (Letterpress Books, WP, DLC).

From William Jennings Bryan, with Enclosures

My dear Mr. President: Washington February 18, 1915.

I enclose three telegrams which have been read to Mr. Lansing and to Mr. Williams of the "Far East." If you will give me your opinion or corrections I will have Mr. Davis put them in cipher tomorrow morning and send them from the White House office.

And while on this subject I would like your opinion as to what it is proper to do in regard to the newspaper men. They hang around the door of my office, interview the Ambassadors and Ministers when they call and occasionally they get an idea of what is being done by glimpses they catch of the clerks at work.

Take, for instance, today—soon after I had prepared these telegrams and before I had a chance to send them over to you, the newspaper men informed me that an afternoon paper had stated that a despatch had been sent today to Tokio. Our despatches are printed on green paper and anyone passing a machine can see that a despatch is being written. If he passes near enough to see the heading, as, of instance, "Amembassy Tokio" he can state that a despatch is being sent and then they can inquire what is being sent.

Do you see any objection to a rule being adopted here, fixing an hour when the newspaper men can come for such news as we have to give out? And then deny to them the privilege of staying in this corridor. There is a press room on the "Navy" side and also on the "War" side and it can be understood that we would send anything that we had to them between these hours.

We need the newspapers, of course, when we want to give out anything and we have to afford them such facilities as can be given, with due regard for the public interest, but it does not seem to me fair to compel the foreign representatives to "run the gauntlet" of a dozen newspaper representatives when they come to the Department, and I do not like to have them moving about through the rooms where the clerks are at work.

I am going to have a typewriter placed in my room and have my Confidential Clerk use this typewriter for any confidential messages so that no one can know what he is doing. While that will help me out on confidential messages such as we have occasion to write nearly every day, it does not protect the foreign representatives who come in here from being cross-examined as to why they call.

I shall be glad to have your opinion.

With assurances of high respect I am, my dear Mr. President,
Yours very sincerely,   W. J. Bryan

Mr Lansing who approves above of above [sic] makes the additional suggestion that diplomats shall not be interviewed in this building

TLS (WP, DLC).

ENCLOSURE I[1]

Amlegation Pekin.   Washington, February 18, 1915.

We have received from the Chinese Minister complete statement of demands. The demands contained in Article Five are not included in the statement which we received from the Japanese Ambassador.[2] We infer that the demands contained in Article Five may have ⟨been tentative and that having⟩ met ⟨with⟩ *with such opposition from the* Chinese ⟨opposition⟩ *government that* they were withdrawn before the shorter statement was handed to us. Please keep us advised as to negotiations, cabling at once whether the demands in Article Five affecting the entire government are being urged. Those demands if they had been made as demands would have aroused serious concern for they would have menaced the political integrity and independence of China and would have materially discriminated against other nations which are entitled to equal treatment.   Bryan

T telegram (SDR, RG 59, 793.94/241, DNA).
   1 Words in angle brackets deleted by Wilson; words in italics, Wilson's. Bryan was responding to P. S. Reinsch to WJB, Feb. 15, 1915, T telegram (SDR, RG 59, 793.94/231, DNA), and P. S. Reinsch to WJB, Feb. 17, 1915, T telegram (SDR, RG 59, 793.94/232, DNA). The first telegram warned that the Japanese memorandum purporting to list the Japanese government's demands on China was incomplete and misleading. The second reported that the Chinese government was distributing to the diplomatic corps in Peking the full text of the demands. The telegram to Reinsch was sent on February 19.
   2 Ambassador Chinda, on February 8, had given Bryan a memorandum which listed most of the demands in the first four groups. On the following day, Baron Katō called Ambassador Guthrie to the Japanese Foreign Office to explain the nature of the Sino-Japanese negotiations. Katō assured Guthrie that Japan's "propositions" were "not contrary to China's integrity or to the rights and interests of other nations." Katō did not mention the demands in Group V. Japanese Embassy to the Department of State, n.d., and G. W. Guthrie to WJB, Feb. 9, 1915, *FR 1915*, pp. 83-85.

E N C L O S U R E   I I

CONFIDENTIAL.

Amembassy Tokio   Washington, February 18, 1915.

We are sending you another telegram which you can present to the Japanese Government. We are informed that the demands contained in Article Five were presented to China although not included in the memorandum handed to us. They may have been informally discussed and, having met with opposition from China, abandoned before the shorter memorandum was sent to us. The fact that they have been published in the press and the further fact that they were not included in the memorandum sent to us by Japan enables us to comment upon them without coming into conflict with the announced position of Japan which, we assume, is fully stated in the memorandum handed us.   Bryan[1]

T telegram (SDR, RG 59, 793.94/241, DNA).
   1 This telegram was sent on February 19.

ENCLOSURE III

Amembassy Tokio   Washington, February 18, 1915.

Press despatches have been announcing that Japan is asking of China:

First: That the Central Government employ only influential Japanese subjects as advisors for conducting administrative, financial and military affairs.

Second: That China and Japan jointly police the important places in China or that China employ a majority of Japanese in her police department.

Third: That China shall purchase from Japan at least half the arms and ammunition used in the whole country or establish jointly in Japan factories for the manufacture of arms.

Fourth: That China shall permit Japan to build certain railroads connecting Wuchang with Kiukiang and Nanchang, Nanchang with Hangchow and Nanchang with Chiaochow.

Fifth: That in case the province of Fukien requires foreign capital for railway construction, mining, harbor improvements and ship building, Japan shall be first consulted.

The above demands if they had been made would have aroused serious concern for they would have menaced the political integrity and independence of China and would have materially discriminated against other nations which are entitled to equal treatment.

We were very much relieved to receive the memorandum delivered by the Japanese Ambassador and likewise forwarded by you for this memorandum is a complete denial of the press reports as above quoted and gives assurance that Japan has no such intentions as the press reports would have indicated. You may express to the Government our appreciation of its action in making known to us its purpose, in accordance with the terms of the Root-Takahira agreement, as stated in the memorandum referred to.   Bryan[1]

T telegram (SDR, RG 59, 793.94/240, DNA).
[1] This telegram was sent on February 19.

From William Jennings Bryan

My dear Mr. President: Washington February 18, 1915.

I am enclosing a statement of the Vicar-General of Mexico,[1] of which we had advance notice in one of Silliman's telegrams.

It is a very interesting statement and I think we ought to

send a copy of it to the three Cardinals, explaining to them that insofar as it makes charges against any of the revolutionists no reference should be made to the Vicar-General for fear it might incite personal hostility toward him, but insofar as it denies the reports of outrages—as in the case of the nuns[2]—it would not hurt him to have his opinion made known and it would certainly relieve the distress of many in this country who have evidently been misinformed on this particular subject.

I think it might be well to send Malone a copy of that part of the statement referring to the nuns in order that he may send it to Father Kelly of Chicago who has shown much interest in the matter and evidently relied upon the statements he had received in regard to the nuns.

With assurances of high respect I am, my dear Mr. President,
Yours very sincerely,   W. J. Bryan

TLS (W. J. Bryan Papers, DNA).
[1] Msgr. Antonio J. Paredes to J. R. Silliman, Mexico City, Jan. 22, 1915, TCL (SDR, RG 59, 812.404/58, DNA). It reviewed recent *Zapatista* murders of priests and the treatment of priests and church property in the archbishopric of Mexico City.
[2] Paredes reported that he knew of no cases of assaults against nuns.

From William Jennings Bryan, with Enclosure

My dear Mr. President: Washington February 18, 1915.

You will find in the afternoon "Star" a copy of the German note.[1] We understand that this is complete except for the omission of a sentence which is supplied by a flimsey herein enclosed. It relates to the matter of "convoys" and the sentence is—

"Germany believes it may act on the supposition that only such ships would be convoyed as carried goods not regarded as contraband according to the British interpretation made in the case of Germany."—

that is, I suppose, not carry food if Great Britain continues to regard food as contraband.

I have just received from Page, in the confidential cipher, a despatch which I enclose.

Mr. Lansing and I have gone over the copy of the German note which we have and the Page telegram together, and feel that the Page telegram offers a *"ray of hope."* Page says that the British Government *may* propose to the German Government, in answer to the Bernstorff note, that it will not put food on the absolute contraband list if Germany will sow no more mines and will attack no more commercial ships by submarines. This, he adds, is not certain and must not be made known.

If Great Britain will make the proposition above suggested, it is possible that some arrangement may be reached. I think it would be worth while for this Government to undertake the distribution of the food, even though it would entail a large amount of labor. But no amount of labor would be too great to avoid the dangers which now menace us. It would be almost a miracle if our ships avoided the dangers necessarily attendant upon the war zone order in view of the increasing bitterness displayed by the belligerent countries. At least it is worth while to attempt negotiations and the German note indicates the willingness of that Government to enter into negotiations.

Whether Germany would be willing to agree that no mines should be sown and that no merchant vessels should be attacked by submarines remains to be seen. I am inclined to think, however, they may agree to that.

Mr. Lansing and I have been going over the proposition together and suggest for your consideration a proposition like this:

Food sent to Germany for the use of non-combatants, to be consigned to American agents and by American agents delivered to retail dealers licensed for that purpose by the German Government—the license specifying that the food so furnished was to be sold to non-combatants and not to be subject to requisition. Any violation of the terms of the license could work a forfeiture of the right of such dealers to receive food for this purpose.

In return, let it be agreed—I suppose Great Britain would have to agree to this as well as Germany—

First: That there shall be no floating mines;

Second: That any other mines should be placed only at the entrance of harbors and then only for defensive purposes; all mines to bear the stamp of the Government placing them and to be so constructed as to become inoperative if detached;

Third: As to submarines—the belligerents to agree that submarines will not attack commercial vessels.

If this agreement is made in regard to submarines it might also be stipulated—

Fourth: That neutral flags shall not be used by merchant vessels of belligerent countries.

We think that an agreement covering these four points—food, mines, the use of submarines against merchant vessels and the use of neutral flags—might be worked out and if so, would be a great triumph for ne ral trade and would be appreciated by all neutral countries besides restoring the combatants to normal lines of attack.

We have not yet received the copy of the German note officially.

With assurances of high respect I am, my dear Mr. President,
Yours very sincerely,   W. J. Bryan

I enclose a cable note from Gerard.[2]

TLS (SDR, RG 59, 763.72/13422, DNA).
[1] Clipping from the *Washington Star* pasted on pages with comments by
Lansing (SDR, RG 59, 763.72/1481, DNA). The German note (J. W. Gerard
to WJB, Feb. 17, 1915, T telegram [SDR, RG 59, 763.72/1481, DNA, printed
in *FR-WWS 1915*, pp. 112-15]) was a reply to the American "strict accountability" note of February 10. It appealed for American understanding, again
reviewed alleged British violations of international law and the consequences
to Germany of acquiescence in these illegal measures by the neutrals, and said
that the German government would do its best to avoid violence to American
ships. It pointed out that there were, however, grave dangers to any ship approaching an area legitimately mined and said that absolute safety to neutral
ships lay in staying out of the war zone. It said that the German government
had announced the destruction only of enemy vessels found within the war
zone, not the destruction of all merchant ships, as the American government
appeared to have erroneously understood. However, the note continued, dangers
remained on account of the British use of neutral flags and because neutral
ships continued to carry contraband through the war zone. The German government appreciated the American protest against British use of the American
flag, and U-boat commanders had been instructed to abstain from violence
against American ships when they were recognizable as such. However, it
would be safest for the American government to convoy ships through the war
zone, but these ships could not carry contraband. The German government,
the note concluded, would welcome an American initiative looking toward
adoption of the Declaration of London as the code governing maritime warfare
because this would guarantee Germany its legitimate supply of foodstuffs and
industrial raw materials.
[2] J. W. Gerard to WJB, Feb. 16, 1915, received Feb. 17, 9 P.M., T telegram
(SDR, RG 59, 763.72/1470, DNA, printed in *FR-WWS 1915*, p. 110), forecasting
the outline of the German note and going into some detail about the German
plan for United States Navy convoys of American ships which did not carry
contraband.

E N C L O S U R E

London February 17, 1915.

1668, Confidential following in Secretary's private code:

Your 1140, February 16, 3 p.m.[1] I have delivered to Sir Edward Gray Bernstorff's note and the substance of your instructions. A frank and full canvass of the whole situation by Prime
Minister[,] Sir Edward Gray, House and me at noon luncheon
today brought out the possibility that the British Government
may propose to the German Government in answer to Bernstorff's note that it will not put food on absolute contraband list
if Germany will sow no more mines and will attack no more
commercial ships by submarines. But this is not yet certain and
must not be made known. The greatest hindrance to an accept-

ance of the proposition is the offensive language in the last sentence of Bernstorff's note.[2]

Meantime I ask your consideration of the following and advice thereon.

First. Is our Government prepared to undertake the distribution of food to non-combatants throughout Germany so as to make sure that it will all be consumed by non-combatants? It requires a large number of men to do this for the commission in Belgium and if we can undertake this service would it be an unneutral act by our Government?

Second. Bernstorff's last sentence about neutrals "compelling" the British Government may prevent any agreement. If it does prevent an agreement, I hesitate, without your definite instructions so to endorse Bernstorff's position as to make it appear that we are trying to "compel" the British Government. I am rather offering our good offices towards an agreement and informing Gray that making food absolute contraband would greatly embarrass our commercial interests and our government and help towards an adverse turn of public opinion. I hesitate to seem to endorse "compelling" him.

American Ambassador, London.

T telegram (SDR, RG 59, 763.72112/1386½, DNA).
  1 See WJB to WW, Feb. 15, 1915 (first letter of that date), n. 3.
  2 "Germany therefore will adhere to the announced method of warfare until England comes to the decision of observing hereafter the generally accepted rules of naval war as laid down in the Paris declaration of Maritime law and in the London Declaration of Naval War law, or is compelled to do so by the neutral Powers." J. von Bernstorff to WJB, Feb. 15, 1915, TLS (SDR, RG 59, 763.72/1519, DNA, printed in *FR-WWS 1915*, pp. 104-105).

From William Charles Adamson

Dear Mr. President: Washington, D. C. February 18th, 1915.

I thank you most deeply for your kind letter of the 17th instant. Your commendation is very sweet to me. Of all earthly things at this time I desire the success of your administration, and that it may be reindorsed by the people. For the House to fail to pass the bill and thereby uphold your hands would have been an irretrievable party calamity.

With high regards and best wishes, I remain,

Your friend,   W C Adamson

TLS (WP, DLC).

From Edward Mandell House, with Enclosures

Dear Governor: London. February 18th, 1915.

Zimmermann's letter and my answer, also a letter from Gerard and my answer are enclosed for your information.

I had a conference with Sir Edward Grey last Tuesday evening, and again yesterday at which the Prime Minister and Page were present.

Both Asquith and Grey thought it would be footless for me to go to Berlin until the present German enveloping movement in the East is determined. It looks, for the moment, bad for the Russians, and they do not want me to be in Berlin at such a time. If this movement fails and things get again deadlocked, they think I should take that opportunity to go there.

As a matter of fact, I could not go just now if I so desired for no boats are running.

I put the matter plainly to both Asquith and Sir Edward asking their advice as to what to do, telling them we were all interested alike in bringing about the desired result, and it was a question of how best to do it. They accepted this position and Sir Edward thought, at the moment, I should write to Zimmermann along the lines that I did.

The idea was that unless they at least conceded these two points, the matter had as well be dropped until they were willing to do so.

Sir Edward said that England would continue the war indefinitely unless those cardinal points were agreed to.

I am having another private conference with Sir Edward this evening in order to discuss Gerard's letter which has just come and which he has not seen.

The postscript to Gerard's letter was written on a small slip of paper and enclosed in the letter. Just why he did it this way I am unable to determine. He seems to have a touch of the general madness. His prediction as to the result is hardly justified, and his idea that a peace proposal can be made by all the Allied Powers in fifteen minutes does not merit serious discussion.

I told them at yesterday's conference that it would not do to close the door too tightly, for we must leave it ajar so it could be widely opened if Germany really desired peace. Asquith smiled and said "You will be a very clever man if you can do that successfully."

The situation grows hourly worse because of the German manifesto in regard to merchantmen and the sowing of mines. I tried hard to get Sir Edward and afterwards Asquith, to meet this situation before today, but with the usual British slowness they put it off until Thursday or perhaps next Tuesday.

The psychological time to have ended this war was around the end of November or the first of December when everything looked as if it had gotten into a permanent deadlock. You will remember we tried to impress this upon Sir Cecil and tried to get quicker action, but without success.

The Germans have waited until the ground in East Prussia and Poland became frozen in order to start this aggresive campaign. It seems, at the moment, as if they might be successful. If they are, it is a serious situation for the Allies.

The sad part of it all is that it might have been settled long ago and to the satisfaction of everyone, provided we could have gotten them to have acted more promptly.

Sir William Tyrrell's son was killed today. He was a boy of about twenty.   Affectionately yours,   E. M. House

I saw Sir Edward alone this evening. I read him Gerards letter. He thought it absurd, and said even if all of his predictions came true England would continue alone until a permanent peace could be made and Belgium's wrongs were righted. He also thought that nothing further could be done for the moment until this new phase of the war developed further. I have access to Sir E. at all times when he is at home and no one knows of our conferences.

TLS (WP, DLC).

ENCLOSURE I

Arthur Zimmermann to Edward Mandell House

My dear Colonel,   Berlin, February 4, 1915.

Your letter of January 3rd reached me yesterday through the kindness of Mr. Gerard.

I read with interest what you were good enough to write with reference to the desired interchange of opinion. While we are quite ready, as I wrote you before, to do our share to bring about the desired termination of the war, at the same time there are certain limits which we are unable to overstep.

What you suggest concerning the paying of an indemnity to Belgium seems hardly feasible to me. Our campaign in that country has cost the German nation such infinite sacrifices of human lives that anything in the form of such a decided yielding to the wishes of our opponents would cause the most bitter feeling among our people.

I hear that you are on your way to England at this moment and that a trip to Germany is in view. I shall be most happy to see you, should you carry out your intention and shall hope for a personal interview more satisfactory than is possible through correspondence by letter.

With kindest regards I am, My dear Colonel,

Sincerely yours, Zimmermann.

ENCLOSURE II

James Watson Gerard to Edward Mandell House

My dear Colonel: Berlin, Germany. February 15th, 1915.

I received your letter from London. I saw Zimmermann and he told me he had written to you saying they would be glad to see you etc. which is, of course, all they can do.

You will find Americans very much hated here. It is felt that we are partial to England.

They are serious here about this submarine blockade, but are willing to withdraw it if food and raw materials are allowed to enter. In other words, if England will adopt either the Declaration of London or of Paris, but they say they will not stand having their civil population starved.

Make no mistake they will win on land and probably get a separate peace from Russia, then get the same from France, or overwhelm it and put a large force in Egypt and perhaps completely blockade England.

Germany will make no peace proposal but I am sure if a reasonable peace is proposed *now* (a matter of days even hours) it would be accepted. (This on *my* authority) The Allies should send a peace proposal for an armistice to talk peace *to me verbally and secretly here.*

If it is accepted, all right, if not, no harm done, or publicity for the proposal, for *I would only make it in case I learned it would be accepted.* But Germany will pay no indemnity to Belgium or anyone else. But I tell you this peace matter is a question *almost of hours.* The submarine blockade once begun a feeling will arise which may make it impossible until after another phase of war.

If you can get such an intimation from the Allies and then

come here, it will go to the best of my belief. I do not think the Kaiser ever actually wanted war.

The feeling as I said just now is very tense against America. The sale of arms is at the bottom and the fact that we stand things from England that we would not from Germany (according to the Germans) is the cause. But it is very real and makes us all very uncomfortable.

Hope to see you soon.

Yours ever,   James W. Gerard.

P.S. I am sure of acceptance of proposal.

E N C L O S U R E   I I I

Edward Mandell House to James Watson Gerard

My dear Judge: London. February 17th, 1915.

I am enclosing you a letter for Herr Zimmermann which please read before sending so that you may be fully informed.

If I get a favorable reply I will go to Germany as soon as practicable. If the reply is unfavorable I shall drop the matter for the moment, and go to the south of Italy and await developements, for there would not be the slightest use of my remaining here longer.

With all good wishes for you all, I am,

Sincerely yours,   [E. M. House]

E N C L O S U R E   I V

Edward Mandell House to Arthur Zimmermann

My dear Herr Zimmermann: London. February 17th, 1915.

Thank you for your kind letter of February fourth.

I thought I should be able to go to Berlin early next week but it now seems best to remain here until I can have another word from you.

All of our conversations with the Ambassadors in Washington representing the belligerent nations were based upon the supposition that Germany would consent to evacuate and indemnify Belgium, and would be willing to make a settlement looking towards permanent peace.

I can readily understand the difficulty which your Government would encounter in regard to an indemnity, therefore if that question might for the moment be waived, may we assume that your Government would let the other two points make the beginning of conversations?

If we could be placed in so fortunate a position, I feel confident that parleys could at least be commenced.

I need not tell you, Sir, what great moral advantage this position would give Germany, and how expectantly the neutral nations would look towards the Allies that they would meet so fair an attitude.

Your favorable reply to this will, I believe, mark the beginning of the end of this unhappy conflict.

I am, my dear Herr Zimmermann,

Sincerely yours,   [E. M. House]

E N C L O S U R E   V

Edward Mandell House to James Watson Gerard

My dear Judge: [London] February 18th, 1915.

Your letter of the 15th came to me yesterday. I immediately saw Sir Edward Grey. He said it was utterly impossible to make any such hasty proposal as you thought the situation required.

If things had gone on quietly for a few weeks longer, I feel sure we could have gotten these belligerents together, but the blockade has, for the moment, brought everything to a standstill.

As far as I can see, there is no prospect now of my getting to Berlin soon, so I take it, we will have to let the matter drift until another period of deadlock ensues.

I sincerely hope that the good relations between Germany and the United States will not be interrupted. I know how earnestly the President desires to be on good terms with all, and I am sure that your every effort is bent in that direction.

It is a great disappointment to me that I cannot be with you at an early date, but this unexpected phase has upset all plans.

With warm regards and good wishes, I am,

Faithfully yours,   [E. M. House]

TCL (WP, DLC).

From Pussy de Spoelberch and E. de Spoelberch

Dear Mr. Wilson: Brussels, 18th February, 1915

Thank you very much for the good bread. The poor people in our villages were starving for they had nothing to eat, but now that you have sent over to our dear little country a big provision of wheat, both rich and poor can live—thanks to the Americans.

Best love and wishes from little

Pussy de Spoelberch
(nine years old)

I join in with my sister in thanking you too, for it is jolly good bread, enough to satisfy any schoolboy's hunger.

E. De Spoelberch
(nine years and seven days)

TCL (C. L. Swem Coll., NjP).

Walter Hines Page to Sir Edward Grey

Personal

Dear Sir Edward: London. Feb. 18, 1915

I am glad to inform you that the order forbidding the publication for 30 days of ships' manifests has been rescinded by the Secretary of the Treasury.

Yours Sincerely,   Walter H. Page

ALS (E. Grey Papers, FO 800/85, p. 102, PRO).

To Joseph Patrick Tumulty

Dear Tumulty,   [The White House, c. Feb. 19, 1915]

I would very much like your advice about what Mr. Bryan suggests as to the newspaper men. Their methods are jeoparding not only the dignity but the very peace and safety of the country.

W.W.

WWTLI (WP, DLC).

Three Letters to William Jennings Bryan

My dear Mr. Secretary,   [The White House] 19 February, 1915.

I am cheered to see the "ray of hope" and we must follow it as best we can.

I would be deeply obliged if you and Mr. Lansing would put the suggestions you here make into shape for immediate use in despatches, against the time when we shall see the full official text of the German note.

Page ought to be told at once that the offensive word complained of was not addressed to Great Britain, but appears only in a note sent to us and confidentially communicated to the British government by us merely for their information and guidance. It ought not to stand in the way of anything that can be done.

Faithfully Yours,   W.W.

WWTLI (SDR, RG 59, 763.72/13422, DNA).

My dear Mr. Secretary,   [The White House] 19 February, 1915.

All your suggestions about the use to be made of this statement[1] seem to me admirable. I hope that you will act on them.

Faithfully Yours,   W.W.

[1] The statement of the Vicar-General of Mexico City.

My dear Mr. Secretary,   [The White House] 19 February, 1915.

Pardon me for not having made myself clear.

I am not willing to consider Senator O'Gorman's suggestions at all. They are all made, I have found, for personal reasons and without regard to the interests of the public service.[1]

With regard to Mr. Walker, I am frank to say that, much as I like him, I think his gifts are those of the newspaper man and are not of the kind that fit him fir [for] responsible pu[b]lic office. This is not in the least degree a reflection on his character, but only a comment on the real character of his gifts.

Faithfully Yours,   W.W.

WWTLI (W. J. Bryan Papers, DNA).
[1] Wilson must have relented about O'Sullivan. In any event, he soon became a confidential clerk to Tumulty in the White House while attending the law school of George Washington University.

From William Jennings Bryan, with Enclosure

My dear Mr. President: Washington February 19, 1915.

I am enclosing a telegram drawn along the line suggested in my letter of yesterday and approved in principle by you.

We have tried to make this telegram as mild and inoffensive as we can make it and yet cover the matters which it was necessary to include. It is submitted for your consideration and criticism.

The only suggestion I have to make is in regard to the question as to whether we shall propose to distribute food from this country only or from *any* neutral country. I am inclined to think that we had better put in parenthesis, after the word "United States," the words "or from any neutral country desiring us to act for it."

My reason for inclining to this is that it might seem selfish of us if our effort was confined to food from this country. It is not likely that any other country would ask us because I think we could persuade Great Britain to let each neutral country distribute food exported by it to Germany. If, however, we confine our offer to our country and Great Britain refuses to extend the same arrangement to other countries, it would create great complaint and the unselfishness of our purpose would be questioned.

However, this is merely a suggestion and relates only to a detail. I am deeply impressed with the importance of this communication. I believe the time is ripe for the proposal and it will be hailed with rejoicing by all the neutral countries if it succeeds —and I think the sober second thought of the belligerent countries would support it, for surely they cannot find any excuse except the sternest necessity for the resort to such unusual, not to say cruel, remedies as they propose.

With assurances of high respect I am, my dear Mr. President,
Yours very sincerely,　W. J. Bryan

TLS (W. J. Bryan Papers, DLC).

E N C L O S U R E

To Ambassadors Page and Gerard[1]

[Washington] February 19, 1915.

You will please deliver to Sir Edward Gray　the German Foreign Office　the following identical note which we are sending England and Germany:

In view of the correspondence which has passed between this Government and Great Britain and Germany respectively relative to the Declaration of a war zone by the German Admiralty and the use of neutral flags by British merchant vessels, this Government ⟨hopes that⟩ *ventures to express the hope that* the two belligerent governments may, through reciprocal concessions, find a basis for agreement which will relieve neutral ships engaged in peaceful commerce from the great dangers which they will incur in the high seas adjacent to the coasts of the belligerents.

⟨For the purpose of furnishing an opportunity to discuss this subject, the United States submits tentatively [[and in the most friendly spirit]] the following terms of an agreement, to which it earnestly invites the careful consideration and comment or suggestion of each government:⟩

The Government of the United States respectfully suggests that an agreement in terms like the following might be entered into. This suggestion is not to be regarded as in any sense a proposal made by this Government, for it of course fully recognizes that it is not its privilege to propose terms of agreement between Great Britain and Germany, even though the matter be one in which it and the people of the United States are directly and deeply interested. It is merely venturing to take the liberty which it hopes may be accorded a sincere friend desirous of embarrassing neither nation involved and of serving, if it may, the common interests of humanity. The course outlined is offered in the hope that it may draw forth the views and elicit the suggestions of the British and German governments on a matter of capital interest to the whole world.

Germany and Great Britain to agree

(1) That neither will sow any floating mines, whether upon the high seas or in territorial waters; that neither will plant on the high seas anchored mines except within cannon range of harbors for defensive purposes only; and that all mines shall bear the stamp of the government planting them and be so constructed as to become harmless if separated from their moorings;

(2) That neither will use submarines to attack merchant vessels of any nationality except to enforce the right of visit and search;

(3) That each will require their respective merchant vessels not to use neutral flags for the purpose of disguise or *ruse de guerre.*[2]

Germany to agree

That all importations of food or foodstuffs from the United States [[(and from such other neutral countries as may ask it)]] into Germany shall be consigned to ⟨American⟩ agencies to be ⟨established⟩ *designated* by the United States Government; that these American agencies shall have entire charge and control without interference on the part of the German Government, of the receipt and distribution of such importations, and shall distribute them solely to retail dealers bearing licenses from The German Government entitling them to receive and furnish such food and foodstuffs to non-combatants only; that any violation of the terms of the retailers' licenses shall work a forfeiture of their rights to receive such food and foodstuffs for this purpose; and that such food and foodstuffs will not be requisitioned by the German Government for any purpose whatsoever, or be diverted to the use of the armed forces of Germany.

Great Britain to agree:

That food and foodstuffs will not be placed upon the absolute contraband list and that shipments of such commodities will not be interfered with or detained by British authorities if consigned to ⟨American⟩ agencies ⟨established⟩ *designated* by the United States Government in Germany for the receipt and distribution of such cargoes to licensed German retailers for distribution solely to the non-combatant population.

In submitting this proposed basis of agreement this Government ⟨has no purpose of⟩ *does not wish to be understood as* admitting or denying any belligerent or neutral right established by the principles of international law, but ⟨considers⟩ *would consider* the agreement, if acceptable to the interested powers, a *modus vivendi*[3] based upon expediency rather than legal right and as not binding upon the United States either in its present form or in a modified form until accepted by this Government.

⟨Robert Lansing⟩
Bryan[4]

T telegram (SDR, RG 59, 763.72/1498a, DNA).
  [1] The italicized words in the following document are Wilson's; words in angle brackets were deleted by him; words in double brackets were inserted by Bryan.
  [2] Italicized in the original draft.
  [3] *Ibid.*
  [4] Dispatched in this revised form to London and Berlin on February 20, 1915, and printed in *FR-WWS 1915*, pp. 119-20.

James Watson Gerard to William Jennings Bryan

Berlin, via Rome. Feb. 19 [1915]

1649. Strictly confidential.

Yours about Colonel House received. Favorable moment is passing. Germans have gained great victory over Russians, are following it up and will soon turn and break through French lines. Germany will never make proposal but if Colonel House can come here bringing secret reasonable proposal it will be accepted in all probability but Germany will never pay an indemnity to Belgium and on contrary will probably expect all or part of Congo and perhaps indemnity from France for portion now occupied.   Gerard.

T telegram (WP, DLC).

From Charles William Eliot

Dear President Wilson: Cambridge, Mass. 19 February, 1915

I see the nature of the quandary, but I do not see that it was the duty of your Administration to put yourself into that quandary. The neutral right to buy ships from citizens of belligerent countries during war may exist; but has it ever been good for anything? Has it ever been a right which a prudent and genuine neutral would want to exercise? You did not propose to exercise that right; because you saw clearly that it was an irritating and, therefore, inexpedient thing to do. Your very pleasant note of the 18th, consequently, leaves me still in doubt as to the object you had in view in risking party unity and success on the Shipping Bill, particularly on the Bill in its original form, for which the Administration was held responsible.

I wonder if the Administration has all the advice it needs about international law and custom about contraband, partial contraband, and the right of seizure to search for contraband. Professor George G. Wilson of Harvard knows much about that subject, having been for many years an acceptable teacher of International Law at the Naval War College at Newport, and having also been a member of the recent Conference at London. He is a quiet, judicious man, who keeps his head.

The War is teaching many things about the best equipment of an army and of a navy. I hope we shall not spend any unusual amount of money on war equipment or forts, until we can learn what sort of munitions, forts, and vessels are the most effective. One of the most curious demonstrations thus far given is the return to the primitive man-to-man collision with what amounts to a short spear or long sword—the bayonet. The efficiency of trenches and the inefficiency of forts seem to be proved. Are all the nations going to give up armored vessels?

One could wish that Brazil, Argentina, or Chile would propose that those three nations, the United States, and Spain should combine to set Mexico in order, each Government contributing an appropriate portion of the military and naval force which would be needed. The South American countries might not favor the inclusion of Spain in such a group; but, historically considered, it would be rather pleasing. An American League to set Mexico, and perhaps Hayti and San Domingo, in order, would be a suggestive precedent for a European League to keep the peace of Europe. Does not the doctrine that Mexico must be

permitted to stew in her own juice leave something to be desired
from the Christian Brotherhood point of view?

Sincerely yours,   Charles W. Eliot

TLS (WP, DLC).

Count Johann Heinrich von Bernstorff
to the German Foreign Office

[Washington] 19. Februar 1915

Nr. 287. Im Anschluß an *Tel. Nr. 281.*

Senatskomitee für auswärtige Angelegenheiten nahm heute
hinter verschlosenen Türen Mitteilungen Herrn Wilsons ent-
gegen, hinsichtlich der durch unsern Unterseebootskrieg geschaf-
fenen Lage. Diese wurde, wie ich unter der Hand hörte, in den
Mitteilungen als "ominous but not alarming" bezeichnet.[1]

Ich glaube nicht, daß hiesige Regierung sich entschließen
wird, in England diplomatische Schritte zu tun, welche die Situation verbessern könnten, da sie immer unbeteilit bleiben will.
Indes würde m. E. die Zerstörung eines amerikanischen Schiffes
eine außerordentlich bedenkliche Erregung schaffen, welche die
schlimmsten Folgen haben könnte. Ich rate dringend, *House*
kommen zu lassen oder wenn er schon dort ist, Lage mit ihm
zu besprechen. Er hat hier mehr Einfluß als irgend ein anderer.

Bernstorff.

T telegram (Weltkrieg No. 2, geheim, Vermittlungsaktionen, 4272 D 955893,
GFO-Ar).

[1] No newspaper printed a report about this meeting. Bernstorff's typist or the
decoder in Berlin must have garbled "ominous but not alarming." Surely Bernstorff wrote "alarming but not ominous."

TRANSLATION

[Washington] 19 Feb. 1915

With reference to my *telegram No. 281.*

Senate Committee on Foreign Relations today received behind
closed doors statements by Mr. Wilson concerning the situation
created by our submarine war. This situation was labeled in the
statements, as I heard it from confidential sources, as "ominous
but not alarming."

I do not believe that the government here will decide to take
diplomatic steps against England that could improve the situation, because it has always desired to avoid entanglements. I
believe, however, that the destruction of an American ship would

create an extraordinarily serious commotion which could have the worst consequences. I advise urgently to have *House* come, or, if he is already there, to discuss the situation with him. He has more influence here than anyone else. Bernstorff

To Edward Mandell House

[The White House, Feb. 20, 1915]

Yours of the 17th received. It will of course occur to you that you cannot go too far in allowing the English government to determine when it is best for you to go to Germany because they will naturally desire to await some time when they have the strategic advantage because of events in the field or elsewhere. If the impression were to be created in Berlin that you were to go only when the British government thought it the opportune time for you to go, you might be regarded when you reached there as their spokesman rather than my own. I think you can frankly state this dilemma to Sir Edward Grey. He will doubtless realize how important it is to learn Germany's mind at the earliest possible moment. No one can be sure what a single day may develop either in events or in opinion. The whole atmosphere may change at any moment.

We are sending today identical notes to the British and German governments. Please say to Page that he cannot emphasize too much in presenting the note to the British government the favorable opinion which would be created in this country if the British government could see its way clear to adopt the suggestions therein made. Opinion here is still decidedly friendly but a tone of great uneasiness is distinctly audible now, and events [and decisions] of the next few days will undoubtedly make a deep impression.

T transcripts of WWsh telegram (WP, DLC; WC NjP).

From Joseph Patrick Tumulty

Dear Governor: The White House. February 20th [1915].

I agree with Mr. Bryan in what he seeks to accomplish, but I do not think the action he is about to take is a wise move.

I will be glad to discuss this matter with you.

The Secretary.

TL (WP, DLC).

A Telegram and a Letter from Edward Mandell House

[London] February 20th, 1915.

The new phase has merely halted negotiations momentarily, and I hope to be able to go to Germany within two weeks. Meantime I am holding frequent absolutely private conferences with Sir Edward Grey who has been working earnestly and sincerely with us.

The Russian situation is not so bad as reported by Germany but a deadlock is again expected there.

The present attack on Dardenelles is serious and it is thought they may be forced within only two weeks. Then Sir Edward Grey believes I should go to Germany.

There is no immediate prospect for compromise on blockade question, but the door is not absolutely shut.

T transcript of WWsh decode (WC, NjP).

Dear Governor: London. February 20th, 1915.

I hope you will not always feel that Page's despatches express my full views.

On Thursday he sent a despatch in regard to a compromise which we thought might be effected between Germany and England concerning the latest phase of maritime warfare.[1]

I thought it misleading and that it did not express the situation as it existed, for while I was urging Grey to bring about such a compromise, and while he regarded it with some favor, I thought it could readily be seen that the Naval and Military Departments would most likely veto it, and the chance of successful negociation was slender.

Then, too, I suggested the modification of Bernstorff's note before sending it to the Foreign Office. This he thought he could not do, while it seemed to me it could only result in making the feeling worse.

I am telling you this without the slightest criticism of Page, for he may have been right in both instances, but I merely want you to know that my views and his are not always the same.

I also want you to know that his name is sometimes signed to the despatches I send you, but he does not know the contents, or even that I have sent them. It is done in the Embassy under the belief that they will be expedited.

Affectionately yours,   E. M. House

TLS (WP, DLC).

[1] It is printed as an Enclosure with WJB to WW, Feb. 18, 1915 (third letter of that date).

From Thomas Dixon, Jr.

Dear Mr President: [New York] Feb. 20, 1915

I must thank you for the gracious and beautiful way in which you received and made happy my friends and associates at the White House Thursday Evening.[1] They had heard much of your "austere and unapproachable" character. They came away wildly enthusiastic. After that evening they hold you the foremost exemplar of true American Democracy.

You made our operators so proud & happy with the cordial handshakes you gave them, I fear the boys will hardly speak to their boss. I wish you could have heard the half of what they have been saying about you—it would cheer you in your moments of weariness.

I must express to you also my pride & pleasure in meeting your lovely daughters—no photograph I have ever seen gives even the remotest idea of the charm & beauty of their personality.

Don't overwork yourself. You have great deeds yet to do for our Nation.

With my best love, Sincerely Thomas Dixon

ALS (WP, DLC).

[1] Dixon and a projection crew showed "The Birth of a Nation" for Wilson and his family and wives of cabinet members in the East Room of the White House on the evening of February 18. There is a tradition, repeated, for example, in Raymond A. Cook, *Fire from the Flint: The Amazing Careers of Thomas Dixon* (Winston-Salem, N. C., 1968), p. 170, that Wilson, after the showing, said to Dixon: "It is like writing history with lightning. And my only regret is that it is all so terribly true." This quotation first appears (without attribution) in all known sources and literature in Milton MacKaye, "The Birth of a Nation," *Scribner's Magazine*, CII (Nov. 1937), 69. Dixon did not use the quotation in his memoirs, "Southern Horizons" (composition date unknown).

Marjorie Brown King, the only survivor among the persons at the showing in the East Room, told the Editor on June 23, 1977, that Wilson seemed lost in thought during the showing, and that he walked out of the room without saying a word when the movie was over.

From Edward Mandell House

[London, Feb. 21, 1915]

Your yesterday's dispatch received. Sir Edward Grey does not so much desire an advantage before I go to Berlin but that there should neither be such a great disadvantage as now. His colleagues, the majority of these people, and both Russia and France do not want negotiations to begin now. Sir Edward Grey looks upon the situation as fairly and dispassionately as we, but he cannot act alone. Germany refuses to indemnify Belgium and has not yet consented to begin parleys on a basis of evacuation of Belgium and a permanent peace settlement. Unless she yields these two points, no start can be made either now or in the future. Even if Germany consents to this basis as a beginning, it would be impossible for Sir Edward Grey to get the Allies to agree at the present moment. Therefore not even the beginning of the end is in sight. We must be patient; to be otherwise is to lose the advantage we have gained here. The general public in England does not like us very well, and Gerard says we are now hated in Germany.

T transcript of WWsh decode (WP, DLC).

To Edward Mandell House

[The White House, Feb. 22, 1915]

I learned yesterday through our friend[1] here that Bernstorff showed great relief when he learned directly from his government that you would receive "a most cordial welcome from them any time you chose to come." He reports Bernstorff as seeming anxious and worried. Do you get it directly from Zimmermann or from Gerard that the terms you suggested as basis for parleys in your letter to Zimmermann would not be considered? I understand the situation but want to be sure of each element in it.

T transcript of WWsh telegram (WP, DLC).
 [1] Hugh C. Wallace to WW, Feb. 21, 1915, ALS (WP, DLC).

From Edward Mandell House

[London, Feb. 22, 1915]

Zimmermann wrote me no indemnity to Belgium would be possible but said nothing about evacuation. Gerard makes it stronger and adds that Germany will not suggest terms but will consider terms if offered by Allies. I have written Zimmermann saying that the whole bases of our conversation have been predicated upon evacuation and indemnity and permanent settlement but that indemnity might be waived for the moment if Germany [would consent] to the other two conditions as a beginning. If I receive a favorable reply I will go to Germany and sound them further although they will have to concede more before any important progress is made. The Prime Minister said to Page yesterday that he hoped that I would not go just now. We are not losing time but simply getting the situation in satisfactory condition for future action.

T transcripts of WWsh decode (WP, DLC; WC, NjP).

Wilson in the Oval Office

At a Baseball Game with Helen Bones

The Secretary of State Is Amused
(Bryan with Albert S. Burleson)

Walter Hines Page

Edward Mandell House

Constantin Theodor Dumba

Count Johann Heinrich von Bernstorff

Jean Jules Jusserand

From William Jennings Bryan

My dear Mr. President: Washington February 22d, 1915.

Our telegram to Tokio had the desired effect. It brought out the fact that the additional concessions[1] were presented as *requests*—not as demands. They were presented at the same times that the demands were made but the Ambassador, who called today, in leaving the memorandum which I enclose,[2] explained that there is a material difference between the presentation of the *requests* contained in this article and the *demands* set forth in the memorandum left with us. He emphasizes the fact that he, himself, did not know of these additional *requests*; but when the papers kept reiterating them he made inquiry of his Government.

You have a flimsey of the telegram just received from Guthrie[3] and from it I think you will draw the same inference that I did, namely, that they will not press these requests. I think our telegram will contribute something toward the disposition on their part not to press the requests.

I tried to get you by phone this morning but had to leave the house before you were able to come to the phone, and, having to go by and call on Solicitor Johnson (who, by the way is improved) I had not reached the office when you called me here.

I was going to ask you whether it would not be well to repeat to Peking our telegram to Guthrie and then give him the substance of our recent communication from Tokio. While these communications are confidential I presume that we are at liberty to communicate them to our representatives who are directly interested, although, in doing so I fear that it will be difficult to keep the Chinese Government from knowing what the Japanese Government has communicated to us.

What answer do you think we ought to make to Guthrie's telegram, now that we have both it and the enclosed memorandum left by the Japanese Ambassador?

It seems to me it might be well for us to present your views on the subject now that these requests have been officially communicated and the following is the way the matter presents itself to me:

(Sections Two and Seven[4] need not be considered since they are not objectionable.)

One: As to the first, it may be assumed that the Chinese Government would not discriminate unfairly in the employment of advisors—an advisor, of course, having no power to compel the acceptance of the advice given.

I do not know of any other Government that asks for the employment of any of its citizens as advisors. Surely this Government does not although it is perfectly willing to have Americans employed by China in any capacity.

Third: The Japanese Ambassador informs us, as does Mr. Guthrie, that the paragraph in regard to the employment of Japanese police officers relates to Manchuria only.

That was the most menacing of the requests because it did not as published limit the area of their employment and left it to be inferred that Japan desired to share in the general police system of the country. Even as it is, it is objectionable unless it is understood that Manchuria is to pass over entirely to Japan. I am not sure but that it would be worth while for China to agree to the cession of Manchuria to Japan if, by doing so, she could secure freedom as to the rest of the country. As China probably would not be willing to give up Manchuria she would rightfully object to being forced to organize joint police control.

Fourth: The proposition that China should buy a certain percentage of her arms of Japan, or establish in China joint Chino-Japanese factories for the manufacture of Chinese arms is, to my mind, quite objectionable.

No other country is asking for any such privilege and it is so closely connected with the control of the country as to impair the political independence of China, not to speak of an infringement of the "open door" policy.

Fifth: The railway concessions asked for in Paragraph 5 ought not to be granted unless China desires to grant them.

In view of the experiences she has had I should think that China would quit granting railroad concessions and build for herself the railroads she needs. If she lets a concession to the capitalists of any country they insist upon extensions and then desire to control the territory through which they go, as, see for instance, the request now being made in the province in which the German road was built.

Sixth: The provision asked for in regard to the province of Fukien would virtually close that province to other countries because Japan would not be likely to allow foreign capital to go in there. This would bring another province under Japanese control.

In other words, there are two objections to the five requests made: First—that they menace the political integrity of China; and, Second—that they interfere with the agreement for the equal treatment of all nations.

If you think it wise to bring this matter to the attention of

Japan we can follow the plan adopted in the last telegram and express gratification that these are not made as demands but merely presented as requests, and, thus, our discussion of them upon their merits will not be objectionable.[5]

With assurances of high respect I am, my dear Mr. President,

Yours very sincerely,   W. J. Bryan

TLS (SDR, RG 59, 793.94/240, DNA).

[1] That is, Group V.

[2] [Japanese Embassy], T memorandum (WP, DLC). It is printed in *FR 1915*, p. 97.

[3] Ambassador Guthrie to WJB, Feb. 21, 1915, *ibid.*, p. 96. Bryan gives its significant details in his letter.

[4] They concerned the right of Japanese hospitals, schools, and churches in the interior to own land and the right of Japanese missionaries to propagandize religious teachings in China.

[5] See WW to WJB, Feb. 25, 1915.

From Joseph Edward Davies

Personal!

Dear Mr. President: [Washington, Feb. 22, 1915]

I cannot permit this occasion to go by without trespassing upon your tolerance a moment that I may express my really heart felt appreciation of your confidence.[1] That is what I value above all else! And it is that, which will insistently stimulate the best I have to give in your service and that of the country in this work, to which you have assigned me.

The Commission[2] you have named is unusually well balanced. It will, I believe justify your confidence. It has a great work ahead of it. Providence helping, it can aid in the solution of the great problem, which you have so clearly stated of the relationship of industry to government, to the end that representative institutions may persist. It holds within it promise of substantial part of that wonderful contribution, which your administration will give to the life of the nation in enduring measure, in those programs which you foresaw, stated and accomplished into law.

Believe me to be deeply grateful that you should have designated me to be one of those to do this work, and believe me further to be always,

Faithfully Yours,   Joseph E. Davies

ALS (WP, DLC).

[1] Wilson had just appointed him chairman of the Federal Trade Commission.

[2] The other commissioners nominated were Edward Nash Hurley, William Julius Harris, Will H. Parry, and George Rublee.

From James Kerney

My dear Governor   [Trenton, N. J.] Feby 22 [1915]

I was engaged this afternoon in the delicate task of informing Geo Record that he was not to go on the Trade Board when the wire brought the news that the Board had already been named. I never saw a better exhibition of good losing. I suppose George has had so many raps on the head that disappointments no longer have any terror for him. Following the inquest we went over to the Sterling for lunch with Matt Ely and Jim Blauvelt and before the others had fully recovered their composure Record was busily engaged seeking our views as to just where was his greatest opportunity for service to the cause for which you have been battling. Not the faintest evidence of soreness or resentment. I felt you would be interested in hearing how this loyal old scout and admirer acted.

You certainly have had your full share of hard fighting and I trust the trip to California will bring you much rest and recreation. Your friends back home think of you often and appreciate the fine work you are doing for America. They are not affected by any snap judgments of the hour

With best wishes for your continued good health and happiness, I am   Always sincerely yours   James Kerney

ALS (WP, DLC).

From Seth Low and Others

Tuskegee Institute, Ala., Feb. 22, 1915.

The board of trustees of the Tuskegee Institute have heard with profound regret that the proposed appropriation of $101,-000 for Howard University has been stricken out in the House of Representatives on a point of order. Assuming that an appropriation which has been made for twenty five years more or less in some amount has been constitutionally made this board earnestly asks you to use your influence to restore this item to the proper appropriation bill, because of training leaders for the ten millions of negroes of the United States will suffer serious injury if this be not done.

> Seth Low, Chairman,
> Booker T. Washington, Principal,
> Frank Trubull [Trumbull], Julius Risenwald [Rosenwald].[1]

T telegram (WP, DLC).

¹ The House reversed its vote on this appropriation on February 23. Concerned about the fate of the appropriation in the conference committee, Wilson wrote to Tumulty: "Please send this to the proper Senator, saying that I have asked you to do so and that the matter has given me some concern." WW to JPT, n.d., TL (WP, DLC).

Remarks at a Press Conference

February 23, 1915

Mr. President, will there be any reply at all to either the note of Great Britain or of Germany?

> I haven't had time to go into that matter, to know whether that—I mean what further talk or not.

The demands that are made by Japan upon China under our treaty rights and obligations—would that become any of our business?

> Well, I don't think it would be wise for me to express an opinion about that, because I haven't gone over it thoroughly enough to be justified in expressing an opinion.

Any conflict as to the exact status?

> Yes, there is a conflict of evidence as to just what demands were made, and in what way they were made.

And we are not yet sufficiently informed to formulate a policy?

> Not sufficiently to adopt a policy.

To return to those notes, there is nothing you know of at this time which would alter our position in either matter?

> Not in the least. The only question, you see, in my mind, is whether it is necessary to state our position again or not.

Mr. President, at the time the English planted mines in the North Sea, it was reported that they had offered to furnish pilots to American vessels going through that area. Do you know whether that practice is being kept up now?

> They did maintain that. They carefully designated the area so that any captain familiar with his chart could keep out of trouble.

Mr. President, in the appointments on the Federal Trade Commission board there is refusal in Congress, on the alleged ground that there is no Republican on that board. Was it your belief that you had named a Republican?

> Certainly. Mr. Parry is a Republican. The act says that not more than three shall be Democrats. I can appoint a Prohibitionist, I suppose, if I want to. But Mr. Parry I have every reason to believe has always been a Republican, and Mr. Rublee too, for that matter.

Can you say anything as to your attitude toward the seamen's bill, Mr. President?

What state is that in? I saw something yesterday in the paper that it is in conference. Is it in conference?

In the House, with the so-called conservative end on its—

You say it's in conference, eh?

Apparently with the House bill being preferred in the Senate.

I am not in touch with it.

The story went out last night that you were likely to veto it.

Nobody was authorized to say that. I haven't considered the bill at all.

Mr. President, even though there should be no action on the ship purchase bill at this session, is the danger of an extra session passed?

I honestly think that there is a possibility of its passing, yes.

Do you anticipate, Mr. President, that that bill will be at all changed in Congress to meet any objections at either end of the Capitol?

No, I do not. It may be changed in Congress to be a little more explicit on some points, but not by way of substantial alteration. . . .

One paper states this morning that you have given some consideration to an embargo on foodstuffs and war ammunitions, with a view to determining whether or not an embargo is constitutional?

No, sir, that is not true. I also learn that I have a bad attack of influenza, which I am happy to deny.

Mr. President, there is a great deal of tension over this war zone situation. Can you give any encouragement on that situation now?

I haven't any new light of any kind on it.

Mr. President, has there been any further inquiry into the complaints of the German and Austrian ambassadors with regard to the manufacture of submarines in this country for shipment abroad?

Oh, yes. When I last met the cabinet, the Secretary of the Navy said he was having a very thorough investigation made. He has not reported to me yet, and I don't know what the result is. But we will follow the matter up very carefully.

JRT transcript (WC, NjP) of CLSsh (C. L. Swem Coll., NjP).

To John Sharp Williams

My dear Senator: [The White House] February 23, 1915.

I hope you will feel that it is never an intrusion for you to write me or to speak about anything you choose to speak about.

I appreciate the reasons urged for an interval between sessions in your letter of February fifteenth[1] and you may be sure that they are very prominent in my own mind and that I want to act upon them.

May I not say how glad I am that you favor a reasonable rule with regard to concluding debate in the Senate. I think that such a rule is not only necessary for the conduct of business in that body, but that it is necessary in order to regain the confidence of the country in the efficiency of the Senate. Such a rule need not prevent the most thorough debate.

Cordially and sincerely yours,   Woodrow Wilson

TLS (Letterpress Books, WP, DLC).
  [1] J. S. Williams to WW, Feb. 15, 1915, TLS (WP, DLC).

To Robert Newton Page

My dear Mr. Page: [The White House] February 23, 1915

May I not thank you very warmly indeed for your letter of February seventeenth?[1]

I hope you know how entirely I respect and honor you. I have been grieved, of course, that you could not support me in such matters as the vote on the ship purchase bill. The fact that you could not has, however, made me question my own judgment more than it made me question your confidence in me or your loyalty to the party. I do feel very strongly that party government is not possible unless the judgment of individuals can yield to the determinations of party councils, but I have no doubt that that consideration is as prominent in your own mind as in my own and that you do not need to have it recalled.

Pray never think that any false impression will be lodged in my mind as to your motives.

Cordially and sincerely yours,   Woodrow Wilson

TLS (Letterpress Books, WP, DLC).
  [1] R. N. Page to WW, Feb. 17, 1915, TLS (WP, DLC).

To Charles William Eliot

Personal.

My dear Doctor Eliot: The White House February 23, 1915

While it is true, as you say, that the right of neutral nations to buy ships from citizens of belligerent countries during war has never proved of much practical value, it would in this case be of very considerable advantage, because we know that it would be quite feasible to buy such ships and put them upon the direct trade between this country and South America. The only complications that would arise would spring out of putting them upon their old trade routes or attempting to operate them between this country and European ports.

You are very kind to suggest the name of Professor George G. Wilson. As a matter of fact, we have constituted and have been consulting for a number of months a little council on questions of international law made up of some of the well-known students of the subject in the country,[1] and have done so greatly to our advantage.

The suggestion you make as to a possible means of settlement in Mexico would commend itself to me more strongly if it did not seem to involve the use of force. I feel that nothing but the extreme necessity would justify that.

Cordially and sincerely yours,   Woodrow Wilson

TLS (C. W. Eliot Papers, MH-Ar).
[1] The Joint State-Navy Neutrality Board, about which see J. Daniels to WW, Aug. 22, 1914, n. 1, Vol. 30.

From Edward Mandell House

Dear Governor: London. February 23rd, 1915.

In reply to your cablegram of the 20th indicating that you thought there was danger of my yielding too far to the wishes of this Government in deferring my visit to Berlin, I tried to give you some explanation in my reply, which I sent yesterday.

Up to now, all we know is that Germany refuses to indemnify Belgium, and also refuses to make any proposition herself. She may or may not be willing to evacuate Belgium and consider proposals looking to permanent peace. But even if she concedes these two cardinal points, it is well to remember that neither Russia nor France is willing to now make peace on any such terms.

When the Russian Minister of Finance and the French Minister for Foreign Affairs were here, Sir Edward told them of your letter and of my presence. He also told them what I thought might be accomplished now, and he asked them whether or not they would like to have a conference with me. They both preferred not doing so, stating that the time was not opportune for peace proposals, for the reason that it was certain that Germany, being so far successful, would not acquiesce in such terms as their governments would demand.

The British public and a majority of the Cabinet would not

look with any greater favor upon the only terms that Germany would now concede, than would France and Russia.

Since the war has begun and since they consider that Germany was the aggressor and is the exponent of militarism, they are determined not to cease fighting until there is no hope of victory, or until Germany is ready to concede what they consider a fair and permanent settlement.

It is almost as important to us to have the settlement laid upon the right foundations as it is to the nations of Europe. If this war does not end militarism, then the future is full of trouble for us.

If there was any reason to believe that Germany was ready to make such terms as the Allies are ready to accept, then it would be well to go immediately, but all our information is to the contrary, and the result of my visit there now would be to lose the sympathetic interest which England, and through her, the Allies, now feel in your endeavors and without accomplishing any good in Germany.

You may put it down as a certainty that Germany will only use you in the event it suits her purposes to do so, and she will not be deterred from this if, at any time, she sees that it is to her advantage to accept your good offices.

Asquith told Page yesterday that he sincerely hoped that I would not make the mistake of going just now. That simply means, if I do go, they will probably cease to consider you as a medium.

If Zimmermann replies to my letter, then I shall go to Berlin and have a conference with him, but it will accomplish nothing for the moment, for he will not now go further, and the Allies will not be willing to begin parleys upon such a basis.

Sir Edward is extremely anxious for England to take the highest possible grounds, and not ask for anything excepting the evacuation and indemnifying of Belgium and a settlement that will insure permanent peace. But, there again, he comes in conflict with Colonial opinion. The South African Colonies have no notion of giving up German Africa which they have taken, as they say it will be a constant menace to them to have so powerful and warlike a neighbor.

The same applies to the Caroline Islands, Samoa, etc. which the Australians have taken.

Sir Edward is trying assiduously to work up an opinion upon broader lines, and he may or may not be successful, but he is not now in a position to say that his wishes will prevail.

There are two things that are possible, not probable. One is that Germany may be successful. If France or Russia give way, she will soon dominate the Continent, and it is not altogether written that one or the other will not give way. Even if the Allies hold together, there is a possibility that the war may continue another year.

It is to be remembered that Europe is not normal now, and what they may or may not do, cannot be judged by the ordinary rules of logic.

I try very hard not to think of it any more than I did at home, and I try to talk of it as little as possible, so that my mind may be clear to look at the situation dispassionately.

The one sane, big figure here is Sir Edward Grey, and the chances are all in favor of his being the dominant personality when the final settlement comes, and I believe it is the part of wisdom to continue to keep in as close and sympathetic touch with him as now.

If I go to Germany I shall try to remain there for a long time, provided I can arrange to have Tyrrell or someone else meet me from time to time in Holland, and with, of course, the knowledge and consent of the German Government.

I note now with interest that occasionally Sir Edward speaks of "that second convention which the President may call." He has come to look upon it as one of the hopes for the future, and if we accomplish nothing else, you will be able to do the most important world's work within sight.

I have reason to believe that this Government will be ready to make great concessions in that convention in regard to the future of shipping, commerce, etc. during periods of war. It is my purpose to keep this "up my sleeve," and when I go to Germany, use it to bring favorable opinion to you by intimating that I believe when the end comes, you will insist upon this being done. In other words, that, with your initiative and with Germany's cooperation, Great Britain can be induced to make these terms. This I think will please the Germans and may go a long wat [way] towards placating their feelings towards us.

Again, I want to suggest, that it might be wise, under certain circumstances, for me to disappear from the war zone altogether and drift into Italy or Spain, and wait a more opportune time. I shall not do this, of course, unless it seems the part of wisdom.

Please remember, too, that my name has never been mentioned, as far as I know, either directly or indirectly, on this side of the water, and it matters but little what they say at home as long as we can keep it out of the European press.

Affectionately yours,   E. M. House

TLS (WP, DLC).

From Francis Clement Kelley

My dear Mr. President: New York, February 23, 1915.

First of all I desire to thank you for the long and very satisfactory hearing of a few weeks ago, in which you gave me an opportunity of expressing the views of the exiled Bishops of Mexico, and of the Board of Governors of The Catholic Church Extension Society on the Mexican situation. I realized that your time was very much taken up, and that many important matters were awaiting your attention. That made my appreciation of your courtesy all the greater.

I promised that I would commit to writing some of the most important points touched upon. I do this now with very great pleasure, feeling confident, after my interview with you, of your desire to know every detail of the Mexican situation and to work out Mexican problems for the best interests of the people of that unfortunate country.

The point that I particularly desired to make was that the troubles in Mexico go deeper down than those which effect the agrarian question; and that any remedy offered for Mexico must reach the root if the cure is to be permanent. . . .

The exiled Bishops of Mexico do not ask, nor do they want, American intervention. What they want is a simple guarantee of liberty of conscience. General Angeles, speaking, I suppose, for General Villa, recently addressed the people of Monterey, assuring them: "We have not come to offend the belief of anyone; but we respect them all. This army, conscious of its duties, is sufficiently disciplined to impart ample protection and respect towards all rights and creeds. We have amongst us Catholics, Protestants, and even men who follow no religion; but all of us, from the first to the last, harbor a feeling of deep respect toward all."

This statement shows a remarkable change in the policy of the Convention forces, but it does not wipe out the fact that from the beginning the entire Constitutionalist move[ment], was, through the influence of such men as General Antonio I. Villareal, made anti-religious and persecuting. This condition is an old one in Mexico. The eighty percent to which you referred in your Indianapolis speech, and who have your sympathy, is religious, and desire liberty of conscience. A minority of even the twenty percent left, refuse it; and have mixed up the anti-religious spirit so much with the name "revolution," that the two have almost become synonymous.

You know, Mr. President, that it is impossible to have peace when laws directed against freedom of worship, are forced upon the people by the will of an atheistic minority. You know that under such conditions, peace cannot exist. An arrangement may be arrived at now, but if the canker is not cured, the arrangement cannot last. The Mexican question will come up again. There will be trouble again, and our Mexican neighbor will be a constant source of disturbance to us. To me it seems the most logical thing that you, as a representative of the American people, and as one who has sympathy for Mexico, should point out to her the radical difficulty, in a friendly and kindly manner. The United States is a successful democracy, after which Mexico has already copied. The trouble is that she has added laws to her Constitution, which she did not take from the United States. If you insist upon liberty of conscience for Mexico, in all respects as it exists in the United States, you are on absolutely safe and solid ground. No one can object; for even a handful of bigots can scarcely attack a policy that is justified by American tradition and by the words of the American Constitution. Such a declaration is all that the Catholic people want; but less than that would promise nothing for the future welfare of Mexico.

It is my sincere conviction, my dear Mr. President, that you will find the parties of Mexico, with the exception of Carranza, perfectly willing to listen and accept your suggestion. The leaders I have seen in the United States are already convinced that the best interests of their country require that Mexico should cast off the fetters of anti-clericalism and pattern its conduct toward religion after its Northern neighbor. I think Villa now realizes the mistakes that were made; and Zapata has never persecuted the Church or murdered her clergy. I am well aware that nothing is to be expected of Carranza, not even respect to the United States which helped him to success. But I do believe that Villa could be reached, and I know positively that Mexican leaders in the United States are favorable. A strong declaration on your part of your own position would be the first step toward giving to Mexico that real liberty which it has not had for fifty years. Indeed, Mr. President, the destinies of Mexico are in your hands, and it is because we know this that we have troubled you; for you cannot expect the sixteen million Catholics of the United States to stand back silently and allow the religious rights of their Mexican brethren to be outraged by a party which claims to have the protection of the American Government. You can scarcely blame us if we stand against having this horrible injustice perpetrated, under what, some have come to think, is protection by the Government of our own country. . . .

I propose to send out another letter in a few days, in which I shall inform the bishops of the sympathetic consid[er]ation you had given to the question. I assure you that I desire to be absolutely fair; and the reason the facts of the persecution have been brought out, has been simply because it was the only way we had to stir up that deep sympathy upon which we relied for securing not only the sympathetic attitude of the Administration, but also its good offices. As you yourself informed me you said to some of the Mexican leaders: "When the time for recognition of a Government in Mexico comes, the American Administration can only act in accordance with the wishes of the American people." I feel sure that in this just demand for Liberty of conscience, the American people will practically be a unit.

As to the method which might be followed for making your position plain and removing all doubt as to your sympathy, perhaps the easiest way would be a letter such as the note Mr. Bryan wrote to Senator Stone on the neutrality of this country in the European war. This letter could be addressed to me by yourself, accompanied by your permission to make it public. I could see to it that the letter is circulated, particularly amongst those interested in the matter. Catholic editors, now worried and disturbed, would be certain to give it publicity and comment upon it editorially in such a way as to remove all doubt as to your desire to do us justice.

In accordance with my promise, and in order to make the matter perfectly clear, I have prepared some statements for your consideration, and forwarded them to Mr. Malone for his criticisms, together with this letter which he will see is delivered to you.

I once more beg to assure you, my dear Mr. President, that in this matter I am only desirous of helping Mexico. I have no temporal interests to guard, and I will be only too glad to place any information or influence at my disposal, to help you in the task of solving this difficult problem for the benefit of Mexico and to the credit of the United States.

Faithfully yours,   Francis C. Kelley

TLS (SDR, RG 59, 812.404/85, DNA).

George Lawrence Record to Joseph Patrick Tumulty

Dear Joe: Jersey City, N. J. February 23, 1915.

While I was talking with Jim Kerney yesterday on the Trade Commission matter, word came in to the office that the names had been sent in. Jim explained to me the difficulties which confronted the President in the matter.

I write now merely to say that apart from the natural feeling of disappointment, I have only the keenest appreciation for your earnest efforts in my behalf from the beginning to the end of this matter, and of the honor done me by the President in giving my name such serious consideration. I can well understand the difficulties which confronted him, and know that in meeting them he acted from the very highest motives. I wish you would give him my respects, and for yourself accept my sincere thanks for the interest you have shown in my behalf.

Very sincerely yours,   George L Record

TLS (WP, DLC).

An Address on Behalf of Berea College[1]

February 24, 1915.

Mr. Chairman, ladies and gentlemen: I am not here tonight in my official capacity as President of the United States. I would deem it an impertinence to patronize a cause like this. I am here because of my profound personal interest in Berea College.

I have spent very many happy days in those great mountains. I have threaded many of their most remote fastnesses. I have felt the charm and the mystery of some of those uplifted valleys, and I have mixed a great deal with the simple, straightforward, sturdy folk who inhabit them. I have learned a great many things from them, and I doubt if they ever learned anything from me. I do not have to call upon my imagination to realize the condition of those people or their needs.

I remember when I first met Doctor Frost, I envied him. I envy him now, because he is going straight at the heart of one of the most interesting problems of American life. The only thing that is worthwhile in human intercourse, after all, is to wake somebody up, provided you wake them up to see the light, provided you wake them up to see something that is worth seeing and to comprehend something that their spirits have not hitherto comprehended.

There are colleges and colleges. I have spent the greater part of my life doing what is called teaching, but most of the pupils of most of our universities systematically resist being taught. I remember being somewhat comforted and reassured some years ago, after I had taught for ten or fifteen years, by being told by a friend of mine at Yale University, who had taught for twenty, that he had found that the human mind possessed infinite resources for resisting the introduction of knowledge.

But here is a college filled with people hungry to learn. If I had anything that I thought was worth their hearing, I should love to address a body of people hungry to learn. I have never done it yet. I have devoted the best energies in me to getting their attention; I have used every resource of knowledge and of speech that I was master of to call their attention to the fact that what I was talking about was worth talking about and worth knowing about. And, after having spent some twenty-five years in that endeavor, I do not know how I could follow these lines of least resistance! It would be a very novel experience to find that they were waiting to hear what I had to say. They are hungry because they have only a vague sense of the great hinterland lying beyond the regions that they know, those primitive regions upon which nature has bestowed infinite beauty, but where her life is in its simplest terms.

This college is, as Mr. Mabie has said, a college of emancipation—taking the limitations off of the spirits of these people, sweeping the barriers away from their understandings, letting them out into that bigger world, which is a commonplace to us but which we do not comprehend, which we look upon so superficially that it would be very difficult for us to interpret it to them. These men at Berea are starting at the right place. They are starting with the simplicities of life, which are the foundations of life, and are leaving out its sophistries which are of no account. Those old maxims, some of them very worldly, contained in *Poor Richard's Almanac* are, after all, at the basis of most sensible living, and I dare say that Benjamin Franklin has suggested to more men their original instincts, and the uses for those instincts in the practical world, than any other man that ever lived. And that book must seem to those mountain people what it seems to a lad when he first reads it, like a sort of manual of worldly wisdom coming out of the great world of which they have only dreamed and of which they have only heard rumors.

The object of Berea College, in other words, is to do what America was intended to do—to give people who had not had it an opportunity, and to give it to them upon absolutely equal terms, upon a basis, not of birth, but of merit; to let every man have access to what he can use, to let every mind get at the things which that mind can make the highest use of in order to elevate the life which it serves. Not only that, but Berea is meant to do the fundamental, democratic thing. A tree does not derive its strength from its flower or from its fruit. It derives its strength from its roots. It derives all the vital sources of its life from the soil and those portions of its structure that draw the vital sources of the soil into them. And so with a nation. The nation is not fed from the top. It is not fed from the conspicuous people down. It is fed from the inconspicuous people up; and these institutions which, like Berea, go into the unexhausted soils and tap their virgin resources, are the best feeders of democracy.

What America has vindicated, above all things else, is that native ability has nothing to do with social origin. It is very amusing sometimes to see the airs that high society gives itself. The world could dispense with high society and never miss it. High society is for those who have stopped working and no longer have anything important to do. Those who can open up the great origins of power are those who feed the nation; and when one thinks of that old stock in storage there in the mountains for over a hundred years, untapped, some of the original stuff out of which America was made, waiting to be used, one ought to bid Godspeed to those men who are going there and using this old capital that has not even been put out at interest, that has been, as it were, kept in a chimney piece until we shall go to it, and use it, and find that the usury from it was that same usury of freedom and of power and of capacity which has been so characteristic of America from the first.

I do not see how anybody can think of Berea and the work it has to do without catching fire. The trouble about the world is that there are so many interesting things to do that one hates to confine himself to one or two of them. I find myself envying missionaries, envying engineers, envying pioneers of all sorts—envying those who touch with the closest possible contact the genuine stuffs, whether of the animate or inanimate world, because they must have the sense, if they have any imagination at all, of some way carrying the great world upon their shoulders and making it serviceable for mankind.

So that, as I began by saying, I have not come here to patronize this cause. I have not come here to lend it such support as it may get from the office that I temporarily occupy. I have come here, as I have come on many other occasions before the American people had put any burdens on me, to help Doctor Frost, if I can, to attract the attention of men and women, thinking men and women everywhere, and men with means, and men with energy, to these great and noble things that need to be done and done well and done at once.

T MS (WP, DLC), with corrections from the complete text in the *Berea Quarterly*, xviii (April 1915), 25-29.

1 Delivered in the Memorial Continental Hall of the Daughters of the American Revolution in Washington. Charles Evans Hughes presided, and Hamilton Wright Mabie, William Goodell Frost, and Frederick Gordon Bonser, Professor of Education at Teachers College, Columbia University, also spoke.

To James Kerney

My dear Kerney: [The White House] February 24, 1915

Your letter about that splendid fellow, George Record, brought tears to my eyes. Such tests of quality are conclusive and I am prouder than ever that he should be my friend.

In haste

Cordially and faithfully yours,   Woodrow Wilson

TLS (Letterpress Books, WP, DLC).

To Lindley Miller Garrison

[The White House]
My dear Mr. Secretary: February 24, 1915

I feel that it is my duty to urge the passage, if it is at all possible at this session of the Senate, of the Philippine bill, because, deeply important as the general power and the conservation bill[s] are, they do not touch, as the Philippine bill does, the general world situation, from which I think it is our duty to remove every element of doubt or disturbance which can possibly be removed. Such communications as that we have received from the Governor General of the Philippines show that a very important element of disturbance indeed will be removed if we can get the Philippine bill through.

If it must be a choice, therefore, among the three bills, I must give my preference to the Philippine bill. I do not see how it is possible to pass all three of them.

Cordially and faithfully yours,   Woodrow Wilson

TLS (Letterpress Books, WP, DLC).

From Edward Mandell House

[London] February 24, 1915.

I have cable from Thomas Page saying important I come to Rome even if only for a few days.

I have had private conference with Sir Edward Grey this morning. He thinks it might be wise to go to Rome and confer with the German Ambassador[1] there whom he thought, perhaps, the most influential German. I shall develop by cable what Thomas Page has in mind. In the meantime, please send me your views.

I strongly urged the adoption of your suggestion regarding maritime compromise. Sir Edward seems favorable, but has not discussed it with his colleagues. He thought difficulty was to make any agreement that Germany will keep. I suggested way to cover this point that may satisfy them.   Edward House.

T transcripts of WWsh decode (WC, NjP; WP, DLC).
    ¹ Bernhard Heinrich Martin Karl, Prince von Bülow, former Imperial Chancellor.

From William Joel Stone

Dear Mr. President: [Washington] February 24 1915.

We had a meeting of the Committee on Foreign Relations this morning with a bare quorum present. Several of those present expressed themselves as opposed to reporting the Colombian Treaty at this session, or until the Committee should act upon amendments that are to be proposed. It seemed to be impossible to get action without a row; and as it requires two-thirds to ratify it seemed to me that it would not be advisable in the circumstances to force a report by a bare majority of a quorum. Such a course would probably stimulate opposition to ratification. So nothing was done.

We then took up the Nicaraguan Treaty with a view to seeing if an understanding could be arrived at by which a vote could be had at this session. Senator Smith of Michigan stated very positively that he, Senator Borah and others would resort to whatever means they deemed necessary to prevent a vote at this session. Plainly we are up against it, and it does not look as if we will be able to secure action now.

With respect to the matter about which we talked this morning, if you are inclined to take the course indicated in our conversation, I think it advisable that you assemble the Democratic members of the Committee for a conference with you at the earliest practicable moment. In view of what the newspapers might say if all of us met you at the same time, it might be better if you could arrange to talk with three or four at a time, taking their opinions. I think Senator Pomerene does not look favorably on the Colombian Treaty, and Senator Clarke of Arkansas is understood to be against it. I think it important that you or Mr. Bryan should go over this latter treaty with Senator Pomerene. Outside of the newspaper phase of the subject it would, I think, be better if all the Democratic members of the

Committee could meet you at the same time to discuss the entire subject, having Mr. Bryan present.

I send these suggestions for your consideration.

Very sincerely,   Wm J Stone.

TLS (WP, DLC).

To William Jennings Bryan

[The White House]

My dear Mr. Secretary,   25 February, 1915.

We have already discussed the matter here referred to, and, as you know, I fully approve of taking advantage of the opening to present to Japan very frankly our views on her "suggestions" or "requests." I think those views can be made very weighty and conclusive. We shall not have uttered a more important state paper.   Faithfully Yours,   W.W.

P.S. It is evident that things are being pressed at Peking. It would be wise to let Tokyo have our views by cable, I think, if it can be managed without the intervention of the Press.

WWTLI (SDR, RG 59, 793.94/240, DNA).

To Edward Mandell House

[The White House, Feb. 25, 1915]

Your cables enable me to understand the situation in all its phases, and I greatly appreciate them. I am of course content to be guided by your judgment as to each step. Is there any danger that your going to Italy would be thought to have anything to do with her neutrality or participation?

T transcript of WWsh telegram (WP, DLC).

To George Lawrence Record

My dear Mr. Record: [The White House] February 25, 1915

I want you to know how sincerely I admire you and value your friendship. You show as fine a spirit in matters of public duty as any man I have ever known and understand where other men seem incapable of understanding. I am proud that you are my friend.

Cordially and sincerely yours,   Woodrow Wilson

TLS (Letterpress Books, WP, DLC).

To William Joel Stone

My dear Senator: [The White House] February 25, 1915

Thank you warmly for your letter of yesterday. I will take up the important matter we consulted about the other day at Cabinet tomorrow and will let you hear from me as promptly as possible.

In haste

Cordially and sincerely yours,   Woodrow Wilson

TLS (Letterpress Books, WP, DLC).

From William Jennings Bryan

My dear Mr. President: Washington February 25th, 1915.

I am sending you flimsey of a telegram which we have just received from Haiti.[1] If you will compare the two paragraphs of the answer to the third question you may be convinced, as I am, that there is some contradiction.

The first sentance says that the Legislature was *not coerced* in the selection of Theodor who received the entire vote.

The second shows that the proclaiming of a successful revolutionary leader as Chief of the Executive Power *is tantamount to his election* as President—and that "upon his entrance into the capital the Chambers are convoked and he is *invariably elected.*"

It seems that the new revolution has been successful and that the successful insurrectionist is likely to be elected for a term of seven years.

The last sentence of the despatch presents Minister Blanchard's opinion—namely, that the sending of a Commission appears to be unwise. He advises delay until the Government is established. I am inclined to differ from him in opinion.

It seems to me that the beginning of this administration is an opportune time for the sending of the Commission and I would respectfully advise that Fort and Smith start at the time arranged—namely, *next Saturday*. If you approve of this it will be necessary to prepare instructions, and I beg to submit the following suggestion:

As we have already sent by Blanchard a copy of the treaty which we would like to have made, and as we gave to the Commission when it went to Santo Domingo instructions covering the condition there, would it not be well to instruct Governor Fort, who will be the President of the Commission, that the Commission should investigate the conditions there and report how nearly the plan employed in Santo Domingo can be used in Haiti.

There is one very marked difference—namely, that there is no popular election of President in Haiti. The people, every three years, elect a Chamber of Deputies and this Chamber of Deputies selects Senators; and the Senators and Deputies together form a National Assembly which elects the President. There is, therefore, no way of securing the opinion of the people in regard to any presidential candidate and it seems likely that any successful revolutionist will be able to control the National Assembly. An election of this kind does not indicate much, so far as national sentiment is concerned, because the members are under duress—as Huerta's congress was.

We cannot, however, change this and we will have to content ourselves with ascertaining whether, so far as public opinion can be learned, the man selected by the National Assembly is really the choice of the people.

We run some risk—considerable risk in fact—when we put the strength of our Government behind any Hatian President without some provision for the control of the customs, such as we have in Santo Domingo, and yet I am not prepared to say that we ought to make that an absolute condition. It may be better, in the interests of order, to support a President if he seems to be generally acceptable and gives promise of capacity and efficiency, trusting to the future to secure such authority as may be found necessary.

We cannot well make the negotiation of such a treaty as we desire a condition precedent to recognition and if our Commissioners there find that the situation is not such as to enable us to secure the treaty now, we might, by rendering assistance, increase our influence and ultimately, by showing the value of our support, secure the necessary concessions to enable us to give stability there as we do in Santo Domingo.

I wish you would let me know your opinion on the subject.

With assurances of high respect I am, my dear Mr. President,
Yours very sincerely,   W. J. Bryan

TLS (W. J. Bryan Papers, DNA).
¹ A. Bailly-Blanchard to the Secretary of State, Feb. 24, 1915 (SDR, RG 59, 838.00/1119, DNA), printed in *FR 1915*, pp. 465-66. Bryan summarizes this telegram below.

From William Joel Stone

Dear Mr. President: [Washington] February 25 1914 [1915].

You may remember that some ten days ago when I had called at your office on some matter I said to you just before leaving that I wanted to talk with you about the so-called Hitchcock Bill, authorizing an embargo on the exportation of munitions of war to belligerent countries, etc, at which time I said to you that at the beginning and up to within a short time I had looked with decided disfavor on any Measure of that character, but that I was becoming more impressed with the idea that a law some-what on the general lines of the Hitchcock Bill, but going further than his bill, might be a wise move for us to make. You stated that you had been opposed to the bill all along and had not changed your opinion, or words to that effect. I told you then that I would like to discuss the matter with you when both of us could find an opportunity to do so. These have been very busy times for all of us as you know, and I have not sought an ap-pointment with you about this matter for I do not like to discuss a matter of such grave importance when either of us should be so pressed with other things as not to be able to go over the sub-ject fully.

I am more and more impressed with the belief that if the President now had the power that such a law would confer on him, he would be armed with a weapon he might use very ef-fectively, if occasion arose, to compel the belligerent powers to respect the commercial rights of neutrals. It strikes me that such power might be used more effectively than any form of physical force to compel a proper recognition of and respect for our rights under international law. It would be a dangerous power to place in the hands of a rattle-head like Roosevelt or in the hands of any impulsive or indiscreet man; but I have faith that you would know how to employ it with the greatest of good judgment. If it were known to the world, as it would be, that you had this power, that you were reluctant to use it, but that you had the nerve to use it if necessary, I feel that it would have in itself a salutary effect and that a warning diplomatically conveyed would prob-ably accomplish the end you sought without an actual resort to drastic means.

I appreciate the fact that you would probably be subjected to the annoyance of constant pressure brought from first one source and then another to persuade you to exercise your power or desist from exercising it; but it occurs to me that if you should give it out pat that you would decline to receive suggestions from the partisans of or sympathizers with any of the belligerents or from any especially interested source you would in large measure escape the annoyance apprehended. But in any event I have suf-ficient faith in you to believe that you would not hesitate to face any trouble of that nature if you thought that you could in the end so exercise your power as to accomplish a great national good with the least possible danger to our peace.

I have refrained from giving any expression of opinion respecting this matter, partly because I am not myself entirely convinced that the plan suggested should be adopted, and partly because, knowing your embarrassments and difficulties, and aware of the fact that you are in possession of a great fund of information of which I know nothing, or but little, I feel that I want to strengthen your hands and be careful about saying or doing anything that might tend to increase your difficulties. It does not seem practicable to discuss the matter with you as I would like and so I am sending you this note as a sort of tentative expression of my views for whatever they may be worth. It is not at all necessary that you should make any response to this communication.

I have the honor to be
                     Very sincerely yours,   Wm J Stone.
TLS (WP, DLC).

To William Jennings Bryan

My dear Mr. Secretary,   [The White House] 26 February, 1915.

My own judgment follows and agrees with your reasoning in this letter altogether. I do not see what other course we can follow in the circumstances.   Faithfully Yours,   W.W.

WWTLI (W. J. Bryan Papers, DNA).

Two Letters from Lindley Miller Garrison

My dear Mr. President: Washington. February 26, 1915.

Since coming from the Cabinet meeting, I have had a conversation over the telephone with Senators Hitchcock and Simmons about the Philippine bill.

I called Senator Hitchcock up in accordance with my understanding with you, and told him that you had communicated with Senator Simmons and suggested that he get in conference with Senator Simmons. Senator Hitchcock said that he had talked to Mr. Jones to-day and that Mr. Jones said that the House would not stand for the Lippitt preamble.[1] He said he had talked with Simmons and it had been suggested that the Senate might agree to the Lippitt preamble and leave the matter to be fixed up in conference, but that he (Hitchcock) thought this was useless if the House would only stand for its own preamble[2] and the

Senate would not stand for that preamble but would insist upon the Lippitt preamble. Hitchcock told me that his idea was to call the bill up on Monday and see what the reaction was and be governed accordingly, he being of the opinion that it would be better to stand by the Senate preamble[3] rather than to accept the Lippitt preamble.

Later Senator Simmons called me up and said that he had just had another talk with Hitchcock and the situation was this: That the Republicans assured him (Simmons) that if the preamble were altered as suggested by Lippitt, with one further concession on their side, namely, the insertion of the word "autonymous" before "self-government," the debate would be confined to two hours or less and the bill could then be passed; that he had seen Hitchcock but Hitchcock was of the opinion that I have attributed to him above, namely, that it would be better to stick to the original "independence" preamble. Senator Simmons desired me to communicate with you so that you would let him know, either through me or directly, whether you thought it best to make the concession above suggested as to the preamble, or whether you thought it best to press the bill with the preamble as now drawn.

I am sending this right to you with the request that you communicate your decision either to me or to Senator Simmons, or to both, as you see fit.

Sincerely yours,   Lindley M. Garrison

P.S. I asked Senator Simmons when they expected to bring the bill up if they reached an understanding, and he said either to-morrow (Saturday) or Monday.

TLS (WP, DLC).

[1] Henry Frederick Lippitt, Republican of Rhode Island, never actually introduced his preamble to the Philippine bill in the Senate; hence, its text is unknown. Lippitt was a member of the Senate Committee on the Philippines and was strongly opposed to the bill as passed by the House. Therefore, it is reasonable to assume that his proposed preamble was even less favorable to Philippine independence than the "Senate preamble," discussed in n. 3 below.

[2] For the preamble of H.R. 18459, passed by the House of Representatives on October 14, 1914, see n. 3 to remarks at a press conference printed at Jan. 5, 1915.

[3] The Senate Committee on the Philippines, on February 2, 1915, had submitted a report on H.R. 18459 which proposed a new preamble for the bill. The report noted that the proposed substitute was "free from certain ambiguities in the House preamble and avoids the references to debatable historical events." It further stated that some members of the committee had wanted to omit the preamble altogether, but that the majority had felt that this would be construed by the Filipinos as meaning that independence would never be granted. The substitute preamble, the report continued, indicated "the purpose to grant independence to the people of the Philippine Islands when in the judgment of the United States the Philippine people have become fitted for its enjoyment." 63d Cong., 3d sess., Senate Report No. 942, p. 3.

My dear Mr. President: Washington. February 26, 1915.

I merely want to add to the letter about the Philippine bill, that Senator Simmons told me that if they pressed the bill with the original preamble, he feared that there would be no chance to get it through this session.   Sincerely yours,   L.M.G.

TLI (WP, DLC).

From Joseph Patrick Tumulty

Dear Governor: The White House February 26, 1915.

I did not have sufficient time this morning to impress upon you the folly of an extra session of the Senate. If I am any judge of public sentiment, it will be overwhelmingly against the proposed session. You will have many delicate matters to handle in the next few weeks and all of your time ought to be given to the consideration of them. By all means get the Senate and House away from here during the next few weeks and do not allow anything to interfere with your consideration of the grave matters that will confront you in the next few weeks. If there was justification for an extra session, it would be to consider the shipping bill. All of the Democratic papers of the country and the independent papers have praised your attitude on this matter and have pronounced your proposed course in refusing to call an extra session on the shipping bill as an act of the highest wisdom. If you have an extra session of the Senate, you will have on your back a crowd of bitter partisans, ready and willing to take advantage of any situation that may arise, growing out of the war.

I would not write this note if I did not feel the importance of the matter and realize the consequences of an extra session.

Yours Sincerely   Tumulty

TLS (WP, DLC).

Herbert Clark Hoover to Edward Mandell House, with Enclosure

Dear Colonel House,   London, 26th February 1915

Please find enclosed a letter for the President, covering the three documents, which I enclose,[1] and I would be grateful indeed if you could get the matter to his personal attention as I believe it would be of interest to him.

Yours faithfully,   H C Hoover.

Dear Governor,

This man seems to be doing a great work in an unselfish and efficient manner. If you have time will you not drop him a line of acknowledgment. Aff.   E.M.H.

TLS with EMHhw note (WP, DLC).
¹ *The Commission for Relief in Belgium* (London, 1915), a brochure describing the organization and work of the commission; printed exchange of letters between Sir Edward Grey and H. C. Hoover, Feb. 22 and 24, 1915, concerning the work of the commission; and Commission for Relief in Belgium, *Report for the Period ending February 22nd, 1915* (London, 1915), all in WP, DLC.

ENCLOSURE

From Herbert Clark Hoover

Dear Mr. President,   London, 26th February 1915

Learning from Colonel House of your interest in the work of this Commission, I take the liberty of sending you herewith a copy of our last fortnightly report, together with some small brochures bearing upon the work of the Commission.

You will appreciate that the American Ambassadors concerned and the Members of the Commission have realised that the survival of the 7,000,000 of people is, aside from the administrative work of this Commission, dependent either upon the support of the charitable world or upon some basis of arrangement amongst the belligerent powers, by which the financial problem of this Commission could be solved. This problem amounts practically to the finding of $7,500,000 per month and, although the flow of charity has been generous and of a volume hitherto unknown in relief work, it is entirely inadequate and we are, therefore, brought to the point of finding some solution in the way of financial assistance from the belligerent Powers themselves. This is not a matter on which we expect to trouble you in any way, except merely by way of an explanation of the activities of this Commission in negotiations with the various Governments concerned.   Yours faithfully,   Herbert Hoover

TLS (WP, DLC).

From the White House Staff

The White House, February 27, 1915

Senator Lafollette telephones that the conference report on the seamen's bill has been agreed to, and he asks an opportunity to be heard in case the President has any intention of vetoing the measure.

Mr. Tumulty thinks the President ought to see the Senator.

Please make engagement with the Senator to see me this afternoon (March first) or evening, as may suit him best—6 o'clock or 8 o'clock   W.W.[1]

TL with WWhw reply (WP, DLC).

[1] The meeting actually took place on the evening of March 2. Senator La Follette decided to bring Andrew Furuseth with him. La Follette later recalled what took place: "Andy went down on his knees to the President. He begged him to make him a freeman who had a right to walk the streets and live his life as other citizens did, which right he did not have as a seaman." La Follette declared that Wilson was moved by this appeal as he had never seen him moved on any other occasion. After Furuseth left the meeting room, La Follette remained to argue the cause for another twenty minutes. Two days later, Tumulty told La Follette that Wilson had commented, just after the meeting: "Tumulty, I have just experienced a great half-hour, the tensest since I came to the White House. That man La Follette pushed me over tonight on the Seamen's bill." Belle Case La Follette and Fola La Follette, *Robert M. La Follette*, I, 535-36.

William Jennings Bryan to John Franklin Fort

My dear Governor Fort: [Washington] February 27th, 1915.

After conversing with the President in regard to the work to be done in Haiti I beg to give the following instructions to the Commission, composed of yourself as Chairman, Minister Bailly-Blanchard as Vice-Chairman, and Mr. Charles Cogswell Smith as Secretary.

Minister Blanchard will show you the draft of the Convention setting forth the President's views as to the arrangement which he regards as most desirable. You will notice that it follows quite closely the terms of the Convention with Santo Domingo, under which it has been possible for this Government to render timely and valuable assistance in the maintenance of a Government capable of enforcing law and order, and administering justice.[1]

Under this Convention we have supervised an election at which more than eighty thousand votes were cast, and have been instrumental in aiding in the inauguration of a President who received a majority of the total votes cast, a majority of the electors, and a majority of the members of both House and Senate. Having the assurance that he is the choice of the people this Government is now supporting him and has, by the promise of its assistance, enabled him to pass successfully two crises which have arisen since his inauguration.

The fact that you and Mr. Smith were members of the Commission and succeeded so admirably in Santo Domingo, suggested the propriety of sending you on this Commission to Haiti where

Minister Blanchard will take the place of Minister Sullivan who acted with you in Santo Domingo.

I enclose herewith copy of the instructions given you when you went to Santo Domingo and they will guide you as far as they can be applied to the Haitien situation.

The fact that the President of Haiti is elected by the National Assembly instead of by popular vote will, of course, make it impossible for such an election to be held as was held in Santo Domingo and you must, therefore, resort to other means of ascertaining whether Vilbrun Guillaume Sam has the support of the people to such an extent as to give reasonable assurance of permanency to his government.

You will inquire, also, as to his past record, qualifications, and as to his views in regard to international matters. Will he recognize and protect the rights and legitimate interests of foreigners residing or doing business in Haiti?

It is the desire of the President to render to Haiti such assistance and disinterested service as are possible under the circumstances, but just what the character of that service is to be, or to what extent this Government can be of assistance cannot be determined until the President is fully informed.

Keeping in mind what has been accomplished in Santo Domingo and the terms of the proposed Convention, the Commission will make inquiry and promptly communicate to this Government such information as it acquires and such suggestions as it may desire to make. Further instructions will be given as the situation develops.

You will please assure the authorities with whom you have to deal of the genuineness and disinterestedness of this Government's friendship for Haiti. We ask nothing in return but the satisfaction which will come to our people from the knowledge that the assistance rendered has contributed to the peace, progress and prosperity of a neighboring republic. Our conduct toward other Latin-American countries ought to make the assurance unnecessary, but that there may be no misunderstanding you will, of course, explain to the Haitien authorities that such guarantees as we ask for citizens of this country we ask also for the citizens of other countries and that any work entrusted to this Government by Haiti will be performed with entire impartiality toward all foreigners, from whatever nation they may come.

Wishing the members of the Commission health and comfort during their stay there, and success in its efforts, I am,

Yours very truly,   W J Bryan

CCL (SDR, RG 59, 838.00/1382, DNA).
¹ Bryan enclosed a copy of Wilson's "San Domingo. Proposed Memorandum," printed at July 27, 1914, Vol. 30.

William Jennings Bryan to Arthur Bailly-Blanchard

Amlegation Port au Prince.   Washington, February 27, 1915.

Have laid your telegram before the President. He believes that under the circumstances it is wise for the Commission to come to Haiti at once. You will be a member of the Commission and act with Governor Fort and Mr. Smith in carrying out the instructions which are sent by Governor Fort. They will leave Santiago de Cuba about March third. Can you arrange for Consul Livingston¹ of Cape Haitien to be at Port au Prince when Governor Fort arrives? You may ask one of our boats to bring him if he cannot reach there by regular boat. Please keep us informed of the situation as it develops there.   Bryan

T telegram (SDR, RG 59, 838.00/1119, DNA).
¹ Lemuel W. Livingston.

A Telegram and Three Letters
from Edward Mandell House

[London, Feb. 27, 1915]

Your cable of the 25th received. Thomas Page had nothing specific in mind but thought the most valuable insight into the situation could be had there. Your point is well taken and I shall not visit Italy unless absolutely necessary. I am still waiting for Zimmermann's reply to my letter. Communication with Germany is a very difficult matter.

T transcripts of WWsh decode (WP, DLC; WC, NjP).

Dear Governor: [London] February 27th, 1915.

It has been in my mind for sometime that our cypher was not secure. Given the blue code, it would not be difficult to work it out. Little as I know about such things, I believe I could do it in a day, and probably an expert could do it within an hour. It is the general belief that many foreign countries, including England and Germany, have this blue code.

I talked to Irwin Laughlin, First Secretary here, about the matter and without telling him what system we used, I got him to work out something with a dictionary as a medium. I found, however, that this would not be satisfactory on account of the lack of words and groups of words we needed.

It occurred to me then that we could make another cypher which would be absolutely safe and a great deal easier to send and receive by changing the numbering of the pages in the blue code.

As soon as you receive this letter, if you approve of this new plan, please cable me under it and we will use it in the future. No one can possibly unravel it unless they know how we have numbered the pages.

I have taken the blue code and numbered backwards, starting with 113 on page 739 and ending on page 100 with 749.

You will notice that each two pages have the same number. It will not take longer than an hour to change it in this way. Care should be taken, however, that it is done correctly for if it is not, it would throw us all out.

After renumbering, look up in the book the word to be encyphered and set down the number at the top of that page and suffix to it the number obtained by counting the words from the top of the page including the word in question. Should the word be found in the first nine words on the page, a zero must be prefixed to it since a completed cypher group must contain exactly five figures.

For example to encypher the sentence "Your cable of the 25th received"

The words "your cable of" will be found on page 620 (as renumbered) number 97. The cypher group representing it therefore would be 62097.

The word "25th" is the ninety-sixth word on page 163 therefore the cypher group would be 16396.

the word "received" is 88 on page 268, therefore the group of figures would be 26888.

The message when coded then reads as follows: 62097-16396-26888.

This cypher cannot possibly be unravelled by anyone not possessing a duplicate of the blue code numbered as we have it.

A thorough explanation of the system is to be found at the beginning of the blue code and it would be useful to read this. The principles upon which it is based are thoroughly understood by the cypher clerks at the State Department and if you are at all puzzled by it you can send for one of them to make it clear to you. This could be accomplished without letting the man know how your pages were numbered or what book you were using, because anyone who got a glimpse of it could easily make a copy, provided he also had a blue code.

I find that departmental despatches are sent in figures and not in words as we have done. This, of course is for convenience and the telegraph companies understand the method thoroughly.

In using this code, I do not believe it will be necessary to also use the different numbers as we have heretofore, but simply take the code as it is and use the numbers opposite the actual words we desire. I am sure you will find this a great convenience for it will not take half the time to either receive or send messages.

Affectionately yours,   E. M. House

Dear Governor: [London] February 27th, 1915.

I have had several talks with White [Grey] since I wrote you. In one of these I told him that I thought I now knew his mind quite well and also that of practically every Member of the Cabinet. In addition I believed I knew what the people of the Empire desired and how far he could go with the Cabinet, the public and with his Allies.

With this information before me, I suggested that it would be well to now go to Zadok [Germany] as soon as I could hear favorably from Wolf [Zimmermann], and that I thought it would be well for me to remain in Zadok or on the Continent and not return to England again excepting when necessary.

When I go, I shall arrange to send confidential messages to him through Page and under a code that will be quite safe. When anything of great importance arises, I suggested that he send someone having his entire confidence to meet me in Holland. I would not do this, however, without the consent and approval of Zadok.

I had lunch with James Brice yesterday and we had an interesting two hours together. He particularly wished to be remembered to you.

Sidney Brooks is preparing a leader for the Times to be published on the 4th of March giving a resume of your two years in office.[1] I hope he will make it as appreciative as his conversations with me now indicate.

Affectionately yours,   E. M. House

[1] This editorial or article did not appear.

Dear Governor: [London] February 28th. 1915.

I lunched with Sir Edward yesterday alone. He is rather a diffident man and he seemed to have some trouble in telling me what he had on his mind.

He met Roosevelt here some three years ago and again last year and they have corresponded spasmodically since. Roosevelt has been writing him in regard to peace settlements and Sir Edward has written in turn rather freely. He showed me some of the correspondence and said he wanted us to know of it, and that in the future, he thought it would be well to "ease off" in that direction since he was now taking up such questions with you through me.

I advised him to do this. He has not written him since I have been here and I think we may count upon his not writing again upon this subject.

It has occurred to me that it might be useful if later I visited some of the neutral capitals in order to work up a sentiment in favor of the convention which I am hoping you will call to sit at the same time, or just after, the peace convention. Of course, I cannot do this if my time is taken up wholly between Berlin and London, but if there is a lapse, I could do it, provided you approve. Before doing so, it would be my idea to get favorable expressions from all the belligerants, just as I feel sure, we will get it from England. I hope you will write me your mind very fully about this.

I still see in it the most certain way in which you can be of service in the final adjustment of international comity and laws. I feel confident that Germany will thoroughly approve after I have once explained the purpose, and with the approval of Germany and England, it is not likely that any dissent will come from elsewhere.   Affectionately yours,   E. M. House

TLS (WP, DLC).

To Edward Mandell House

[The White House, March 1, 1915]

An intimate friend[1] just returned from Berlin reports that the German Foreign Minister told him in person that Russia was listening to suggestions of peace and that Germany was willing to obtain for her the outlet she desires at the Dardanelles; that Belgium also was listening to proposals of separate peace on a basis of indemnity for her losses; and that even France was being confidentially approached with offers of money indemnity as the price of peace with her, no peace with England being in mind in any circumstances short of victory.

He also stated that he had himself seen camps in which Russian prisoners of war had been placed practically without guards because of their perfect willingness to remain prisoners rather than fight, thus giving credit to what you had heard from Austrian officials to the effect that Russians by the thousands were offering to surrender whenever they got a chance.

He reports that his own observations while in Germany convince him that she has supplies enough of all kinds and means and resources enough to carry the war on with perfect confidence of ultimate triumph.

This is also Gerard's information and opinion.

My friend also reports that the Germans heatedly disapprove of the Emperor's preference of counselors, and that they thoroughly despise America and Americans.

T transcript of WWsh telegram (WC, NjP).
[1] Melvin A. Rice.

From William Jennings Bryan

My dear Mr. President: Washington March 1, 1915.

I am sending you a copy of the notice delivered to us this morning in regard to the retaliation which the Allies propose against Germany.[1] I also enclose a copy of another memorandum which indicates that Great Britain does not regard this notice as affecting the matter referred to in the identical notes.[2] I also enclose a flimsy of a telegram received from Mr. Gerard.[3] There was another despatch from Gerard,[4] of which I presume you have a flimsy, in which he suggested that this government warn Great Britain that it would put an embargo on arms if an embargo is put on food. I do not know whether he sent that with his approval or whether he simply meant to communicate it as a suggestion from the Foreign Office, but I presume it was not his own idea, for he could hardly expect a threat as effective in securing any understanding.

With assurances of high respect, I am, My dear Mr. President,
Very sincerely yours, W. J. Bryan

TLS (WP, DLC).
[1] CC T press release, March 1, 1915, announcing that the British and French governments, in view of the flagrant illegality of unrestricted submarine warfare, were contemplating retaliatory measures and would detain and take into port ships carrying goods of presumed enemy destination, ownership, or origin. However, the goods would not be confiscated unless they would otherwise be liable to confiscation. The notice is printed in *FR-WWS 1915*, pp. 127-28.

² E. Grey to C. A. Spring Rice, Feb. 28, 1915, TC telegram (SDR, RG 59, 763.72/1552, DNA), printed in *FR-WWS 1915*, p. 128.

³ J. W. Gerard to WJB, Feb. 26, 1915, T telegram (SDR, RG 59, 763.72/1521, DNA), printed in *FR-WWS 1915*, p. 126. It said that Germany would probably ask for free passage of such raw materials as rubber, cotton, and copper, as well as food.

⁴ J. W. Gerard to WJB, Feb. 27, 1915, T telegram (SDR, RG 59, 763.72/1517, DNA), printed in *FR-WWS 1915*, p. 126, saying in part, "Respectfully suggest . . . that you then say that if Germany accepts the proposition contained in the identical note that the United States will put an embargo on the export of arms unless England and her allies agree to accept the same proposition."

From William Jennings Bryan, with Enclosure

My dear Mr. President: Washington March 1, 1915.

I am sending you a memorandum on the Seaman's bill prepared by Mr. Lansing. I feel sure that those who supported the bill could not have given due consideration to the confusion that would follow the denunciation of all these treaties at this time. In view of the fact that ten days are given the Executive for the consideration of bills might it not be well to allow this to die in your hands for lack of time, rather than to veto it, if you have any doubts as to the wisdom of a veto?

With great respect, my dear Mr. President, I remain,

Very truly yours,   W. J. Bryan

TLS (WP, DLC).

ENCLOSURE

Robert Lansing to William Jennings Bryan

Dear Mr. Secretary: [Washington] March 1, 1915.

I enclose herewith a memorandum,¹ prepared in this office, relative to the features of the so-called "Alien Seamen's Bill," now before the President, which would in my opinion cause serious difficulties in our foreign relations at the present time.

It is not my intention to criticise the expediency of this legislation from the domestic standpoint, but to direct attention to the embarrassments which would undoubtedly result in our intercourse with foreign nations in case the bill became a law.

In any circumstances the provisions of the bill would involve us in numerous controversies with other governments and require the negotiation of new treaties in conformity with such provisions, a negotiation which would be very difficult in view of the well-established practice of nations in regard to seamen on vessels in foreign ports.

At the present time, when the commerce of the whole world is disorganized by the war in Europe, governments would be in no temper to discuss this legislation deliberately or to enter into a negotiation to modify existing treaties.

The chief objections to the bill are, first, the failure to make proviso for the continuance of treaty stipulations, and, second, the direction to the President to denounce portions of treaties in conflict with the provisions of the bill. A treaty cannot be denounced in part. To carry out the direction in Section 16 would require the denouncement of our most important commercial treaties which cover many subjects other than those dealt with in the bill. It seems to me that this would cause endless confusion. I have not had time to see how far it would affect commercial privileges secured by these treaties, but I am sure it would be most serious.

If the treaties were denounced, our commercial intercourse would have to be regulated by international law. In view of the fact that some of the provisions of the bill (as indicated in the enclosed memorandum) appear to be in direct conflict with the accepted rules of international usage, the denouncement of the treaties would be only one phase of the controversies which would be precipitated by this bill becoming a law.

I sincerely hope that this Department will not have imposed upon it new difficulties, which are so far reaching, at a time when our foreign affairs present so many grave questions.

Faithfully yours, Robert Lansing.

TLS (WP, DLC).
¹ RL, "THE ALIEN SEAMEN'S BILL," T MS (WP, DLC).

From Edward Mandell House

Dear Governor: [London] March 1st, 1915.

The King's Private Secretary, Lord Stamfordham, came yesterday to bring an invitation to me from the King to call today at eleven o'clock for a private audience. I was curious to know what he wanted.

I was with him for nearly an hour. He is the most bellicose Englishman that I have so far met. I had hopes that he might want to talk concerning peace plans, but he evidently wanted to impress me with the fact that this was no time to talk peace. His idea seemed to be that the best way to obtain permanent peace was to knock all the fight out of the Germans, and stamp on them for awhile until they wanted peace and more of it than any other nation.

He spoke kindly of the Germans as a whole, but for his dear uncle[1] and his military entourage, he denounced them in good sailorlike terms. He is the most pugnacious little monarch that is loose in these parts.

He told me a good deal about the Navy and its operations and also of what they hoped to do on land. He seemed more certain than anyone I have met that France and Russia would stick to the last man. He said what would happen to Germany when the French got in there, if they ever did, would be a plenty, and he said his cousin, the Czar had written him that Russia was aflame from one end to the other and was determined to win if they had to put in the field twenty million men.

As for England, he said she was sending the flower of the nation to the front, and that the world would be forced to acknowledge, before the spring and summer were over, that her army was equal to her best traditions.

He spoke of our relations and expressed the greatest gratification that we were on such good terms. He said the hope of the world lay in their continuance.

He asked me to convey to you his most respectful compliments and assurances of distinguished consideration.

Someone had evidently given him a glimpse of your character, for he voiced almost all I said of you before I could say it myself. He talked in a loud and excited manner and though he said he spoke German indifferently, yet he spoke English somewhat as a German would.

I had hoped that he might be useful to us as an instrument of peace, but he will have to change his attitude before that hope can be realized.   Affectionately yours,   E. M. House[2]

TLS (WP, DLC).
  [1] George V and William II were actually first cousins.
  [2] House summarized this letter in E. M. House to WW, March 3 [2], 1915, T telegram (WP, DLC).

From Andrew Furuseth

Mr. President: Washington, D. C., March 1st, 1915.

In your address to Congress on December 2nd, 1913, you gave expression to your kindly sympathy with the efforts being made to improve the conditions of seamen in the following language:

"An International Congress for the discussion of all questions that affect safety at sea is now sitting in London at the suggestion of our own Government. So soon as the conclusions of that Congress can be learned and considered we ought to address ourselves, among other things, to the prompt alleviation of the very unsafe, unjust, and burdensome conditions which now surround the employment of sailors and render it extremely difficult to obtain the services of spirited and competent men such as every ship needs if it is to be safely handled and brought to port."

In an interview which you granted to the members of the Executive Board of the American Federation of Labor, you renewed your expressions of sympathy but expressed some apprehension with reference to some possible complication that might arise over one section of the bill dealing with the right of a seaman on a foreign vessel to demand and receive one-half of his earned wages in a port of the United States. I understand your apprehension has special reference to the domestic law of the Republic of France dealing with the payment of seamen and forbidding such payment except at the home port. I have observed French vessels in many ports of the world and particularly on the Pacific Coast, and I have found in other ports, as well as in ports on the Pacific, that part of the wages earned by French seamen are often paid to them in presence of the consul, and very often outside of the presence of the consul.

The practical operation of the French law does not seem to differ materially from that of other nations. Sometimes the law is used to prevent men from deserting by depriving them of the means to obtain board and lodging on shore while looking for other employment. Sometimes it is used to drive men to desert when the master wants to get rid of them, and a refusal to pay them part of the money earned seems the best means of attaining that end.

It is very difficult for us seamen, Mr. President, to understand how any nation can justly make any complaint because the United States chooses to make the seaman a freeman, to guarantee to him in ports of call one-half of the wages that he has earned in order that he may protect and exercise such freedom, and to make such laws not only applicable to our own seamen but also to foreign seamen while within the jurisdiction of the United States. I therefore most earnestly urge you to approve this bill.

With profound respect, I beg to remain,

Faithfully yours,   Andrew Furuseth

TLS (WP, DLC).

From Jessie Woodrow Wilson Sayre

Williamstown Massachusetts

My dearest, precious, Father,   March 1st [1915].

Here we are safe and sound in Williamstown! How it snowed and how hard the wind blew when we arrived; but that blessed baby slept without stirring and kept as warm as toast! Our nurse seems to be a treasure, capable and gentle and a comfort generally, and our routine is already fairly well established. We are having the kind of weather I love best. I am beginning to take walks again and to recover from my first tiredness. It was hard to tell Miss Harkins 'good bye' this morning. I can't tell you how much it has meant to us to have her here to get things started. Every detail is so well arranged here now for convenience in caring for the baby and it gives one such confidence to know that things are *right*. She has been lovely in every way.

Oh Father, dearest Father, how can I ever find words to express our gratitude for all you have done. I couldn't say a word when I left and now I find it equally hard to write, for it has meant more than you can ever know to me to have a father's tender love and care and thoughtfulness at this time. You seemed to be giving me all mother's love combined with your own, so that I felt her very close and you most wonderfully dear.

Those were blessed hours, dear Father, when you sat and talked with me in your busy hours and I shall cherish them always. They and you and your love are bound up for always in my new happiness with the little son. I *wish* we were not so far away, or that if I were nearer I could give you a fraction of all the happiness you have given me. How I hope that Frankie will grow up to know and love and be like you.

With dearest love from us both to all but especially to my darling Father,   devotedly   Jessie.

ALS (WP, DLC).

Remarks at a Press Conference

March 2, 1915

Do you expect to be in the city after the fourth of March, Mr. President?

Yes.

Will you tell us whether you have decided definitely whether you will go to 'Frisco?

Unfortunately, I cannot decide definitely. I am waiting to see if there is rope enough.

Mr. President, the big question this morning is the British note and our attitude toward it. Can you give us any light on it?

> I cannot define our attitude toward it yet, because I have not had a chance to digest it—I mean to canvass the whole situation.

As you understand it, does the British note merely declare a blockade, or does it go farther than that?

> That is just the question I cannot answer. Apparently, it seeks to establish a blockade, but I cannot answer that question with confidence.

If England establishes a blockade, it would be her right or alleged right to seize neutral ships in the waters of the blockaded ports, but under this order Great Britain would go a great deal farther than that, wouldn't she? She would arrogate to herself or claim the right, at least, to seize a neutral ship, no matter in what waters it may be.

> The precise meaning I have not got at yet. It will need further correspondence to get at it.

Any attempt to send ships in there would involve merely a risk then, rather than a violation of neutrality?

> Oh, yes, that would be true of a strict blockade.

Do you mean, Mr. President, that the note does not define Great Britain's position clearly, or that you have not yet studied it?

> Both are true. I have not had time to study it. As I read it, it merely defines in general terms a policy without defining the means by which they intend to enforce that policy, whether that means is a definite blockade or not.

Mr. President, submarines seem to have changed the rules of warfare considerably. Has any information come to you that a blockade under modern war conditions is a very different condition than what it has been, and that therefore the lines are made broader?

> Yes, sir, but no nation has the right to change the rules of war. I think that it would be more precise to say that the conditions of war have changed radically; the rules of war have not.

Can you say anything with reference to the seamen's bill, Mr. President?

> I am in executive session on that.

Can you say whether or not you have heard from the State Department on that?

> Yes, I have heard from the State Department concerning the degree to which it affects treaties with foreign nations.

Can you say anything about that?

I would rather not say anything just at present, because I am studying the matter.

You know, Mr. President, there are always some leaks in executive session.

But not until after they are over.

Is the rural credits situation satisfactory to you now?

I don't know what it is this morning. It changes kaleidoscopically.

Mr. President, when that matter was up before it was understood that you were opposed to any form of federal aid in the rural credit plan. Is that true still?

Yes, sir.

One statesman informed me that the Hollis bill was the only one you would sign, Mr. President.

Oh, well, there are a great many people who know my mind better than I do myself.

Mr. President, I thought it was the Hollis-Bulkley bill that was laid aside because it had federal aid in it.

Yes, it was.

Federal aid is out of the bill?

Out of the most recent form.

The House put it back in at 1:30 this morning?

Did it?

Mr. President, could you say anything about this passport investigation. It is reported to have been brought to your attention.

It was, of course, but I immediately directed that there should be a full investigation. I haven't had time to follow the testimony.

Do you expect, Mr. President, that an extra session of the Senate will be necessary?

No, sir, I don't expect it.

Mr. President, have you any plan of doing anything further with regard to the southern Ohio coal strike?

Well, the Department of Labor is seeking to do everything that the law permits us to do. I merely said to one of the representatives from Ohio the other day that I would be pleased to play any part in it that I could play. Of course, I am interested in a settlement.

Did he suggest any definite course?

No, he did not.

Didn't he suggest that you might receive the representatives of the miners and the operators? Have you agreed to that?

I haven't been asked to do it. The representatives of both sides were to be in Washington, I think it was, yesterday, to see the Secretary of Labor; they were invited by him, I believe, to a conference.

Mr. President, have you given any consideration to the suggestion—I don't know that it has been made to you personally—of a special session of Congress in the fall?

    No.

Mr. President, have you heard that Ambassador Bernstorff from Germany was expected to be recalled by his government?

    No, sir.

T MS (C. L. Swem Coll., NjP).

To Andrew Furuseth

My dear Mr. Furuseth: [The White House] March 2, 1915

I have your interesting letter of yesterday.

My interest in the relief and protection sought to be afforded in the seamen's bill is no less deep than it was, and some of my apprehensions with regard to the bill that has just been passed have been removed. But what is troubling me just at this moment is that it demands of the Government what seems a truly impossible thing, namely, the denunciation of some twenty-two commercial treaties.

I am advised by the State Department that the denunciation of a particular clause of a treaty is not feasible, that to denounce any of it would be to denounce all of it unless it in terms permits a partial denunciation, which none of our existing treaties does. To throw the commercial relations of the country into disorder and doubt just at this juncture might lead to the most serious consequences, and upon that ground I am debating very seriously whether it is possible for me to sign the bill or not.

    Cordially and sincerely yours,   Woodrow Wilson

TLS (Letterpress Books, WP, DLC).

From William Jennings Bryan

My dear Mr. President: Washington March 2, 1915.

I am sending you the supplementary abstract prepared by Mr. Lansing.[1]

I receuved[2] a visit this afternoon from Senators La Follette and Owen who were accompanied by a Mr. Foruseth. Senator La Follette, as you know, has had a great interest in this bill. He says it is the result of a fight that has carried on for twenty-one years. It passed the last Congress just after the Baltimore Convention and he says that if there was objection to the clause in regard to the renunciation of treaties it ought to have been brought to the attention of Congress before the bill was passed.

While I was talking with them this thought occurred to me—I did not mention it to them but I suggest it to you—namely: that if this clause is the only thing that stands in the way you might propose to the advocates of the bill that they call the bill back and amend it so as to give you three months (or six months) *after the close of the war* to denounce these treaties.

I confess I am very much impressed by the arguments in favor of the bill on its general merits and but for the two objections—

1st: the denunciation of these treaties at this time; and,

2d: the putting of the bill into operation during the war; I would be inclined to favor the bill.

If you propose to them this change and they are not able to make the amendment it will strengthen your position if you you [sic] veto it or allow it to die in your hands. If, on the contrary, they are able to make the amendment it will then postpone operation of the bill until after the war, when it can be tried under more favorable circumstances than now exist.

With assurances of high respect I am, my dear Mr. President,

Yours very sincerely,   W. J. Bryan

TLS (WP, DLC).

¹ RL to WJB, March 2, 1915, TLS (WP, DLC), enclosing RL, untitled T memorandum (WP, DLC), on the treaty arrangements of the United States with various governments relating to the treatment of seamen.

² That is, "received."

From David Wark Griffith[1]

Mr. President: New York March second 1915

Please pardon this intrusion; as Mr. Dixon had already expressed his own and our thanks to you, I didn't know whether it would be quite the thing for me to trouble you with anything additional. But the honor you conferred on us has brought to me so much happiness that I cannot refrain from expressing my deepest and most sincere gratitude.

In the big picture world, of which I am only a small part, and in those channels through which the pictures reach all the American people, I shall in every way do all in my power to show my practical appreciation of your generosity.

If we carry out the proposed series of motion pictures dealing with matters historical and political, of which I spoke to you,

I should be most happy to have someone representing your views to pass upon our ideas before beginning the initial work.

Again thanking you profoundly, I am

Most sincerely,   David W Griffith

TLS (WP, DLC).
¹ Producer of "The Birth of a Nation," pioneer of the modern motion picture form.

From William Jennings Bryan, with Enclosure

My dear Mr. President: Washington March 3d, 1915.

Mr. Lansing and I have decided to submit to you the enclosed telegram which we think ought to be sent to Great Britain.

You will notice it asks for information which seems necessary to enable us to understand the purport of the declaration which you have under consideration. If you agree with us that a telegram ought to be sent will you please make such corrections as you think best in this and send it over to the State Department Telegraph Office to be sent out tonight.

With assurances of high respect I am, my dear Mr. President,

Yours very sincerely,   W. J. Bryan

TLS (SDR, RG 59, 763.72/1551, DNA).

E N C L O S U R E

American Ambassador, London.   Washington, March 3, 1915.

British-French declaration regarding commerce to and from Germany delivered by British and French Ambassadors on March first appears to contemplate a blockade of German coasts but fails to announce establishment of such blockade or to use the word in declaration.

You will please inquire at once of British Government whether they consider a state of blockade exists.

If they reply in the affirmative, you will ask by what means they intend to make it effective, and what will be the radius of activity of the blockading squadron, and what particular ports or coastal area they intend to blockade.

You will further ask, in case of a reply in the affirmative, what is meant by the sentence: "It is not intended to confiscate such vessels or cargoes unless they would otherwise be liable to condemnation."

If they reply in the negative, you will ask under what principle of international law or practice the proposed total interruption of commerce will be enforced and to what extent it is proposed to apply the rules of contraband in dealing with vessels and cargoes detained, which are going to or coming from Germany. You will further ask, in case the reply is in the negative, how the right of immunity from seizure of neutral-owned cargoes is affected by its origin and what rule of international law prevents free passage of a cargo of German origin in a neutral vessel bound to a neutral port.

It is necessary for a proper consideration of the British-French declaration that the foregoing questions be answered categorically and clearly in order that this Government may determine to what extent its rights as a neutral are affected by the declaration. Report as promptly as possible.   Bryan

T telegram (SDR, RG 59, 763.72/1551, DNA).

From Robert Marion La Follette

Dear Mr. President: Washington, D. C. 3 March 1915.

Permit me this one further suggestion on the bill for the Freedom of American Sailors and for the Safety of Human Life at Sea:

By its terms, you have three months within which to give notice for the denunciation of the treaty provisions in conflict with it. You have twelve months thereafter in which to adjust differences with foreign nations,—fifteen months in all.

Congress meets in nine months. The treaties continue in force for six months thereafter.

Should you require additional time to adjust all differences with the nations concerned, I will pledge myself to aid to the uttermost in passing a joint resolution extending the time limit on the treaties. Indeed such action by Congress would follow at once as a matter of course.

Congressional action continuing existing treaties in force for whatever time is necessary under conditions then prevailing removes every possible risk of foreign complications, touching which you have expressed apprehension.

Sincerely yours,   Robert M. La Follette

TLS (WP, DLC).

Walter Hines Page to William Jennings Bryan

London. March 3 [1915]

1734. Following is in the cipher of the Secretary of State.

Very confidential. For the Secretary and the President.

In view of the decisive effect of the British reprisals which brings the war into its final stage, in view of the unparalleled power with which the British will be left when peace comes, and in view of this government's courteous regard for us and for our rights, and in view of British public opinion which is more than thoroughly aroused and firmly united than ever before in English history, I most earnestly recommend the following:

That we content ourselves for the present with a friendly inquiry how the proposed reprisal will be carried out and with giving renewed notice that we hold ourselves free to take up all cases of damage to our commerce and all unlawful acts on their merits as they occur. This will enable us to accomplish all that we can accomplish by any sort of note or protest. It will leave us perfect freedom for any action that events make proper and it will not inflame public opinion in England, France and Japan.

The Spanish Ambassador here tells me that this is practically what his government will do; and I hear the same from other neutrals.　　　　　American Ambassador, London.

T telegram (WP, DLC).

An Unpublished Statement on the Ship Purchase Bill

[c. March 4, 1915]

The shipping bill has failed because the Republican Senators and their unexpected allies from the Democratic side were unwilling to permit the business of the country to be served and relieved at a time of extraordinary crisis and necessity,—when all the rest of the world needed what America produces, and America was ready to supply the need,—when the whole foreign trade of the country was threatened with a disastrous congestion and the fortunes and opportunities of thousands of her people put at jeopardy.

The war, with the extraordinary circumstances which have attended it, has removed from the sea nearly one-half of the tonnage of the world. The owners of the ships that remain free to traverse the sea have taken advantage of the situation to raise the freight rates from four to ten fold—to what figures they please,—to such figures that in many instances the freight charges for a single voyage exceed the value of the vessel itself. Many sorts of cargo they refuse altogether. They will carry only what is most profitable to them and and [sic] what can be conveyed at the greatest convenience and smallest cost to themselves. Foodstuffs get slowly out. Cotton is carried in considerable quantities because high prices are to be had on the other side of the water for it, but not high prices on this side the water. The increase above the low price which the farmer in the South receives for it goes chiefly to the ship owner, whose profits are enormous. Lumber the ships will not take at all; nor coal; nor many another a commodity which the ship owners are not interested at present to carry. Contracts are ignored; all engagements made before the war are off; they discriminate as they choose. More bottoms must be had and fair rates obtained or the export trade of rich America, for which the rest of the world impatiently waits, will be partially paralyzed and what part of it moves will be unconscionably taxed by the ship owners. No one can break their monopoly as things stand. They have long operated upon agreement with one another. There is no reason why they should bid against one another when there is more than enough for them all and to spare. Whether their owners are Americans or foreigners, it is all the same. They have the same interest and they stand together.

Through several generations of legislation we have starved and hampered and destroyed our merchant marine and Americans have put their money into ships carrying the flags of other nations. We have managed to make both the cost of building ships and the cost of operating them as great as possible and have put ourselves in every way at a disadvantage in the competition of the seas; and now our sins have found us out. We are reaping the full harvest.

Something had to be done or, at least, attempted. Private capital would do nothing. Foreign built ships were admitted to American registry; the Government undertook insurance against the risks of war at sea. Some Americans bought ships; some transferred those they already owned from foreign flags to the American flag. But the result did not affect the freight rates in the least. There were only a few more ships to reap the harvest of inordinate gain and select the most profitable cargoes. Nobody proposed to do anything unless the Government would advance the money or furnish the financial guarantee to make the enterprise profitable. Every measure proposed turned out to be some form of subsidy under which private owners were to have the use of the public moneys to make their profits certain.

To the men now in control of the Government every such proposal seemed only to lead back to the very things the party now in power had been elected to alter and prevent. Has the public not had examples enough and to spare of the use of the money of the Treasury of the United States through private hands, through small groups of bankers, to secure advantages in which the public had no share and from which it derived no direct benefit, and by means of which it was made to pay again and again? If private capital would not or could not come to the assistance of the public and the relief of the congested foreign trade of the country, if the money of the taxpayers must be used, it was plain that the Government itself ought directly to control the use of it and see that the benefit of its use got as directly as possible to the people who paid the taxes, to the industries upon which private ship owners had put such extraordinary burdens, and to the hundreds of thousands of men employed in those industries.

Hence the ship purchase bill providing for a corporation the majority of whose stock was to be owned by the Government of the United States and whose business was to be controlled by considerations of public interest under the direction of a government board. It would have supplied many ships, more and more as the months to come disclosed the necessity. But, more than that, it would have broken the control of the shipping monopoly and brought the freight rates down and cut short the present riot of unconscionable charges. It would have broadened the old lines of trade and would have developed new ones. It would have come just when the flags hitherto free upon the seas are in danger of being driven from it and only the flag of the United States represents the neutral trade of the European world.

Seven Democratic Senators united with the Republican Senators to defeat the plan, by filibuster when they realized the weakness of debate, and they have achieved their object. The members of that ill-omened coalition must bear the whole responsibility for it, the very grave responsibility for infinite damage to the business of the United States, to farmers, to laborers, to manufacturers, to producers of every class and sort. They have fastened the control of the selfish shipping interests on the country and the prospect is not a little sinister. Their responsibility will be very heavy, heavier and heavier as the months come and go; and it will be very bitter to bear.

I shall not call an extra session of Congress. I have promised the country that there should be as long a period as possible of accommodation to the new conditions which have been created by recent important legislation. Unless circumstances arise which I cannot at present foresee, I cannot in good faith deny the business of the country this time of adjustment in many large matters, even to remedy the perhaps irremediable damage this unnatural and unprecedented alliance has brought upon our business. Their opportunity to rectify their grievous disloyalty has passed.[1]

CLST MS with WWhw and WWT emendations (WP, DLC).
[1] There is a WWsh draft of this statement in WP, DLC.

A Statement

[March 4, 1915]

A great Congress has closed its sessions. Its work will prove the purpose and quality of its statesmanship more and more the longer it is tested. Business has now a time of calm and thoughtful adjustment before it, disturbed only by the European war. The circumstances created by the war put the nation to a special test, a test of its true character and of its self-control. The constant thought of every patriotic man should now be for the country, its peace, its order, its just and tempered judgment in the face of perplexing difficulties. Its dignity and its strength alike will appear not only in the revival of its business, despite abnormal conditions, but also in its power to think, to purpose, and to act with patience, with disinterested fairness, and without excitement, in a spirit of friendliness and enlightenment which will firmly establish its influence throughout the world.[1]

T MS (C. L. Swem Coll., NjP).
[1] There is a WWsh draft of this press release in WP, DLC.

To William Jennings Bryan, with Enclosure

My dear Mr. Secretary,   [The White House] 4 March, 1915.

The green paper despatch attached hereto[1] seems to me abrupt in expression and also a bit difficult to interpret as it stands. I therefore beg that, in its stead, you will send to Ambassador Page at London Mr. Lansing's letter to you (also attached), as I have taken the liberty of altering it. It is both lucid and conveys the matter in just the right tone of inquiry.

Faithfully Yours,　W.W.

WWTLI (SDR, RG 59, 763.72/1554½, DNA).
1 The Enclosure printed with WJB to WW, March 3, 1915.

ENCLOSURE[1]

⟨Dear Mr. Secretary:⟩　　　　　　　　　　⟨March 2, 1915.⟩
American Ambassador, London.

In regard to the recent communications received from the British and French governments concerning restraints upon Commorece with Germany, please commu[n]icate with the British foreign office in the sense following: The difficulty of determining action upon the British and French declarations of intended retaliation upon commerce with Germany ⟨is⟩ *lies in* the nature of the proposed measures in their relation to commerce by neutrals.

While it appears that the intention is to interfere with and take into custody all ships both outgoing and incoming, trading with Germany, which is in effect a blockade of German ports, the rule of blockade, that a ship attempting to enter or leave a German port regardless of the character of its cargo may be condemned, is not asserted.

The language of the declaration is "the British and French Governments will therefore hold themselves free to detain and take into port ships carrying goods of presumed enemy destination, ownership or origin. It is not intended to confiscate such vessel or cargoes unless they would otherwise be liable to condemnation."

The first sentence claims a right pertaining only to a state of blockade. The last sentence proposes a treatment of ships and cargoes as if no blockade existed. The two together present a proposed course of action previously unknown to international law.

As a consequence neutrals have no standard by which to measure their rights or to avoid danger to their ships and cargoes. The paradoxical situation thus created should be changed and the declaring powers ought to assert whether they rely upon the rules governing a blockade or the rules applicable when no blockade exists.

The declaration presents other perplexities.

The last sentence quoted indicates that the rules of contraband are to be applied to cargoes detained. The rule covering non-contraband articles carried ⟨to⟩ *in* neutral bottoms is that the cargoes shall be released and the ships allowed to proceed. This rule cannot under the first sentence quoted be applied as to destination. What then is to be done with a cargo of non-contraband goods detained under the declaration? The same question may be asked as to conditional contraband cargoes.

The foregoing comments apply to cargoes destined for Germany. Cargoes coming out of German ports present another problem under the terms of the declaration. Under the rules governing enemy exports only goods owned by enemy subjects in enemy bottoms are subject to seizure and condemnation. Yet by the declaration it is purposed to seize and take into port all goods of enemy "ownership and *origin*."[2] The word "origin" is particularly significant. The origin of goods destined to neutral territory on neutral ships is not and never has been a ground for forfeiture except in case a blockade is declared and maintained. What then would the seizure amount to in the present case except to delay the delivery of the goods? The declaration does not indicate what disposition would be made of such cargoes if owned by a neutral or if owned by an enemy subject. Would a different rule be applied according to ownership? If so, upon what principles of international law would it rest? ⟨But⟩ *And* upon what rule if no blockade is declared and maintained could the cargo of a neutral ship sailing out of a German port be condemned? If it is not condemned, what other legal course is there but to release it?

While ⟨I am⟩ *this government is* fully alive to the possibility that the methods of modern naval warfare, particularly in the use of the submarine for both defensive and offensive operations, may make the former means of maintaining a blockade a physical impossibility, ⟨I think⟩ *it feels it can be urged with great force* that there should be also some limit to "the radius of activity," and especially so if this action by the belligerents can be construed to be a blockade. It would certainly create a serious state of affairs if, *for example*, an American vessel laden with a cargo of German origin should escape the British patrol in European waters only to be held up by a cruiser off New York and taken into Halifax.[3]

⟨These are some of the questions which suggest themselves from a hasty examination of the British and French declaration. It seems to me that the documents require careful scrutiny before action is taken by the Department as the whole matter of "blockade" under modern methods of naval warfare must be analyzed and some idea reached as to what is proper and right for belligerents to do and to what extent the previous rules should be modified.

Faithfully yours,   Robert Lansing⟩

Respectfully submitted to the President   W.J.B.

T telegram (SDR, RG 59, 763.72/1551, DNA).
  ¹ In the following document, Wilson deleted words in angle brackets and added those in italics.
  ² Emphasis here in Lansing's text.
  ³ This dispatch was sent as WJB to WHP, March 5, 1915, T telegram (SDR, RG 59, 763.72/1551, DNA). It is printed in *FR-WWS 1915*, pp. 132-33. The British censor intercepted this telegram. The decode is filed with FO 382/2, No. 26336, PRO. A minute attached and initialed by Grey reads: "The note on the whole distinctly gives the impression that the U. S. government will not seriously oppose our action in holding up German shipments."

To William Jennings Bryan, with Enclosures

My dear Mr. Secretary,   [The White House] 4 March, 1915.

My judgment is against this, as yours is. It would seem like bargaining away some of the rights of China in exchange for relief from some of our own difficulties.

I think we ought to go straight at the matter of the requests, in the way you and I agreed was opportune and best when we conferred on the subject.

I hope that this may be done as soon as possible, so that we may deal with the matter while it is vital and warm.

Faithfully Yours,   W.W.

WWTLS (W. J. Bryan Papers, DLC).

E N C L O S U R E   I

Edward Thomas Williams to William Jennings Bryan

Dear Mr. Secretary: [Washington] February 26, 1915.

Before the Department decides definitely to make no objections to the "demands" as distinguished from the "requests" which Japan has presented to China I respectfully suggest the propriety of obtaining a quid pro quo since we shall be surrendering valuable treaty rights.

There are however certain other considerations that also deserve attention.

  1. The demands with respect to South Manchuria and East-

ern Mongolia would undoubtedly, if granted, be an infringement of our treaty rights and a violation of Article IV of the
Treaty of Portsmouth which stipulates that

> "Japan and Russia reciprocally engage not to obstruct any
> general measures, common to all countries, which China may
> take for the development of the commerce and industry of
> Manchuria."

This demand and others, which, if granted, will give Japan a
preferred position in Manchuria, is a dangerous precedent since
it is almost certain to be followed by Russia in North Manchuria
and Mongolia, by France in Yunnan, and by Japan herself in
Shantung and Fukien and we shall be face to face with the partition of China. Even should it result in nothing worse than the
renewal of the policy of spheres of interest, it would certainly
injure our commerce and to a certain extent hamper our missionary and educational work.

At the same time it is necessary to recognize that Japan has
special interests in Manchuria.

Moreover, she needs the sparsely settled and fertile lands of
that region for her surplus population which is not disposed to
settle in any large numbers in Formosa.

The diversion of the tide of Japanese emigration towards
Manchuria may somewhat relieve the situation on our own
Pacific Coast.

In September, 1912, when Secretary Knox was in Japan attending the funeral of the Emperor it was suspected that he
would discuss with the Japanese Foreign Office the questions of
the internationalization of railways in Manchuria, Japanese immigration into the United States and other matters then pending
between the two Governments, but Mr. Knox felt that it would
scarcely be proper under the circumstances to open such discussion. The Minister for Foreign Affairs had already prepared a
memorandum which he handed to Mr. Knox and which it was
decided should not be made a matter of official record. This
memorandum is interesting as showing what, in the opinion of
the Japanese Government, the effect of Japanese settlement in
Manchuria would be upon Japanese emigration to America.

Viscount Uchida said in the document mentioned:

> "It became apparent some years ago, that it would be neces-
> sary for the Imperial Government, in order to relieve the situa-
> tion of embarrassment and friction, to adopt some efficient
> means to turn the tide of Japanese emigration from the con-
> tinental territory of the United States. But considering the
> pressure of population in Japan, it was felt that no measures

would be regarded as efficient that did not at the same time provide some suitable outlet for the Japanese people desiring to emigrate.

"Accordingly, the Imperial Government on the one hand, put into force the existing arrangement regarding Japanese emigration to America, and, on the other, took steps to encourage Japanese to go to Korea and the adjacent regions.

"They have been so far successful in their endeavors that there are now over 80,000 Japanese subjects, exclusive of Koreans, resident in South Manchuria and the eastern portion of Inner Mongolia, which is geographically and administratively appurtenant to South Manchuria, and the question of Japanese emigration to America has wholly ceased to be acute.

"These circumstances combined, coupled with the necessity to safe-guard her own frontiers, have given to Japan a title to special rights and interests in the region of South Manchuria and eastern Inner Mongolia which the Imperial Government believe is entirely unassailable."

Possibly a better understanding with respect to the California land question might be brought about by a reference to this statement in connection with our acquiescence in the Japanese demands as to Manchuria.

There is, however, a question of some importance now pending which ought to be settled before acquiescence in the Japanese demands is expressed.

The South Manchuria Railway with the approval of the Japanese Government is discriminating against freight brought into Manchuria in other than Japanese vessels and against goods sent to Newchwang rather than Dairen or Antung.

The Japanese Government would probably agree to rectify this discrimination and bind itself once more to maintain the "open door" in Manchuria.

I do not think we should protest against the action of the Japanese in Manchuria or in Shantung, but we have just received a series of resolutions adopted by the Cotton Goods Export Association of New York, requesting the Department to obtain a reaffirmation of the principle of the "Open Door." The American cotton goods trade has suffered severely from Japanese methods of competition in Manchuria and what can be done to assist that trade ought of course to be done. I believe the removal of the discrimination in freight rates will help to a considerable degree.

There is one other demand that deserves our attention, i.e. the demand concerning the Han Yeh Ping coal and iron company. The demand as stated in the Japanese Memorandum is quite incomplete according to the text received from China. That text contains a second article which requires Japanese consent to the opening or operation of other mines in the *neighborhood* of the Han Yeh Ping properties. This is a very elastic term and may be made to include the provinces of Hupeh, Kiangsi and Hunan in which their properties are located and thus may be employed to exclude Americans from opening and working the valuable mineral deposits of those three provinces to which we could not at all consent.

I suggest that we ask Japan about the discrepancy between the demands as expressed in the memorandum and that published in the press.   E.T.W.

TLI (W. J. Bryan Papers, DNA).

E N C L O S U R E   I I

Robert Lansing to William Jennings Bryan

Dear Mr. Secretary: [Washington] March 1, 1915.

It seems to me that the suggestions made by Mr. Williams in his memorandum of February 26th, which is enclosed, are worthy of careful consideration.

This Government could take the position that, while, it has reason to complain of the Japanese "demands" on China on the ground that they infringe the treaty rights of the United States and are contrary to the formal assurances heretofore made by the Japanese Government, it appreciates the internal pressure of the increasing population of the Empire and the necessity for oversea territory to relieve this pressure by emigration.

It could be stated that in the opinion of this Government this necessity for expansion has been in a large measure the cause of Japanese emigration to the United States, and the underlying reason for the controversies which have taken place over exclusion laws and California land-legislation.

I would suggest for your consideration whether it would not be well for this Government to state that if it refrains from urging its undoubted treaty rights relative to Southern Manchuria and Shan Tung, it would do so as a friend of Japan who is solicitous for her welfare, recognizing her economic situation and the relief which would doubtless result from an opportunity to develop Southern Manchuria through Japanese emigrants into that region.

It could be further stated that, if this Government adopts such a policy out of friendship for Japan and with an earnest desire to see her wishes accomplished, it may justly expect reciprocal friendly treatment on the part of the Japanese Government, and similar evidence of good will on their part.

It could be pointed out that this spirit of friendship could be shown by Japan by a declaration that in view of the announced attitude of the United States in regard to Southern Manchuria and Shan Tung that the Japanese Government:

(1) Will make no further complaint in regard to legislation affecting land tenures in the United States unless such legislation is confiscatory in character, or materially affects vested rights;

(2) Will reaffirm explicitely the principle of the "Open Door," making it particularly applicable to the territories affected by the demands;

(3) And will prevent any monopolization by Japanese subjects of particular trades in these territories, and any preferential rates or treatment by Japanese railways or other transportation concerns for the benefit of Japanese subjects or their merchandise.

If a bargain along these lines could be struck it would relieve us of the vexatious California land controversy, and prevent in large measure future disputes which seem almost inevitable if the "demands" of Japan are permitted at the present time to pass unchallenged.

In any event can there be any harm in attempting to reach a reciprocal understanding, such as the one outlined above? We would certainly be no worse off than we were before; and I think, even if our proposal is rejected, we would be in a far better position to discuss Japan's conduct when a more propitious time comes to take up with other interested powers the question of the "Open Door" and the respective rights of the Powers secured through the application of that principle.

In view of the situation it has seemed to me advisable to wait until this matter could be considered before preparing a memorandum on the subject of the Japanese "requests."

Very sincerely yours, Robert Lansing.[1]

TLS (W. J. Bryan Papers, DNA).

[1] In spite of Wilson's veto of the proposed bargain, Lansing, as late as April 2, informed the British government that the administration favored it: "Counsellor of State Department, who is now President's chief adviser, told me to-day he thought wisest course would be for United States simply to enter caveat and make no formal protest, and for other Powers to await developments, and see if agreements are really violated. All United States Government have done hitherto is to ask for explanations. His impression is that Japan is contemplating action which comes very near violation of agreement with United States,

but so long as said action is limited to Manchuria and Mongolia, United States Government were inclined to think this would be useful as outlet to Japanese energies, thus diverting them from this continent.

"United States Government will do what they can to moderate action of State Governments on Pacific slope.

"They are evidently rather alarmed at possibility of a secret understanding with Russia, and even eventually with Germany." C. A. Spring Rice to E. Grey, April 2, 1915, printed telegram (FO 371/2323, No. 38669, PRO).

To Frank Irving Cobb

My dear Mr. Cobb: [The White House] March 4, 1915

I can't let the day pass without expressing my profound gratification in the generous editorial in this morning's World.[1] Its judgment is so generous that I cannot pretend to feel in the least deserving of its praise and confidence, but I can say that it will steady my hopes and purposes for the great tasks that are in hand and that lie immediately ahead of us. Such things make me feel stronger just because of the feeling they give me that thoughtful men are back of me.

May I not say that I so value the judgment of The World that I find myself questioning my own judgment when it runs contrary to yours?

Cordially and sincerely yours,   Woodrow Wilson

TLS (Letterpress Books, WP, DLC).
[1] "Two Years of Wilson," New York *World*, March 4, 1915, praised Wilson's political independence, noting that "he and he alone is President," and called his "the sanest mind to-day that is intrusted with the responsibilities of government anywhere in civilization."

To Newton Diehl Baker

My dear Mr. Mayor: [The White House] March 5, 1915

Mr. Tumulty placed your telegram of the third[1] before me and you may be sure that it made a great impression on me, notwithstanding the fact that I signed the Seamen's Bill. I shall be very much grieved if the law has the effect you fear. I sincerely hope that those who are interested are mistaken in their forecast.

I debated the matter of signing the bill very earnestly indeed, weighing the arguments on both sides with a good deal of anxiety, and finally determined to sign it because it seemed the only chance to get something like justice done to a class of workmen who have been too much neglected by our laws.[2]

With warmest regard,

Cordially and sincerely yours,   Woodrow Wilson

TLS (Letterpress Books, WP, DLC).
[1] N. D. Baker to JPT, March 3, 1915, T telegram (WP, DLC).
[2] Wilson had signed the bill on March 4.

To David Wark Griffith

My dear Mr. Griffith: [The White House] March 5, 1915

Thank you sincerely for your generous letter of March second.

I am very much interested in what you intimate as to your plans with regard to future motion pictures and if it is possible for me to assist you with an opinion about them at any time, I shall certainly try to do so, though, of course, you realize that there is always a violent probability that I shall be absolutely absorbed and my attention preempted.

      Cordially and sincerely yours,   Woodrow Wilson

TLS (Letterpress Books, WP, DLC).

To Ewing Charles Bland[1]

My dear Mr. Bland: [The White House] March 5, 1915

Your letter to the Attorney General, of which you were kind enough to send me a copy,[2] distresses me very much. I have desired only to honor you and yet I seem to have succeeded, to judge by your feeling as expressed in your letter, only in bringing mortification to you. Nothing could have been further from my thought or intention.

My decision was based entirely upon the feeling that while I no doubt had the legal power to renew former recess appointments which had been opposed by the Senate, it was clearly inconsistent with the spirit of the Constitution that I should do so. It was a contest in my mind, therefore, in this case between my desire to honor you and my desire to live up, not only to the letter, but to the spirit of the Constitution. I think that you will see in such a case how my conscience was bound.

This whole case has perplexed and distressed me. I cannot believe that the community will fail to realize how sincerely I have endeavored to show my confidence in you or that my expressions of that confidence will fail to offset any disadvantage which may have come to you through your generous cooperation with the administration.

      Cordially and sincerely yours,   Woodrow Wilson

TLS (Letterpress Books, WP, DLC).

[1] Judge of the South Side municipal court of Kansas City, Mo., son of Representative Richard P. ("Silver Dick") Bland of Missouri; former associate of Frank P. Walsh; and a leader in various reform movements in Missouri. Wilson had given him a recess appointment as United States marshal for the western district of Missouri in December 1914, whereupon he had resigned his judgeship. Senator James A. Reed had blocked his confirmation in early January 1915 after Wilson had sent his name to the Senate for regular appointment.

2 This copy is missing. However Bland's letter to Gregory must have been similar to E. C. Bland to WJB, Feb. 27, 1915, TLS (W. J. Bryan Papers, DNA), saying that the President had not stood by him in the fight against his confirmation in the Senate. He went on: "All of the above facts are well known to the public here and if I am let out I will be humiliated and disgraced and made the object of ridicule."

From William Jennings Bryan

My dear Mr. President: Washington March 5th, 1915.

I am sending you flimsies of two despatches which bother me very much.[1] The last one is dated yesterday at six p.m.

Obregon, whether he intends it or not, is using language to arouse opposition to foreigners, and it is impossible, of course, for anyone to guess what may be the result. We are unfortunate in not having any Special Representative in Mexico City. We have a man, and I believe an excellent one, recommended by Senator Mark Smith, but he took sick on reaching Washington and is now in the hospital. He is the one who was intended for Mexico City and adjoining country.

I am wondering whether it may not be necessary to speak more emphatically than we have done. I have used all the adjectives that properly go with persuasion but things seem to grow worse instead of better and the representatives of other nations are very much concerned.

Mr. Lansing has suggested it might be worth while to notify carranza and Obregon that in view of the language which is being employed by Obregon to excite hatred of foreigners, thus greatly increasing the risks, and in view of the interruption of traffic and communication by Carranza, thus further increasing the risks, that we would hold Carranza and Obregon personally responsible for injury that resulted from the methods which they are employing.

We have no soldiers nearer than Texas and are not in a position to protect Americans and other foreigners from riot, in case Obregon should succeed in stirring up riot—which he promises in advance not to resist—and I am not sure but we may be justified in bringing this pressure to bear upon Carranza.

They are proposing to evacuate, but before doing so they may create a condition there which will result in violence. The fact that the people of Mexico City are ready to welcome Zapata, whom they formerly so greatly feared, or Villa, who was also a terror to them, as a substitute for Carranza and his best general, Obregon—for Obregon seemed to stand highest among those supporting Carranza—this fact contrasts strangely with the predictions and fears expressed by the people of Mexico City before Huerta left.

Will you please let me know whether you have any instructions to give?

With assurances of high respect I am, my dear Mr. President,
Yours very sincerely,   W. J. Bryan

TLS (SDR, RG 59, 812.00/14496A, DNA).
[1] These were J. M. Cardoso de Oliveira to WJB, March 3, 11 a.m. and March 4, 6 p.m., 1915, T telegrams (SDR, RG 59, 812.00/14496 and 14488, DNA). The telegram of March 4 is printed in *FR 1915*, p. 657. The first reported that the *Carrancistas* were stepping up their campaign against foreigners, with demonstrations of workers, incendiary statements from Obregón, and, from one speaker, a threat to set up a guillotine "to finish with them." The second repeated a military order to all merchants, demanding that they open their shops for business immediately and accept Constitutionalist money, under threat of severe penalty.
Wilson undoubtedly saw as well the telegrams of March 4, 5 p.m. and 11 p.m., 1915, *FR 1915*, pp. 656-58. The first quoted a speech by Obregón against foreign control of Mexican resources; he also threatened to publish more alarming decrees and incited hungry citizens to loot: "If my children had no bread I would go out and look for it with a dagger in my hand." The second explained the merchants' dilemma: Constitutionalist money would lose all value as soon as Mexico City changed hands and the punishment for failing to do business would be "authorized looting." The telegram also contained Carranza's warning to the diplomatic corps that Mexico City would soon be evacuated.

From Edward Mandell House

Dear Governor: [London] March 5th, 1915.

I have not written in the past few days for the reason there has been no boat leaving for America for ten days.

I have had several conferences with Sir Edward and I have persuaded him that the time has come for me to leave England and go to Berlin. In the meantime, I have seen many public men of both parties, and I have laid, I think, the foundation for their approval of our future plans.[1]

During the past few days, I have gone into the Conservative camp and have talked with such men as Arthur Balfour,[2] who thoroughly approves of the second convention and also tentatively approves the plan in regard to the limiting of the manufacture of munitions of war.

I want it to be thoroughly understood that these suggestions come from us so, if they are adopted, the credit will be yours. I find that these proposals have done as much or more than anything else to make them feel that we can be helpful in the final solution. Balfour says both proposals are entirely original and, at the moment, he could see no flaws in them. I am to lunch with him again on Wednesday so we may discuss the matter further.

It will be a great help to Sir Edward to have not only his own party, but the leaders of the Conservatives working in accord with him.

I have seen many editors, both of the daily press and of such publications as the Quarterly Review, the Economist, etc. etc. whom I thought might be helpful.

And this reminds me that Northcliffe refused to publish Brooks' article about you because he thought it too eulogistic. He wanted Brooks to tone it down, but he refused to do so and will publish it in the Nation and another article of like tenor in the English Outlook.[3]

Please remember that it will be very difficult to either write or cable after I reach Germany.

Affectionately yours,   E. M. House

TLS (WP, DLC).

[1] House summarized his letter to this point in EMH to WW, March 5, 1915, T telegram (WP, DLC).

[2] Arthur James Balfour, at this time a member of the War Council, soon to become First Lord of the Admiralty in the coalition cabinet formed in May 1915.

[3] Sydney Brooks, "President Wilson," London *Outlook*, xxxv (March 6, 1915), 298-99, and "President Wilson's Record," London *Nation*, xvi (March 6, 1915), 709-10. House sent tearsheets of these articles to Wilson (they are in WP, DLC), and his note is the only indication that Brooks wrote the anonymous article in *The Nation*. In the first, Brooks praised Wilson's decisive leadership in domestic legislation but dwelt on the failure of his Mexican policy. How could a man of "rare and discriminating intelligence" behave as Wilson did while Mexico experienced "all the horrors of a seemingly perpetual anarchy"? Brooks found the answers in Wilson's "terrible conscience" and in his pedagogic traits: "a habit of authority, a stubborn pride of opinion, and a certain impatience of opposition that make it exceedingly difficult for him to reverse or depart from any policy which he has once persuaded himself possesses the essential sanctions of justice and right." In *The Nation*, Brooks emphasized Wilson's successful legislative record and steered clear of his international policies, except to suggest a role for Wilson in establishing contact among the belligerents and formulating "some scheme for insuring peace in the future."

From Paul Samuel Reinsch

PERSONAL AND CONFIDENTIAL.

Dear Mr. President: Peking, March 5, 1915.

In my letters to you I have repeatedly alluded to the need of a more effective organization for American investments in China. What is needed is a broadly representative institution or group that could take the lead in financing American enterprises in China and directing American investments into the safest and most fruitful activities. Such an organization should have no monopoly, but it would be its function to lead the way so that minor ventures might safely follow. I dealt with this matter somewhat at length in a despatch (No. 294), dated July 3rd last, to the Secretary of State, of which I enclose a copy:[1] the

underlying situation and the needs there described are un-
changed.

I may say in strict confidence that the development of independent and effective American enterprise in China is at present
impeded and the credit of your Administration compromised
by a peculiar situation. The firm of J. P. Morgan & Company or,
more exactly, the American Group appears to be in somewhat of
a sulking humor, insisting upon blaming your Administration
for having, as they put it, made active American enterprise in
China impossible through the withdrawal of support from the
Group. They count for nothing the very positive evidences your
Administration has given of a desire to encourage and foster
American enterprise in China. As another element in the situation, it appears that the member of the firm of J. P. Morgan &
Company who is most conversant with Chinese affairs[2] is now
generally considered to be desirous of later becoming American
Minister or Ambassador to China. While he has every right to
this ambition and possesses, undoubtedly, excellent qualifications of experience and ability, the result of all these facts upon
the present action of the firm of J. P. Morgan & Company would
seem to be that they are not desirous that the present Administration should receive any credit for developing American enterprise and prestige in China. Not only do they hold aloof from
giving assistance here, but they cultivate a general pessimism
with respect to American interests in China. The worse the state
of American affairs can be made to appear at present, the more
likely are these interests to be looked upon as the saviors later on
and therefore to be given control of the situation.

In thus stating the conclusions to be drawn from the prone-
ness and general attitude of indifference of this firm, I am not
actuated by any hostile feelings towards them; in fact, as you
know, I have endeavored to keep them actively interested in
China, as having every reason to go ahead with Chinese enterprises. But it would be a great pity if the resentment and the
ambitions of this firm were allowed to stand in the way of Americans holding and developing that place of influence and fruitful
activity which rightfully belongs to us in China.

If the Morgan firm could be made to see that their active and
present participation in China's development would be a good
and necessary thing from the point of view of their own interests,
they could of course be of great assistance to American enterprise here. It would appear not unlikely that they would certainly
increase their activities should any other strong organization
show any desire to enter this field; but whether or not the
Morgan firm or the old American Group persist in their attitude

of indifference and hostility, it is in any event desirable that there should be formed *a broadly representative American investment organization*.[3] Without exclusiveness or tendencies to monopoly, such an institution could pave the way for American industrial and commercial enterprises in China and could take advantage of the unusual opportunities that are now being offered. Whether this corporate body should have a semi-public character, similar to that of the Federal reserve banks, or whether it were to be a widely inclusive private institution: the main consideration is that only through such an organization can American commerce get a secure footing in China under present conditions. Opportunities are offered for your Administration to lay the foundations of a great development of American enterprise in the Far East—a development which will soon be a life necessity to our industries and for which future ages will give their thankful recognition.

There is an abundance of capital and energy in the United States for this purpose: if the men who formerly took the lead are for various reasons holding back, others should take their places. With your encouragement, they are ready to come forward.

With the highest regard and the best wishes for your continued well being, I am, dear Mr. President,

Faithfully Yours,   Paul S. Reinsch.

TLS (WP, DLC).
  [1] For a summary of P. S. Reinsch to WJB, July 3, 1914, see WW to W. G. McAdoo, Nov. 9, 1914, n. 1, Vol. 31.
  [2] Willard Dickerman Straight.
  [3] Wilson's emphasis.

To Francis Burton Harrison

[The White House] March 6, 1915.

Secretary of War has already told you of the impossibility of passing Philippine Bill at the session of Congress just closed. It was constantly pressed by the Administration, loyally supported by the full force of the party, and will be pressed to passage when the next Congress meets in December. It failed only because blocked by the rules of the Senate as employed by the Republican leaders who were opposed to the legislation and who would yield only if we withdrew the assurance of ultimate independence contained in the preamble. That we would not do. The bill will have my support until it passes and I have no doubt of its passage at the next session of Congress. Please express to the people of the Philippine Islands my deep and abiding interest in their welfare and my purpose to serve them in every possible way.

In this I am expressing the spirit and purpose of the majority of the Congress and of the whole government of the United States. Please accept my congratulations upon the success of your administration and my earnest assurance of belief in a happy and prosperous future for the islands. The people of the Islands have already proved their quality and in nothing more than in the patience and self control they have manifested in waiting for the fulfillment of our promises. Continuance in that admirable course of action will undoubtedly assure the result we all desire.

Woodrow Wilson.

T telegram (WDR, RG 350, BIA, No. 4325-157, DNA).

To William Jennings Bryan

My dear Mr. Secretary,   [The White House] 6 March, 1915.

I had seen these despatches[1] and they had given me deep anxiety and perplexity, as they have given you.

Nothing better than what Mr. Lansing suggests occurs to me, and I hope that you will act at once on his suggestion.

In addition, I hope that you will say to Carranza that the extraordinary and unpardonable course pursued by General Obregon, under his command, has renewed the talk of joint action by several of the chief governments of the world to protect their embassies and their nationals at Mexico City, and that he is running a very serious risk.

Will you not be kind enough to ask Daniels if he has ships with long range guns (not necessarily battle ships) which he could order at once to Vera Cruz, and, if so, to let me know?

Faithfully Yours,   W.W.

WWTLI (SDR, RG 59, 812.00/14504½, DNA).
[1] That is, the dispatches cited in WJB to WW, March 5, 1915.

To José Manuel Cardoso de Oliveira[1]

Washington, March 6, 1915. 9 pm

508. Your number 383, March 4, 5 P.M., and 386 March 4, 11 P.M.

We have been anxious and perplexed over the statements in your dispatches and have concluded that the best course at present is for you immediately to see General Obregon and present to him a most earnest and emphatic note in the following sense.

The Government of the United States has noted with increasing concern the reports of General Obregon's utterances to the residents of Mexico City. This Government believes they tend to incite the populace to commit outrages in which innocent foreigners within Mexican territory, particularly the City of Mexico may be involved. The Government is particularly impressed with General Obregon's suggestions that he would refuse to protect not only Mexicans but foreigners in case of violence and that his present decree is a forerunner of others more disastrous in effect. In this condition of affairs the United States Government is informed that the City of Mexico may soon be evacuated by the Constitutionalist forces, leaving the population without protection against whatever faction may choose to occupy it, thus shirking responsibility for what may happen as a result of the instigation to lawlessness before and after the evacuation of the city.

The United States Government is led to believe that a deplorable situation has been wilfully brought about by Constitutionalist leaders to force upon the populace submission to their incredible demands and to punish the city on account of refusal to comply with them. When a factional leader preys on a starving city to compel obedience to his decrees by inciting outlawry and at the same time uses means to prevent the city from being supplied with food, a situation is created which it is impossible for the United States to contemplate longer with patience. Conditions have become intolerable and can no longer be endured. The Government of the United States therefore desires General Obregon and General Carranza to know that it has, after mature consideration, determined that if, as a result of the situation for which they are responsible, Americans suffer by reason of the conduct of the Constitutionalist forces in the City of Mexico or because they fail to provide means of protection to life and property, the Government of the United States will hold General Obregon and General Carranza personally responsible therefor. Having reached this determination with the greatest reluctance, the Government of the United States will take such measures as are expedient to bring to account those who are personally responsible for what may occur.

A similar message has been sent to Vera Cruz for delivery to General Carranza.[2]   Bryan

T telegram (SDR, RG 59, 812.00/14501, DNA).

[1] The only surviving copy of the following document is the telegram that was sent. The phrasing and vocabulary are so Wilsonian that the Editors have concluded that Wilson wrote it. At the very least, in view of the personal threat against Carranza and Obregón, Wilson must have read and revised a draft before the one printed below went to Mexico City and Veracruz.

[2] WJB to J. R. Silliman, March 6, 1915, T telegram (SDR, RG 59, 812.00/14501, DNA).

From William Jennings Bryan

My dear Mr. President: Washington March 6, 1915.

I have had three copies made of the two confidential notes from Japan.[1] One copy I have given to Mr. Lansing who is at work on the note about which we have conferred; one copy I am sending to you; and the original I am keeping in my safe. You can keep this copy over there for your own reference.

With renewed assurances of high respect I am, my dear Mr. President,   Yours very sincerely,   W. J. Bryan

TLS (WP, DLC).

[1] T memoranda (WP, DLC) from the Japanese Embassy listing the demands made by the Japanese government on China regarding Shantung Province, South Manchuria and eastern Mongolia, engagement by the Chinese government not to alienate or lease any port, bay, or island along the coast of China, and agreement in principle to reorganize the Han-ye-p'ing Iron and Coal Co. a Sino-Japanese enterprise. They are printed in *FR 1915*, pp. 83-84.

From Andrew Furuseth

Mr. President: Washington, D. C. March 6, 1915.

In the name of the liberated seamen of the United States and of the partly liberated seamen of the world, I would like even to try to express some of the feeling that now is ours.

In signing the Seamen's Bill you gave back to the seamen, so far as the United States can do it, the ownership of their own bodies, and thus wiped out the last bondage existing under the American flag. The soil of the United States will be holy ground henceforth to the world's seamen, and if you should need them you will not have to draft them; you would only have to call on them. It is my prayer that you may not need them. I am saying, them, because I realize that I am a little too old.

Much important and far-reaching legislation has been enacted since you have been President, but when time shall have tested it all, your greatest and most courageous act will be deemed your signature to the Emancipation Proclamation of the Seamen.

The moral greatness of this act will silence opposition in foreign countries and compel them to follow your lead.

Thanking you again, I beg to remain, on behalf of the freedmen,

Respectfully and faithfully yours,   Andrew Furuseth

TLS (WP, DLC).

To Nancy Saunders Toy

Dearest Friend,   The White House 7 March, 1915.

Congress has adjourned, and part of the strain is off. When I can get a little rest I am sure I shall feel better, though perhaps there will come this along with it, that I shall feel the loneliness a little more poignantly, when my attention is less dispersed. Of course my main anxieties lie in a field with which Congress has little to do, in which, I mean, it could do little either for better or for worse, the field of foreign affairs. Both sides are seeing red on the other side of the sea, and neutral rights are left for the time being out of their reckoning altogether. They listen to necessity, not to reason, and there is therefore no way of calculating or preparing for anything. That is what makes the situation such a strain on the nerves and on the judgment. One waits for he does not know what, and must act amidst a scene that shifts without notice, without precedent. In such circumstances it is clearly impossible for me to get away from Washington to go to the Pacific coast or anywhere else. I must stay where I can, as nearly as possible, be in touch with all the elements all the time.

But I can regulate my days now so as to be at my own disposal rather than at the disposal of others all the day through; and that will be an immense relief, if for no other reason, because I can take time to look into things and comprehend them thoroughly and think them through! And no doubt I shall be able to get a *little* rest at intervals, instead of spending my strength on trifles all the week through. I am well, singularly well. My only trouble is with my spirits, which are distinctly bad, when I allow them time to be.

Your letters give me a great deal of pleasure.[1] It was generous of you to think of any part of Wordworth's Happy Warrior as applying to me. I seem to myself so unheroic a figure (just a man who intends right things and looks for them every day with a steady mind, uncommon in nothing except that it is at his command when he wishes, as the result of long discipline) and with none but common tools to work with. If there is anything that can infuse the heroic into me it is the trust and confidence of those whom I honour and who know the right from the wrong. Any heroism I may be vouchsafed will come from the outside, not from within. Do not hesitate to give me any opinion with which you may chance to come in contact. That is the only atmosphere in which the mind of a man charged with public duties can properly or successfully function, the atmosphere of opinion. One must not be wholly dominated by it, but one can at least learn what is practicable and what is not. And the opinion you come into contact with (though, perhaps, not quite so typically American as that which cimes [comes] from further West!) is very stimulating and suggestive, because it comes from thoughtful sources and from men who have knowledge of many things from which I am for the present cut off. I want to know what it is, and to profit by it when possible.

The dear young people have carried the baby home to Williamstown and are happily settled there in their little nest. The climate of Williamstown agrees famously with both Jessie and Frank. Jessie has never been better and stronger than she is there, under the stimulation of that keen northern air. She writes in fine spirits, seems to have secured an excellent nurse, is near a doctor who knows what children thrive best on, and the baby apparently shows not the slightest signs of having been transplanted. All of which is a source of great happiness to me.

Helen and Margaret have been having hard colds which have made them very miserable, but are on the mend now. Spring should be here presently with its kind and healing airs. Our home life may be as quiet as we choose to make it and that, too, will heal.

All join me in affectionate messages. Please give our warmest regards to Mr. Toy. I hope that he is feeling much better, and that your Spring may not be too long delayed!

Your devoted friend, Woodrow Wilson[2]

WWTLS (WP, DLC).
[1] Her most recent one was Feb. 22, 1915, ALS (WP, DLC).
[2] Wilson wrote an almost identical letter to Mrs. Hulbert on the same date. It is WW to Mary A. Hulbert, March 7, 1915, WWTLS (WP, DLC).

From Edward Mandell House

[London, March 7, 1915]

I have seen many more people since last cabling and if Germany is really in a responsive mood there is hope ahead.

I will leave here next Thursday reaching Paris Friday and hope to arrive Berlin 17th.

Sir Edward Grey now advises seeing French Minister for Foreign Affairs.

If Germany will evacuate and help indemnify Belgium, and will make permanent peace settlement, we shall soon be able to begin.

There will be great difficulty though in satisfying France and the African colonies.[1]

T transcripts of WWsh decode (WP, DLC; WC, NjP).
[1] That is, the Union of South Africa.

To William Gibbs McAdoo, with Enclosure

Dear Mac. [The White House, March 8, 1915]

I am returning this with suggested changes W.W.

ALI (W. G. McAdoo Papers, DLC).

E N C L O S U R E[1]

Washington, D. C., March 8, 1915.

Secretary McAdoo said:

Senator Lodge is quoted as felicitating the country upon the defeat of the shipping bill, because he says it was "the intention, if the bill had passed, to buy the German ships imprisoned in our ports to avoid capture. Of this fact there can be no doubt, and the refusal to put in a clause prohibiting the purchase of belligerent owned ships, which might have passed the bill, demonstrated it."

The shipping bill never did have in view the purchase of the interned German ships, or any specific ships. The purpose of the bill was to give the Government authority to buy or to build any kind of suitable ships for the purposes of American trade and commerce. Had the bill passed the President would not have sanctioned the purchase of any ship that would have caused complications with any Power⟨,⟩. ⟨and⟩ This assurance was given to ⟨various⟩ *every* Senator⟨s⟩ who made inquiry, and was conveyed to the Senators in the Chamber as coming from the President himself. Moreover, as a concession to the timid, the bill was amended by the Democrats so as to provide that the President should do nothing "to disturb the conditions of neutrality." Even this was unnecessary, because the country knows that the President, more than any other citizen of this country, has stood strongly for peace and can be depended upon to use none of the powers of his great office to involve the country in needless war.

Senator Lodge knows that the only reason the administration would not agree to the insertion of a clause in the bill "prohibiting the purchase of belligerent owned ships" was that this would have been a surrender of a vital American right—a right which this nation has consistently and inflexibly upheld since the foundation of the Government. To preserve this vital right did not mean that it must be asserted. *but it did mean that this Government felt keenly its responsibilities as the chief representative and trustee of neutral rights*

How does the Senator explain his fear that the President might exercise the power to buy belligerent owned ships so as to produce foreign complications, when he and Senator Root and all of the Republicans voted unanimously for the ship registry bill in August, last,[2] which authorized any American citizen to buy a belligerent owned ship and transfer it to the American flag, and thus ⟨raise⟩ *permit private individuals to raise* the very issues which the Senator pretends to fear if the ship bill had passed? This is exactly what has already happened in the DACIA case. An American citizen purchased a German ship and transferred it to the American flag by virtue of the ship registry act, for which Senator Lodge and his Republican associates voted. The very controversy which the Senator pretends to apprehend is raised by the DACIA case.

The American nation has always been the chief champion of the rights of neutrals. It would have been an inexcusable surrender of the rights of this nation, as well as of its position as the defender of neutral rights throughout the world, for the Government to have adopted the amendment to the ship bill which Senator Lodge says "might have passed" it. The administration would not pay for the passage of the shipping bill by such a ⟨betrayal⟩ *disavowal* of American rights as was involved in the adoption of Senator Lodge's amendment.

How does Senator Lodge reconcile his vote in favor of the ship registry bill last August, which was a reassertion and reaffirmation by Congress of the American principle of the right to transfer a belligerent owned vessel to a neutral flag, with his support of a proposed amendment to the shipping bill in February, last, to surrender this very right?

The Republican opposition to the shipping bill upon these grounds is mere ⟨hypocracy.⟩ *make-believe.*

⟨There never has been the least basis for the claim that the passage of the shipping bill would endanger the peace of the country.⟩

Senator Lodge says the Republicans "won a very great victory" by defeating the bill.

Had the bill passed American ship yards would have received orders promptly for cargo ships aggregating 300,000 to 400,000 tons, deadweight, thereby giving employment to labor, stimulating manufacturing industries and providing vessels for our foreign trade. If it ⟨was⟩ *is* a "very great victory" to defeat these ends, the Republican Senators are welcome to all the joy and credit they can get out of it.[3]

T MS (W. G. McAdoo Papers, DLC).

[1] Wilson's deletions in the following document are in angle brackets; his additions and substitutions, in italics.

[2] Lodge and Root, who were both absent when the vote was taken on August 17, 1914, were paired in favor of the bill.

[3] Most of this statement appeared as "Ship Bill Attack on Lodge by M'Adoo," *New York Times*, March 9, 1915.

To Edward Mandell House

[The White House] 8 March [1915]

There is nothing special to report from this side and you need no instructions. Your admirable letters and telegrams keep me posted in just the right way. Your cable of today gives me the feeling that there is at last some real hope. This is just a message of personal greeting and to express the hope that the journey you are [now] about to undertake may be accomplished without misadventure and in perfect health. The way you manage all the rest I have no anxiety about.   Wilson.

T transcript of WWsh (WC, NjP).

From William Jennings Bryan

My dear Mr. President: Washington March 8th, 1915.

The Brazilian Government has reported in favor of your proposition excepting the matter of arbitration upon which it is still deliberating.

Argentine has reported enthusiastically in favor of all the propositions.

We have not yet heard from Chile. You remember it was the Chilean Ambassador who expressed the most objection both to the arbitration feature—that is compelling the arbitration of differences within a certain time—also to the guarantee of republican form of Government and the guarantee of integrity.

The Argentine Ambassador is quite anxious that we shall proceed with the treaty among the republics of the western hemisphere in order to produce an effect upon the European belligerents.

I asked the Brazilian Ambassador today to request the Chilean Ambassador to urge his Government to give us its opinion with a view of proceeding as soon as possible.

The Argentine Ambassador thought it might be well to have the plan presented to the other representatives soon so that they could consult their Governments. My own opinion is that the small countries will be very glad to approve and accept the plan in toto.

There are two questions:

First: How long should we wait on Chile?

Second: What we shall do if Chile postpones answer or answers unfavorably to some of the important parts of the plan.

Would the objection of one of the larger countries compel an abandonment of the plan, or would you want it presented to the others?

I think the treaty should be so drawn that those that do not sign now would be permitted to sign at any future time. If some of the countries are willing to accept the main propositions but are not willing to accept one or more of the minor provisions would it be best to so frame the treaty that each would bind itself to the others to such an extent as it is willing? I think this would be better than allowing the opposition of a few on some details prevent the securing of such advantages as might come from agreement of all the nations on some of the provisions and of some of the nations on all the provisions.

I have referred to a number of questions which have arisen in the discussion of the subject with the three Ambassadors, but the most important thing to find out is whether we should wait on Chile before submitting the plan to the other countries. In submitting it we need not say that any of the nations have been consulted but send identical notes to all of them at the same time, submitting the plan as you have prepared it.

With assurances of high respect I am, my dear Mr. President,
Yours very sincerely,   W. J. Bryan

TLS (SDR, RG 59, 710.11/198½ B, DNA).

To William Jennings Bryan

My dear Mr. Secretary,   [The White House] 8 March, 1915.

This is very good news indeed.

I think that we need not wait for Chile's reply after we have got the full assent of Brazil and Argentina; but I think we should have the cordial support of those two governments before laying the plan before the other governments. I am assuming that Brazil already knows that we are quite willing to entertain and discuss any modification of the arbitration clause that she may wish to suggest, provided we can be assured of the acceptance of the principle.

So soon as that is accomplished it is my idea that we should lay the plan before all the other governments (except, of course, Mexico) at one and the same time in identical notes, and that it would be well at that time to state to their representatives, unofficially and confidentially, that Brazil and Argentina had assented (and Chile, if by that time she had), for that would constitute a most influential argument for its universal acceptance.

I agree with you that it would be wise to draw and conclude the treaty in such a way that those not accepting it now would have an opportunity to accept and ratify it at any future time. But it is my present judgment that it would not be wise to let some enter upon other terms than the rest. I think the understanding should be the same for all who come in, otherwise some very confused responsibilities might arise. With several of the big States in and a number of the smaller ones, we could await the outcome with confidence.

With very happy expectations in this great matter,

Faithfully Yours,   W.W.

WWTLI (SDR, RG 59, 710.11/199½, DNA).

From Edward Mandell House

Dear Governor: [London] March 8th, 1915.

I was with Sir Edward Grey this morning for a last interview but one before leaving for Berlin.

I thought it was well to tell him of my different interviews with Liberals, Conservatives and those who are not closely affiliated with either party. I explained to him that the purpose of these interviews was not only to get at the bottom of British opinion, but to also aid him when the time comes to act. He seemed to appreciate it and was good enough to say that it would be of service to both of us.

Since I last wrote, I have been seeing something of the peace party, headed by such men as the recent Lord Chancellor, Lord Loreburn, Mr. Hirst of the Economist[1] and others.

Northcliffe is of the ultra set on the other side. He remarked to one or two friends of mine that if you had sent me over here to discuss peace, I should be run out of England. This, of course, was said half humorously, but it really voices his opinion. I mention this to show the extreme difficulties of the situation. Sidney Brooks told me, however, that he had found no one with whom I had talked, now antagonistic to our purposes.

I shall find this anti-peace feeling much stronger in Germany among the military party, but if I can get directly at the Kaiser, I hope to be able to make some impression. The great question is, who really controls in Germany. This is something I am afraid I shall have to find out for myself. I have been utterly unable to get Gerard to correspond with me freely since I have been here. He writes hurried notes and sends cablegrams urging me to come, but never tells anything of value.

I have arranged with Sir Edward to keep in close communication by sending cables to Page which Page, in turn, is to show him, unless indeed I mark them confidential. We further arranged to send confidential messengers to Holland, as I wrote you before.

If things get started at all in Berlin, it will be necessary for me to have someone take messages to Holland and perhaps to England. I have in mind a man by the name of Frazer of the Paris Embassy.[2] My son-in-law, Gordon, has been unable to come which makes it necessary for me to have someone else, provided, after looking them over, I feel I can trust them to a measurable degree. There is no one here or in Berlin that I think would answer this purpose.

Sir Edward thinks now it would be well for me to see Delcasse, and I shall also call upon the President,[3] for he might think it discourteous if I failed to do so, as he knows that I have been in touch with the British Government and am going to Berlin.

I am asking Mr. Sharp to arrange this. The final trouble will be with France and the African Colonies, the one wanting Alsace and Lorraine and the other the German Colonies.

I think constantly of the great part I feel sure you are to play, and my desires go no further than to have you preside over the convention composed of all nations.

I am sure that America would be filled with enthusiastic pride to have you play this part, and there would be no voice raised against your leaving our country for such a purpose.

If Germany receives this suggestion as cordially as it has been received here and nothing arises to disturb the existing relations, we can put it down as being humanly certain.

This Government has used much bad judgment in presenting their case in the press, both here and in America. They might have done it worse, but I doubt it. I suggested to Sir Edward that he let Sidney Brooks handle this feature for the Foreign Office and he has consented.[4] I believe this will make it easier for both you and for them.   Affectionately yours,   E. M. House

TLS (WP, DLC).
[1] Robert Threshie Reid, Earl Loreburn, Lord Chancellor, 1905-12; and Francis Wrigley Hirst, editor.
[2] Arthur Hugh Frazier, second secretary.
[3] That is, Raymond Poincaré.
[4] Brooks was never associated with the official British propaganda organization or the Foreign Office. In fact, Sir Edward Grey positively refused to permit Brooks to represent himself as an official or unofficial spokesman of the Foreign Office in the United States. E. Drummond to S. Brooks, Nov. 1, 1915, CCL (*The Times* Archives).

From Frank Irving Cobb

Dear Mr. President,   New York, March 8, 1915.

Your compliment to The World is more than generous. Whatever support we have given to you, you have abundantly earned, and we could not have done otherwise without repudiating all the political principles for which The World has battled these thirty years.

Mr. Pulitzer, who had more afflictions than blindness, once cynically remarked that "every reporter is a hope and every editor a disappointment." I used to feel that way about candidates and Presidents, but you have restored my faith. You have brought the government of the United States back to first principles, and such an administration must inevitably bulk large in American history.

With my best wishes and sincere regards,

Faithfully yours,   Frank I. Cobb.

ALS (WP, DLC).

Sir Cecil Arthur Spring Rice to Sir Edward Grey

Washn March 8 1915

A friend who saw President today says he is quite conscious of condition of affairs and is really in earnest. All preparations are made in order to enforce compliance with message to Carranza.[1] At same time he is determined not to allow intervention on a large scale.

Cruiser "Tacoma" is ordered to Vera Cruz.

I let President know message of newspaper correspondents. He said, American colony's one object was to bring about American invasion and this he would not have.

President knows that outrages on a large scale in Mexico City would make intervention inevitable.

Repeated to Hohler.

Hw telegram (FO 115/1922, p. 193, PRO).
    [1] To J. M. Cardoso de Oliveira, March 6, 1915.

Remarks at a Press Conference

March 9, 1915

Mr. President, the main thing seems to be Mexico this morning; can you tell us anything of the government's intentions?

> The government has no intentions. We have represented our views to them on what appears to be the danger in Mexico City. Of course, you have to discount a great deal that comes from Mexico City because there are certain persons down there who are determined to have us intervene, even if they have to manufacture the facts on which the intervention takes place.

Mr. President, are our representations in anything like the shape of an ultimatum?

Oh, we don't utter ultimata; we represent our views and act accordingly.

Are any new naval vessels required there?

I don't think there are any required. There are a couple that are going down preparatory to coming home for the annual repairs. I mean a couple going from Guantánamo.

Mr. President, could you tell us something about the views that we have presented to Carranza in this note?

We haven't presented any views. We have simply told him what we have heard of the situation in Mexico City, how serious it seems to be, and have called upon him to take the necessary steps to protect the foreign population of the city. That is all.

Have we been requested by any foreign governments to urge—

The representatives of one or two foreign governments have informally expressed their anxiety to us, but no request of any sort has come.

Mr. President, they are depending upon us, are they not, to handle the situation, and are not figuring on doing anything themselves, so far as you know?

Oh, no; there has been no suggestion about their doing anything themselves. They have depended upon us all along.

Does that apply also to South American countries? There has been some suggestion of Pan-American action—some of the South American countries getting together with the United States in joint representation.

That has not reached me. I had not heard that suggestion. Where did you learn that?

It was printed in the papers the latter part of last week. The story was that the Pan-American countries were considering this proposition of eventual intervention by joining with the United States.

I don't think that can have a substantial foundation. It has not come to me at all.

Mr. President, have any outrages actually been committed in Mexico City, or is it just the fear that there will be?

Just the fear. The fear is that the city will be evacuated and left without protection. For some reason, they all want to get out of it; I don't understand why.

Have you any information of a new movement of Felix Díaz?

Yes, I have had such an intimation about once a month. I don't take Felix Díaz seriously.

Mr. President, what is the situation in Mexico in that territory that is supposed to be controlled by Villa? Has there been any complaint in recent weeks, any outrages?

None at all in recent weeks.

How about the famine conditions?

Well, I have been told that for about seventy-five miles south of the border—the border between the United States and Mexico—there is distress and some fear of famine. That is the only part of the country in which I have heard of that.

Mr. President, have you begun to hear from Mr. West[1] yet?

Oh, yes, but simply of his movements.

Anything as to his conclusions?

No.

With which side has he been conferring?

With all sides. I will not attempt to enumerate them!

Mr. President, do you know where he is right now, whether he is with Carranza or not?

My latest information is that he is on his way to Mexico City. . . .

Mr. President, this Government has been discussing recently with the belligerents of Europe various issues arising out of the war. Can you tell us anything about the status of those questions?

All that I know is that the final notes in the matter have not been received.

Mr. President, has this government made any inquiry for a more explicit statement of the last British note?

Yes, sir.

As to the policy aimed at by the British?

No; as to the particulars of the policy.

Have you received any word yet when the Orders in Council contemplated by Great Britain will be issued?

No; it was supposed to be yesterday, but apparently they were not issued. Still, I was merely gathering that from what I had heard. I have not had any official news

Mr. President, there has been a great deal said about the number of treaties which will be violated by the passage of the seamen's bill. Have you heard anything from the State Department as to what the status is?

Yes, I have a detailed statement as to what treaties would be affected by the bill. You notice we are given plenty of time to deal with that matter.

It gives you ninety days in which to give notices, and a year from the time the bill goes into effect.

No, it is a year from the time that the notice takes effect. Each treaty, of course, provides a time for notice, how many

[1] That is, Duval West.

months or whatever period it is in which notice shall be given, and then a year is allowed after that, so that in most instances it will be about fifteen months after the ninety days.

Great commercial treaties are not affected in every instance, are they?

No, and in many of the most important instances—I mean in cases of countries with which we have the largest commercial dealings—they are not affected at all—the commercial treaties are not affected at all.

Mr. President, is the point with regard to the detention of deserters the only one raised in connection with the treaties?

That is the only one.

Foreign governments, Mr. President, do not object to meeting our lifeboat requirements?

Those requirements are identical with those in the Convention of London, which three governments have ratified—our own, the English, and the German.

Our own conditionally?

Yes, conditionally, on being understood that we have the privilege of exacting further safeguards in our own ports.

As to the manning of the ships, Mr. President, the requirements are not alike?

Not identical in all respects.

Had you heard that some American ship lines that have recently taken the flag were to go to foreign registry again because of the seamen's bill?

That would not be very intelligent unless they were going to stop using our ports, because the requirements apply to users of our ports, under whatever registry.

They could use Chinese crews and fly the Chinese flag; that is the principle objection they have to it.

No, I had not heard that. . . .

Mr. President, have we made any representations to China or Japan recently with reference to the situation in China?

No.

Mr. President, Senator Lodge came out the other day with a statement on the shipping bill; have you any comment to make on it?

No, sir.

T MS (C. L. Swem Coll., NjP).

From Ambrose White Vernon

Brookline, Massachusetts

My dear Mr. Wilson: March 9, 1915.

Your delightful reply to my recent letter about our civic forum was just like you and made me very happy.[1] I have just written to Secretary Lane and Senator Underwood and hope that your generous commendation may persuade them to come to us. I am very glad that Mr. Taft is coming. Mr. Roosevelt will not be invited; nobody here seems to desire him.

You were good enough to say that you wished you might have a part in the forum. And if at any time or for any reason things break so that you would like to address the people of Boston and New England informally thro' the medium of our forum on the real rewards or problems or difficulties of the public service on some Sunday evening of the fall or winter, we would of course be greatly honored and would at once cancel any engagement that we had made.

What a crisis you have been Providentially called to lead us through. That you have been chosen for so vast a task must mightily humble and exalt you! If an honorable way may be found to lead us through these days without war, I believe you will be enabled to find it. We seem to be living in the war; everything else is a side-issue. And I cannot see how we are to continue trade with England in arms, because international law requires that trade of a neutral, and at the same time to allow Engla[n]d to cut off our trade in food-stuffs with Germany, which international law also requires of a neutral. We pray for you who bear the burden of this epoch making decision. I cannot see how the neutral nations can allow food-stuff, which certainly is conditional contraband to be treated as though it were absolute contraband or—which may Heaven forbid—to be proclaimed as such. That might mean starvation to a multitude of women and little children!

With affectionate regards,

Devotedly Yours   A. W. Vernon

TLS (WP, DLC).
[1] A. W. Vernon to WW, Feb. 16, 1915, ALS (WP, DLC), and WW to A. W. Vernon, March 1, 1915, TLS (Letterpress Books, WP, DLC).

From Venustiano Carranza

Vera Cruz, Mexico, March 9, 1915.

I am in receipt of a communication of the 8th instant from the Hon. John R. Silliman, in which is transmitted to me the following from the text of his instructions from the Department of State: . . .

Although the terms in which this note is worded would afford me cause for not answering it, it is my wish notwithstanding that my silence be not construed as a justification of the charge contained in the statement. I have tried to put aside for the moment the reference[s] which are made to my personal responsibility and looking only for the good of my country and for the benefit of the cause which the Mexican people have trusted to me, I thought it my duty to answer it at once. On the other hand, in view of the unusual importance of the subject contained in the aforementioned note, I have thought myself authorized not to follow for this time the customary channels but to address you personally concerning a matter which may involve the success of the Mexican revolution. In the note that I am answering it is taken for granted that the imputations made against General Obregon by an international committee of foreign residents in the City of Mexico, the substance of which had been also communicated to me by Mr. Silliman in his note of note [sic] 1st inst., are true and this assumption has been indulged in, when the answer to those imputations was being prepared reserving the privilege of answering more fully and in detail through the customary diplomatic channels the note referred to lately, take this opportunity to state in an earnest and emphatic way that General Obregon has never intended to incite the hungry populace of the City of Mexico to commit outrages of any character. He has not prevented in any way the entrance of food supplies in Mexico City, but on the contrary he has facilitated such importation. He has not created wilfully the distressing conditions which prevail at present in the City of Mexico but he has done everything in his power to alleviate them. Such situation is the consequence painful but unavoidable of the state of war in which we are in and which for the first time has really reached the City of Mexico, but it has been aggravated by the conduct of the merchants who openly defiantly and with concert of action closed their commercial establishments in the moments of greatest public distress. As a protest against the humanitary relief tax that General Obregon imposes in the face of the charges expressed by the international committee in their complaint [to] the State Department I point you to the fact that General Obregon has been in possession of the City of Mexico since the 26th of January until to-day without mobs assassinations lootings or any other of the outrages which are apt to occur and which frequently do in times of war; during all this time large amounts of food supplies have been taken into Mexico City and large quantities of supplies have been distributed among the distressed people and besides other important measures have been taken looking to further relief which I will mention in detail at the proper time. While it is proper to state to your Excellency that the right to occupy or to evacuate Mexico City or any other place in the Republic must at all times be reserved and to be exercised when deemed by the responsible military authority to be in furtherance of the cause of the revolution. The obligation on the Constitutionalist to safeguard the lives of foreigners is nevertheless fully understood and realized. You will therefore permit me to assure you that at the time of the evacuation of Mexico City every facility within my power will be afforded to all foreign residents in that city to depart the country or to go other and safer places in the republic. I have always tried to give and have given the largest protection that has been possible to the lives and interests of Americans and other foreigners, even during the most difficult periods of our struggle. I have the purpose of continuing the same line of conduct and have decided to take all measures possible to avoid all damages to foreign residents. With this purpose solely in view, I addressed a note to the diplomatic corps in the City of Mexico which I have repeated twice, inviting them in case of evacuation to come to either to this port or to any of the cities, for instance, Puebla[,] Jalapa or Orizaba, which are under the control of the Constitutionalists forces, where they can be assured perfect protection. It was only three days ago that the State Department at Washington directed the attention of the American residents in the City of Mexico to your former advice that they should retire from the country until the conditions should be settled.[1] It is my most earnest wish that the other foreign residents will follow a line of conduct similar to the one suggested by you to the American residents, for the adoption of such a course would be the wisest measure that can be taken to avoid the consequences so much feared. I wish I could adequately convey to your Excellency the political and economic conditions in the City of Mexico and their causes as they are understood and known here to be concerning which representations by an international committee have been made to the State Department. Perhaps the last effort is now being made by the Reactionaries to bring about complications which may cause the failure of the ideals of the Mexican Revolution after having encountered and disposed of other and much more difficult and embarrassing situations in the past when there were larger num-

[1] In WJB to J. M. Cardoso de Oliveira, March 5, 1915, FR *1915*, p. 658.

ber of foreign residents scattered all over the territory of Mexico. It will prove to be most unfortunate if now when the City of Mexico is alone involved a situation shall arise that will destroy the hopes and purposes of the Mexican people. Because of this consideration, permit me to repeat the hope elsewhere expressed that the foreign residents may be induced to save your government and the Republic of Mexico from embarassments, by temporarily leaving the City Mexico.

Allow me to avail myself of this opportunity to reiterate you the assurances of my highest consideration and personal regards.

V. Carranza.

T telegram (SDR, RG 59, 812.00/14573, DNA).

From Edward Mandell House

[London, March 9, 1915]

Letter from Zimmermann[1] indicates Germany is not ready for peace upon lines suggested by Bernstorff. Letter from Gerard says a Melville Rice having letters from you is making the situation there more difficult [for me].

I shall be in Paris from 11th to 15th inclusive.

I deeply appreciate your cable of the eighth.   House.

T transcript of WWsh decode (WP, DLC).
[1] It is printed as an Enclosure with the following letter.

From Edward Mandell House, with Enclosures

Dear Governor: London. March 9th, 1915.

Senator Beveridge has just come back from Germany and France. He seems to have met a great many people of importance. He is distinctly pro-German, but what he has to say is interesting nevertheless. He tells me that he saw the Kaiser around the first of February and he was in fine health and all reports of his being careworn and sick were false.

He saw many people in France and he reports that the officials or ruling class have no idea of peace but want to continue the war until Prussian militarism is crushed. They feel that peace will not be worth while under any other condition. They are also obsessed with the idea of regaining Alsace-Lorraine.

Beveridge is returning to the United States and I think it might be interesting to talk to him for a half hour.

I am enclosing you copies of letters from Gerard and Zimmermann. Neither of them seem encouraging. However, I am not downhearted and trust there may be more light when I am once there.

I met John Burns[1] at Lord Loreburn's last night. He had some diagrams which astonished me. He is at the head of the British Relief Committee. This Committee has to do with the care of the unemployed and indigent, and the diagrams (which by the way are confidential for the moment) showed the fluctuations for different years. There is less poverty and less unemployment now in Great Britain than within the memory of man.

Burns is all for peace and he showed me these diagrams to let me know that he was not influenced in the slightest by the condition of the working people.

Sir Edward had already spoken to me about this and had said that one of the conditions they expected to be confronted with was industrial depression and the unemployment of labor, and their troubles were now coming from just the reverse condition.

Just a last word to say that I leave everything here in admirable shape. It could not be better.

Page told me yesterday that he was afraid that our country would not be able to play a big part in peace negociations because of the irritation that was constantly arising between the State Department and the Foreign Office. He said Tyrrell told him some months ago that he believed when peace finally came, it would be through the mediation of the Spanish King. He had a feeling that I had not gotten far in my endeavors here, and that I was leaving with but little more accomplished than when I came.

Of course he does not know anything about the situation. As far as he knows, I have only seen Sir Edward twice and with him. He has not the faintest conception of the people I have met and what I have done, or the active cooperation of Sir Edward. I enlightened him but little, for it seems best not to endanger our very warm and cordial relations by telling him of my activities in which he has not participated.

I want to say this about Page, and that is, he is so open frank and honest that he believes everybody is as much so as himself. He is inclined therefore to put too much trust in the people with whom he is thrown. They have the highest regard for him here in official circles, and Sir Edward has spoken of his liking for him time and again. And yet Sir Edward has joined me in keeping our present negociations entirely secret. He never indicates to Page that we have met other than at the two visits mentioned.

I merely want to tell you this so you may understand the true situation. I think this liking for Page here is of great value to our two countries at the present moment.

Affectionately yours,   E. M. House

TLS (WP, DLC).
[1] M.P. for Battersea and chairman of the committee to advise the Government Commission for Prevention and Relief of Distress on conditions in London.

E N C L O S U R E   I

Arthur Zimmermann to Edward Mandell House

My dear Colonel: Berlin, March 2nd, 1915.

Many thanks for your letter of February 17th. I regret to see that you consider giving up your trip to Berlin which I had counted on as offering a much more satisfactory opportunity for an interchange of ideas than has been possible up to now.

I read with interest what you believe to be a possible beginning to the desired end. It seems to me however, that you are taking as a basis a more or less defeated Germany or one nearly at the end of her resources. It is hardly necessary for me to show in how far this is not the case. Although I can assure you that Germany has the welfare of Belgium very much at heart still she is not able to forget what a terrific cost was paid for the resistance our men encountered there.

You may be sure, as I said before, that Germany's wish for a permanent peace is as sincere as your own. If England would consent to give up her claim to a monopoly on the seas together with her two to one power standard, I think it might be a good beginning.

I remain, my dear Colonel,
                    Sincerely yours,   Zimmermann.

E N C L O S U R E   I I

James Watson Gerard to Edward Mandell House

My dear Colonel: Berlin, Germany. March 6th, 1915.

I hope you are coming here soon. Von Jagow said he hoped you were coming and while I see no prospect of peace now you could acquaint yourself with the general situation and be in a better position to talk in the other capitals.

One Melville Rice,[1] with letters from the President, has been here for three weeks. He never came near me and had interviews with the Chancellor, Von Tirpitz etc. and they do not understand exactly who he is. This makes it more difficult for you, as they all thought you were the one and original.

Rice had letters to me, but never presented them, and I learn, tried to send telegrams to one McLean, 156 Broadway, New York, for transmission to the President about peace, etc. These telegrams were not sent. It may be all right but I think he has made matters more difficult for both you and me. Von Tirpitz and the Chancellor were both very much surprised when I said I had never seen or even heard, of Rice.

The feeling against America is in abeyance waiting to see what happens with relation to the latest English declarations about the blockade of Germany. I have as yet no official information.

The Chancellor is not "boss" now. Von Tirpitz and Falkenhayn (Chief of Staff)[2] have more influence especially as the Chancellor bores the Emperor. There are great intrigues going on among all these conflicting authorities.

The people who were in favor of accepting a reasonable peace proposal were, strange to say, the military General Staff end. And it was Von Tirpitz who did not want our last proposal accepted. Zimmermann and the Chancellor were in favor of simply saying "Yes" (that is to our proposal in the identical note to England and Germany.)

I hate to write in these spy times and do most earnestly hope you are coming soon, or if you are going to Italy, I will run down and report to you there if you want.

With best wishes to you and Mrs. House,

Sincerely yours,   James W. Gerard.

TCL (WP, DLC).
  [1] That is, Melvin A. Rice.
  [2] Grand Admiral Alfred von Tirpitz, Secretary of State for the Imperial Navy Department; General Erich von Falkenhayn, formerly Prussian Minister of War, now Chief of the General Staff.

To William Jennings Bryan

My dear Mr. Secretary,   [The White House] 10 March, 1915.

I do not think that this[1] ought to be published. If its publication would do its authors the least bit of good, I would say by all means give it to the papers. But of course it would accomplish nothing.

I do not altogether credit what these persons say. We have no reason to credit them, in view of what they have done and said at previous stages of this perplexing business in Mexico. Did you know that they sent a statement like this to Sir Cecil Spring Rice the other day, asking him to publish it? Of course he did nothing of the kind. But it shows their spirit towards their own government and the courses to which they are willing, in their disloyalty, to resort.

But their message ought to be replied to. I think they should be told simply that we understand and sympathize with their situation and with their quandary in all its aspects and that we are doing everything in our power to improve that situation. They might be told also that in his gessage [message] of yesterday to me (which I assume you have seen) General Carranze himself, after giving us assurance that everything within his power will be done to proptect the lives and rights of foreigners, repeats our advice that they should temporarily remove to Puebla, Jalapa, or Orizaba where they can be more effectually protected.

Faithfully Yours,   W.W.

WWTLI (W. J. Bryan Papers, DLC).
¹ J. M. Cardoso de Oliveira to WJB, March 9, 1915, T telegram (W. J. Bryan Papers, DLC), conveying a message from a "committee of American citizens" explaining why it would cause great hardship for them if they had to leave Mexico, reminding the State Department "of the obligation it had assumed by its treaties with Mexico to see that their persons and property were protected," and calling for "effective guarantees" of their "rights."

To William Jennings Bryan

My dear Mr. Secretary,   [The White House] 10 March, 1915.

I am anxious to know whet[h]er our note to Japan about the "requests" she made of China has gone forward or not. The twelfth (Thursday of this week) is the day named in the despatches on which China must yield or—? It would be well to have our note in Japan's hands by that date.

Faithfully Yours,   W.W.

WWTLI (SDR, RG 59, 793.94/240, DNA).

From William Jennings Bryan

My dear Mr. President: Washington March 10, 1915.

I am sending you a copy of a letter from Mr. Sullivan to Mr. Gray, which was put into the record at New York. I did not notice any mention of it in the paper.¹ I have not read all of the three volumes of testimony and, therefore, had not seen it.

It has been printed, or, at least, most of it, in Santo Domingo and has aroused intense criticism there as it naturally would. Senator Phelan thinks that it has very much increased the feeling against the Minister and there are phrases in there so offensive to the people of Santo Domingo—both public officials and the masses—that it seems to me deserve serious consideration. I can talk over this matter more fully when I see you but I thought you would be interested in seeing this letter.

Senator Phelan says that some of the members of the Cabinet[2] expressed a desire to come here and confer with the Government in regard to Santo Domingo affairs and the Senator agreed to bring their request and give them an answer. I think he spoke with you about this when he called at the White House yesterday. I see no objection to it—neither does General McIntyre. In fact, I think it might be a good thing to have them come up here and become convinced of the disinterestedness of our nation and its determination to support the Government and put an end to insurrections.

If you will send me word in the morning, indicating your opinion of the coming of these delegates I will send a telegram at once in Senator Phelan's name and confirm it through a despatch to the Legation.

With assurances of high respect I am, my dear Mr. President, Yours very sincerely,   W. J. Bryan

TLS (W. J. Bryan Papers, DNA).
   [1] James M. Sullivan to John G. Gray, Jan. 31, 1914, had, in fact, been quoted extensively in "Religion Bryan Aid in Affairs of State," *New York Times*, Jan. 22, 1915. Sullivan characterized the people of the Dominican Republic as "unmoral" and of "gross and crass ignorance," the Roman Catholic Church as too weakened "to cope with the savage and brutal tendencies of semi-civilization" on the island, and the current generation of leaders as "hopeless." Concerning his belief that the United States should use the Church to reclaim the country and the people, he remarked: "It would be mighty good politics, John, as well as a glorious philanthropy."
   [2] The Dominican cabinet.

To William Jennings Bryan

My dear Mr. Secretary,   [The White House] 10 March, 1915.

This letter, now that it has been made public, is certainly a *very* serious matter. I do not see how it is possible for Mr. Sullivan to overcome the impression it must have made.

The other matter you speak of Senator Phelan spoke to me about. I see no objection at all to the sending of the delegation suggested from San Domingo. I would be glad to see and talk with the delegates. I would like them to get their own direct impression of our purpose and spirit as regards their troubled country.   Faithfully Yours,   W.W.

WWTLI (W. J. Bryan Papers, DNA).

From William Jennings Bryan

My dear Mr. President: Washington March 10, 1915.

I enclose two documents which have been handed to me to-day.[1] Two men called upon me this morning—one a Mr. Henry R. Hall of Mexico City,[2] and the other Mr. Joseph R. Wilson of Philadelphia[3] whom he has associated with him.

I have questioned Mr. Hall and Mr. Wilson as to their pecuniary interests in the matter. Mr. Hall says he has a ranch near the City of Mexico but has never been attorney for any corporation or any foreign interest in Mexico. Mr. Wilson's only connection with Mexico was representing an estate of a Spaniard who died in Mexico leaving some property both there and in Spain.

I have not been able to learn, from questioning them, any reason for suspecting them of ulterior or pecuniary motives.

Now for the proposition: Mr. Hall comes as the representative of General Benevides,[4] who says he has canvassed the situation and reports that the Generals whose names he gives,[5] commanding something like one hundred thousand soldiers, are in favor of peace. They are willing he reports to support the United States in any effort it may make to use its moral influence for the establishment of peace and orderly government in Mexico. Their plan contemplates the elimination of both Carranza and Villa—which was the plan proposed by the Convention.[6] They would favor the recognition of Gutierrez until an election could be held, but they do not make this a condition. They say Gutierrez would resign in favor of some man more acceptable to the United States.

In talking with them I found that they had a favorable opinion of Doctor Silva who seems to be very generally praised, or General Angeles,[7] although I think from what they said they would regard Silva more acceptable than Gutierrez.

They have drawn up a pledge which they say General Benevides will have signed by all the persons named if given assurance that it will be acceptable to you. They are afraid to act separately for fear of punishment being inflicted upon them by either Carranza or Villa, but they believe that with the moral support of the United States they can, by standing together, support the Government selected. They say that the people there are tired of fighting and that the Generals are willing to make this offer in behalf of restoration of peace.

It is evident from the statement made that they regard Villa as the one who must be deposed, Carranza having agreed to retire if Villa would. If it was certain that Benevides represented all the Generals whose names are given it would indicate that Villa has really a small following but as Benevides is a supporter of Gutierrez his statements must be taken as the statements of an advocate rather than as the statement of an impartial judge.

You will notice that the plan proposed does not go beyond pacification. No mention is made of the matter of land or of any other reforms. They seem to be in a mood to listen to suggestions but we have nothing but the word of Benevides as to the number of those who are favorable to their proposition. Mr. Hall says he has seen several of them but did not know the men well enough to be able to give a list of the names.

I do not know that you will think this worth considering— surely not to the extent of authorizing anybody to act for you in ascertaining the views of these people or giving assurances to them, but you may be interested in reading the proposals.

I send it over to you in order that you can be revolving it in your mind tonight. Can see you either in the morning or later, at your convenience if there is anything in connection with the matter you desire to discuss.

I leave at five o'clock to speak to the students at Annapolis tonight and will return early in the morning.

With assurances of high respect, I am, my dear Mr. President,
Yours very sincerely,   W J Bryan   H.E.S.

TLS (W. J. Bryan Papers, DNA).
    1 Eulalio Gutiérrez *et al.* to WW, n.d., TL, and Eugenio Aguirre Benavides to WW, n.d., T MS (W. J. Bryan Papers, DLC). Bryan summarizes them below.
    2 Lawyer of Mexico City.
    3 Lawyer of Philadelphia.
    4 He was a general in the Division of the North.
    5 These included José I. Robles, Division of the North; Pablo González, of the Northeast; Pánfilo Natera, of the Center; Álvaro Obregón, of the Northwest; Lucio Blanco, of his own division; and more than twenty generals under their commands.
    6 The Aguascalientes Convention.
    7 Dr. Miguel Silva, *Villista* officer, and General Felipe Angeles, Villa's chief of artillery.

To William Jennings Bryan

My dear Mr. Secretary,   [The White House] 10 March, 1915.

I am inclined to be very sceptical about this. I may do the Mexicans involved an injustice, but, as you evidently see, this might easily turn out to be merely a scheme to get us behind the ambition of a particular group of leaders. I think it safest to have nothing to do with such plans until the situation has developed itself a little further.

Might it not be well to drop a hint to these gentlemen, for the benefit of their principals, that the patience of this country was all but exhausted; that we could not wait for peace much longer; and that there was still in my hands the very effective weapon of an embargo on shipments of arms and ammunition from this country to Mexico?   Faithfully Yours,   W.W.

WWTLI (W. J. Bryan Papers, DNA).

To Andrew Furuseth

Personal

My dear Sir: [The White House] March 10, 1915

Allow me to acknowledge the receipt of your kind letter of March 6th and to thank you for your generous expressions.
                     Sincerely yours,   Woodrow Wilson

TLS (Letterpress Books, WP, DLC).

From Walter Hines Page

Dear Mr. President: London [c. March 10, 1915].

The net tightens, and the struggle becomes more desperate. It is not "a war": it is the break-down of civilization. The continent will be a bankrupt graveyard about which sorrowful women will live—not a few of them outraged women. Germany, disappointed at the failure of her first plans, has reduced the desperate struggle to the level of a ravaging cut-throat. Along the battle-line the Red-Cross flag is a joke, the white flag is laughed at. In German prisons the verminous underclothes of English prisoners are searched for concealed money. England is thoroughly aroused. She has mobilized her Empire—its men and its treasure. She is spending nearly 10 millions of dollars a day. The whole annual expenditure of our National Government would last her only 70 days; and she can keep this up a very long time. Nobody complains. She has bound the Allies to her by financial as well as other bonds, and for the first time she absolutely knows they are secure to the end. She has 3 million men trained or in training, and she will soon be making enough new ships a year to duplicate our navy. When the war ends, she will have the most colossal debt in history, but she will also be incomparably the strongest naval and military power the world has ever seen or dreamed of. She will be able to dictate, if need be, to her Colonies and Allies. No fort in the world can withstand her 2,400-pound shells shot 28 miles from her *Queen Elizabeths*.

With all this the best traits of English character come out. They are not boastful. They are not naturally war-like. They are not aggressive. They will hold to what they have, but they will misuse their vast power less, I think, than any other nation would. And to us they are considerate and most friendly. They are even pathetic in wanting our sympathy.

But we have made two mistakes—the effort to make them accept the Declaration of London entire (they do not forget that, as an instance of our bad judgment), and our recent suggestion to the British and German Governments which included our proposed supervision of the distribution of food to the civilian population of Germany. That wd. be an impossibility, and we shd. surely have a row if we were permitted to undertake it. The English see by that suggestion how ill we understand the Germans and the conditions in Germany.

I myself can form some judgment of this by the infinite difficulty of the work of the Commission for the Relief of Belgium —met continually by German duplicity and evasion. Besides, while the Germans have the best blockade of these islands that they can make, the English are not going to admit food to them. Both these suggestions of ours have been conspicuously favourable to the Germans. The English do not question our good faith, but they see very clearly that we do not understand the nature of the struggle nor the character of the Germans; and they conclude that the German propaganda in the U. S. is succeeding in its main purpose—namely to cause us to misunderstand England and, if possible, to have a serious difference with her. The German method is to stir up trouble for England in Ireland (the English had to shoot 8 Irishmen the other day for supplying a German submarine with oil), in India (where there has been local trouble), in South Africa (where the practically suppressed Boer revolt took place)[,] in Japan (where they hope to make trouble with the U. S.), in the U. S., where they hope to make trouble with England, and in Turkey, where they did bring the poor Turk in to his own destruction. They work on the French and on the Russians to make a separate peace—with utter failure. Yet every visitor to Berlin brings away the story that the French and Russians are about to yield: we've heard that here every week for four months. There never was such a world-wide intrigue since men discovered themselves on this planet.

The comment on our suggestion to England and Germany is very damaging to us here. By it Germany wd. get free of an effec-

tive blockade in exchange for relinquishing a ludicrously ineffec-
tive one. The plain, bald truth is: they regard us as 'simple' for
thus playing, or trying to play, into the Germans' hands. . . .

The submarine, in German hands, wh. carry blood and iron
but no manuals of international law, has got the English into
their present embarrassing situation. The Germans undoubtedly
have so commandeered the food-supply as to make all food
subject to army use if need be. But the one great achievement of
the submarine has been to make a literal blockade as defined in
the books impossible. But I think they will yet have to call it a
blockade and do their best to make it conform to the definitions.
But several things are certain—

(1) They are going to cut off trade with Germany.
(2) They are going to put us to the very least trouble and
     annoyance that they can. For instance, they will go a
     long way towards buying our cargoes—etc. etc.

Did you ever hear that early in the war a proposal was made
in the Cabinet that the British Government shd. buy the whole
American cotton-crop? The member of the Cabinet who made
the suggestion told me that he thought it failed for this reason:
Cotton was then very low. The English Government wd. almost
surely have made much profit. Instead of pleasing the Americans, therefore, this wholesale purchase wd. probably have
provoked their criticism because of the profit.

If we register our objection to the reversion in the conduct of
the war to methods that antedate the rules of the game—that's
all we can do; and they'll treat us in case after case as it comes
up with consideration—provided we don't play further into the
German hand and plans. The Declaration of London wd. have
brought down the censure of Parliament on the Gov't and w'd
have prevented them from adding copper, petroleum, rubber etc.
to the contraband list, and our latest suggestion wd. give the
Germans food while—or after the Germans had done their best to
starve out England.

I can but write you the truth: The Government once definitely
concluded that when the time for peace-talk shd. come they wd.
ask the good offices of the Spanish Gov't, because our State Dp't
seemed so likely to be taken in by the Germans. . . .

And peace? Yes, when a message comes direct and *clearly
authenticated*, that the Germans will restore Belgium and pay
for its devastation: then *talk* may begin—not before. Until that
starting point be made perfectly clear, several million more men
from England and the Colonies will be got ready and a new navy
will be built every year and the manufacture of steel nets to

catch German submarines will go on, and submarines will continue to be fished up and *nothing said about it*. The Germans don't know how many of them are captured.

I'm afraid it sounds insulting to keep saying that it is impossible for the State Dep't to form a right conception of the war (and of many questions growing out of it) at a distance. But half the requests that I am instructed to make of Sir Edward Grey provoke merely a tolerant smile these days, as you'd smile at a child who shd. ask you to take your automobile and run back 10 miles to look for a marble he had lost. They have had—I mean the English —about 1000 merchant ships impressed into service to carry men and supplies to France, to Servia, and to the fleet. Now they are sending a large force and ammunition and supplies to the Dardanelles and to East Africa—more impressed ships of course. Presently they will send great stores of ammunition to Russia— more impressed ships of course. They need more and more ships as mine-sweepers and submarine-fishers—more impressed ships of course. Now, it so happens that one British ship has been impressed wh. the owners had agreed to charter to an American firm. Here come instructions to see to it that this important private contract is carried out! Probably the ship is by this time far into the Mediterranean or on its way to East Africa. It is as if a man in a big hotel had given a boy a dime and sent him to buy a pair of shoe-strings and the hotel had caught on fire and in the loss of life and property the man shd. insist on having the boy compelled to bring those shoe-strings!

This colossal Empire is throwing all its undreamed of wealth, many times more men and better men that it ever before sent to war—war on three continents at once and on the sea—but we ask it to guarantee a suspension of hostilities in the Mediterranean till an American ship (in ballast) may make its escape from Smyrna. Mr. President, we thus throw away, fritter away, our influence and discredit our judgment. And Sir Edw. sends for me and says that numbers of telegrams about trading with the enemy—private telegrams—wh. w'd be stopped by the censor if the names of the real senders were signed to them regularly come and go between continental American diplomatic and consular officers and the State Dp't. Can I not give a hint? he asks. I swear they are very polite and considerate of us. . . .

You will not wonder, then, that House leaves here for Berlin empty-handed of peace material. No peace-material will be ready here till Belgium is given up and compensated. If the Government were disposed to do otherwise, the people wd. not permit it. Public opinion in England is going to insist on starving out the

Germans as well as on the utmost effort to whip them. Sir Edw. Grey himself put it to me in this way yesterday in a long general talk: "If we are defeated, it will be worse with us than it can be with Germany if she is defeated. The German people in any event will remain—remain on land that can practically feed them. We— if Germany shd. win—wd. have our overseas dominions cut off and we shd. be an island people without the means of self-support—utter obliteration of Great Britain and of English influence. That is why we all prefer to die before disaster, if it need be, rather than after. That is why we must starve the Germans, lest we and our civilization starve afterwards." He told me that the Government wd. be considerate of us and of all neutral rights just as far as possible—"if possible, further than possible"—but about cutting off supplies from Germany they now have no choice, after Germany's own actions.

As I came away, the queer feeling came over me—here we are on this little island with war on and under the waters all about us; and we don't know what is happening. We know neither how many English boats the German submarines are sinking nor how many submarines the English are catching, nor where either is putting new mines. All that *I* know is that there is an air of great cheerfulness and satisfaction at the Admiralty. I said to Churchill[1] a few days ago: "It is good to see you so cheerful." "It's better," said he, "to have good reason for cheerfulness." "How many captive submarines does that mean?" I askd. He laughed and brought up another subject. . . .

Look at it in any way you will, the chief result of the war will be the strengthening of British influence in the world—to a point of danger to the world if they were really a warlike people. But they are not, and (if one may venture a prophecy) they will be even less aggressive in the future, for several reasons—*eg.* (1) the wider development of democracy here will keep back any warlike or aggressive spirit; and, (2) if there be no aggressive navy in the world, the English will at least endeavor to make seapower more sensible. Sir E. Grey is in favour of so changing the sea war-rules as to make all merchant ships immune from capture in any future war. He said this at my table the other day. And he has several times made the prediction that we shd. live to see most of the European Governments controlld. by the Labour Party—which I do not believe. But there's going to be a mighty shaking-up of privilege and of all habits as a result of this war. I look for the display of unexpectedly generous impulses— so many men will be dead that the survivors will do or give any-

[1] Winston Spencer Churchill, First Lord of the Admiralty.

thing for security from a return of these times. And of one thing I am very sure—if we look at the thing in a big way and do not waste our influence in piddling little contentions, our most generous impulses will be met in a sympathetic way.

In this belated and rambling letter, I pray you read nothing that I have written either as a criticism or as a complaint. I have meant only to illustrate the fear that sometimes overtakes me lest we fritter away our influence on trifling things. And the weariness and the sadness and the difficulty of it pass all preceding experience and all belief. I had an evening's talk last week with Bonar Law,[2] the razor-tongued leader of the Opposition. (There is no Opposition now.) "We're working out our plan of blockade," said he, "with especial reference to giving you as little trouble as possible. We've got to end this thing. We are going to end is [it] vigorously. We are going to end it with all possible regard to neutral rights. But we may have to ask your patience now and then. If you trust us, we'll not forget it."

And the two (almost silent) days I spent with the Prime Minister in his country place left the same impression on my mind. Mr. Asquith at times looks older than he ought and tired. He gets away from London all he can—away from people. He's not a very communicative man in normal moods and less communicative now than usual. He blurts out things & relapses into silence. He does not carry on a conversation; and he seems to be seeking ways of escape from himself. He will sit for 3 hours and play bridge after dinner—hardly speaking. During a whole game of golf he spoke only ejaculations now and then. He seems to me to become greyer and silenter.

And think of the lonely figure of Sir Edw. Grey last Sunday walking alone about Kew gardens, seeing what the Spring was starting into colour and bloom—and back home again to see the dispatch boxes with their endless telegrams from all corners of the world!

It's well these English have no nerves. They are the most impertur[b]able folk that ever made a nation. They are now planning to lay-off a region along & behind the German lines in France, say, 25 miles long and 10 or 15 deep,—to lay it off in squares; to mass 1000 or more big guns; to assign a square to every gunner; to command him to plough it with shells—every foot of it—and to keep this up by relays for 3 or 4 days, day and night; and then, when there is nothing alive in this area, to push an army through. They tried this on a small scale a week ago; they killed 10,000 Germans and advanced 5 miles for a short

2 Andrew Bonar Law, leader of the Conservative party.

part of the line. And they are now sending men & guns over all the time and sending word to all the hospitals to increase their staff and the number of their beds. The men that are going know that half-a-million of them will be rushed into such a Dantean channel of death. Yet they are all eager to go.

They are doing everything they can to induce the Germans to send out more submarines. They catch the submarines, many of them "alive," and suppress the news; but they ostentatiously report the sinking of ships by the submarines. This is the Englishman's idea of a joke. I told Bonar Law that they were making much of the "war zone" about these islands in their correspondence with us, while they were actually keeping the zone pretty peaceful by quiet fishing for submarines. "Your efficiency kills your argument," said I.

The rumour comes, Mr. President, that you, too, are tired and not quite well. Let the worst worries mend themselves rather than weary you: we can't afford that. We can afford almost anything else—at least for a time. Get the golf clubs. Keep them active. (I've played twice in six months, but I've kept pretty well, even indoors.)

My gratitude for your kindness to Mrs. Page. She brings back much interesting news and a fresh spirit. And this latter is now the most desired of all things here—in this weary devastation.

Very heartily Yours,   Walter H. Page

ALS (WP, DLC).

To John Reid Silliman[1]

Washington, March 11th, 1915. 1 p.m.

Please deliver the following message from the President to General Carranza: Quote. I thank you for your message of the ninth of March, for the assurances it conveys, and for your kind personal words. I beg that you will understand that if our messages are occasionally couched in terms of strong emphasis it is only because they concern some matter which touches the very safety of Mexico itself and the whole possible course of her future history. We seek always to act as the friends of the Mexican people, and as their friends it is our duty to speak very plainly about the grave dangers which threaten her from without whenever anything happens within her borders which is calculated to arouse the hostile sentiment of the whole world. Nothing will stir that sentiment more promptly or more hotly or create greater dangers for Mexico than any, even temporary, disregard for the lives, the safety, or the rights of the citizens of other countries resident within her territory, or any apparent contempt for the rights and safety of those who represent religion, and no attempt to justify or explain these things will in the least alter the sentiment or lessen the danger that will arise from them. To warn you concerning such matters is an act of friendship, not of hostility, and we cannot make the warning too earnest. To speak less plainly or with less earnestness would be to conceal from you a terrible risk which no lover of Mexico should wish to run. Unquote.   Bryan

T telegram (SDR, RG 59, 812.00/14573, DNA).
  ¹ There is a WWsh draft of the following telegram in WP, DLC, and a WWT draft in SDR, RG 59, 812.00/14573, DNA.

From William Jennings Bryan

My dear Mr. President: Washington March 11, 1915.

The Argentine Ambassador has made a suggestion which I think it worth while to report to you. It is a personal suggestion and has not been communicated to his Government. He is one of our most devoted friends and no one is more interested in everything that concerns Pan-America. He asks for your opinion on the following proposition, namely:

That *all* of the American republics join in an appeal to *all* of the factions in Mexico to adjust their differences and agree upon some means of establishing and maintaining a stable and orderly government in Mexico.

This is the thing which we desire and I believe that great force would be added to our appeal if all of the Latin-American countries joined in the appeal.

With assurances of high respect I am, my dear Mr. President,
                    Yours very sincerely,   W. J. Bryan

TLS (W. J. Bryan Papers, DNA).

To William Jennings Bryan

My dear Mr. Secretary,   [The White House] 11 March, 1915.

My own opinion is, that such action as this would be without effect and might lead only to irritation. I saw an interview (or statement) in this morning's paper purporting to come from the Archbishop of Mexico in which he said that joint action by this government and the governments of Latin America would be resented. I rather think they would stand more from us than from a group of American states from which they are not accustomed to expect admonition.

Faithfully Yours,   W.W.

WWTLI (W. J. Bryan Papers, DNA).

From William Jennings Bryan

My dear Mr. President: Washington March 11, 1915.

Dudley Field Malone was in a few moments ago and said Father Kelly had written you a letter suggesting the advisability of giving out some statement to the effect that no government would be recognized in Mexico unless it gave assurances of religious liberty.[1]

We have had a great many letters, petitions and resolutions on that subject from Catholic societies. This seems to be the main thing that they agree upon asking, although they differ in the language employed in the denunciation of what has occurred—some of the communications being couched in language very unfriendly to the administration.

As no government would be recognized without giving assurances desired I am inclined to think it might be well if you would give out a statement, or, if you prefer to do so, authorize it to be given out from here, to the effect that the question has not been reached because we have not taken up for proper consideration the recognition of any government down there but that the question of protection of religious liberty has always been in mind and that there has never been any intention of recognition of any government until such assurances were given. No government that refuses to promise protection of religious liberty and religious rights would have any promise of stability.

Some such statement would, as we are informed, satisfy the Catholics and it would offend no one else, since the statement would include all religions.

With assurances of high respect I am, my dear Mr. President,

Yours very sincerely,   W. J. Bryan

TLS (W. J. Bryan Papers, DNA).
[1] It is printed at Feb. 23, 1915.

To William Jennings Bryan

My dear Mr. Secretary,   [The White House] 11 March, 1915.

I am at work on a solution of this matter, and shall wish to discuss it with you very soon.   Faithfully Yours,   W.W.

WWTLI (W. J. Bryan Papers, DNA).

From Thomas William Hardwick

Personal.

My dear Mr. President: [Washington] March 11, 1915.

I had hoped to see you before leaving for Georgia, but find it impossible, so I am dropping you a line. I am leaving this afternoon.

Of course it was a matter of deep personal regret to me that I was unable to support you on the shipping bill, but my opinion on that measure is matured and my judgment that it would have proven a mistake is so fixed as to amount to a profound conviction, which I was compelled to follow or to absolutely stu[l]tify my own mentality. I merely refer to this matter, however, to express the hope that you fully understand how unpleasant it was for me to be placed in an attitude of even *apparent* opposition to you, and to express the *hope* that this honest difference of opinion between us may make no difference in the close personal & political relations that have heretofore existed. Certainly my own feelings are just as warmly friendly towards yourself, and I think I know you well enough to know that I have lost neither your friendship nor your respect by an honest inability to concur in all your views. Somehow, I *can not* support a government ownership proposition. I could not do it, as you recall on the Alaskan railroad bill. If you feel like it I would be glad to have a line from you, on this matter, at my home in Sandersville Ga. Wishing you, personally, a happy & helpful recess & praying for our country at this trying time, I am,

Very sincerely,   Thos. W Hardwick.

ALS (WP, DLC).

To Edward Mandell House

[The White House] 12 March [1915]

Melvin Rice went to Europe on business carrying a letter from me[1] which could by no stretch of construction be construed as constituting him my spokesman about anything, and he did not so use it, but he did act very unwisely, I am afraid.

I infer that you will proceed to Berlin, notwithstanding Zimmermann's letter.

T transcript of WWsh telegram (WP, DLC).
   [1] WW to Whom It May Concern, Jan. 14, 1915, CCL (WP, DLC).

To William Jennings Bryan

My dear Mr. Secretary,   [The White House] 12 March, 1915.

Since the discussion in the cabinet this morning of the situation at Progresso[1] I have been giving a great deal of serious thought to the questions then raised and have come to this conclusion:

I think that we are justified, in all the circumstances, in saying to Carranza that we cannot recognize his right to blockade the port to the exclusion of our commerce; that we must beg him to recall his orders to that effect; and that we shall feel constrained, in case he feels he cannot do so, to instruct our naval officers there to prevent any interference with our commerce to and from the port. He should be told, at the same time, that we are doing this in the interest of peace and amity between the two countries and with no wish or intention to interfere with her internal affairs, from which we shall carefully keep our hands off. I hope that your thinking has led you to a similar conclusion.

Faithfully Yours,   W.W.

WWTLI (W. J. Bryan Papers, DNA).
  [1] Carranza had recently closed the port of Progreso in the Yucatan to prevent the export of the sisal hemp that American manufacturers of binder twine for reapers desperately needed. See Link, *Struggle for Neutrality*, p. 457.

To William Jennings Bryan

My dear Mr. Secretary,   [The White House] 12 March, 1915.

This note[1] seems to me thorough and satisfactory, and I hope that it may be possible to despatch it promptly.

I have suggested a few verbal changes.

Faithfully Yours,   W.W.

WWTLI (SDR, RG 59, 793.94/240, DNA).
  [1] WJB to Viscount Chinda, March 13, 1915, CCLS (SDR, RG 59, 793.94/240, DNA), printed in *FR 1915*, pp. 105-11, and summarized in Link, *Struggle for Neutrality*, pp. 283-85. Wilson made only four verbal changes, none of them important. A long summary of the note was sent by wire on March 13: WJB to American Embassy, Tokyo, March 13, 1915, T telegram (SDR, RG 59, 793.94/240, DNA).
  The note expressed gratification that the proposals in Group V were "requests" and not demands and reviewed Japan's commitments to equality of opportunity for all foreigners in China, as well as America's duty to uphold the "broad and extensive" rights and privileges of Americans in China. It then conceded an important point: "While on principle and under the treaties of 1844, 1858, 1868 and 1903 with China the United States has ground upon which to base objections to the Japanese 'demands' relative to Shantung, South Manchuria, and East Mongolia, nevertheless the United States frankly recognizes that territorial contiguity creates special relations between Japan and these districts. This Government, therefore, is disposed to raise no question, at this time, as to Articles I and II of the Japanese proposals." The note concluded with a restatement of the Open Door policy and a warning to

Japan that the United States could not "regard with indifference the assumption of political, military, or economic domination over China by a foreign Power."

To William Jennings Bryan, with Enclosure

My dear Mr. Secretary,   [The White House] 12 March, 1915.

This seems to me very serious. It mages [makes] it all the more desirable that our note to Japan should go forward at the earliest possible moment.   Faithfully Yours,   W.W.

WWTLI (W. J. Bryan Papers, DLC).

E N C L O S U R E

Edward Thomas Williams to William Jennings Bryan

Dear Mr. Secretary: [Washington] March 12, 1915.

I call particular attention to the statement of the Japanese Minister in Peking reported in this telegram[1] that "the Japanese fleet has already sailed under sealed orders" and also to the fact that the "requests" of group five are being pressed. A Japanese fleet in Foochow or Amoy will create a serious situation in China.

This coupled with the orders to send more troops to Shantung and Manchuria, already reported both by Peking and Tokyo[2] shows Japan's determination to get what she wants without delay and before opposition of other powers can express itself diplomatically.

They are apparently willing to abandon the "request" for joint policing (Group V item 3) if they can get police advisers.

China is apparently willing to ask Japan's approval in case of railway construction and loans in Manchuria and eastern Mongolia.

The article two, group three is the one which the Japanese have never reported to us and which seriously affects the right of Americans to operate mines in Kiangsi, Hupeh and Hunan.

E.T.W

TLI (W. J. Bryan Papers, DLC).
[1] P. S. Reinsch to WJB, March 12, 1915, T telegram (W. J. Bryan Papers, DLC).
[2] E.g., P. S. Reinsch to WJB, March 8, 1915, T telegram (SDR, RG 59, 793.94/245, DNA).

To Manuel Luis Quezon

My dear Mr. Quezon: [The White House] March 12, 1915

May I not wish you a safe and pleasant voyage and a happy return when you resume your duties here again?

I will be very much obliged if you will take some occasion when you are at home to express the admiration I have felt for the self-respecting behavior of the people of the Philippines in the midst of agitations which intimately affect their whole political future. Nothing is needed to establish their full reputation with the people of the United States as a people capable of self-possession and self-government but a continuation in the moderate and constitutional course which they have pursued.

Cordially and sincerely yours,   Woodrow Wilson

TLS (Letterpress Books, WP, DLC).

From William Jennings Bryan, with Enclosure

My dear Mr. President: Washington March 13, 1915.

I am sending you a copy of the telegram in regard to Progresso. I feel as reluctant as you do to take such positive action, but I believe it as real a kindness to Carranza as it was to Huerta and I think the Huerta incident furnishes a very strong precedent. While Carranza *may* take offense at it, the chances are he will not, and we can assure Villa and Zapata of our purposes, and in case we come in conflict with Carranza we are in a position to restrain the employment of force within the smallest possible limit just as we did at Vera Cruz. At Progresso there would be no reason for landing a force or taking charge of the port. The people of Progresso are against Carranza, while at Vera Cruz Huerta was in possession.

As Mr. McAdoo told you, I am preparing to leave for Atlantic City at four o'clock this afternoon. Mr. Davis will telephone me if anything comes up that might require my presence here.

I am, my dear Mr. President,

Sincerely yours,   W. J. Bryan

TLS (WP, DLC).

E N C L O S U R E

Washington, March 13th, 1915. 3 PM

You will please call upon General Carranza and present a request that he recall his order blockading the port of Progreso.

If the request respectfully and earnestly presented is not sufficient to induce him to recall the order, you may say to him that in case the order is not recalled the President will feel constrained to instruct our naval officers at Progreso to prevent any interference with our commerce to and from the port. In case you are obliged to communicate the President's intentions, explain to Carranza that this is done in the interest of peace and amity between the two countries and with no wish or intention to interfere with the internal affairs of Mexico, which we shall carefully avoid. In case he enters into a discussion of the matter you may, upon your own initiative and not as if under direction from us, remind him that when Huerta attempted to blockade Tampico this government informed Huerta that it could not allow the interruption of commerce at Tampico. The constitutionalists approved this action.[1]   Bryan

T telegram (SDR, RG 59, 612.1123/119a, DNA).
[1] Carranza, in conference with Silliman, agreed to lift the blockade, and Silliman did not need to deliver Wilson's message. J. R. Silliman to WJB, March 15, 1915, *FR 1915*, p. 824.

To Jessie Woodrow Wilson Sayre

My darling Jessie,   The White House 14 March, 1915.

I am ashamed of myself when I think I have been so long acknowledging the dear letter from you that made me so happy, and touched me so deeply. You cannot know, I fear, what it meant to me to have you say that I had in some sort taken your incomparable mother's place when you were here! Ah! how little I knew how! and how impossible it was to do more than just let you feel as well as I knew how the infinite tenderness I felt and the longing that was at my heart to make up for what can never be made up for either to you, my sweet daughter, nor to me nor to anyone who ever had a chance to know how sweet and loving and infinitely rewarding she was. I cannot yet trust myself to speak much of her, even in writing. My heart has somehow been stricken dumb. I felt so dumb when you were here, dear. I did not know how to *say* the things that were in my heart about you and the baby and all the crowding thoughts that made my heart ache with its fulness. I had to trust you to *see* them; and your dear letter makes me hope that you did. I can talk about most things but I always have been helpless about putting into words the things I feel most deeply, the things that mean most to me; and just now my heart is particularly voiceless. But I do love you and yours, my dear, more than words can say, and there *is* added to my love now the mother tenderness which I know the depths and beauties of in *her* heart. She was beyond comparison the deepest, truest, noblest lover I ever knew or ever heard those who knew the human heart wish for!

It is delightful to hear how well everything goes with you. God bless you. You will have heard of Mac's operation.[1] He has come out of it finely: and is doing as well as anyone could in the circumstances. Nell is here with us, of course, and as steady and brave as usual. Nothing happens to the rest of us except daily crises in foreign affairs.

Love beyond measure from us all to you all.

Your loving Father

WWTLS (photostat in RSB Coll., DLC).
[1] McAdoo underwent surgery for appendicitis on March 12.

To Mary Allen Hulbert

Dearest Friend,   The White House 14 March, 1915.

I wonder if my letter of last Sunday, which I addressed to Gloucester Street, found you. I take it for granted that someone there would tell the postman what to do with it. I hope so,— not because the letter was important or interesting (I seem to have lost the gift for writing anything vital, if I ever had it; or is it only the freshness that it is necessary to have if one would write a letter worth reading?), but only because when the rare moments come nowadays when I *can* write a few lines to those to whom my thought turns so often I do not like the poor thing to go astray and be wholly lost. It is at least a real token of affection! Have you taken up quarters at The Brunswick with the idea of staying there indefinitely, or only until you can get away to Nantucket? Tedcastle told me you were thinking of taking a little house near Sandanwede and settling down again to the life that refreshed you so much down there where one can be as nearly as may be indifferent to the vexatious world that seems likely just now to drive some of the rest of us crazy. Scarcely a day so poor as not to produce its complication in foreign affairs, its "delicate situation,"—a good many more than the public knows of or the newspapers invent. I am getting almost used to them! Some of these days, when peace comes (if it ever can!) and the world has grown sane again, or too worn out with folly to persist in it for a season (like Society in Lent), it may be that I shall find the days dull and stale and tedious, having eaten so long of highly spiced food and subsisted on excitement and perplexity! You never can tell what habit will do to you. Mexico got us in training and Europe has only quickened the pace. We have been at the problem business now for two years! And think of what one would do with the leisure that would be involved, if Congress were not in session. Think of being able actually to sit down with a friend now and again and have a chat about personal matters without having despatches brought you every few minutes and the tug of things that cannot wait perpetually pulling at your mind. After all, I do not want time to think about myself and my own affairs. I am bereft and do not know how I shall ever restore the ruin that has been wrought in my private life. It is best that I should be absolutely compelled and commanded to other duties. I do not like any longer to sit down and think. If there is not an immediate task at hand (for that happens for half an hour at a time even now sometimes) I look at once for something to read a scrap of or turn to some friend for a talk, preferably about them, not myself. I want letters all about yourself, so that I can think about *you* and turn away from

Your devoted friend,   Woodrow Wilson

WWTLS (WP, DLC).

From Edward Mandell House[1]

Dear Governor: Paris, March 14th, 1915.

We arrived here Thursday night. A submarine destroyer accompanied our boat a good part of the way, and we passed one floating mine about one hundred yards away. Otherwise the trip was without incident.

Mr. Sharp has been extremely kind. He seems to be a level headed, plain American of the Western type. He knows but little concerning diplomatic usages, but he will learn, and will perhaps prove more satisfactory than his immediate predescessor.

And this reminds me that he says Herrick treated him very badly. He is getting up data to prove this. I have urged him not to make any use of it for the moment, but to leave it until the campaign of '16 or before, when the republicans will doubtless mention your superceding Herrick as one of your shortcomings. If Sharp can prove what he says he can, it will be a great boomerang.

[1] House conveyed the gist of the following letter in a telegram to Wilson on March 13, 1915. There is an EMHhw copy in the House Papers.

In my last conference with Sir Edward, the night before I left, it was agreed that he should telegraph Delcasse apprising him of my coming and suggesting that it would be well to get in touch with me. We agreed that it would not be advisable for me to go into any details, but to mention the subject of peace with the lightest possible touch.

I have just returned from my interview with Delcasse. The interpreter was the Assistant Secretary for Foreign Affairs.[2] I let him read your letter and told him I came to present your compliments, but that you did not desire to intrude yourself upon them or to hurt their sensibilities in any way by making an immature suggestion of peace.

I said this before he had a chance to say anything for I knew quite well what was in his mind. He was visibly pleased when this suggestion was made and it placed us on a good footing.

I then told him that you had foreseen for a year or more that unless something was done to prevent it, some spark might cause the present conflagration and you had sent me to Europe last May for the purpose of seeing what could be done to bring about a better understanding. That I had gone to Germany and had come to France, but they were changing governments at the time and it was impossible to talk to them.

I wanted to let him know that you had had the threads in your hands from the beginning, and that you understood the situation thoroughly.

I also told him you had refused to let me leave America until Bernstorff had tentatively suggested that I would be welcome in Germany and that a discussion of peace could be taken up upon a basis of evacuation and indemnity for Belgium and a permane[n]t settlement. I said that you did not desire me to go to any capital without first having the assurance that my presence would be welcome and that I had this assurance from von Jagow direct.

In reply he said that France greatly appreciated your keen interest and noble desire to bring about peace, and he was glad I had come to Paris and would look forward with interest to seeing me when I returned from Germany. He said he would then tell me in the frankest way what France had in mind and was willing to do. I did not press him to tell me this then, because I happened to know what they have in mind and I did not want to get into a footless and discouraging discussion.

I had accomplished more than I anticipated, for it was not certain that I would be received cordially. Even Sir Edward was

2 Pierre de Margerie.

a little worried. The main thing accomplished was that France has at least tentatively accepted you as mediator, and that, I think, is much.[3]

I feel that you know enough of my disposition to realize that I am much more likely to move too quickly than too slowly, for I am eager beyond measure to being [bring] about the much desired end. Do not therefore think for a moment I am not pushing just as hard as it is safe to do. I have the greatest difficulty in restraining myself, but I am very sure that if I go too quickly you will lose all that you have so far gained.

I am leaving Wednesday morning for Germany and should be there on the 18th.

I told Delcassé, if he thought it best for me to present your compliments to Poincaré, I would be glad to do so, or if he thought I should mention the purpose of my visit to France, I would do that, but I would be guided entirely by his advice. He is to let me know by Monday or Tuesday concerning this.

Gerard's secretary, Winslow,[4] came over from Berlin to bring some information that Gerard thought I should have before my arrival there. He will travel with us in order to facilitate our trip which is not without some difficulties.

Gerard tells me, through Winslow, that he does not believe the Germans would hesitate a moment to go to war with us. On the other hand, Winslow says that when you sent them the note to Germany which was almost an ultimatum,[5] he saw a distinct change for the bestter [better] at the German Foreign Office the very next day. They had been insolent before, but were all right afterwards.

They all seem to think that the Germans have literally gone crazy. I am not so sure of it myself. I can see gleams of sanity in much they are doing.

I shall be exceedingly careful about cabling you or even writing from Berlin, for it is dangerous to the last degree. Winslow tells me that their system of espionage is something beyond belief, and that one can never be sure that papers have not been tampered with.

I find that the ruling class in France do not desire peace, but that a large part of the people and the men in the trenches would welcome it. This, I think, is also true of Germany.

Another thing I have found and that is the soldiers on both

[3] A somewhat optimistic report. There is no evidence, even in the House Diary, that the French had tentatively accepted Wilson as a mediator, or that they had the slightest interest at this time in mediation by anyone.
[4] Lawrence Lanier Winslow.
[5] The "strict accountability" note of February 10, 1915.

sides are far less bitter than the politicians at the seats of government. The Allies expect to throw the Germans back to the Rhine by the late spring or early summer, and they expect to drive them out of Belgium by the Autumn, provided the war continues that lone [long].

There is no evidence that there is a shortage of food in Germany, or that she will be considerably hampered by a stoppage of her imports of foodstuffs.

I shall probably be back here around the first of April for if there is to be an exchange of thoughts or a beginning of parleys, it will not do to remain there too long. I shall of course determine this after I reach there.

Affectionately yours,   E. M. House

Gerard also sent me word that he thought Dante [the Kaiser] would be deposed, in the event Zodak [Germany] was not successful in this contest.

TLS (WP, DLC).

To Thomas William Hardwick

My dear Senator: [The White House] March 15, 1915

I am sincerely obliged to you for your letter of March eleventh. You are right in thinking that differences of opinion upon public questions cannot alter my personal feeling towards men whom I respect and with whom it is a pleasure for me to work and I thank you for judging me so truly. I must in frankness say, however, that the recent situation in the Senate distressed and disturbed me not a little. I do not see how party government is possible, indeed I can form no working idea of the successful operation of popular institutions, if individuals are to exercise the privilege of defeating a decisive majority of their own party associates in framing and carrying out the policy of the party. In party conference personal convictions should have full play and should be most candidly and earnestly presented, but there does not seem to me to be any surrender either of personal dignity or of individual conviction in yielding to the determinations of a decisive majority of one's fellow workers in a great organization which must hold together if it is to be serviceable to the country as a governing agency.

This conviction on my part lies back of and supports every conclusion that I have come to in years of study not only, but in recent years of experience, with regard to the feasibility and efficiency of party government, and I beg, my dear Senator, that you will allow me to press this view upon you with the earnestness of a conviction which underlies all others.

      Cordially and sincerely yours,   Woodrow Wilson

TLS (Letterpress Books, WP, DLC).

Two Letters from Edward Mandell House

Dear Governor: Paris, France. March 15th, 1915.

I want to tell you some of the difficulties of the situation over here. One is the impossibility of keeping my mission secret.

Where an Ambassador knows it, one or two of the secretaries are sure to know it and it creeps around insidiously. It is the same with the Foreign Offices. When the Chief knows it, it dribbles through to the under secretaries, and they in turn, repeat it.

The capitals of Europe are full of Americans, mostly antagonistic to your Administration. They are habitues of these capitals and know officialdom intimately, therefore they get a measure of it. Things are constantly coming back to me that some American has said derogatory to you and your purpose to inject yourself, for political advantage, into this situation. Roosevelt's friends are particularly active.

I have denied unreservedly that you have any desire to act as mediator and that it is probable that you would refuse to act in this capacity even if asked. I also say that I am here merely to find what is in the minds of the belligerents and to report to you for your information, and that you are not urging or insisting upon anything.

Your letter of instructions to me tells this in a wonderful way, but of course, it cannot be shown to anyone excepting the heads of the governments.

The thing I am always most afraid of is the press. My name has not been mentioned here and I have not thought it worth while as yet to ask the Foreign Office to censor anything that might be said. At the first intimation, however, I shall do this.*

I mention these things merely to let you know with what circumspection it is necessary to move.

I would appreciate it if you would write me upon receipt of this, if you have not already done so, concerning your views upon the second convention. Everyone I have talked to seems delighted with that thought. I have not heard a single objection to it. If Germany receives it kindly I would like your permission to discuss it with some of the neutral nations through our Minis-

* I have since done this.

ters or Ambassadors, so as to have the ground fallow when the time comes for you to act.

I have been staying here for a few days merely to sow some seed which I hope may later bear fruit.

These people believe that final victory is certain and they are in no mood for peace talk. I have been cautiously trying to let them know what a gamble they are taking. I have told them that Germany realizing what an effort the Allies will make this spring, seems willing to discount some chance of success and begin parleys.

Another interesting feature here is that the Government is not nearly so disposed to let Russia have Constantinople as is England. Grey told me this, but I could scarcely credit it. It is another indication of their excessive confidence of final success.

I want to again tell you that Mr. Sharp has been as kind and friendly as possible. In other words, he is disposed to let me do as I please and without intruding himself. In this respect he has used unusual tact and good judgment.

Affectionately yours,   E. M. House

Dear Governor: Paris, France. March 15th, 1915.

De Casenave came to see me today. He is at the head of the Press Bureau and his principal duties are to see that the French papers contain the proper kind of reading matter in regard to England, America and other nations.[1] In other words he is connected with the Foreign Office in that capacity.

I asked him to be very frank and to tell me of French opinion. He said the French people at large thought that America had nothing in mind further than a dollar. He said a few Frenchmen had gone to America, had stayed there some weeks, not knowing the language, had visited such places as the pork packeries of Chicago and had come away to write books concerning the avarice of our people. He said this had been done to such an extent that the opinion was fixed in France that we were guided entirely by mercenary motives.

He said when he gave to the French papers directions as to what to say in regard to America, they smiled and shrugged their shoulders.

I asked him what they thought of the munificent contributions and services that Americans were giving to aid France in this her hour of trial. He said they thought it was confined to a noble few who knew and appreciated France.

I told him that France was not alone in this opinion, that England shared it to a lesser degree and Germany to a larger one. He admitted that this was true.

I am trying to make a friend of de Margery of the Foreign Office. He has lived in America, speaks English well and is said to be almost as much of a force in the Foreign Office as Delcasse, besides being in Delcasse's confidence. I have some mutual friends on this job and I will remain here long enough upon my return to try and clinch it.

I shall attempt the same thing in Germany, probably using Zimmermann as a medium. If I can establish such relations, the situation can scarcely get away from us.

There is one other thing about my interview of Saturday and that is while they decried any thought of peace for the moment, I felt a note of interest in your endeavors and I shall be surprised if they do not look forward with very keen concern to my return from Germany.   Affectionately yours,   E. M. House

TLS (WP, DLC).
¹ Jean Marie Maurice Casenave had retired from the French diplomatic service with the rank of Minister Plenipotentiary before taking up his position in the Foreign Ministry.

Walter Hines Page to William Jennings Bryan

London. March 15, 1915. Recd 11 p.m.

1795. Following is the full text of a memorandum dated March 13, which Gray handed me today:

"On the 22nd of February last I received a communication from Your Excellency of the identic note addressed to His Majesty's Government and to Germany respecting an agreement on certain points as to the conduct of the war at sea. The reply of the German Government to this note has been published and it is not understood from the reply that the German Government are prepared to abandon the practice of sinking British merchant vessels by submarines and it is evident from their reply that they will not abandon the use of mines for offensive purposes on the high seas as contrasted with the use of mines for defensive purposes only within cannon range of their own harbours as suggested by the Government of the United States. This being so it might appear unnecessary for the British Government to make any further reply than to take note of the German answer. We desire however to take the opportunity of making a fuller statement of the whole position and of our feeling with regard to it. We recognize with sympathy the desire of the Government of the United States to see the European War conducted in accordance with the previously recognized rules of International Law and the dictates of humanity. It is thus that the British forces have conducted the war and we are not aware that these forces either naval or military can have laid to their charge any improper proceedings, either in the conduct of hostilities or in the treatment of prisoners or wounded. On the German side it has been very different.

1. The treatment of civilian inhabitants in Belgium and the north of France has been made public by the Belgian and French Government and by those who have had experience of it at first hand. Modern history affords no precedent for the sufferings that have been inflicted on the defenseless and non-combatants population in the territory that has been in German military occupation. Even the food of the population was confiscated until in Belgium an International Commission largely influenced by American generosity and conducted under American auspices came to the relief of the population and secured from the German Government a promise to spare what food was still left in the country though the Germans still continue to make levies in money upon the defenseless population for the support of the German army.

2. We have from time to time received most terrible accounts of the barbarous treatment to which British officers and soldiers have been exposed after they have been taken prisoner while being conveyed to German prison camps, one or two instances have already been given to the United States Government founded upon authentic and first hand evidence which is beyond doubt. Some evidence has been received of the hardships to which British prisoners of war are subjected in the prison camps contrasting, we believe, most unfavourably with the treatment of German prisoners in this country. We have proposed with the consent of the United States Government that a commission of United States officers should be permitted in each country to inspect the treatment of prisoners of war. The United States Government have been unable to obtain any reply from the German Government to this proposal and we remain in continuing anxiety and apprehension as to the treatment of British prisoners of war in Germany.

3. At the very outset of the war a German minelayer was discovered laying a minefield on the high seas. Further minefields have been laid from time to time without warning and so far as we know are still being laid on the high seas and many neutral as well as British vessels have been sunk by them.

4. At various times during the war German submarines have stopped and sunk British merchant vessels thus making the sinking of merchant vessels a general practice though it was admitted previously, if at all, only as an exception. The general rule to which the British Government have adhered being that merchant vessels, if captured, must be taken before a prize court. In one case already quoted in a note to the United States Government a neutral vessel carrying foodstuffs to an unfortified town in Great Britain has been sunk. Another case is now reported in which a German armed cruiser has sunk an American vessel, the WILLIAM P FRYE, carrying a cargo of wheat from Seattle to Queenstown.[1] In both cases the cargoes were presumably destined for the civil population. Even the cargoes in such circumstances should not have been condemned without the decision of a prize court much less should the vessels have been sunk. It is to be noted that both these cases occurred before the detention by the British authorities of the WILHELMINA and her cargo of foodstuffs which the German Government allege is the justification for their own action. The Germans have announced their intention of sinking British merchant vessels by torpedo without notice and without any provision for the safety of the crew. They have already carried out this intention in the case of neutral as well as of British vessels and a number of noncombatant and innocent lives on British vessels unarmed and defenseless have been destroyed in this way.

5. Unfortified, open and defenseless towns such as Scarbotough [Scarborough], Yarmouth and Whitby have been deliberately and wantonly bombarded by German ships of war causing in some cases [c]onsiderable loss of civilian life including women and children.

6. German aircraft have dropped bombs on the east coast of England where there were no military or strategic points to be attacked. On the other hand I am aware of but two criticisms that have been made on British action in all these respects: (1) It is said that the British naval authorities also have laid some anchored mines on the high seas. They have done so but the mines were anchored and so constructed that they would be harmless if they went adrift and no mines whatever were laid by the British naval authorities till many weeks after the Germans had made a regular practice of laying mines on the high seas. (2) It is said that the British Government have departed

---

[1] About the *Frye* case, which ended in friendly agreement between the American and German governments about the treatment of American merchant vessels and cargoes by German naval forces, see Link, *Struggle for Neutrality*, p. 454.

from the view of International Law which they had previously maintained that foodstuffs destined for the civil population should never be interfered with, this charge being founded on the submission to a prize court of the cargo of the WILHELMINA The special considerations affecting this cargo have already been presented in a memorandum to the United States Government and I need not repeat them here.[2] Inasmuch as the stoppage of all foodstuffs is an admitted consequence of blockade it is obvious that there can be no universal rule based on considerations of morality and humanity which is contrary to this practice. The right to stop foodstuffs destined for the civil population must therefore in any case be admitted if an effective "cordon" controlling intercourse with the enemy is drawn, announced and maintained. Moreover, independently of rights arising from belligerent action in the nature of blockade some other nations differing from the opinion of the Governments of the United States and Great Britain have held that to stop the food of the civil population is a natural and legitimate method of bringing pressure to bear on an enemy country as it is upon the defence of a besieged town. It is also upheld on the authority of both Prince Bismarck and Count Caprivi and therefore presumably is not repugnant to German morality. The following are the quotations from Prince Bismarck and Count Caprivi on this point. Prince Bismarck in answering in 1885 an application from the Kiel Chamber of Commerce for a statement of the view of the German Government on the question of the right to declare as contraband foodstuffs that were not intended for military forces said, "I reply to the Chamber of Commerce that any disadvantage our commercial and carrying interests may suffer by the treatment of rice as contraband of war does not justify our opposing a measure which it has been thought fit to take in carrying on a foreign war. Every war is a calamity which entails evil consequences not only on the combatants but also on neutrals. These evils may easily be increased by the interference of a neutral power with the way in which a third carries on the war to the disadvantage of the subjects of the interfering power

[2] In order to test British policy concerning food shipments to Germany, a group of Germans, backed by German officials in the United States, had purchased *Wilhelmina*, a ship of American registry, and sent her on her way to Hamburg on January 22 loaded with food specifically destined for civilian firms. While *Wilhelmina* was at sea, the Bundesrat of the German Empire issued a decree forbidding private transactions in major food staples and appropriating all stocks of corn, wheat, and flour. The German government quickly assured the State Department that the decree would not apply to imported foodstuffs. However, the British seized *Wilhelmina* at Falmouth on the ground that all food going to Germany was destined for the armed forces. See Link, *Struggle for Neutrality*, pp. 187-190.

and by this means German commerce might be weighted with far heavier losses than a transitory prohibition of the rice trade in Chinese waters. The measure in question has for its object the shortening of the war by increasing the difficulties of the enemy and is a justifiable step in war if impartially enforced against all neutral ships." Count Caprivi during a discussion in the German Reichstag on the 4th March 1892, on the subject of the importance of International protection for private property at sea made the following statements, "A country may be dependent for her food or for her raw procuce [produce] upon her trade. In fact it may be absolutely necessary to destroy the enemy's trade"—"The private introduction of provisions into Paris was prohibited during the siege and in the same way a nation would be justified in preventing the import of food and raw produce." The Government of Great Britain have frankly declared in concert with the Government of France their intention to meet the German attempt to stop all supplies of every kind from leaving or entering British or French ports by themselves stopping supplies going to or from Germany for this end. The British fleet has instituted a blockade effectively controlling by cruiser "cordon" all passage to and from Germany by sea. The difference between the two policies is, however, that while our object is the same as that of Germany we propose to attain it without sacrificing neutral ships or non-combatant lives or inflicting upon neutrals the damage that must be entailed when a vessel and its cargo are sunk without notice, examination or trial. I must emphacize again that this measure is a natural and necessary consequence of the unprecedented methods repugnant to all law and morality which have been described above which Germany began to adopt at the very outset of the war and the effects of which have been constantly accumulating."   American Ambassador London.[3]

T telegram (SDR, RG 59, 763.72/1588, DNA).
[3] There is a printed copy of this telegram in WP, DLC.

To William Jennings Bryan, with Enclosures

My dear Mr. Secretary,   [The White House] 16 March, 1915.

I have read this paper very attentively and with a great deal of interest. Thank you.   Faithfully Yours,   W.W.

WWTLI (W. J. Bryan Papers, DNA).

ENCLOSURE I[1]

GENERAL VILLA

FIRST INTERVIEW—GUADALAJARA—MARCH 4, 1915.

Met C.,[2] D–L,* and Dr. de la Puento, Tax Collector, proceeding by auto to General Villa's car at the station, for luncheon and conference with him. D–L had previously presented my credentials for inspection, though not requested.

Car under station shed—one side a crowd of gazers at the General, who sat on a lounge, talking to occasional visitors. Attired in very heavy sweater—bad cold. Rough and ready ranchero type, good round head, heavy square jaw. Almost none of the suaviter common to all natives. Had six-shooter right hip, Colt's .45, old style, pearl handle.

Ushered into car by D–L and Dr. de la Puento, C. following. Met secretary, Colonel Perez Ruel, and Colonel Trillo; also Colonel Dario W. Silva present, and General Banda, who made a report.

Villa continued his conference with the party with whom he was talking, we taking seats and chatting until party left, when I was presented—1:10 P.M. He proceeded without formality to express his obligation to President Wilson in preventing war in this country, and in preventing war between Mexico and The United States. He hoped to be recognized by The United States, and thought he ought to be, because he had demonstrated his ability to enforce law and order throughout Mexico, and was actuated solely by a desire to promote the welfare of his country, disclaiming any personal ambition whatsoever. Also thought that it would be unnecessary for me to go to Vera Cruz.

There can be no doubt of his good hard common sense, and he weighed his words well, talking slowly and distinctly. He stated that an embargo was placed upon his right to receive coal from the United States by The Santa Fe', after he had paid about $600,000. gold for coal; and he presumed, now that he was about to get his supplies from the Coahuila fields, that The United States railroads and coal owners would complain that he no longer patronized them. He felt aggrieved at the misrepresentations continually made against him and his character, and appearing in the papers, and stated that he was willing to be judged by results—since, unlike Carranza, it was not his practice to conduct his campaigns in the newspapers.

Concerning the question of religion, stated that there would

* Diaz Lombardo, Minister of Foreign Affairs and Justice.

be no denial of right to worship, but that all denominational (religious) schools would be abolished, and that, so far as the catholic clergy was concerned, he believed in the expulsion of the foreign priests; and, so long as there was no meddling in politics, there would be no restriction of rights. On the other hand, if there were bad men among the religious, who disregarded law, they would be punished. He favored an equitable and just partition of the great landed estates among the common people.

On the question of education, said that he believed that the great progress in The United States was founded on the education of the masses, and he hoped to multiply and increase the schools so that every ranch might have its school. He stated that he had picked up, on the streets of Mexico, more than two hundred gamins, and sent them to Chihuahua, for instruction in the school of arts there—and would continue to do so, as opportunity afforded.

During the progress of our talk, General Fierro[3] came to make a report, and I was introduced to him. He was not so unprepossessing as one might think. His greeting was cordial, and his talk businesslike and short.

During lunch, there was more ease, and less stiffness in the talk, quite a deal of quiet banter passing around. I had the head of the table, C right, Colonel Silva left; Villa next to C, D–L next to Silva; then Dr. de la Puento and Secretary Perez Ruel, and Colonel Trillo next to General Villa. At the foot of the table was a lady in black, Mrs. T., to whom there was no introduction. The meal was served in the observation, or office end of the car. Limeade and ice-water, fruit, soup, macaroni, meat, salad, cafe au lait, and cakes. No smoking. Villa cut up bananas in his soup, using tortillas instead of knife and fork, where practicable. Ate sparingly, and made no pretense of table manners.

With reference to the military campaign, stated that General Angeles advised of the capture of important coal fields in Coahuila, and a defeat of the enemy; that General Chao had won an important "combate," and was now within 100 kilometres of Tampico; that he, Villa, was sending 10,000 troops, mostly cavalry, to the North, and asked if I did not think that sufficient to clean up the country to the Rio Grande, and take Tampico. He expressed the opinion that in fifteen days Angeles would reach the Rio Grande, and that in twenty days, Tampico and the oil fields would be taken; that then he would direct his attention to the subjection of Mexico City, Puebla, and Vera Cruz.

Concerning the resources of the country, said that there were abundant supplies of beans and corn in storage, and that there was no danger of shortage.

He excused himself for siesta at 3:15 P.M.

1 All of these reports were by Duval West. Preceding these Enclosures was a seven-page report dated Feb. 10, 1915 (T MS, SDR, RG 59, 812.00/14622, DNA) entitled "The Villa Government," which listed the principal officials of Villa's administration; described the Villa government's extensive confiscations of property of the well-to-do; related plans for land reform; discussed the attitude of the Villa government toward the Roman Catholic Church; and emphasized that the "socialistic idea, without definite expression," seemed to prevail everywhere concerning large landowners and great mercantile companies. This report continued:

"The people en masse, having reference to the seven or eight millions of the peon type, are densely ignorant and may be considered as being without sufficient knowledge or education to have any desires except those elemental, and are practically without ambition to better themselves. In the mass, their only wish is for little food, little money, little work, and are content with the extreme minimum of actual necessaries. Increase of wage to them only means longer periods of idleness and more pulque. To elevate this mass of humanity to a higher plane is the work of a future generation, but the reforms to be instituted must have an early beginning. The Villa Government promises these, but looking to the present governing class, I should say that the possibilities for substantial aid and assistance to the mass of people will be negligible for a long time. The reason for the inertia of the body of people has existed from the time of Cortez, and even before. The Spaniards, generally speaking, merely held them to their original places in the scheme of government.

"The uniform use of spiritous liquors by the population, pulque, mescal and distillates from cane and other products of the soil, being had at nominal cost and slight exertion, has been, perhaps, the greatest single factor in holding them to their low level. In this connection it is stated that General Villa, personally, hopes to inaugurate widespread reforms to make it impossible for the lower classes to obtain spirituous drink. Undoubtedly, if no other reform was brought into effect, than this, the cost of years of warfare would be amply repaid.

"The mass of the people will be educated through the establishment of schools, but a greater educational factor is their employment in industrial and manufacturing enterprises.

"An estimate of the personal character and political aspirations and ambitions of General Villa and of General Angeles, may be put in the clearest way by giving verbatim notes taken by me immediately following personal conference with each of them. Therefore my estimates of the two leaders will be put in a clearer light by inserting those notes in this report."

In addition, West sent a two-page memorandum (T MS, SDR, RG 59, 812.00/14622, DNA) entitled "General Angeles–Interview–Monterrey–February 26, 1915," a highly flattering portrait emphasizing Angeles' ability, patriotism, lack of political ambition, and the fact that he had not permitted any confiscations, much to the displeasure of *Villista* partisans.

2 George C. Carothers.

3 Rodolfo Fierro, who had the reputation of being one of Villa's more bloodthirsty lieutenants.

ENCLOSURE II

SECOND INTERVIEW—ENROUTE NORTH—MARCH 6, 1915.

Villa, sans ceremony, came aboard in shirt-sleeves, and hatless, as usual. He sat with us for half an hour, and talked casually and unreservedly, commencing by statement that he was only a common, rough, uneducated man, who had spent the great portion of his life in the mountains, alternately fighting Don Pofirio,[1] and in hiding. That he did not know, but that, because Mr. Wilson seemed to understand him, he felt sure that Mr. Wilson must have at one time been a poor boy who had to struggle for himself and depend upon his own exertions, and so achieve success. Incidentally, the shots were fired by Villa at a telephone pole, all taking effect, as George[2] said. Had taught himself to read and write, but was well aware of his shortcomings in that regard. He believed he was a good judge of men, and that General Angeles was, in his opinion, the man for the Presidency—the provisional Presidency, at any rate. It was his desire and intention to urge General Angeles to accept the Presidency, administering its civil functions, while he retained control of the military arm until peace and order had been secured over the country; that when this was accomplished, he would be entirely content to retire to his small ranch near Chihuahua, and, if desired, to separate himself entirely from official connection with the Government.

At this point, he remarked that his life and its experiences with all conditions of men, had caused him to be suspicious of all men, but that he hoped I would believe him in the statement that he was honest, truthful, and sincere in the statement that he only desired peace and happiness to his people, but for himself personally he wished for nothing. That it was not true, as frequently charged, that he was storing away money for his own ends. All revenues and returns were being devoted by him to prosecuting the war and in establishing the government. Personally, this country should have his all. It was true that he had at a certain place considerable stores of bullion. He first had thought best to mint this into coin for the people, but had found, upon issuing some money, that it was at once hidden away, and none except coppers remained in circulation; therefore concluding that it was useless to attempt to replace the paper money by metal issues, and accordingly had discontinued, though he still held his stores of bullion, and intended to have some coined for the benefit of the country when peace prevailed.

I told General Villa that, while true that his lack of experience in the administration of the civil affairs of government might raise the question as to his ability to conduct them, still, he could, and should, call to his aid men of matured judgement and ex-

[1] That is, Porfirio Díaz.
[2] Carothers.

perience in those matters in which he was deficient—men upon whose loyalty, patriotism, and honesty he could rely that the problems to be solved might be successfully worked out; that brains and experience and knowledge of technical or special matters were easily secured, if there were such men in his following—*which I doubted*. He said, "Yes, I have them—and can get them," though gave no names.

An increase in speed of our train brought out few premonitory jiggles from the Cricket, which caused a rolling of Villas's eyes, and the inquiry to C. as to what was the matter—later promising a more confortable car than the box.

Bringing up the question of Zapata's influence on the establishment of peace, he said that he was sure he could control Zapata personally, because he had promised, and intended to act as God-father for one of Zapata's children; that this, when done, would make them compadres, and indissolubly bind them together. Zapata was well-meaning, patriotic, and entirely devoted to the good of his people, who inhabited the mountain country embracing the State of Moreles, and parts of the States of Puebla, Guerrero, Mexico, and Michoacan. That Zapata, however, was surrounded by men of bad influence, of some ability, who would have to be disposed of eventually, which he was sure could be done. Argumedo, a renegade Villista, being one of the men referred to—admitted to be a good fighter, with ability, but bad. (Apropos of this, rumor has it that Villa, upon requesting Zapata to deliver up Argumedo to him, stated that he would exchange him for Angeles, the latter being Huerta's artillery commander during very severe fighting around Cuerna Vaca against Zapata during Madero's time).

Zapata has no flag, but his men carry as their banner or insignia, the image of the "Virgin of Guadalupe." I noticed that many of Villa's soldiers also carry pictures of this Virgin on their hats.

Villa, through Carothers, had previously advised that it was impossible to arrange for a safe conduct for me from Zapata through the lines, because of lack of communication with Zapata except by occasional messenger through the mountains.

Recurring to the military campaign, stated that in forty days he was confident he would be in complete control of Northern Mexico from the Rio Grande south down to and including the Port of Tampico, the oil fields, and Manzanillo. While moving out a good many of his troops to the north—all cavalry—he was leaving in Jalisco and Colima some five thousand men, and had ordered the enlisting of a sufficient number there to make ten thousand. These forces would be ample to take care of the scattered camp of Carranzistas in that territory, who, with Dieguaz, their commander, was still at large.

I directed his attention to the activities of Salazar along the border, expressing the opinion that he should be arrested, that there was no effort being made by his men to run him down. He was quite amazed, and seemed unaware that Salazar was giving trouble. Said it was *very* hard to catch Salazar, but that of course he could not personally undertake it, because of the larger operations. He would, however, direct his officers to take more vigorous and energetic measures.

Upon being questioned as to what extent foreigners would be encouraged to develope the country, stated that there would be no disposition to prohibit such developement, except that in the case of lands foreigners should not, or would not, be permitted to own lands. That it was his idea that the country should be developed by Mexican capital, and that this capital should be compelled or required—did not say what, or how, or when—to employ itself in the establishment of the usual industrial enterprises.

I get the idea, from the foregoing statement, and from the failure of General Villa to take the opportunity afforded by the question to make clear the wish of his followers to encourage foreign capital, that he is standing upon the popular demand that "Mexico should be for the Mexicans," and that an open door to foreign investors means ultimate danger to the nation. Vide the various checks and conditions and demands made by the foreign countries, growing out of their investments and the presence of their nationals. Carrothers does not agree altogether with me in this conclusion; but, in any event, there should be a clear statement, positive and definite, to which the declarants may be held—as to foreign policy.

Instancing his efforts to protect foreign investments, declared that he "has, since the revolution, paid to The North Western Railroad about a Million and a quarter Dollars." The statement was not made with any air of cheerfulness.

Villa was much more at ease, and much less on guard, than at our prior formal interview, giving better opportunity of studying and estimating him. He is much stronger in native mentality than given credit for. His schooling has been in the open, and his wits keenly sharpened by playing a game, the stake being his existence. So, as to all matters involving physical safety of the individual or in mass, his judgement is so trained by years of constant use as to be almost intuitive; this being the foundation upon which rests those attributes that make him a great military leader of his kind. On the other hand, because of lack of exercise of those faculties by experience and education and study necessary to high statesmanship, meaning a knowledge of the administration and operation of the civil government of peoples, he is wholly a stranger. His views of important governmental plans and policies to be undertaken by way of civil administration must be, for the present, considered as entirely amateurish and tentative.

Villa rode with us about three-quarters of an hour. As before stated, he was hatless and coatless, wearing light straw-colored shirt, with limp collar, dark khaki trousers, and the usual six-shooter, old style .45 Colt's, cut off, with belt of cartridges.

He is well and strongly built, weight about 175 pounds; height 5 ft., 10½ in.; age 38. Black hair, and very dark, small brown or black eyes that are the expression features of his face. An unusual lot of white is shown, and the eyes have unusual glint and sparkle. He has a characteristic way of slightly lowering his head and looking upward in questioning pose. The nose is small, straight, and well formed. Large, rather coarse mouth, and firm heavy jaws; the neck being short, thick and massive, which, together with his solid, compact, muscular figure, gives him a decidedly bull-like appearance. He is quick and active in his movements, and is of the vaguero type, appearing much more at home on horseback than on foot, or in his private car.

He bade us a cordial invitation to lunch or dine with him whenever we pleased, and dropped off to board his own car, about 5:30 P.M.

TS MSS (SDR, RG 59, 812.00/14622, DNA).

E N C L O S U R E   I I I

CONCLUSIONS

The conclusions reached are based upon investigation of the Villa territory alone. Not having the benefit of similar study of leaders and conditions in Carranza and Zapata territories, they must be taken as tentative, subject to modifications where comparison is necessary in order to form a surer judgement.

ORDER

Admirable order is preserved throughout Villa territory, which embraces the major portion of the Republic, both as to territorial

area and population. There is no complaint of disregard by subordinates of any orders issued by Villa. It is my opinion that Villa
will continue to maintain order within territory dominated by
him.

LAW AND JUSTICE

The law administered by the Military commanders is in most
cases harsh and unfair, being based upon ex-parte statements of
interested persons, without trial or inquiry. The existence of this
method is responsible for great wrongs, still existent, and serves
as authority for many executions and confiscations of property,
summary and without trial. These will continue to a lessening
degree until civil courts are established and the right of trial
guaranteed. Mr. Lombardo informed me that Villa at Torreon on
March 9th authorized him to prepare the orders necessary to put
into effect the suspended functions of the Courts of First Instance, and that he would at once proceed to do so.

SETTLEMENT OF DIFFERENCES

The only settlement taken into account is one involving complete physical control of the whole country. Both Villa and
Angeles are absolutely confident that they can bring this about,
speedily if recognition by The United States be given, a longer
period if not given. Both at my request entered into the military
features of their campaigns in great detail, giving their strategy,
numbers of troops, where disposed, and outlined in a very clear
manner their plans, already mentioned in the interviews. I
believe that they will ultimately succeed, but having no knowledge of similar facts as to Carranza, Obregon, Gonzales, Zapata,
and others, my opinion should be so weighed.

DIFFICULTIES OF THE VILLA GOVERNMENT

The chief danger to the stability of the government established
by Villa, assuming complete ultimate control, will be those of
civil administrations having reference

(1) To the adjustments of claims and demands of foreign
governments arising out of disorders of the last four years.

(2) To the adjustment of the claims of foreign industrial
enterprises already established, and the passage of fair laws
regulating same; and formulating a policy as to foreign immigration and foreign investors.

(3) The establishment of a stable currency having a fixed
value; and provisions for the validations of outstanding paper
issues. There already exists grumbling and discontent among

the masses at the small purchasing power of the peso, now worth 10 cents gold.

(4) The widespread idea that the property of the rich is to be divided amongst the people, promises difficulties, involving as it does the popular cry of "Mexico for the Mexicans," which, by some, is considered to mean the exclusion and prohibition of foreigners.

(5) A serious difficulty arises from personal characteristics attributed to General Villa, having special reference to several authenticated instances wherein he is charged with having forcibly taken respectable women, and compelled them to submit to his wishes. These instances have not been verified by me, and the statement may not be considered as conclusive.

Finally, I wish to say that I have talked with a great many most reputable people concerning conditions in Mexico during the last thirty days, confining myself, as far as possible, to persons in Mexico having first-hand knowledge. The conclusions reached are stated, for lack of time, without logical order, and the degree of care that should be employed, being partial and tentative, and incomplete. A conference touching its various subjects would more nearly reach the actual situation, as I understand it. Trusting, however, that it may serve to be of some assistance in reaching a just and fair judgement of the questions involved, I remain   Very respectfully,   Duval West.

To William Jennings Bryan

My dear Mr. Secretary,   [The White House] 16 March 1915.

No doubt a confidential print of our note to Japan ought to be made, if it can indeed be preserved from publicity as confidential; but my judgment is that the confidential circle should be as small as possible.

I think that the note should be communicated in strict confidence to the Governments of Great Britain and France and perhaps to the Government of the Netherlands (if we can without offence thus limit the circle); and of course it should be communicated in the same way to Reinsch (that he may let the authorities at Peking know what we are attempting in their support); but, as I have said, every effort should be made to safeguard it for the present and it should pass through as few hands as practicable.   Faithfully Yours,   W.W.

WWTLI (SDR, RG 59, 793.94/267½, DNA).

From William Jennings Bryan

My dear Mr. President: Washington March 16, 1915.

I enclose the statement which Bishop Currier promised,[1] but I notice in reading it over that he has omitted the most important fact—namely, that the Church is supporting this movement.

Will you please indicate the line that the answer should follow? I assume that we shall remain neutral as between all factions but do not know whether you would care to express an opinion as to the wisdom of a movement founded entirely upon the proposed lines. I do not know to what extent the movement is supported by Cienfuegos. You will notice that no reforms are outlined—it is merely *pacification*. Would you think it worth while to suggest the wisdom of incorporating a plan of reform in the party program?

With assurances of high respect I am, my dear Mr. President,
Yours very sincerely,   W. J. Bryan

Later—I find that the Gamboa who signs this paper with Bishop Courier was Huerta's Sec of Foreign Affairs.

TLS (SDR, RG 59, 812.00/16810, DNA).
    [1] Charles Warren Currier, Federico Gamboa, and Gabriel Fernandez Somellera to WJB, March 15, 1915. TLS (SDR, RG 59, 812.00/16810, DNA), announcing a new counterrevolutionary movement to pacify Mexico and asking the United States to promise not to oppose it and not to favor "factions actually in the field." Bishop Currier had just resigned as Bishop of Matanzas, Cuba, and was living in Washington. Gamboa has been identified in this series; he was, among other things, the leader of the Catholic Party of Mexico. Somellera is unidentified.

To William Jennings Bryan

My dear Mr. Secretary,   [The White House] 16 March, 1915.

I do not like the possibilities lurking in this. I am clear that we cannot in conscience countenance or give the least encouragement to any counter revolution. We have never in any other case been asked to do what we are asked to do in this paper. Some of the names given are certainly not the names of friends of any conceivable people's plan. And in any case what is contemplated is not revealed. It is a pig in a poke. I think that we should very respectfully reply that this Government does not feel warranted in giving countenance to any plan which involves (at any rate by possibility) the multiplication of revolutionary elements. And the reply should, if possible, be made orally, not in writing. It is so difficult to give a true impression in writing of our real feeling.   Faithfully Yours,   W.W.

WWTLI (SDR, RG 59, 812.00/16810, DNA).

From Edward Mandell House

[Paris, March 16, 1915]

Will leave tomorrow for Germany, reaching Berlin Friday morning. My visit here has been useful. I am now eager to develop the situation there. Edward House

Transcript of WWsh decode (WC, NjP).

To William Jennings Bryan, with Enclosure

My dear Mr. Secretary, The White House. 17 March, 1915.

The enclosed letter from Father Kelley explains itself.[1] I have written to him that I would refer it to you and ask you if you would not reply to it for me, in order to set forth what the Administration has done in behalf of religious freedom in Mexico in a way that, it may be hoped, will set at rest the serious misunderstandings that have been created.

I am taking the liberty of enclosing a suggested form of answer. I do not think that it would be wise, or possible, to give a definite assurance that we would not recognize any government in Mexico which did not give us satisfactory guarantees of a fair treatment of the Church (too much Mexican history lies back of and complicates that matter), but we can and should promise the exercise to the full of our influence in that behalf. Please let me know what you think of the reply I have drafted. I am anxious to avail myself of every opportunity to remove the false impressions which have got abroad among the Catholics of the country. Faithfully Yours, Woodrow Wilson

WWTLS (photostat in W. J. Bryan Papers, DNA).
[1] It is printed at Feb. 23, 1915.

ENCLOSURE

Draft of Letter.

The President has referred to me your important letter of the twenty-third of February concerning the present distressing situation in Mexico, with the request that I tell you very definitely what the attitude and acts of the Administration have been in the matter of the protection of the rights of conscience and of worship there, a matter in which the Administration is, I need not say, deeply interested as all true Americans must be.

The question which has bulked largest in political discussion in connection with the present revolution in Mexico, and in connection with the revolution which preceded it, is the land question, because upon a people's economic relations to the land everything else, it would seem, that is to determine its institutions and secure its freedom must depend. There can be no permanent pacification in Mexico, no stable settlement of her political troubles, until the land question is justly and wisely settled and the land made the basis of the independence of her citizens, rank and file, and the foundation of her family life.

But of course economic questions are settled, if the matter be thought through to its real heart, only in order to give leave to the deeper things that are spiritual. A democracy must be sustained by education, by the education of the people, and her schools will be as valuable to Mexico as her acres of fertile land. It will be as necessary that she have them as that she break the monopoly that has controlled her land.

And, above and beyond all, the full flower of democracy, lies religious freedom, the principle which the builders of our own Republic made the crown of the whole structure. To this freedom political liberty has seemed, at many of the most important crises of history, to be only the handmaiden and servant. There can be no doubt in the minds of Americans about these things.

The Administration has not felt at liberty to play any part in the internal affairs of Mexico except that of friend and adviser. It realizes that, by reason of geographical proximity and many historical circumstances known to all the world, it is in some peculiar degree charged with the duty of safeguarding, so far as it may within the limits of international privilege, the lives and rights of foreigners in Mexico, and it has again and again made the strongest possible representations with regard to such matters to those who have from time to time assumed responsibility for affairs in Mexico during the troubled months through which that country has been passing. At every turn of affairs there, moreover, and upon every report of persecution, it has advised and warned those who were exercising authority of the fatal effect any disregard for the lives or rights of those who represented religion or any attack upon liberty of conscience or of worship would have upon the opinion of the people of the United States and of the world.

Here quote pertinent despatches and efforts on our part.

This Administration is of course the servant of the American people. It seeks to be governed by their convictions and by the principles which have governed their political life. It has felt it to be its duty to urge upon the leaders of Mexico, whenever an opportunity offered, the principles and methods of action which must underlie all real democracies, as they have supported ours. These principles will, in the same way, govern the Administration in handling every question that affects its relations with Mexico, including the final question of the recognition of any government that may issue out of the present revolution and give promise of stability and justice. It cannot dictate laws or forms of government to Mexico; but it can, and will, bring to bear upon Mexican affairs, wherever it may legitimately do so, the pressure of American opinion and American example. The Mexican leaders will certainly know that in order to command the sympathy and moral support of America Mexico must have, when her reconstruction comes, just land tenure, free schools, and true freedom of conscience and worship. We know of no other foundation stones upon which to build the economic and spiritual life that makes political freedom a reality and a blessing.[1]

WWT MS (photostat in W. J. Bryan Papers, DNA).
[1] There is a WWsh draft of this draft in WP, DLC.

To William Jennings Bryan

My dear Mr. Secretary,   The White House. 18 March, 1915.

I think it is clearly our duty to reply[1] to the following effect:

We cannot refrain from expressing our grave concern at the plan disclosed. To encourage, or even to countenance, any interference in the internal affairs of an independent country with which we are at peace when that plan plainly involves the possibility of the use of armed force would be a manifest violation of the sacred obligations of neutrality. We feel it to be our plain duty to say that no plans for controlling the politics or government of Mexico should emanate from or be guided, directed, or assisted from the United States or by any of its citizens. With every effort to bring peace and orderly government, with liberty, to that distressed country every thoughtful American must of course sympathize; but citizens of the United States are not at liberty to take any part in such efforts, either directly or indirectly, beyond the limits of the moral support of public sentiment.

This can be said with entire respect to Bishop Currier, for of course we are neither questioning his motives or even suggesting a criticism of his conduct. The matter having been brought to our attention, this is the answer we must make: this is the course we must take. It is only fair to these gentlemen that they should be told thus frankly beforehand.

But I am sure you will know how to make all this very clear in your reply.[2]   Faithfully Yours,   Woodrow Wilson

WWTLS (SDR, RG 59, 812.00/16810, DNA).
  [1] To Bishop Currier.
  [2] WJB to C. W. Currier, March 19, 1915, CCL (SDR, RG 59, 812.00/16810, DNA), repeated Wilson's letter almost verbatim.

To William Jennings Bryan

My dear Mr. Secretary: The White House March 18, 1915

I write this to reach you on your birthday tomorrow.

We have now been associated for two years and I feel that I have greatly profited by the association. I have learned not only to value you as a friend and counsellor, but, if you will let me say so, I have found a very strong affection for you growing in my heart. Your high motives and constant thought of the public interest have been an example and stimulation to me throughout these years. I can, therefore, send you a greeting on your birthday which comes from the heart. May there be many, many returns!

Cordially and faithfully yours,   Woodrow Wilson

TLS (W. J. Bryan Papers, DLC).

To Edward Mandell House

The White House. Mar. 18, 1915

I approve the change of code. I shall understand difficulty of sending messages from Germany. You may find it wise to retire to neutral territory before sending full reports of conferences and results. I shall be especially interested to know what impression the suggestion of a conference of all nations on questions of war and neutrality seems to make at Berlin. I do not gather that you broached it at Paris. We know nothing new that would help you.

Transcripts of WWsh telegram (WP, DLC; WC, NjP).

To Nicholas II

Your Majesty: [The White House] March 18, 1915

May I take the liberty of calling your Majesty's attention to a matter in which the Government and many disinterested citizens of the United States of America would be very happy, and even thankful, to be of service in assisting to moderate the sufferings and difficulties incident to the present war?

It is the desire of the Government of the United States and of the American Red Cross Society to be of service whenever and wherever it is possible to render a service which can have no color of partisanship or of officious suggestion. The field that seems most open for this purpose is the care and support of prisoners. I take it for granted that, no matter how great the generosity of your Majesty's Government may be in caring for the prisoners in Siberia, many severe hardships will necessarily attend life in the concentration camps there. I venture, therefore, to inquire whether your Majesty would be willing to vouchsafe to representatives of the American Red Cross Society, or to any other impartial agency this Government might be able to supply or vouch for, the right to distribute to the prisoners in Siberia, either military or civil, money, medicines and supplies sent by their friends or by philanthropic people in this country or elsewhere?

I make this inquiry and request very earnestly, not as the chief official of my Government, but only as a servant of humanity, with no political purpose, of course, and as a friend who would help if he could, and who shares with millions of his fellow-countrymen the desire to assuage, wherever it is possible to do so, the inevitable miseries of the present war.

My suggestion is made in conformity with a general plan for prisoners relief which the Government of the United States is now trying to arrange at the request of the several belligerent nations whose interests in enemy territory are entrusted to its care; and your Majesty will understand that the only reason why I do not include in my suggestion an offer of similar services on behalf of Russian subjects held as prisoners, is that the Government of the United States does not represent diplomatically the interests of Russia in any of the belligerent countries.

May I not take this opportunity to express my sincere friendship for the great Russian people and their Government, and my high personal regard for your Majesty?

Your Majesty's good friend,   Woodrow Wilson[1]

TLS (Letterpress Books, WP, DLC).
[1] There is a WWsh draft of this letter, dated March 16, 1915, in WP, DLC.

To Francis Clement Kelley

My dear Father Kelley: [The White House] March 18, 1915

Dudley Field Malone handed me the other day your letter of February twenty-third. I read it with the closest attention and with a great deal of interest, and thank you for it.

Since it concerns matters with which we have dealt through the Department of State, I have taken the liberty of referring it to the Secretary of State with the request that he send you a very full statement of the attitude and purposes and acts of the administration in the important matter to which it refers, giving you information which will set the whole matter in its true light very clearly indeed.

I have spoken to the Secretary and am sure that he will comply with this request at an early date.

With much respect,

Cordially and sincerely yours,   Woodrow Wilson

TLS (Letterpress Books, WP, DLC).

To William Jennings Bryan

My dear Mr. Secretary,   The White House. 18 March, 1915.

This is an important memorandum,[1] and supplies much to think about. I do not yet allow myself to think of intervention as more than a remote *possibility*; but I suppose I must admit that it is at least a possibility, and, if it is, the possibility is worth preparing for.

On the whole, I like the suggestion Mr. Lansing makes. It is in thorough accord with what we are hoping for in the Americas. It would be, as it were, anticipating some of the things we are preparing the way for. At any rate, let us keep it in mind. Should the possibility loom a little nearer, I can well imagine that Mr. L. has pointed out the wisest and most practicable course.

Faithfully Yours,   W.W.

WWTLI (SDR, RG 59, 812.00/14665½, DNA).

[1] RL to WJB, March 18, 1915, TLS (SDR, RG 59, 812.00/14664½, DNA), proposing joint action with Argentina, Brazil, and Chile as the surest way to demonstrate respect for Mexican territorial integrity and political independence, if the United States needed to take military action against Obregón and Carranza.

To William Jennings Bryan, with Enclosure

My dear Mr. Secretary,   The White House. 19 March, 1915.

I am sending you herewith an outline sketch of the substance of a reply to the British note which accompanied the recent Order in Council.[1]

It is intended as a suggestion, and as the basis upon which we may be shaping our thoughts in this important matter. You will see that what I have done is little more than to reduce to writing what I roughly indicated in Cabinet to-day.

Faithfully Yours,   Woodrow Wilson

WWTLS (W. J. Bryan Papers, DLC).
[1] The British Order in Council of March 11, 1915, interdicting all trade to or from Germany, issued in retaliation against the German submarine campaign. It is printed in *FR-WWS 1915*, pp. 144-45.

ENCLOSURE

Outline Sketch of a Note to Great Britain.

The White House. 19 March, 1915.

Note in reply to ours received, notifying us of the establishment of a blockade of the coasts of Germany which it is intended to make in all respects effective.

The cordon of blockading ships which it is intended to maintain is, however, of such an extent, the blockade as indicated in the plan announced covers so great an area of the high seas, that it seems that neutral vessels must pass through it in order to approach many important neutral ports which it is not Great Britain's privilege to blockade, and which she of course does not mean to blockade.

The Government of the United States takes it for granted, in view of the anxiety expressed by His Majesty's Government to interfere as little as possible with neutral commerce, that the approach of American merchantmen to neutral ports situated upon the long line of coast affected will not be interfered with when it is known that they do not carry goods which are contraband of war or goods consigned to a destination within the belligerent territory affected. The Government of the United States assumes this with the more confidence because it is manifest that His Majesty's Government has undertaken a very unusual method of blockade which it will be difficult to confine within the limits required by the law of nations; and it is natural to infer that the commanders of His Majesty's vessels of war engaged in the blockade will be instructed to be very careful that the blockade is not made to involve consequences to the trade of neutrals greater and more burdensome than those which have hitherto been regarded as inevitable when the ports of one belligerent are blockaded by the ships of another.

The Government of the United States of course appreciates the existence of the unusual conditions of modern warfare at sea upon which it understands His Majesty's Government to rely to justify methods of blockade and practices of search and detention which His Majesty's Government, like the Government of the United States, has so often and so explicitly held to be inconsistent with the best usages of warfare in the dealings of belligerents with neutrals at sea; but it does not understand His Majesty's Government to claim exemption from the hitherto accepted principles and obligations in these matters because of those unusual conditions; and it should regard itself as failing in its duty, because failing to maintain the principles for which it has always contended, were it not very earnestly to call the attention of His Majesty's Government to the grave responsibilities it is incurring in its effort to meet a novel situation.

The Government of the United States notes with gratification the assurances conveyed in the note of His Majesty's Secretary of State for Foreign Affairs that special care will be taken to invade neutral rights no further than the necessities of the blockade make unavoidable; but the possibilities of serious interference are so many, the methods and circumstances of the blockade are so unusual and are likely to constitute so great an impediment and embarrassment to neutral commerce, that the Government of the United States feels that it is only candid and in the interest of avoiding future misunderstandings to say that it apprehends many interferences which may involve His Majesty's Government in heavy responsibilities for acts of His Majesty's naval officers which may make the methods of blockade which are now being adopted clearly obnoxious to the well recognized rights of neutral nations on the high seas. It therefore assumes that His Majesty's Government has considered these possibilities, will take every practicable step to avoid them, and stands ready to make reparation wherever it may be shown to have been in the wrong.

The Government of the United States, in brief, does not understand His Majesty's Government as claiming the right to set aside any accepted principle of international law, or to plan to act in contravention of any such principle; and therefore understands His Majesty's Government to assume full responsibility in case its present course of action should unexpectedly draw its representatives into acts for which it would be responsible in law and in comity.[1]

T MS (SDR, RG 59, 763.72112/976½, DNA).
[1] There is a WWsh draft of this draft, dated "March 1915," in WP, DLC.

To Herbert Clark Hoover

My dear Mr. Hoover: The White House March 19, 1915

Mr. House has kindly sent me the documents you were kind enough to place in his hands for my inspection.

May I not take this occasion in thanking you for the documents to express my sincere appreciation of the work that you have been doing? It has commanded the admiration and confidence of every one who has had a chance to know of it and I am sure that every American who has had any part in the work of relieving suffering in Belgium will feel, when the whole story is told, that the part you have played is one of distinguished service.

Cordially and sincerely yours,   Woodrow Wilson

TLS (H. Hoover Papers, CSt-H).

From William Jennings Bryan

My Dear Mr President   Washington March 19 1915

Your gracious and cordial note of yesterday was the first birthday greeting to reach me and is, I assure you, most heartily appreciated. It is a genuine satisfaction to be associated, personally and officially, with one who sees so clearly the fundamental distinctions between democracy and aristocracy, and so bravely stands for the rights and interests of the masses.

Your openmindedness makes conference with you a delight, while your firmness in action gives constant evidence of your "faith in the wisdom of doing right." To have been of assistance to you in the trying times through which we have passed is compensation for the trials and restraints incident to a cabinet position.

In thanking you for your generous words allow me, my dear Mr President, to reciprocate most fully your expressions of confidence and affection.   Very truly yours   W. J. Bryan

ALS (WP, DLC).

From Edward Mandell House

Dear Governor: [Berlin] March 20th, 1915.

Mr. Stovall met me at Bale, where I stayed for a day in order to discuss with him and Consul General Wilbur[1] conditions in Switzerland, and their bearing upon the international situation.

I asked Stovall to feel out the Swiss authorities concerning the second convention so we could confer again when I pass through Bale.

Consul General Harrison[2] met me at Frankfort and I had a half hour's talk with him that was of some value.

I arrived in Berlin yesterday morning and Gerard immediately arranged for a private conference for me with Wolf [Zimmermann]. Wolf's greeting was almost enthusiastic in its cordiality. I let him read your letter which impressed him favorably, as it does everyone. I told him frankly what I had done in Zenobia [England], whom I had met there and in Warren [France], and my conclusions. He was surprised to hear of the lack of bitterness in Zenobia towards Zodak [Germany], and was equally surprised when I told him that the difficulty was with Warren. They have evidently tried to cultivate good relations with both Winter [Russia] and Warren for the purpose of making separate terms with them.

I think I convinced him that Zenobia did not desire to crush Zadok, and that in the final analysis terms would have to be agreed upon between the two countries. This is so patent that I wonder they do not recognize it. It is fortunate this is true, for the difference between the two is not great, and they could get together now if it were not for the fact that the people in both Zadok and Warren have been led to expect much more than is possible to realize. Neither Government can fulfil these expectations.

If they attempted to make peace upon a different basis from that which the people have been led to believe will ultimately come about, there is a possibility that the governments would be overthrown. This is really the trouble now. Just how it can be overcome is the question. I am trying to get everyone to soften down through the press and create a better feeling.

Wolf said that the main thing Zadok wanted was a settlement which would guarantee permanent peace. It is the same cry in each of the belligerent states.

I showed Wolf the different points where our interests and theirs touched, and expressed a desire that we work together to accomplish our purpose. I brought up the second convention in this connection and he received it most cordially. I told him that we, as well as Zadok, desired that some guaranty should be had in the future as to the protection and uninterruption of our commerce both as neutral or belligerent. I told him that we recognized that Zenobia had a perfect right to possess a navy sufficient to prevent invasion, but further than that she should not go.

He was exceedingly sympathetic with this thought, and I think it will have a tendancy to put us on a good footing here.

The Chancellor is out of town for a few days, but Wolf is to arrange a meeting as soon as he returns. He also suggested that Dante [the Kaiser] might want to see me. Gerard says this is impossible, that he has not seen him for months because of his intense feeling against us on account of our shipment of munitions of war to the Allies. It is not important now whether I see him or not, and I shall leave it to Wolf's judgment.

I arranged with Wolf that my name should not be mentioned in the German press or sent out by cable. It looks as if we had this covered now in England, France and Germany. While I am talking the second convention, I have in the back of my mind a single convention with you as its head, the neutrals taking part in it to have no vote or voice upon questions strictly concerning the belligerents. When I have them well committed to the second convention, I think it will not be difficult to show them that one convention would be more workable.

If nothing arises to disturb the relations we are establishing in these several belligerent countries, I feel hopeful that your influence will dominate to a larger degree than it ever seemed possible.

I am somewhat at a loss as what to do next, for it is plain at the moment that some serious reverse will have to be encountered by one or other of the belligerents before any government will dare propose parleys.

I can foresee troublous times ahead, and it will be the wonder of the ages if all the governments come out of it intact. The world is upon a strain as never before in its history, and something is sure to crack somewhere before a great while. It looks as if our best move just now is to wait until the fissure appears.

Affectionately yours,   E. M. House[3]

TLS (WP, DLC).
  [1] David Forrest Wilber.
  [2] Heaton W. Harris, not Harrison.
  [3] House conveyed the gist of this letter in EMH to Wilson, March 19, 1915, T telegram (WP, DLC).

From William Jennings Bryan

My dear Mr. President: Washington March 20, 1915.

I am submitting to you the letter to Father Kelley prepared in accordance with your instructions.[1] You will notice that I have quoted the despatch sent to Villa and Carranza, with the addition which was made to it when it was sent to Gutierrez and Garza. I have also quoted the despatch sent to Carranza in regard to the imprisoned priests. These will, I think, give sufficient evidence of the interest that we have taken in the church and clergy there. You will notice from the date that the telegram was sent to Gutierrez and Garza after the charge was made in regard to the violation of the nun and therefore a paragraph was added construing the original communication to cover both sexes. If the letter is satisfactory you can mail it there and thus save a day's time. If you have any corrections to make, please return the letter with corrections so that the corrections may be made in the copy which we keep here.

With assurances of high respect, I am, My dear Mr. President,
Very sincerely yours,   W. J. Bryan

TLS (W. J. Bryan Papers, DNA).
[1] WJB to F. C. Kelley, March 20, 1915, CCL (WP, DLC), using Wilson's text with the additions that he enumerates.

From Lindley Miller Garrison, with Enclosure

My dear Mr. President: Washington. March 20, 1915.

The fact that Cabinet discussion is necessarily so hurried and that I did not have the copies of the various notes[1] makes me feel that I did not express myself clearly upon the important subject discussed yesterday.

Upon returning to the Department, I gathered the notes together and read them, and herewith hand you a memorandum which expresses my state of mind concerning the existing situation.

My purpose in sending you this memorandum is not to burden you with reading it if you are already acquainted with all of the implications I had in mind, but to place them before you more clearly if you are not.

Sincerely yours,   Lindley M. Garrison

TLS (WP, DLC).
[1] Wilson or Bryan had had the following notes printed for distribution to the cabinet before its meeting on March 19: the American notes to Great Britain of December 26, 1914, and to Germany of February 10, 1915; the American note to Great Britain of March 5, 1915; WHP to WJB, March 15, 1915, conveying

Sir Edward Grey's memorandum of March 13; and WHP to WJB, March 15, 1915, transmitting the Order in Council of March 11, 1915. Printed copies of all but the note to Great Britain of December 26, 1914, are in WP, DLC.

ENCLOSURE

Washington. March 20, 1915.

Memorandum respecting diplomatic exchanges between the United States, Germany, and Great Britain.

For the purpose of being able to state more clearly the situation as it appears to me that it is, I have gone over the notes exchanged between us and the Powers involved, and herein refer to such as I think relevant. . . .[1]

I think that the striking things to be observed are that Great Britain first announces that she proposes as a *retaliatory* act to prevent all supplies going to Germany or from Germany. She makes this declaration in such a way as to indicate that she proposes carrying it out by roving over the high seas and picking up neutral vessels carrying goods of enemy destination, origin or ownership. This being plainly in contravention of clearly established principles of international law, we called her attention to this. We told her that we felt that she should either declare a blockade or should confine herself, so far as neutral commerce was concerned, to dealing with contraband. Her reply to this is the order in council, which certainly does not in any way declare a blockade and does, I think, very plainly indicate the contrary of a blockade and the duties, obligations and responsibilities arising therefrom. The order in council orders the subordinates of the king to prevent vessels from going to Germany, from Germany to any neutral port with goods for Germany, and from any neutral port with goods of Germany—in other words, the continuation of just what she has been doing and which we had said was unwarranted.

The two latter things she contemplated doing, of course, have nothing to do with blockade, which of necessity is confined to the ports of the blockaded country and not the neutral ports. I cannot escape the conviction that when Sir Edward Grey refers to the "cordon" of cruisers and when he refers to "measures of blockade authorized," etc., he is merely giving a name to what the order in council declares shall be done. In other words, as it

[1] In the excised portions, Garrison reviewed the American note to Great Britain of December 26, 1914, and to Germany of February 10, 1915; the American note to Great Britain of March 5, 1915; the Order in Council of March 11, 1915; and Grey's message of explanation of March 13, 1915.

strikes me, the order in council is a municipal enactment telling the British authorities what they must do. And what they must do is plain. They must stop these ships wherever they are, without any regard to a "cordon" of cruisers, or to a blockade, which words are entirely inapplicable to the goods going from neutral countries or to neutral countries. The order contains no language whatever such as would certainly have been used by so eminent and experienced diplomatists as Earl Grey and Mr. Asquith, if they had intended it to be a blockade in legal fact. It will be recalled that we distinctly told England that we could not permit her, by legislative enactment, to make or alter international law; that we distinctly told Germany that the sole right of a belligerent with respect to neutral commerce was to visit and search and deal with contraband unless a legal blockade were proclaimed.

I think it extremely significant that in view of all the correspondence and of the circumstances, that the order in council, which is the effective thing in this respect, absolutely refrains, as if by most determined purpose, from using any word or expression indicative of the fact that a blockade was thereby being established, or orders with respect to such blockade were being issued.

It is also significant that on the 13th of March, before the order in council was issued and without the slightest suggestion that the subject-matter had ever been dealt with in any other government proclamation or statement, Sir Edward Grey talked about a blockade controlled by a "cordon" of cruisers. I think that what Sir Edward Grey then had in his mind and what the draftsmen of the order in council had in mind was such a blockade or "cordon" of cruisers as results from individual vessels sent over the high seas, sufficient in number perhaps to pick up the vessels of any nation sailing the high seas. This is not and cannot possibly be construed as a blockade; and the fact that the word "cordon" whenever used is put in quotation marks seems to me indicative of the meaning they intended to ascribe to it, namely, not a blockading squadron within a fixed and declared area but roving cruisers going anywhere. It is also noteworthy that nowhere does she speak of blockading German ports by a cordon or otherwise. She speaks of preventing passage to or from, of preventing vessels from going to and fro, of blockading Germany, but she nowhere designates ports and declares them blockaded.

What I endeavored to express in Cabinet and fear that I failed to do and what I now wish to sum up in as few words as possible is this:

Great Britain has not in any proper fashion declared a blockade. She has no right to do the things that she orders her own
authorities to do in the order in council, even if she had declared
a blockade. She would have the right to prevent commerce with
blockaded ports but she would not have the right to prevent commerce between neutral nations, excepting in contraband of war
destined to an enemy. Until therefore she proclaims a blockade,
I think that her whole order in council contravenes international
law and she should be so notified and be told that we will hold
her to "strict accountability," that being the same phrase which
we used to Germany when we informed her of the inadmissibility
of her departure from international law and the consequences
therefor. Of course if Great Britain should now plainly declare a
legal blockade, then our protest would only be proper with
respect to so much as is left of the order in council, which contravenes international law, which is that portion of it which
endeavors to restrict non-contraband commerce between neutrals. Incidentally it is interesting to note that our Supreme Court
in The Peterhoff case, against our own interest by the way,
decided that a belligerent blockading an enemy's port had not the
right under the most well settled principles of international law
to interfere with the commerce between neutrals, although one
of such neutrals owns contiguous territory to the enemy and the
supplies being taken into such contiguous neutral territory were
readily transportable by inland water or land transportation to
such enemy.

The gravity and importance of the treatment of the existing
situation, among other reasons, arises out of its effect upon our
own people when the stress of the contemplated policy of the
allies begins to be felt, out of the assurance of position which
we secure by standing upon clearly settled principles of international law and out of the necessity of our taking this stand if we
are to remain in our present position of strict neutrality, which,
in this instance, means a similar ruling upon a similar subject-
matter.

I merely want to mention, without expatiating upon the same,
my idea that the introduction of submarines does not alter the
rules of warfare in so far as the subject-matter we are dealing
with is concerned and does not justify either nation in abandon-
ing the settled principles of international law in so far as neutrals are concerned. I cannot admit as a matter of argument or
fact that because a submarine makes it more dangerous to maintain a blockade, that the law respecting a blockade has or should
be changed; certainly not by the action of any one party to the

conflict. The fact that the Spanish fleet was in Santiago harbor made it much more dangerous and difficult for the American fleet to blockade that harbor than if there had been only merchantmen therein but I cannot conceive that it altered the rules of international law with respect to such blockade or gave the United States any right whatever to claim any release of obligations or duties from those which it must assume if it should get the privileges of a blockade. In similar conditions I cannot conceive the propriety of admitting that because submarines or naval vessels of any sort within a harbor or along the seacoast make it more dangerous than it used to be to maintain a blockade, the affected enemy is released from any of the duties or obligations theretofore enjoined upon a blockader or invested with any other rights and privileges than theretofore enjoyed by a blockader.   Lindley M. Garrison

T MS (WP, DLC).

To Pussy de Spoelberch and E. de Spoelberch

My dear little Friends: The White House. 20 March, 1915

Your letter touched me very deeply and I thank you for it with all my heart. It makes me very happy to think that what generous Americans have done to relieve the hunger and distress in your country has brought you the help you needed and given you a little happiness in the midst of these terrible days of war. I hope that you will grow up to be strong to do the work that will have to be done in the days of peace that are coming. It would be a great pleasure to me if some day I might see you both when those happier times have come.

                    Your sincere friend,   Woodrow Wilson.

TC of ALS (C. L. Swem Coll., NjP).

To William Jennings Bryan

My dear Mr. Secretary,   The White House. 21 March, 1915.

This is very friendly of President Menocal,[1] and I appreciate it very much indeed.

Do you not think that it might be well, by the way, speaking of Carranza, to go into the Yucatan situation rather fully with him and explain very frankly how indispensable the sisal is, not merely to the United States, but to the world, inasmuch as the food supply of the world may be said in a large measure to depend on it; and that we are therefore justified, as friends of

Mexico, in keeping her out of the deep trouble that would ensue if he interfered with the trade, with the crops, or with anything upon which the trade depended, and if he, moreover, did not cooperate with us to safeguard to [the] supply at Progreso? What do you think? It *might* impress him. And could President Menocal serve us in any way in this matter?

Faithfully Yours,   W.W.

WWTLI (W. J. Bryan Papers, DNA).
¹ WJB to WW, March 19, 1915, TLS (W. J. Bryan Papers, DNA), conveying the offer of General Mario García Menocal, President of Cuba, to exert influence on Carranza and Zapata to follow whatever policy Wilson suggested.

To Edward Mandell House

The White House, March 22, 1915

The new British Order in Council in effect seeks to alter the hitherto recognized international law with regard to blockades by including within the blockade the coasts of neutral as well as belligerent countries.

Do you think it would be wise to intimate in our reply now that we think this should not be done without such a conference as we have been calling the second conference [convention].

Transcript of WWsh telegram (WC, NjP).

From William Jennings Bryan, with Enclosure

My dear Mr. President: Washington March 22, 1915.

The enclosed flimsy of a despatch from London would indicate that they do not give much weight to our despatches. They seem to think they are intended for home consumption, rather than for serious consideration.

With assurances of high respect I am, my dear Mr. President,
Yours very sincerely,   W. J. Bryan

TLS (W. J. Bryan Papers, DLC).

E N C L O S U R E

London. March 21, 1915. 5 p.m.

1816. CONFIDENTIAL. FOR THE SECRETARY AND THE PRESIDENT.

Investigation in as many departments of the Government as possible and many unofficial talks with the best informed men form the basis for the following conclusions.

The blockade differs from previous blockades and from a blockade as defined in the books only in two particulars. (1) It is made by moving cruisers instead of warships stationed at blockaded ports and (2) it permits and contemplates exemptions of neutral ships and cargoes from confiscation. The submarine has, in spite of the book definition, made the first change inevitable in all future blockades. The second change is made to leave the fullest opportunity to favour neutral trade and especially American trade.

The only practical difference that the blockade will make will be the shutting out of cotton and foodstuffs from Germany. Most foodstuffs had already been shut out and the English will buy the cotton they stop. The American lawyer who has come here representing the Chicago meatpackers is making good progress at satisfactory settlement and arrangements.

The American trade with the Allies is, I am told, increasing rapidly and will grow by leaps till the war ends.

I have the promise of the Government of greater promptness in dealing with stopped ships and cargoes.

The Government is publishing as a White Paper all the correspondence about shipping between the American and British Governments since December twenty-eight. Unofficial critics praise the courtesy and admit the propriety of our communications. But they regard them as remote and impracticable. They point out that we have not carried our points, namely that copper should not be contraband, that ships should be searched at sea, that to order cargoes should be valid, that our export trade had fallen off because of the war. They point out these in good natured criticism as evidence of the American love of protest for political effect at home. While the official reception of our communications is dignified the unofficial and general attitude to them is a smile at our love of *letterwriting* as at Fourth of July orations. They quietly laugh at our effort to regulate sea warfare under new conditions by what they regard as lawyers' disquisitions out of textbooks. They (#) [receive] them with courtesy, pay no further attention to them, proceed to settle our shipping disputes *with any* effort at generosity and quadruple their orders from us of war materials. They care nothing for our definitions or general protests but are willing to do us every practical favour and will under no conditions either take our advice or offend us. They regard our writings *as addressed* either to complaining shippers or to politicians at home.

For these reasons complaints about concrete cases as they arise are more effective than general communications about rules of sea warfare, which must be revised by the submarine, the aeroplane, the mine and our own precedents.

The German submarine blockade is a practical failure. Its chief effect has been to provoke the English blockade of Germany which is effective.

American Ambassador London.

T telegram (W. J. Bryan Papers, DLC).

From Edward Mandell House

Dear Governor: [Berlin] March 22nd, 1915.

I am gradually getting at the bottom of things here and while I cannot write with perfect freedom, I can tell enough to give you a fair idea of it.

I am seeing a great many people, just as I did in London, and hope to soon have a composite picture that may be of value.

I met last night an able and sane man by the name of Dr. Rathenau.[1] I am told he is a great power in commercial Germany. He has such a clear vision of the situation and such a prophetic forecast as to the future that I wondered how many there were here that thought like him. It saddened me to hear him say that, as far as he knew, he stood alone. He said he had begun to wonder whether the rest were really mad or whether the madness lay within himself.

He told me it would be a mistake to push matters now, and that perhaps we would have to wait until the Autumn before an opening came. He thought it would not be long before others would begin to think as he does and later the percentage would grow until in the Autumn or in the spring of next year, all would come to the same view. He told me how this change of thought would come about and the cause. I shall keep in touch with him for he has promised to inform me when it is advisable to return.

It was almost pathetic to hear him urge us not to cease in our efforts to bring about peace. He said it was the noblest mission that was ever given to man, and that he would pray that we would not become discouraged. I hear this note struck in all the countries. Mothers and wives, fathers and brothers have spoken in the same strain and they seem to feel that the only hope lies in your endeavors.

Affectionately yours,   E. M. House

P.S. March 26th.

I find that Rathenau is mistaken in believing that he is alone in his opinion concerning conditions. I find many intelligent, fairminded Germans with the same private views, although they dare not express them to one another.

TLS (WP, DLC).
[1] Walther Rathenau, head of Allgemeine Elektricitäts-Gesellschaft and organizer of a board of the War Ministry to control and allocate raw materials.

From William Jennings Bryan

My dear Mr. President: Washington March 22, 1915.

I sent you, earlier in the day, a memorandum which Mr. Lansing prepared before he received your outline.[1]

I am now sending you his views on the subject,[2] embodied in the form of a suggestion for an answer. It is accompanied by some general comments on the order.

The difference between you and him seems to me rises first from a failure of the British Government to use the word "blockade" in the Orders in Council. I cannot see that it makes a great deal of difference, because it does not really change the situation and I cannot believe that so much importance can be attached to a single word.

The word "blockade" describes a method of procedure. If the method of procedure is described in other words that mean the same, the difference cannot be material.

If by insisting upon the use of the word blockade Mr. Lansing means to insist upon the rules originally governing the blockade, it seems to me that your position is the better sustained. We cannot, I think, ignore the change in methods of warfare. If we recognize the submarine as a legitimate engine of war, we cannot ignore the change in the location of the blockade line made necessary by the use of the submarine. *So far as the blockade of enemy's ports are concerned, I believe the use of the submarine justifies the withdrawing of the cordon to a sufficient distance to protect the blockading ships.*[3]

The third point is one that gives me most difficulty—namely, their right to interfere with goods going into, or coming out of, Germany through a neutral country. *Unless a belligerent nation has a right to extend its contraband list at will so as to include if it desires to do so every article of merchandise*, I do not understand how Great Britain can assert the right to stop non-contraband goods shipped to neutral ports. It seems to me that this is quite a different thing from the right to withdraw its ships from the immediate vicinity and yet establish an effective blockade of German ports. I do not understand that any nation has ever asserted the right to blockade a neutral port merely because non-contraband goods may come out of the enemy country through that neutral port, or enter the enemy country through that port. Unless a blockade can be extended to neutral ports I do not see how merchandise can be stopped *unless it is contraband* and I do not understand that *all* merchandise may be declared contraband.

The statement which is appended to Mr. Lansing's suggestion[4] very clearly points out the different propositions covered by the Orders in Council.

It occurs to me that in the note as you propose it you assume that interferance with non-contraband goods destined for a neutral port is not intended. The language of the Orders in Council is so clear that I am not sure that we are justified in making such an assumption. If the assumption is clearly inconsistent with the language of the Orders in Council, would it not lead to a contradiction that would embarrass us?

The matter is so important that I would like to go over the situation with you after you have read what Mr. Lansing says.

With assurances of high respect I am, my dear Mr. President,

Yours very sincerely,   W. J. Bryan

TLS (SDR, RG 59, 763. 72112/981½, DNA).

1 "Memorandum by the Counselor . . . ," *FR-LP*, I, 280-281, arguing that the American government should not be led into the trap of admitting that a blockade had been established by the Order in Council, and should insist that, if it was to be considered a blockade with its attendant belligerent rights, the British government should conform strictly to the rules of blockade promulgated in its Order in Council of October 29, 1914, namely, the rules laid down in the first twenty-one articles of the Declaration of London.

2 RL to WJB, Mar. 22, 1915, TLS (SDR, RG 59, 763.72112/981½, DNA), enclosing "SUGGESTION FOR AN ANSWER," TS memorandum, with the same file number (printed in *FR-LP*, I, 282-85). Lansing's draft of the note of reply called the new British maritime practices unprecedented in international relations; denied that the British had instituted a legal blockade; declared that the new Order in Council was a flagrant violation of the Declaration of London's provision governing blockades; asserted that retaliation should not injure the rights of neutrals; and concluded: "The Government of the United States, in view of the foregoing considerations, to which it earnestly invites the attention of His Majesty's Government, confidently expects that the provisions of the Order in Council which place illegal restraints upon the commerce between neutral ports will be so modified as to remove their objectionable features, and that in the maintenance of a blockade of German ports and coasts, if a blockade is declared, the British officers charged with the maintenance will observe strictly the rules of blockade recognized by civilized nations and refrain from improper interference with neutral vessels plying between neutral ports.

"In case the practices, which seem to be contemplated by the Order in Council, are persisted in by His Majesty's Government despite their manifest infraction of neutral rights, the Government of the United States reserves the right to make further representations to His Majesty's Government upon this subject and to hold them responsible for any loss or damage which citizens of the United States may incur by reason of any interference on the part of the British authorities with their trade with the neutral countries of Europe.

"In making this communication to His Majesty's Government, the Government of the United States does so in that spirit of amity and good will, which has happily for a century characterized the relations between the two countries and which it is the sincere desire of this Government to preserve."

³ All emphases Wilson's.
⁴ He referred to Lansing's covering letter, cited above.

To William Jennings Bryan

My dear Mr. Secretary,   The White House, 22 March, 1915.

I have read this memorandum with a great deal of interest; but I think it practically useless to ask such question of Great Britain or to argue with her questions of consistency, as between one Order in Council and another, for example.

The note might be drawn in this way, however, following the general lines of the sketch I sent you the other day:

After the introductory portion, we might speak, as I did in the sketch, of the unusual character of the blockade, and then say that, reading this Order in Council in connection with the former Order (of such and such a date) in which His Majesty's Government announced its adoption of the Declaration of London except with regard to questions of contraband, we would take it for granted that this, though in appearance a blockade of neutral as well as of hostile coasts, was not meant to be so in effect, and that the instructions given the commanders of His Majesty's ships of war engaged in the blockade would be very explicit in this sense, etc., etc.,—as in other memorandum which I sent.

Faithfully Yours,   W.W.

WWTLS (SDR, RG 59, 763.72112/980½, DNA).

From William Jennings Bryan, with Enclosure

My dear Mr. President: Washington March 22, 1915.

I am sending you—(1) flimsy of a telegram received from Guthrie;¹ (2) Mr. Williams' comment on the telegram with his suggestion as to what may be done;² (3) a confidential memorandum of an oral statement made to me this afternoon by Ambassador Chinda.

The telegram from Tokio, as you will notice, suggests a way out so far as Fukien is concerned. This matter is treated at some length in the memorandum left by Chinda. The Tokio telegram throws some light upon the Japanese situation. It is evident that the suggestion made by Secretary Hay as to a coaling station has been in the back of the Japanese head ever since, and they have construed everything we have said in connection with this coaling station suggestion. They doubtless had that in mind last year when they expressed so much concern about the contract which China was reported to have made with the Steel Company for an improvement of a harbor in Fukien.

I believe it would be possible to smooth out a good deal of our difficulty by an exchange of notes which would relieve the anxiety of the Japanese people on that point.

This Government has no desire to secure a coaling station on the border of Fukien, especially not with a knowledge of Japan's feeling on the subject—a feeling not so unnatural when you remember that Fukien is opposite Formosa.

You will notice on page eight of the memorandum that the Japanese Government seems willing to reconsider the proposal so far as it affects Fukien if it is understood that we will not be a party to any development on the coast which could be construed as a menace to Japan. It is possible that it could be so worded as not to seem to affect the United States, but, rather, be an agreement with China, our nation consenting to the agreement, by which all investment of foreign capital in harbor improvement, or the establishment of coaling stations or naval bases, should be prevented. How does it impress you?

I am surprised to learn from the memorandum that Great Britain, France and Germany have already secured agreements identical with those asked by Japan, in Fukien, if not even more restrictive, and at least one of them has been secured since the establishment of the "open door" policy.

You will notice that as to the advisors it is only suggestive and Japan disclaims any attempt to coerce China to accept the proposal. There is no objection to the offering of such a suggestion by Japan, and it would naturally produce irritation if China, in selecting advisors, ignored Japan.

In the matter of arms, the Ambassador explains that they did not insist upon any particular amount or proportion, but as all arms made in Japan are made by the Government they wanted to know in advance something about how much they would need so that they could make preparation for furnishing them. I believe that this can be obviated by language to the effect that Japan shall not be discriminated against in the purchase of arms and that she should receive notice a certain time in advance of the purchase.

In talking with Chinda I believe I discovered the reason for this particular request—namely, that China has been buying her arms of Germany and Austria and I think there was some discussion of plans for the establishment of armor plants by Germans and Austrians. It is not unnatural that they should object to having an enemy providing arms for China.

You will notice in Section 3, on page 4, the police proposal had reference only to Manchuria especially, and to Mongolia also in certain contingencies.

While I hope to have a moment's time with you tomorrow to consider this matter I thought I would better send these papers over to you tonight so that you will have time to think over them.

With assurances of high respect I am, my dear Mr. President,
Yours very sincerely,   W. J. Bryan

This dispatch[3] has just been rec'd since letter was written.

TLS (W. J. Bryan Papers, DLC).
[1] G. W. Guthrie to WJB, March 21, 1915, T telegram (W. J. Bryan Papers, DLC), printed in FR 1915, pp. 113-15, reporting on a conversation with Baron Katō. The latter indicated that Japan could not simply withdraw its opposition to the Bethlehem Steel Company's proposed contract to improve the port at Fukien; proposed that Japan and the United States agree on a frank and friendly statement about the future of Fukien before the demand was withdrawn; and regretted that word of the American government's objections to the Japanese demands had leaked out since his government maintained the position that no protests had come from Washington.
[2] E. T. Williams to WJB, March 22, 1915, TLI (W. J. Bryan Papers, DLC), recommending an exchange of notes between Chinda and Bryan pledging Japan and the United States not to request the lease from China of any port or territory in Fukien and not to seek for their nationals any exclusive commercial or industrial privileges in the province.
[3] P. S. Reinsch to WJB, March 22, 1915, FR 1915, p. 115: "Your telegram of March 18, 2 p.m. Chinese Government today informed of arrival of twelve hundred new Japanese troops along Shantung Railway and six thousand in Manchuria."

ENCLOSURE

Unofficial Memorandum left by Ambassador Chinda March 22, 1915 at my request after he had delivered its contents as an oral communication. Strictly Confidential[1]

Pending the receipt of the full text of the note of the United States Government addressed to me under date of March 13, 1915, the Japanese Government would not naturally be in a position to give definite reply as to the full particulars of the communication. I am, however, instructed to lay before you candidly and without reserve the views of my Government regarding the considerations of the United States Government, as far as they were ascertained through my telegraphic report and the conversation Baron Kato had with the American Ambassador on the subject.

Before doing so, however, it is deemed advisable to observe at the outset that in confidentially communicating to the United States Government the proposals advanced by Japan in her

[1] WJBhw.

present negotiations with China, the Japanese Government were actuated not by a sense of obligation imposed upon them by the provisions of the Takahira-Root agreement of 1908, but by a sincere desire to act in the matter with a due regard to the American interests in China, and in full conformity with the great importance which my Government attach to the particularly friendly relations existing between Japan and the United States.

It is a matter of unfeigned gratification to the Japanese Government to note that the Government of the United States, in frank recognition of Japan's special position in South Manchuria, Eastern Mongolia and Shantung, are disposed to raise no question as to the proposals relating to those regions.[2]

The views of the United States Government, when summed up, appear to address themselves to four of the proposals, viz., those regarding (1) the advisers, (2) the arms and ammunition, (3) the policing and (4) the Province of Fukien, all of which are contained in the "requests."

It hardly requires to be stated that the Japanese Government entertain no design whatever to impair the sovereignty or independence of China, or to encroach upon her territorial integrity, or violate the principle of equal opportunity. In formulating the bases of the present negotiations, they had, in fact, taken the most scrupulous care in the above respect.

Taking up those proposals to which the observations of the United States relate, it may be stated:

(1) That, while the Japanese Government desire earnestly to see the proposed employment of advisers agreed to by China, they disclaim any attempt to coerce China to accept the proposal. It was formulated with a sincere hope and expectation that it would, if carried out, result in the improvement of the domestic administration of China. The conviction that the proposal would contribute towards the promotion of good relations between Japan and China, also entered into consideration.

(2) That the proposal relative to arms and ammunition is not regarded by the Japanese Government to be, in any manner, in conflict with the principle of equal opportunity. In framing the proposal, this point was very carefully considered. It is to be pointed out that the amount of the purchase from Japan by China of arms and ammunition is left indeterminate in the proposal, thus allowing an ample latitude for adjustment in course of the negotiations. The suggestion of Japan to have the amount fixed in advance is explained by her desire to be better prepared to meet the orders. The advantage of such an arrangement will

2 See WW to WJB, March 12, 1915 (second letter of this date), n. 1.

enure as much to purchaser as to the supplier. In fact, it is to be regarded as a pure and simple business proposition, so far as this particular phase of the question is concerned. This nature of the proposition would be more evident in case it be decided upon to adopt the plan of establishing in China a joint Chino-Japanese factory for the manufacture of arms, as provided in the latter part of the proposal advanced.

The attention of the United States Government is also invited to the fact that hitherto Germany and Austria-Hungary have been furnishing China with the greater portion of her arms and ammunition and that the two Powers went so far as to contemplate, in the course of last year, the establishment of factories for the manufacture of arms and ammunition at Sha-ho-chen in the vicinity of Chang-chia-kou and other places, arousing no small measure of misgivings in the Japanese mind. It is self-evident that Japan finds it impossible to acquiesce in the continued activities of the agents of her enemy Powers in supplying arms to China. In formulating the proposal in question, therefore, the Japanese Government had to meet this particular situation.

(3) That, with regard to the question of policing, the proposal as intended by the Japanese Government, is to have its practical application nowhere except Manchuria and possibly Mongolia in certain contingency. Though the Japanese Government had already an occasion to confidentially explain this point to the American Government, Baron Kato now charges me to reiterate this statement in the confident hope that the true nature of the proposal will prove satisfactory to the Government of the United States in view of the friendly attitude which they take in regard to Manchuria and Mongolia.

(4) That the proposal relating to the right of priority in the Province of Fukien has parallel instances in other regions, of which the following may be cited as examples: the preferential right in respect to investment enjoyed by England regarding the mining industry in Shansi Province (vide annex, I);[3] that enjoyed by France in the Provinces of Kuantung, Kuangsi and Yunnan (vide annex, II); that enjoyed by England relating to railway in the Provinces of Hunan and Hupeh; and that enjoyed by Germany in relation to enterprises in the Province of Shantung (vide annex, III). All these claims are in every respect as much pronounced in their preferential character, if not more so, as what is now being sought for Japan in Fukien.

In this connection, I learn that, in the interview of March 16, Mr. Guthrie called the attention of Baron Kato to the deffer-

---

[3] All the annexes are missing.

ence between the preferential right as held by a private corporation and that vested in a government, using the argument in explaining the American right of priority concerning the loan contract relative to the petrolerm industry in Shensi. When considered, however, from the point of view of a third Power, it would be wholly immaterial whether the exclusive right belongs to a private corporation or to a government.

Again, it might be argued with some plausibility that a line of distinction ought to be drawn between the provisions dictated by political exigencies and the undertakings of purely commercial or industrial nature, and that an attempt on the part of a foreign government to secure directly from China an agreement whereby certain preferential right is created in the latter case, is unjustifiable in the light of the principle of open door and equal opportunity. But, when the peculiar conditions actually prevailing in China are carefully considered, the extreme difficulty, if not the utter impossibility, of acting on such distinction, if it could be drawn at all, would become apparent. One may safely state that, as things actually exist in China, the matters of political, commercial and industrial nature are so interlocked one with the other, and every commercial or industrial undertaking of any note is invariably supported politically by the interested government, particularly when it is a question securing some right or privilege from China. It should also be well noted that not only do the commercial and industrial undertakings in turn become the factors of international politics as understood in ordinary sense, but they are very often conceived with such purpose at the very inception particularly on the part of China, and are so engineered as to add still more disquieting element to the situation.

Turning to the case in question, the peculiar relation in which Japan stands in the Province of Fukien should be borne in mind. In view of the geographical propinquity to Taiwan, Japan secured from China an engagement of non-alienation in respect to that particular province, a fact which has often been brought to the notice of the United States Government. This circumstance is sufficient to explain why it is absolutely impossible for Japan to view with indifference the establishing of any influence other than Chinese in that particular Province.

In the face of the above situation, however, there have not been lacking in the past various reports regarding attemprs [attempts] on the part of some foreign nations to interest themselves in the undertakings connected with harbor works, public means of communication and other works in Fukien. It has even been rumored that the lease of a certain part of the province has been under contemplation. Such reports and rumors have not failed to cause extreme irritation and misgivings in the public mind of the Japanese, and have sorely tried its susceptibilities. Especially the feeling of the people of Japan has assumed a delicate aspect regarding the relation of the United States with Fukien in consequence of the various reports, which have, for the past two or three years, been persistently circulated concerning American activities in Fukien, such, for instance, as the projected loan regarding the establishment of a naval station at San-tu-ao.

To state frankly, any intrusion of foreign influence in Fukien would lead the people of Japan to entertain fear that the defence of Taiwan would thereby be directly or indirectly manaced. Nothing is more natural than that their feeling should reach a high tension at any news of such purport. The present proposal to China concerning the right of priority for Japanese capital was, primarily, conceived in the hope of setting at rest in certain measure this constant feeling of uneasiness among the Japanese people.

In the circumstances, should the Japanese Government withdraw the proposal in question in compliance with the desire of the United States Government, it would *ipso facto* be sufficient to engender a serious irritatiin in the mind of the Japanese public. What the feelings of the Japanese people would be, in case the United States themselves should, after the withdrawal of the Japanese proposal, engage in enterprises in Fukien tending to arouse such apprehension as described above, is too evident to need any comment. Accordingly, if it be the desire of the United States Government, the Japanese Government, for avoiding any possible misunderstanding, may not be opposed to the reconsideration of the proposal in question. But in that contingency the Japanese Government will have to desire that the American Government enter into an engagement to make the citizens of the United States refrain from any undertaking in Fukien which may directly or indirectly cause the above-indicated fear on the part of the Japanese people, and that the engagement be strictly and effectively carried out.

The Japanese Government hope that the United States Government would, in view of the relation above referred to of Fukien to Japan, fully understand the inexorable nature of the situation with which Japan is confronted. Considering that the engagement above alluded to would be in full accord in spirit with the attitude assumed by the United States Government in

December, 1900, in relation to the plan of leasing the islands in the San-sah-ao for a coaling station, and with the steps taken by them in the month of May last year concerning the alleged loan with regard to San-tu-ao, the Japanese Government feel confident that the suggestion of such an arrangement would not be regarded as unwarranted by the United States Government.

T MS (W. J. Bryan Papers, DNA).

From Paul Samuel Reinsch

Personal

My dear Mr. President: Peking, March 22, 1915.

I thank you sincerely for your letter of February 8th and for the words of appreciation which it conveys. The knowledge that you are giving your personal attention to the difficult situation out here and that your hand is at the helm gives us courage and confidence. Whatever America can accomplish towards enabling China to resist the attempts now so craftily made to undermine her national independence will not only be in line with the best traditions of our action in the Far East, but will serve in the future as a discouragement of all attempts to settle the destiny of great nations by means of secret diplomacy backed by force.

The Governor of Chekiang Province recently send me little silk flags bearing your portrait and that of the President of China, which were made by pupils of Higher Government Industrial School of Chekiang. I am enclosing them, as they may be of interest to you.

With the highest regard and sincere wishes for your continued well being, I am,   Faithfully yours,   Paul S. Reinsch.

TLS (WP, DLC).

From William Jennings Bryan

My dear Mr. President: Washington March 23d, 1915.

I am enclosing a flimsy of a despatch from Gerard. This is the most interesting communication we have received from him lately.[1]

I also enclose an additional suggestion by Mr. Lansing[2] (by the way, I learned from one of the messengers in the White House that the envelope which I sent over yesterday evening about half past seven, was laid upon your table and I presume it was while you were at dinner. It contained notes on several subjects.) In the enclosed note Mr. Lansing calls attention to the difference between the law governing blockades and the law governing contraband. This is one of the points to which I called attention in my note of yesterday.

In the matter of the blockade we can make allowance for the use of new implements of warfare, but the changing of conditions does not affect the laws in regard to contraband. Unless a belligerent has a right to add *everything* to the contraband list we cannot concede their right to interfere with shipment through neutral countries of such merchandise as is not contraband. In refusing to recognize the right we do not necessarily resort to force. My own idea is that we cannot afford to make merchandise a cause for the use of force. If we have any disputes about merchandise which cannot be settled during the war, they can be settled afterwards, and if we have any disputes which cannot be settled by agreement between the parties, they can, in due time, be submitted to investigation and arbitration, but it seems to me that we must distinguish between the rules applicable to blockade and the rules applicable to non-contraband goods shipped to neutral ports, reserving for future consideration any questions which may arise, first, concerning the effectiveness of the blockade, and second, concerning the interference with non-contraband goods.

With assurances of high respect, I am, my dear Mr. President,
Very sincerely yours,   W. J. Bryan

TLS (W. J. Bryan Papers, DNA).
¹ J. W. Gerard to WJB, March 21, 1915, *FR-WWS 1915*, pp. 354-55, suggesting that Germany placed so many obstacles in the way of trade with the United States that it hardly seemed worthwhile to go to war with England to keep up trade relations with a country, Germany, which did not seem to wish to trade with the United States; listing the items, such as potash, carbolic acid, machinery, and surgical instruments, on which an absolute embargo already existed; and noting that American ships bearing cotton to Germany returned home empty.
² RL to WJB, March 23, 1915, TLS (SDR, RG 59, 763.72112/982½, DNA), printed in *FR-LP*, I, 286-87, explaining that if the Order in Council were acknowledged to create a blockade, two points remained to be made to Britain: that the blockade, as established, would be differentially applied to neutral nations, and that noncontraband consigned to a neutral port, whatever its ultimate destination, should be allowed free passage.

From Edward Mandell House

[Berlin, March 23, 1915]

Your cable under new code just received. All the ministers to whom I have spoken agree that Germany will stand with us for a second convention. Minister of Foreign Affairs of France also agrees, in tentative way. However, this may not be as important as it now appears. I will explain why later. I have got at the bottom of things here and leave Saturday or Sunday for Switzerland, where I will cable fully. It is my intention to confer with the American Ambassador to Italy, and the American Ambassador to Spain in the South of France, so that they may create sentiment in Italy and Spain regarding a second convention. Cablegram in care of our Minister to Switzerland will reach me from 28th to 30th inclusive. After that I will keep in touch with the American Embassy at Paris.   Edward House

T transcript of WWsh decode (WP, DLC).

Edith Bolling Galt[1] to Annie Stuart Litchfield Bolling[2]

Dearest Annie:

[Washington] Tuesday,
March the 23rd, 1915

You have been so in my thoughts all this evening that I won't go to bed until I tell you of my real genuine wish that for once you & I could have changed places and you had what came to me.

It is that I am just home from the White House where I spent the evening and dined informally with the President.[3]

He is *perfectly* charming and one of the easiest and most delightful hosts I have ever known.

You know Miss Bones and I have gotten to be great friends & we walk together 3 or 4 times a week, and last Thursday I had her come to lunch with me. And Dr. Grayson invited himself to come too.

It seems at breakfast a day or so afterwards something was said about it, and the President said Why don't you ask her here sometime say Tuesday, but not to lunch, for I always have to leave, but ask her for dinner when I can spend the evening

They sent the big car for me, & I picked up Dr. Grayson, and there were no other guests, but Col. Brown from Atlanta, who was staying there. I sat by the Pres. right, & Dr. Grayson next to me, and we had the most delightful dinner, right after which we went up in the Oval Room where, before a big wood fire we had coffee and all sorts of interesting conversation. Dr. G. had to go to see Mr. McAdoo, and Col. Brown was going on the 9 ock train so Miss Bones & I had the Pres. to ourselves and he was full of interesting stories and a fund of information, and finally, at Miss B's request, read us three English poems, and as a reader he is unequalled.

Of course I kept thinking of you & how you would have loved it, and I do hope you will have the same pleasure some day. . . .

Yours always   Edith.

ALS (EBW Papers, DLC).

¹ Born in Wytheville, Va., on October 15, 1872, the seventh child of William Holcombe and Sallie White Bolling. Her father was a lawyer and circuit court judge. After brief attendance at Martha Washington College and the Powell School for Girls in Richmond, she moved to Washington to live with her older sister, Gertrude, the wife of Alexander Hunter Galt. She married Norman Galt, a cousin of her brother-in-law, in 1896. Norman Galt became sole owner of Galt's, a well-known Washington jewelry and silverware store. Widowed in 1908, Mrs. Galt managed the business herself for a number of years and traveled annually to Europe. She was largely self-educated and lived apart from the social and political life of the capital.

For accounts of her early life, see Edith Bolling Wilson, *My Memoir* (Indianapolis, 1938) and two biographies, based heavily on her unreliable autobiography—Alden Hatch, *Edith Bolling Wilson: First Lady Extraordinary* (New York, 1961) and Ishbel Ross, *Power with Grace: The Life of Mrs. Woodrow Wilson* (New York, 1975).

² Mrs. Rolfe E. Bolling, sister-in-law of Edith Bolling Galt, who lived in Panama City, Panama. She had been an active Wilson supporter in 1912.

³ The many accounts of how Wilson first met Mrs. Galt, some of which conflict with the version in this letter, have in common an accidental encounter at the White House, when Helen Bones insisted that Mrs. Galt have tea with her after one of their walks and assured her guest that Wilson was out playing golf with Dr. Grayson. The four met at the elevator door, the women with mud-covered shoes and the men in golfing attire. This led to invitations to tea, rides in the automobile, and, eventually, to dinner at the White House. For variations on this theme, see Edith B. Wilson, *My Memoir*, pp. 56-58, and Cary T. Grayson, *Woodrow Wilson, An Intimate Memoir* (New York, 1960), pp. 50-51.

Five Letters to William Jennings Bryan

My dear Mr. Secretary,   The White House. 24 March, 1915.

This is indeed most interesting. I have referred to it in the memorandum attached to Mr. Lansing's note about the Order in Council. Of course, as you say, these facts do not alter our duty with regard to our rights of trade.

Faithfully Yours,   W.W.

WWTLI (W. J. Bryan Papers, DNA).

My dear Mr. Secretary,   The White House. 24 March, 1915.

These notes by Mr. Lansing are admirable and convincing; but they lead only to debate, and debate with the British Government (which for the time being consists of the War Office and the Admiralty) is at present of no practical avail.

Inconsistencies in the Order and inconsistencies between the Order and Sir Edward Grey's note accompanying it are neither here nor there, as it seems to me; neither is the lack of the ordinary forms of notice of blockade. We are face to face with *something they are going to do,* and they are going to do it no matter what representations we make. We cannot convince them or change them, we can only show them very clearly what we mean to be our own attitude and course of action and that we mean to hold them to a strict responsibility for every invasion of our rights as neutrals. In short we must make them understand that the discretion which their officials are vested with must be exercised in such a way that the extraordinary "blockade" they are instituting will *not* in fact violate our rights as neutral traders on the seas.

Take an instance (in the field of argument). It is true that a previous Order in Council adopted all the the [*sic*] Declaration of London except the portions defining contraband, as a temporary code of warfare at sea; but that previous Order did not constitute an agreement with any other nation. It was a piece of domestic legislation; and a subsequent Order no doubt repeals it so far as it is inconsistent with it. So *that* line leads nowhere, I fear.

If, then, we speak only to the facts, is not this our right course? Ought we not to say, in effect: You call this a blockade and mean to maintain it as such; but it is obvious that it is unprecedented in almost every respect, but chiefly in this, that it is a blockade of neutral as well as of belligerent coasts and harbours, which no belligerent can claim as a right. We shall expect therefore that the discretion lodged by the Order in Council in the administrative officers and courts of the crown will be exercised to correct what is irregular in this situation and leave the way open to our legitimate trade. If this is not done we shall have to hold you to a strict accountability for every instance of rights violated and injury done; but we interpret Sir Edward Grey's note to mean that this is exactly what will be done.

Note, by the way, the sentence in Page's despatch in which he says that they will heed none of our arguments, but that they will be careful not to offend us in act.

Note, also, that, as a matter of fact, our export trade shows no sign of slackening and that there is little left, by the action of Germany herself (See Gerard's recent de[s]patch and several preceding) for us to trade with Germany in. Our cotton ships bring nothing away on their return voyage.

I hope that Mr. Lansing will be kind enough to try his hand at a note such as I have indicated, and then we can get together (perhaps all three of us?) and put the thing into a shape that will thoroughly hold water (and exclude it, too, as a maritime paper should). Faithfully Yours, W.W.

WWTLI (SDR, RG 59, 763.72112/982½, DNA).

My dear Mr. Secretary,   The White House. 24 March, 1915.

It seems to me that it is very clear that the difficulties with regard to Fukien can now be easily cleared away; and I think the suggestions made by Mr. Williams, which as I read them are practically the same as those outlined in your letter, show the way. I am happy to think that we can easily come to an understanding on this point, and remove an impression which ought not to have been [permitted] so long to exist: I mean the impression created by Mr. Hay's suggestion as to a coaling station in Fukien.

The other matters give me more trouble. Frankly, I do not think that the explanations of the other "requests" which are offered in Ambassador Chin[d]a's note are convincing, and I hope that a candid discussion of them by the two governments may result in putting them in a more satisfactory light. I quite understand the motives disclosed. I do not feel like criticising the Japanese Government in regard to them. But I think that the remedies and safeguards proposed in the "requests" go too far. Whatever the intention, they do, in effect constitute a serious limitation upon China's independence of action, and a very definite preference of Japan before other nations, to whom the door was to be kept open.

I shall look forward with pleasure to discussing these points with you when we get Japan's direct and official reply to our note of inquiry.

Perhaps we need not wait for that reply before supplying Guthrie with the answer and the representations he may make in the matter of Fukien.   Faithfully Yours,   W.W.

WWTLS (W. J. Bryan Papers, DNA).

My dear Mr. Secretary,   The White House. 24 March, 1915.

I had already seen a copy of this despatch. I am sure that Page is a very penetrating and accurate assessor and reporter of the state of opinion inside and outside official circles in England. We need not quarrel with the facts: we need not even comment on them in our own minds. Whatever they do or think, we can at least keep cool and keep our own mental powder dry. You will notice that I refer to this despatch in the memorandum I have attached to Mr. Lansing's note about the Order in Council.
          Faithfully Yours,   W.W.

My dear Mr. Secretary,   The White House. 24 March, 1915.

I think you take absolutely correct and defensible ground about this matter.[1] We cannot give publicity to what is in effect an attack on every faction now operating in Mexico, even if it does emanate from our own nationals who are suffering.

But I have read this morning a long statement, handed me in flimsy form last evening, transmitted by the faithful Brazilian minister from the same source, about the food supply of the country which I think ought to lead to action on our part.[2]

I mean that I think we ought to send messages to Villa and Carranza very promptly making inquiries about the prospective food supply and pointing out what will inevitably be the opinion, and what will very possibly be the action, of the whole civilized world if wholesale famine fall on the land as a result of the inability of the factions there to get together and form a government under which the ordinary occupations of life can be resumed.   Faithfully Yours,   W.W.

WWTLI (W. J. Bryan Papers, DLC).
[1] WJB to WW, March 22, 1915, TLS, enclosing J. M. Cardoso de Oliveira, March 20, 1915, T telegram (W. J. Bryan Papers, DLC). The enclosure conveyed a message from a mass meeting of five hundred Americans in Mexico City, which dismissed the possibility of any fruitful negotiations with any of the warring factions, warned that Mexico was "drifting toward total destruction from which a mistaken altruism is powerless to save it," and asked that their message be published to expose the evasion and repression of truth about Mexico in the United States. Bryan's covering letter recommended that, if the message were to be published, the administration should issue a reply, since its authors not only condemned Wilson's policies in Mexico but took sides, contrary to the obligations of foreigners to remain neutral during a civil war.
[2] J. M. Cardoso de Oliveira to WJB, March 22, 1915, FR 1915, pp. 674-76, transmitting a message from the International Relief Committee in Mexico to the effect that the civil war had so disrupted the agricultural economy that there would be a shortage of thirty-nine million bushels of corn by November. The committee calculated that it would need $1,000,000 in gold to purchase and distribute this desperately needed corn.

From William Jennings Bryan, with Enclosure

My dear Mr. President: Washington March 24, 1915.

I am sending you another memorandum from Mr. Lansing. He hopes to have ready for your consideration tomorrow a memorandum to be used in framing the reply.

With assurances of high respect I am, my dear Mr. President,
          Yours very sincerely,   W. J. Bryan

TLS (W. J. Bryan Papers, DLC).

E N C L O S U R E

Memorandum on Reply to British Note
and Order in Council of March 15, 1915.

March 24, 1915.

In formulating a reply to the British note of March 15th transmitting the Order in Council of the same date, I think that it is important to consider the following:

1. *The general effect on public opinion in this country.* Unless the reply contains a declaration of the legal rights of the United States based on the principles of international law, with which the press has made the public more or less familiar, the American people will consider the Government either indifferent to or ignorant of its rights. Furthermore, the declaration must be urged with sufficient vigor to remove any impression that the Government is submitting without objection to violations of such rights.

2. *The political effect of a strong declaration of rights in contrast to a general statement based on expediency rather than legality.* A general statement, I am afraid, which amounts to a practical acceptance of the right asserted by Great Britain to interrupt commerce to Germany passing through neutral ports, regardless of its contraband character, would invite strong criticism and furnish the opponents of the Administration with a plausible argument as to the weakness of our foreign policy.

3. *The benefit of asserting legal rights upon any claims arising from the enforcement of the Order in Council.* If the reply of this Government is so worded that it can be construed into an admission that the measures adopted by Great Britain are justified by the conditions and possess, therefore, a degree of legality, it will make the recovery of a claim very difficult. This will also affect public opinion.

4. *The necessity of declaring neutral rights as heretofore recognized in order to be able after the war to assert that such rights exist and their legality has not been impaired by any admission of justification for the Order in Council.* The United States in the present war is the guardian of neutrality. For the sake of the future it ought to assert firmly the rights of neutrals. I have the impression that Great Britain after the war is over will be glad to recede from certain positions now assumed and admit that the position taken by the United States was legally correct. If

this Government does not declare its rights as a neutral, Great Britain will have no opportunity to recede, and the future rights of neutrals will be materially curtailed.

5. *The declaration of neutral rights will amount to a reservation rather than cause a relaxation of the enforcement of the Order in Council.* While the assertion of legal rights may have no practical effect on the present commercial situation, it will in the future be of extreme value to those who suffer by reason of the Order in Council and to neutrals in general in case of another maritime war.

6. *The avoidance of asserting legal rights in such a way as to force this Government to employ drastic measures to compel their recognition.* The idea is to file a *caveat,* to permit their violation under protest deferring settlement until peace has been restored.   Robert Lansing.

TS memorandum (W. J. Bryan Papers, DLC).

From Edward Mandell House

[Berlin, March 24, 1915]

I would suggest your doing nothing until I can cable you from Switzerland on Monday. I have just had another conference with Zimmermann. He is enthusiastic concerning the idea of a second convention. However, the situation here as a whole is most discouraging. The civil government has absolutely no power at present. I am leaving Sunday morning.   Edward House

T transcript of WWsh decode (WP, DLC).

An Address to the Annual Baltimore Conference of the Methodist Episcopal Church, South[1]

March 25, 1915.

Bishop Candler,[2] ladies and gentlemen: It is with sincere pleasure that I find myself here tonight. I would be more gratified if I were sure that I knew anything to say to you that was worth saying. My days are so filled with matters which demand my attention that you will understand how it was impossible for me to prepare to say anything to you such as I would have wished to say. I was—I hope Judge Chambers[3] will forgive me for saying —amused that, when I took his arm at the door and proceeded up the aisle, he told me I was expected to address you on missions. I know something about missions but quite too much to recollect in the length of an aisle; and it is utterly impossible, of course, for me to send my mind upon such an excursion on so short notice, much as my thoughts have been turned in recent months to some of the missionary stations of the Christian church because of their danger, because of the complications that surround them. All I can do is to say that I am privileged to be here, that I am heartily glad to see a conference like this in the City of Washington. The City of Washington needs a great many good influences. I am not meaning to intimate that it is more in need of such good influences than other places that might be mentioned; but we are in Washington, and we are thinking only of Washington in this respect at the present time.

I have the feeling as I look upon you that I have had in many other church conferences—that I am looking in the faces of men and women who are not interested in the temporary things but are interested in the permanent things, that give very little thought, I hope and believe, to the things that separate us and give a great deal of thought to the things that unite us—things that are good for the healing of this nation, not only, but for the healing of all the nations. This is a council of peace, not to form plans of peace—for it is not our privilege to form such—but to proclaim the single supreme plan of peace, our relation to our Lord and Savior, Jesus Christ, because wars will never have any ending until men cease to hate one another, cease to be jealous of another, get that feeling of reality in the brotherhood of mankind, which is the only bond that can make us think justly of one another and act righteously before God Himself.

I value the churches of this country as I would value everything else that makes for the stability of our moral processes. There are a great many people—not so many that they give me any particular concern—but nevertheless a great many people who, in the language of the day, are trying hard "to rock the boat." The boat is too big for them to rock. They are of such light material that they cannot rock it very much, but they are going through the motions. And it is just as well for them to look around once in a while and see the great steadfast body of self-possessed Americans not to be hurried into any unconsidered line of action; sure that, when you are right, you can be calm; sure that when the quarrel is none of yours, you can be impartial; sure that the men who spend their passion most will move the body politic the least; and that the reaction will not be upon the great body of American citizens, but upon themselves. So that I look upon you in the present circumstances as a great part of the stabilizer of the nation. You know that some-body has just invented a thing called a stabilizer that is used in connection with airplanes, and by some process, the mechanics of which I have not had explained to me, and perhaps could not understand if I had, this corrects the erratic movements of the machine, so that it, when adjusted, determines the plane upon which the machine is to move, and the machine cannot depart from it. Something like that is the function of the great moral forces of the world, to act as stabilizers even when we go up in the air.

I have come to you tonight, therefore, may I say, for reassur-ance—to look upon an undisturbed body of men who have their compasses and know the moral charting of the world. We know what haven we are bound for. We know the only legitimate processes by which one can work his way against the trade winds of evil in the world to the haven desired. So I am sure that I shall go away from here reinforced. I need not tell you that the Presi-dent by himself is absolutely nothing. The President is what the American nation sustains, and if it does not sustain him, then his power is contemptible and insignificant. If I can speak for you and represent you and in some sense hand on the moral forces that you represent, then I am indeed powerful. If I cannot, then I am indeed weak. I shall hope and believe that I go away from here sustained, as Bishop Candler has so generously said, by your prayers. I hope I shall feel that I am also sustained by your confidence.

T MS (WP, DLC).
   1 It met at Mount Vernon Place Church in Washington.
   2 The Rev. Dr. Warren Akin Candler of Atlanta, Bishop of the Methodist Episcopal Church, South.
   3 William Lea Chambers of Washington.

To William Jennings Bryan, with Enclosure

My dear Mr. Secretary,   The White House. 25 March, 1915.

This is certainly a very remarkable message, as coming from the *Mexican* representative at Rome,[1] and quoting his South American colleagues. I would like to follow it up a little.

Do you not think it would be well to have the Mexican minister at Rome looked up, to ascertain his Mexican and other affilia-tions and his standing?

And do you not think that it might be well to let the A.B.C. men see this message and ask their comment on it?

The opinion of the representatives of the European powers we could have guessed ourselves.

Faithfully Yours,   W.W.

WWTLI (W. J. Bryan Papers, DLC).
¹ Gonzalo A. Esteva.

ENCLOSURE

Rome, Italy. March 23, 1915

220. Mexican Minister has suggested to me that the time has arrived for the United States to intervene in Mexico with view to ending intolerable conditions existing there. He says that he has letters from many friends there urging this view. I asked him if he knew what the views of South American Republics were. He said that their representatives thought as he did and that such was opinion of all European powers.   Nelson Page

T telegram (W. J. Bryan Papers, DLC).

From William Jennings Bryan

My dear Mr. President: Washington March 25, 1915.

I am sending you the telegram drafted by Mr. Lansing.¹ I have just had time to read it but not time to go over it with a view to digesting it sentence by sentence. He has worked in nearly, if not all of your language but the impression it makes upon me is that the tone of it is a little more severe than the tone of your memorandum.

If, after you have had an opportunity to consider it, you desire any exchange of views I am at your service, as is Mr. Lansing.

With assurances of high respect I am, my dear Mr. President,

Yours very sincerely,   W. J. Bryan

TLS (SDR, RG 59, 72112/990½, DNA).
¹ For what remains of this document, see the Enclosure printed with WW to RL, March 28, 1915.

Two Letters to William Jennings Bryan

My dear Mr. Secretary,   The White House. 25 March, 1915.

Thank you for having let me see this note by Mr. Lansing. Its suggestions have great weight; but I have proposed nothing necessarily inconsistent with them in what I have suggested as to our reply to Great Britain. It all depends on how the thing is done, whether argumentatively or merely as a statement of rights.

Argument in the circumstances, I feel, is a waste of time. So would be any suggestion as to the way in which Great Britain *ought* to have announced and established her "blockade." My idea all along has been that, accepting the facts as they are, we state our well known rights as neutral traders and say that of course we should feel at liberty to hold Great Britain responsible for any violation; but that, at the same time, we should do this not only in friendly language (that of course) but with the explicit statement that we take it for granted that Great Britain means to respect these rights and will instruct her officers to see to it, in the use of the wide discretion lodged in them, that they are respected.

The statement of rights can be made very brief and succinct (as if of universal and matter of course recognition) and not in the least controversially, as if they were in question, and will be all the stronger, more persuasive, and of plainer implication if so set forth, not as part of an argument, but as part of a lucid statement of a position.   Faithfully Yours,   W.W.

My dear Mr. Secretary,   The White House. 25 March, 1915.

This despatch troubles me not a little.[1]

Do you not think that, in view of the always cordial and confidential relations always existing between you and Ambassador Chin[d]a, you might take the matter up with him very frankly, say how these things puzzled and disturbed us, and ask if we are to fear that the negotiations between China and Japan, about which correspondence is even now pending, unfinished, between this Government and the Government of the Mikado, are to be interrupted or superceded by the exercise of force?

Faithfully Yours,   W.W.

WWTLI (W. J. Bryan Papers, DLC).

[1] P. S. Reinsch to WJB, March 24, 1915, T telegram (W. J. Bryan Papers, DLC), reporting on extensive Japanese military preparations in and around Manchuria and concluding: "All such indications point to probability that military partly under cover of negotiations is repidly fortifying Japan's positions in China with a view to passing from diplomacy to force when the situation is ripe and when ready pretexts will be found. The Chinese Government is confronted by dilemma of letting these preparations proceed or of breaking off the negotiations.

"At an interview for the purpose of presenting military attache President Yuan stated to me that while it was his policy to reach a peaceful settlement with Japan for which he was prepared to make all possible concessions he foresaw the possibility that a different policy would be forced on him by Japan.

"The Japanese here are attempting to discourage the Chinese by reports that America has given the assurance to Japan through the Embassy at Tokyo that it will not protest or interfere with contemplated action China."

From William Jennings Bryan, with Enclosure

My dear Mr. President: Washington March 25, 1915.

In the telegram which I have prepared on Fukien I only mention the one "request" which Japan has made of China—namely, the request in regard to Fukien.

I am submitting for your consideration another telegram in regard to advisors, arms and police supervision. As Japan and China must remain neighbors it is of vital importance that they should be neighborly, and a neighborly spirit cannot be expected if Japan demands too much, or if China concedes too little. It is very evident that each country is suspicious of the other. China is afraid that Japan has ulterior motives, and Japan thinks that China is secretly plotting with her enemies. It is quite natural that the Germans should do all in their power to create in China a prejudice against Japan, and it is equally natural that Japan should resent any partiality shown to Germany.

It occurrs to me that an agreement might be reached on the propositions if, instead of demanding the appointment of any specific number of advisors, or advisors in any particular capacity, there was an understanding that in the selection of advisors, both as to number and importance, Japan should not be discriminated against as compared with the other leading nations.

In the same way, instead of agreeing that Japan should furnish a certain percentage of the arms purchased, China could promise not to discriminate against Japan in the purchase of arms, but fairly apportion the purchases among the leading nations or their nationals; sufficient notice—the time to be agreed upon—to be given in advance so as to permit proper arrangements to be made for the fulfilling of the contract.

In the matter of joint police supervision, the difficulty seems to lie in a failure to specify either the places or even to limit them to manchuria and eastern Mongolia.

In the verbal explanation it has been stated that this only relates to these provinces and to only certain places in the provinces, but these restrictions do not appear in writing.

In the telegram which I enclose, which, like the telegram in regard to the coast of Fukien, has been submitted to both Mr. Lansing and Mr. Williams, I have included a suggestion in regard to police supervision. I am only putting these suggestions in the form of a telegram in order that you may have the idea fairly before you and be in a position either to disapprove it entirely, or to amend the language if the idea is approved.

With assurances of high respect I am, my dear Mr. President,
Yours very sincerely, W. J. Bryan

Mr Williams suggests that Reinsch might make these suggestions to China if you approve of sending them to Japan

TLS (W. J. Bryan Papers, DNA).

E N C L O S U R E[1]

Amembassy Tokio   Washington, March 25, 1915.

⟨While⟩ Until our full communication has been received and answered we are not in position to consider definitely the requests relating to advisors, arms, and police supervision, [but] you might tentatively discuss the subject in the following sense if inquiry is made of you in regard to the subjects.

First: As to advisors, Japan disclaims any desire to insist upon an undue or unfair representation, as compared with other countries, and China, ⟨of course,⟩ *we may assume*, does not desire to discriminate against Japan in the employment of advisors. It might be possible for the two countries to reach an agreement whereby China would promise that in the selection of advisors no discrimination would be made against Japan as compared with other leading countries, either as to the number of advisors employed, or as to the subject matter concerning which the advisors are selected.

Second: In the matter of arms a similar arrangement might be made. As Japan does not desire to insist upon the purchase from her of an unfair proportion of the arms, and as China has no reason ⟨or⟩ *to* desire to discriminate against Japan in the purchase of arms, the agreement might be so worded that in the purchase of arms China would not discriminate against Japan as compared with the other leading powers, either in the amount or kind of arms purchased, [due notice to be given of intended purchase.]

Third: ⟨In the matter of⟩ [If China is disposed to concede] police supervision language should be employed *explicitly* limiting the application of this request to Manchuria and eastern Mongolia, and to such places in these provinces as have a considerable percentage of Japanese subjects. It might be definitely based upon proportion—that is, the provision for [joint] supervision might automatically become operative when a certain percentage of the population was made up of Japanese subjects.

The above suggestions are made for your use in case the

subjects are brought up for discussion before the matter can be fully treated in the correspondence between the two countries.

Bryan

25 March 1915

My dear Mr. Secretary:

I like this message and hope that it will be sent.　W.W.[2]

T telegram (SDR, RG 59, 793.94/294a, DNA).

[1] This was sent as WJB to G. W. Guthrie, March 26, 1915, 4 P.M., T telegram (SDR, RG 59, 793.94/294a, DNA). In the following document, words in angle brackets were deleted either by Bryan or Wilson; those in italics were added by Wilson; those in square brackets were added by Bryan, perhaps at Wilson's suggestion. The words "First," etc. were italicized in the draft sent to Wilson.

[2] Copied on a carbon of this telegram in the W. J. Bryan Papers, DLC.

From William Jennings Bryan

My dear Mr. President:　　　　　　[Washington] March 25, 1915.

I have put into the form of a telegram the proposition in regard to Fukien, which you approved.[1]

You will notice that it is suggested that the arrangement be made between Japan and China, and that this arrangement be then approved by the United States. I submit this idea for your consideration. It seems to me it would be better for us to approve an arrangement between Japan and China than to have this depend entirely upon an agreement between Japan and ourselves. If Japan makes an agreement with China it prevents all other nations from securing concessions on the coast of Fukien, whereas, if it was simply an arrangement between us and Japan it would seem to be a discrimination against us by preventing us while the way would be left open to other nations.

I take it for granted that Japan does not want any other nation to establish a naval base there, and by making the arrangement with China all other nations can be excluded.

I have had in mind the following addition to the telegram, but, not having had your opinion on the subject I have not included it. If it embodies your wishes, the paragraph can be added. It is as follows:

"If the Japanese Government has any uneasiness as to the development of the interior of Fukien you might inquire whether it would not be advisable to propose that no railroad concession be granted to any foreign power, with the understanding that the Chinese Government shall, itself, build, own and operate any railroads that may be deemed necessary for the development of Fukien, such railroads, if built with borrowed money, not to be mortgaged or in any way pledged to the creditors."

Experience has shown that foreign governments demand a sphere of influence whenever they build a railroad, and these spheres of influence are a menace to the political integrity of China. The arrangement above suggested would probably be welcomed by China as a means of protecting herself from any further complication with foreign powers.

With assurance of high respect I am, my dear Mr. President,
Yours very sincerely,   [W. J. Bryan]

CCL (W. J. Bryan Papers, DLC).
[1] WJB to G. W. Guthrie, March 25 [26], 1915, T telegram (SDR, RG 59, 793.94/258, DNA), printed in *FR 1915*, pp. 116-17. It affirmed the American government's willingness to approve any agreement between China and Japan to the effect that China should not make any concessions to foreign powers along the coast of Fukien, and the Washington administration's hope that Japan would not feel it necessary to insist on special advantages in developing the interior of the province. Wilson made only three verbal changes in Bryan's draft and approved the inclusion of the concluding paragraph suggested by Bryan.

From William Jennings Bryan

My dear Mr. President: [Washington] March 25, 1915.

I am sending you for your approval, or correction, a telegram, prepared in accordance with your instructions, to the Brazilian Minister in regard to the resolutions passed at the American meeting;[1] and also a telegram to Port au Prince.[2] I am making inquiry of the French Ambassador and I have learned this afternoon from Mr. Farnham that a French firm—not the French Government—has made a loan to the Hatien Government of a million dollars.

I am asking Mr. Farnham to come down for a conference in regard to American interests.

With assurances of high respect I am, my dear Mr. President,
Yours very sincerely,   [W. J. Bryan]

CCL (W. J. Bryan Papers, DNA).
[1] WJB to J. M. Cardoso de Oliveira, March 26, 1915, *FR 1915*, p. 680, replying to the Americans in Mexico City that the United States was doing "everything in its power" to provide protection for them and would contribute toward relief of hunger, but it would not publish "the language employed in the resolution concerning the leaders of the various factions."
[2] WJB to A. Bailly-Blanchard, March 25 [26], 1915, T telegram (SDR, RG 59, 838.00/1151a, DNA): "The President regrets to learn that the American Minister to Haiti has disregarded the instructions given him by this Government and has not only failed to perform his duty as a member of the Commission but has, on the contrary, used his influence to obstruct the work entrusted to the Commission. A full and immediate explanation of his attitude and the reasons therefor is requested.
"The Government is not ready to consider at this time the question of recognition."

To William Jennings Bryan

My dear Mr. Secretary, The White House. 25 March, 1915.

I take pleasure in approving both of these messages.

I am glad you are going to see Mr. Farnham. I hope that you will go into the Haitian situation very fully with him and find out all that he knows.

I think it very likely that you will find that, while in form it is a private French firm that is lending the money, it in fact has the backing of the French Government. It may be, indeed, that it is only serving that Government as an *alter ego.*

Does it not strike you as singular that a loan can be had out of France at this time? Faithfully Yours, W.W.

WWTLI (W. J. Bryan Papers, DNA).

From Edward Mandell House

Dear Governor: Berlin, Germany March 26th, 1915.

While I feel I have accomplished much of value here, I leave sadly disappointed that we were misled into believing that peace parleys might be begun upon a basis of evacuation of France and Belgium.

I have been cordially received and have added many new friendships to the old.

I find the Civil Government here as reasonable and fair-minded as their counterparts in England, but they are for the moment, impotent. It is a dangerous thing to inflame a people and give them an exaggerated idea of success, and this is what has happened and is happening in almost every country that is at war.

I have talked of the second convention to everyone worth while and without exception, it has been cordially received. If those that are in charge of the Civil Government now hold their power when peace comes, there will be no doubt of their cooperation, provided of course, our relations grow no worse, and without actual war, they could not be worse.

This is almost wholly due to our selling munitions of war to the Allies. The bitterness of their resentment towards us for this is almost beyond belief. It seems that every German soldier that is now being killed or wounded is being killed or wounded by an American bullet or shell. I never dreamed before of the extraordinary excellence of our guns and ammunition. It seems they are the only ones that explode or are so manufactured that their results are deadly.

I have pointed out the danger of such agitation against us, and have tried to show how much it would lessen our influence in helping Germany when our help was needed. I have indicated where our our [sic] interests touched at various points, and how valuable it would be to both nations to work in harmony rather than at cross purposes.

I have drawn particularly upon our desire for the freedom of the seas, and how in the second convention they would find us standing firmly by Germany to bring about this desired result.

I have said that our thought went far beyond the Declaration of Paris, or the proposed Declaration of London, and that we have in mind the absolute freedom of commerce in future warfare, and that navies should be used almost wholly for protection against invasion.

This thought has been enthusiastically received and it has done more to bring about a better feeling than anything that has been said or done.

There is a general insistence here as elsewhere that when a settlement is made it must be an enduring one, but ideas as to how this may be brought about are as divergent as the poles.

I am leaving Sunday, the 28th, for a conference with Stovall in Switzerland, with Page at Nice and Willard at San Sabastian. Penfield comes here tomorrow. We will soon have them all working for the same purposes and I shall keep in constant touch with them so they may be informed and working in harmony.

When peace does come we will have a sentiment prepared in each country to help accomplish the great things we have in mind to be done.

Gerard has been exceedingly helpful here. He has not interfered in any way and has insisted upon my seeing the different Ministers and influential Germans alone. He is very courageous and is different from some of our representatives, in as much as his viewpoint is wholly American.

Affectionately yours,   E. M. House

TLS (WP, DLC).

From William Jennings Bryan

My dear Mr. President: Washington March 27, 1915.

I am enclosing two statement[s] given this morning by Mr. Farnham, who came down at my request. One gives the attutide of the Bank and the other states the condition of the railroad.[1]

We have expressed a desire to these people that they should not surrender the American interests in the Bank, and yet we can hardly expect them to retain their interests there which they can now dispose of without loss, unless we are prepared to give them protection against the influence which is evidently being brought to bear from German and French interests.

There are some matters he did not want to put in writing, and after you have had a chance to digest the statements he has prepared I think I had better have a few minutes with you to go over the situation. The British Ambassador has asked what we had decided to do in the matter of recognition and why recognition was delayed. It seems that the German and French Ministers acted simultaneously—if not together—and there seems to be some sympathetic cooperation between the French and German interests in Haiti. There are some indications that their plans include taking advantage of Mole St. Nicholas.

With assurances of high respect I am, my dear Mr. President,
Yours very sincerely,   W. J. Bryan

TLS (W. J. Bryan Papers, DNA).
[1] R. L. Farnham, "Confidential Memorandum in Respect to American Interests in the National Bank of Haiti," and "Confidential Memorandum Concerning the National Railroad of Haiti," March 27, 1915, T MSS (W. J. Bryan Papers, DNA). In the first, Farnham explained that the Americans who controlled a one-half interest in the bank had little choice but to pull out in light of the financial chaos brought on by repeated revolutions, the failure of the Fort mission to find a formula for Haitian stability, and the recent and growing prominence of French banking interests on the island. The second statement predicted that European bondholders, whose coupons were unpaid since construction had been halted, would soon take over the railroad and eliminate American interests in the enterprise. As a result, Haiti's business would revert entirely to French and German interests.

Two Letters from Edward Mandell House

Dear Governor: Berlin March 27th, 1915.

Penfield has been here today. He has told of conditions in his section. They could not well be worse. Bankruptcy and defeat are staring them in the face, and zadok [Germany] will soon have to carry her ally. Not only this, disease is rampant all along the eastern frontier and that may soon wreak greater havoc than the war has. Smallpox, meningitis and typhus are doing their deadly work and there is no way to better conditions while the war continues.

As a matter of fact, it looks as if Europe would be ravaged by disease, for even in England some of these scourges have been brought back by the wounded.

Penfield tells me that the people in that section are exceedingly anxious for peace, but those in authority do not altogether share in this desire.

I have talked to him about the second convention and its purposes. He is pleased with the thought and will work up a sentiment for it. I have also made arrangements with him to keep me informed, even to the extent of sending a special messenger to London, if its importance justifies it. As it is now, he has no way of safely communicating with anyone. It is only in this manner that I can keep you properly informed and know the situation myself, otherwise we would not know when to act or in what direction.

We will soon have a fairly reliable bureau of information in each belligerent capital, and there will not be as much guesswork as in the past. It would surprise you to learn how loosely information is gathered by the different belligerents, even from one another.

We should be in a position to know the situation better than all others and unless we do we will not be able to intelligently do the work we have undertaken.

Affectionately yours, E. M. House

Dear Governor: Berlin March 27th, 1915.

Some way has to be thought out to let the governments down easy with their peoples. That is almost if not quite our hardest problem.

It occurred to me today to suggest to the Chancellor that through the good offices of the United States, England might be brought to concede at the final settlement, the freedom of the seas and to the extent that I have indicated to you.

I told him that the United States would be justified in bringing pressure upon England in this direction for our people had a common interest with Germany in that question. He, like the others I have talked to, was surprised when I told him the idea was to go far beyond the Declaration of Paris or the proposed Declaration of London.

I said someone would have to throw across the chasm the first thread so that the bridge might have its beginning and that we knew of no suggestion that was better fitted for that purpose than this. That if England would consent, this Government could say to the people that Belgium was no longer needed as a base for German naval activity, since England was being brought to terms.[1]

I have sown this thought of the freedom of the seas very widely since I have been here and already I can see results. I am enclosing you a translation of an item that appeared this morning.[2]

I believe I can show England that in the long run and looking at the matter broadly, it is as much to her interests as it is to other nations of the earth.

The Chancellor seemed to think, and so does Zimmermann, that we have offered in this suggestion the best idea as a peace beginning. They understand that I am to go to Switzerland to confer with Stovall, to Nice to confer with Page and to Biarritz to confer with Willard and all to the one purpose.

They know that I am then to go to Paris and to say that I see no prospects for immediate parleys unless everyone softens in their demands. Afterwards I have told them I would take this matter of the freedom of the seas up with the British Government, and that we would thresh it out with them to a finish. That if we succeed in bringing them to a reasonable view I would communicate at once with them, and that we would expect them to make as great concessions.

The Chancellor told me to say to you that he appreciated your disinterested and splendid purpose to bring about peace between the warring nations, and that he understood that you were actuated only by the highest motives.

I have told them frankly and with emphasis that they could not expect us to lift the embargo[3] on the export of munitions of war, and that they must soften their press and people on this point. They have promised to do this. I have told them that we would help them in the big things later and that they must be content with our efforts in that direction.[4]

I leave here fairly satisfied, as we now have something definite to work on, and as the warring nations have tacitly accepted you as their Mediator.

I am writing hastily to catch the mail before it closes.

Affectionately yours,   E. M. House

P.S. I shall probably cable you concerning the treatment of German prisoners in Russia. It would have a splendid effect here if you could do something to better their condition.

I do not believe that Mayre [Marye] is equal to his job. I do not hear good things of him.

TLS (WP, DLC).

1 T. von Bethmann Hollweg, T memorandum, March 28, 1915 (Der Weltkrieg, geheim, Vermittlungsaktionen, Vol. 5, D 956261, GFO-Ar), is the Chancellor's memorandum of this conversation.

2 A translation of an editorial from the Berlin Tageblatt, March 27, 1915, saying that Germany was fighting, not only to preserve her independence, but also to free the world "from the terrorism of the English fleet."

3 House obviously dictated "to impose the embargo" and Miss Denton misread her notes. The Gregg outlines for impose and lift are nearly similar and can easily be confused.

⁴ Jagow gives a different version (our translation): "I spoke up then to Mr. House about the American supplies of munitions. According to his statement, America wants peace. However, she only prolongs the war by furnishing the weapons for waging it; and since only our enemies can profit by American deliveries, they stand in contrast to true neutrality. To that Mr. House presented the following: America had almost (or not at all) no state-owned ammunition factories for her army and would have to rely upon private industry in the event of war. If the President now forbade the export, he would ruin the domestic munitions and weapons industries. This would mean danger for the nation. He, House, talked the matter over with the President, and Mr. Wilson had considered declaring that the state should take over private factories. Then he would be able to prohibit the export of arms. House has expected such a declaration from the President in the course of this month. If it has not come, he believes that the reason is that the President in the meantime has become convinced by soundings that he could not secure the approval of Congress for such a measure." G. von Jagow, TS memorandum, March 23, 1915 (Der Weltkrieg, geheim, Vermittlungsaktionen, Vol. 4, D 956200-202, GFO-Ar).

To Robert Lansing, with Enclosure

My dear Mr. Lansing,   The White House. 28 March, 1915.

Will you not be kind enough to look over the enclosed and tell me what you think of it?

You will see what I have done. I have recast the note as a *statement* and *interpretation*: so that there is no argument involved, but it is meant to mean: We have the Order and the note accompanying it. We cannot understand these as notice of illegal action. We shall assume the contrary until actual things done compel us to look upon the matter differently. Then we shall hold the British government responsible in accordance with the well known principles of international law, of which we now remind her, so that she may know just what we understand them to be.

Please make any comment you please either on the statements or the language of what I have written.

Sincerely Yours,   Woodrow Wilson

WWTLS (SDR, RG 59, 763.72112/986½, DNA).

E N C L O S U R E¹

DRAFT.

The White House [March 28, 1915].

Your Nos. 1795 and 1798, of March fifteenth.

The Government of the United States has given careful consideration to the subjects treated in the British notes of March

¹ The roman text in the following document is WWT; the text in italics is that of portions of Lansing's draft, the latter pages of which Wilson added to his own text. Words in Lansing's text in angle brackets were deleted by Wilson; Wilson's substitutes are printed in square brackets. There is a WWsh draft of Wilson's text in WP, DLC.

thirteenth and March fifteenth, and to the British Order in Council of the latter date.

These communications contain matters of grave importance to neutral nations. They appear to menace their rights of trade and intercourse not only with belligerents but also with one another. They call for frank comment in order that[2] misunderstandings may be avoided. The Government of the United States deems it its duty, therefore, speaking in the sincerest spirit of friendship, to make its own view and position with regard to them unmistakably clear.

The Order in Council of the fifteenth of March would constitute, were its provisions to be actually carried into effect as they stand, a practical assertion of unlimited belligerent rights over neutral commerce within the whole European area and an almost unqualified denial of the sovereign rights of the nations now at peace.

This Government takes it for granted that there can be no question what those rights are. A nation's sovereignty over its own ships and citizens under its own flag on the high seas in time of peace is, of course, unlimited; and that sovereignty suffers no diminution in time of war except in so far as the practice and consent of civilized nations has limited it by the recognition of certain now clearly determined rights which it is conceded may be exercised by nations which are at war.

A belligerent nation has been conceded the right of visit and search, and the right of capture and condemnation if upon examination a neutral vessel is found to be engaged in unneutral service or to be carrying contraband of war intended for the enemy's government or forces in the field. It has been conceded the right to establish and maintain a blockade of an enemy's ports and coasts and to capture and condemn any vessel taken in trying to break the blockade. It is even conceded the right to detain and take to its own ports for judicial examination all vessels which it suspects for substantial reasons to be engaged in unneutral or contraband service and to condemn them if the suspicion is sustained. But such rights, long clearly defined both in doctrine and practice, have hitherto been held to be the only permissible exceptions to the principle of universal equality of sovereignty on the high seas as between belligerents and nations not engaged in war

It is confidently assumed that His Majesty's Government will not deny that it is a rule sanctioned by general practice that, even

2 Here Wilson crossed out "serious."

though a blockade should exist and the doctrine of contraband as to unblockaded territory be rigidly enforced, innocent shipments may be freely transported to and from the United States through neutral countries to belligerent territory without being subject to the penalties of contraband traffic or breach of blockade, much less to detention, requisition, or confiscation.

His Majesty's Government, like the Government of the United States, have often and explicitly held that these rights represent the best usage of warfare in the dealings of belligerents with neutrals at sea. In this connection I desire to direct attention to the opinion of the Chief Justice of the United States in the case of the PETERHOF, which arose out of the Civil War, and to the fact that that opinion was unanimously sustained in the award of the Arbitration Commission of 1871, to which the case was presented at the request of Great Britain. From that time to the Declaration of London of 1909, adopted with modifications by the Order in Council of the twenty-third of October last, these rights have not been seriously questioned by the British Government. The rules of the Declaration of Paris of 1856, among them that free ships make free goods, will hardly at this day be disputed by the signatories to that solemn agreement; and no claim on the part of Great Britain of any justification for interfering with these clear rights of the United States and its citizens as neutrals could be admitted. To admit it would be to assume an attitude of unneutrality towards the present enemies of Great Britain which would be obviously inconsistent with the solemn obligations of this Government in the present circumstances.

The note of His Majesty's Principal Secretary of State for Foreign Affairs which accompanies the Order in Council, and which bears the same date, notifies the Government of the United States of the establishment of a blockade which is, if defined by the terms of the Order in Council, to include all the coasts and ports of her present enemies and every port of possible access to their territory. But the novel and quite unprecedented feature of that blockade, if we are to assume it to be so defined, is that it embraces many neutral ports and coasts, bars access to them, and subjects all neutral ships seeking to approach them to the same suspicion that would attach to them were they bound for the ports of her enemies,—to similar risks and in large measure to the same penalties.

It is manifest that such limitations, risks and liabilities placed upon the ships of a neutral power on the high seas, beyond the right of visit and search and the right to prevent the shipment of contraband already referred to, are a distinct invasion of the sovereign rights of the nation whose ships, trade, or commerce is interfered with.

The Government of the United States is of course not oblivious to the great changes which have occurred in the conditions and means of naval warfare since the rules hitherto governing legal blockade were formulated. It might be ready to admit that the old form of "close" blockade with its cordon of ships in the immediate offing of the blockaded ports is no longer practicable in face of an enemy possessing the means and opportunity to make an effective defence by the use of submarines, mines, and air craft; but it can hardly be maintained that it is impossible to conform, ⟨in⟩ whatever form of effective blockade may be made use of, at least to the spirit and principles of the established rules of war. If the necessities of the case should seem to render it imperative that the cordon of blockading vessels be extended across the approaches to any neighboring neutral port or country, it would seem clear that it would still be easily practicable to comply with the well recognized and reasonable prohibition of international law against the blockading of neutral ports by according free admission and exit to all legal traffic with neutral ports through the blockading cordon. This traffic would of course include all outward bound traffic from the neutral country and all inward bound traffic to the neutral country except contraband in transit to the enemy. Such procedure need not conflict in any respect with the rights of the belligerant maintaining the blockade since the right would remain with the blockading vessels to visit and search all ships either entering or leaving the neutral territory which they were in fact, but not of right, investing.

If His Majesty's Government should follow any other course, it would not only incur very grave responsibilities and enter upon practices for which every neutral government affected would feel obliged to hold it strictly accountable in damages, but it would also abandon and set at naught principles for which it has itself consistently and earnestly contended in other times and circumstances.

The Government of the United States notes that in the Order in Council His Majesty's Government gives as its reason for entering upon a course of action which it is aware is without precedent in modern warfare the necessity it conceives itself to have been placed under to retaliate upon its enemies for measures of a similar nature which they have announced it their intention to adopt and which they have to some extent adopted; but the Government of the United States, recalling the principles upon which

His Majesty's Government have hitherto been scrupulous to act, interprets this as merely a reason for certain extraordinary activities on the part of His Majesty's naval forces and not as an excuse for or prelude to any unlawful action. If the course pursued by the present enemies of Great Britain should prove to be in fact tainted by illegality and disregard of the principles of war set upon among the nations, it cannot be supposed, and this Government does not for a moment suppose, that His Majesty's Government would wish the same taint to attach to its own actions or would cite such illegal acts as in any sense or degree a justification for similar practices on its part.

It is thus that the Government of the United States interprets the language of the note of His Majesty's Principal Secretary of State for Foreign Affairs which accompanies the copy of the Order in Council which was handed to the Ambassador of the United States near the Government in London and by him transmitted to Washington.

This Government notes with pleasure that *"wide discretion is afforded to the Prize Court in dealing with the trade of neutrals in such manner as may in the circumstances be deemed just, and that full provision is made to facilitate claims by persons interested in any goods placed in the custody of the Marshal of the Prize Court under the Order"; that "the effect of the Order in Council is to confer certain powers upon the executive officers of His Majesty's Government"; and that "the extent to which these powers will be actually exercised and the degree of severity with which the measures of blockade authorized will be put into operation are matters which will depend on the administrative orders issued by the Government and the decisions of the authorities especially charged with the duty of dealing with individual ships and cargoes according to the merits of each case." This Government further notes with ⟨peculiar⟩ [equal] satisfaction the declaration of the British Government that "the instructions to be issued by His Majesty's Government to the fleet and to the customs officials and executive committees concerned will impress upon them the duty of acting with the utmost despatch consistent with the object in view, and of showing in every case such consideration for neutrals as may be compatible with that object, which is, succinctly stated, to establish a blockade to prevent vessels from carrying goods for or coming from Germany."*

In view of these assurances formally given to this Government, it is confidently expected that the extensive powers conferred by the Order in Council on the executive officers of the Crown will be restricted by "orders issued by the government" directing the exercise of their discretionary powers in such a manner as to modify in practical application those provisions of the Order in Council which, if strictly enforced, would violate neutral rights and interrupt legitimate trade. Relying on the faithful perform-ance of these voluntary assurances by His Majesty's Government the United States takes it for granted that the approach of Amer-ican merchantmen to neutral ports situated upon the long line of coast affected by the Order in Council will not be interfered with when it is known that they do not carry goods which are contra-band of war or goods destined to or proceeding from ports within the belligerent territory affected.

The Government of the United States assumes with greater confidence that His Majesty's Government will thus adjust their practice to the recognized rules of international law, because it is manifest that the British Government have adopted an extraor-dinary method of "stopping cargoes destined for or coming from the enemy's territory," which, owing to the existence of unusual conditions in modern warfare at sea, it will be difficult to restrict to the limits which have been heretofore required by the law of nations. Though the area of operations is confined to "European waters including the Mediterranean," so great an area of the high seas is covered and the cordon of ships is so distant from the territory affected that neutral vessels must necessarily pass through the blockading force in order to reach important neutral ports which Great Britain as a belligerent has not the legal right to blockade and which, therefore, it is presumed she has no in-tention of claiming to blockade. The Scandinavian and Danish ports, for example, are open to American trade. They are also free, so far as the actual enforcement of the Order in Council is concerned, to carry on trade with German Baltic ports, although it is an essential element of blockade that it bear with equal severity upon all neutrals ⟨alike⟩.

This Government, therefore, infers that the commanders of His Majesty's ships of war engaged in maintaining the so-called blockade will be instructed to avoid an enforcement of the pro-posed measures of non-intercourse in such a way as to impose restrictions upon neutral trade more burdensome than those which have heretofore been regarded as inevitable when the ports of a belligerent are actually blockaded by the ships of its enemy.

The possibilities of serious interruption of American trade un-der the Order in Council are so many, and the methods proposed are so unusual and seem liable to constitute so great an impedi-ment and embarrassment to neutral commerce that the Govern-ment of the United States if the Order in Council be strictly en-

forced, apprehends many interferences with its legitimate trade which will impose upon His Majesty's Government heavy responsibilities for acts of the British authorities clearly subversive of the rights of neutral nations on the high seas. It is, therefore, expected that His Majesty's Government having considered these possibilities will take the steps necessary to avoid them, and, in the event that they should unhappily occur, will be prepared to make full reparation for every act, which under the rules of international law constitutes a violation of neutral rights.

As stated in its communication of October 22, 1914, "this Government will insist that the rights and duties of the United States and its citizens in the present war be defined by the existing rules of international law and the treaties of the United States, irrespective of the provisions of the Declaration, and that this Government reserves to itself the right to enter a protest or demand in each case in which those rights and duties so defined are violated, or their free exercise interfered with, by the authorities of the British Government."

WWT and CC MS (WP, DLC).

From Robert Lansing

Dear Mr. President,   Washington March 28, 1915.

I return the draft which you sent me this afternoon, and which I have, in accordance with your request, examined critically and suggested without reserve certain changes. These are verbal, being chiefly "pluralizing" pronouns relating to the British Government.

I believe that the reply as drafted fully protects our legal rights, so that in the event of claims arising out of the enforcement of the Order in Council no admission by this Government can be urged by Great Britain in denying liability. It was that feature, which it seemed to me, was of special importance.[1]

I do not believe the method of treatment could be improved upon.   Very sincerely yours   Robert Lansing.

I have just been handed by a reporter of the N. Y. Tribune the enclosed clipping from its issue of today, which may be the line of defense which will be offered by Great Britain. If you have not read Mr Balfour's statement, I am sure you will find it interesting.[2]   R.L.

ALS (SDR, RG 59, 763.72112/985½, DNA).
[1] A week later, in an interview with Arthur Willert, Washington correspondent of *The Times*, Lansing explained the true meaning of the American note for the

benefit of the British government and public. Willert's dispatch appeared in
The Times on April 7, 1915. "Please read carefully 'Times' telegram dated April
7th about United States view as to Order-in-Council," Spring Rice wired the
Foreign Office. "It is based on conversation with principal legal adviser of
United States Government." C. A. Spring Rice to the Foreign Office, received
April 9, 1915, T telegram (E. Grey Papers, FO 800/85, p. 133, PRO).

Although Willert's reports and letters to *The Times* do not mention this
episode (no doubt for reasons of security), there can be no doubt that the
"principal legal adviser" was Lansing. Willert's dispatch follows:

"Washington, April 7. In the estimation of cool observers the publication of
the American Note and its reception here and at home puts it in the power of
the British Government to write *finis* to the first and most troubled chapter
of the history of Anglo-American trade relations during the war. The situation
is felt to be as follows: The American Government recognizes the right of Great
Britain to carry out 'a long-distance blockade?' on terms which do not quite
tally with the old conception of international law. It has done this because it
realizes that the adjustment of precedent to new conditions is the basic principle
of Anglo-Saxon law, and because, as a matter of policy, it is deemed inadvisable
for the United States, which herself is a maritime nation, to enunciate new
principles unduly harassing to the operations of a Maritime Power.

"Except in Germanophil quarters, which describe the Note as a surrender
to British high-handedness, the Government's decision has got a good Press.
So have the broad-minded and friendly comments on the Note to which you
and various of your contemporaries are reported to have given expression. There
remains, however, one important thing to be cleared up. The American Government is unable to accept the British claim to the right arbitrarily to interfere with neutral shipments to neutral ports, because the shipments are suspected to be of eventual enemy destination. To avoid further controversy Great
Britain must yield that point. But if current comment goes for anything, she
need yield it only in theory and not in fact.

"This, it is felt, we can do by enlarging as much as may be necessary our
list, not of absolute but of conditional contraband, for the American Civil War
decisions, while explicit upon the illegality of the application of the continuous
voyage doctrine to non-contraband, allow its application to conditional contraband. Were this to be done it is unlikely that the United States would enter
more than a perfunctory protest. If, however, we insist upon seizing non-contraband shipments to neutral ports, there is bound to be a sharp protest, followed
probably by an agitation about infringement of American rights, which the
German agitators well know how to exploit to the injury of our prestige and to
the embarrassment of the President in following the difficult course of neutrality. Such a compromise would not, of course, apply to German exports, but
it is still hoped that some arrangement will be reached about German dyestuffs
while, in regard to German exports in general, it is generally expected that the
question will be rather academic.

"Neither the public nor public men demand unreasonable concessions. It is
hoped by our well-wishers that some sort of compromise will be reached. It is
felt that it would be a thousand pities if full advantage cannot be taken of the
atmosphere of friendly understanding and compromise created by the American
Note. Especially is this the case in view of the general situation as between the
United States and Great Britain and the United States and Germany. Never
since the beginning of the war has feeling against Germany been more bitter,
or the real significance of Teutonic methods better understood. Never, perhaps,
has the official attitude of Berlin been more worrying to those responsible for
American foreign policy. . . .

"The stage in fact seems, as far as the United States is concerned, to be set
for a fuller Anglo-American understanding over the various issues of the war
than at one time seemed possible, and there will be much regret if London
fails to take the cue. This regret will be due to two causes—first, to the feeling
that a solid Anglo-American understanding is of the greatest importance at
this juncture; secondly, to the realization that the German propagandists, while
discredited, are by no means finished with."

2 "Balfour Defends British Blockade Order in Council," *New York Tribune*,
March 28, 1915, quoting an interview with Balfour. He argued that Britain had
"conclusive moral justification" for its blockade and urged American critics
to forego "the most rigid technical standards" of international law and to regard
the "equity of the Allies' case rather than the law." The obligations of inter-

national law were conditional, he continued, and one of its conditions was reciprocity: once Germany had violated the spirit and the letter of the law, Britain, in self-defense, had no choice but to violate the letter.

To William Jennings Bryan

My dear Mr. Secretary,   The White House. 28 March, 1915.

Here is the note as I have rewritten it. I would be very much obliged if you would read it and tell me when I get back from Annapolis just what you think of it. I have tried to con[s]truct it in the spirit of our recent discussion in the Cabinet.

Since I had built it chiefly on Mr. Lansing's note, I sent it to him this afternoon, and his note is attached (I mean his comment).

I shall be back Tuesday morning early.

Faithfully Yours,   W.W.

WWTLI (SDR, RG 59, 72112/987½, DNA).

From William Jennings Bryan

[Washington, March 29, 1915]

New York parties very anxious to have opinion on matter submitted Friday   They are receiving urgent dispatches from Paris.[1]

Bryan

ALS (W. J. Bryan Papers, DNA).
  [1] This concerned a one-year loan of $50,000,000 to France. J. P. Morgan and Co. and two other New York banks wanted to issue French treasury bonds at 5 per cent interest as collateral for the loan, the proceeds of which would be used to finance French purchases in the United States. For the background of this loan, see Link, *Struggle for Neutrality*, pp. 132-36.

To William Jennings Bryan

USS Mayflower Via Annapolis Mar 29 1915

Quote Do not think we can sustain objection signed Wilson unquote

T telegram (W. J. Bryan Papers, DNA).

An Address on Board *Moreno*[1]

March 29, 1915.

Mr. Ambassador, gentlemen: It is with great pleasure that I find myself in this interesting company and in this interesting place. There has obtained a custom of the United States, which has seemed to amount almost to a superstition, that the President of the United States should not leave its territory. I do not know whether that was out of distrust of the President or out of precaution for the country—whether there was fear that he would not behave himself outside of his own jurisdiction or whether it was thought that he was absolutely necessary to the country and its administration. I shall try on this occasion, at any rate, to relieve the country of the fear of his misbehavior.

I am particularly glad that this great vessel, which I have so much admired, should represent some part of the reciprocity and connection between the United States of America and the great Republic of the Argentine. We have been the more glad to be instrumental in supplying you with this great arm of war because we are so sure that neither of us will ever use such an arm against the other. I feel that I am speaking the sentiments of my fellow countrymen when I say that there is with us a growing warmth of affection, as well as understanding, for the other countries of the great American hemisphere, which we are coming daily to understand better and which are, I hope, daily coming to understand us better, and to which we are drawn by feeling as well as by interest, by the desire to be comrades in some common undertaking for humanity as well as neighbors. It is not always that neighbors understand one another. I remember a very witty passage from an English writer, who says that you may talk of the tyranny of Caesar and Tiberius, but the real tyranny is the tyranny of your next door neighbor, the obligation to be like him and to do what he does, and to remember what he will say of you if you do not act as he does. But there is no such tyranny in international affairs. The rivalry there is in the kind of actions that will commend a nation to the respect and affection of other nations.

It is a fine thing to believe, and I believe it in the midst of this period of war, that the real ground of respect is justice and fairness and good will, that you cannot respect a man or a nation for which you cannot sooner or later acquire an affection. The great advantage of intermixture, not only of actual intermixture of blood, but of constant intercourse between nations, is that there grows up a common understanding. We speak different languages, we have followed to some extent different customs, we have to some degree different national traditions, but at the bottom we have got just the same sort of polity and understandings and the same essential interests, and, when we mix with one another and touch hands, we are apt to touch hearts also. I believe that the modern world is preparing us for this understanding and comradeship by its extraordinarily increased means of intercommunication. There is a very delightful saying ascribed to the English writer, Charles Lamb. He spoke very harshly of a man who was the subject of conversation but not present, and someone said, "Why, Charles, I didn't know that you knew him." Lamb stuttered a little; he said, "I-I-I d-dont know h-him; I-I can't h-hate a man I-I know." I think that is true between nations just as well as between individuals.

I want to congratulate you upon the completion of this ship and upon all that she stands for in the way of reciprocity between ourselves and the great country you represent, and I want to express my feeling as President of the United States that we are rapidly approaching a day when the Americas will draw together as they have never drawn together before, and that it will be a union, not of political ties, but of understanding and of mutual helpfulness.

I want to drink to the health and success of your President, your government, and, if I may, I wish to include your Ambassador, for whom we have the greatest respect.

T MS (WP, DLC).
¹ At a luncheon in Annapolis harbor given by Ambassador Romulo S. Naón in Wilson's honor, on board the battleship *Moreno*, just completed by the New York Shipbuilding Co. for the Argentine navy.

From William Jennings Bryan

My dear Mr. President: Washington March 29, 1915.

I am sending you the note to Page, drawn in accordance with your instructions, with a few changes so indicated that you can either approve them or cross them out.

The note from Mr. Lansing, which I enclose,¹ explains those which he has suggested.

The three which I suggest—(I might add with Mr. Lansing's approval)—are as follows:

1. About the middle of page 5 of your notes, I beg to suggest the substitution of the following: "*unusual risks and penalties,*" instead of "similar risks and in large measure to the same penalties."

It would not be quite accurate to say that the risks and penalties are *similar, or in a large measure the same*, because the Orders in Council clearly discriminate between the treatment of merchandise destined to an enemy country through a neutral country, and the treatment of merchandise that attempts to run the blockade. It is correct, however, to say that the risks and penalties are *unusual*.

2. On page 8 of your notes, about the middle of the page, I suggest the addition of the words—"insofar as they affect neutral rights."

We are speaking of acts of retaliation and I take it for granted that your language is intended to refer to retaliation only insofar as retaliation affects neutral rights.

3. Upon reading the concluding paragraph of the note it struck me as ending rather bluntly, and I suggested to Mr. Lansing a little sweetening in the form of a reiteration of the friendly spirit in which the answer is made. Mr. Lansing and I have gone over it together, and the following is the result of our collaboration:

"In conclusion you will reiterate to His Majesty's Government that this statement of the views of the Government of the United States is made in the most friendly spirit, and in accordance with the uniform candor which has characterized the relations of the Governments in the past, and which has been in large measure the foundation of the peace and amity existing between the two nations without interruption for a century."

I am sure you will pardon me for making these suggestions, in compliance with your request. They are not very material, but are submitted for your consideration.

Allow me to say in conclusion what I possibly should have said in the beginning of this note, namely that I am very much pleased with the note and believe that it will find popular endorsement. The position which you take is very clearly and strongly stated and yet due consideration is given to the exegencies that call forth the Order in Council and to the promises which they make in regard to its enforcement.

With Assurances of high respect I am, my dear Mr. President,
Yours very sincerely, W. J. Bryan

TLS (SDR, RG 59, 763.72112/988½, DNA).
¹ RL to WW, March 28, 1915.

From Warren Forman Johnson, with Enclosure

[The White House] March 29th [1915].

The Secretary wishes to know the opinion of the President in the matter of the attached. WFJ.

Please say I have expressed no opinion about it W.W.

TL with WWhw reply (WP, DLC).

ENCLOSURE

Margaret Blaine Damrosch[1] to Joseph Patrick Tumulty

Dear Sir: [New York] March 27, 1915.

It has been stated to me on excellent authority that Mr. Aiken,[2] the owner of the film "Birth of a Nation" says that before it was given publicly, President Wilson, and Chief Justice White saw it, and saw nothing objectionable in it.

I know of no method but this of direct appeal to ascertain the truth or falsity of Mr. Aiken's claims, so after hesitating some time before troubling you I am finally impelled to do so, because of the lively discussion which the presentation of the "Birth of a Nation" is causing in this city.[3] I shall be most grateful for the courtesy of a reply.

Very truly yours,   Margaret Blaine Damrosch.
(Mrs. Walter Damrosch).

ALS (WP, DLC).
   [1] Daughter of James Gillespie Blaine and wife of Walter Johannes Damrosch, conductor of the New York Symphony Orchestra.
   [2] Harry E. Aitken, pioneer financier of motion pictures and president of the Epoch Producing Co., which owned "The Birth of a Nation."
   [3] About the furor caused by the showing of this film in New York and elsewhere, see Link, *The New Freedom*, pp. 252-54; and Thomas Cripps, *Slow Fade to Black: The Negro in American Film*, *1900-1942* (New York, 1977), pp. 55-61.

From Edward Mandell House

[Bern, March 29, 1915]

The situation in Germany is this: Peace is desired generally, but not having actual facts given them, the people would overthrow the government and perhaps the throne if parleys should now be commenced on the basis of having any chance of success. The civil government would listen to proposals based on evacuation of Belgium and France, and about half the military government would consent to this; but the people generally would not permit it. The problem is to save the face of the authorities and to enlighten the people. I have proposed a way to do this, and it was cordially received by von Bethmann Hollweg and Zimmermann. In substance it is for us to try to induce England to consent to the freedom of the seas as one of the peace conditions. If they yield, as we have reason to believe they will, then Germany can say to the people that the great cause they have been striving for has been won, and there is no need to retain Belgium and her coast in order to be in a position to wage a more successful maritime war at some future time; that to hold an alien people would be a source of weakness rather than strength and would bring future trouble.

After seeing Thomas Page and Willard I shall go to England to take the matter up with Sir Edward Grey. If you approve please cable Thomas Page permission to meet me at Nice.

The blockade is pinching Germany, and, while there is no suffering, there is a great and growing inconvenience. This tends to increase peace sentiment. The feeling against us still runs high because of export of war ammunition to Allies. In governmental circles this is allayed because of our proposed aid in securing the freedom of the seas, but the people are very bitter and unforgiving. Zimmermann asked if we would permit Germany to buy up all munitions of war and hold them. I told him yes if it could be so arranged. I regard this as impracticable. I would advise doing nothing to upset our amicable relations with the Allies consistent with our position of neutrality. Germany will use us, but they will continue to dislike us. I judge my visit to Germany has been successful on account of the unusual courtesies extended me upon leaving which was not in evidence on arriving.

Cables to Paris will reach me from now. The United States Minister at Bern reports that second convention idea is very well received in Switzerland and they expect you to take the lead.

Edward House

Transcripts of WWsh decode (WP, DLC; WC, NjP).

Remarks at a Press Conference

March 30, 1915

Mr. President, could you tell us whether the note to Great Britain is in final shape?

> I think it is about in final shape and is to go—probably go within the next twenty-four hours. Let me revert just a moment to what I was saying to you gentlemen, and beg that you will assist me to observe the courtesies on correspondence. Of course, so soon after the note reaches Great Britain, it will be given out just as their note was given out by arrangement after it had reached here. And I ask for your cooperation in not speculating as to its contents until it is given out at its destination. Things are very much more effective when they are managed according to etiquette of the precedents.

Mr. President, has any tentative draft of a proposed treaty with Russia been submitted to you?

> No, sir. . . .

Mr. President, going back to Haiti for a moment,[1] has there been any correspondence with these particular nations when recognition should be accorded?

> No. None at all. Of course, they are perfectly free, legal agents. Hadn't heard of any such thing mentioned.

Is there anything with reference to the situation in Japan and China that you can discuss with us?

> No, there is nothing new at all since I saw you last.

Is there anything new in Governor Fort's report on Haiti[2] that would keep us from recognizing the government?

> No, he just reported on the conditions that he had found there. He didn't draw any conclusion at all.

Mr. President, in his address the other night, Mr. Taft said that the Harrison administration in the Philippines had substituted incompetency for efficiency. . . . Are you familiar with that?

> I am, but I hope that when I get out of office, my successors will not express an opinion with regard to what I said about them. I have no opinion to express about what my predecessors say about me. It is not often that there are two ex-Presidents living, and we are trying to invent an etiquette.

Have you gotten anywhere with your effort on that line?

> Well, I am trying to make it up all by myself. . . .

Can you say anything, Mr. President, as to Mr. Phelan's report on Santo Domingo?

> I haven't seen it. He hasn't made it yet.

Mr. President, is there anything you can say about the Colonel's visits? Have you had any communications from Colonel House?

> A great many. There seems to be a lot of notions as to what he is up to. He isn't up to anything. That is the answer to that question. He is on a tour of information entirely.

JRT transcript (WC, NjP) of CLSsh (C. L. Swem Coll., NjP).

[1] There is no earlier reference to Haiti in Swem's notes of this press conference.

[2] Fort had reported on the failure of the commission to Port-au-Prince, which he had headed, to Bryan on March 13. J. F. Fort, A. Bailly-Blanchard, and C. C. Smith, to WJB, March 13, 1915, CCL (WP, DLC). About this matter, see Link, *Struggle for Neutrality*, p. 529.

To William Jennings Bryan

My dear Mr. Secretary,   The White House. 30 March, 1915.

This note is entirely satisfactory to me with the alterations you have suggested, and I entirely approve of adding the paragraph you have drawn as the concluding passage of the note.[1]

I hope that the encyphering and all the ha[n]dling of this note will be under the safeguards as to privacy which we agreed upon,[2] so that there may be no garbled versions of it current before it reaches London. I assume that it will be agreed between Washington and London that it will be published here upon its receipt and delivery there.   Faithfully Yours,   W.W.

WWTLI (SDR, RG 59, 763.72112/989½, DNA).
¹ It went to London as WJB to WHP, March 30, 1915, T telegram (SDR, RG 59, 763.72/1588, DNA), and is printed in *FR-WWS 1915*, pp. 152-56.
² See WW to WJB, Feb. 8, 1915, and WJB to WW, Feb. 12, 1915, printed as addenda in this volume.

To William Jennings Bryan

My dear Mr. Secretary,   The White House. 31 March, 1915.

This whole matter¹ has a most sinister appearance. The more we go into it the more unpleasant and unpropitious it looks.

I think that the American interests should stay in and that we should sustain and assist them in every legitimate way.

I think, too, that it is evident we shall have to take a very decided stand with the government of Haiti, and demand certain things as a condition p[r]ecedent of recognition.

You know much more of the detail than I do. Will you not be kind enough to think out a plan of controlling action which we can take, and take before the tangle gets any greater,—while the threads can be pulled apart rather than cut?
                             Faithfully Yours,   W.W.

WWTLI (W. J. Bryan Papers, DNA).
¹ See WJB to WW, March 27, 1915.

From Edward Mandell House

[Bern, March 31, 1915]

Zimmermann says their reports indicate that German prisoners in Russia are being badly treated. He said that Germany would greatly appreciate your asking American Embassy at St. Petersburg to give the matter attention. I would suggest having the Secretary of State communicate with American Ambassador. This courtesy would please Germany.   Edward House

Transcripts of WWsh decode (WP, DLC; WC, NjP).

From William Jennings Bryan, with Enclosures

My dear Mr. President: Washington March 31, 1915.

I am sending you copy of a telegram which we have received from our Minister at Peking, together with my reply to it. If the reply does not conform to your wishes will you please indicate the changes you desire to have made and return it to me tomorrow so that I can have it enciphered by Mr. Davis—this is being done out of greater caution.

With assurances of high respect I am, my dear Mr. President,
Yours very sincerely,   W. J. Bryan

TLS (W. J. Bryan Papers, DNA).

E N C L O S U R E   I

Peking March 30, 1915, three p m. Recd. 1 p m.
Strictly confidential.

Embassy at Tokyo has repeated to me your instruction of March twenty six, four p m. to it: I have not received a repetition of the other telegram referred to in your March twenty-seven, one p m[1] nor any word as to the reply understood to have been given by Japan to your memorandum nor any indication whether use has been made of the suggestions embodied in your telegram of March twenty-six, four p m. to Japan.

From my knowledge of the attitude of the Chinese government and people I feel it my duty to inform you that the compromises suggested in that instruction are such as the Chinese feel would irrevocably derogate from the principle of administrative independence and, with no return even in the form of an assurance that they had bought peace by such concessions, would definitely set a term to the existence of China as a free country. Should they become aware that the American government favors an adjustment by which China would forego its freedom to choose advisers whom it trusts, to buy munitions according to its needs and without foreign supervision of its military organization and to exercise police functions independently in the territory still under its sovereignty, I fear that such knowledge would produce in the minds the Chinese a conviction that United States had betrayed its historic friendship and its moral responsibility in respect to principles of China's administrative integrity and the Open Door. If it is not the policy of the United States to take any preventive action in the present crisis I beg to submit that it would at any rate be more expedient to follow a course of passive acquiescence rather than to intervene in such a manner as could scarcely fail to cause revulsion of Chinese feeling against the United States and put an end to our influence here and our opportunities either of assisting the Chinese government or of preserving our own rights in China.

I therefore beg to urge that if there is still time Embassy at Tokyo be instructed to make no use of the suggestions referred to which if once communicated to the Japanese government would serve to render its attitude towards China more inexorable and could not of course be prevented from coming eventually to the knowledge of the Chinese.   Reinsch

T telegram (SDR, RG 59, 793.94/275, DNA).
1 That is, WJB to G. W. Guthrie, Tokyo, March 26, 1915, concerning Fukien, summarized in WJB to WW, March 25, 1915 (3rd letter of this date), n. 1.

E N C L O S U R E   I I

Amlegation Peking (China)   Washington, March 31, 1915.

Answering your March thirty, three p.m.

It is evident that you had not yet received the telegram which we sent Guthrie in regard to Fukien. We will cable Guthrie to forward that at once although you have probably received it before this. In that you will notice how carefully we have protected China's interests, assuming that China does not desire to grant a concession on the coast of Fukien. We have assured Japan that we do not desire any concession on the coast of Fukien, and we are sure that any concession granted to any other country would be very objectionable to Japan on account of her interests in Formosa.

The suggestion in regard to the railroad development of Fukien was also intended to protect China from the dangers that are attendant upon the granting of spheres of interest.

The suggestions to which you refer were not to be volunteered by Ambassador Guthrie but only to be made in case of inquiry, and they were worded as they were for the purpose of removing the friction between the two countries. China does not of course desire to discriminate against Japan either as to advisors or as to the purchase of arms, and that was all that was suggested.

The suggestion in regard to joint police was confined to specific places in Manchuria and eastern Mongolia and was conditioned upon China conceding such joint policing. We have not recommended joint policing but if joint policing is conceded, the fairest basis would seem to be the proportion that Japanese residents bear to the entire population.

We are very sorry if the advice that we have given in a spirit of friendliness to both nations should prove unacceptable, but, being given as advice it is no more binding upon China than upon Japan. Our original communication was sent by mail and has not yet reached Japan. You have received a copy of the abstract which we sent to Japan and we will ask Guthrie to send you a copy of the cabled reply to the abstract if it has not already been done.   Bryan

T telegram (SDR, RG 59, 793.94/275, DNA).

To William Jennings Bryan

My dear Mr. Secretary,   The White House. 31 March, 1915.

I am glad you are sending this.

I had read Rensch's message, in the flimsy sent me, and it had given me a good deal of concern.

I sincerely hope that this telegram will set the matter in the right light alike in Reinsch's mind and in the mind of the Chinese, when they learn of our interchange of views with Japan.

Faithfully Yours,   W.W.

WWTLI (W. J. Bryan Papers, DNA).

Paul Samuel Reinsch to William Jennings Bryan

Peking March 31, 1915.

Strictly confidential.

The Japanese at the conference held yesterday adopted an attitude of uncompromising exigence, the Minister stating that as the Chinese are now fully aware of the Japanese demands further discussion of the details is unnecessary and China is now expected to make categorical answer and be prepared for the consequences of refusal.

The demands as to the right of residence in the interior of Manchuria in addition to the opening of seventeen treaty ports there also those concerning Hanyehping and the right of Buddhist propaganda were insisted upon in toto. In regard to the last point it was stated that Japanese Buddhist monk[s] had given Count Okuma special support in the last election and that therefore their claim to missionary rights in China could not be ignored. The Chinese fear injection of political intrigue into the entire Buddhist system of China.

The most serious matter is the insistence of Japan upon the second portion of Hanyehping demand the effect of which would be to give Japanese interests the right of veto over competitive mining developments in the Yangtze region.

An ultimatum backed by force is momentarily expected.

Reinsch

T telegram (SDR, RG 59, 793.94/276, DNA).

To Edward Mandell House

[The White House, April 1, 1915]

Your full cable of Monday received and read with deep satisfaction and approval. The suggestion you are to carry to London seems to me very promising and may afford the opening we are looking for. Willard and Page have been given leave as requested. I warmly admire the way in which you are conducting your conferences at each stage. You are laying indispensable groundwork and sending me just the information I need.

In reply to your cable of the thirty-first, representations had already been made by the American Ambassador at Petrograd such as Zimmermann suggests, and I myself wrote a personal letter to the Czar at the request of the Austrian Ambassador here. Anything that has not been done will be done up to the limit of diplomatic privilege.   Wilson

Transcripts of WWsh telegram (WC, NjP; WP, DLC).

From Jean Jules Jusserand, with Enclosure

Dear Mr. President,   Washington April 1st, 1915.

I take the liberty of including herewith a translation of the telegram sent to the *Temps* by Mr. Alphaud[1] after he had the honour of being received by you. He gave it me to read and I do not think that there is in it anything which might be the cause of any trouble of any sort. If, contrary to what I believe, anything inscribed in it ought to have been erased, I cannot say how sincerely I would regret it, but I am confident such is not the case.[2]

I beg you to receive my sincere thanks for the great kindness you had of receiving this representative of the French press yesterday, and I beg you to believe me, dear Mr. President,

Very respectfully yours,   Jusserand

TLS (WP, DLC).
    [1] Gabriel Alphaud, an editor of *Le Temps* of Paris, accompanied by Jusserand, called upon Wilson at the White House on March 31.
    [2] On the evening of April 1, a White House spokesman, undoubtedly Tumulty, issued a statement declaring that the President had not given an interview or expressed any opinion on current affairs to Alphaud. Alphaud, it continued, had merely called at the White House to pay his respects, and it was understood specifically that he was not to discuss the war with the President or interview him. The following day Alphaud replied with a statement of his own:
    "I regret exceedingly having caused any annoyance to President Wilson, for whom I have the greatest respect both officially and personally. But the truth is the truth. Mr. Wilson was aware of my intention to send to the Temps the statements which he so graciously made to me. Moreover, I offered to submit to him an outline of my dispatch before sending it to my paper. But he very

courteously assured me in the presence of M. Jusserand. . . that he was willing to rely entirely upon my judgment in the matter. . . . I can only formally maintain both the text of my interview and the bona fide authorization which I had to publish the statements of the President." *New York Times*, April 2 and 3, 1915.

It is possible, of course, that Tumulty issued the White House statement without consulting Wilson. There is no correspondence in the Wilson Papers concerning this matter.

We may be sure that Wilson read Jusserand's letter because he wrote the notation, "Personal," in shorthand at the top of the first page. He did not acknowledge the letter.

E N C L O S U R E

Summary of What the President said:

I am glad to see on American soil Frenchmen who come to ascertain by themselves what is the state of public opinion in this country. I feel confident that you will not consider that there is for you any reasonable ground of complaint. Some particular facts and special cases give sometimes to the press of each of the opposed parties the impression that the American Government might favour at one time the one, and yet at another time, the other of the belligerents, but if both are thus impressed, is it not a sign that the United States conscienciously observe the rules of neutrality.

Belligerents may hold, at times, that we are too exacting and that we too strictly adhere to those rules: War will not last for ever; when it is finished, those nations will perhaps be glad that we have maintained the rules to which they may now take exception. France will certainly avoid the mistake of many who, in conflicts of such sorts, choose to consider that one who is not actively for us is necessarily against us.

For what concerns my own sentiments with regard to France, I have written to the President of the French Republic a letter in which I have clearly stated them.[1] Be assured that I do not think less than the letter says.

Being asked about the increase of the American Army and Navy presently mentioned by the papers, the President answered that such an augmentation had rather been slackened than hastened by present events owing to a desire to avoid false interpretations.

Being asked whether there was hope of a speedy termination of the Mexican trouble, the President said: The answer is a difficult one. Favourable symptoms, however, may be noted; the most recent information received here show, among the principal Mexican Chiefs, a better inclination to understand the reasons they have to respect the life and interests of foreigners. Nothing will be neglected by the American Government to confirm them in these tendencies.[2]

T MS (WP, DLC).
[1] WW to R. Poincaré, Dec. 7, 1914, Vol. 31.
[2] The French text appeared in *Le Temps*, April 2, 1915; a translation of the French text, with the dateline Paris, April 1, appeared in the *New York Times*, April 2, 1915.

From William Jennings Bryan, with Enclosure

My dear Mr. President: Washington April 2, 1915.

I am enclosing a memorandum by Mr. Lansing in regard to the Thrasher case.[1] The matter has been reported to us by Page and Consul-General Skinner[2] but we have not yet the details. It may be worth while to be considering the matter in advance.

It seems to me that the doctrine of contributory negligence has some bearing on this case—that is, the American who takes passage upon a British vessel knowing that this method of warfare will be employed, stands in a different position from that occupied by one who suffers without any fault of his own.

The first question raised is, What kind of a demand shall we make, if we make a demand? We can hardly insist that the presence of an American on a British ship shall operate to prevent attack unless we are prepared to condemn the methods employed as improper in warfare.

If we are to make a demand, shall we recognize the warfare as proper and ask indemnity for the loss of life? Can an American, by embarking upon a ship of the allies at such a time and under such conditions impose upon his Government an obligation to secure indemnity in case he suffers with others on the ship? I confes[s] I have not yet been able to reach a conclusion which is entirely satisfactory to me, but I send this memorandum that you may revolve it in your mind as the question will probably arise.

With assurances of high respect I am, my dear Mr. President,
Yours very sincerely,   W. J. Bryan

TLS (SDR, RG 59, 462.11 T 41/14½, DNA).
[1] On March 28, the German *U28* sank a small British passenger ship, *Falaba*, outward bound from Liverpool for West Africa, in Saint George's Channel. Among the passengers killed was an American citizen, Leon Chester Thrasher, who was returning to his post as a mining engineer in the Gold Coast. Accounts of the circumstances of the attack differ, but it is clear that the submarine commander fired his torpedo knowing that it would cause the death of many passengers. See Link, *Struggle for Neutrality*, pp. 358-59.
[2] Robert Peet Skinner, Consul-General at London.

E N C L O S U R E

Dear Mr. Secretary: [Washington] April 2, 1915.

The case of the death of an American citizen through the sinking of the British s.s. FABALA presents a question which will have to be decided and the decision will determine our policy in this case and in the event other Americans meet death in the same way.

I assume that, if the sinking of the FABALA had been the result of an attempt of the vessel to resist or to escape when summoned to stop or to surrender by a German submarine, there would be no ground of complaint for the loss of an American life as a result of the submarine's frustrating such attempt.

In that case the submarine would be exercising a belligerent right recognized by international law.

But the sinking of the FABALA, when no attempt is made to resist or escape, without giving the crew and passengers adequate time to leave the vessel is a different matter. It is a practice unwarranted by international usage.

Now the question is this: Ought we not to hold the German Government responsible for the death of an American through the act of their naval forces, when that act is in violation of the established rules of naval warfare?

An American taking passage on a belligerent merchant vessel is entitled to rely upon an enemy's war vessel conforming to the established rules of visit and search and of protection of non-combatants. He should not be exposed to greater dangers than the enforcement of the rules impose. If this is a correct statement, duty would appear to require a complaint and a demand for damages.

On the other hand, to enter complaint on account of the death of an American in these circumstances would compel this Government to denounce the sinking of merchant vessels in the manner referred to as a flagrant violation of international law. In fact it would be a denunciation of the German "war zone" plan, or at least of the method of carrying it out.

While as yet we are not fully advised as to the facts of the case I think that the policy of the Government should be determined in order that we may act promptly if action seems advisable and necessary, as delay in entering complaint and denunciation would be, in my opinion, a matter of just criticism.

I would like to be advised as to the policy of the Government in order that preparations may be made to act in case it is decided to act.   Faithfully yours,   Robert Lansing.

This editorial from the N. Y. Herald of today[1] came to my attention after this letter was written. I believe that it indicates the attitude of many other newspapers.   RL

TLS (SDR, RG 59, 462.11 T 41/14½, DNA).
   [1] "To a Strict Accountability," saying that Thrasher's death raised the issue outlined in the State Department's note to Berlin of February 10. It called the killing of Thrasher and other passengers "cold blooded murder" and asked in conclusion: "What is the government of the United States going to do about it?"

From William Jennings Bryan

My dear Mr. President: Washington April 2, 1915.

When I sent you the Sullivan letter which was put in evidence by Mr. Gray, you replied that the language of the letter made it impossible for him to remain there. I feel that this is the only conclusion that can be reached unless we intend to discard the rules that govern diplomatic relations.

Of course Santo Domingo is not in a position to demand the recall of Minister Sullivan, but since his language has been published it would seem to be ungenerous in us, to say the least, to insist upon his remaining there.

Assuming that you have not changed your opinion on the subject, there are two questions which I beg to submit:
   1. In what manner shall the matter be brought to his attention?
   2. When shall it be done?
With assurances of high rexpect I am, my dear Mr. President,
          Yours very sincerely,   W. J. Bryan

TLS (W. J. Bryan Papers, DNA).

From William Jennings Bryan, with Enclosures

My dear Mr. President: Washington April 2, 1915.

I have prepared, with the aid of Mr. Williams' suggestions, two telegrams, one to Ambassador Guthrie, making inquiry in regard to the terms of the proposed agreement in regard to the Han-yeh-ping corporation and one to Minister Reinsch in regard to the rights of Buddist missionaries.

If you approve of sending them please return the despatches

with any corrections you wish to make to the State Department telegraph office so they can go tonight.

With assurances of high respect I am, my dear Mr. President,

Yours very sincerely,   W. J. Bryan

TLS (W. J. Bryan Papers, DNA).

E N C L O S U R E   I

Amembassy Tokio.   April 2, 1915.

The newspapers report that the proposal in regard to Han-yeh-ping Corporation includes a provision which would give to the Japanese interests in that section the right of veto over any competing mining developments in the Yangste region. Will you please ascertain whether anything is contemplated which would discriminate against the nationals of other countries and if so what territory is understood to be included in the area thus described. In the confidential communication submitted to us the language used is quote Agreement in principle to have the Han-yeh-ping Iron and Coal Company become a Chino-Japanese corporation at an appropriate time in the future unquote. There is no suggestion in the memorandum of anything that would discriminate against the nationals of other countries.

T telegram (W. J. Bryan Papers, DLC).

E N C L O S U R E   I I

Amlegation Peking.   Washington, April 2, 1915. 9 pm

We are making inquiry in regard to the newspaper reports that the proposal in regard to the Han-yeh-ping corporation includes provisions which would discriminate against nationals of other countries. *For your personal guidance we would say that*[1] We do not see how China can justify refusing to grant to Buddist missionaries from Japan the same rights which she grants to Christian missionaries from other countries. It would seem necessary to grant the same religious privileges to representatives of all religions and all nations.   Bryan

T telegram (SDR, RG 59, 793.94/276, DNA).
[1] WWhw.

From William Jennings Bryan

My dear Mr. President: Washington April 2, 1915.

I am sending you a telegram which I have prepared.[1] I did not have opportunity to take this matter up with you this morning but it occurs to me that something ought to be done to bring to all factions the importance of getting together before the situation is further complicated. Possibly it might be better for me to see the Washington representatives of Villa and Carranza and bring the matter to them verbally and let them deal with their respective governments. What do you think? I am apprehensive as to the result of Huerta's presence on this side of the Atlantic.[2] We found him to be a strong man when backed by the interests which supported him and he may, if he re-enters the contest, prolong the situation indefinitely.

With assurances of high respect I am, my dear Mr. President,
Yours very sincerely,   W. J. Bryan

TLS (W. J. Bryan Papers, DNA).
   [1] It is missing.
   [2] Victoriano Huerta sailed from Cadiz, Spain, on March 31, allegedly bound for the West Indies. Rumors that he was planning a counterrevolutionary expedition to Mexico began to circulate immediately. As it turned out, he landed at New York on April 12 and spent most of his time there for the next several months. *New York Times*, April 1, 11, and 13, 1915. His subsequent movements, arrest, and detention by United States officials will be related in future volumes.

Four Letters to William Jennings Bryan

My dear Mr. Secretary,   The White House. 3 April, 1915.

I sent these over to the telegraph office at your Department last evening about eight, or a little after, to be transmitted at once.

I added a few words to the message to Reinsch, to say that it was sent for his information, so that he would not feel bound to communicate it to the Chinese government unless he thought it opportune and wise to do so.

Faithfully Yours,   W.W.

WWTLI (W. J. Bryan Papers, DNA).

My dear Mr. Secretary,   The White House. 3 April, 1915.

I do not like this case. It is full of disturbing possibilities.

But it is clear to me that this American citizen came to his death by reason of acts on the part of German naval officers which were in unquestionable violation of the just rules of international law with regard to unarmed vessels at sea; and it is probably our duty to make it clear to the German Government that we will insist that the lives of our citizens shall not be put in danger by acts which have no sanction whatever in the accepted law of nations.

I think it would be wise for Mr. Lansing to draw a brief and succint note in the matter for mature consideration, so that we may formulate our position in precise terms.

Faithfully Yours,   W.W.

WWTLI (SDR, RG 59, 462.11 T 41/15½, DNA).

My dear Mr. Secretary,   The White House. 3 April, 1915.

I feel as you do about this; but I think that it would be wiser for you to see the representatives of the factions who are here, than to send this message. You could go into the matter more fully with them and make the whole situation so clear that they would see that it was really imperative for them to act.

Faithfully Yours,   W.W.

My dear Mr. Secretary,   The White House. 3 April, 1915.

I think that the best way is to bring the matter very frankly to the attention of the Minister just as it lies in our minds. He will, I feel sure, see that his only right course is to resign.

But I think it is fair to await the report from Senator Phelan, and when we have it to let Mr. Sullivan's resignation be as much disconnected from it as possible.

Faithfully Yours,   W.W.

WWTLI (W. J. Bryan Papers, DNA).

From William Jennings Bryan, with Enclosure

My dear Mr. President: Washington April 3, 1915.

I am sending you a telegram to Minister Long which has been drafted in accordance with your instructions. Will you please send it to the State Department Telegraph Office with such changes as you desire to make.

With assurances of high respect I am, my dear Mr. President,
Yours very sincerely,   W. J. Bryan

TLS (W. J. Bryan Papers, DNA).

E N C L O S U R E¹

Amlegation San Salvador.   Washington, April 3, 1915.

Your telegram in regard to the possibility of securing from Salvador the lease of land for a naval base in return for certain advantages to be afforded in the establishment of a university there² has been considered by the President and you are directed to communicate with the Foreign Office and secure from them the outline of such a proposition as would be favor⟨able to⟩ed by them. This Government is disposed to give favorable consideration to the plan and appreciates the high purpose which actuates the Salvadorean Government. While we are not in a position to give financial assistance as a Government we ⟨have no doubt⟩ hope that American financiers will, when their attention is called to the matter, be willing to furnish the capital necessary for the bank and for the reorganization of the financial system of the country. The President is disposed to favorably consider a treaty having in view the acquiring of the site for a naval base, this Government, in return, to establish a College or University open and free to the young men of Salvador. Please inquire whether Salvador would have any objections to our making the same provision with Honduras in case that country desired to enter into a similar treaty. Also as to whether there would be any objection to having young men from other Latin-American republics admitted to the institution. We take it for granted that Salvador would not object to others being admitted, provided accomodations were sufficient. We shall be pleased to receive an outline of the plan which the Government of Salvador has in mind.³   Bryan

T telegram (SDR, RG 59, 817.812/123, DNA).
¹ Words in angle brackets deleted by Wilson; those in italics added by him.
² B. W. Long to WJB, March 26, 1915, T telegram (SDR, RG 59, 817.812/123, DNA). Long reported that President Carlos Melendez of Salvador had recently told him that he would like to see a working partnership between the Central American countries and the United States, in which the former would agree to the building of a United States naval base in the Gulf of Fonseca in return for the assistance of the United States in economic development. In particular, the President wanted to see Salvador "put on a gold basis," to have "an American bank of large capital" opened there, and to have established at the proposed naval base "an American school free to certain male students of Central America where the English language, industrial, agricultural, economic and business courses would be taught and possibly elementary military training given." Melendez promised to sound out the governments of Costa Rica and Guatemala about the plan; however, he thought that any official initiative should come from the United States.
³ Bryan, highly enthusiastic about the proposal, soon instructed Long to conduct personal discussions in all the Central American capitals. Long reported favorable reaction in Nicaragua, Honduras, and Salvador on June 5 and urged that the State Department take quick action. Bryan's resignation as Secretary of State on June 8 and the Lusitania crisis with Germany caused the tem-

porary shelving of the project. It was revived in November, and Long, at Secretary Lansing's direction, drafted treaties to be proposed to Guatemala, Salvador, Costa Rica, and Nicaragua. However, they were never presented to the Central American governments. Instead, the United States Senate proceeded, on February 18, 1916, to approve the Bryan-Chamorro Treaty with Nicaragua. In spite of a Senate amendment to the treaty protecting the rights of Costa Rica, Honduras, and Salvador, the ratification of this treaty provoked a storm of protest in Central America. See Link, *The New Freedom*, pp. 343-46.

From William Jennings Bryan

My dear Mr. President: Washington April 3, 1915.

I have conferred with Mr. Lansing in regard to the Hatien situation. It presents a number of embarrassments and I am not sure that I know just what your wishes are in the matter. I therefore present my view of the subject in such form that you may give your opinion upon the several propositions, and a despatch can then be prepared. I think it is important that early action be taken.

First: As to our Minister there. I am disappointed in Bailly-Blanchard. This is the only case in which we have selected a secretary for promotion, but owing to his diplomatic experience, and owing also to the fact that he spoke the French language perfectly I thought he was the man for this particular work and recommended him to you. Mr. Lansing, who knew him in Paris, thinks that he is an excellent man for secretary but is as disappointed as I am with his conduct as Minister. It is my opinion that he should be recalled.

In appointing him I told him that when he had finished his work in Haiti we would give him a position as secretary and would, if possible, send him to Paris. He served for many years in Paris, but was first secretary in Japan when we made him Minister. There is no position among the first secretaries open at this time and I do not know how we can restore him to his rank until we are ready to send a secretary to Mexico, and then we can make some rearrangement of the secretaries that would give him a place. I send you flimsy of the despatch in which he replied to the complaint made by Governor Fort—in wiring the rebuke we did not, of course, mention Fort's name.[1]

Second: In case you think it wise to recall Bailly-Blanchard have you anyone in mind for the place? This is about the only place except Liberia to which we could send a colored man—but I am not sure that it would be wise to send a colored man there at this time. The other nations have white men and I think that they have more influence with the President than a colored man would have. Those with whom I have talked believe that they would have more respect for a white man than for one of their own color.

If we send a colored man I think Bishop Walters is the best man we have, but I am inclined to think we would better have a white man there until we get things in better shape.

Third: If we send a white man have you anyone in mind for the place? We might as well recognize the fact that the prejudice of the country is against us and this prejudice is not likely to grow less as long as the French Minister is the advisor of the President, and as long as the German merchants have eighty-five per cent of the local business. It is desirable, of course, that the Minister shall speak French, but I have found that the language is not so important as the *man* and, therefore, I would not consider the knowledge of the language as indispensible.

Fourth: As to the course to be pursued in dealing with Haiti. The man who is now acting as President[2] desires recognition, and Bailly-Blanchard telegraphed that he thought if we gave recognition we could secure, at the time of giving recognition, certain agreements—one in respect to Mole St. Nicholas.

I take it for granted from what you have said, that you have not changed your mind as to Mole St. Nicholas and that it should not be permitted to pass into the hands of other foreign governments, or foreign capitalists. I think we have to decide as to the attitude of the Government toward the whole Hatien situation. As long as the Government is under French or German influence American interests are going to be discriminated against there as they are discriminated against now. A Frenchman named Reine, who has a Hatien wife, has come back and has been put in charge of the Bank. The German holdings and the American holdings together constitute one-half the stock, but as the German holdings are not allowed to vote now, the French are in control although they have only half the stock. The American interests are willing to remain there, with a view of purchasing a controlling interest and making the Bank a branch of the American bank—they are willing to do this provided this Government takes the steps necessary to protect them and their idea seems to be that no protection will be sufficient that does not include a control of the Customs House.

I have been reluctant to favor anything that would require an exercise of force there but there are some things that lead me to believe it may be necessary for us to use as much force as may be necessary to compel a supervision which will be effective. Following the line of your Mobile speech we have as much reason to object to the control of a Latin-American Government by foreign financiers as by a foreign government, and there is no doubt that the foreign financiers have been a controlling interest in the politics of Haiti.

Then, again, Haiti shares the Island with Santo Domingo and it has been customary for these two governments to aid revolutions against each other. The revolutions of Haiti, therefore, are a constant menace to the stability of Santo Domingo.

If, for the two reasons mentioned—namely, that foreign capitalists are controlling the government, and that the Hatien Government is disturbing the peace of Santo Domingo—it should be decided to insist upon some more active supervision in the government, the two questions remaining are the *time* and the *method*.

I am inclined to think that this would be a better time than later although there are two sides to the proposition and I recognize that arguments can be made in favor of delay as well as in favor of early action.

As to method—I have wondered whether it would be wise to propose a plan similar to that which The Netherlands adopts in Java—namely, having a resident Advisor. I am not sure but the same plan is employed in some of the provinces of India. The government is in the hands of natives but a representative of the outside Government resides at the capital and *advises* the native officials. That might not be so offensive as to have foreign officials actually collecting the customs, as in Santo Domingo. Even if it were not regarded as permanently sufficient it might be the means of making a beginning. I am inclined to think it worth trying before demanding such a control as we have in Santo Domingo.

I have presented above the various propositions involved in the problem. When I have your answer to these I can then prepare the necessary telegrams. I do not think it would be necessary for us to go further than to make a demand, with a good sized ship there ready to enforce the demand; but we must, before acting, take into consideration all the possibilities.

With assurances of high respect I am, my dear Mr. President,
Yours very sincerely,   W. J. Bryan

TLS (W. J. Bryan Papers, DLC).

1 A. Bailly-Blanchard to WJB, March 27, 1915, T telegram (W. J. Bryan Papers, DLC), insisting that he had done everything in his power to cooperate with the commission to Haiti headed by Governor Fort.

2 Vilbrun Guillaume Sam.

From William Jennings Bryan, with Enclosure

My dear Mr. President: Washington April 3, 1915.

I send you a flimsy of a despatch just received from Santiago. The Chilean Ambassador notified me yesterday afternoon that he had received an answer from his Government which he would be able to submit Monday. He said that it was in the nature of a *counter proposition* and I think eliminates the guaranty of territorial integrity and the guaranty of republican government.

He also said that he understood from Mr. House that *the plan would not be presented to the other countries unless it had the approval of the three large countries*[1]—Brazil, Argentine and Chile to whom Mr. House confided the plan. The Chilean Ambassador also gathered the idea that the chief purpose was to have the South American countries join in the Monroe Doctrine and he did not seem favorably inclined to the idea of protecting each South American country against other South American countries.

The flimsy presents Chile's proposals in regard to the settlement of disputes between Chile and Peru. I wonder if it would not be well to take up this subject with Peru and see if any progress can be made toward settlement.

With assurances of high rexpect I am, my dear Mr. President,
                         Yours very sincerely,   W. J. Bryan

TLS (SDR, RG 59, 710.11/199½A, DNA).
[1] Emphasis by Wilson.

E N C L O S U R E

                                   Santiago April 2, 1915.

Your March thirty-one, seven p m.[1]

The Foreign Office informs me that reply was telegraphed to the Chilean Ambassador thirtieth ultimo. Strictly confidential. In connection with the above Sub-Secretary of State for Foreign Affairs[2] stated that the Chilean government willingly complies with your wishes to know their proposals in regard to Tacna-Arica[3] and that they are as follows:

First. Plebiscite to take place at the end of one year.

Second. Voters must have lived in that territory at least one year and must know how to read and write; further that the Chilean government accepts that the winning country pay to the other country an amount even in excess of the amount named in the treaty of Ancon.[4]   Summerlin[5]

T telegram (SDR, RG 59, 723.2515/300, DNA).

1 WJB to H. P. Fletcher, March 31, 1915, printed as an addendum in this volume.

2 Carlos Castro Ruiz.

3 Two former Peruvian provinces occupied by Chile as a result of its victory in the War of the Pacific, 1879-1884.

4 The Treaty of Ancón, signed by Peru and Chile in 1884, which provided that, following ten years of occupation by Chile, the permanent ownership of Tacna and Arica would be decided by a plebiscite of their inhabitants. The nation which thus gained the two provinces would pay the loser ten million silver pesos. However, the plebiscite had never been held.

5 George Thomas Summerlin, Secretary of the United States embassy in Santiago.

From Edward Mandell House

[Paris, April 3, 1915]

Your cable of the second received and makes me very happy.

Thomas Page has given me much information of value. When Italy thinks the war will end in a few months she will go in on the side of the Allies. She is not prepared for a long contest but could have assisted the Allies only a little had she entered sooner. When the Dardanelles fall it is probable that Greece and Rumania will both enter. Should we attempt to force matters further than I have already suggested, we would probably lose the advantage we have gained. If our people grow impatient, I would suggest that you tell them that you are doing everything possible to bring about peace and that they must accept your assurance of this without asking for details.

Thomas Page now understands the whole program and will work on it and report later.

I go to Biarritz on Monday to meet Willard; then back to Paris by the 15th.

It is practically impossible to send letters except from embassies.   Edward House

Transcripts of WWsh decode (WC, NjP; WP, DLC).

To Mary Allen Hulbert

Dearest Friend,   The White House 4 April, 1915.

It has been very good of you to write while I was unable to answer. For I really have been unable to answer. I do not suppose that the work has in fact been harder and more constant and exacting in its demands on me of late; it has seemed so, but probably only because it was more exacting in its kind and put such a strain on my judgment and thought that it "took it out of me" more than usual. And then the strain has now lasted so long! That no doubt makes it tell on me more than before. This is what happens, every day. After the work of the long forenoon, and after I have had the game of golf in the early afternoon by which I keep myself physically fit, I find a thick bundle of despatches and other papers awaiting me which have been sent over from the Department of State, marked "Private and Important" or "Confidential and Immediate," which when opened prove to contain a miscellany of just about every sort of problem that can arise in the foreign affairs of a nation in a time of general questioning and difficulty: from Japan, China, the Philippines, Mexico, Chile, San Domingo, Haiti, England, Germany, and Turkey. It is not uncommon for matters to turn up from every one of these within a few hours; and often it is necessary for me to work far into the night to give them prompt and careful attention. They will not wait to be pondered upon these days. Delay may mean misunderstandings or deeper difficulties. I must form and express an opinion within a few hours. So down I sit and attach to each of them a memorandum of suggestion or instruction which I write out on this machine, sign, and put all together into a big envelope which I seal (literally, to make sure that it is not opened in transit from me to the Secretary) and send by messenger to the Secretary, wherever he happens to be, so that subordinates may not handle and delay in delivery. And after this is done (it has to be done on Sunday as well as other days) there seems to be nothing left in me. It would be impossible to write a letter such as one would be willing to ask to pass as one!

And yet how happy I should be to repay you in kind for the letters I am so glad to see, especially now that they give me reason to hope that you are better and that things go a little more hopefully for you. My heart sank when I learned that Allen had bought a business (which I take it for granted he knew nothing about) so soon after reaching Los Angeles, but your later letter reassures me. I suppose the moving picture business requires as little working capital as a business could require that involved rentals and equipment and salaries to employees, and that energy and personal attention to it is the way to success. And you are simply splendid! Nothing can conquer you, or break that spirit that I so much admire and that seems to bring you untouched out of everything,—I mean untouched in anything that is essential. I wish you could be out with Allen now! It would be like additional capital to him, and better.

Is there any way I can help in finding a publisher for the cook book? Did I give you a letter of introduction that would help you with the publishers?

Alas! No: I shall not be able to go to New York at any time soon that I can foresee, or anywhere else that is more than a few miles away from my desk and the despatches. I say "alas," not because I want to go to New York; there is no place I would rather stay away from; but because, if you are going to be there, it would be so refreshing to get a glimpse of you. Talks are so much better than letters. I have not forgotten how to talk, but I have forgotten how to write letters, or anything else except memorandum for the State Department. I wonder if I could make a speech now, or have altogether and unalterably turned into a writer of despatches! My letters are only messages. They only say (and I hope say in the tone in which I feel them) that my thought is constantly of the friends I love, and that all my little household joins in affectionate messages.

Your devoted friend,   Woodrow Wilson

WWTLS (WP, DLC).

To William Jennings Bryan

My dear Mr. Secretary,   The White House. 5 April, 1915.

I had already seen this memorandum of Mr. Lansing's.[1] I appreciate its force to the full. But it ought not to alter our course so long as we think ourselves on the firm ground of right.

It has, as Mr. Lansing points out, its bearings on the Thrasher case. That case, as I said the other day, troubles me. I should very much like to know what Mr. L's view of it is. We must compound policy with legal right in wise proportions, no doubt.

Faithfully Yours,   W.W.

WWTLI (SDR, RG 59, 462.11 T 41/13½, DNA).
[1] "Relations with Germany and Possibilities," Feb. 15, 1915, TS memorandum (SDR, RG 59, 462.11 T 41/12½, DNA), printed in *FR-LP*, I, 367-68. Lansing briefly outlined the possible advantages and disadvantages to Germany of war with the United States. He believed that such a conflict would produce little change in Germany's military and naval situation. Therefore, he concluded that the advantages of a free hand in disrupting United States trade with the Allies and possible civil strife created by German Americans in the United States would outweigh the disadvantages of the cessation of the already very limited United States trade with Germany and the loss of capital tied up in German ships already interned in American ports.

From William Jennings Bryan

My dear Mr. President: Washington April 5, 1915.

A man called this morning to inform me that he had just talked with one of our Americans residing in Mexico City, who told him that a plan was on foot for an uprising on the part of the foreigners, who wanted to take Mexico City, establish a government and hold the City until the United States would be forced into intervention.

I told him I could not regard such a plan as really entertained and that we would be sure to hear about any such movement from our representative down there, but I communicate this to you for whatever it is worth. I will inquire of the Brazilian Minister if he has heard of any such plot.

With assurances of high respect I am, my dear Mr. President,
Yours very sincerely,   W. J. Bryan

TLS (W. J. Bryan Papers, DNA).

Three Letters to William Jennings Bryan

My dear Mr. Secretary,   The White House. 5 April, 1915.

I think it would be well to tell this gentleman, in case he should have some channel of communication with the foreigners of whom he speaks, that any action on their part of the sort indicated would have just the opposite effect to that intended. It would absolutely outlaw them and put them at the mercy of the Mexicans outside the pale either of domestic or of international law.   Faithfully Yours,   W.W.

It may have been a feeler.

WWTLI (W. J. Bryan Papers, DNA).

My dear Mr. Secretary,   The White House. 5 April, 1915.

I shall await the note from Chile with deep interest.

Will you not be kind enough to have a talk with Ambassador Naon and ascertain whether he got the impression from House that the Chilean Ambassador seems to have got, that we would not propose our treaty to the other countries of South and Central America unless all three of the A.B.C. approved. I remember nothing of the kind, and think Mr. Suarrez must be mistaken.

I think it would be wise, as you suggest, to approach the Peruvian government very tactfully and ascertain whether they are willing to treat matters in dispute between them and Chile as the enclosed despatch suggests.

Faithfully Yours,   W.W.

WWTLI (SDR, RG 59, 710.11/200½, DNA).

My dear Mr. Secretary,   The White House. 5 April, 1915.

I wish that I were clearer in my judgment about this perplexing case, and were more confident that I am right in what I say
in reply to the queries of this letter.[1] I can only speak with hesitation, and speak now because reflection does not seem to do much
towards leading me to firm ground.

May I take your points in a different order, so as to begin
where I am clearest?

First. The time to act is now.

Second. We must make certain demands and make them as
conditions of recognition, backed by the intimation that we will
not take No for answer:

1) The use and control of Mole Saint Nicholas, or, at the
least, the exclusion there of foreign control;

2) An advisor, who must be regarded as our spokesman and
who must be understood, in his advice, to speak the conditions upon which this Government will support the government of Haiti, our object being, not merely to safeguard
foreign interests on the island with entire impartiality, but
also to prevent the constant recurrence of revolution there
and the assistance thence of revolution in San Domingo. Our
support and countenance to be depended on so long as the
government there honestly sought to represent and serve the
people of the Republic.

In this connection we ought to let them know that the
management of the customs was the point of danger which we
would watch, and through our Advisor control, with the greatest
vigilance.

Third. Let us select now some able and trustworthy man,
thoroughly conversant with French, whom we would in all
likelihood eventually make our Advisor there, to be sent at once
as our special agent and spokesman to make these demands
known and carry the new arrangement through by negotiation.
Unfortunately, I do not know of such a man. Is it not possible
that Mr. Fuller could put us in the way of finding one, the Cou-
derts being French, though of course it should not be a Frenchman, in the circumstances?

Fourth. When this is over (Bailly-Blanchard having been set
aside in these negotiations) find another place for B.-B. and
send Bishop Walters to act as Minister, alongside the Advisor.

I shall be very much interested to know what you think of
these suggestions.   Faithfully Yours,   W.W.

WWTLI (W. J. Bryan Papers, DLC).
[1] Bryan's letter of April 3 about the Haitian situation.

From Edward Mandell House

Dear Governor: Nice, France. April 5th, 1915.

I am taking a chance upon sending this letter to you by hand through a friend of Mr. Page's whom he met today and who sails on the 6th via the southern route.

I have had word from England since we arrived here that sentiment is hardening against Germany because of the submarine depredations upon passenger ships. I shall doubtless find it more difficult to proceed now than before I left there.

I am enclosing you a copy of a letter which I have just sent to Gerard and which is for the consumption of Zimmermann and the Chancellor.[1]

I do not think it safe to write fully and will not do so until I return to Paris.

Stovall told me that the Swiss authorities would like to know something further concerning the purposes of the second convention. I outlined its intentions only in a general terms and I think we had better stick to that for the present.

I am leaving here in a few minutes for Biarritz to meet Mr. Willard. I am afraid that things will go slowly from now unless something decisive happens. Wilmot [the Allies] is evidently having a harder time forcing the Dardanelles than anticipated. When that is done, if it is done, something is likely to happen.

Affectionately yours,   E. M. House

TLS (WP, DLC).
[1] The enclosure is missing, but it was EMH to J. W. Gerard, April 5, 1915, TCL (E. M. House Papers, CtY), the significant portions of which follow:
"Will you not kindly say to Herr Zimmermann that I cabled the President immediately upon reaching Switzerland and that I have a reply here saying that he has written the Czar a personal letter, and that he will do everything that is diplomatically possible. . . .
"I have letters from England which indicate that the sentiment there is hardening towards Germany because of the sinking of passenger boats by submarines. These letters indicate that I will not find, upon my return to London, a spirit as receptive as that which I left. My opinion has always been that this war might have been more easily ended earlier than now and the longer it continues, the more bitter the feeling will grow and the more difficult the problem of adjustment will become.
"If it continues many months longer, with the ever increasing tendency on both sides to disregard international usage, there will soon arise an uncontrollable sentiment in each belligerent nation for complete destruction of the enemy.
"One of the worst features of this contest is the hate that it has engendered and which may breed trouble and disaster for a century to come. It is all too bad that the sensible people of all countries cannot get together in a fair spirit of compromise looking, not so much to their immediate selfish interest, but to the larger good which would come from such an attitude."

From Henry White

Personal & Confidential

Dear Mr President   Washington [April 5, 1915].

Pray forgive me for not having answered more promptly the note, in which you did me the honor to suggest that I sketch you a digest of certain opinions contained in letters which I have received from Berlin recently.

The delay has been for the most part unavoidable but I am also somewhat embarrassed by conflicting feelings; i.e. a desire to comply with your wishes as well as to be of any use to you within my power; coupled with a strong disinclination to put in writing anything savoring of criticism—much less complaint—of a high official who finds himself in a position of exceptional difficulty and delicacy, for which he has not only had no previous training, but is also I fear not adapted by temperament.

My letters contain a series of reasons for the feelings of antagonism to our Ambassador which, I am afraid, undoubtedly exist in German and American circles at Berlin. They are chiefly based upon a series of tactless remarks to individuals some of them verging upon discourtesy and even incivility. One such for instance being to a personage of considerable importance who had come to discuss with the Ambassador the expenditure of money sent from this country for the relief [of] Russian Poles. "You can take my conditions or leave them but they shall stay as I have said" and also to the same individual: "you are merely wasting my time in discussing matters of that kind until I hear from home as to whether money will be given for that purpose at all and let me add that I am very adverse to any of our good American money being spent in Germany any way." These remarks standing by themselves would not of course be of much importance; but a considerable number of them, made during a series of months, to people who are in a condition of extreme sensitiveness as to public opinion in the country represented by the Ambassador, and who compare notes with each other, are not unlikely to produce feelings the reverse of sympathetic towards him.

This of course is unfortunate, but I do not see that you can do anything to remedy the situation; as it is impossible to impart a conciliatory and sympathetic manner to one who is not naturally gifted therewith, and I very much doubt whether the Ambassador realizes the causes of his unpopularity. I have no actual reason to know—or even to suspect—that he is really anti-German in this war, but such is unfortunately the feeling which he has undoubtedly produced and by which he is irritated and is not always able to disguise his feelings of irritation. Moreover I have little doubt that his recent candidacy for the Senate had an unfortunate effect upon his position in Germany, where it was known, or believed, that a large majority of those whose votes he was seeking, are anti-German in their feelings, and it was not unnaturally suspected that he would make efforts to show them that his views and theirs were identical. He also probably does not realize what you understand so well and have recently furnished evidence thereof, (if I may venture to say so) in your admirable note to Great Britain just published; namely: that absolute firmness can be combined with perfect courtesy.

Let me add however that whatever may be thought of the Ambassador there is but one opinion—and that an entirely different one—of the tact, sympathy, gentleness and courtesy of his charming wife, who does much to counteract the conditions which have been described to me and who is really, I believe, loved in the circles to which I am referring.

And with regard to the last paragraph of your note, let me add furthermore that I do not suppose anyone in this country, now that Rockhill[1] is dead, appreciates as fully as I do, the extent to which you are overwhelmed with work "in these crowded and rushing days." For that reason I did not ask you to see me on a matter respecting which there is no action which I could suggest you taking. Knowing as I do—many of them, intimately, ever since we were colleagues as young men at different diplomatic posts—those who are conducting the affairs of the nations now at war, I often wish I could be of some assistance to you in your heavy labors but I do not see how I could be just now. I hope you know however that I am always at your disposal.

Believe me, dear Mr President

Very Sincerely Yours   Henry White

Private & Confidential

P.S. The enclosed extract from a private letter which I have received from London may be of interest to you and possibly of some use:

"I wish the stethoscope could be applied, as —— could apply it—to British French & German chests and, by expert auscultation, it could be discovered what chances there are of a deal being made before ruin stares *everybody* in the face. The pleasing fiction that Germany is on the verge of exhaustion in food & men & that Asquith's campaign bluster about smashing German militarism is likely soon to be realized, deceives people less and less."

I may add that my butler who has just returned from a visit to England reports a very strong desire among the people of his class for a cessation of the war and also that the troops to be seen about England are for the most part now below the average size—"quite small men & boys" as he expresses it.

Doubtless you will receive interesting information soon from Colonel House, whose name I was very sorry to see had got into the newspapers, doubtless through no fault of his own, as it is likely to nullify his efforts even at getting information; as those in authority will fear being suspected of seeking peace by talking to him. In spite of the above quotation from my London letter, I do not believe any "honest broker" from this country or elsewhere can yet be of any use towards peace.

ALS (WP, DLC).
1 William Woodville Rockhill, distinguished American career diplomat, died Dec. 8, 1914.

Robert Lansing to William Jennings Bryan, with Enclosure

Personal and Confidential.

Dear Mr. Secretary: [Washington] April 5, 1915.

In compliance with the President's note to you of the 3rd, I have drafted a memorandum for an instruction to Ambassador Gerard in the Thrasher case.

The tone of the instruction is not conciliatory, and the language is plain almost to harshness. Probably it can be softened without weakening it.

I feel this: If it is decided to denounce the sinking of the FALABA as an act indefensible legally and morally, we will have to say so, and I do not see how we can say it in a pleasant way. We are dealing with a tragedy. It seems to me that we must assert our rights, condemn the violation and state the remedy which we expect. If we do this without evincing a firm determination to insist on compliance, the German Government will give little heed to the note and may even show contempt for its weakness.

Furthermore, American public opinion will never stand for a colorless or timid presentation of a case, in which an American has been killed by an atrocious act of lawlessness.

If the note is weak or uncertain, it had better not be sent. The situation does not seem to me to be one for compromise. We can not take the position that Thrasher should have kept out of the war zone. To do so would amount to an admission of Germany's right to perform lawless acts in that area. This would unquestionably arouse a storm of criticism, and I think that it would be justified.

On the other hand, the consequences of a strong, vigorous note may be most momentous.

In spite of the critical situation which may result I do not see how we can let the matter pass without protest.

As I said to you, I think that this case is pregnant with more sinister possibilities than any with which the Government has had to deal. After mature consideration from various points of view, I can not advise against a firm demand, and yet I feel the gravest anxiety as to the results of such a course. It by no means means war, but it means intense hostility and the charge of open support of the enemies of Germany.

Faithfully yours,   Robert Lansing.

TLS (WP, DLC).

ENCLOSURE

Confidential Memorandum for Instruction to
American Ambassador at Berlin, April 5, 1915.

THRASHER CASE. The Government of the United States has received a report, confirmed by substantial evidence, that Leon C. Thrasher, a native born American citizen, came to his death by reason of the act of the German naval authorities in sinking the British passenger steamer FALABA on the high seas on the 28th of March, 1915, outward bound from Liverpool, and the failure of the commander of the German submarine U-28 to give ample time for the crew and passengers of the FALABA to leave the vessel before sinking her by means of torpedoes. It is further reported that, at the time when the FALABA was torpedoed and sunk, she was lying to, making no attempt to escape and offering no resistance.

The circumstances of the sinking of the FALABA, by which Thrasher with scores of other non-combatants, irrespective of age and sex, met their death, indicate a wantonness and indifference to the rules of civilized warfare by the German naval officer responsible for the deed, which are without palliation or excuse. This is aggravated by the fact that the vessel was departing from and not approaching British territory. So flagrant a violation of international law and international morality requires from a neutral government, whose citizen has been a victim of the outrage, an unequivocal expression of its views as to such conduct and as to the duty of the belligerent government, whose officers are guilty of the violation.

The Government of the United States considers that a United States citizen is entitled to rely upon the practice, heretofore universally observed by belligerent warships, of visiting and searching merchant vessels of enemy as well as of neutral nationality and of protecting the lives of their crews and passengers whatever disposition may be made of the vessels and their cargoes. No notice by a belligerent government that it intends to depart from this practice within a certain area of the high seas can deprive justly a neutral of his rights or relieve the government disregarding those rights from full responsibility for the acts of its naval authorities performed in accordance with such notice.

The Government of the United States is loth to believe that the German Imperial Government authorized, much less directed, the officers of the Imperial Navy to perpetrate acts as ruthless and brutal as the sinking of the FALABA before her helpless crew and passengers had been removed, or that that Government will pass over the offense without condemnation and permit the offenders to remain unpunished.

The Government of the United States, in view of the death of a United States citizen through the wanton act of an officer of the German Imperial Navy, which was in direct violation of the principles of humanity as well as of the law of nations, appeals earnestly to the Imperial Government to disavow the act, to punish the perpetrator, and to make just reparation for the death of Leon C. Thrasher.

It is with extreme reluctance and with a full appreciation of the exceptional conditions, in which Germany is placed in the present war, that the Government of the United States makes these representations and presents this appeal to the justice and humanity of the Imperial Government. This Government owes a duty to itself, to its citizens, and to civilization, which is imperative and which it cannot as a sovereign power ignore. No other course, consonant with its dignity, is open to it. Were the rights at stake those which relate to property, it might continue to show that patience and forbearance which it has manifested so often during the progress of this deplorable conflict, but

when a United States citizen is killed through an act of lawlessness and cruelty, committed under the orders of a commissioned
officer of the German Imperial Navy, and other citizens are
threatened with a like fate if they continue to exercise their just
rights, this Government can not remain silent. It sincerely hopes
that the Imperial Government, recognizing the justice of these
representations, will promptly disavow the act complained of and
take the steps necessary to prevent its repetition.

Robert Lansing.

TS MS (WP, DLC).

Edward Douglass White to Joseph Patrick Tumulty

Dear Mr. Tumulty: Washington, April 5, 1915.

After talking with you the other day on the subject of the
picture show[1] I wrote to the gentleman in New York[2] and had
an answer from him. In writing him I told him that I was so
situated that if the rumors about my having sanctioned the
show were continued that I might be under the obligation of
denying them publicly and say, it might be, that I do not approve
the show, and therefore if the owners were wise they would stop
the rumors. Incidentally in the letter I said: "I have reason to
know,—although not authoritatively so—that the name of the
President also has been used[3] and that he might perhaps be
obliged to take the same course that I have indicated if the
rumors are not stopped. I do not speak with any authority, but
only by way of rumor."

I quote a passage from his letter, as it may be well for you
to see it:

"I have heard that it has been stated on more than one occasion that the President and the Chief Justice, who had seen a
private performance of the production in Washington, regarded
it as unobjectionable. On the strength of my associate's acquaintance with Mr. Aitken, I will have an interview with him and
strongly urge him, not only as an act of fairness, but in his own
interest, to see to it that no further currency is given to this in-
correct report. I have no doubt that this caution will be heeded."

I don't send this letter to be put upon the files, but only for
your information.

I trust your Easter was a happy one and that every blessing
may arise along the way of you and all of yours during this
Easter Season.   Faithfully yours,   E. D. White

TLS (WP, DLC).

1 "The Birth of a Nation."
2 Unknown.
3 About Dixon's use of Wilson's and White's alleged approval of "The Birth of a Nation," see Link, *The New Freedom*, p. 253.

To William Jennings Bryan

My dear Mr. Secretary, The White House. 6 April, 1915.

This is frank and satisfactory, too, as far as it goes;[1] but I think that the sooner we get our plans going in Haiti for a stable arrangement that will preclude anxieties such as we have recently felt the better. Faithfully Yours, W. W.

1 WJB to A. Bailly-Blanchard, April 6, 1915, T telegram (SDR, RG 59, 838.61331 T 55/20a, DNA), stating that the President desired that he come to Washington at his earliest convenience to report on the situation in Haiti. Bryan also requested that he lay before the current Haitian regime, without recognizing it, the American objections to a proposed tobacco monopoly.

From William Jennings Bryan

My dear Mr. President: Washington April 6, 1915.

I am trying to get my ideas in shape on this Thresher question but am not able to send them tonight. As we are not yet fully informed in regard to the case the time for action has not arrived, but, as I told you today, I am very much worried about it— the troublesome question being whether an American citizen can, by putting his business above his regard for his country, assume for his own advantage unnecessary risks and thus involve his country in international complications. Are the rights and obligations of citizenship so one-sided that the Government which represents all the people must bring the whole population into difficulty because a citizen, instead of regarding his country's interests, thinks only of himself and of his interests.

I hope by tomorrow night to be able to send you a note on the subject.

With assurances of high respect I am, my dear Mr. President,
Yours very sincerely, W. J. Bryan

TLS (WP, DLC).

To William Jennings Bryan

My dear Mr. Secretary, The White House. 6 April, 1915.

Thank you for showing me these.

I will keep Lansing's note about the Thrasher case until we get the information we have asked for and until I can see and meditate upon what you are to put in writing of your own views; and will give my thoughts time to settle before allowing myself to form a conclusion. I feel, as you do, the greatest anxiety about the matter.   Faithfully Yours,   W.W.

WWTLI (W. J. Bryan Papers, DNA).

To the Newsboys of Baltimore

My dear Boys: [Washington] April 7, 1915

I am very glad to hear about the way in which you youngsters are beginning to take care of yourselves and stop the things that you are sure to be sorry for afterwards, and I want to send you this message of hearty good will and express the hope that the things you are learning now will make you not only more successful men, but happier men. The right road is the straight road and it is the only road that will carry any man where he would care to go, because I am sure that you feel as I do, that it isn't worth while to go anywhere if you cannot go with honor and self-respect. My message is God bless you and guide you!
                    Sincerely yours,   Woodrow Wilson

TLS (Letterpress Books, WP, DLC).

From William Jennings Bryan

My dear Mr. President: Washington April 7, 1915.

In leaving with you the tentative draft prepared by Mr. Lansing I stated that I would submit a note on the subject. I have been considering the questions involved and find that the facts are so incomplete as to make it impossible to reach a satisfactory conclusion as to the representations that should be made.

We do not know yet whether the merchant vessel was armed, or whether, if not armed the fact that the vessel was unarmed was known to the commander of the submarine.

We are informed that Great Britain has permitted the arming of some of her merchant vessels and we have received a note from the British Ambassador saying that if her vessels are permitted to arm it is because of the action of the German submarines. The German government seems to assume that British merchantmen are armed, and gives that as a reason why her submarines cannot insure the rescue of crew and passengers.

The facts, when fully disclosed, may enable us to make a claim without announcing a position on the entire question. While, however, we are waiting for the facts we can be revolving in our minds the various propositions that may be involved:

First: The use of submarines in attacking merchant vessels;

Second: The right of merchant vessels to arm themselves to resist the submarine; and

Third: The effect of such arming on the rules that govern the conduct of the submarine as to the rescue of passengers. Does the arming of a merchant vessel so change the character of the vessel as to increase the risks of passengers and crew?

It seems to me that the third question may become a very important one and I shall confer with Mr. Lansing in regard to the authorities on this subject.

If the arming of a merchant vessel so changes its character as to effect the rights of those who travel on it, the risks assumed by an American passenger would necessarily be greatly increased and he might occupy the position of a foreigner who goes into a fortified city, or exposes himself when a battle is on.

I feel that this is the most delicate question we have had to meet—not only because it involves the loss of a human life, but because we are dealing with a nation whose people have been made sensitive by the course we have pursued in the matter of the export of arms—a course not only entirely consistent with neutrality, but a course compelled by neutrality. We are aware, however, that a large element of our population, influenced by sympathy with the German side, has criticized us violently, and this criticism has been communicated to the other side until there is widespread evidence of unfriendliness. Whatever we do in this Thrasher case will be viewed with suspicion and we must, therefore, be the more careful to take a position which will be not only defensible but, if possible, so obviously defensible as to appeal to the judgment of the entire country.

I am sure that the almost unanimous desire of our country is that we shall not become involved in this war and I cannot help feeling that it would be a sacrifice of the interests of all the people to allow one man, acting purely for himself and his own interests, and without consulting his government, to involve the entire nation in difficulty when he had ample warning of the risks which he assumed. The world has notice of the bitterness of the struggle in which the belligerents are engaged, and each side has issued warning. While we may regard the belief that both sides have overstepped their international rights, the citizens of our country ought to allow these questions to be decided by governmental action and not attempt to decide the questions themselves.

I hope that by the time action is necessary a course may be found which will satisfy the requirements of the case, without increasing the tension already sufficient to cause anxiety.

With assurances of high respect I am, my dear Mr. President,
Yours very sincerely,   W. J. Bryan

TLS (WP, DLC).

From William Jennings Bryan, with Enclosures

My dear Mr. President: Washington April 7, 1915.

I am sending you with my note another memorandum which Mr. Lansing has prepared, and a memorandum prepared by Mr. Anderson with Mr. Lansing's comments on Mr. Anderson's memorandum.

With assurances of high respect I am, my dear Mr. President,
Yours very sincerely,   W. J. Bryan

TLS (WP, DLC).

E N C L O S U R E   I

MEMORANDUM ON THE THRASHER CASE.

Under the hitherto generally accepted rule of international law unresisting merchant vessels, whether belligerent or neutral, may not be destroyed, even when they are liable to seizure, without first placing the passengers and crews in a place of safety, and without becoming responsible for all damages illegally inflicted.

The German Government disputes the application of this rule to its submarine warfare in the naval war zone which it has proclaimed around Great Britain. The United States Government insists that the rule is in force and that a failure to observe it will be regarded as "an indefensible violation of neutral rights" for which the offender will be held to a strict accountability. It is possible that the note of warning on this subject addressed by the Government of the United States to the German Government on February 10th may be interpreted by the German Government as applying this rule only to American vessels, and therefore by implication acquiescing in its non-application to belligerent vessels. Presumably the Government of the United States did not intend, and will not admit, that its note should be given this interpretation.

The circumstances surrounding the sinking of the FALABA have not yet been fully ascertained, but assuming that they justify the United States Government in asserting that the German submarine failed to observe this rule, and that it was in consequence of this failure that Thrasher lost his life, his death clearly would be attributable, in the opinion of this Government, to an illegal act for which the German Government is responsible.

It may fairly be assumed that the presence of an American citizen on board the FALABA was not known to the German submarine, and consequently that its action was not directed specifically against an American citizen. No question, therefore, of a deliberate attack against an American citizen or the American flag is presented in this case.

The attack was directed against a British vessel and the death of an American citizen was merely one of the incidental results of an act which the United States Government regards as a violation of international law.

It is true that the German Government gave notice of its intention to destroy enemy merchant vessels in the waters in which this vessel was destroyed, and announced that it might not always be possible to save the crews and passengers of such vessels, and knowledge of this notice must be attributed to Thrasher.

Notice of an intention to commit a wrongful act, however, does not relieve the wrongdoer of the responsibility for the consequences of that act.

Furthermore, the fact that Thrasher was willing to take the chance that the German Government would not succeed in carrying out its purpose in the case of the FALABA is not a bar to a claim for indemnity in this case.

It appears, therefore, that the case does not present a question of national affront, but merely the question of whether a German submarine was acting lawfully or unlawfully in sinking the FALABA without taking every precaution to save Thrasher's life.

The Government of the United States contends that the act was unlawful, and the German Government will contend that the act was lawful, thus presenting a difference of a legal nature between the two Governments on this point.

If the act was lawful, the Government of the United States cannot hold the German Government accountable for any of the consequences.

If the act was unlawful, the German Government is accountable, but its accountability is measured at the utmost by a pecuniary indemnity.

This view of the case reduces it to a pecuniary claim for indemnity involving merely a disputed question of liability.

Chandler P. Anderson

Washington   April 5, 1915.

ENCLOSURE II

Comments on Mr. Anderson's
Memorandum of April 5, 1915.

THRASHER CASE.

April 7, 1915.

The fundamental difficulty in following the argument of the memorandum appears to me to be the necessity of admitting that the illegality of the method employed by the German naval officer in sinking the FALABA is open to question. I do not think that this Government can, even for the sake of argument, assume that position. It seems to me that we go as far as we ought when we leave open for discussion the legal right to sink a merchant vessel on the high seas after the persons on board have been given time to reach a safe distance from the vessel. Debating the legality to destroy life and the legality to destroy property are very different things.

Now if we hold rigidly to the view, which I think we are bound to do, that the sinking of the FALABA with innocent non-combatants on board, is an illegal and indefensible act, I do not see how we can avoid asking the German Government to disavow responsibility for the act, punish the offender and respond in damages for the death of Thrasher.

Of course the German officer in command of the submarine did not know that an American citizen was on board, but he was bound to know that he was committing an act contrary to the law of nations. He is in the position of a man who commits a crime, say grand larceny or destruction of property, and by that act unintentionally kills another. He is of course liable for murder, although the death was caused without malice aforethought. He cannot plead want of intent nor ignorance of the presence of an American on the vessel. He is liable for every consequence which results from his illegal act.

It seems to me that it is very much as if the German military authorities, in order to prevent supplies reaching the enemy's front, should, through spies or otherwise, poison the wells on the routes by which the supplies would be furnished. If an American lawfully within the French lines should drink of the poisoned water and come to his death in that way, I do not believe we could consider pecuniary damages as sufficient adjustment for the man's life. In such a case it would seem to me that this Government would be in duty bound to denounce the poisoning of the wells as an inhuman act and in direct violation of the rules of civilized warfare, and also to demand of Germany the disavowal of the act and the meting out of proper punishment to those guilty of putting poison in the water.

While I would be inclined, as far as possible, to avoid a demand upon Germany, which would undoubtedly be rejected, I do not think that we ought to admit that the illegality of the method employed in the sinking of the FALABA is a subject for argument. We must start out our consideration of the course to be taken in this case on the proposition that the act of the commander of the submarine was illegal, inhuman and indefensible.

Robert Lansing

TS MSS (WP, DLC).

From John Palmer Gavit

Dear Mr. President: [New York] April 7, 1915.

Many thanks for the autographed photograph of you and your Boss,[1] which comes to me in this morning's mail. I shall prize it very highly; I am not quite sure but that I care more for it as the picture of two Good Fellows whom it has been my pleasure to know in a man-to-man way, than for any of the official and professional implications involved!

Anyway, I am glad of the opportunity it gives me to express my personal appreciation of the magnificent fashion in which you have borne and are bearing a personal and official load that would stagger if it did not crush any but a Man.

God bless you!   Faithfully   John P. Gavit

ALS (WP, DLC).
[1] Tumulty.

From Jessie Woodrow Bones Brower

Dear Cousin Woodrow: Winnetka, Illinois [c. April 7, 1915]

It is safe to say I never enjoyed a vacation more than the one I have just spent with you.[1] It seemed to carry me back to the days at Fort Lewis[2] & those spent in your home before my marriage. And it was perfectly delightful to find you the same charming small boy as of yore. All the cares of an exalted position have not been able to kill that wonderful youth & sense of the ridiculous that is yours. I haven't laughed as much in years as over your fun, & I still insist the world is the poorer for not knowing this side of you. If it were only possible for this great country to know Woodrow Wilson—the man, as he is to his family!

And how I enjoyed my games of golf with you. I know full well I would not have a "look in" on a game, if you were not so burdened with care & work. Some day I hope to be able to play with you again—when you are just plain Mr. Wilson once more. Thank you so much for the happy times you gave me. . . .

Please tell that nice doctor of yours that I still believe him a friend. He was too polite to beat a woman, and I shant forgive him. There is only one way for him to right himself with me, & that is to lick me to a finish.

If you ever come this way, bring your clubs, & I can get a pleasant partner who will show you our most interesting course.

Lots & lots of love my dear cousin. How I wish I lived a bit nearer to you.   Affectionately   Jessie

ALS (WP, DLC).
    [1] She had been a visitor at the White House from March 26 to April 4.
    [2] In Bath County, Va., where members of the Wilson and Bones families had spent a vacation in the late summer of 1880.

Remarks to the Maryland Annual Conference of the Methodist Protestant Church[1]

April 8, 1915.

Mr. President,[2] ladies and gentlemen: Apparently the President is regarded in Washington as a sort of host to the bodies that assemble here, and certainly it is a very agreeable function that he is occasionally called upon to exercise of bidding great assemblages like this welcome to the capital of the nation. Not that I own an undivided or a divided share in the capital, but that, presiding here at this time, it is my privilege to meet bodies like this and to welcome them.

As I was thinking today over the purposes for which you assemble and comparing them with the purposes for which, for example, the Congress of the United States assembles here, and

    [1] Which was meeting in the Rhode Island Avenue Methodist Protestant Church of Washington.
    [2] The Rev. Dr. John S. Bowers, pastor of the Allnutt Memorial Methodist Protestant Church of Baltimore and president of the conference.

we who are entrusted with the executive functions do our work here, at first it seemed to me that there was a considerable contrast—that we were engaged in the things that were temporary and ephemeral, while bodies like this, conferences of a great church, were engaged in things that were permanent, that had to do with the interests of the human race and with human souls, whether they lived under one government or under another, whether their polity, their civil polity, was of one kind or of another kind. Yet, as I reflected upon the matter, it did not seem to me that this difference was fundamental, after all. In transacting the business of a great church, you are handling the facet of the day. You are handling the affairs of the church as they stand under the treatment of the men of your generation. Back of them lie the eternal principles which you are trying to exemplify in the life of the work; back of us here in the government lie the eternal principles of justice and of righteousness, which, in my conviction, at any rate, we do not derive from ourselves, but from the same source from which a great church derives its inspiration and authority. It seemed to me that it was worth saying something like this: These are days of very great perplexity, when a great cloud of trouble hangs and broods over the greater part of the world. It seems as if great blind material forces had been released which had for long been held in leash and restrained. And, yet, underneath that you can see the strong impulses of great ideals. It would be impossible, ladies and gentlemen, for men to go through what men are going through on the battlefields of Europe and struggle through the present dark night of their terrible struggle if it were not that they saw, or thought they saw, the broadening of light where the morning should come up and believed that they were standing each on his side of the contest for some eternal principle of right. Then, all about them, all about us, there sits the silent, waiting tribunal which is going to utter the ultimate judgment upon this struggle—the great tribunal of the opinion of the world. And I fancy I see, I hope that I see, I pray that it may be that I do truly see, great spiritual forces lying waiting for the outcome of this thing to assert themselves, and asserting themselves even now, to enlighten our judgment and steady our spirits. No man is wise enough to pronounce judgment, but we can all hold our spirits in readiness to accept the truth when it dawns on us and is revealed to us in the outcome of this titanic struggle.

So it is of infinite benefit that in assemblages like this, and in every sort of assemblage, we should constantly go back to the sources of our moral inspiration and question ourselves as to what principle it is that we are acting on. Whither are we bound? What do we wish to see triumph? And if we wish to see certain things triumph, why do we wish to see them triumph? What is there in them that is for the lasting benefit of mankind? For we are not in this world to amuse ourselves with its affairs. We are here to push the whole sluggish mass forward in some particular direction, and unless you know the direction in which you want to go, your force is of no avail. Do you love righteousness is what each one of us ought to ask himself. And if you love righteousness, are you ready to translate righteousness into action and be ashamed and afraid before no man? It seems to me, therefore, that it is worth suggesting to you that you are not sitting here merely to transact the business and express the ideals of a great church as represented in the State of Maryland, but you are here also as part of the assize of humanity, to remind yourselves of the things that are permanent and eternal which, if we do not translate into action, we have failed in the fundamental things of our lives.

You will see that it is only in such general terms that one can speak in the midst of a confused world, because, as I have already said, no man has the key to this confusion. No man can see the outcome, but every man can keep his own spirit prepared to contribute to the net result when the outcome displays itself. That is the reason I said to a body similar to this only a few nights ago that I welcomed the atmosphere which these solemn assessments of the human spirit bring to Washington, for this is the place of assessment. In one sense Washington is not even a part of the United States. It is where everybody else comes and sooner or later speaks his mind about the United States, and about many outlying parts of the world. Mr. Bryan[3] and I are constantly auditors to what I dare say is a large part of the opinion of the world; to judge by the time it takes to express it, I think a very large part, and, to judge by the variety and contrariety of it, I dare say it is a fair cross section of what men are thinking about. But, for my part, I am very happy to hear all of this, provided I can be sure that I am the right kind of sensitive registering machine and will register it, excluding its contradictions and embodying its harmonies which, after all, is a very difficult thing to do. Because our day has only twenty-four hours in it, and not everybody can be heard in the twenty-four hours; and yet everybody, if I may judge by certain indications, is wishing to be heard every twenty-four hours, I therefore, would rather hear what comes as the combined counsel of great bodies

<hr>

[3] Bryan spoke following Wilson.

like this and let that sink into my consciousness as part of the contribution to my conception of what the great sober first and second thought of America is. For by that we are guided. That is the atmosphere in which we live. We should wish, if successful, to express that. You can see, therefore, with what deep sincerity I bid bodies like this welcome to Washington, for I know that it is for our benefit, and I hope that it is for theirs.

T MS (WP, DLC).

To William Jennings Bryan

My dear Mr. Secretary,   The White House. 8 April, 1915.

The Thrasher case is constantly in my mind. I received your letter of yesterday and the accompanying papers from Mr. Lansing and Mr. Anderson, and have of course read them with the closest attention.

Unless you think it premature or unwise to do so, I shall bring the matter up for discussion to-morrow morning at the meeting of the Cabinet.

Meantime, one suggestion for your consideration, in the light of the authorities:

If *some* British merchantmen were known to be armed, and the British Government had in fact authorized or advised all merchantmen to arm themselves against submarines, and, assuming it to have been impracticable for the German commander to ascertain whether the FALABA was armed, was he justified in the circumstances in acting upon the theory that the British authorization had in effect transformed all British merchantmen into public armed vessels and made them liable to attack as such?   Faithfully Yours,   W.W.

WWTLI (W. J. Bryan Papers, DNA).

From William Jennings Bryan

My dear Mr. President: Washington April 8, 1915.

I am sending you flimsy of a report from our Consul General at London on the FALABA case.[1] While it seems almost certain that Thrasher was among the lost it is not known as a fact but as a conclusion drawn from the fact that he is not reported among those saved.

I am sending the following inquiry:

"Answering your April seven, report on FALABA please make following additional inquiries:

"*First*: Number of passengers on FALABA and number rescued.

"*Second*: Whether there was any communication by signals or otherwise between commanders of FALABA and submarine before or after firing torpedo.

"*Third*: Please report any other facts brought out at inquiry as to time when submarine flew British flag."

Mr. Lansing and I will see what authorities we can find on the proposition which you submit.

Allow me to submit this proposition for your consideration:

An American citizen, after being warned of the dangers involved, takes passage on a British ship and loses his life with other passengers as a result of an attack by a submarine—the attacking Government not knowing that the American was on board—not having any intention therefore of doing harm to an American citizen, and having notified this Government of its intended action against British ships:—

QUERY: What claim can this Government rightfully make for unintended loss which ordinary diligence would have avoided?

The above question, it seems to me, presents the problem with which we have to deal, unless we take the position that the method of attack is so contrary to international law that a neutral is justified in ignoring the warning and relying upon his government to vindicate his right to travel on the belligerent ship, notwithstanding the risks involved.

In view of the importance of the subject I am inclined to think it would be well to bring the matter up at the Cabinet meeting so that we can get the opinions from as many angles as possible.

With assurances of high respect I am, my dear Mr. President,
Yours very sincerely, W. J. Bryan

TLS (WP, DLC).

[1] It is not with this letter. However, Lansing sent it to Wilson on April 10. It was R. P. Skinner to WJB, April 7, 1915, T telegram (WP, DLC), printed in *FR-WWS 1915*, pp. 359-60. Skinner verified that Thrasher had been a passenger on *Falaba* and had been lost, and summarized the sworn testimony of three surviving passengers as to the circumstances of the sinking of the vessel.

To John Palmer Gavit

My dear Gavit: [The White House] April 9, 1915

I cannot let your letter of April seventh go unanswered. I do not know when I have received a letter which has made me happier and I thank you for it from the bottom of my heart.

Let me say that for my part I would rather have you think of Tumulty and me as men whom you like and believe in than as officers of a Government, and when you believe in us so generously and throughly I can only say, God bless you!

    Cordially and sincerely yours,   Woodrow Wilson

TLS (Letterpress Books, WP, DLC).

To William Arnold Shanklin

My dear President Shanklin: [The White House] April 9, 1915

Nothing could gratify me more than the desire on the part of the trustees of Wesleyan to confer upon me the honorary degree of Doctor of Laws. I look back upon my connection with Wesleyan as upon a time of great happiness when I was associated with men whom I greatly admired and with whom it was a privilege to serve.

I wish that I could accept this honor offered me, but I have this scruple in the matter: I do not think that while in office a President of the United States should accept honorary degrees. I think that he should forego all tokens of this kind and forget himself in the work that he has to do.

It is with a pang of genuine regret that I state this conclusion in this particular case, but I am sure that you and the trustees associated with you will understand and pardon.

    Cordially and sincerely yours,   Woodrow Wilson

TLS (Letterpress Books, WP, DLC).

From William Jennings Bryan, with Enclosure

My dear Mr. President: Washington April 9th, 1915.

I am enclosing a copy of the telegram just sent to Peking. Before we had an opportunity to send the telegrams which we talked of this morning, the Japanese Ambassador came in and asked whether we were willing for his Government to say to the Chinese Government, in case it was found desirable to do so, that we had no objection to the agreement prohibiting the granting of a concession for a naval base or a coaling station along the coast of Fukien to any foreign power. I had told him in person that we have no objection to Japan knowing that we were making no objections. I stated to him that in case it was communicated to Japan by the Chinese Minister, our Minister should be authorized to confirm it in case of inquiry. The other telegram, of which a copy is enclosed, deals with the disclosures that have been made at Peking.[1] If you read the enclosed press despatch[2] you will see that somebody must have been permitted to see our note and the reply, for no one could have guessed all the facts stated.

    With assurances of high respect, I am, my dear Mr. President,
Very sincerely yours,   W. J. Bryan

TLS (W. J. Bryan Papers, DNA).
  [1] WJB to American Legation, Peking, April 9, 1915, T telegram (SDR, RG 59, 793.94/333B, DNA). Bryan reported that Ambassador Chinda had twice recently called upon him to complain about leaks to the press, apparently originating in Peking, of important diplomatic documents relating to Japan's demands upon China. One was the memorandum handed by Chinda to Bryan on February 22 (about which see WJB to WW, Feb. 22, 1915); the others were the note handed by Bryan to Chinda on March 13 (see WW to WJB, March 12, 1915, [2nd letter of that date], n. 1) and the Japanese reply handed to Bryan on March 22 (printed as an Enclosure with WJB to WW, March 22, 1915). Bryan asked if the legation could suggest any possible source of the leaks.
  Reinsch, in his reply (P. S. Reinsch to WJB, April 12, 1915, T telegram [SDR, RG 59, 793.94/293, DNA]), said that he did not know how the leaks had occurred but that the information might have come ultimately from Japan. He added: "These statements find confirmation in the fact that during the recent conferences the Japanese negotiators have repeatedly impressed upon the Chinese the view that the communications of the American Government have indicated its acquiescence in the present Japanese policy towards China. It seems reasonably clear that the motive of Japanese Ambassador in making the inquiries referred to in your telegram April 9, 9 P.M. was to force the agencies of the United States into an attitude of defense and explanation in regard to the leakage of confidential information, some of which has been discovered and made public by those interested in behalf of China and some of which has been made known through judicious indiscretions on the part of the Japanese themselves with a view to furthering the impression that the Chinese cannot build any hopes upon the attitude adopted by the United States. I trust that I am justified in dismissing from consideration a construction of your telegram which would indicate that you countenanced any insinuations on the part of Japanese Ambassador that this Legation is giving out or that it ought to assist the Japanese Government in detecting the sources of such publicity as may prove inconvenient to that Government.
  "At Saturday's conference the Chinese endeavored to secure a definite acceptance of concessions which they have made in regard to Manchuria but the Japanese Minister stated that he had not yet received instructions authorizing him to make final settlement. He then attempted to discuss articles four, five and six of group five: the Minister for Foreign Affairs insisted that he could not consider these demands in principle since they conflict with China's sovereignty and treaty obligations; the Japanese Minister thereupon stated that he could not see the force of these arguments in view of what the Chinese had already found it possible to grant in Manchuria."
  [2] Missing.

ENCLOSURE

Amlegation, Peking.   [Washington] April 9th, 1915.

    Japanese Ambassador informs me that his Government may desire to communicate to the Chinese Government contents of our note stating that this Government would have no objection to an agreement between China and Japan that no foreign power should be permitted to establish a naval base or coaling station on the coast of Fukien. It is not certain that Japan will desire to communicate this but if it is communicated by the Japanese Government and the Chinese Government asks you for confirmation of it you are hereby authorized to confirm it by the despatch which you received at the time. This relates not to the interior of Fukien but to the sea coast.

CCT telegram (W. J. Bryan Papers, DNA).

From Josephus Daniels

Dear Mr. President: Washington. April 10, 1915.

It is probable the newspaper men will ask you what about Congressman Gardner's statement[1] that you ordered the Joint Board of the Army and Navy to hold no further meetings.[2] You may not recall the facts and so I write to say that, after publications of their actions, during the delicate Japan situation, which you disapproved, you directed me to say to the naval members not to attend another meeting until you gave orders for such meeting. A few days thereafter you told me to say that meetings might be held but you wished no action decided upon in the Pacific pending the Japanese land discussion. This merely to refresh your memory if the incident has escaped you. My own view is, since Gardner's statement at the White House,[3] that it is not necessary to give answer to any statement he makes. But your judgment will be better than mine.

Sincerely,   Josephus Daniels

ALS (J. Daniels Papers, DLC).
[1] Augustus Peabody Gardner made his statement in a speech delivered on the evening of April 10 at the New Willard Hotel. *New York Times*, April 11, 1915.
[2] See n. 1 to the extract from the diary of J. Daniels printed at May 17, 1913, Vol. 27.
[3] Daniels apparently referred to a statement that Gardner made at the time of his interview with Wilson at the White House on December 7, 1914 (about which see the news report and statement printed at Dec. 7, 1914, Vol. 31). However, all newspaper accounts agree that Gardner refused all comment immediately after the interview except to confirm that he had asked the President if he intended to have Gardner's resolution for an investigation of the nation's preparedness for war quashed in the House, and if he would allow army and navy officers to testify at congressional hearings. Gardner also reaffirmed that he would continue to press for the passage of his resolution. Daniels was probably thinking of a comment which Gardner made to the press on the evening of December 7. Among other remarks critical of Wilson's stand on an investigation of preparedness, he said: "It may be easy enough to chloroform my resolution and it may not be difficult to chloroform me, but all the anaesthetics in the world can never lull to sleep the demand of an alarmed public sentiment that the truth must be revealed." *New York Tribune*, Dec. 8, 1914.

From Benjamin Howell Griswold, Jr.[1]

Dear Mr. President: Baltimore, Maryland, April 10th, 1915.

The matter referred to in my letter of the 8th instant[2] which I wanted to discuss with you, is as follows:

President Goodnow has just received from Willoughby, who succeeded him at Peking, an inquiry as to the possibility of the Chinese Government placing a loan of from one hundred to two hundred millions of dollars in the United States. The purpose of the loan is to reform the banking and currency system of China and the security offered is the land tax which is also to be reorganized. The amount doubtless would be made available to the Chinese Government in relatively small amounts at agreed dates covering a fairly long period.

Both of the reforms mentioned appear to be of great importance to the welfare of the Chinese. The Government officials have assured Willoughby that they were now in a frame of mind to adopt these reforms under the direct supervision of representatives of the bankers. As we now understand it, the loan would be arranged by and be under the control of United States bankers only.

Mr. Willoughby has laid great stress upon the necessity of treating this matter with the greatest confidence and discretion. Mr. Goodnow has asked me to undertake the necessary banking negotiations. My interest in the matter, however, as a banker, is secondary to my desire to be of service to the Government.

The "Six Power Group" proposition, as I understand it, practically required the United States to become a party to an agreement with foreign nations. At all events our Government's direct sanction was required. Furthermore, the proposed "Six Power" loan was to be based upon an obsolete salt tax and not upon the greatly needed reform of the land tax.

As we view the present suggestion, it seems that a loan by United States bankers would not necessarily need the *sanction* of our Government and we might proceed as bankers, to negotiate directly with the Chinese Government. But we do not want to undertake any negotiations which might indirectly cause embarrassment to the State Department.

I should like very much to discuss the matter with you. Mr. Goodnow is to be in Washington on Thursday morning next. Would it be convenient for you to see us then?[3]

Faithfully yours,   B. Howell Griswold Jr.

TLS (WP, DLC).
[1] Partner in the Baltimore banking firm of Alexander Brown and Sons.

2 It is missing.

3 Wilson conferred with Griswold and Frank Johnson Goodnow, President of The Johns Hopkins University, at the White House on April 15.

Two Letters from Robert Lansing

Confidential.

Dear Mr. President: Washington April 10, 1915.

I enclose the telegrams received from Consul General Skinner regarding the sinking of the *Falaba*.[1]

The significant fact to my mind is that the submarine's commander allowed ten minutes for the crew and passengers to leave the vessel, showing that he did not act on the suspicion that the vessel was armed and might attack him. If he had allowed no time for escape, he might enter that plea, but, since he gave *some* time, he should have given sufficient.

It seems to me that the question of arming British vessels, or Germany's belief that it is being done, disappears from the *Falaba* case.   Very sincerely yours,   Robert Lansing.

TLS (WP, DLC).

[1] Skinner's telegram of April 7 has already been noted. The other enclosures were R. P. Skinner to WJB, April 9 and 10, 1915, T telegrams (WP, DLC), printed in *FR-WWS 1915*, pp. 362-64. Both gave further details of the sinking of *Falaba*, including the numbers of passengers and crew and those saved, signals given by the submarine, and affidavits that the liner had no guns aboard and no ammunition "for ships purposes."

Confidential.

Dear Mr. President: Washington April 10, 1915.

As you are considering the Thrasher case I enclose a report which I have received on the subject from the Joint State and Navy Neutrality Board.[1] I have not approved the report because there are certain features in it as to which I am doubtful.

Very sincerely yours,   Robert Lansing.

TLS (WP, DLC).

[1] J. B. Scott *et al.* to RL, April 8, 1915, TLS (WP, DLC). After briefly summarizing the known details of the sinking of *Falaba*, the authors proceeded to discuss the "legality" of submarine warfare against merchant shipping. They summarized their findings as follows:

"1. Visit by a belligerent vessel of war to a merchant vessel encountered by her is a necessity to establish the nationality of that merchant vessel, whatever that nationality really be, before capture can be made.

"2. Capture is illegal unless enemy character be established, or, in the case of a neutral vessel, unless that vessel has offended against international law in some recognized ways.

"3. Capture is necessary before the vessel of war making the capture has any legal right whatever to do more than visit and search.

"4. A submarine, by its nature, is incapable of conducting visit.

"5. The destruction, therefore, of a vessel presumed to be an enemy vessel by a submarine, without visit, is an illegal act.

"6. If neutral interests suffer by such illegal act, the neutral government interested is within its rights and is pursuing its duty in seeking redress.

"Applying these remarks to the case of Thrasher under the assumed circumstances, and answering the question of the Counselor in the last paragraph of his letter, the Board considers that there is no justification for the acts of the German naval authorities cited. In this particular instance, the acts appear to the Board to be especially reprehensible. Had the personnel on board the FALABA been given time to leave that ship and get well clear of the dangerous area about her before the ship was torpedoed, the Board would regard the action as illegal; but if, as it appears, the personnel had not all had a chance to leave the ship and the FALABA was torpedoed with some of the personnel on board and others in boats in the immediate vicinity, the action of the commanding officers of the German submarine appears to the Board not only illegal but revoltingly inhuman.   James Brown Scott
                                                                        H S. Knapp.
                                                                        James H. Oliver"

A Telegram and a Letter from Edward Mandell House

[Paris, April 11, 1915]

American Ambassador to Spain thinks Spain will cordially accept the proposal for the second convention. The King[1] is exceedingly desirous of playing some part in the peace negotiations and would probably be willing to follow your lead if he could even play second part. I told him that I regarded this as impracticable unless the situation changes and that such an idea better be discouraged. Spain wishes closer relations with America. Believe this sentiment should be fostered, for it would have a beneficial effect upon our relations with Latin America.

I will see French Minister of Foreign Affairs Monday or Tuesday and will cable result. Our relations with France bearing on my mission need some cultivation, which I shall endeavor to accomplish. I shall get in touch with Sir Edward Grey from here and determine when best to go to London.

I have now in mind a distinct plan of campaign about which I will write you and which you will receive April 24th.

                                                                        Edward House

T transcript of WWsh decode (WP, DLC).
[1] Alfonso XIII.

Dear Governor: Paris, France. April 11th, 1915.

This is the first time I have had an opportunity to write you freely since I left here.

My visit in Berlin was exceedingly trying and disagreeable in many ways. I met there no one of either high or low degree who did not immediately corner me and begin to discuss our shipment to the Allies of munitions, and sometimes their manner was almost offensive.

Upon the streets one hesitated to speak in English for fear of being insulted. Harrison, our Consul at Frankfort, Morgan of Hamburg and Lay of Berlin,[1] all told me of disagreeable incidents they had had or knew of. At one time, in the early stages of the war, it was sufficient to say one was an American, but now this has disappeared.

I feel, however, that with the Government and with the influential people with whom I talked, a better understanding of our purposes was brought about and I hope this feeling will sooner or later reach the people at large.

One of the most intelligent and fair-minded Germans I met was Herr Solf,[2] Minister for the Colonies. I had several long conferences with him and he expressed the general feeling of bitterness that Germany had no colonies and was deprived of securing them. I told him that colonies in themselves were not sources of strength to a country, but were oftentimes a weakness. That German citizenship was of such a high character that they were welcomed everywhere. I suggested that they might colonize in South America to any extent and pointed out the vast possibilities of Brazil.

He thought this would come in conflict with the Monroe Doctrine. I told him that no one would object provided they had no ulterior design upon the governments of the countries. That Brazil, for instance, would doubtless welcome German immigration and German capital in the developement of her great resources, and that it would be of benefit to both Brazil and Germany. This would be equally true of other sparsely settled countries. I thought in this way German citizenship and character could make itself felt just as strongly as it could by holding colonies in Africa or Asia.

To my surprise, the idea seemed to be new to him. I also pointed out that in the future there would be far less segregation of interests throughout the world than there had been in the past, that intercommunication had become so general that a new and better outlet for expansion would probably take place.

The trouble with Germany is that it is antiquated in some of its ideas. They started upon the rule of force at a time when the most advanced nations were going in the opposite direction.

I endeavored to make it clear to the German Government that

---

[1] Heaton W. Harris, Henry Hays Morgan, and Julius Gareche Lay; all held the rank of consul-general at this time.
[2] Wilhelm Solf.

their best interests could be served by working along harmoniously with us. If we can keep this view before them, they will probably want you as mediator, for they are narrowly selfish in their purposes and have no broad outlook as to the general good of mankind.

I found a lack of harmony in governmental circles which augurs bad for the future. They are divided amongst themselves. You would have thought that Germany was the easiest place in Europe to establish a censorship, and yet I found my name mentioned both in the papers and in cablegrams after an absolute assurance from the Foreign Office that it would not be done. It was not their fault, but rather because the military and civil forces are not working in harmony.

The Emperor is still in absolute authority, although he is criticized pretty generally by both the civil and military branches of the government. Falkenheyn and von Tirpitz seem to have more influence with him than anyone, but Falkenheyn is not popular with the army in general.

The Crown Prince seems to be left out of all important councils, and is generally ignored by both the Civil and Military Governments, though he seems to be more popular with the people than his father, because he is said to be without egotism and more democratic in his manner.

Hindenberg[3] is the popular hero and is the only one that dares assert himself against the Emperor. I believe there are troublous times ahead for the Kaiser and that one denoument of the war may be a more democratic Germany.

There is another thing that may interest you and that it [is] that outside of Belgium, Serbia and Poland, there is no great change in the comfort, or living of the inhabitants in the different belligerent nations. There is less distress from actual poverty than ever before. The loss of life has been stupendous, but outside of that the soldiers themselves are far better cared for in every way than were the Northern soldiers in the Civil War, to say nothing of the Southern soldiers.

In the South there were inadequate supplies of food, clothing and medicines and the people suffered beyond measure because of the blockade and because of the devastation that occured. There is nothing of that sort in this war. The soldiers are well fed, well clothed and sixty percent of the wounded are able to return to the front.

[3] Paul von Hindenburg, who had become a popular idol and had been appointed field marshal and commander in chief on the eastern front as a result of the great victory at Tannenberg for which he was given popular credit and his subsequent successful eastern campaign in the fall and winter of 1914.

Travelling, however, because of the ever tightening restrictions, has grown to be almost impossible. In fact, unless I had had someone like young Winslow, who speaks both German and French, I would have had the greatest possible inconvenience.

There is much that is good that will come out of the war; such, for instance, as the temperance movement. Russia led the way and France and England are following. Then, too, there has been a sobering down of all the peoples, and there has now come to them a patience and fortitude that could never have come otherwise.

If at the end, the belligerent governments adopt the suggestion I have made in regard to the cessation of the manufacturing of munitions of war, the saving would be sufficient to cover the interest on the war debts and perhaps leave a sinking fund sufficient in time to meet the principal.

Affectionately yours, E. M. House

TLS (WP, DLC).

From William Jennings Bryan

My dear Mr. President: Washington April 12, 1915.

I enclose flimsy of a despatch just received from Mr. West.[1] You will notice that Zapata feels hurt at having received no answer to his letter sent by Jenkinson.[2] We have looked the matter up and find that the letter is in the hands of Mr. Ingling at the White House.[3] Not knowing the nature of the Zapata letter I cannot prepare any telegram, but in view of the urgency I suggest that you prepare a telegram this evening if you have time, and send it to the State Department for transmission, so that West can proceed to Cue[r]nevaca. I think it important that he should see Zapata as soon as possible.

With assurances of high respect I am, my dear Mr. President,
Yours very sincerely, W. J. Bryan

TLS (W. J. Bryan Papers, DLC).
[1] D. West to WJB, April 10, 1915, T telegram (WP, DLC). West stated that, because of Zapata's feeling "hurt," he needed an explanation of what had happened to the Zapata letter (see n. 2 below) and what, if any, reply had been made to it before he could call upon the agrarian leader.
[2] See C. Jenkinson to WW, Sept. 8, 1914, n. 2, Vol. 31.
[3] Clarence E. Ingling, clerk at the White House.

To William Jennings Bryan

My dear Mr. Secretary,   The White House. 12 April, 1915.

I am sending a despatch to-night to Mr. West which I hope will straighten this matter out.

Faithfully Yours,   W.W.

WWTLI (W. J. Bryan Papers, DLC).

To Duval West

The White House. 12 April, 1915.

Mr. Jenkinson duly delivered General Zapata's letter to me and I read it with the deepest interest. I am deeply sorry that it was not acknowledged as I had instructed and can only ascribe this to a misunderstanding. The letter gave me a new and gratifying insight into the purposes of General Zapata and a new understanding of the revolution. I was very glad indeed to receive it. It was just because I wished to know how the whole situation now lies in his mind and what his present view of the outlook and plans of the revolution is that I asked you to see General Zapata. He may regard you as deputed to discuss the very matters he set forth in his letter and to hear any suggestions he may have to make that he would wish conveyed to me in the light of recent and existing circumstances.   Wilson.

WWT telegram (WP, DLC).

To William Jennings Bryan

My dear Mr. Secretary,   The White House. 12 April, 1915.

Thank you for these papers.

Have you had time to read the long message sent us by a group of American missionaries in China?[1] I shall be very much interested to learn what you think of it.

Faithfully Yours,   W.W.

WWTLI (W. J. Bryan Papers, DNA).

[1] C. A. Hubbard et al. to WW, April 8, 1915, T telegram (WP, DLC). This twenty-page telegram, signed by seven American religious and educational leaders in China, contained both a petition and a memorial to the President. The petition urged that the United States, preferably in conjunction with Great Britain and the other European powers, but alone, if necessary, demand to be represented at a conference between Japan and China to discuss Japan's demands upon China. It also suggested that the American government request the suspension of the Chinese-Japanese negotiations in progress and the withdrawal of "excessive contingents" of Japanese troops from Chinese territory pending the assembling of the conference. The memorial, which made up the bulk of the telegram, discussed the present situation in China, strongly con-

demned alleged Japanese imperialism and militarism in that country, and stressed the peaceable attitude of the Chinese and their capacity to govern and, given time, even to defend themselves. The memorialists interpreted the struggle in the Far East as a reflection of the war in Europe: they were both part of a conflict to determine whether militarism would predominate or be crushed. Japan really needed to be saved from herself, for her momentary success in China would ultimately lead only to countermilitarism in China and a bitter struggle for many years in the future. If Japan was now effectively checked by American intervention, the memorialists foresaw a great future development of the entire Pacific region in which China, Japan, and the United States would share leadership. Thus, it was to America's self-interest, as well as her moral duty, to intervene in the present situation. Moreover, as the only country not distracted by the European conflict, the United States alone could act effectively.

One or more of the signers must have given copies or summaries of this document to the press corps in Peking a few days later. It is briefly summarized in a news report, datelined Peking, April 17, in the *New York Times*, April 18, 1915.

To John Knox Coit[1]

My dear Mr. Coit: [The White House] April 12, 1915

I have your letter of April seventh[2] and in reply will say that it gives me real pleasure to renew the subscription which Mrs. Wilson made last year in order that Miss Bulgin[3] may continue her studies.

May I not thank you for the personal words of your letter?
In haste

Cordially and sincerely yours,   Woodrow Wilson

TLS (Letterpress Books, WP, DLC).
[1] Superintendent of the Nacoochee Institute, a co-educational school for mountain children in Sautee, Ga.
[2] J. K. Coit to WW, April 7, 1915, TLS (WP, DLC).
[3] Myra Bulgin, a student at Nacoochee Institute. A newspaper clipping enclosed in the letter cited in n. 2 above tells the story of Ellen Axson Wilson's interest in and subscription to the school.

From William Jennings Bryan, with Enclosures

My dear Mr. President: Washington April 12, 1915.

I am sending you a draft of a note prepared by Mr. Lansing. It is accompanied by his note and by the communications answered.[1] I have no changes to suggest; the question in my mind is whether we should answer him by letter or call him to the Department and explain the situation to him verbally. If we make an answer in writing I suppose it would be necessary to give it to the public, as his memorandum was given to the press yesterday. If you have any doubt in your mind as to what it is best to do, I can talk with you after Cabinet meeting tomorrow. The paper has just come into my hands and I am sending it over with only a moment's time for consideration.

With assurances of high respect, I am, my dear Mr. President,
Very sincerely yours,   W. J. Bryan

¹ J. H. von Bernstorff to WJB, April 4, 1915, TCL and TC memorandum, both in translation (W. J. Bryan Papers, DLC), printed in *FR-WWS 1915*, pp. 157-58. Bernstorff's memorandum strongly attacked the alleged failure of the United States government to protect the trade of its citizens in noncontraband goods with Germany against the British ban on such trade, stating: "The Imperial Embassy must therefore assume that the United States Government acquiesces in the violations of international law by Great Britain." It went on to denounce the arms trade of the United States, commented acidly on the rapid buildup of the American arms industry, and declared that it could "in no event be in accordance with the spirit of true neutrality" to permit the export of munitions when in fact they could go only to the Allies. In this connection, Bernstorff recalled a statement attributed to the President at the time of the lifting of the embargo on arms to Mexico in February 1914, in which Wilson was reported to have said that "the true spirit of neutrality as compared with a mere paper neutrality" required that both sides in the Mexican conflict have access to arms.

E N C L O S U R E   I

Robert Lansing to William Jennings Bryan

Confidential.

Dear Mr. Secretary: [Washington] April 11, 1915.

I enclose a draft reply to the note and memorandum of the German Ambassador of the 4th instant.

The memorandum impresses me as couched in language, which is unpardonable in the insinuations which it contains as to the motives of this Government, and which therefore deserves some rebuke. The fact is that Count von Bernstorff, by making this memorandum public without seeking your consent, has acted in a manner almost as improper and offensive as did Rustem Bey. I believe that it should be seriously considered whether he ought not to be called personally to account for this breach of diplomatic etiquette.

In any event our reply, in my opinion, should show displeasure at his criticisms and should decline to debate the subject with him. Any treatment more moderate than this would, I believe, displease the American people who are jealous of our national dignity and expect our Government to maintain it.

The course which the Ambassador has taken in this matter indicates to my mind that the memorandum was prepared with the intention of publishing it as an arraignment of the Administration in order that German sympathizers in this country may be aroused to stronger political hostility to the Government. It is in entire accord with the Dumberg-Münsterberg-Fatherland propaganda.

Neither the dignity of the Government nor political expediency seems to me to warrant a conciliatory reply to the memorandum.

It is with these thoughts in mind that I drafted the reply.

Faithfully yours,   Robert Lansing.

TLS (W. J. Bryan Papers, DLC).

E N C L O S U R E   I I

Excellency: April 12, 1915.

I have given careful consideration to Your Excellency's note of April 4, 1915, enclosing a memorandum of the same date, in which is discussed the action of this government relative to trade between the United States and Germany, and the attitude of this Government in regard to the exportation of arms and ammunition from the United States to the nations at war with Germany.

While I am not unmindful that a consequence of the naval war waged between Germany and her enemies has been to deprive the German people of the commercial privileges which they previously enjoyed, and has prevented intercourse between them and neutral nations across the seas, I am unable to perceive any justification for Your Excellency's unfavorable comments upon this Government's failure to insist upon an equalization of American trade conditions with all belligerent nations which the fortunes of war have made unequal.

Since, however, Your Excellency in your memorandum has seen fit to take this view of the course taken by this Government in the matter of the interruption of trade between the United States and Germany by the enemies of Germany, I cannot permit the comments to pass without remark, as they appear to impugn the good faith of the United States in the performance of its duty as a neutral. It should be understood, however, that the views herein expressed are not advanced by way of apology or excuse, but for the purpose of showing that the memorandum is based on an idea of a neutral's conduct and on a conception of a belligerents privilege to pass judgment upon that conduct, when the commercial rights of the neutral are affected by another belligerent, which this Government considers to be erroneous.

In connection with the conduct of this Government in maintaining its trade I note that Your Excellency has failed to make any reference to the attempt of the United States to secure from the German and British Governments mutual modifications of the measures proposed by each respectively in regard to the interruption of trade on the high seas, which attempt, though unsuccessful, indicated its impartial good will towards the belligerents. Such an omission of reference to a fact which exhibited so friendly a spirit to both parties in the present conflict, was made presumably through inadvertence, but in view of Your Excellency's comments is especially unfortunate.

Furthermore no reference is made to the diplomatic correspondence in which the United States has set forth its attitude toward the unlawful molestation of its trade by Germany's adversaries. These omissions do not comport with Your Excellency's assumption "that the United States Government acquiesces in the violations of international law by Great Britain.["]

As to the course, which has been pursued by this Government in the matter of detentions or seizures by Great Britain of American vessels and American cargoes, I believe that it is my duty to state frankly to Your Excellency that the interference with the rights of American citizens in regard to their property on the high seas is a matter between this Government and the government interfering with those rights, and that criticism of this Government's course in general as to such interference, or in a particular case, made by another government, which cannot be fully informed as to the facts, and which can not know the reasons for the course taken, is an assumption of a privilege which does not appear to be in accord with international custom and usage.

The Government of the United States is not required by duty or courtesy to explain to a third party the reasons for the attitude which it may take in any case involving the effect of the acts of a belligerent upon American rights, and it cannot recognize the propriety of another belligerent government to invite discussion of such attitude, especially when the language used appears to impute to the Government of the United States motives at variance with its character of an impartial neutral power. Whatever conclusion may be drawn from the course adopted by the Government of the United States in relation to its rights as a neutral, is a subject which it is unwilling to discuss with any government other than the one which invades or threatens to invade them.

I have stated the views of the Government of the United States frankly, not only because it is my duty to remove from the field of controversy a subject which this Government does not consider proper for diplomatic discussion, but also because it is for the mutual interest of the two Governments to avoid disputes which can accomplish no good purpose and which tend to arouse irritation and impair the spirit of friendship which has characterized their past relations, and which it is my sincere hope may continue to influence their intercourse in the future.

The memorandum also adverts to the question of the sale and exportation of arms by citizens of the United States to the enemies of Germany, and implies that the continuance of that trade manifests an unneutral spirit by this Government and an unfair attitude on its part towards Germany.

This Government, as Your Excellency I believe is fully aware, holds the opinion that any change in its laws of neutrality during the progress of a war, which would affect unequally the relations of the United States with the belligerents, would be a departure from the principle of strict neutrality, by which it has consistently directed its actions. The placing of an embargo on the trade in arms at the present time would constitute such a change, and be a direct violation of the neutrality of the United States. It is well known that several bills or resolutions were introduced by individual members in the last session of the Congress purposing, in one form or another, to prohibit the exportation of war material. The Congress, however, declined to place such legislation upon the statute books. In view of the attitude of this Government as to its neutral obligations, and the manifest approval of the Congress of that attitude by its refusal, while a state of war exists, to amend the laws affecting the neutrality of the United States, this Government can perceive no practical benefit to be gained by traversing the arguments advanced in the memorandum of Your Excellency, or by continuing further a discussion of this subject.

Accept, Excellency, the renewed assurances of my highest consideration.

CCL (SDR, RG 59, 763.72111/1930, DNA).

From Edward Mandell House

Dear Governor: Paris, France. April 12th, 1915.

I have just written Sir Edward in part as follows:

"I did not find conditions in Berlin favorable for any discussion looking towards peace, consequently I did not remain long or say much.

The visit, however, had great value and I feel that I now know the true conditions there, making a more intelligent line of action possible.

I found but few points where our interest and theirs touched strongly enough for me to create a sympathetic feeling, but one of these was what we might term the freedom of the seas. It was upon that subject alone that I awoke sufficient enthusiasm to warrant the hope that in it lies the way to peace.

Looking at the matter from a narrowly selfish standpoint, they could not believe that England would concede enough in this direction for Germany to consent to those things, without which no peace can ever be possible. But from my conversations with you, I knew that you saw a future more secure and splendid for England in this new direction than in the old. I gave no sign of this, but left them thinking what concessions they might make in order to reach so promising an end.

While I am eager to discuss this and other matters with you, still I feel that it is well to move leisurely, and to assume a certain indifference as to time. In the meanwhile, I beg of you to meet as far as possible the American position concerning the question of blockade, for the President has gone as far in your direction as public opinion and our duty as neutrals would permit, and I should regret a seeming unwillingness on your part to meet him half way."

What I want to do is to get Sir Edward's consent to what might be termed a paper campaign. If he agrees to this I will write to him even though in London, and have him reply. Copies of this correspondence will be sent to either the German Chancellor direct, or to him and Zimmermann through Gerard.

This will necessitate replies, and we may have them talking to one another before they realize it.

If this plan fails, then I think it would be well for you to write me concerning the second convention and its purposes. I will send copies of your letters to both Sir Edward and to the Chancellor, and ask for such additions or eliminations as may occur to them. This correspondence will at first necessarily be far flung, but we will narrow it from time to time, until again we will have them discussing terms of peace.

I feel sure that your thoughts upon that subject and the felicity with which you express them, will help beyond measure to convince these warring peoples.

Please let me know what you think of this.

Your affectionate,   E. M. House

TLS (WP, DLC).

From Robert Lewis Waring

Mr. President, Sir: New York City, April 12, 1915.

May 26th, 1914, I took the liberty to address you on behalf of myself and other Negro democrats who felt at that time, and who still feel the slight the present administration has put upon us by simply ignoring us out of existence. In reply to that communication, under date of June 1st, 1914, I received a personal letter from you,[1] a copy of which I herewith enclose, together with a copy of my letter of May 16th [26th], 1914, both of which explain themselves.

I appreciate the fact very much that the President refered my matter [letter] to the Attorney General for his consideration. I have been informed by the Department of Justice that my letter was duly received and noted.

I have been further informed, from a source heretofore reliable, that after the adjurnment of the Congress the President would adjust the matter of federal appointments among Negro democrats. I beg leave to suggest that the Congress has adjurned; that the "difficult situation" is removed and should it be the purpose of the President to recognize Negro democrats, particularly those who have sacrificed in his behalf, now is the time for action.

I cannot believe, that in the face of your pre-election utterances, you will, as President, now that the Congress is out of your way, leave us to be held up to the scorn and ribaldry of any and all stump speakers, lecturers, preachers, newspaper editors and "what-nots" who choose to point a finger at us and cry, "I told you so. 'Nigger democrats'? No body wants them!"

I, personally, am in the most humiliateing situation before my people in all my life's experience.

I fight hard in all my endertakings. I faught hard for the Wilson and Marshall ticket. I am now being called to account for MY utterances in 1912. I am still fighting, but dying by inches as I have absolutely no foundation upon which to stand.

I will never believe that the President made a promise, even by inference, which he will not keep.

I have the honor to remain,

         Respectfully yours,   Robert Lewis Waring

TLS (WP, DLC).
[1] These letters are printed in Vol. 30.

Remarks at a Press Conference

April 13, 1915

Mr. President, is there anything to be said at this time with reference to the memorandum recently left at the State Department from the German Ambassador?

No, sir. Nothing just now.

Mr. President, can you tell us when it was you received the assurance that the Holy See would cooperate with you in any move you might inaugurate for peace?[1]

That intimation has been conveyed to me a number of times. I can't recollect just what, individually, is referred to, but the matter referred to any one of several.

Could you tell us the form in which it came?

It didn't come in any formal way at all.

Have there been any intimations to you, official or unofficial, which would indicate the basis on which peace negotiations might be pressed?

No, none whatever, I am sorry to say.

This peace gathering,[2] from the viewpoint of the United States Government, hasn't any official standing or sanction?

No. I don't wish, by saying that, to discountenance it in any way, but it has no official sanction of any kind. Indeed, so far as I know, they didn't ask for any.

It has been intimated in some of the press dispatches I have seen, Mr. President, that the delegation had a preliminary meeting of the peace conference at The Hague and had adopted a program in line with the American idea. Were any inquiries made as to the attitude of this government at this time?

No, sir, none whatever. I dare say they meant by that only the attitude of the American people, for whom there is no exclusive spokesman. . . .

Mr. President, Congressman Gardner, at a dinner here, made the assertion, having made certain suggestions to you, that the joint Army and Navy Board was dissolved?

I have no comment whatever to make upon anything Mr. Gardner said.

Mr. President, have you anything regarding the plans of General Huerta?

No, sir. I am not in his confidence.

Mr. President, would you care to say whether the German note came from the Ambassador or from the government?

I don't know. You mean whether the text was sent over? Whether it was authorized by the government?

It said it was authorized, at least it said so in the newspapers. I don't know whether it said so to the State Department or not. I haven't conferred with Mr. Bryan about it yet.

Mr. President, have we any, or received assurances that the Japanese-Chinese negotiations are progressing satisfactorily to the United States?

No, we haven't received any assurances one way or the other. We have simply tried to keep in touch with them.

The announcement from Peking, that the United States has given assurances, or rather has asserted or has told China she could rely upon any representation from the United States, is not correct?

All those are without foundation. We haven't entered into that sort of business at all.

JRT transcript (WC, NjP) of CLSsh (C. L. Swem Coll., NjP).
1 This question was inspired by an exclusive interview granted by Benedict XV to Karl H. von Wiegand, a special correspondent of the New York *World*, on April 6. The Pope urged the American people to pray and work for peace. He declared that the United States was the one neutral nation with sufficient influence to bring an early end to the conflict in Europe. Von Wiegand quoted him directly as saying: "America, when the favorable moment comes for the initial step for a peace suggestion, may be certain of the utmost support of the Holy See. SO I HAVE ALREADY LET YOUR PRESIDENT KNOW THROUGH ONE OF HIS HIGHEST FRIENDS." New York *World*, April 11, 1915.
2 A reference to the International Congress of Women, held at The Hague, April 28-May 1, 1915. Jane Addams, who had agreed to serve as president of the conference, and over forty other American participants sailed from New York on April 13, amid much controversy in the press. For accounts of the congress, see International Congress of Women, *Report* (Amsterdam, n.d.), and Marie Louise Degen, *The History of the Woman's Peace Party* (Baltimore, 1939), pp. 64-91.

To Ida Houston Nelson[1]

[The White House] April 13, 1915.

May I not express my deep sympathy with you in the loss of your husband. The whole country will mourn the loss of a great editor and citizen.   Woodrow Wilson.

WWT Telegram (Letterpress Books, WP, DLC).
1 Wife of William Rockhill Nelson, who had died on April 13.

From Annie Josephine Wilson Howe

My precious Brother,   New York, April 13th 1915

I should have written this letter some days ago but could not get my courage up to the point.

We will give up our rooms here the last week in April and go south, where Annie will give a recital, hoping to make enough money to pay the expenses of the trip. We will go to Columbia and to Chapel Hill. Mr David[1] says that next fall Annie will be ready to go out on a tour, giving several recitals, and we therefore hope, dear brother, to make expenses lighter for you next winter. If I had known how much it would cost I do not think I could have made up my mind to begin Annie's musical education. Mr. David says, however, that she has done in one year what it has taken *all* of his other pupils two or three to accomplish. We have been as careful about spending money as we knew how to be, doing the greater part of our washing and ironing in our rooms, and spending *nothing* on pleasure in any form. I tell you this not complaining, dear, but for fear you will think I have been extravagant when I tell you that I will have to have the two hundred and eighty dollars I have paid Mr. David, out of the two thousand you gave me, before I can go south. You gave me eighty dollars at one time and seventy at another which has been used for the sight singing teacher, the italian teacher, *Miss David*[2] and the music we have had to buy.

Now, dear, I would *rather* borrow this money from the bank than bother you about it, but you said in Cornish when I told you I thought I would need six hundred more than I did last year and could borrow it from the bank, that you did not want me to do that. If my checks from the south had come in I could have managed with what you have given me, but I was notified that because of the hard times I would have to wait for them.

I am sorry to bother you with all this but could not be content without explaining matters to you. Please forgive me and do not hesitate to tell me if it is inconvenient to help me any further. I hope we will be out of the woods before long.

I am so glad to hear that you are well and not quite so tired as you were when we saw you last.

I am prouder and prouder of you each day and love you with all my heart, and our gratitude to you is beyond words. With warmest love from us both,   Your devoted sister Annie.

I believe Annie is going to make a success of her music and you will not regret what you have done.

ALS (WP, DLC).

[1] Her singing coach, Ross David, who also taught Margaret Wilson.

[2] Marion L. David, vocal teacher and piano accompanist of New York, who also had worked with Margaret Wilson. Miss David married Ralph Kingsbury in 1915.

From William Jennings Bryan, with Enclosures

My dear Mr. President: Washington April 14, 1915.

I enclose flimsy of a despatch from Peking. I think it might be well to authorize him to make a statement not quite in the language he uses, but similar to that in the enclosed despatch. What do you think?

With assurances of high respect I am, my dear Mr. President,
                Yours very sincerely,   W. J. Bryan

TLS (W. J. Bryan Papers, DNA).

E N C L O S U R E   I

STRICTLY CONFIDENTIAL.   Peking. April 14, 1915. Rec'd 11 A.M.

Referring to my cable of April 8, 4 P.M. It is reported to me from trustworthy sources that during the conference on Saturday when Fukien was under discussion Japanese Minister observed that Japan's real aim was to protect China against the pretensions of America in that province, and he urged that it would be highly expedient for China to take advantage of the opportunity afforded by the disposition of the present administration to withdraw from such pretensions. In this connection he again took occasion to make disparaging reference to the alleged complaisance of the Government of the United States and the futility of China's basing any hopes upon American support.

There has just come to my attention, as a first evidence of the success of Japanese efforts to alienate Chinese confidence in the United States, an article in the vernacular peculiar to TIENTSIN TIMES which quotes "a prominent Japanese" as publicly declaring the absurdity of anticipating any action by the United State[s] in opposition to Japanese policy since "the Secretary of State is so much under the influence of Baron Chinda that he is not saying a word against the wishes of Japan" and comments bitterly that the facts seem to warrant this view inasmuch as the American Government seems to have abandoned its championship of the open-door policy.

It is to be feared that unless our Government unmistakably dissociates itself from the appearance of acquiescence in the unconscionable demands of Japan, persistent flagrant misrepresentations of its motives, such as above cited, will embitter Chinese public opinion against it. With a view to offsetting such propaganda, I beg to request authorization to give informally, impersonally and unofficially, publicity to the view that the American Government has not abandoned either its material interests or its moral obligations in respect to China and, while of course, awaiting the results of the present negotiations in confident expectation that these rights and obligations will remain unimpeachable, it may be expexted to take appropriate action if that belief should prove likely to be disappointed. Meanwhile I am taking appropriate steps through friendly Chinese to prevent the spreading of misrepresentations.   Reinsch.

T telegram (W. J. Bryan Papers, DNA).

E N C L O S U R E   I I[1]

Amlegation Peking   Washington, April 15, 1915. 3 pm
    Answering your April fourteenth, seven p.m.
    You are authorized to give out informally and unofficially something in the following sense—quote The American Government has not surrendered any of its treaty rights in China or abated one iota of its friendly interest in all that concerns the industrial and political welfare of China. It is awaiting the results of the present negotiations in the confident expectation that the rights and obligations of the United States will not be affected or its interests impaired. unquote For your own information will say that you have received copies of all our communications from which you will see that we have not acquiesced in anything that violates China's rights or disregards this Nation's interests.
                                                                Bryan

T telegram (SDR, RG 59, 793.94/294, DNA).
    [1] The following document is the telegram sent. The draft that Bryan sent to Wilson is missing.

To William Jennings Bryan

My dear Mr. Secretary,   The White House. 14 April, 1915.
    I hope that you will send this telegram.
    I am very uneasy about what is going on, as reported by Mr. Reinsch, and must frankly admit that I do not credit the assurances the Japanese have sought to give us. I wish that you might find an opportunity to express to the Japanese ambassador the grave concern we feel at hearing that his government is insisting upon the acquiescence of the Chinese government in the "Requests," because they are so clearly incompatible with the

administrative independence and autonomy of the Chinese Empire and with the maintenance of the policy of an open door to the world.

In short, I feel that we should be as active as the circumstances permit in showing ourselves to be champions of the sovereign rights of China, now as always, though with no thought of seeking any special advantage or privilege for ourselves. In this way only can we make good this message to Reinsch.

Has Reinsch been told definitely that it is not true that we have acquiesced in any of Japan's demands? Count Okuma has been quoted in the newspaper despatches as saying that we had acquiesced.   Faithfully Yours,   W.W.

WWTLI (W. J. Bryan Papers, DNA).

A Telegram and a Letter from Edward Mandell House

[Paris, April 14, 1915]

In a private conference with French Minister for Foreign Affairs he was good enough to express his satisfaction at the way negotiations have been carried on up to now. He said that I had given Berlin a correct idea of France's attitude and he approved what I had said and done there. I discussed with him the World interview with the Pope and indicated that it was not altogether friendly. I feel that our relations here have distinctly improved. He wished me to convey to you the appreciation of France for the fairness with which you have maintained relations with the belligerents. I shall see the President of France before I leave.

Edward House

T transcript of WWsh decode (WC, NjP).

Dear Governor: Paris, France. April 14th, 1915.

I saw Delcasse yesterday and I have cabled you the substance of the interview.

He told me frankly of France's position which was merely one of self protection. He said this war had been hanging over them for many years, and that France had done what she could to avoid it, but now that it had come, they were determined to make an end of it.

I do not think he has any more feeling against the Germans at large than the English have. All their efforts are directed towards the Prussian military autocracy. They feel here, as they do in England, that until that is broken, there can be no certitude of permanent peace. Even if the Kaiser should enter into a pact with them now, who is to tell whether when the Crown Prince comes to the Throne, that pact will not be broken and another military oligarchy, with another purpose, be built up.

I am giving you this as the general feeling in Europe, outside of Germany.

I showed Delcasse van Weigand's interview with the Pope as published in the New York World, and drew his attention to the inference that if we refused to sell munitions of war to the Allies, peace might be brought about.[1] In Germany, they told me that the Allies would not last a month if this were done, and that the war was being prolonged by our Government.

I suppose you know that the Pope was elected through Austrian influence, and that he is largely guided by it. Berlin evidently used Austria to get this interview for van Weigand, and for the purpose of, not only stirring up resentment, but to bring pressure upon you through the Catholic world.

The Pope desires very much to be mediator, and the Dual Alliance may so want to use him, but I am trying to make sure that the Allies will never accept him.

Page told me that if Italy entered the war, she would not consent to the Pope's mediation, or to his being put forward in any pronounced way. He also told me that the Italian Government hoped that you would not send an American Delegate to the Vatican, as some of the other nations have done, although the Italian Government did not express this hope in so many words.

Delcasse desires me to meet Poincare which I shall do before I leave. I shall also see Delcasse again and talk to him more particularly about the second convention and its purposes. I touched upon this but lightly yesterday, for the reason I wished to get on better terms with him, which I feel I have done.

It may interest you to know that the British attack at Neuve Chapelle is supposed to have been a mistake, and that the losses there were largely caused by their own guns. Several of the Generals have been recalled.

You may also be interested in the fact that Joffre[2] is in supreme command of the French mil[i]tary forces. Any decision of his can only be reversed by the unanimous vote of the Cabinet, plus that of the President. He has no political ambition, and is the only man that all political parties feel that it is safe to trust. He has great ability, but as you know, there has not been a genius developed anywhere in this war.

The French were not well prepared, and largely because of

corruption. The same might be said of the Russians. However, France is now in the hands of competent and patriotic officials, and some of our military observers think that she has the most efficient army in the field.

The English seem to lack well trained officers. They have not only lost many of their best, but their army has grown far beyond any supply that they are able to make in this direction.

It is rumored, and I give it only as a rumor, that within a month there will be a general move by all the Allies along the lines. That is the movement will commence in both the east and west throughout the entire field. This could give the advantage to the army having the greatest number of men, and that is what the Allies now claim to have. They also claim that the Germans are losing in morale because of the evident lack of success. They expected to reach Paris within three weeks from the day war was declared, and when they failed and had to retreat at the Marne, they lost hope of ultimate complete victory.

I am giving you all this as gossip and not as facts.

Your affectionate,   E. M. House

TLS (WP, DLC).
  ¹ House referred to the following direct quotation of the Pope: "If your country avoids everything that might prolong this struggle of nation against nation, in which the blood of hundreds of thousands is being shed and misery untold inflicted, then can America, by its greatness and its influence, contribute much toward the rapid ending of this terrible war."
  ² Joseph Jacques Césaire Joffre, commander in chief of the French armies, hero of the first Battle of the Marne.

To Edward Mandell House

[The White House, April 15, 1915]

It is fine how you establish just the right relations and just the right understanding at each capital, and I am sure it will bear rich fruit at the right time.

I am particularly gratified by what you report concerning your conference with the French Minister for Foreign Affairs. Please express to the Minister and to the President my feeling of warm gratitude that they are so generous as to receive our offers of friendship in just the spirit in which they are offered and with such full and sympathetic comprehension of the part we wish to play.

America will remember these things as she remembers many another generous attitude of France in her relations with the United States.

Has the text of Walter's [Bernstorff's] note about our neutrality been cabled to France? If so do you think it possible he is speaking as the Berlin Foreign Office would speak or only in his own voice and manner?

T transcript of WWsh (WC, NjP).

From William Jennings Bryan, with Enclosure

My dear Mr. President: Washington April 15, 1915.

I am sending you copy of a telegram which we have just received from the Department of Justice. This has been communicated to the Army and the Navy departments. I think we are justified in making inquiry. If you approve I will bring it to the attention of the Japanese Ambassador.

Mr. Hoover informs me that you have already received a copy of the letter sent by the Missionaries in China. I told him I did not think it proper for us to give out a document like that, attacking as it does the Japanese Government, and emphasizing our material interests in preventing the carrying out of Japan's program.

It seems to me that it is quite unwise for representatives of the United States to take so active and outspoken an interest in the matter. It is liable to put all of our Missionaries in Japan, as well as in China under suspicion and it will not help China because it will be regarded by Japan as an expression of China's animosity.

The Chinese Minister[1] was here yesterday and inquired very confidentially whether we had consented to China's proposals in regard to Fukien. I told him that we had no objection to an agreement between China and Japan that would exclude concessions to *any* foreign power, but that we had not surrendered any treaty rights that we had. I suggested to him that his Government might say to Japan that wherever we were quoted as favoring or consenting to anything, China would claim the privilege of communicating with us directly in order to avoid any possible misunderstanding with us.

Japan could hardly object to China inquiring of us in regard to any matter concerning which Japan presumes to quote us.

In other words—Japan could not expect to speak for us in dealing with China. China would expect to speak to us and have our position directly from us.

I made this suggestion to the Chinese Minister in the belief that it would give China an excuse for asking us about matters with which we are connected, and thus enable us to speak directly to China without violating confidence with Japan.

    With assurances of high respect I am, my dear Mr. President,
                Yours very sincerely,   W. J. Bryan

I also asked Chinese Minister to inquire how much China has spent for arms for past 5 years and from whom purchased   This will show whether there has been discrimination

TLS (W. J. Bryan Papers, DNA).
1 Kai Fu Shah.

E N C L O S U R E

Washington, April 15, 1915.

Following telegram received from special agent Los Angeles, California: Quote—Interviewed A. F. Nathan, reporter for Times who just returned from Turtle Bay, Mexico. States five Japanese cruisers, three colliers and three British colliers moored in Bay when he left nine days ago and armed Japanese being landed, and camps erected. Also large number boxes were transferred from Asama, which he was told contained ammunition, also heard that guns on Asama were to be landed. From investigation Asama in soft mud. Witnessed two mines taken from Bay. Mines scattered. Agent shown large number negatives of pictures taken by Nathan party verifying statements.[1]
T. W. Gregory.

TCL (W. J. Bryan Papers, DNA).
1 About this, the so-called Turtle Bay, incident, see WW to WJB, April 16, 1915 (third letter of that date), n. 1.

From Nicholas II

Mr. President,   Koristovka, 15 April 1915.

    The Ambassador of the United States has handed me Your letter of March 18th 1915.

    In this letter you ask me to allow representatives of the United States Government and of the American Red Cross to render assistance to prisoners of war of hostile armies interned in Russia, by personally distributing various gifts.

    I highly appreciate and share the philanthropic feeling of the citizens of the United States in view of which you addressed yourself to me with the above request. Wishing to meet this feeling, and deeply appreciating your initiative, I have instructed my

Minister of Foreign Affairs to enter into negotiations with the Ambassador of the United States of America and to communicate to him the conditions on which a distribution of gifts among Austro-Hungarian and German prisoners in Russia can take place.

I avail myself of this opportunity to express my sincere friendship to the Great American Nation and its Government and my personal high respect for yourself,

Your good friend, Nicholas[1]

T translation (SDR, RG 59, 763.72114/551, DNA).
[1] The ALS has the same file number as the translation.

Two Letters from William Jennings Bryan

My dear Mr. President: Washington April 16, 1915.

I am sending for your consideration two drafts which Mr. Lansing has prepared in case you wish to shorten the note to von Bernstorff.[1] I am inclined to think, however, that the longer one which you have been revising will be better.[2]

I am especially pleased with the addition made in the closing paragraph to soften the blow. I believe on reflection it would be well to leave out reference to the action of Congress. It may provoke an answer and we do not care to invite discussion. The German-Americans are quote [quite] sure to reply that the Resolution would have been passed but for the Administration's opposition, and von Bernstorff might even venture to suggest that Congress would have passed the Resolution if you had asked for such legislation. This is merely a suggestion but I feel that I should communicate anything that may help in the consideration of these matters.

The only other question I have is in regard to his suggestion that the right to sell arms to belligerents contemplated only the utilization of existing factories. That position, while unsound, is legitimate argument and I am wondering whether we might not answer it in a word by saying that there is no support in international law for the suggestion which he makes.

With assurances of high respect I am, my dear Mr. President,

Yours very sincerely, W. J. Bryan

[1] T MSS dated April 16, 1915 (SDR, RG 59, 763.72111/1930, DNA). Both stated simply that, since the matters discussed in Bernstorff's memorandum of April 4 were improper subjects of diplomatic discussion, the Secretary of State therefore declined to reply to the memorandum.
[2] It is printed as an Enclosure with WJB to WW, April 12, 1915 (second letter of that date).

My dear Mr. President: Washington April 16th, 1915.

I am enclosing a despatch which we have received from Berlin.[1] It presents quite a different report. You will notice that they claim, first, that the vessel tried to run away and made rocket signals calling for help. According to the report the chase lasted a quarter of an hour. Second, it is claimed that from the time the command to leave the ship until the torpedo was fired it was twenty-three minutes. Third, they make as an excuse for not giving more time that England arms her merchant vessels, etc.

We have not heard anything from Thrasher's relatives yet. A newspaper man told me some days ago that he heard they were likely to settle with the German Government without bringing the matter to the attention of the State Department. Do you think that we can wait until the matter is brought to our attention by the relatives of the deceased man, or should we take the initiative in making the representations?

With assurances of high respect, I am, my dear Mr. President,   Yours very sincerely,   W. J. Bryan

TLS (W. J. Bryan Papers, DLC).
[1] J. W. Gerard to WJB, April 14, 1915, T telegram (W. J. Bryan Papers, DLC). Bryan summarizes the telegram below.

To William Jennings Bryan

My dear Mr. Secretary,   The White House. 16 April, 1915.

What are we to believe? This version is absolutely in contradiction of that given by both passengers and petty officers of the FALABA!

I fear we cannot base our action in this case upon any demand of Thrasher's relatives, or delay action until we hear from them. I am still mulling the questions over, and hope in a short time now to have a suggestion to make as to a note.

Faithfully Yours,   W.W.

WWTLI (W. J. Bryan Papers, DLC).

From William Jennings Bryan, with Enclosure

My dear Mr. President: Washington April 16th, 1915.

I am sending you a telegram to Rein[s]ch in line with my conversation with the Chinese Minister yesterday. If you approve of it please send it to the State Department telegraph office for transmission.

    With assurances of high respect, I am, my dear Mr. President,
                Yours very sincerely,   W. J. Bryan

TLS (W. J. Bryan Papers, DNA).

E N C L O S U R E

Amlegation, Peking.   Washington, April 16th, 1915.

    A confidential conference held yesterday with the Chinese Minister suggests the following: In conferring with the Chinese Government you may, on your own initiative, suggest that whenever during negotiations the Japanese representative assumes to state the views or position of the United States the Chinese Government would be justified in saying that to avoid any possible misunderstanding it would be advisable for the Chinese Government to confer directly with the United States as to the position of this Government on the subject. This would enable us to make clear our position on any matter involved in the negotiations and thus exclude the possibility of mis-interpretation or misunderstanding. The United States and Chinese Governments do not of course need to communicate with each other through any third power on matters affecting their relations with each other or their treaty rights or obligations.
                                   Bryan

T telegram (SDR, RG 59, 793.94/333C, DNA).

Three Letters to William Jennings Bryan

Dear Mr. Secretary,   The White House. 16 April, 1915.

    I thoroughly approved the telegram which was enclosed with this, and sent it over this evening to the telegraph office of the State Department to be forwarded.
                        Faithfully Yours,   W.W.

My dear Mr. Secretary,   The White House. 16 April, 1915.

    I hope that you will make a very frank inquiry about this news from Turtle Bay. I do not like the look of it at all. At the least it looks as if the weakness of Mexico were being presumed upon and her neutrality violated.[1]

I agree with you entirely about the giving out of the message from the missionaries in China. They have been most unwise in giving it out themselves on the other side.

I note what you say about the way in which China should keep herself informed as to our attitude, and of course concur in your judgment.   Faithfully Yours,   W.W.

WWTLI (W. J. Bryan Papers, DNA).
1 On December 14, 1914, the Japanese cruiser *Asama* ran aground on rocks in Turtle Bay (Bahía Tortugas) on the west coast of Baja California. Refloating the vessel proved very difficult; it was still stuck fast by mid-April. At that time, news reports originating in Los Angeles stated that the Japanese had established a coaling station or naval base in Turtle Bay and had mined the bay. The Japanese embassy and officials of the Navy Department in Washington ridiculed the reports on April 15. However, Secretary Daniels, on April 16, did order the commander of the Pacific Fleet to have the matter investigated. Commander Noble E. Irwin of *U.S.S. New Orleans* paid a courtesy call on *Asama* on April 18 and afterwards radioed that he had found in Turtle Bay, in addition to the disabled cruiser, a Japanese navy supply ship, a Japanese repair ship, three Japanese fishing vessels, and two British colliers, and that the sole reason for the Japanese naval presence was the salvaging effort. The cruiser was finally refloated about May 10. *New York Times*, April 14-19 and May 11, 1915. See also William Reynolds Braisted, *The United States Navy in the Pacific, 1909-1922* (Austin, Tex., 1971), pp. 164-65.

My dear Mr. Secretary,   The White House. 16 April, 1915.

It helps my thought on this matter to have you think aloud in such letters as this. You are probably right about mentioning the fact that the Congress did not act.

I return the proposed note because I think, with you, that the other is on better lines, and that we can build on it.
          Faithfully Yours,   W.W.

WWTLI (W. J. Bryan Papers, DLC).

From William Jennings Bryan

My dear Mr. President: Washington April 16, 1915.

I am sending you a communication from Reinsch which gives a comparison of the demands and requests as they were presented to China, and in a parallel column the demands as presented to us.[1] You will notice that there is some discrepancy.

At the time this was made Mr. Reinsch had not received the copy of the requests submitted in addition to the demands. You will notice that fifty per cent of the arms is tentatively suggested. We have already submitted a suggestion in regard to that.

In looking over the Article in regard to the Han-Yeh-Ping Iron Mines I am wondering whether it is in keeping with the "Open

Door" policy for Japan to insist: *First*—upon having her mortgage changed into a joint ownership; and *second*—upon having a refusal on new mines in that neighborhood, even though the neighborhood is restricted.

As they state it in their communication to us it does involve to some extent the granting of a sphere of influence, not willingly but under compulsion. While Japanese have loaned some 30 millions—(I think that is the sum)—to this Chinese Company, China is anxious, so I am informed, to pay that off and thus avoid a joint ownership in that section. These mines are near Hang-Chow [Hankow], which is almost the center of the Chinese Empire. If China desires to pay off this mortgage and thus leave these mines free from any foreign influence I think she ought to be allowed to do so.

I have stated to you what is running through my mind and I am wondering whether we ought not to make some representation to Japan in regard to the matter—an inquiry as to whether her interests would not be properly protected by a repayment of this mortgage, leaving a Chinese company in entire charge so that all countries dealing with the corporation would deal upon the same footing. This might be strenuously objected to because Japan seems to have her eye upon that particular spot and we are informed that the ore deposits are very valuable. In fact, I think that Japanese companies, if not the Japanese Government, have a long-time contract with the Company for the purchase of ore and pig-iron.

Have you anything to suggest along this line?

I shall speak to the Japanese Ambassador about the Turtle Bay matter.

With assurances of high rexpect I am, my dear Mr. President,
                    Yours very sincerely,   W. J. Bryan

TLS (SDR, RG 59, 793.94/292, DNA).
    1 P. S. Reinsch to WJB, March 6, 1915, TLS (SDR, RG 59, 793.94/292, DNA), enclosing a typed memorandum which placed in parallel columns a translation of the "demands" and "requests" given to President Yuan Shih-k'ai by the Japanese Minister on January 18 and the version handed to Reinsch by the Japanese Minister on February 14. The letter and its enclosure are printed in *FR 1915*, pp. 98-103. Bryan's comment that the parallel columns revealed "some discrepancy" was a considerable understatement. The version given to Reinsch on February 14 was at best only an outline of the document presented to the Chinese President in January, and it did not mention at all the "requests" included in Group V—in fact demands that China employ "influential" Japanese political, financial, and military advisers, appoint Japanese to police departments in particular localities, agree to purchase a certain portion of its arms from Japan, and so on.

To William Jennings Bryan

My dear Mr. Secretary,   The White House. 16 April, 1915.

The aspects of this matter between Japan and China change so often as our information grows more complete that I am convinced that we shall have to try in every practicable way to defend China.

Her position in the matter of the Han-Yeh-Ping iron mines is certainly justified by every consideration; and I believe that you ought, as you suggest, to have a very candid talk with the Japanese Ambassador about it.

I think you will be justified in showing him that we take it very seriously and are very much concerned, seeing in such things a very decided infringement of the principle of the open door and also of China's administrative and economic integrity.

We shall have to be very chary hereafter about seeming to concede the reasonableness of any of Japan's demands or requests either, until we get the whole of the situation in our minds by hearing from Peking as well as from Tokyo.

Faithfully Yours,   W.W.

WWTLI (SDR, RG 59, 793.94/292, DNA).

From Edward Mandell House

[Paris, April 16, 1915]

I deeply appreciate your cable.

The text of Bernstorff's interview has appeared here. He undoubtedly represents the attitude of his government. Germany's methods are so unaccountable that it is difficult to understand their purpose. A firm reply may make them less offensive in the future.

I have had a delightful interview with the President. He said that he well understands our relations, and thanked you for sending me to France. He complimented us upon the tact and judgment used. He was stirred by your message and said France reciprocated the friendly feeling of America and believed our cordial relations would continue to grow.

France greatly appreciates your note and regrets that the policy of the Allies caused us so much inconvenience. However the control of the seas was absolutely necessary in order to bring the war to a more speedy end. This control he promised would be exercised to cause the minimum inconvenience to us. He wished me to express to you the gratitude felt by France for the splendid donations which Americans were making in the aid of her sick and wounded. I shall see the French Minister for Foreign Affairs again soon to discuss the second convention.

Edward House

T transcripts of WWsh decode (WC, NjP; WP, DLC).

From Seth Low

Dear Mr. President: New York, N. Y. April 16th, 1915.

I have just had a call from Mr. Cyrus W. Phillips,[1] who, by invitation of the Speaker of the House of Representatives, has been in Colorado representing The National Civic Federation for the purpose of co-operating in securing the passage of a suitable industrial commission bill for the State, and a suitable compensation bill. Mr. Phillips has left with me a copy of the law in regard to the Industrial Commission, which is certainly clothed with ample powers. It consists of three members to be appointed by the Governor to serve for three years, one member retiring each year. Provisions for workmen's compensation are embodied in a separate law; but this law also is administered by the Industrial Commission, which is also to supervise the enforcement of labor laws; prescribe safety devices and methods for every employment; collect statistics and information; inquire into labor conditions, wages, sanitation, health and safety, and causes of industrial disputes; suggest remedial legislation; promote voluntary arbitration so as to avoid necessity for strikes and lockouts. Strikes and lockouts are forbidden pending arbitration before Commission. The Compensation Act, broadly speaking, contains the Michigan schedule of payment.

Mr. Phillips reports that a good foundation is laid, and that the disposition among both employers and workmen is to co-operate in carrying out the spirit of the law and aiding in its success. Mr. Phillips thinks that this legislation means industrial peace and development in Colorado—a condition desired by employers, workmen, and the people generally.

Mr. Phillips reports that the correspondence between the Colorado operators and The President's Coal Commission, and also our Report of Progress to you, were published in the Colorado papers, and that, so far as he could judge from expressions which he heard from both sides, the action of your Commission was approved. He thinks that there is a distinct purpose on the part of the operators to improve conditions as much as possible between now and the time of our visit to the State, towards the end of the year. In other words, so far as I can judge from Mr. Phillips, events are moving there precisely as we had hoped.

Respectfully,   Seth Low, Chairman,
President's Colorado Coal Commission.

TLS (WP, DLC).

[1] Cyrus William Phillips, lawyer of Rochester, N. Y., and an expert on workmen's compensation legislation.

ADDENDA

To Charles Wesley Wisner, Jr.[1]

Princeton, New Jersey,

My dear Mr. Wisner,   5 December, 1899.

I do not quite believe in "lists" of books. The best way, it seems to me, is to read one or two standard works on a given subject and let those be, through their foot notes and the various subjects they suggest but do not fully treat, your guides to further and wider reading, following lines of suggestion.

The best book for American constitutional study is, perhaps, Judge J. I. Clark Hare's "Constitutional Government" in two vols.;[2] and the best for a compendious view of International Law is W. E. Hall's "International Law,"[3] published by the Clarendon Press at Oxford.

In Government and Diplomacy it is very hard to find anything comprehensive in English except my own very dry "The State," which D. C. Heath & Co. publish. No doubt you have that, and I would suggest that you look up such parts of the subject as you become interested in by the aid of the lists of books at the ends of its several chapters. It however has nothing on Diplomacy, and I do not know of anything that covers that field. Perhaps you could not do better than begin with Eugene Schuyler's "American Diplomacy,"[4] and read from that out.

I hope that you are well and prosperous.

Mrs. Wilson joins me in kindest regards,

Sincerely Yours,   Woodrow Wilson

WWTLS (WC, NjP).

[1] Princeton 1896, a former student of Wilson's.

[2] John Innes Clark Hare, *American Constitutional Law* (2 vols., Boston, 1889).

[3] William Edward Hall, *A Treatise on International Law*, 4th edn. (Oxford, 1895).

[4] Eugene Schuyler, *American Diplomacy and the Furtherance of Commerce* (London, 1886).

To Cyrus Adler[1]

My dear Dr. Adler: Princeton, N. J. June 23rd, 1902.

Thank you very cordially indeed for your kind letter of congratulation.[2] I believe my predominant feeling just now is one of very great diffidence because of the magnitude of the responsibility and of the tasks that lie ahead of me. You may judge, therefore, of the value to me of such words of confidence as you sent. It is like supplying a man with capital to trade on, to assure him that men who know what they are talking about, believe in him, and I thank you for your part in the capitalization.

Most sincerely yours, Woodrow Wilson

TLS (C. Adler Papers, Jewish Theological Seminary of America-Ar).
[1] Fellow student of Wilson's at the Johns Hopkins University. A student of Semitic languages, archeology, and the history of religions, he was at this time librarian of the Smithsonian Institution.
[2] On his election as President of Princeton University. Adler's letter is C. Adler to WW, June 13, 1902, TLS (WP, DLC).

Lindley Miller Garrison to Francis Burton Harrison

[Washington] January 11, 1915.

The President directs that execution Noriel be suspended until case can be investigated.[1] Garrison.

[1] Mariano Noriel, a general in the Philippine insurrectory army and one of the most powerful caciques in the islands, who had long maintained a reign of terror in Cavite. He and two accomplices had been convicted of murder and sentenced to hang, and the sentence of the lower court had been confirmed by the Philippine Supreme Court. Most leading Filipino politicians, including Emilio Aguinaldo, had put pressure upon Harrison to commute the sentence upon Noriel. When Harrison refused, the Filipino leaders had appealed to Wilson through Manuel Quezon. Francis B. Harrison, "About It and About" (MS in the possession of Verna Hobson), pp. 249-53.

Francis Burton Harrison to Lindley Miller Garrison

Manila, January 12, 1915.

I beg to acknowledge receipt of your telegram of January 11th and in accordance with the President's instructions the execution of Noriel has been suspended.

I have the honor to submit herewith my resignation as Governor General. As the President's representative, I felt myself competent to pass upon the question of executive clemency in this case. After the most careful consideration extending over several weeks, I came to the conclusion that Noriel and his companions were guilty of the murder for which they were convicted; that there were no mitigating circumstances whatever; that they were not deserving of any clemency. I have been subjected to tremendous pressure from the most prominent Filipino politicians to change my opinion, and have refused. Without consulting me, the President has directed suspension of the sentence. Had I been consulted I would have advised that suspension casts doubt upon the courts in this most crucial case and impairs the administration of justice. The issue really was whether the government was strong enough to execute this criminal Noriel with all his political influence. Not having been considered in this question, so vital to my power to administer the laws here, and feeling that my opportunity for usefulness is now greatly impaired, I herewith resign. I have made no statements upon this subject here excepting that I had informed those interested that I had decided not to grant clemency, but that the President had directed this morning the suspension of the sentence.

Harrison.

Lindley Miller Garrison to Francis Burton Harrison

[Washington] January 12, 1915.

Confidential. The President can not think of accepting your resignation which is based upon a complete misunderstanding upon your part of his attitude in the matter. He has entire confidence in you. He will send you as soon as possible a full statement of the matter.   Garrison.

To Francis Burton Harrison

[Washington] January 12, 1915.

Am deeply disturbed by your message. My action was taken hastily and without knowledge of the circumstances because told that it was a question of hours only. I knew nothing of the case and merely wished time to inquire. I am ready to stand by you and sustain your judgment at every point. Matter brought to me when it was impossible for me to consult either Secretary of War or General McIntyre within the time named. Beg that you will withdraw resignation and await letter which follows.[1] I find that I have no legal right or responsibility in this case and should have left it entirely to you. I hope that you will regard my request for delay as withdrawn and act as you think right.[2]

Woodrow Wilson.

T telegrams (WDR, RG 350, BIA, Noriel Case, DNA).

[1] Wilson must have written Harrison a personal letter, no copy of which can be found.

[2] Noriel and his accomplices were hanged on January 27, 1915, at Bilibid Prison. Harrison withdrew his resignation. There is a WWhw copy of Wilson's telegram in the possession of Harvey Mortimer.

From Nancy Saunders Toy

My dear Mr. President   Cambridge. 13 Jan. 1915

I smile to myself as I write this and recal[l] what a Spaniard once said to me—something like this: "You Anglo-Saxons have a trick of putting your ideals always just at the end of the road you are traveling; we Latins hitch ours to a star beyond our grasp or even *reach*, and go on our way unheeding, content that they are so high." Thus I, after addressing you with the utmost correctness, dash ahead with the utmost disrespectfulness like the Latins.

Isn't it disrespectful to say that your Indianapolis speech took my breath away? I look at these little shorthand hieroglyphics[1] and wonder why their dynamic quality didn't blow me up before. But "Te duce, Caesar." When you are philosophical, we your friends are. When you are political, we are. The height of my ambition is to follow the example of Mr. Tumulty. "He often combats my point of view," you once said, "and presents his own vigorously, but when once my point of view becomes a decision, he accepts it and stands staunchly behind it as if it were the only possible one."

And yet the little curlicue which I have picked out as "Woodrow chuckles"[2] grins at me defiantly and I should have rubbed my hand softly over its face could I have guessed its meaning. These Western folk have a strange spell over you, Mr. President. You know and said that I resent it. It is, I think, because you idealize their spirit. It may be, however, that you truly *realize* it. But one of these days when we are seventy or thereabouts, I wish we could meet sometime at a corner by the fireside and see if the spell still holds. I myself frankly prefer the Easterners. The refusal of the West to "grow up," like T.R.'s, bores me. But I am ready for a fight as are all your Eastern friends, and you will find when the time comes that our loins are girded up as securely as the apparently more brawny ones of the West. Seriously—and here I *must* interpolate a story— *Later.* Our doctor interpolated himself here. He came to see Mr. Toy who has been suffering Job-wise since my return and declined more skilful treatment than that I could give him. But today I summoned the doctor, a shrewd man of 60, the best surgeon in the State and generally considered hard and unsympathetic, but today when he heard I had been visiting at the White House, he said: "I wish you would tell your President that I consider him the grandest man, politically and personally, that I've ever known or read about. I told somebody the other day that I haven't one patient that could stand what he has had to stand and come out of it alive, and dyed-in-the-wool old Republican that I am, I laughed aloud over his Indianapolis speech just because I was so glad he had that much fight in him. He's a grand man and I'll vote for him every time I get the chance." And this was what *my* "serious" was to be, too, to tell you that though I should have liked other people to make your political speeches for you, as I read on and on, I saw the inevitableness of it; the sheer necessity that *you* should say these things at [and] say them just at this time. And it was splendidly done—clear cut, each sentence thrust home by the sheer conviction behind it, full of hope and cheer, and leading the way with flags flying. And yet as *I* read, I was far nearer crying than laughing. It is a strange world you are inhabiting now—"so many worlds, so much to do" and you standing like "a pillar steadfast in the storm," with your own foundations swept all away. And it is true—isn't it?—that in spite of the universality of death, people seem to take it little into account, *seem* to understand so little the devastation left behind.

I had a blessed visit with you all, and to you all I send many messages of affection.

Your much daring but much admiring friend   Nancy Toy

P.S. I have just been telephoning to Mrs. Hulbert and arranged for her to take Mr. Toy's ticket to the Symphony Concert out here tomorrow evening. Miss Wambaugh[3] will have mine, for I musn't leave him, and do the honors of our little theatre. Mrs. H. tells me that she has just finished her cook-book and I told her I should try to help her find a publisher.   N.T.

ALS (WP, DLC).
  [1] Wilson had obviously given Mrs. Toy the shorthand outline of his Indianapolis speech as a memento.
  [2] The symbol in Graham shorthand for humor. It looks like a beehive.
  [3] Sarah Wambaugh of Cambridge, Mass., daughter of Eugene Wambaugh, distinguished lawyer and author and professor of law at Harvard University.

A Memorandum by Henry Skillman Breckinridge

Thursday, February 4th [1915]

MEMORANDUM: Re interview with the President.

On Monday, February 1st, the Secretary of War communicated to me his intention to resign. He imparted as his reason a combination of public and private considerations. First he alleged that his continuous disagreement with the views of the President and others of his Cabinet was a source of embarassment to him and he felt that he should not go along with them as a hindrance. Furthermore, he felt that his private interests demanded his return to private life; that in the period which would intervene between the present and the normal duration of his powers he could improve the condition of his private fortune to a degree adequate to provide for those dependent upon him. At my special instance, the Secretary of War consented that I should go and have a talk with the President before he should communicate his intention in person to the President. I sought an interview with the President and was told to come to the White House at 8 o'clock, Monday night, which I did.

I told the President the circumstances that led to my visit, to-wit, that at my special request the Secretary of War consented that I should go and have a talk with the President before he, the Secretary, made known his intentions. I then recounted the development of the situation in which the Secretary found himself; that he found himself continually in disagreement with the President and his colleagues as to the course to be pursued in matters of governmental policy and that he had come to feel himself embarrassed by being a continually dissenting minority; that he felt that his continued disagreement must imply a certain fundamental incompatibility and that therefore his presence must be a hindrance rather than a help and the only thing left for him to do would be to retire; furthermore, that the state of his personal finances was such that the expense of public life inconvenienced him and impressed him with the necessity of a return to private life and attention to his private affairs; that the Secretary had nothing but appreciation for the courtesy and consideration that had always been extended him and of course felt great regret at having come to the conclusion that he must withdraw.

The President expressed the highest estimation of the Secretary's capacity, character and service; stated that though he had often been in disagreement with the rest of the Cabinet, nevertheless his colleagues had nothing but respect for his opinions and independence of judgment and that his service in council had been a real service; that his administration of the duties of his office had been eminently effective and that his loss would be a very real one. He asked me my opinion of the consequence of his resignation.

I told him in frankness I thought there were about five million people who would vote the democratic ticket irrespective of changing circumstances and that there were two million voters who must be secured by other attractions than that of unquestioning loyalty; that the withdrawal of Mr. Garrison from the

Cabinet at this time perhaps would render it impossible to secure these two million voters for the democratic party and certainly would make them very much more difficult to obtain. He said, "I agree with you fully. What would you advise?" I said that my advice would be largely negative; that I considered this to be a crisis in the affairs of his Administration and that one thing I was sure of, to-wit, that such advice as would normally come to him from his hot partisans that were in continual association with him would be worse than useless. He spoke again in high commendation of the Secretary and stated that he had no other desire than to see him and talk with him in the same spirit in which he had talked with me. I had explained to the President previously that the Secretary of War had desired that the first intimation of his intention to resign should come from himself; that as long as the matter was in the shape of a tentative conclusion, he had not seen fit to worry the President with his private affairs; that the fact of the matter coming to the attention of the President through other channels than direct from the Secretary was a source of regret to the Secretary and that as soon as he heard that the matter had come to the attention of the President, he had insisted on coming immediately to see the President, and only on my insistent urging that he permit me to go first and give my view of the situation and of the steps that led up to the present situation did he refrain from going himself and permit me to go first.

I went from the White House to the residence of the Secretary of War and laid before him my interview with the President. After consideration of the view held by the President, that the withdrawal of the Secretary would be an injury to the Administration and the party, the Secretary wrote to the President stating that he had not attached this significance to his withdrawal; that the last thing he desired to do was to injure either the President or the party and that if I correctly interpreted the attitude of mind of the President, he, the Secretary, desired to consider the matter a closed incident for the present. The Secretary suggested in this letter that the President send for him to talk over the matter if there was anything he desired to communicate. I delivered this note at the White House at 10:30 p.m.

Henry Breckinridge

TS CC memorandum (H. S. Breckinridge Papers, DLC).

To William Jennings Bryan, with Enclosure

My dear Mr. Secretary: The White House February 8, 1915

Here is the memorandum of which I spoke to you some time ago and which at that time I had misplaced. I submit these suggestions for safeguarding the more important diplomatic proceedings for your consideration.

Cordially and faithfully yours,   Woodrow Wilson

TLS (R. Lansing Papers, NjP).

E N C L O S U R E

MEMORANDUM.

One person to draft all despatches which it is thought wise to keep safe from publication.

One (and the same) stenographer to transcribe *all* such despatches and their ciphered or deciphered versions.

One (and the same) official to do *all* the enciphering and deciphering of such despatches.

No flimsies of such despatches; only one or two copies; a copy of the most important despatches to be sent to the President, to be returned for file always.

In brief, a single, clearly defined inner circle to handle these matters always, without variation of method or personnel, with the most carefully guarded exclusiveness, so that it may always be possible to fix the responsibility for a leak definitely and at once.

The only person outside this circle allowed even the [to] *handle* such despatches unsealed to be the head of the Index Bureau.

The despatches sent to the President to be sent always in sealed envelopes to *the White House*, never to the Executive Offices, where it is impossible to prevent their passing through several hands.   W.W.

WWT MS (R. Lansing Papers, NjP).

From William Jennings Bryan

My dear Mr. President: Washington February 12, 1915.

I have your letter of February 8th, enclosing your memorandum of suggestions for safeguarding the more important diplomatic proceedings of the Department. I think it will be entirely feasible to confine the matters of which you speak within the circle of you and myself and Mr. Davis, the Chief Clerk of the Department. Mr. Davis has been looking after these matters for some time, is familiar with the various ciphers used by the Department, and can also attend to the necessary typewriting of the dispatches. This will seem to keep these most important matters within a very circumscribed circle which will be most advisable.

I am, my dear Mr. President,
                                    Very sincerely yours,   W. J. Bryan

TLS (WP, DLC).

William Jennings Bryan to Henry Prather Fletcher

Amembassy Santiago (Chile)   Washington, March 31, 1915.

The Chilean Ambassador, some weeks ago, submitted to his Government several propositions which are being considered in connection with a proposed treaty. Argentina has responded endorsing all the propositions submitted. Brazil has endorsed all except one and we are daily expecting favorable answer in regard to that. So far no answer has been received from Chile. All these communications are confidential. Will you please confer with the Chilean Government and ascertain whether they are likely to send an answer to their Ambassador in the near future? The President is very anxious to take up the matter with other countries but is delaying doing so in the hope of receiving favorable answer from Chile.   Bryan

T telegram (SDR, RG 59, 723.2515/299a, DNA).

INDEX

NOTE ON THE INDEX

THE alphabetically arranged analytical table of contents at the front of the volume eliminates duplication, in both contents and index, of references to certain documents, such as letters. Letters are listed in the contents alphabetically by name, and chronologically within each name by page. The subject matter of all letters is, of course, indexed. The Editorial Notes and Wilson's writings are listed in the contents chronologically by page. In addition, the subject matter of both categories is indexed. The index covers all references to books and articles mentioned in text or notes. Footnotes are indexed. Page references to footnotes which place a comma between the page number and "n" cite both text and footnote, thus: "624,n3." On the other hand, absence of the comma indicates reference to the footnote only, thus: "55n2"—the page number denoting where the footnote appears.

We have ceased the practice of indicating first and fullest identification of persons and subjects in earlier volumes by index references accompanied by asterisks. Volume 13, the cumulative index-contents volume is already in print. Volume 26, which will cover Volumes 14-25, will appear in the near future.

The index supplies the fullest known form of names and, for the Wilson and Axson families, relationships as far down as cousins. Persons referred to by nicknames or shortened forms of names can be identified by reference to entries for these forms of the names.

All entries consisting of page numbers only and which refer to concepts, issues, and opinions (such as democracy, the tariff, the money trust, leadership, and labor problems), are references to Wilson speeches and writings. Page references that follow the symbol Δ in such entries refer to the opinions and comments of others who are identified.

INDEX

WITHDRAWN